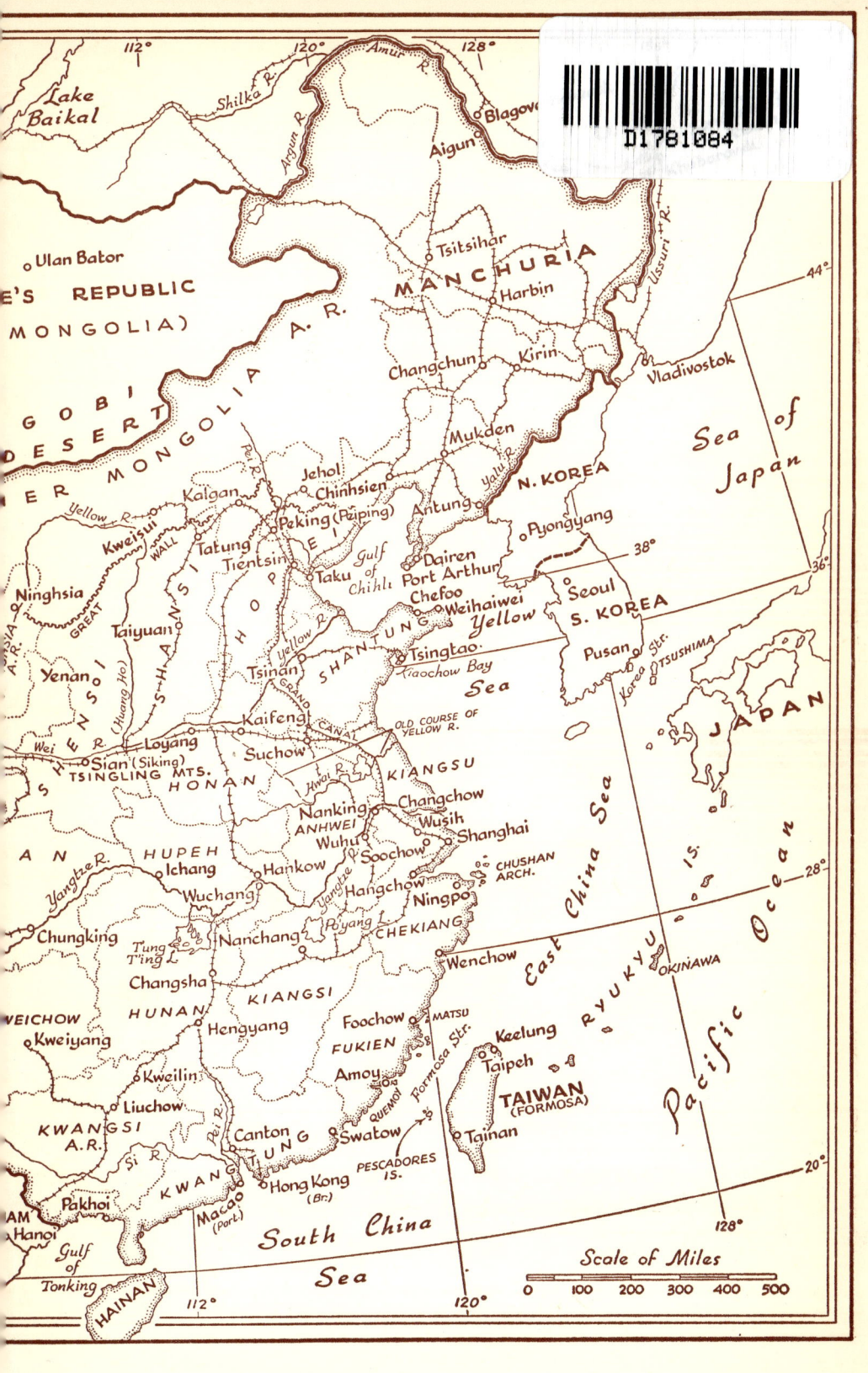

CHINA, JAPAN AND THE POWERS

A History of the Modern Far East

MERIBETH E. CAMERON
PROFESSOR OF HISTORY
MOUNT HOLYOKE COLLEGE

THOMAS H. D. MAHONEY
ASSOCIATE PROFESSOR OF HISTORY
MASSACHUSETTS INSTITUTE OF TECHNOLOGY

GEORGE E. McREYNOLDS
LATE PROFESSOR OF HISTORY
THE UNIVERSITY OF CONNECTICUT

WITH A FOREWORD BY
KENNETH SCOTT LATOURETTE

Second Edition

THE RONALD PRESS COMPANY · NEW YORK

Copyright © 1960, by
THE RONALD PRESS COMPANY

Copyright, 1952, by
THE RONALD PRESS COMPANY

All Rights Reserved.

No part of this book may be reproduced in any form without permission in writing from the publisher.

Library of Congress Catalog Card Number: 60-7761

PRINTED IN THE UNITED STATES OF AMERICA

To

Miriam McReynolds

Leonard Paul Mahoney

and

the memory of *Anne Appleby Elliott*

FOREWORD

It is a pleasure to greet the revised edition of *China, Japan and the Powers*. The fact that it is called for is evidence both of the usefulness of the original edition and of the growing interest in the United States in its trans-Pacific neighbors. Events in China, Japan, and Korea have moved so rapidly in the brief years since the book first appeared that it has been no small achievement to summarize them in a few pages while keeping a sense of perspective in stressing the more important over the ephemeral trends. In accordance with their purpose in the initial edition the authors have emphasized the political aspects of the story and the relations with other powers, especially with the United States. Yet they have also given some hints of other aspects of the story, including particularly the economic factors. The book can be heartily recommended to those who wish background for an understanding of the situation in that part of the world.

For several decades the United States government and Americans have had a more active and continuous interest in the internal and foreign affairs of China and Japan than, until recent years, they have had in those of Western Europe. At first sight this seems strange, for by race and culture most Americans are much more closely related to Europe than to China and Japan. However, viewed from the perspective of history, the contrast is understandable. Coming from Europe as the ancestors of most Americans did, and for the most part to escape conditions which bore hard upon them, they tended to think of the Old World as evil and wished to avoid entanglement in its affairs. Such, indeed, was the warning of the first President of the United States to his fellow countrymen, a conviction which again and again across the years found expression in other mouths.

On the other hand, the westward urge which carried Americans across the continent caused them to cast interested eyes onward across the Pacific and led them to view hopefully and longingly the opportunities for trade and investment in the Far East. They also developed early a benevolent concern for the peoples of those lands. Although fearing a large influx from these Far Eastern nations, Americans wished to provide an opportunity for them to share on their own soil whatever advantages Christianity and Western culture had to offer, and to help preserve their freedom from the aggression of both neighboring and distant powers.

This combination of motives led to an increasing involvement of the United States in the Far East. Beginning with the occupation of the Philippines in 1898, the United States has held territory in the western Pacific. For about forty years after 1900 American armed forces were continuously in China. It was by way of the Far East that the United States was drawn into World War II. With the end of hostilities, the United States assumed a larger share of the responsibility for the occupation of Japan than she did for any country in Europe, with the exception of Greece. It was in China late in the 1940's that, through the triumph of the Communists, the United States suffered the greatest defeat in her history. In Korea she bore the brunt of the resistance of the United Nations to Communist aggression.

In spite of these facts, the majority of Americans still know less about China and Japan than they do about Western Europe. It is gratifying, therefore, that this survey of the history of China and Japan, and especially of those phases which bear most directly upon the entanglement of the United States in their affairs, has now been brought up to date. Here is a volume which can be used either for courses in colleges and universities or by the thoughtful general reader.

As will be obvious to all who give the book more than cursory examination, the authors have consistently sought to tell the story in the fashion and from the perspective epitomized in the title. They have given in brief but admirable proportion a summary of the pre-nineteenth century history and culture of the two countries which are their primary concern. Some understanding of that background, it need scarcely be said, is essential to any intelligent appraisal of recent and current events. The authors then sketch the impact of the Occident upon the Far East in the nineteenth and the fore part of the twentieth centuries and the revolutions wrought by that impact. As is proper for an American audience, they pay special attention to the participation of the United States. As is also right, with the coming of World War II they expand their account to narrate in greater detail those events in which the United States played a part fraught with decisions and deeds momentous for the future for Chinese, Japanese, and Americans, as well as for the other peoples of the world.

True to the implications of their chosen title, the authors have concerned themselves primarily with the policies and actions of governments. This is where the interest of most Americans is centered, and to that emphasis newspapers, radio, and the American government contribute. As to the importance of this aspect of the story, there can be no debate. I find myself wishing, however, even while recognizing that no book can be all-inclusive and that much factual information is unavailable, that the authors could have carried through the proportion maintained in the pre-nineteenth century section of their book and told us more of what the impact of the West has meant in such matters as religion, thought, education, customs, and social institutions, especially the family. They have given us some of this, more than is to be found in many surveys of the history of the Far East. Also, they have been able only to hint at the extra-governmental contacts between Americans and the peoples of China—the activities of merchants, the thousands of American Christian missionaries, the effects of American movies, the vast flood of Chinese and Japanese students that has poured through American colleges and universities and then has eddied back to East Asia. Much of this story has yet to be written in either detailed or comprehensive fashion, but it is of major importance to both the Far East and the United States. Consequently, we are not yet in a position to appraise fairly the full range of the impact upon China and Japan of the Occident and of the United States as a part of the Occident.

The authors have packed the book with information. Here one finds the names of the chief actors and many of the minor ones, with thumbnail sketches of their share in events. To the uninitiated who wish to be told the story quickly and are unwilling to read slowly, this may at first be irritating. Yet it is time that Americans realized that if they are to act wisely in their relations with the Far East, more than a cursory knowledge is necessary.

The authors have made the details palatable with a most alluring literary style. The book is not simply informative. It also beguiles the restive reader with a turn of phrase, an aptly chosen word, or a vivid descriptive passage which arrests attention if, annoyed by some unfamiliar name, his mind may be tempted to wander.

Underneath and behind the refreshing use of English is sound scholarship. Some of this is to be detected in the bibliographies and the footnotes. The authors have not encumbered their volume with complete bibliographies or with the apparatus of full references to the authority for each of their statements. Remembering that this is not a treatise for specialists but a book for those who wish an introduction to their subject, the authors have been selective, choosing those books deemed best suited to the purposes of the student who wishes to go further into this interesting history. Several of the volumes chosen are other comprehensive accounts. Others are detailed studies. Here the authors have shown admirable judgment. Specialists may wonder why some books are included and others omitted, but that is the lot of all bibliographies which do not aspire to be exhaustive. In general, the reader can trust the bibliographies as giving him the essential works. So, too, with the footnotes. Some of these are explanatory of items in the text which otherwise might be mystifying. Others refer to books where pertinent documents or more detailed treatment can be found. These, too, will be welcomed by the reader who wishes to go more deeply into the subject.

Many of the topics dealt with, especially those of the later years, have been the occasion for debate, much of it bitter and highly emotional. On several of these, full agreement will probably never be reached. In general, the authors have avoided becoming embroiled in controversy. They are familiar with the issues, but they have endeavored to be objective. Full objectivity is impossible; historians who claim to have attained it are either dishonest or self-deceived. Yet an approach can be made to the ideal. This the authors have succeeded in doing. In telling their story they have displayed both frankness and admirable sobriety in their treatment of subjects and incidents where opinions of observers have differed.

Here is a book which the reader can trust as a competent, informed, reliable, and engaging introduction to an area in which, for better or for worse, the people of the United States are inextricably involved.

KENNETH SCOTT LATOURETTE

Sterling Professor of Missions and Oriental History, Emeritus
Yale University

PREFACE

Since the First Edition of this book appeared in 1952, the great revolution in Eastern Asia has proceeded at a rapid pace. The two countries specified in the title of this work continue to be the major centers of change, as China under a Communist regime drives toward industrialism and socialism and Japan, released from foreign occupation, seeks her place in the postwar world. Their development in the years ahead will have immense influence on international affairs not only in Asia but throughout the world.

Americans therefore stand more than ever in need of sound understanding of these Asiatic peoples, their cultures, history, past role in international politics, and present dramatic growth. Only with such a background can there be any hope of meeting successfully the many difficult issues which arise from rapid social change in an area so long thought of as "the unchanging East."

This book, originally written to furnish this background, has now been revised to include treatment of the remarkable events of the 1950's. Its main themes are still the relations of the West with Eastern Asia and the revolutionary ferment set up in Eastern Asia by those contacts. The introductory chapters sketch the traditional cultures of China and Japan in their geographic settings. Later chapters trace and seek to explain the processes by which the self-sufficiency and isolation of these two countries were broken down and the development of resulting cultural changes, both planned and spontaneous. The authors have written primarily for the college student but have also sought to interest and serve the general reader. While avoiding elaborate documentation and footnotes, they have attempted to provide sufficient bibliographical aids to introduce the reader to the literature of the field.

The writers wish once more to thank Professor Kenneth Scott Latourette of Yale University for his generosity in reading the manuscript and preparing an introduction both for the original and for the revised edition, and to Professors Earl H. Pritchard of the University of Chicago, Claude Buss of Stanford University, and Edwin Reischauer of Harvard University for their helpful criticisms of portions of the narrative. Full responsibility for errors of fact or of interpretation of course rests with the authors.

The death of George E. McReynolds before this revision was undertaken is a matter of deep regret to his co-authors. His contributions, revised where necessary in the light of later events, remain an integral part of the Second Edition.

MERIBETH E. CAMERON
THOMAS H. D. MAHONEY

January, 1960

CONTENTS

CHAPTER	PAGE
1. China's Land and People	3
2. China's History and Political Institutions	22
3. China's Economic and Social Foundations	46
4. China's Intellectual and Aesthetic Tradition	58
5. Japan: Land and People	78
6. Japanese History and Government to 1867	91
7. Japanese Economic and Social Institutions	118
8. Japanese Religion and Culture	132
9. Sino-Japanese International Relations—Pre-Treaty	149
10. Treaty Pattern for China	163
11. Treaty Pattern for Japan	181
12. China in Rebellion, 1844-1878	206
13. Reaction and Reform in China, 1861-1894	222
14. Japan: The End of an Era	238
15. Japan: Reform by the Few, 1867-1894	252
16. Japan's Emergence as a Modern State	269
17. The Attack Renewed by the West	283
18. China: The Failure of Reform, 1894-1911	306
19. The United States as a Pacific Power	326
20. Russia's Asiatic Interest and Policy	345
21. The Far East in World War I	358
22. China, 1911-1926: Republic, Militarism, and Renaissance	381
23. The U.S.S.R. in the Far East	399

CONTENTS

CHAPTER	PAGE
24. China, 1923-1937: Triumph of the Kuomintang	413
25. Sino-Japanese Relations Between the Two World Wars	441
26. United States Far Eastern Policy, 1919-1941	462
27. Japan: Political Development	499
28. Japan: Economic and Social Progress	521
29. The Far East in World War II and a New Balance of Power	545
30. China 1937-1949: The War and the Triumph of the Communists	556
31. Japan Since Pearl Harbor	577
32. International Relations and the Far East, 1945-1950	598
33. The Korean War and Its Aftermath	620
34. International Relations and the Far East, 1955-1960	642
35. Communist China: The First Decade	658
Index	691

MAPS

	PAGE
China and Her Neighbors	*(Inside front cover)*
Population Density in China	16
A Comparison of the United States and China	19
The Agricultural Regions of China	47
Old Japan	79
Mineral Resources of Japan	87
Tokugawa Japan	109
Population Density in Japan	121
Foreign Possessions, Leases, and Spheres of Influence, About 1900	292
The Japanese Empire in 1933	451
Japan Today	500-501
Korea in 1951	622
Taiwan and the Nationalist Offshore Islands, 1959	643
Communist China	662-663
The Far East	*(Inside back cover)*

China, Japan and the Powers

1

CHINA'S LAND AND PEOPLE

A century and a half ago, one of the greatest states in the world was the Ta Ch'ing Empire, the vast domain in East Asia which had been conquered in the seventeenth and eighteenth centuries by the Manchus. It extended from north of the Amur River in what is now Siberia to Tongking in what is now French Indo-China, and from central Asia to the Pacific Ocean. It was tremendous in size, larger than the United States of today; in 1800 only the Russian Empire surpassed it in land area. In this great empire lived upwards of 300,000,000 people; in population only the decaying Mogul Empire could compare with it. The chief lands included in this empire were Tibet, Sinkiang, Mongolia, Manchuria, and, important above all the others, China, which the Manchus had brought under their control in the mid-seventeenth century. The Manchus recognized the primacy of China in their empire. They had adopted a dynastic name in the Chinese style and were known as the Ch'ing (or Pure) ruling house. They ruled from the traditional Chinese capital of Peking, used the Chinese political system, and in many ways testified to the superiority of Chinese culture. They were the Visigoths to China's Rome, but went even farther in adopting the ways of the conquered.

The Chinese in 1800 could still use with assurance the name by which they traditionally called their country—*Chung Kuo,* the Middle Kingdom, the center of the civilized world. Chinese civilization had a history of 3,500 years, and was unique in its continuity, in the quality of its human achievement and in the number of people included in its orbit. Not only was it the way of life for the 300,000,000 Chinese, but such neighboring peoples as the Koreans, Japanese, and Annamese had imitated it; even its perpetual antagonists, the nomadic peoples of the steppes and forests of central and northern Asia (among them, the Manchus) were perpetually drawn to it, and when conquering China tended to succumb to Chinese ways. Even the Westerners who had seen something of China in the seventeenth and eighteenth centuries were impressed, and their accounts of the virtues of Chinese society had made it the model of the eighteenth-century philosophers, while the charm of Chinese *objêts d'art* had occasioned in fashionable Europe a craze for Chinoiserie. Probably the greatest historical process of today is the revolution in what was the Ta Ch'ing Empire. The Manchus of course are gone, swept away in the great changes which are still continuing in China. China, once the synonym for tradition and stability, is now a byword for rapid social change. It was the impact of the West on China in the mid-nineteenth century which unintentionally and accidentally initiated this process. What China was before the revolution, how that revolution began and developed, and where it is tending today constitutes one of the major themes of this book.

The first step in getting some understanding of China's traditional culture is to assess the physical setting in which the Chinese created their great civilization and in which new China is developing. Resources and climate have been basic conditioning factors in shaping Chinese life; it has been the special reaction of the Chinese to the peculiarities of their physical environment which has made Chinese culture distinctive. Chinese culture, primarily agricultural and developed by very careful and direct adaptation to its physical resources, can perhaps be rather more nearly explained in terms of geographic factors than can the cultures of the technically more elaborate West.

Natural Boundaries and Their Cultural Effects

China has fairly clear geographic boundaries which have defined its limits of expansion, given it comparative security, and cut it off from the rest of the world.[1] To the south and west rise the great Himalaya Mountains and the high Tibetan Plateau. To the north and west are the steppe lands, which are too dry for Chinese agriculture and which shade off into real desert. And to the east the ocean provided until very late in Chinese history a formidable barrier. The land thus enclosed is large, similar in size to the United States east of the Mississippi, and, while neither fully arctic nor fully tropical in its extremes, is influenced by wide variations in climate and qualities of soil.

From the Chinese point of view, these natural frontiers protected them and provided the opportunity to develop a unique civilization, relatively free from interference except by the nomads from the steppes of central

---

[1] For additional information on the geography of China, see such standard works as G. B. Cressey, *China's Geographic Foundations* (New York, 1934) and *Asia's Lands and Peoples* (New York, 1944), chaps. 3-9.

Asia who periodically plundered China but were unable to transform it.[2] Reversing the viewpoint, China was relatively isolated from the rest of the world. The nearness of India to China on the map was an illusion. The ocean, which might have been a channel of communication, was much more truly the salt estranging sea. The Chinese were not a seafaring people, and for centuries Japanese pirates made more effective use of the waters around China than did Chinese traders. Chinese culture did make its way across the narrow straits from Korea to Japan, but on the whole the sea was a boundary, until sea-borne commerce with the Occident became important. This sense of separateness and seclusion gave the Chinese a very exalted sense of their own creativity and originality, which by 1800 had set into smugness and egocentricity.

Yet this isolation and immunity, physical and spiritual, had never been complete. From very far-off times the weak spot in China's defenses, and the channel for interchange of ideas, was what came to be called the Silk Route; this ran out through the panhandle of Kansu Province in northwest China, along the edge of the Tarim Basin in Sinkiang, and so on westward. Barbarian invasions of China came in through the northwest, but so did ideas and techniques, though on the long-term balance sheet it may well prove that China gave more than she got via the Silk Route. Kipling to the contrary, East and West met for many centuries in central Asia, the melting pot of cultures. Just as Chinese silk, paper, and printing made their way to the West via this central Asia clearinghouse, so China in turn received additions to her culture, running all the way from alfalfa to Buddhism. The Chinese throughout their history were not particularly aware of their cultural vulnerability on the northwest; they were more conscious of the northwest frontier as a danger to China's physical security, which they tried to guard by building the Great Wall and by controlling the peoples of the steppe. Sometimes the Chinese dominated the nomads, at others the nomads penetrated China, but in any case the nerve center of old China was in the Northwest, as the traditional location of the capital in such northern cities as Hsianfu or Peking shows. Only when Chinese ruling houses lost control of the North to invaders and retreated below the defense line of the Yangtze River, did Nanking become the political center. When the Occidental "sea-barbarians" exerted pressure on China in the nineteenth century, Chinese economic and political life had to perform another about-face, and China's seacoast replaced the northwest frontiers as China's front door.

[2] For a discussion of the effects of geographic isolation on Chinese culture see K. S. Latourette, *The Chinese, Their History and Culture* (2 vols., New York, 1946), Vol. I, pp. 27-30.

River Systems

Within these well-defined natural frontiers, China as a whole slopes downward from the great Tibetan highland on the west into mountainous territory, then hilly land, and then the seacoast. Through China run three major rivers, rising in the western highlands and running to the Pacific. Of such tremendous importance are these drainage systems that China can almost be described as a land of rivers. Even today Chinese civilization is the child of its great watercourses, much as were the early cultures of Mesopotamia and Egypt.

The Huang Ho. The great historic river of China is the Huang Ho, or Yellow River, in the North. Along its banks and those of its tributaries, Chinese communities first emerged from the Stone Age into the Age of Bronze. The Huang Ho, 2,700 miles in length, rises in the Tibetan highlands, drops into Kansu Province, makes a great north bend around the Ordos grasslands, then flows east only to turn sharply south again to form the border between Shansi and Shensi. In that part of its course, it is a stream of torrents and rapids cutting through the loess highlands. After being joined by two tributaries, the Fen and the Wei, it emerges from the highlands upon the great alluvial plain which it has created and on which Chinese farmers have been living for forty centuries. As it flows across the plain, it carries with it a great burden of soluble loess soil, so that it is literally yellow, a river of mud. It is navigable only for small river steamers; its great significance is in relation to farming. It is a difficult, obstreperous river, which has repeatedly earned its title of China's Sorrow. From the silt which it carries, the Huang Ho builds for itself a bed which is actually above the level of the fields. The Chinese have exercised great vigilance in trying to keep it in bounds, but when floodwaters come, the river may jump or cut its banks, inundate the countryside, and perhaps even completely change its course. Chinese history records at least eight major shifts of course by the Huang Ho. In 1852 the river, which had reached the sea south of the Shantung Peninsula, made a new channel to the north, and during the second Sino-Japanese war, Chinese patriots cut the dykes and let loose the waters. The Communist regime has announced a long-range project to make the Huang Ho tame and navigable by the construction of a great series of dams. Each flood means disaster to the farmers whose lands are inundated and whose crops may be washed away, although the subsiding waters leave behind a layer of fresh rich loess topsoil—a sort of blessing in disguise.

A smaller river of North China is the Pei Ho, on which is located the important port city of Tientsin. Southward from the plain of the Huang Ho is the region of the Huai River. This area, between the two regions of the Yellow and the Yangtze rivers, has been the no-man's land and battleground of Chinese history. It has been fought over not only by man but by the rivers themselves. Long ago that disorderly river, the Huang Ho, pre-empted for a time the lower course of the Huai, which as a result has no proper mouth but finds its outlet in the Grand Canal and so on into the Yangtze.

The Yangtze River. The second of the three great river systems, in order of length of time during which they have been significant in Chinese history, is the Yangtze. The Yangtze is one of the world's great rivers. It is 3,200 miles in length, and is navigable by light craft for 1,600 miles and by good-sized steamers for 600. It rises in the Tibetan highlands. In western China it cuts through famous gorges, which are beautiful to look upon but obstructive to navigation. Then come the great lakes, T'ung-t'ing and P'o-yang, which really act as reservoirs in the summer when the river is at its height. Like the Yellow River, the Yangtze is laden with silt from which it has long been building an elaborate delta, one of the few sizable flat areas in China. As Chinese settlers moved south from the early centers of Chinese culture, the Yangtze area developed in the first millennium A.D. into the great food-producing area of China. In the nineteenth century it assumed new significance as China's commerce with the Occident grew. Shanghai, near its mouth, became the greatest port in China, to which down the Yangtze came the produce of the interior, and from which up the Yangtze foreign goods and ways could penetrate the hinterland.

Rivers of the Canton Delta. Still further south is the third river area important in Chinese agriculture and commerce. Three rivers come together to the sea, and create the Canton Delta. They are the Pei, T'ung and Si rivers. Canton is older as a port for foreign commerce than Shanghai, and the concentration of population on the rich rice lands of the Canton area is great.

The three great Chinese river systems cut down through mountainous and hilly country and eventuate in alluvial plains of their own making, which are virtually the only level areas in China. The Chinese can always lift up his eyes to the hills; China has almost no great plains like those of the American Middle West. The Chinese have terraced far up the hillsides and have gone a long way toward bringing under cultivation all lands fit to cultivate. In area China is vast, but the conformation of much of the land makes it more suitable for mountain goats than for agriculturalists. Population inevitably is very unevenly distributed, with great densities per square mile in the coastal plains and in the Red Basin of Szechuan, and relatively sparse settlement in the mountainous areas which constitute so much of China's territory. In general, the further east one goes, the more low flat land there is and the greater the concentration of people upon it. It is almost as though the great mass of human beings on the seaward edge of China had flattened the land and pressed it down toward sea level.

Mountains

However, although population density varies from east to west, the lines of cleavage in Chinese culture are even more north-south than east-west. This is to a good extent the result of climatic differences. The great conditioning factor which differentiates climate in north and south, and as a result affects agriculture in north and south, is the location of the mountains of China. Of all the many mountains and hills which dominate the Chinese landscape, the decisive group is the Tsingling Range, which crosses the center of China from Kansu to Honan. Like the other mountains of China, the Tsingling Range is an eastward extension of the highlands of central Asia, in this case of the great K'un Lun Range. At their highest, in western China, the peaks of the Tsingling rise well above 12,000 feet; to the east they shade down to heights of about 5,000 feet. A traveler crossing China by air looks to the north on the brown dry land of the yellow earth, and to the south on a green moist world. It is remarkable that the genius of Chinese culture, originating in the comparatively arid north, was able to operate also in the wet and humid south, and that one cultural world and not two resulted from Chinese expansion below the Tsingling barrier. Nevertheless there are marked regional differences which reflect geographical and climatic factors, and which, though they have not permanently split China, have given variety and diversity to its history and culture.

Climate and Regional Divisions

China's climate is the consequence of its location on the Pacific edge of Eurasia. Different weather influences reach it from two directions. The ocean on the east is a source of moisture and heat. The central Asian highlands to the west are a sending area for dry cold masses of air. In the summer come the water-laden monsoonal winds from the Pacific; in the winter come the winds from the west. This means an east-west division; the rainfall so essential to agriculture falls heavily along the coast, while greater aridity and severity of weather characterize the western regions. The Tsingling Range, however, throws across this vertical line of climate demarcation a sharp horizontal. It blocks off the cold winds of the west from South China and deflects from North China the monsoonal rains which bear up from the southeast. Therefore China can be divided into climatic and agricultural regions, with quantity and distribution of rainfall the distinguishing features. A rather elaborate pattern of such regional divisions may be worked out, but perhaps a brief characterization of a few major areas will demonstrate the variations of Chinese climate and agriculture. Each of these regions is larger than any European state. Indeed, granted its local geographical and climatic characteristics, each might have become a separate state. Up to a point, China's history shows the regionalism which reflects the differentiations of topography and climate, but in the long run it reveals the triumph of the centripetal forces in Chinese culture over the obstacles which physical factors have tended to put in the way of unity.

North China

North China may be divided into two regions. In the Northwest along the upper course of the Yellow River are the semiarid loess highlands. In the Northeast is the alluvial plain of the river from which jut the highlands of Shantung; these long ago formed an island, later the silt from the river filled in the gap and made them a part of the mainland. Both regions are drier than the lands south of the Tsingling, but the Northeast is considerably less arid than the Northwest. Both regions are the products of long interaction of two great natural elements, wind-blown loess soil which lies like a blanket over northwest China, and spasmodic irregular rainfall. The Yellow River comes pouring down out of the loess highlands, carrying in solution its burden of loess, ready by flood or irrigation to renew the fertility of the alluvial plain of the Northeast.

Although it may be divided into these two regions, one relatively high and dry, the other relatively low and wet, North China as a whole has certain general characteristics which distinguish it from the South. It has limited and irregular rainfall and is peculiarly liable to drought or flood, and in consequence to famine. It has a continental climate, rather like that of the American Middle West; its winters are cold and dry, its summers hot and humid. Its crops, too, are continental. There is a short growing season for wheat, millet, kaoliang (a kind of sorghum), and beans. In the North, people travel by land on roads which are either dry ruts or wet mud tracks. Everywhere, when it is not the rainy season, there is dust, which wheels through the air in storms and which people taste in their mouths and feel on their skins. The loess dust gives to the North its characteristic color. This is the land of the yellow earth and the yellow river.

The North is not the richest farming region in China today—long ago the rice-producing lands to the south stole that title—but it is the birthplace of Chinese civilization. In the North the Chinese seem to have discovered the secret of perpetual cultivation; they have been farming this land for four millennia or more. This astonishing achievement is the Chinese response to the challenge which the loess soil and the river presented to human ingenuity, and it was on the border line between the two regions of the North, the highlands and the plains, that the Bronze-Age culture of the Shang arose and civilized life in China began.

Northwest China. The dominant natural forces in the shaping of North China have been wind and water, but in each of the two regions of the North one of these two forces has had primacy. In the Northwest the barren mountains rise out of a sea of the crumbly wind-blown soil called loess. The loess covers about 120,000 square miles, including Shensi and Kansu provinces, and parts of Shansi and Honan. Ages ago the loess was blown in from central Asia. It slices like cheese, stands in great walls, and forms a sort of crust, so that the inhabitants of some parts of the loess region live in caves cut out of the sides of the loess walls and farm fields on top of their dwellings. The loess is full of phosphorus and lime and soaks up water like a sponge. The water reaches the minerals, takes them into solution, and makes them available to the roots of plants. Given water, the loess is virtually self-fertilizing and self-renewing, but in the Northwest water is lacking. Rainfall is not only spasmodic but slight,—fifteen inches a year or less,—and irrigation is necessary for agriculture.[3]

The loess area has been the weak spot in China's natural frontier. There is no sharp barrier in the Northwest between China and non-China. Arable land gradually shades off into pasture land, and pasture land into desert. Over these relatively dry lands China, through most of its history, has had its chief contacts with the outside world, until in modern times the sea became a highway and the loess highlands a back country.

Northeast China. In northeast China, loess soil, combined with water, has provided the basis for long-term agriculture. The Yellow River Plain is an area of about 125,000 square miles, one of the few large tracts of arable land in China. The Northeast has more rainfall than the Northwest, an average of 20-25 inches a year. For the farmer on the Yellow River Plain, everything depends on how much rain there is and how it is distributed. If the rain comes in sufficient quantity and at a fairly even

---

[3] See Cha'o-ting Chi, *Key Economic Areas in Chinese History* (London, 1936), pp. 23-26.

pace, the crops will be good. If there is not enough rain, the farmer faces drought and famine. And if the rain comes in a summer torrent which swells the Yellow River to the bursting point, the river will break its banks and pour from its high channel over the fields, and the farmer faces flood and famine. The desire to secure the maximum benefit from the Yellow River while avoiding the curse of flood was one of the causes of the development of organized society in North China, and eventually of the great empire which embraced the whole Yellow River area. Flood could not be counted on to devastate only the fields of strangers or enemies, and "dykes and ditches" had to be maintained by some over-all authority if they were to be effective.

South China

South of the Tsingling barrier, the country is different—lush, green, and wet. South China is a beautiful region, with scenery which has been the inspiration of painters and poets, and with richer agricultural land than the North. The great problem for farmers in the Yangtze area has been not irrigation but the reclamation of lake-bottom land and swamp by drainage. Here canals serve not only to distribute water but also for transportation. The South is a region of rice, tea, mulberry trees, and bamboo. The growing season is long, and more than one crop is possible in many areas. The winters are fairly cool; but in the summer, monsoonal rains and typhoons mean humid, steaming weather. The usable areas of South China are chock-full of people. Labor is in such long supply that men, not beasts, carry and drag loads.

The Lower Yangtze Region. The South may be divided into several subregions. Most important in Chinese economic life is the lower Yangtze region, embracing the great lakes, T'ung-t'ing and P'o-yang, and the Plain of the Huai and Yangtze rivers. The Yangtze Plain is an area of 75,750 square miles and is crowded with people. Many of China's great cities are in the area. Six hundred miles from the mouth of the river is the "Wuhan" cluster—Wuchang, Hankow, and Hanyang—which, because they developed Western factories before any other urban center in China, have been called "the Chicago of China." Other great cities of this region, beautiful and historically important, are Hangchow and Soochow, and the great modern metropolis of Shanghai which in the late nineteenth century sprang from almost nothing at the behest of Occidental traders, and which now has, under the Communist regime, a problematic future. The Yangtze Plain is interlaced with thousands of miles of canals and dotted with thousands of grave mounds. To the North, the Yangtze Plain and the Plain of the Huang Ho shade into each other with no sharp dividing line. In this area the Grand Canal has for centuries connected the Yangtze River with the Yellow River and served to bring the rice tribute of the South to the capital. Southward the Yangtze Plain rises into hilly country with high summer temperature, cool winters, and abundant rainfall.

Southeast China. The southeastern coastal provinces of Chekiang and Fukien have an irregular shore line and a very hilly configuration. They have the heaviest rainfall in China, fine stands of timbers, and handsome scenery. Further south, the two Kwang provinces, Kwangtung and Kwangsi, are not as flat as their names ("Broad East" and "Broad West") suggest. Actually they are hilly and rolling. These southern provinces are nearly tropical in climate and vegetation, with high summer temperatures and as much as 70 inches of rain a year. In Kwangtung, three rivers converge in an elaborately formed delta on which is the great southern metropolis of Canton, and close off shore is the island of Hong Kong on which the British have developed a great port of transshipment to Canton. The Canton Delta, cut off by mountains from the back country and late in coming into the orbit of Chinese civilization, has developed its own special version of Chinese culture, with a distinctive dialect, taste in art and architecture, and cookery. It has a special importance in the history of China's relations with the West, for Chinese trade with Occidentals was virtually confined to Canton before 1842, and the great majority of the overseas Chinese who have prospered all over the world are from the Canton area.

Southwest China. Southwest China, on the other hand, has been almost as much cut off from the outside world as southeast China has been accessible to it. Many times in Chinese history, the Red Basin of Szechuan, far up the Yangtze River beyond the gorges and surrounded by high mountains, has been the seat of a separate satrapy. It was first developed by the Chinese over two thousand years ago during the imperial expansion of the Ch'in dynasty. The Red Basin is a rich region, well suited to agriculture and endowed with resources. It is a land of moderate temperature, rather heavy rainfall, and almost perpetual mist and fog, as its residents discovered during World War II, when Chungking was China's capital. The other southwestern provinces, Kweichow and Yünnan, are exceedingly mountainous; less than 5 per cent of their surface is level. Their natural outlet is south into Indo-China, with which Yünnan has railroad connection. During the war, when access to southwest China from Indo-China was cut off, the Burma Road and airplane flights over "the Hump" were developed as two other means of access to China's interior provinces.

Outlying Regions

The regions around China proper require characterization and comment, since they play their parts, in some cases very important ones in China's recent history. These regions have for centuries had close relations with China; at times they have been under Chinese political control or have, together with China, been parts of a huge empire.

Manchuria. Most closely akin to China is Manchuria—indeed today it may be considered as virtually a part of China proper. Manchuria is the name which Westerners have used for the area which Chinese have called the Three Eastern Provinces. Lying east of Mongolia, it is bounded on the north by the Amur River, and on the east by the Ussuri. It is separated from Korea by the Yalu River, and on the south juts into the sea. In many ways southern Manchuria is like the Yellow River Plain, but it is free from the danger of flood which haunts that area. From Han times on, Chinese edged up into southern Manchuria, forming a Chinese pale. The dominant people in Manchuria in the past, however, were not the Chinese farmers in the South, but the seminomadic peoples who from time to time invaded China. In the twelfth and early thirteenth centuries the Nüchên or Chin people from Manchuria ruled North China; in the seventeenth century their descendants, the Manchus, emulated and surpassed their exploit by conquering all of China. From the mid-seventeenth century until the beginning of the twentieth, Manchuria was almost a vacuum. Most of the Manchus moved down into China to enjoy the conquest, leaving only a few garrisons to watch their homeland. But Manchuria is a rich area, well supplied with good farmland, timber, and mineral resources, and its wealth and strategic location have made it in the twentieth century the center of a great power struggle which will be discussed later.

Mongolia. Mongolia, to the west of Manchuria, is a high tableland. It is divided into Inner Mongolia, that portion near China, and Outer Mongolia. Inner Mongolia is mostly grazing land. Outer Mongolia includes grazing land, forest and the real desert of the Gobi. One of the persistent themes in Chinese history has been the push and pull of Chinese farmers and nomad tribesmen along the line where agricultural land meets grazing land. This struggle, reminiscent of the contest between farmers and stock raisers in the American West, continued until quite recently. The Mongols have been chronically suspicious of the encroachments of Chinese farmers upon their tribal lands and have tried to play the neighboring powers of China, Japan, and Russia against each other to save themselves. Today Outer Mongolia is a republic in the orbit of the U.S.S.R., and Inner Mongolia is being drawn into Communist China.

Sinkiang. Sinkiang or Chinese Turkestan, in central Asia, was given its name of the "New Dominion" by the Manchu conquerors, but its recorded relations with China go far back in Chinese history indeed, to the second century B.C. Sinkiang is rather like a picture frame around a blank canvas. Surrounding it is a ring of high mountains; in the center, in the Tarim Basin, is the Takla-makan Desert. Streams running down from the mountains disappear into the sands, but before they do so, they provide the water to sustain a ring of oasis cities at the foot of the mountains. Through the Tarim Basin, following either the oasis cities of the north edge or those of the south, ran the Silk Route, China's traditional line of contact with the West. Today Sinkiang occupies a strategic position, between China and Russia, and may be one of the testing grounds of the relations between Communist Russia and Communist China.

Tibet. Tibet, "the land of the Gods," is a high plateau, more than half of it at altitudes of over 15,000 feet. It is still perhaps the most remote region on earth. High mountains surround it, the Himalayas to the south, the K'un Lun to the north. From the Tibetan Plateau mountain spurs reach into China, and in the Tibetan highlands China's great rivers have their origins. Tibet first established contact with China about 1,300 years ago. It was a part of the Ta Ch'ing Empire, and has been claimed by Chinese republican governments as a part of China, but Chinese influence there has been slight, even in those border areas of Tibet which have been organized into Chinese provinces as Ch'ing Hai and Hsi K'ang. In 1951 Tibet submitted to the control of the Chinese Communist regime.

Natural Resources

How adequately China was or is endowed with natural resources is a question which can be answered only in terms of the sort of material culture the Chinese have developed. China's natural endowment was quite adequate to sustain for millennia a brilliant civilization of the agricultural, nonindustrial type. For many centuries the Chinese have used metals for weapons, tools, ornaments, and coins, purposes for which their metallic resources were ample. The first modern judgments of China's mineral wealth were favorable. Later estimates were somewhat chilling, but the Chinese Communist regime, which has carried on extensive prospecting in connection with its first Five Year Plan, now makes more optimistic claims. In the past China's use of her resources has been at a snail's pace: if she consumes them at the rate characteristic of modern industrial states, they may, with the exception of coal, not last very long.

Of the three types of power—coal, petroleum, and water—China has only coal in significant quantities. There seems to be little or no petroleum in China proper, though oil deposits have recently been found in Sinkiang and the Tsaidam Basin. Chinese water has in the past been little developed. In coal, China is rich beyond other Asiatic countries. Her coal supplies rank fourth among those of the nations of the world, although coking coal is limited in supply and poor in quality. Even so, China has only one-tenth as much coal as the United States, and a population perhaps almost four times as large. Most of this coal is in the loess highlands and in Sinkiang province, regions which in the pre-Communist period were without modern transportation. Until very recently, only Manchuria and Shantung had combined adequate coal reserves with good transport. Coal has been used for heating in China for a long time, as Marco Polo revealed in his reference to the black stones which the subjects of the Great Khan burned, but it has been used relatively little for industry.

Iron ore, the companion to coal in modern industry, is seriously lacking in China. China has a few iron-ore deposits, some of low grade, and they are not located near coking coal. They would have lasted a long time at China's former consumption rate, which has been estimated at three pounds a year for each Chinese, compared with 350 pounds for each American, but in an industrialized society they will not go far. The best iron ore in China proper is in Chahar, Hupeh, and Anhwei. In Manchuria, the Anshan Works, developed by the Japanese, have been well known. China's supply of such metals as copper, vanadium, nickel, and chromium is small. China consumes great quantities of silver, but produces little. On the other hand, China is rich in tin and tungsten and dominates the world market in antimony. Despite the commitment of the Communist regime to the development of heavy industry, it may well be that China is better fitted for the growth of light industry, since she does not have within her own borders the wherewithal for development into another United States or U.S.S.R.

The Chinese People

One resource China has in almost excessive abundance—people. Just how many Chinese there are is difficult to determine. For centuries Chinese dynasties gathered census returns, but since the census data were used for taxation, there probably were always evasion and misreporting. The general census which was completed in 1953 set the number of Chinese at approximately 600,000,000, far above the Communist government's own earlier estimate of 475,000,000, but in line with estimates made

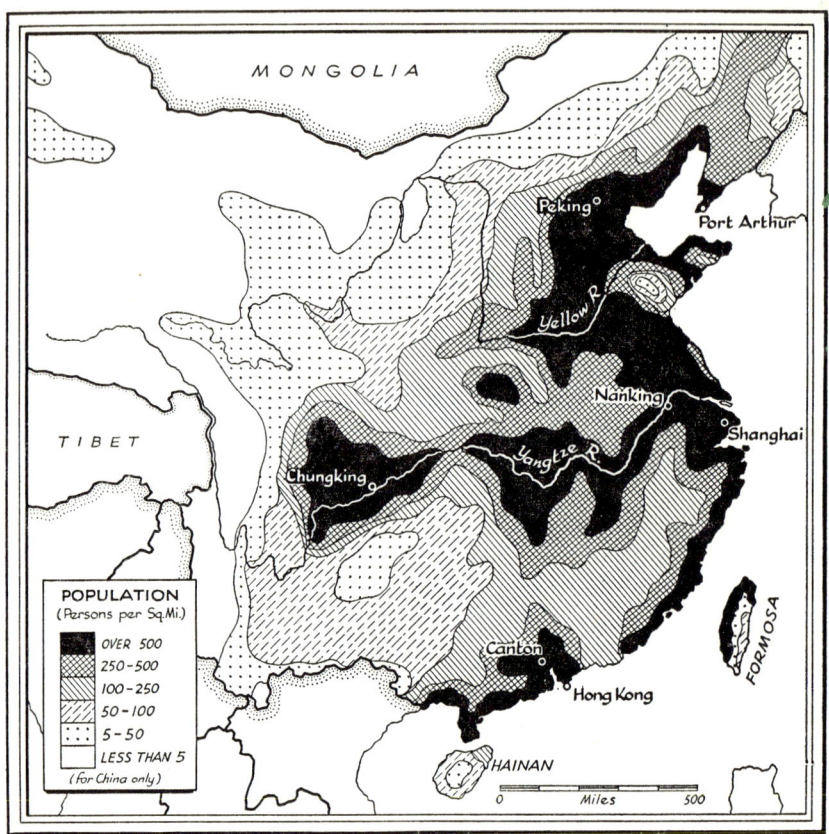

Population Density in China

by J. L. Buck in connection with his studies of Chinese land utilization. Careful students of Chinese demography believe that this huge population with its rapid rate of growth may be a comparatively recent thing.[4] During the past 280 years, China's population seems to have grown greatly. In 1710 there were perhaps 140,000,000 Chinese, a population comparable to that of the United States in 1950. By 1800, there were 300,000,000, more than twice as many as in 1710. By 1850 the number had risen to 342,000,000, and during the past hundred years there has been a tremendous increase, following a curve of population development like that of western European countries during the early stages of the Industrial Revolution. Experts

---

[4] See J. K. Fairbank, *The United States and China* (Cambridge, Mass., 1948), pp. 39-43.

gloomily project this continued increase into the future. Indeed, the Chinese Communists, who have estimated the annual increment of population at close to 15,000,000, were therefore, in 1957, contemplating the rather un-Marxist position of advocating birth control.

There is no simple explanation of this phenomenon, of course. In the earlier Manchu period several factors were at work to produce population increase. The Chinese had learned the use of sorghum, maize, the sweet potato, and the peanut, crops which added to the variety of the diet and could be grown on poorer land or in rows between other crops.[5] Once the Manchus had established themselves, the eighteenth century was a period of peace and order, during which the Malthusian check of war was hardly operative. Later, trade with Westerners, and improvement in medical care and sanitation as a result of contact with the West, helped still further to increase the population. The Chinese death rate has declined but the birth rate has not, and despite war, flood, famine, and disease, the number of Chinese continues to increase steadily and rapidly.

As already suggested, the population of China is very unevenly distributed. A small portion of China's area is packed with people, despite the fact that China is predominantly a rural rather than an urban community. Probably not more than 20 per cent of the population live in cities. There are four Chinese cities with populations of over a million— Shanghai, Peking,[6] Tientsin, and Canton. The British Crown Colony of Hong Kong and the city of Mukden in Manchuria, outside of China proper, also have populations, mostly of Chinese, which run into seven figures. In addition to these great metropolitan centers, there are many cities of second rank, such as Hankow, Foochow, and Soochow, and in each agricultural area there is a fair-sized market town as a nucleus. Even with all this, the vast majority of Chinese are farmers, living in tiny villages and working the soil. If they are crowded in some areas of China with a density which surpasses that of many Western urban areas, it is because the extent of arable land in China is limited. The general average of about 120 people to the square mile for China as a whole is not remarkable, but in the fertile river deltas and in the Red Basin the crowding is extreme. It has been estimated that on every square mile of cultivable land in China there are about 1,500 Chinese.

In physical makeup the Chinese, despite their huge number, appear today to be a relatively homogeneous people. Their general physical

---

[5] L. C. Goodrich, *A Short History of the Chinese People* (New York, 1943), p. 217.

[6] Peking means "northern capital." In 1928 the capital was moved to Nanking, "southern capital," and the name Peiping, which means "Northern Peace," was substituted. The Communist regime has changed the name back to Peking (Pei-ching).

characteristics put them in the Mongoloid group: they have straight black hair, scanty beard, black or brown eyes, long, slender hands and feet, and the Mongoloid eyefold, which Westerners think of as a slant in the set of the eye but which is really a fold in the eyelid. The earliest skeletal remains which have been found, going back far into the prehistoric periods, suggest to many anthropologists that the inhabitants of China in very remote times were of the same physical type, though evidence of physical continuity between those early "pre-Chinese" and the Chinese of today is still lacking.

Granted certain general characteristics which make it fairly easy to identify a Chinese, the people themselves display regional physical differences corresponding roughly to the districts into which the country can be divided. Northerners tend to be taller, longer-headed, and fairer in skin than southerners. Whether these differences are "racial" is not certain; they may be the result of differences in climate and diet. However, the history of the Chinese people certainly shows the possibility of mixture of physical types. In fact, two of the chief processes of Chinese history may well have made the Chinese a very mixed people.[7] One is the steady southward expansion of the Chinese people from the Yellow River region. This expansion was carried on at the expense of the aboriginal inhabitants of the South. Today, especially in Kweichow and Yünnan, there are non-Chinese groups such as the Lolo and the Miao, who are now backward hill folk, pushed into the uplands long ago during the advance of the Chinese. However, exogamous marriage and the reckoning of the family through the male line made it easy to take barbarian wives and concubines, and the Chinese undoubtedly intermarried and intermixed with the aborigines. Even so, it would be difficult to prove that all the barbarians whom the Chinese met and conquered in their southward progress were racially different from the Chinese. They may have been simply backward cousins who had failed to develop the higher culture of the Chinese. It is also possible that the Hakka, a distinct group in Fukien and Kwangtung, are descendants of early Chinese invaders, for their dialect still resembles the Mandarin speech of the North.

Another cause of physical mixture may be found in the long-term relations of the Chinese with the nomadic peoples to the north and northwest. The Chinese have made no careful ethnographical study of their perpetual opponents to help us define their physical character. They appear in Chinese history at various times under various names, but their behavior toward the Chinese has not changed much for two thousand years or more. They were the people of steppe or forest, who

[7] See Chi Li, *The Formation of the Chinese People* (Cambridge, Mass., 1928), p. 275.

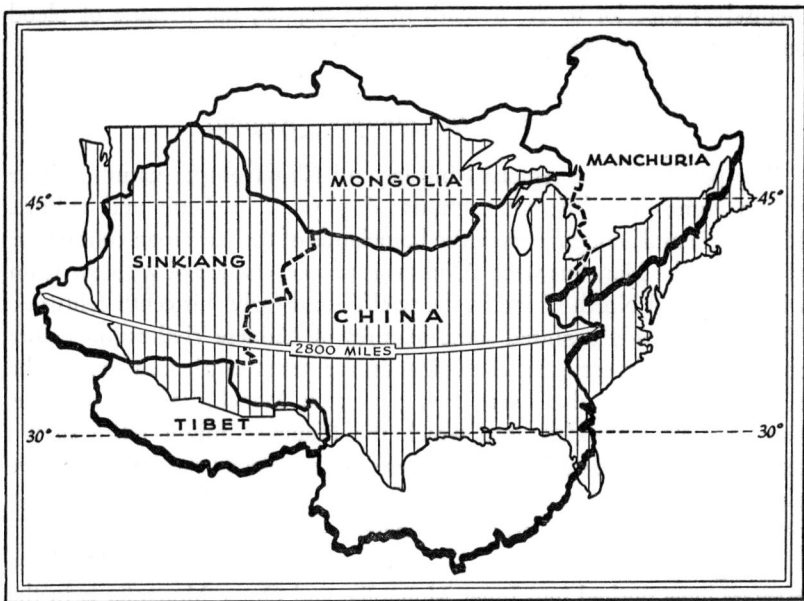

A Comparison of China and the United States, exclusive of Alaska and Hawaii

had evolved a distinct way of life in adjustment to their environment. Sometimes they raided and conquered in China; at other times they were kept at bay or brought to heel by strong Chinese dynasties. These peoples, the Hsiung Nu, Hsien Pei, Hsi Hsia, Liao, Chin and Mongols, must all have added something to the physical makeup of the Chinese. The Manchus, when they became rulers of China, tried to prevent intermarriage, which they felt had sapped the military strength of early non-Chinese ruling groups. In recent decades, Manchus have been intermarrying with the Chinese and have largely lost their identity as a people. The large Moslem group in northwest China shows some distinctive physical characteristics which indicate a strain of non-Mongoloid blood from central Asia. However, far more important than finding any answer to the beclouded question of race, is recognition of the durability and continuity of Chinese culture, which has made the Chinese, physical mixture though they may be, a remarkably unified people. The Chinese themselves have long recognized the relative unimportance of race and the overwhelming importance of culture. They have accepted as a civilized human being, as one of themselves, anyone who has understood Chinese ways and behaved like a Chinese. The Chinese have felt themselves superior to the nomads of the steppes, not because of blood but because of superior social and ethical wisdom.

Peoples of the Outlying Regions

The peoples of the regions lying beyond China proper naturally have shown somewhat different patterns of physical makeup and culture. Manchuria and Mongolia were the homelands of the barbarian conquerors of China. The Manchus were a Tungusic people, connected with the Chin who had ruled North China in the twelfth and early thirteenth centuries. They had already acquired some features of Chinese civilization before completing their conquest of China in the seventeenth century. In the nineteenth century they were trying to keep Manchuria as a preserve, very sparsely populated, into which the Manchus might retire should the Ta Ch'ing dynasty lose the Chinese throne. Today the Manchus have almost vanished as a distinct people, and Manchuria has more than 30,000,000 inhabitants, nearly all Chinese.

Mongolia is still inhabited largely by the original Mongols, but Chinese farmers have pushed into Inner Mongolia, and Outer Mongolia is in the Soviet orbit. The Mongols will certainly never be world conquerors again; they may even have great difficulty in maintaining their nomadic way of life. Sinkiang, as one might expect from its location as a crossroads, contains a melange of peoples, the majority of whom are Moslems, many of whom are of non-Mongoloid stock. The Chinese appeared in Sinkiang as outsiders and overlords. In the eighteenth century, the Manchus acquired Sinkiang and in 1884 established it as a nineteenth province. The people of Tibet are of various physical types, some closely related to the South Chinese. Their geographic isolation has put on them the mark of a distinctive culture, in which the dominating institution has been the Lamaist Buddhist faith.

No sketch of the peoples of China is complete without some reference to the overseas Chinese. Most of them or their ancestors emigrated from South China, from the vicinity of Canton, Swatow, or Foochow. They are found in large numbers in southeast Asia and adjacent islands, and in smaller numbers elsewhere. They have usually remained closely knit groups with a strong sense of continued connection with China. They have shown a keen interest in Chinese politics and have had the money to back up that interest. In southeast Asia where they have been successful, efficient, prosperous businessmen, they have not been beloved, and the nationalist movements of that area have usually turned against them as one of the foreign, even semi-imperialistic elements, in the local scene.

SUGGESTED READINGS

The standard works on geographical characteristics and natural resources, on which the author has especially relied, are two books by George B. Cressey, *China's Geographic Foundations* (New York, 1934) and *Asia's Lands and Peoples* (New York, 1946). Other useful studies are L. Dudley Stamp, *Asia* (London, 1933) and *Asia, a Regional and Economic Geography* (London, 1938); Hans W. Weigert and Vilhjalmur Stefansson (eds.), *Compass of the World, A Symposium on Political Geography* (New York, 1944); Chi Ch'ao-ting, *Key Economic Areas in Chinese History* (London 1936); Daniel R. Bergsmark, *Economic Geography of Asia* (New York, 1944); David N. Rowe, *China Among the Powers* (New York, 1945); Walter H. Mallory, *China, Land of Famine* (New York, 1928); J. L. Buck, *Chinese Farm Economy* (Chicago, 1930); F. H. King, *Farmers of Forty Centuries* (Madison, Wis., 1911); H. F. Bain, *Ores and Industry in the Far East* (New York, rev. ed., 1933). The best historical atlas of China is A. A. L. Herrmann, *Historical and Commercial Atlas of China* (Cambridge, Mass., 1936).

The following works deal with population problems and the physical characteristics of the Chinese: Ta Chen, *Population in Modern China* (Chicago, 1946); Chi Li, *The Formation of the Chinese People* (Cambridge, Mass., 1928); L. H. D. Buxton, *The Peoples of Asia* (New York, 1925) and *China, the Land and the People* (Oxford, 1929).

On the outlying regions, see Owen Lattimore, *Manchuria, Cradle of Conflict* (New York, 1932), *Pivot of Asia, Sinkiang and the Inner Asian Frontiers of China and Russia* (Boston, 1950), and *The Desert Road to Turkestan* (London, 1928); Langdon Warner, *The Long Old Road in China* (New York, 1926); Sven Hedin, *The Silk Road* (London, 1938); Sir M. Aurel Stein, *On Central Asian Tracks* (London, 1933); R. C. Andrews, et al., *The New Conquest of Central Asia* (New York, 1933); Charles Bell, *Tibet, Past and Present* (Oxford, 1924); Schuyler Cammann, *The Land of the Camel. Tents and Temples of Inner Mongolia* (New York, 1951).

2

CHINA'S HISTORY AND POLITICAL INSTITUTIONS

The Origins of Chinese Civilization

No existing country has a longer or more impressive history than China. Because the Chinese themselves, as venerators of their ancestors, early developed an interest in the writing of history, the past 2,500 years of Chinese history are recorded and preserved for us more satisfactorily than is the corresponding history of Europe.[1] Unfortunately, but not surprisingly however, reliable Chinese historical records do not take us back to the beginnings of Chinese civilization. How did Chinese culture, for centuries the inspiration of all eastern Asia, originate? How did the Chinese emerge from relatively simple and undifferentiated Stone Age life to the particular path which they traveled for so many centuries?

Chinese myth, legend, and literary tradition provided a circumstantial account of beginnings, which older generations of Chinese accepted as their Book of Genesis. According to these stories, early cultural heroes who invented such essentials as writing and agriculture, were succeeded by model emperors who served later generations as examples of benevolent governance. The first hereditary dynasty, the Hsia, was supposedly inaugurated late in the third millennium B.C. Eventually its rulers lost their virtue, and righteous rebellion brought to the throne the House of Shang, which ruled from 1766 to 1122 B.C. when, having undergone corruption in its turn, it was replaced by the virtuous House of Chou. These stories of the days before the first millennium B.C. become more human and believable as they advance in time, but they still bear the marks of legend more than of history. Indeed, throughout Chinese history there have always been a minority of "doubters of antiquity," whose efforts until recent times were thwarted by its venerators. In late decades the

---

[1] Among the more scholarly general accounts of Chinese history in English are L. C. Goodrich, *A Short History of the Chinese People* (New York, 1943), and K. S. Latourette, *The Chinese, Their History and Culture* (3d ed., New York, 1946). A longer list of histories of China will be found at the end of this chapter.

doubters have been reinforced by scholars trained in modern techniques of critical scholarship. They have put down the ancient worthies and model emperors from their high estate as historical truth incarnate and have revealed them as compounds of folklore, later utopian philosophizing, and scraps of historical fact. The legends retain importance, not as credible pictures of the beginning of things in China, but as revelations of the problems, attitudes, and standards of the first millennium B.C. when they seem to have taken shape. During the turmoil and civil strife of the late Chou period (c. 550 to 200 B.C.), advocates of reform and reunification bolstered their proposals by claiming for them the support of antiquity, and thus built up a moralized idealized past to which for centuries conventional Chinese looked back as the noblest period of human life.

The doubters' re-evaluation of traditional accounts of early Chinese life knocked a good 2,000 years off knowledge of or supposed knowledge of ancient China, but modern archaeology is beginning to fill this void and reveal to us the people of early China, long forgotten, or remembered only in devitalized moral tales.[2] The archaeological record is full of gaps —work has been interrupted by war and civil strife—and the exact dating of many finds is controversial, but even so the most ancient China begins to emerge from the mist. Only half a century ago, critical scholars regarded real knowledge of Chinese history before the ninth century B.C. as slight: now there is evidence of neolithic, paleolithic, and chalcolithic man, and impressive material evidence of the great Bronze Age culture of the Shang. We now know that the ancient worthies of the high and far off times in China were not benevolent sages, ruling all under heaven by virtue and righteousness, but chariot-riding warriors, who used magnificent bronze vessels, consulted their dead ancestors by scapulimancy and practiced human sacrifice.

It is only comparatively recently that anything has been known of paleolithic and neolithic life in China. It used to be generally assumed that the Chinese had migrated into North China, perhaps from central Asia, at a more advanced stage of cultural development. In 1927 came the discovery which located in China one of the earliest human types— the discovery in a cave near Peking of the remains of a hominid subsequently named Sinanthropus Pekinensis, or Peking Man. Peking Man stands somewhere in the scale between Pithicanthropus Erectus and Neanderthal Man. To some anthropologists he appears to have been

---

[2] The most readily available and interesting accounts of archaeological research and what it has done for our knowledge of Chinese civilizaton are H. G. Creel, *The Birth of China* (New York, 1937), and J. G. Andersson, *Children of the Yellow Earth: Studies in Prehistoric China* (London, 1934).

Mongoloid, which might make him the very remote ancestor of the present-day inhabitants of North China and give the characteristic Chinese physical stock 500,000 years in its present location. Peking Man was on the paleolithic level of existence: he knew how to build a fire in his cave and he had a few crude stone implements, but he lived precariously in a land of saber-toothed tigers, rhinoceri, and other formidable animals which no longer inhabit North China. After Peking Man there is a long gap in our knowledge. Evidences of paleolithic culture, presumably much later than Peking Man, have been found in the Ordos region of northwest China in the gravel under the thick blanket of loess which overlies the region. Another long blank follows, and then there are late neolithic sites which seem to precede fairly immediately the Age of Bronze. Subsequent discoveries may bridge this gap, but it is possible that during the depositing of the great layer of loess, northwest China was too arid for human life.

The two late neolithic cultures which are especially significant in analyzing the beginnings of Chinese civilization are the "painted pottery" culture of northwest China and the "black pottery" culture of northeast China. The human beings who developed the painted pottery culture were physically Mongoloid, but the culture which they developed shows affiliations with western Asia and even eastern Europe. However, the painted pottery did not persist as a feature of later Chinese styles, while the black pottery culture of the Northeast in many ways foreshadows the first full-blown Chinese culture of the Shang. These neolithic, black-pottery-making people of the Honan-Shantung Plain were already at least proto-Chinese in that they lived in walled towns, used pounded earth in construction, made pottery in a distinctive tripod style with fat, hollow legs which the Chinese have used ever since and carried on divination by cracking animal bones—all practices found in the much more elaborate and truly Chinese Shang Bronze Age.

The origins of this bronze culture are debatable and debated. We first see it in full maturity about 1400 B.C., when there lived, near the Yellow River in Honan, the Shang people who made magnificent vessels of bronze, grew wheat, drove chariots with two horses yoked abreast, wrote questions to the dead and the gods, and built elaborate and well-planned towns. Is this culture descended from the black pottery culture? Or are its special features—knowledge of the wheel, a system of writing, and the working of bronze—the result of invasion by a people of superior culture who brought to China the great cultural discoveries of the ancient Near East?[3] Some Shang techniques and patterns seem almost certainly

[3] Carl Bishop inclines to this point of view in *Origin of the Far Eastern Civilizations* (Washington, 1942).

to trace back to the black pottery culture. The skeletons in the great royal graves of the Shang show no non-Mongoloids who might have come in from the Far West. On the other hand, no primitive writing or crude bronze casting has yet been found in China, and the earlier discovery of the wheel, writing, and the use of metals in the Near East opens the possibility of the gradual transference of those skills to China. Some scholars, many of them Westerners, incline to see in the Shang a belated provincial echo of the Bronze Age of the Near East; other Western scholars and many Chinese, determined to preserve for the Chinese a greater claim to originality, have pointed out that Shang bronzes in no way resemble Sumerian bronzes, and that Chinese writing is not a derivative of cuneiform or Egyptian hieroglyphics. Perhaps the most reasonable theory is a compromise. The essential idea of the use of bronze, for example, may have filtered into China from the West. When it reached the black pottery people, sufficiently advanced to make use of it, it was rapidly brought to a distinctive maturity. But whatever their origins, the position of the Shang people at the beginning of Chinese history, and their role as the progenitors of Chinese civilization, are clear.

Shang

There is much in recent discoveries about the life of the Shang which has come as a surprise, even as a shock, to their well-bred Chinese descendants. Their great bronze vessels covered with elaborate interlaced patterns of fragmented animals are the most formidable testimony to the nature of their culture. It was not one of sweetness and light. The Shang rode to war in great chariots to overcome their neighbors who still fought on foot. Their deities (some were deified ancestors of the royal line, others natural forces) were propitiated by great sacrifices of produce and war captives. The Chinese ideographic script, already well developed, was used to write questions on animal bones, which were cracked with heat to determine, from the shape of the crack, the answers of the gods: these questions on "oracle bones" constitute in a sense the archives of the Shang kings. The Shang rulers and the warriors who surrounded them lived in considerable material splendor, on the necks of the mass of the population who still tilled the soil in Stone Age style. Bronze was too precious for tools. It was reserved for weapons, and especially for the great sacrificial vessels which were buried with the dead, for was it not probable that the support of one powerful dead Shang ruler, treated well by his descendants, would be of even greater value in battle than armor and weapons? The pre-moral, harsh flavor of the Shang repels later generations of Chinese bred in Confucian ethics and courtesy, but to their descendants the Shang bequeathed the Chinese system of writing, the worship of ancestors (later inspired with greater moral content), and styles of construction, form, and artistic taste. The Chou Chinese transformed the story of the Shang into a moral tale of the reward of virtue and the punishment of vice; now divested of these legendary trappings, they are revealed as formidable founders who launched a civilization which, though it later became distinguished for its strong moralistic emphasis, continued to owe much to them.

Chou

In about 1050 B.C. the Shang ruling house was overthrown by the Chou, who came from the valley of the Wei and had been under the influence of Shang culture for some time. The Chou kings, eager to give their rule some sanction besides force, announced that they ruled as sons of Heaven, which had withdrawn its mandate from the wicked Shang rulers and bestowed it upon the virtuous princes of Chou. The Chou rulers set about the consolidation of their kingdom by the development of a feudal structure somewhat like that of medieval Europe, but much more deliberately organized and pyramiding more systematically toward the king at the apex. Society was divided into two classes. The mass of the population were peasants tilling the soil; the aristocrats were warriors who, like the medieval European fighting men of a much later day, amused themselves by tournaments (of archery), banquets, feuds, and battles which were conducted, in theory at least, according to an elaborate knightly code. The feudal age in China was lacking however in one of the distinctive features of its analogue in Europe. There was no great all-embracing church with its learned priesthood. Ancestor veneration, the cult of the aristocrats, precluded the growth of a professional priestly class. Each descendant venerated his own ancestors, and the feudal aristocrats were their own priests and men of learning.

By the sixth century, this feudal system showed signs of decline and the late Chou period is a time of troubles, an age of civil war. A gradual and profound economic change was proceeding which outmoded feudalism and pointed forward to a large-scale bureaucratic empire. This economic revolution contributed such elements as the ox-drawn plough, iron tools and weapons, manure as fertilizer, new domesticated animals, and the widespread construction of great irrigation works. These changes, especially the last mentioned, accelerated the rise of independent "national" states in China. As the yield of land increased, surplus man power beyond the needs of farming was turned into labor battalions to construct public works and to build fighting forces for the struggle among the chief principalities. The old feudal pattern of land tenure, and the relations based on it, gave way to individual land ownership and direct responsibility to the state. Merchants developed as a class; new men pushed their way into government office. The atmosphere was not unlike that of late medieval Europe when the national monarchies emerged, shattering the medieval ideal of unity.

The authority of the Chou kings steadily declined. Four great states had developed at the margins of the Chinese world: Ch'i in Shantung; Chin in the north; Ch'u in the south reaching down into the new lands of the Yangtze Valley; and Ch'in to the west. In the center, surrounded by these giants, were the domain of the Chou kings and the territories of the smaller feudal states, which regarded themselves as the custodians of cultural orthodoxy but which were swallowed up as the Period of the Warring States (481-221 B.C.) reached its climax. The successful competitor which eliminated the other major combatants and brought unity to China by the sword was the very unorthodox and semi-barbarian western state of Ch'in, whose ruler in 221 B.C. assumed the vaunting title of Shih Huang Ti, First Exalted Ruler.

The ordeal of Chinese society, from the sixth to the third centuries B.C., was a powerful stimulus to thought, and the Period of the Warring States is also the classical period of Chinese philosophy. The philosophers were not armchair theorists, but physicians full of proposals to cure what looked to them like a diseased social order, however much it may look to us like a society in growth. The chief philosophic schools of China—the Confucian, Taoist, Mohist, and Legalist—took shape in this period of conflicting ideas and conflicting armies. Their original ideas and their subsequent evolution will be discussed later. All were concerned to give advice on statecraft in the hope of winning employment by powerful princes. Most radical and successful in a practical sense were the Legalists who became prime ministers of the state of Ch'in. Rejecting the idealization of the past and the ethical emphasis characteristic of other schools, the Legalists evolved a philosophy of power, uncomfortably like that of modern totalitarianism. The government was to emphasize only two activities, agriculture and war. Freedom of thought, family feeling, mental cultivation and the like were maggots which would destroy the monolithic strength of the state. Legalist statesmen introduced great changes in Ch'in; individual land ownership, taxation levied by the state on every farmer, the use of cavalry, and the development of irrigation works gave Ch'in strength. Ch'in disregarded the amenities and decencies of the old feudal code, made war "like a wild beast," and won.

Ch'in

The attempt to extend the Ch'in system of government to all China was short-lived, but drastic while it lasted. Ch'in Shih Huang Ti and his Legalist prime minister, Li Ssŭ, tried to destroy the feudal nobility and substitute the rule of a professional bureaucracy. They instituted a harsh system of laws, standardized weights and measures, secured the use of a uniform written script, extended Chinese authority to the south, and linked the walls of the individual states into the Great Wall. The reaction against the Ch'in program was in direct proportion to its rapidity and radicalism. Ch'in Shih Huang Ti died in 209 B.C., and Li Ssŭ was executed in 208 B.C. as a result of a court intrigue. The Ch'in dynasty faded out, and the country was once more ravaged by civil war. Later Chinese historical works, written by orthodox Confucians, have execrated the Ch'in and have stressed "the Burning of the Books," by which the dynasty tried to eliminate "private thoughts" such as those of Confucian scholars, and the Building of the Great Wall, in which intellectuals who did not conform were sent into hard labor. But despite the harshness, narrowness, and brutality of Ch'in rule, many Ch'in administrative devices were better suited to the organization of a large territory through which ran an unruly river than were the particularist ideas left over from feudalism, and in some ways the Chinese imperial state for centuries was the lengthened shadow of the short-lived Ch'in Empire.

Han

The new Son of Heaven, victor in the civil strife, certainly represented the rise of the common man, for he had worked his way up from village constable turned bandit. Under the ruling house which he founded, the Han, China became a vast, prosperous empire to which Chinese long paid tribute by calling themselves sons of Han, *han jên*. The Former or Western Han dynasty ruled from 202 B.C. to 9 A.D., the usurper Wang Mang, reigned until 23 A.D., and the Han house returned to power and ruled as the Later or Eastern Han house until 220 A.D.

At the outset the Han rulers, denouncing the wickedness of Ch'in, attempted a sort of revival of feudalism but found it meant disruption. The gutted skeleton of the Ch'in imperial structure still seemed to offer the best framework for the new, larger, more complex Chinese community. The Han, then, in effect adopted the Ch'in governmental system but carried it on in a different spirit and eventually not in the name of Legalism but of Confucianism.

During the Han period, Confucianism absorbed ideas from rival philosophic systems and became a state cult. There was great activity in reconstruction of the Confucian texts, which had suffered during the Ch'in dynasty and the subsequent civil war. Officials were chosen for their knowledge of Confucian teaching. Formal historical writing began under the Han, with Ssŭ-ma Ch'ien whose great work, the *Shih Chi* or *Historical Memoirs,* covers Chinese history from the beginnings to the first century B.C. During the Later Han, the Pan family composed the *History of the Former Han Dynasty,* setting the pattern for a great series of dynastic histories.

Another great theme in the centuries of Han rule was expansion into central Asia. In the third century B.C. the Hsuing Nu, or Huns, had formed a nomadic confederation as a sort of counter empire of the steppes, antagonistic to the Han. A Han mission into central Asia, 136 to 126 B.C., failed to secure allies against the Huns but brought back knowledge of central Asia which led to the establishment of Chinese overlordship in the Tarim Basin. Chinese control in that area had chiefly military and strategic purposes, but the trade route out to the northwest and through the oasis cities of Sinkiang became the "Silk Route," as Chinese silk started on the long and indirect road to Rome. In time the Hun Empire was broken up, and a portion of the Huns made their way west and erupted into European history.

The Han Empire at first grew tremendously in population until in 2 A.D. it may have been close to 60,000,000. However, it eventually ran through the social and economic sequence which some students of Chinese history have come to regard as a sort of pattern of dynastic rise and fall. Large estates developed, and the social pressure of peasant revolt began to grow. The radical measures of the usurper Wang Mang were meant as a cure for the disease, but like the Ch'in reforms, they brought revolt to a head and led to a tremendous bloodletting. The later Han went through a similar cycle of revival, overconcentration of wealth, and collapse.

The Three Kingdoms and the Six Dynasties

The great Han Empire invites comparison with its contemporary, the Roman Empire, in size, in population, and in achievement. To use Toynbee's terms, it was the universal state of the ancient Chinese world, as the Roman Empire was the universal state of the Graeco-Roman world. Like the Roman Empire, the Han Empire weakened, was preyed upon by barbarians, and broke into a crop of succession states; not until the end of the sixth century did China again achieve lasting unity. The Chinese call the mid-third century the period of the Three Kingdoms, because of the three succession states of the time, and the period from 265 to 689 the age of the Six Dynasties. Actually many more than six ruling houses exercised noticeable control over some sizable portion of China during these four centuries, but in a legitimist spirit Chinese historians recognize as true dynasties only the ruling houses of Chinese blood, whose control during most of the time was limited to the South. In the North, various barbarian dynasties appeared, the most notable of which was the Wei dynasty which ruled in North China from the late fourth to the mid-sixth century.

During this prolonged period of political confusion, Buddhism emerged to play in the Far East a role analogous to that of Christianity in the West. Gibbon might well have called the period of the Six Dynasties another time of "the triumph of barbarism and religion." Buddhism had been imported to China during the Han dynasty but did not achieve widespread popularity until the Six Dynasties period. Buddhism as a doctrine will be discussed later. It is sufficient to say here that during the centuries before its arrival in China it had changed from a severe and austere teaching into a great popular religion of mercy and salvation, and had developed a priesthood, scriptures, temples, and all the appurtenances of mass appeal. Taoism, imitating Buddhism, continued its evolution from metaphysic to magic to popular religion, and became a widespread cult. Confucianism survived as the official doctrine and way of life of the intellectuals. Indeed the comparison with the West does not hold good here: Buddhism did not drive its rivals from the field, and the Chinese came to recognize three complementary and useful teachings as their religious system: Buddhism, Taoism, and Confucianism. It is noteworthy that Buddhism developed no elaborate church government, no authoritarian head, no official definitions of orthodoxy and heresy; while it was occasionally persecuted as antisocial, it was never a serious rival of the state and produced no Innocent III or Boniface VIII.

The political confusion of the Six Dynasties period should not obscure the fact that this was a great time of growth and expansion. As barbarian dynasties occupied the north, many Chinese migrated to the region below the Yangtze River and accelerated the process of occupation and conversion of the south which had been going on ever since Chou times. Buddhism greatly enriched many aspects of Chinese life, and this new version of Chinese culture with a strong Buddhist flavor penetrated to other parts of Asia. Chinese influence in Korea was very strong, and the Japanese received the light of Chinese civilization with tremendous effect upon their development.

Sui and T'ang

At last, in 589, the short-lived Sui dynasty reunited the empire, much as the Ch'in had done long before. The extreme policies of the second Sui emperor—especially the building of the Grand Canal and a series of costly campaigns in Korea—brought widespread revolt such as had overwhelmed the Ch'in. The new ruling house, the T'ang, was to hold the throne for nearly three hundred years (618-907) and to recreate the glory of the Han. The country was pacified and reorganized into provinces, education was encouraged, and a system of civil service examinations was put into effect. The T'ang became a great cosmopolitan empire. Its power reached far into central Asia until, in the eighth century, it was driven back by the spread of Islam. In its capital Ch'angan (the modern Hsianfu), one might find people from all parts of Eurasia and churches of many denominations—Nestorian Christian, Zoroastrian, Manichaean, Moslem—to serve their religious needs. Taoism and Buddhism both had dynastic patronage for a time, but Buddhism was later persecuted as withdrawing both allegiance and wealth from the imperial government. Confucianism continued to be the doctrine of the scholar-officials.

The T'ang age was a great period in Chinese literature, especially in poetry, essay writing, and historical writing. The painting of landscapes is reported to have matured into great beauty, though almost no T'ang originals survive, except Buddhist paintings. Block printing, one of the great inventions, was perfected, and employed chiefly for Buddhist and Taoist works. By the later eighth century, the T'ang dynasty had passed its zenith, but its first century was so brilliant that South Chinese long called themselves sons of T'ang.

Sung

After a short period during which five brief dynasties came and went, the Sung dynasty was established in 960. Some of the greatest expressions of the Chinese mind and spirit date from the Sung—in painting, in poetry, and in the Neo-Confucian philosophy which made Confucianism into a philosophic system comparable to Buddhist metaphysic. But politically the Sung period brought a series of disasters, as barbarians invaded and took over control in the north. The Hsi Hsia people seized the Northwest; the Liao, or Khitans, took the Northeast. In the twelfth century the Chin, or Juchên, from Manchuria took possession of the North, and in the thirteenth century the Mongols, in a series of campaigns, conquered all of China; by 1280 the Sung dynasty had come to an end. The menace of barbarian conquest stirred one great Chinese reformer Wang An-shih

(1021-1086) to propose a radical reorganization of Chinese intellectual, social, and economic life, but his program was shouted down by orthodox Confucians.

The Mongol Empire

The Mongol conquerors looked upon China as the richest part of their vast empire, which extended from eastern Europe to the Pacific. Kublai, as Grand Khan, set the capital of the Mongol Empire in Cambaluc, near modern Peking. During the earlier Mongol period, while the "Pax Tartarica" was maintained throughout the Mongol lands, China and Europe drew closer than ever before. A few Chinese went to Europe, or the eastern end of the Mediterranean, and a good number of Europeans came to China, drawn by the opportunity for Christian missionary work or, more often, by the possibilities of trade with a country infinitely richer than Europe. Marco Polo, who became a civil servant in China during the reign of Kublai, is the classic representative of these Europeans. His famous book tells much of the empire of the Great Khan, but by implication it tells even more of the relative smallness and insignificance of even such a bustling trading city as Venice when measured by the Chinese scale. Marco Polo, as an official in China, will also serve as a symbol of the methods by which the Mongols ruled China, interrupting the tradition of choice of officials by examination and employing instead "bearded men"—non-Chinese. The Mongols did not last long. The great continental empire broke up about 1330, contact with Europe ceased, and in 1368 the Mongols left China and returned to their tents.

Ming

The succeeding dynasty, the Ming (1368-1644), not unnaturally was nationalistic and conservative. The Ming period is one not of cultural creation but of cultural summing up. Its characteristic achievements were the building of grandiose palaces, the compilation of huge encyclopedias, the manufacture of elaborate porcelains, and the application of a very orthodox set of civil service examinations based squarely on the classics according to the Sung Neo-Confucian commentaries. China was *Chung Kuo,* the Middle Kingdom, surrounded by a ring of dutifully obedient vassal states that paid material tribute in kind and rendered the even more valuable tribute of imitation of Chinese civilization. The only clouds on the horizon were continued trouble with the Mongols, incursions of Japanese pirates, the appearance of Europeans by sea, and the rise of the Manchus to the north.

The Manchus

In 1644 the Manchus, taking advantage of dissension within China, seized the throne. The Manchu house was to reign in China as the Ta Ch'ing dynasty until 1912. It spent its first few years overcoming resistance and consolidating its power. During the eighteenth century it reached its height, and China knew a period of peace and prosperity. The Manchu house was fortunate in having long reigns of men of ability in the seventeenth and eighteenth centuries. The K'ang Hsi Emperor occupied the throne from 1661 to 1722. After the comparatively brief reign of his son, his grandson the Ch'ien Lung Emperor reigned from 1736 to 1796 and continued to direct affairs from retirement until his death in 1799. The earlier Manchu rulers accepted cultural assimilation with the Chinese while banning physical assimilation. K'ang Hsi and Ch'ien Lung were vociferous, pompous, and energetic patrons of Chinese culture. The Manchus employed the traditional Chinese governmental system, reserving certain posts at the top for Manchus. On the other hand, they kept the Manchu military organization of hereditary banners intact, supported the bannermen by rice pensions, and controlled intermarriage of Chinese and members of the "banners" to prevent the disintegration of this military force. Chinese were required to wear their hair in the queue as a sign of submission; but on the whole the conquest once accomplished did not bear too heavily, and the Manchus ruled as much by tact and adjustment as by force.

At the close of the long reign of Ch'ien Lung, China seemed mighty, secure, and self-sufficient. Indeed the Ch'ien Lung Emperor could in 1793 say blandly to George III through his ambassador Lord Macartney:

> Swaying the wild world, I have but one aim in view, namely, to maintain a perfect governance and to fulfill the duties of the state; strange and costly objects do not interest me. If I have commanded that the tribute offerings sent by you, O King, are to be accepted, this was solely in consideration for the spirit which prompted you to despatch them from afar. Our dynasty's majestic virtue has penetrated unto every country under Heaven, and Kings of all nations have offered their costly tribute by land and sea. As your Ambassador can see for himself, we possess all things.[4]

By the mid-nineteenth century no Chinese could speak thus to a representative of His Britannic Majesty, for Britain had defeated China in battle, civil war ravaged the country, and the Manchus were uncertain how long they could hold the Dragon Throne. However, the sad decline

---

[4] Ch'ien Lung's mandates to George III are quoted in H. F. MacNair, *Modern Chinese History, Selected Readings* (Shanghai, 1927), pp. 1-11.

of China in the nineteenth century was probably not entirely the result of the drastic change in foreign relations. Internal decay was under way behind the impressive façade. Both internal decline and external pressure were at work, and the Middle Kingdom of the 1790's was to become by 1890 the Sick Man of Asia.

Chinese Political Institutions

The political system through which, one hundred and fifty years ago, the Manchus were governing China was no invention of their own. It was essentially and traditionally Chinese. In some ways the Chinese imperial bureaucratic state was one of the great political achievements of mankind. Each dynasty had learned early in its rule that it could not "govern the empire on horseback" and had revived the examination system and the use of scholar-officials. The even flow of Chinese life had been interrupted periodically by revolution, but these risings were crude attempts to exercise the popular mandate in the selection of a new group of governors rather than a new sort of government, and each new dynasty tended to use the old system with new personnel. This type of government, bureaucracy tempered by revolution, was suited to the old agricultural, relatively self-sufficient China. It showed up badly in the nineteenth century as China had to face new problems, and by the mid-twentieth century the Chinese enjoyed among Westerners an undeserved reputation for inherent political incompetence because they had not yet found a new political system to fit the new conditions of their existence. Actually any political arrangements under which 300,000,000 people could live peaceful, reasonably satisfying lives deserve respectful study.

In comparison with European feudalism, traditional Chinese government was centralized. As Karl Wittfogel has pointed out, the necessity of water-control to maintain agriculture led to the establishment in China of a typical "hydraulic society," in which a strong central government commanded the labor of the masses on public works.[5] But the traditional Chinese political structure was more amorphous than its European counterpart. Despite Wittfogel's thesis, it is still arguable that Chinese society was stronger than the Chinese state. The essence of China's success in organizing its society was a community held together not so much by power and law as by ethics, ideas, and customs. Ethics and politics were one. The state was conceived of as a vast family.

The Emperor. The emperor, who was the Son of Heaven, was the father of his people and exercised his parental authority through a vast

[5] See Karl A. Wittfogel, *Oriental Despotism—A Comparative Study in Total Power* (New Haven, 1957).

bureaucracy of "superior men." He lived in Peking in the Forbidden City, a walled and moated area, the northern part of which contained the residence quarters of the emperor, empress and imperial concubines, and the southern part state buildings. Later emperors of the Manchu line seldom went farther afield than the Summer Palace, eight miles outside Peking, or the Imperial Hunting Lodge in Jehol.

According to ancient Chinese political theory, the emperor ruled by virtue; if he was unvirtuous, the country would cease to enjoy well-being. Then the word would go round that Heaven was withdrawing its mandate, rebellion would break out, and eventually a new ruling house would mount the throne, incarnating ruling virtue and recognized by Heaven as its legitimate representative—during good behavior. The reality, of course, was not precisely like the theory. The Manchus were emperors by foreign military conquest, not Chinese popular rebellion. However, they chose to subscribe to the "mandate of Heaven" theory and their edicts were full of conventional expressions of the emperor's responsibility to his people. They performed the ceremonies by which the emperor maintained proper diplomatic relations on behalf of the community with Heaven, Earth, the Sun, the Moon, and other natural forces.

Like the Chinese dynasties before them, the Manchus had no rule of primogeniture. The only rule of succession strongly held to was that the new ruler should be of a younger generation than his predecessor so that he could perform the ancestral rites for the deceased emperor in a spirit of filial piety. Palace intrigue and unnatural death often accompanied succession to the throne. (We shall see how in the later nineteenth century the Empress Dowager Tz'ŭ Hsi manipulated the succession so that she could keep her power as regent.) The later Manchu emperors were on the whole effete and feeble palace-bound specimens who gave substance to the theory that Heaven was growing weary of the Ch'ing house. The early Manchu emperors, by ability and energy, were real political leaders; but, in general, custom and tradition circumscribed the freedom of action of Chinese rulers, and the late Manchu rulers did little more than affix the vermilion seal which made an edict official.

Metropolitan Administration. Above all, the emperors ruled through the scholar-bureaucracy, recruited by examination and arranged in an elaborate hierarchy of posts in the metropolitan and provincial administrations. The most dignified body in the Peking administration was the Grand Secretariat, which under the Manchus was chiefly honorary and decorative. The Grand Council, theoretically inferior to the Secretariat, was used by the Ch'ing as a sort of cabinet. It consisted of four or five elderly and seasoned officials who met with the emperor at dawn. Its composition was watched to see that the Manchus, as the ruling people, had a strong voice in it. Next in line came the Boards, traditionally six in number, though in the last years of the dynasty new departments of government were added. Under the Ch'ing, each board had two presidents—one Manchu and one Chinese—and four vice-presidents—two Manchu and two Chinese. The traditional boards were those of (1) Civil Office, which recommended officials for appointment; (2) Rites, which had charge of the civil service examinations as well as important ceremonials; (3) Revenue, which looked after the receipt and disbursement of the revenue which the provinces transmitted to Peking; (4) War, which was in charge of the provincial Chinese forces, but not the Manchu banners; (5) Punishments, a board of appeal from the decisions of provincial courts; and (6) Public Works, which constructed and maintained imperial palaces and important dikes and canals.

The responsibilities of the boards were not elaborate or searching. The chief task of the metropolitan officials was to check up on their subordinates and those in the provincial service. The chief instrumentality for such supervision was the Censorate ("eyes and ears" officials), the members of which were supposed to report without fear or favor on the conduct of all in public office—including the emperor. This feature of the old regime impressed the modern Chinese revolutionary, Sun Yat-sen, so favorably that he made it one of the units of his five-power government.

There were at Peking a number of lesser government offices, among which might especially be mentioned the Hanlin Academy. To it were appointed the highest ranking graduates of the examinations, who found in the literary functions of the Academy steppingstones to other positions. The lack of any office of foreign affairs coordinate with the other major governmental offices is conspicuous, but to the Chinese a century and a half ago this was entirely natural. China had no dealings with other states on terms of equality. The neighboring states were regarded as dutifully obedient vassals (except for the Japanese, and even they had paid tribute on occasion). The vassal states were not under direct Chinese control, but they used the Chinese calendar, aped Chinese ceremonies and customs, notified the Chinese Court of change of ruler or dynasty, and sent valuable gifts in return for which they received gifts of even greater value. Europeans and Americans trading at Canton were supposed to fit into this pattern of overlord and vassal and to be suitably grateful for the opportunity to enjoy contact with Chinese civilization.

The Provinces. China proper was divided into eighteen provinces, increased to nineteen in 1884 when Sinkiang was given provincial status. The provinces in turn were divided into *fu* or prefectures; *t'ing,* which were subprefectures independent of *fu;* and ultimately into districts (*chou* and *hsien*), of which there were about 1,500. In twelve of the provinces the chief dignitary was the Tartar General, commander of the Manchu bannermen stationed there. The actual administrative direction of the province was in the hands of the viceroy or governor or both, and the other major provincial officers were a treasurer, a judge, and, in some provinces, a salt comptroller since salt was a government monopoly, and a grain intendant since tribute was paid in grain. The provinces were grouped in a rather complex pattern. There were eight viceroys, presiding over the following provinces or combinations of provinces (1) Fukien-Chekiang, (2) Hupeh-Hunan, (3) Kwangtung-Kwangsi, (4) Yünnan-Kweichow, (5) Shensi-Kansu, (6) Kiangsu-Anhwei-Kiangsi, (7) Chihli,[6] (8) Szechwan. Except for the last two, each of these provinces also had a governor, and viceroys and governors, who had virtually the same powers, served as a check upon each other. Shansi, Honan, and Shantung had only governors. The provinces had considerable autonomy, so much that they were sometimes referred to by Western political scientists as "satrapies." Below the central administration of the provinces were circuit officials, known as *tao-t'ai* in charge of a group of *fu*, prefects in charge of *fu*, and district magistrates at the head of *hsien*. The district magistrate was usually an official of the seventh rank, and was assisted by officials of the two lowest ranks in the hierarchy, the eighth and ninth. The district was the lowest unit for which officials were appointed by Peking. The district magistrate, who was presumed to be all competent, was the key figure in the governmental system. He was government as the mass of the population met it.

Good district magistrates could do much to persuade the people that Heaven was still with the dynasty, bad ones, the reverse. In fact, in the whole system, which was conceived of as a government of men rather than of laws, the personal quality and behavior of each official were of great importance. There were only about 10,000 officials, or mandarins to use the term which Europeans coined for them, under the Board of Civil Office. About a third of them were concerned with the examination system, the rest with actual government.

The whole situation raises sharply Rousseau's question, "Why do the many obey the few?" Perhaps the answer lies in the Chinese tradition that government should be rather laissez faire in tone. Both Taoism and Confucianism taught that good government was unobtrusive. Very little was expected of or done by the higher levels of government: the collection of taxes, which went chiefly to maintain the court and the officials; the preservation of internal order and security from attack from without;

---

[6] Chihli Province is now called Hopei.

and the maintenance of a few public works—such as canals and dikes—which contributed to the welfare of the basic activity, agriculture. The ordinary man thought of government as something far away, and tended to avoid officials and courts as much as possible. The cement which held Chinese society together was that of family feeling and family organization: in Sun Yat-sen's phrase, China was "a federation of families."

Dependencies. The dependencies were organized somewhat differently than was China proper. Manchuria, the homeland of the dynasty, was divided into three provinces and had a government more like that of China than did the other outlying territories. In Mongolia, old tribal patterns were followed. Chinese control in Tibet operated through Chinese approval of the Dalai and Panchan Lamas, the heads of the Lamaist hierarchy in Tibet, and through an imperial resident stationed in Lhasa.

Law. The contrast between Chinese and Western theories of government was particularly marked in the low value which the Chinese placed on law and the relatively small role which it played in Chinese life. The Confucians had always decried law as an evidence of degeneracy in the community. Only when men lost *li,* or moral standards, did law (*fa*) appear. The Occidental exaltation of law, whether common or Roman, has no parallel in Chinese thinking. There was a code of laws in effect under the Manchus, but it was chiefly criminal and administrative, and represented an echo of Ch'in and the Legalists. Until the nineteenth century, Westerners accepted Chinese laws and courts with comparative equanimity, but as Occidental laws and courts underwent reform, the Chinese system began to seem barbarous and distasteful. Punishments were harsh. Witnesses were often detained and tortured to extort testimony. Torture was also used to extort a confession of guilt which was necessary for conviction. There were no lawyers and no juries. Particularly disturbing to Occidentals was the doctrine of mutual responsibility which contravened the concept of individual responsibility so strongly established in Western law. The Chinese emphatically was his brother's keeper: ". . . nothing which occurs goes unpunished; if the guilty person cannot be found, convicted and punished, then the responsible person must accept the consequences—father, family, employer, village, magistrate, or viceroy." [7]

Equally confounding to Europeans and Americans was the unlegalistic outlook of the Chinese. Not the letter of the bond, but the rule of reason and compromise was the Chinese way. The Occidental who tried to get the full ounce of flesh in the name of his legal rights was regarded by

---

[7] H. B. Morse, *International Relations of the Chinese Empire* (London, 1910-18), Vol. I, p. 115.

the Chinese as a thorough barbarian. Adjustment and fellow-feeling were the means by which the Chinese had achieved a durable and remarkably harmonious social order under conditions of crowding and pressure; and compromise, a somewhat shabby word to Westerners, was to the Chinese the way to survival. As the West became dominant in China in the course of the nineteenth century, this conflict between *li* and *fa* became increasingly significant, with the Chinese under the necessity of producing codes of law copied from the West in order to convince the West that they had any social order worthy of the name.

Finance. The financial system of the Chinese government also stressed adjustment rather than mathematical precision. Government by gentlemen was apparently inconsistent with precise accounting. The basic income of the government was the land tax, paid in cash. This the Ch'ing dynasty had promised in the eighteenth century not to increase. There was also tribute in kind—grain, silk, and copper—which could be commuted to cash. By ancient practice going back to the feudal states of the Chou period, salt was a government monopoly. The collection and transmission of these taxes were characterized by "squeeze." Official salaries were low, really only retaining fees, and it was expected that each official would take from the revenues which came into his office an amount suitable to maintain him and his personal and official dependents in the style to which Chinese society felt they should be accustomed. As the tax revenue passed from hand to hand on its way up through the lower levels of government, it of course shrank, and the metropolitan government received from each province a customary amount, sometimes smaller than usual in bad years, but almost never larger. This rule-of-thumb financial system was to handicap the Manchus in their belated efforts at reform. They did not dare increase taxes for fear of provoking rebellion, and they found no way to persuade officials to put less in their own pockets and remit more to Peking.

Army. The military establishment of the Ch'ing Empire was also in marked and peculiarly unfortunate contrast to that of Western states. The Manchu banners did maintain their integrity as an hereditary fighting force and kept up their military exercises. There were eight banners, each with three subdivisions, totaling perhaps 300,000 soldiers. Not all bannermen were Manchus; some were descendants of Mongols and Chinese who had taken part in the conquest. In the seventeenth and eighteenth centuries, the banners were formidable against other Asiatic armies, as Manchu victories in Nepal and central Asia showed. In the nineteenth century, against troops drilled and equipped in Occidental style, they were ineffective. Besides the banners, of which there were contingents in twelve provinces with the larger number concentrated near Peking, each province was supposed to have a body of "green standards" recruited from the Chinese population. These forces existed largely on paper; the officers pocketed the money for their maintenance and lined up waifs and strays to be counted on review days. The central government winked at the practice, since it was not eager to see provincial officials build up efficient military forces which might be used for rebellion. In emergencies, such as the Anglo-Chinese War, irregular levies called "braves" were formed. They proved able only to turn and run.

This state of things reflected a general Chinese attitude toward soldiers and the use of force. The Manchus were a warlike people, but their Chinese subjects were not. Although the Manchus were encamped in China as a conquering force, they realized that they would last longer if they governed through the traditional Chinese system of civil service examination and bureaucracy; under that system the writing brush was uniquely mightier than the sword, and the civil official looked down on his military counterpart. The Manchus set up military examinations, which involved trials of strength as well as knowledge of military literature, but ambitious Chinese families preferred to head their sons toward careers in the civil service. Common soldiers were regarded as virtually the lowest form of life. One of the most noteworthy and perhaps not one of the happiest changes which has come as a consequence of Chinese contact with the West is the altered status of the military.

Corruption. One more contrast in government, not as great perhaps as self-righteous Westerners tried to make out, was in the matter of corruption in official life. By Chinese standards, many practices at which Westerners looked askance were not corrupt. Presents, percentages, and family understandings were all part of the Chinese social system. An official had obligations to the government, to be sure, but he had other and perhaps even more important obligations to his family. Nevertheless, there were unwritten but well understood limits on the business of plundering the public to enrich the family, and by the nineteenth century there were many officials who overstepped those limits and were extortionate and unethical. Such relative depravity among officials was a usual portent of dynastic decline.

As conscienceless officials squeezed their subordinates and the population under their rule and invested their takings in land, bitter dissatisfaction arose against the interlocking directorate of officials and landed gentry, antidynastic organizations developed, and revolution was on the way. In the nineteenth century the Manchus passed into this period in their evolution as a ruling power. The government even contributed to the increasing degeneration of official standards by selling official titles.

On the whole, however, the dynasty was aware that an unduly greedy officialdom could ruin the dynasty by bringing on rebellion. It took time-honored measures to block officials from developing centers of personal influence. All appointments from that of district magistrate up were made directly from Peking. No official was allowed to serve in his own province, and three years was the normal term in any post. The censors watched for evidences of malpractice, and officials jealously checked on each other. The real danger signals of corruption and oppression came from below. An extortionate official who got far out of bounds in his demands and in his inequities might be faced with a popular boycott as a gesture of protest, and the government would promptly transfer or demote him. In this case and in the ever-present possibility of rebellion, there was in the Chinese government an element of crudely expressed but real popular control, and wary officials kept one ear to the ground to listen for rumblings of popular discontent.

Civil Service Examinations. Despite these weaknesses and the many differences from Western practice which were not necessarily weaknesses in the abstract but proved to be handicaps in dealing with powerful Occidental states, the Chinese politico-social scheme was in many ways an impressive achievement. One of its more distinctive features was the civil service examination system; this implemented the Confucian idea of the social responsibility of the educated man. Government was the noblest human activity, superior men should participate in it, and the examination would select the superior men. The examination system was the matrix in which was shaped the greatest of all bureaucracies. It was based on the somewhat questionable but natural assumption that thorough knowledge of Confucian writings would lead to thorough practice of Confucian ethics. What the examinations sought to detect was not technical skill, which the responsibilities and functions of Chinese government hardly called for, but high human quality. The curriculum for the prospective official was the corpus of Confucian literature, dating back to before the Christian Era, and the Sung Neo-Confucian commentaries.

The examination mill was an elaborate one which ground slow but exceeding fine. There were four series of examinations, in each of which the candidate must pass before being admitted to the next. First came the district tests, then examinations in the prefectures, and then, once every three years, very rigorous examinations in the provincial capitals. At the climax were the triennial examinations in the national capital, including a special examination in the presence of the emperor. The man who passed the prefectural tests received the degree of *hsiu tsai* (flowering talent) and might fill certain minor posts, the graduate of the provincial examinations was a *chü jên* (promoted man) and was eligible for more important posts. Those who passed the metropolitan examinations were *chin shih* (entered scholars), fully qualified to enter the *cursus honorum* of public office; and those who did well before the emperor went into the Hanlin Academy. The whole process was very rigorous. On the average during the Ch'ing dynasty, 1,810 Chinese and 254 Manchus passed in each session of the provincial examinations, and 234 secured the *chü jên* degree at each triennium.

Few places are more impressive than the courtyard of the Confucian Temple in Peking where stand the tablets with the names of the metropolitan graduates of many centuries. It is no wonder that the eighteenth-century Western philosophers praised China as the land where philosophers ruled. Government service, and learning as the key to it, had tremendous prestige. Those who failed the examination tried again and again in the hope of getting the red strip on the door, the flag on the pole, and the button on the cap which were the marks of scholarly success. However, the Chinese examination system did not create an ideal republic of letters. That it really sifted out the men of highest intelligence and greatest public spirit is open to question. It certainly put a premium on good memories, fine calligraphy, feeling for the niceties of conventional literary style, and nervous stamina. But the examinations were stereotyped: the candidate had to compose in a rigid literary form the eight-legged essay, and what brought success was scrupulous adherence to this form and a wealth of literary allusion. The system tended to eliminate the original and creative, some of whom probably would not have been happy in the civil service anyway. What emerged from the examinations was a standardized group, all the members of which had the same mental furnishings, a singularly homogeneous upperclass united by knowledge and tradition.

Theoretically, access to this charmed circle was open to all except for the scum of the earth, such as actors, servants, private soldiers and convicts. Actually, the scholar-gentry could perpetuate itself, since official families could give their sons better education and a better chance to pass the examinations. Yet the examination system was, in theory at least, a sort of protodemocratic element, worthy of note in the debate as to whether any peoples except those of Europe and America can achieve democracy. Confucian theory stressed individual development through education and the chance for anyone to become a superior man. The examinations provided a ladder by which the individual could climb from bottom to top by his ability. The examination system was thus the great element of social mobility and the great safety valve in China: it provided equality of opportunity, the career open to talents, the chance for intelligence to get into government. When, as in the nineteenth century, the safety valve ceased to work and the examination system became corrupt and office-holding was in practice more and more limited to the sons of officials, the pressure for revolution would pile up rapidly.

The Right of Revolution. The tradition of revolution may be regarded as another protodemocratic element in the old Chinese governmental sequence. Chinese political theory was at variance with the doctrine of divine right. The emperor was the Son of Heaven and the first servant of the state. He ruled by the will of Heaven and "Heaven sees as the people see, Heaven hears as the people hear." Long before John Locke formulated the concept for Western political thought, the Chinese had believed in government by the consent of the governed and the right of revolution; but they failed to evolve the idea of majority rule and the techniques of balloting and of legislative assemblies. Their only way of expressing lack of consent was boycott or rebellion, their only way of getting a new government, a successful rebellion. Armed rising was a crude alternative to a general election, but the Chinese used it over and over again as a means of getting, if not a new system of government, at least a new deal in governors. This tendency periodically to resort to force to change the personnel but not the system won for the Chinese the title of the most rebellious but least revolutionary of peoples. Chinese revolution, old style, was essentially an agrarian rising. When in the course of Chinese events too few people had too much wealth, the signs of trouble began to appear—boycotts, secret societies, local risings—a ferment in the countryside. Until recently there has been no burgher-merchant group or urban proletariat to play a significant revolutionary role in the Marxist sense. The peasant, when pressed too hard, has become bandit and then rebel, a point which is worth remembering in considering the Chinese revolution in the mid-twentieth century. In the early nineteenth century the Manchus were losing the support of many of their subjects. Even if there had never been the crisis with Britain, which in so many ways marks the beginning of a new period in Chinese history, the Manchus before long would probably have been forced off the Dragon Throne by old-fashioned Chinese rebellion.

SUGGESTED READINGS

There are a number of general histories of China in English, some of the better of which are: L. Carrington Goodrich, *A Short History of the Chinese People* (New York, 1943), which stresses cultural rather than political development; K. S. Latourette, *The Chinese, Their History and Culture* (3d ed. rev., New York, 1946), reliable and substantial, and *The Development of China* (Boston, 1929), a shorter account; C. P. Fitzgerald, *China, a Short Cultural History* (London, 1935); René Grousset, *Civilizations of the East, China*, trans. from the French by C. A. Phillips (rev. ed., New York, 1941); Richard Wilhelm, *A Short History of Chinese Civilization*, trans. from the German by Joan Joshua (New York, 1929); Owen and Eleanor Lattimore, *China, a Short History* (New York, 1947); Wolfram Eberhard, *A History of China from the Earliest Times to the Present Day* (Berkeley and Los Angeles, 1950); H. F. MacNair (ed.), *China* (Berkeley and Los Angeles, 1946), a symposium on different phases of China's history and culture; Sophia H. Chen Zen (ed.), *A Symposium on Chinese Culture* (Shanghai, 1931), which contains essays by well-known Chinese scholars; E. T. Williams, *China Yesterday and Today* (New York, 1923), a discursive but interesting account by an American Foreign Service officer; S. Wells Williams, *The Middle Kingdom* (2 vols., New York, 1901), pioneer American account of China, first published in 1848. L. C. Goodrich and H. C. Fenn, *A Syllabus of the History of Chinese Civilization and Culture* (4th and rev. ed., New York, 1947) contains a useful outline and suggestions for reading.

A few works of the many which deal with special periods or problems in Chinese history: Carl W. Bishop, *Origins of the Far Eastern Civilization: a Brief Handbook* (Washington, 1942); H. G. Creel, *The Birth of China* (New York, 1937) and *Studies in Early Chinese Culture* (Baltimore, 1937); J. G. Andersson, *Children of the Yellow Earth: Studies in Prehistoric China* (London, 1934); Henri Maspero, *La Chine Antique* (Paris, 1927); Chi Ch'ao-ting, *Key Economic Areas in Chinese History* (London and New York, 1936); Derk Bodde, *China's First Unifier: a Study of the Ch'in Dynasty as Seen in the Life of Li Ssŭ* (280?-208 B.C.) (Leiden, 1938); C. Martin Wilbur, *Slavery during the Former Han Dynasty* (Chicago, 1943); Nancy Lee Swann, *Pan Chao The Foremost Woman Scholar of China, First Century A.D.* (New York, 1932) and *Food and Money in Ancient China* (Princeton, 1950); Homer H. Dubs (trans.), *The History of the Former Han Dynasty*, by Pan Ku (2 vols., Baltimore, 1938, 1944); Owen Lattimore, *The Inner Asian Frontiers of China* (New York, 1940); Marcel Granet, *Festivals and Songs of Ancient China* (New York, 1932); Woodbridge Bingham, *The Founding of the T'ang Dynasty* (Baltimore, 1941); Karl A. Wittfogel and Feng Chia-sheng, *History of Chinese Society: The Liao* (907-1125) (Philadelphia, 1949); H. R. Williamson, *Wang An-shih* (2 vols., London, 1935-37); Franz Michael, *The Origins of Manchu Rule in China* (Baltimore, 1942); Arthur W. Hummel (ed.), *Eminent Chinese of the Ch'ing Period, 1644-1912* (2 vols., Washington, 1943, 1944), a biographical dictionary; Carroll B. Malone, *History of the Peking Summer Palaces under the Ch'ing Dynasty* (Urbana, Ill., 1934).

On traditional governmental institutions see Pao Chao Hsieh, *The Government of China, 1644-1911* (Baltimore, 1925); H. B. Morse, *The Trade and Administration* of the Chinese Empire (London, 1908); S. Wells Williams, op. cit.; H. S. Brunnert and V. V. Hagelstrom, *Present Day Political Organization of China* (Shanghai, 1912). The most comprehensive account of the civil service examinations is that by Etienne Zi, *Pratique des Examins Litteraires en Chine* (Varietés Sinologiques No. 5, Shanghai, 1894). The legal code of the Ch'ing dynasty was translated by Sir Thomas Staunton, *Ta Tsing Leu Lee* (London, 1810). A good study of Chinese law is Jean Escarra, *Le Droit Chinois* (Peiping, 1936). Wittfogel, Karl A., *Oriental Despotism, A Comparative Study in Total Power* (New Haven, 1957) is an elaborate statement of an interesting theory of "hydraulic societies" with particular reference to Chinese government and economics.

3

CHINA'S ECONOMIC AND SOCIAL FOUNDATIONS

Chinese Agriculture

One hundred and fifty years ago, Chinese society was predominantly agricultural, industry was at the craft-guild level, and capitalism was only a latent potentiality. Most of the people were farmers in blue cotton, the *lao pai hsing* ("old hundred names"); land was the essential form of wealth. This description would still hold good for the early twentieth century, though by that time Western economic enterprise had modified Chinese life in various ways, such as the building of a few thousand miles of railway, the growth of such great foreign trade cities as Hong Kong and Shanghai, the development of a class of Chinese middlemen handling business between foreigners and Chinese, and the westernization of the tastes and methods of certain groups in the port cities. But even with these changes, the great mass of the Chinese were still, before the establishment of the Communist regime, farmers in the old manner; their chief concerns were flood and famine, landlords and money lenders, and grasping officials.

The Chinese Communists have been engaged in a great effort to transform Chinese agriculture by collectivization, which will be described later in this book. What will be attempted in this chapter is a characterization of traditional Chinese agriculture. It is difficult to describe it in specific terms, for here, as in other phases of Chinese life, adequate statistical data are lacking. However, an understanding of the historical problems and achievements of Chinese agriculture is fundamental, for these problems, which the Nationalists failed to solve, the Communists are now trying to resolve in their own peculiar way. Even today, about 80 per cent of the Chinese are farmers, while of the remaining 20 per cent many live in market towns and are really closely supplemental to the farm population. This presents a marked contrast to modern Western states, where a much smaller percentage of the population is engaged in raising food.[1]

[1] For material on Chinese agriculture the author has made particular use of G. B. Cressey, *China's Geographic Foundations* (New York, 1934) and *Asia's Lands and Peoples* (New York, 1946) and Gerald Winfield, *China, The Land and the People* (New York, 1948).

The Agricultural Regions of China

Adapted by permission from George Cressey, *Asia's Lands and Peoples*. Copyright 1944 by the McGraw-Hill Book Company, Inc.

This overwhelming proportion of the Chinese people has been most unhappily distributed. Since the greater part of China's surface is unsuitable for farming, the greater part of China's population has been jampacked into perhaps 10 per cent of China's area. Farms were tiny—perhaps four acres on the average, somewhat larger in the North where the land is less productive, smaller in the South where an even tinier area can support the same number of people because of double-cropping. At that, farms were often in strips, rather than in one strip, with some land wasted as balks. The land was most intensively cultivated. Chinese farmers carried the use of marginal land to the limit of their method of farming. In the

South the fields were terraced far up the hillsides; in the North, Chinese farmers pushed out into the semidry lands of the steppe. It has been estimated that one-fourth of China's farm land has been terraced and one-half irrigated.

In this situation of many people and little land certain economic and social problems developed. The most conspicuous was poverty, almost unbelievable poverty by American standards of material well being, but poverty, too, by Chinese standards. The average family income was perhaps the equivalent of $150, which customary heavy spending on weddings and funerals cut to an even lower figure. It is not surprising that one of Sun Yat-sen's Three Principles was "the nourishment of the people."

Landownership also constituted a problem. The popular impression, strongly endorsed in the Marxist camp, has been that tenancy was almost universal in China and was a social ill of the worst order. Some careful students of old fashioned Chinese agriculture in certain areas, however, have produced figures to show that in North China, the typical Chinese farmer owned his land, and that in the South, while tenancy was more conspicuous, it was by no means universal and was not necessarily in itself an evil.[2] Taking China as a whole, perhaps one half to two thirds of all Chinese farmers were landowners. This, however, does not dispose of the fact that there was a serious agrarian problem in China, centering around the relations of the relatively large landowners on the one hand and the tenants and small farmers on the verge of tenancy on the other. The landlords occupied a distinctive position in the life of the countryside. They were in a position to take advantage of sharp competition for land. They were often the moneylenders, and since most Chinese farmers operated with a very narrow margin and could be ruined by one bad year of flood or drought, borrowing was frequent and rates of interest were very high. Rents, too, were high. The large landlord was also closely tied in with officialdom—both in the days of the empire and under the republic—and was able to manipulate taxation and recruiting to the disadvantage of the poorer farmers.

Chinese farming was not mechanized and is not apt to be in any very elaborate way. Except in Manchuria, there are no vast areas of open cultivable land on which to operate tractors, as in the United States or the U.S.S.R. Indeed, there were very few farm animals. Chinese farming was virtually market-gardening, carried on in very small plots of land with tremendous expenditure of human energy and time. In some ways the results of the meticulous use of the soil were impressive, for the yield per acre in such crops as rice or wheat was even better than it is in the United

[2] For a summary of these ideas, see Gerald Winfield, *China, The Land and the People* (New York, 1948), pp. 279-83.

States. On the other hand, the yield per farmer was very low, a natural consequence of limited land and almost unlimited human beings. It has been estimated that the American farmer has been about sixteen times as productive as the Chinese farmer. Nevertheless, the Chinese farmer has been a skilful and seasoned agriculturalist, with the accumulated wisdom of forty centuries to draw on. He has not known why he follows the practices that he does, except that they seem to have resulted in good crops year after year. Under this empirical practical technique, Chinese soil has been producing the wherewithal to feed a huge population for many centuries.

The key to China's agricultural success has lain in the use of water. Chinese farmers have had to live with and learn to manage the Yellow and Yangtze rivers. The use of wells, irrigation, and drainage goes far back in Chinese history and has provided one of the great incentives to political unity on a large scale. Even rivers on the rampage have helped to keep Chinese agriculture going by leaving in their wake a layer of fresh topsoil. Crop rotation, with the use of legumes, has been a standard practice. Fertilizer, both human and animal, has aided in maintaining the soil and producing crops, but ironically has also killed many of the human beings who have eaten the food thus produced. Human feces from the big cities are saved, dried, and put on the fields. Every family has saved its own excreta and that of its few animals, including the ubiquitous and useful pig, who, Winfield suggests, is to the Chinese farm as the snail is to the balanced aquarium.[3] All this, put on the soil, has resulted in the prevalence of dysentery, hookworm, and kindred ills. The product is composed largely of vegetables and grains, plus tea, silk, and cotton. The Chinese have never been dairy farmers and have been unenthusiastic about cheese and milk. There has been little raising of animals for meat. It is after all cheaper and more direct to eat the grain than to feed it to animals and then eat their flesh and milk.

So much for the general characteristics of old style Chinese farming. In agriculture, as in climate and geography, there have been marked differences between North and South. North China is a great grain-growing region where the standard crops are wheat, millet, and kaoliang, with soybeans and corn as supplementary summer crops. Rice is, in the North, an imported luxury. The area of the Yellow River Valley and Manchuria to the north is a region of very irregular and comparatively slight rainfall, averaging about 25 inches in the alluvial plain and not more than 15 inches in the loess highlands. The winter is long and cold, the growing season short and hot. Here, wells and irrigation are important. This is the land of yellow earth, yellow silt-laden water, and yellow houses built

---

[3] Winfield, *op. cit.,* p. 64.

of mud. The flatness of the alluvial plain is broken by gravemounds rising in the fields and, in the background, by the bare mountains. In the South, by contrast, rice is king. The environment is the hot moist one which rice culture requires, though on the border line, where the Plains of the Yellow and the Yangtze Rivers shade off into each other, wheat is grown in the winter and rice in the summer; this same sort of mixed agriculture can be found also in Szechwan. On the Plains of the South, the technique of rice growing is one of flooding and drainage. On the hillsides it is terracing to hold water. As one goes farther south, the growing season becomes longer, and two and even three crops of rice are possible. Tea is an important crop in the highlands of the coastal area.

This, then, is the general pattern of Chinese farming by which the vast majority of Chinese used to live. Farmers are customarily viewed as conservatives, but Chinese history indicates that the Chinese farmer, carrying on under tremendous economic and social pressure with little margin of protection against disaster, was easily pushed into banditry or rebellion. To cure his ills the Chinese peasant sought elementary and obvious remedies. He did not try new methods of farming to increase the efficiency of his operations. Instead he wanted more land, lower rents, and release from indebtedness. In a recent phase of the Chinese revolution, the Chinese Communists became the leaders of this agrarian discontent and for a time sponsored measures of the sort traditionally popular with the peasants, such as limitation of rents, limitation of interest rates, and redistribution of land. These measures could be only palliatives—they of course did not increase the amount of arable land. The Communists eventually turned to a policy of thoroughgoing agricultural collectivization, like that enforced in the Soviet Union, except that the large population of China has made mechanization inappropriate. The greatest riddle of the Chinese sphinx, what to do about the unhappy relation between population and food supply, still remains unanswered.

Industry and Commerce

Until the coming of the Communists with their Five Year Plans, industry and commerce in China remained at a much less complex level of development than has been attained in the West. With the exception of a few Western-controlled or Western-style enterprises, Chinese industry remained in the craft-guild stage, and commerce was limited largely to direct sale over the counter by the maker of the article. The Chinese craftsman in the old days had great skill and taste, and for centuries the quality and beauty of China's luxury products exerted a magnetic attraction on traders even from remote parts of the world. In large cities, arrangements for craftsmen resembled those of a medieval Western town. The practitioners of each craft were concentrated in one area—Embroidery Street or Brass Street, for example—with workshops and retail outlets under the same roof. Craftsmen were grouped in guilds to maintain standards, limit membership, and restrict competition. There were provisions for apprenticeship under which lads could learn the trade. The craft guilds were also social and religious organizations and benevolent societies. One of their particular functions was to present a united front to officials and to engineer a boycott if it seemed necessary to resist official exactions.

There were commercial guilds as well as craft guilds. Small villages often had no real shop, but on market days and at the time of fairs, traveling vendors would come to display and sell their wares. The process of bargaining to arrive at a price was characteristic of Chinese business operations and was another indication of the general Chinese tendency to avoid rigid and legalistic precision and to practice compromise and adjustment. The Chinese are skilful traders and shrewd bargainers, as their business successes in southeast Asia and other parts of the world have demonstrated. Nevertheless, capitalism failed to take shape in China, for a number of reasons.[4] From very early times the merchant was regarded as a parasite and a menace. The landlords, who included the scholar-gentry, were the leading economic group; land was wealth. Some of the situations that might have facilitated the rise of capitalism did not arise naturally out of the Chinese social structure. The family operated as a unit in business, and certain types of family favoritism acted against the efficiency of business enterprise. Joint-stock companies did not develop; modern banks did not appear until the nineteenth century. Money, weights, and measures were not adequately standardized.

Transportation

The strong localism of the farmers, centering around the market town, provided little incentive for the development of good transportation. In the North, roads were ruts in the dry season, mud holes in the wet. In the South, boats and canals provided slow transport. In the North a few draft animals were in use; in the South most loads were pulled or carried by human beings. Transport of goods in bulk was not easy, and articles of widespread commerce had to be of small bulk and large value. Until the 1840's, foreign trade was of comparatively minor importance. The Chinese thought of themselves as quite able to satisfy their own needs without importation from abroad. The official view of foreign trade was that the "barbarians" came as humble petitioners in great need of Chinese goods,

[4] See J. K. Fairbank, *The United States and China* (Cambridge, Mass., 1948), pp. 47-53.

and were benevolently permitted to secure them on Chinese terms. The later nineteenth century saw changes in Chinese trade and transport. China lost wars and Western states rose to the ascendant; Chinese economic life became reoriented, as the great port cities on the Pacific seaboard indicated. China ceased to be a supplier of luxuries to the West and became an exporter of raw materials and a potential but poverty-stricken market for Western manufactured goods. In the early twentieth century, buses, steamers, railways, and planes were beginning to improve Chinese internal transport. But these changes came slowly, and it is still easy to appreciate the nature of traditional Chinese economic life—the life of a predominantly agricultural society with a relatively high degree of local and national self-sufficiency—in terms of a relatively simple material standard of living.

Standard of Living

The Chinese standard of living was acceptable enough by eighteenth-century Western canons. Under it a few enjoyed a very comfortable life, although the great mass had little. By twentieth-century Western standards, however, the Chinese lived at a very low level. The great majority existed in poverty, undernourished and ill-housed.[5] In the North, dwellings were built of pounded earth or of brick; in the South, of bamboo wattle, with few windows in either type. The fire from the cookstove ran under the *k'ang* or bed platform and kept it warm. Floors were of dirt. Sanitary arrangements consisted of a sump pit to receive all human and animal excrement. City life offered no greater comfort than that of the country. Clothing was for most people a matter of layers of cotton, with so many cotton-padded garments piled on in the winter that the population seemed to change shape and size completely. The wealthy, however, wore luxurious fur-lined garments. Little meat was eaten except pork and chicken, fish and eggs. In fact, bean curd was the meat of the poor. Vegetables and grain made up the bulk of the diet, and tea was the chief beverage. It was no wonder, under these conditions, that good food was greatly appreciated and feasting was one of the chief forms of pleasure and display.

The shortage of calcium in the usual Chinese diet contributed to the wide incidence of tuberculosis. In fact, the general state of health in China has been very bad, although reliable statistics are lacking. The death rate has been very high, about 27 per thousand compared to 11.3 per thousand for the United States. Infant mortality has accounted for a large part of this death rate. In the old days, measures to promote public health and sanitation were almost unknown. Fecal-borne diseases were rampant, plus tuberculosis, smallpox, diphtheria, malaria, typhus, and diseases of child-

[5] See Winfield, *op. cit.*, chap. 3.

birth. Most Chinese died of ailments which are under control in the United States.

But if the Chinese death rate has been high, so has the birth rate. It has been about 38.3 per thousand as against 18.9 per thousand for the United States. The present average annual increase in the population of China may be as high as 15,000,000, which poses in severe style the great problem of increasing pressure of population on means of subsistence. China's population has been growing ever since the eighteenth century, even before modern contacts with the West. The processes first of westernization and then of communization, as they proceed, mean introduction of health measures which reduce the death rate without corresponding shrinkage in the birth rate, and thus intensify the problem. In the past the Malthusian controls of war, famine, and plague have been obviously and brutally at work in China. The Chinese Communists have talked of birth-control in an effort to stabilize the population, but the case of Japan with its westernized death rate and only moderately restricted birth rate raises serious questions about the efficacy of this proposed solution.

Social Structure

In theory at least, this social pressure, which has periodically resulted in the rising of the poor against the rich, should have been relieved by the relative mobility of Chinese society. Chinese culture has not evolved a rigid caste division like that of India. Confucian doctrine strongly emphasized individual self-cultivation; and the examination system carried into reality the concept of superior status as a reward of merit and achievement, not as a perquisite of birth or wealth. The only bearers of titles of nobility in China in the Ch'ing period were some of the Manchus, plus occasional Chinese who had been ennobled for especially valuable service to the dynasty. At the other end of the social scale, there was slavery for a comparatively small group of house servants. The Chinese peasants who made up the great bulk of the population were not serfs bound to the soil, but landowners or renters. Since the civil service examinations opened the highest positions to all, the social ladder was unbroken, however difficult it was for the poor to climb it.

The Chinese themselves thought of society as divided into groups, ranked in order of their value to society and their consequent prestige. First came the scholar-officials, then the farmers, who were the backbone of society, then the craftsmen, and then the merchants, who were regarded as parasites. The actual class structure was not quite so neatly arranged.[6] Unquestionably the scholar-gentry stood at the top of the scale. Public

[6] See Fairbank, *op. cit.*, pp. 32-41.

office, secured by prowess in book-learning, led to access to the public purse and to political influence which might be very lucrative. The official who prospered from his post bought land and established or consolidated his position among the landed gentry. He saw to it that his sons had the sort of education which might enable them to repeat his success in the examinations and thus preserve the family's status. In many cases this did not come to pass; the ambition and determination of the father did not appear in sons who were spoiled and indolent, and a cycle of from blue cotton to blue cotton in three generations was not uncommon.

The landed gentry, who were officials in another manifestation, provided the key to the entire Chinese political and social system. The officials used the gentry in many ways—to collect taxes, gather recruits for the army, and maintain stability. *They* were public opinion. The peasants, the other significant social group, rented land from the gentry or paid them high rates of interest on loans. The gentry lived in style, though sometimes they found it necessary to have their own armed guards for protection against bandits. As they grew too greedy and rich, and ambitious boys from the lower social levels could no longer make their way up through a corrupt examination system, rebellion would break out. The merchants occupied a relatively insignificant part in this picture. They were little more than hangers-on of the scholar-gentry. Long-continued government policy, shaped by the official-landowner group, had helped to keep the middle class in a distinctly inferior position. From the Chou period on, government had controlled the irrigation works which increased agricultural production, and had held a monopoly in such products as salt, iron, and wine. In some ways Chinese government was laissez faire in spirit, but Chinese officials were chronically suspicious of large fortunes made from trade or industry as being inimical to the interests of the public (i.e., the gentry). The situation was not unlike that in early medieval Europe, but in China there developed no alliance between the monarch and the burghers against the landowners.

The Family System. No sketch of Chinese social life can omit a characterization of the family system. It is easy to oversimplify such a description. Actually there have been many kinds of family in China, and in many cases the size and structure of the Chinese family have been more like those of the Western family than has been realized. However, the distinctive type of family organization, found especially among the well-to-do, was the large family which was virtually a self-sufficient social unit and performed functions which in the West today are often in the hands of other agencies. This type of family was a sizable affair, grandfather and grandmothers, their sons and the sons' wives, and the sons' children, plus other relatives and a good number of servants. It was a closely knit group, with great authority in the hands of the head of the family, who was honored as elder and progenitor. Women were theoretically inferior, but since they were entirely capable of achieving the two great grounds for respect, old age and parenthood, the old grandmother, surviving her husband, was often the most important person in the household.

The family was the cushion which protected the individual against a hard world. For the old and the ill, it provided sustenance and care. It arranged marriages which were essentially socioeconomic arrangements between families. It was a religious institution, the only possible center for the most generally accepted and deeply held of all cults, that of the veneration of ancestors. It was a miniature court, which settled disputes between its members. The village, which might be occupied by families many of whom possessed the same surname, would be governed by a council of family heads. Marriage was exogamous, the family name preceded the personal name, interest in genealogy was keen, and the preservation of the family line was of major importance. Concubinage was common only among the wealthy and was looked upon askance unless the wife was childless and the taking of a concubine might mean the birth of an heir. Adoption was also resorted to in order to continue the family name. Family feeling and grouping of this sort were bedrock for the old Chinese social structure. The free or isolated individual was in an exposed position.

Nothing has been more significant in modern China as a social portent than the crumbling of the old-style family system. Economic changes and the disruption of war struck it hard blows. The tendency of the younger generation to withhold their allegiance from it was a conspicuous part of the general revolt, early in this century, against Confucian teaching, which sanctioned family integrity, filial piety, and respect for old age.

Secret Societies. Another set of social groupings found in China have been the secret societies. In some ways they resembled American fraternal orders. They were characterized by secret vows, ritual observances, and religious features. Two well-known organizations of this sort were the Ko Lao Hui (Elder Brothers) and the San Ho Hui (Triad Society). Originally religious and benevolent associations, these societies readily took on political coloration and became anti-dynastic.

Social Attitudes. One of the surest clues to an understanding of traditional Chinese behavior and attitudes is to be found in an understanding of the Chinese ideas of the significance of *li* and *fa* (law) in human relationships. Westerners in China in pre-Communist days were usually impressed by the formality of Chinese manners and the smoothness of social intercourse. By contrast Occidentals seemed abrupt, direct, and even crude. They inclined to face directly issues which the Chinese coped with by avoidance or diplomacy.

The key concept in all Chinese technique of social relations was *li,* a term which is difficult to translate without distortion, but may perhaps be described in the words of the *Book of Common Prayer* as "the outward and visible sign of an inward and spiritual grace." To say that a man was without *li* was to condemn him as a creature unfit for social life. A part of *li* was a proper self-esteem which showed itself in careful regard for the "face" or self-esteem of others. Quarrel and conflict were indications of undue assertiveness. A rigid stand for one's legal rights showed lack of social perception. Such attitudes went far to produce a flexible social order, in which few differences were irreconcilable and few people were subjected to the humiliation of utter defeat. This skill in preserving the appearance by which men live may well have been the product of centuries of living in large family groups and in a congested country, where the way to survival was through consideration for others rather than by tooth and claw struggle. The use of middlemen, the tendency to bargain, the desire to keep out of the law courts were all a part of this prevailing climate of Chinese society which Occidentals found so strange and which the Chinese Communists wish to change beyond recognition. To the Chinese, *li* used to be what distinguished the civilized man from the barbarian, and the Mongol and the Englishman, both being without it, were equally in outer darkness.

SUGGESTED READINGS

On Chinese agriculture, the author has found most useful George B. Cressey's two books, *China's Geographic Foundations* (New York, 1934) and *Asia's Lands and Peoples* (New York, 1946), and Gerald Winfield, *China, The Land and The People* (New York, 1948). Other valuable studies are J. L. Buck, *Chinese Farm Economy* (Chicago, 1930) and *Land Utilization in China* (Chicago, 1937); F. H. King, *Farmers of Forty Centuries* (Madison, Wis., 1911); Walter H. Mallory, *China, Land of Famine* (New York, 1926); R. H. Tawney, *Land and Labour in China* (New York, 1932), an excellent brief survey; Chen Han-seng, *Landlord and Peasant in China* (New York, 1936); two works by Hsiao-tung Fei, *Peasant Life in China* (London, 1939) and, in collaboration with Chih-i Chang, *Earthbound China: A Study of Rural Economy in Yunnan;* Martin Yang, *A Chinese Village: Taitou, Shantung Province* (New York, 1945), a study of his home village by an American-trained sociologist; D. H. Kulp, *Village Life in South China* (New York, 1925); A. H. Smith, *Village Life in China* (New York, 1899); Pearl Buck, *The Good Earth* (New York, 1931), is a good piece of sociological reporting as well as a good novel.

On industry, commerce, and various aspects of city life, see S. D. Gamble, assisted by J. S. Burgess, *Peking, A Social Survey* (New York, 1921); H. B. Morse, *The Guilds of China* (London, 1909), and *The Trade and Administration of the Chinese Empire* (London, 1908); L. K. Tao, *Livelihood in Peking* (Peking, 1928); Richard Wilhelm, *Chinese Economic Psychology,* translated from the German by Bruno Lasker (New York, 1947).

There have been several recent studies of the Chinese family and the changes which are taking place in it: Marion J. Levy, Jr., *The Family Revolution in Modern China* (Cambridge, Mass., 1947); Olga Lang, *Chinese Family and Society* (New Haven, 1946); Frances L. K. Hsu, *Under the Ancestors' Shadow: Chinese Culture and Personality* (New York, 1948); Han Yi-feng, *The Chinese Kinship System* (Cambridge, Mass., 1948); Lin Yueh-hwa, *The Golden Wing* (New York, 1947), a family chronicle in the form of a novel; J. S. M. Ward and W. G. Sterling, *The Hung Society, or the Society of Heaven and Earth* (2 vols., London, 1925), describes in detail one of the important secret societies. Lewis Hodous, *Folkways in China* (London, 1929), is a good study.

4
CHINA'S INTELLECTUAL AND AESTHETIC TRADITION

The intellectual and aesthetic aspects of Chinese life are notable. It is hazardous to select the greatest achievements of various cultures, but if a very rash generalization is in order, one can profitably contrast the growth of science and the application of scientific knowledge to daily life in the West with the rich development in China of the technique of human relationships and of the arts. The West has sought a precise knowledge of the physical world with the aim of mastering it and using it for man's purposes; China has sought an intuitive, emotional perception of the physical world with the aim of adjusting to it and thus creating a harmonious social order. This desire for harmony, if necessary through adjustment, is deep-rooted in Chinese thinking and feeling. It shows itself in the pervading concern of Chinese literature with ethical problems and the pervading concern in Chinese art and poetry with the forms and patterns of nature.

The Language

Chinese Script. The first clue to the nature of Chinese intellectual life comes with a basic knowledge of the Chinese language.[1] The Chinese written script and the spoken language are both far from the normal linguistic experience of Westerners. Moreover, the two are relatively separate from each other, at least in principle. Spoken Chinese could conceivably be written with an entirely different script, while the Chinese written script could be used to write any other language. This situation results from the fact that the Chinese written character is a pictorial, ideographic script, which is primarily designed to represent meanings rather than sounds, in sharp contrast to the alphabetic system which is meant to spell out sounds on paper. Each system has evolved during its long history: the Chinese written script certainly contains phonetic

---
[1] See Bernard Karlgren, *The Chinese Language, An Essay on Its Nature and History* (New York, 1949).

elements and English spelling is often a far cry from contemporary English pronunciation. Nevertheless, in essence they represent two different means of writing which have different advantages and disadvantages as tools. In the Chinese character, the Chinese possess perhaps the most beautiful, most meaningful, and most difficult of all systems of writing in use today. This system is not the exclusive property of the Chinese. As Chinese culture spread to neighboring lands, unsophisticated peoples who had evolved no system of writing of their own adopted the Chinese method; the Koreans have used the Chinese character except for everyday purposes, and the Japanese employ it in a written script which combines Chinese characters with syllabaries which render sounds.

The Chinese script is an ancient system which goes back to the very beginnings of Chinese civilization to the inscriptions on the Shang oracle bones. Although the number of characters used on the oracle bones is small, they already show a knowledge of every way of composing new characters which the Chinese have used since that time. In their earliest form, some of the characters are clearly pictures: the sun is represented as a disc with a dot in the middle, the "moon" is a drawing of the crescent moon. Other characters combined pictorial elements to convey an idea: "east" is the sun seen behind a tree, for example. More complex principles of forming characters also developed. The result was a written script in which each word was rendered by a distinct pattern made up of meaningful pictorial elements and, in some cases, indicators of pronunciation. The process of learning to read and write is one of memorizing character after character, piling block on block, rather than of learning to sound out new words through knowledge of an alphabet. A reasonable working vocabulary contains perhaps 3,000 characters, but a scholar or specialist will need to know more, and to keep a dictionary close at hand.

To add to the difficulty, long ago Chinese literary style hardened and set into a style (or group of styles) known as *wên li*. This literary style was quite distinct from everyday speech even in the Han dynasty, and by the later Ch'ing period it constituted almost a separate language known only to the educated. In fact, it is possible to write or read *wên li* with virtually no knowledge of colloquial Chinese. This traditional style was extremely terse. Auxiliary parts of speech were almost entirely lacking, and key words were packed close together in what has been described as an endless series of ten-word telegrams, over the interpretation of which the experts could—and frequently did—disagree. Punctuation was almost nonexistent, and would have been scorned by old-fashioned scholars as a crutch which the able-minded did not need. The consequence of the nonalphabetical character of the script and the formidable difficulty of *wên li* style was that real knowledge of the written character became almost a monopoly of that small group who could afford or were determined to manage years of formal study. Literacy became a "mystery," the special knowledge of a small group consisting largely of officials and would-be officials. Thus, the linkage of book-learning with public office through the examination system meant that education had become virtually a professional preparation for public office.

In recent years, Chinese governments have gone over to the Western ideal of mass education, but the written character has been a formidable stumbling block on the road to 100 per cent literacy. There have been numerous attempts to make it easier to learn to read and write in Chinese. The movement to write in the vernacular, sponsored forty years ago by the well-known philosopher and educator Hu Shih, has prevailed. Today all writing is done in the *pai-hua,* the style which follows the grammar and word order of everyday speech, and *wên li* has been relegated to a position similar to that in which Latin was placed in Europe when the vernaculars developed as literary languages. The "1000 Character Movement" of Y. C. (James) Yen was an effort to solve the problem through the selection of a basic vocabulary of the thousand most commonly used characters which adult illiterates could learn fairly easily. A radical course of action would be to substitute for the old system of writing the Western alphabet. The Communists have subscribed to this course by announcing plans for the gradual adoption of an alphabetic script. To be successful, this drastic solution will have to overcome various technical difficulties which stem from the character of spoken Chinese, the opposition of many illiterate Chinese who, ambitious for themselves and their children, think of "reading and writing" as being able to use the beautiful formal patterns of the traditional script rather than the tadpole wiggles of foreign writing, and the unwillingness of educated Chinese, even under the Communist regime, to cut themselves off from their cultural tradition.

Indeed, the Chinese written script is not altogether a liability. It is in some ways *the* link of continuity throughout China's long history, the key to all the past. Diversity of dialect in the spoken language has worked for disunity, but the script was a centripetal force. Everyone throughout China who could read at all read the same script and the same style. Educated Chinese of the late Ch'ing had direct access to the great classics of their culture in the language in which they were written. The change to the vernacular is already making it harder for educated Chinese to use that key, for while they will know the individual characters used in classical Chinese, they will not be familiar with the conventions of *wên li* style. But as long as the characters themselves are retained even though the literary style has changed, Chinese will feel the same sort of kinship to their literary past which modern Italians can feel to the Latin tradition. The Communists, however, are apt to weigh lightly these values of historical continuity and aesthetic significance against the need for a script which will facilitate general literacy.

Spoken Chinese. The Chinese spoken language is likely to be just as surprising to Westerners as is the Chinese written script. Speakers of Indo-European languages can shift stress in a sentence by changing the direction of their voices. In Chinese each word has its own "tone" or inflection, and to direct one's voice down instead of up is to say not the same word with different emphasis but an entirely different one, as many Westerners in China have discovered to their dismay, and to the amusement, politely dissembled, of their Chinese auditors. Tones were probably developed in Chinese as a device to cope with the poverty of the Chinese repertory of sounds and the consequent abundance of homophones. The Peking dialect, known to Westerners as Mandarin and now accepted as the *kuo yü*, or national speech, uses a very limited range of monosyllables, avoiding all consonant endings except "n" and "ng." As a result, even a rather small dictionary may contain several pages of words pronounced alike. Inflection fortunately helps to differentiate them from each other. In addition the Chinese make great use of compounds, so that in practice the language is considerably less monosyllabic than it is in theory. *K'an* for "look" may be confused with many other words pronounced *k'an:* the compound *k'an-chien* (literally "look-see"), bringing together two words which are similar in meaning, eliminates ambiguity. Since each word has its special written character, spoken Chinese is more wordy than the written character needs to be, but vernacular written style tends to follow the redundancies of the spoken word. Grammatically, spoken Chinese is rather free and easy in comparison with many Western languages.

These general hallmarks—(1) inflection, and (2) monosyllables, homophones, and compounds to offset them—characterize spoken Chinese throughout the land. However, there are sharp differences of dialect in different parts of China and though Chinese from Canton and Peking speak the same language, they do it so differently that they can hardly understand each other. The existence of this regionalism in speech has been a factor working against national unity. The Peking dialect already prevails throughout a large part of China, all across the North and down into the Southwest. The speech of the lower Yangtze is noticeably different from that of the North, however, and Cantonese is certainly something else again. The greatest diversity of dialects is found in the hilly country near the southeast coast. In the old days, this Tower of Babel situation was offset by the fact that the written script was one and indivisible and known to all the members of the ruling group, all of whom also learned the Peking dialect, which was the speech of the court. During World War II, the development of radio and the shifting and piling together of refugee Chinese from all parts of the country helped to rub off the rough edges of dialect. This and the recognition of the Peking dialect as the national language may lead to a greater standardization of Chinese speech.

Education

In the past the aims of education in China were very different from those in the West today. The Chinese had no idea of formal schooling as a process by which all inhabitants could be initiated into their cultural heritage and prepared for citizenship. The peculiar nature of the Chinese written language and literature, which was suited to be the property of a few rather than of the many, and the close connection between literacy and public office shaped the Chinese educational process for many centuries. There was no public school system, unless one counted the colleges set up to coach relatively advanced scholars who were already fairly well along in the examination system. The government generally confined its activity to setting examinations for public office and judging the results. Schooling was a local problem, met locally. A benevolent and wealthy inhabitant of a village might endow a school; a clan or a group might employ a teacher; a wealthy household could have tutors for its sons. Girls, of course, did not receive much consideration, since they could not be officials. In ordinary families the girl received from her mother such an education in the domestic arts and skills as would enable her to be a good wife and daughter-in-law. In wealthy families, daughters were often educated by the same tutors who taught the sons. Most boys from poor families had very little schooling. Even if there was a village school, their families might not feel able to afford to dispense with their labor on the farm, or they might go for a year or two and get a mere sample of formal learning. Sometimes a family with meager economic resources might nevertheless be extremely ambitious for a bright son and would make great sacrifices, or else find a patron, to see him through his schooling.

These boys who hoped (or whose families hoped for them) some day to be officials stayed at the business of study, although it was fairly rigorous and dull work. Despite the spontaneous, local character of educational arrangements, the curriculum was remarkably uniform and the method of teaching painfully standardized. Since the purpose of education was to be able to pass the civil service examinations, the content of education was that body of literature upon which questions were asked in the examinations. Therefore the Confucian classics and the Sung Neo-Confucian commentaries upon them became the sum and substance of formal education.

Teaching was not inspired. The teachers, only too often, were unsuccessful scholars who had failed to get through the examinations and were reduced to directing the education of other and perhaps more successful candidates—sad illustration of the idea that those who can, do and those who can't, teach. The technique of learning was rote memory. Often the pupils did not understand the meaning of the words which they repeated parrot-wise, because of the obscurities of *wên li*. Yet despite the formality and rigidity of the process many of the youths who went through certainly had "motivation," to borrow from the vocabulary of American educationalists. The prize was a great one, the chance to enter the most admired and best rewarded of all careers, the official service.

The ambitious and diligent scholar emerged from this process and entered the examination halls literally stuffed with classical learning. The examinations in turn put a premium upon retentive memory, good *wên-li* style, and an aptitude for literary allusions. In Chinese theory at least, the typical scholar, old style, was a frail and bookish creature. Actually a survivor of the examination mill was apt to have good nerves, a vigorous if not an original mind, and energy and ambition. Nevertheless the whole process was a standardizing one: young Chinese of every shape, size, province, dialect and social class went in; at the other end came out a type, the members of which had imbibed a common learning, a common set of professional attitudes and ambitions, and a great self-assurance and inflexibility. This sort of Chinese scholar-official was the bulwark of the old regime until the West hit China amidships; thereafter he became increasingly outmoded and even a liability, like a prehistoric creature whose environment had changed and who could not adapt himself.

Literature

Chinese literature is extensive in quantity and varied in type. After all, the Chinese, or at least the educated among them, have been a reading and writing people for millennia. Even with losses from war, flood, and fire, works of literature in China have been somewhat more likely to survive than they have in the West. The prestige of learning and tremendous respect for the written word have meant an unwillingness to destroy any piece of writing. The discovery of printing and its use for many centuries have kept many literary works from disappearing, especially since filial piety suggested the committing to print of one's deceased father's essays and poems. As a result the accumulation of books in China is tremendous and sets a major task for the scientifically trained cataloguers and librarians of this generation.

Chinese have written in almost every genre. Filial piety and a strong feeling of continuity with the past have particularly disposed them to historical writing. The father of Chinese history, Ssŭ-ma Ch'ien, was a court official of the Former Han whose *Shih Chi*[2]—an account of Chinese history from the beginnings—is remarkable for breadth of view and judicious use of evidence. The Pan family, in the Later Han period, composed the first history of a single dynasty, the Former Han.[3] Thereafter, each dynasty pronounced the judgment of history upon its predecessor by designating a board of historians to prepare its history. The last of these dynastic histories is the draft history of the Ch'ing, written by a group of historians named by the Republic after the fall of the Manchus. The dynastic histories stress biography and annals of events. The twenty-five of them, side by side on library shelves, are an immensely impressive sight. For no other culture is there so continuous and systematic a record over so long a period of time. In addition to the official dynastic histories, there are many historical narratives by individual scholars, and a vast number of gazetteers giving data on the history and antiquities of different localities.

Perhaps the greatest of all Chinese literary achievements is poetry which, with painting and calligraphy, makes up the trivium of scholarly arts. The earliest Chinese poetry which we possess, the collection of poems in the *Shih Ching*,[4] is folk verse, but the great Chinese poetry of later centuries was a sophisticated and fully developed art, involving patterns which surpassed the sonnet in complexity. Chinese poetry is difficult to translate, but there are some English versions which can give Western readers the feeling of the Chinese originals. Chinese poetry has been traditionally an intensely individual expression of mood and feeling, full of a Taoist-Buddhist sense of quietism and identity with nature.

From T'ang times on, the Chinese were writing short stories and, in Mongol times, full-length novels became extremely popular. Some of them, especially long historical narratives, are full of vigor and interest. However, since these later were written in the vernacular rather than in *wên li,* the scholars regarded them as vulgar stuff, were apologetic when they read them, and used pseudonyms when they wrote them. It

---

[2] A portion of the *Shih Chi* has been translated by E. Chavannes in *Les Memoires Historiques de Se-ma Ts'ien* (5 vols., Paris, 1895-1905).

[3] See H. H. Dubs (trans.), *The History of the Former Han Dynasty, by Pan Ku* (2 vols., Baltimore, 1938, 1944).

[4] Translated by Arthur Waley as *The Book of Songs* (Boston, 1937).

is only recently, when vernacular has prevailed and when Chinese have felt the influence of Western literature, that novels and short stories have achieved prestige. Recently the Communists have been manifesting their characteristic aversion to "art for art's sake" by conferring praise or blame on the literary works of the past in proportion as they do or do not display a sense of the class struggle.

The great adjunct to Chinese literary output, and the great means to its preservation, was printing,[5] which matured as a technique in China in T'ang times. At first used chiefly to reproduce religious materials, by Sung times printing was used for all sorts of literature and for the production of paper money. Chinese printing was and remained blocked printing. The Chinese discovered the use of movable type but it was far less well adapted to an ideographic script than to an alphabetic one. During the Sung dynasty, the Chinese did printing of great beauty and on a wide scale. It seems clear that knowledge of printing made its way from China slowly across Asia, through the Islamic world, and finally into Europe, where the so-called "invention of printing" was in actuality chiefly the introduction of the printing press. However, the use of printing in China wrought no such literary and intellectual revolution as accompanied its expansion in Europe. Printed or not, the Chinese written character remained extremely difficult to master, and the consumers and producers of printed matter were still the scholar-officials.

Philosophy and Religion

Confucianism. Perhaps the key body of Chinese literature to which Westerners should be introduced, if they are to understand China's reaction to the West in the nineteenth century, is the collection of miscellaneous early writings known as the Confucian Classics. The principal literary works associated with Confucius and the Confucian were early gathered into a canon. Its makeup varied from time to time, but under the Ch'ing it consisted of the so-called *Four Books* and *Five Classics*. The body of Confucian literature somewhat resembles the Bible, being an accretion of centuries and containing documents of debatable date and authorship. It is consequently subject to the same sort of higher criticism which has been applied to the biblical texts. In fact, throughout Chinese history there has been a minority of "doubters of antiquity" who scrutinized the classical texts with a wary eye and developed efficient methods of textual criticism. However, most Chinese scholar-officials accepted the Classics as valid documents of the dates traditionally

[5] See T. F. Carter and L. Carrington Goodrich, *The Invention of Printing in China and Its Spread Westward* (2d ed., New York, 1955).

assigned to them, either endorsed and edited by Confucius or written by him or his followers. The Five Classics [6] were (1) *The Book of History*, much of which is now regarded by critical scholars as singularly unhistorical; (2) *The Book of Changes*, a work of divination by hexagrams; (3) *The Book of Poetry*, formerly regarded solemnly as poems of allegorical and didactic value selected by Confucius, but now recognized as a collection of early folk poetry; (4) *The Ch'un Ch'iu*, or *Spring and Autumn Annals*, a sparse listing of events which seems to be a record of affairs in Confucius' native state of Lu, no longer regarded by most scholars as a work in which Confucius himself passed moral judgment upon history; and (5) the *Li Chi*, a work on ritual, which is certainly post-Confucius in actual composition. Besides the Five Classics there were the Four Books, works by the master or his disciples. They were (1) *The Analects*, or *Sayings of Confucius*, which contains for the most part what seem to be Confucius' actual teachings as recorded by his disciples—one of the most influential of Chinese books; (2) the *Book of Mencius*, who next to Confucius is the greatest figure in the school, St. Paul to his Christ; and (3) and (4) two short treatises, the *Chung Yung* or *Doctrine of the Mean*, and the *Ta Hsüeh* or *Great Learning*.

In Manchu times, Confucianism was regarded by the officials and gentry as the chief of the *San Chiao* (Three Doctrines), Confucianism, Taoism, and Buddhism, which all had merit and value as ways of life. In its origins, however, Confucianism was simply one of the philosophic schools which took form in the fermenting time of the later Chou period when the land was full of itinerant diplomats and philosophers, each trying to persuade the princes of the day to adopt his special "way."

K'ung Fu Tzŭ [7] (551-497 B.C.) was the son of a family of small gentry who entered the service of the small state of Lu, eventually lost favor with the prince of Lu, became a wandering philosopher, found no prince willing to rule by his methods, and eventually returned to Lu where he spent the concluding years of his life teaching his doctrines to a group of disciples. Confucius was not a cloistered metaphysician: he was an active teacher who regarded public office as the highest career and teaching as an equivalent of it. Living in a degenerate day, he praised the earlier years of the Chou dynasty and tried to initiate his disciples

---

[6] The standard translation into English of the Five Classics is that of James Legge, *The Chinese Classics* (2d ed. rev., 5 vols., Oxford, London, 1893, 1895). Translations of considerable portions of the classics are conveniently available in E. R. Hughes (ed. and trans.), *Chinese Philosophy in Classical Times* (London, 1942), and Lin Yutang (ed.), *The Wisdom of China and India* (New York, 1942).

[7] Confucius is a Latinized version of his name. The most effective study of Confucius is H. G. Creel, *Confucius, The Man and the Myth* (New York, 1949).

into the sort of humanistic culture which he believed had then existed. Later generations of Chinese viewed Confucius as a conservative who sought to preserve and revitalize the social and intellectual values of the high feudal period. He endorsed many of the institutions which were already well established in China, such as ancestor veneration, the family system, and the rites and ceremonies associated with each important act of life.

Yet Confucius was much more than an earnest conservative bent on returning to "the good old days." He and his followers put new wine in old bottles and led the way in China from the older amoral state of Chinese society to a new ethical age. A reading of *The Analects* [8] leaves a distinct impression of the great teacher, a man of courtesy, poise, considerateness, and wisdom. It was natural that his followers should place great value upon education, by which each human being might develop his personality and become "a superior man." The Confucian ideal of government resembled that of the rival Taoist school in being one of naturalism and noninterference. According to it, the ideal monarch ruled by virtue, pacifying and ordering society by good example and employing superior men in office. A government of men was far preferable to a government of law (*fa*), which became necessary only when men were no longer governed by conscience and social standards (*li*). The state was the family writ large with the ruler as its father, and proper human relationships were the means to a harmonious social order. Society should achieve "the rectification of names": let the father behave like a true father, the son like a true son, the ruler like a true ruler and all would be well.

The early Confucians were redoubtable idealists, advocates of righteousness for righteousness' sake. Of no one was this more true than of Mencius (Mêng Tzŭ, c. 371-289 B.C.), the St. Paul of Confucianism. Mencius was something of a mystic and much more of a metaphysician than were the earlier Confucians. In his teachings [9] the protodemocratic element in Confucianism stands out sharply. He endorsed and gave new force to the old idea of "the mandate of Heaven" first put forth by the founders of the Chou dynasty to justify their triumph over the Shang. A wicked ruler was not a rightful ruler; revolution against him was righteous. Mencius believed in the inherent goodness of men which could be developed and made effective through education, but he insisted that before the people could be educated they must first be fed. Like Confucius before him, he found no patron among the greedy and ambitious princes

---

[8] One of the best translations is that by Arthur Waley, *The Analects of Confucius* (London, 1938).

[9] See Lin Yutang, *The Wisdom of Confucius* (New York, 1938), chap. 11.

of his time, but he did much to strengthen Confucian doctrine and extend its influence.

The other eminent early Confucian, Hsün Tzŭ (c. 298-238 B.C.) was a man of quite different outlook.[10] He was a tough-minded Aristotelian realist, who regarded man as essentially evil. It was his belief, however, that through education good habits could be made to overlay evil impulses, and man could be delivered from a state of nature much like that which Hobbes pictured centuries later. Hsün Tzŭ was closely linked with both Taoists and Legalists, and it was his sort of Confucianism, with its stress on ritual and form as the means to improvement, which triumphed during the Han period. In the long run, however, Mencius, not Hsün Tzŭ came to be reckoned first among the disciples, and the standard interpretation of Confucian doctrine in Ch'ing days derived from Mencius more than from Hsün Tzŭ.

During the short, drastic rule of Ch'in, Confucianism fell into great disfavor. The Confucians with their emphasis upon education, conduct, history, and culture flew in the face of the dominant Legalists, and the "Burning of the Books" and the "Burying of the Scholars" bore hard on them. Han statesmen eventually discovered, however, that a Confucianism broadened to include ideas from other philosophic schools and interpreted in the spirit of Hsün Tzŭ could be an excellent instrument for the ideologic unification of a state of unprecedented size and population. Confucianism became a cult, with sacrifices performed by the emperor at the tomb of the sage.[11] Scholars searched frantically for the texts of the Confucian books which had suffered under Ch'in, edited them, and apparently even composed them anew if originals could not be recovered. Knowledge of this literature, tested by official examinations, became the open sesame to public office. Thus Confucianism made the strange and ironic transition from its beginnings as the teaching of a true gentleman who valued courteous and humane understanding as the way of life to the position of state cult for a tremendous bureaucratic empire. In subsequent centuries, Taoism and Buddhism, both at once more philosophic and more popular in their appeal, became rivals of Confucianism for general favor, but Confucianism remained the doctrine of the scholar-officials par excellence, and dynasty after dynasty discovered that although it could win the Dragon Throne with the sword it could hold it only through the writing brush in the hands of the Confucian literati.

In Sung times, a great reassessment and reinterpretation of Confucianism took place. Buddhist metaphysics, which concerned itself with

---

[10] See H. H. Dubs (trans.), *The Works of Hsüntze* (London, 1938).

[11] The history of Confucianism is well told in J. K. Shryock, *The Origin and Development of the State Cult of Confucius* (New York, 1932).

questions of the ultimate meaning of the universe, became a serious challenge to Confucianism which had remained empirical and disinclined to deal with ultimates. The Neo-Confucians,[12] of whom Chu Hsi (1130-1200) is most notable, developed for Confucianism a respectable and logical metaphysic, and it was this more philosophic version which was standard in the Ch'ing dynasty. Confucianism was not in the beginning and did not really become a religion, though there were times in Chinese history when it approached that position. Confucius was the great teacher, and all educated men were, however remotely, his disciples who paid him the tribute of respect. Under the Manchus, Confucianism was strongly endorsed as the state cult. Its injunctions laid down a pattern of life, urbane, gracious, conscientious, and devoted to the public service—the way of the ethically superior man; and detailed knowledge of these injunctions (though not necessarily the practice of them) led through the examinations to the status of the socially and economically superior man. Confucianism was a pillar of the Manchu dynasty and an important instrument of social control. However, as we shall see, before the end of the nineteenth century scholars came forward to claim that Confucius was not a reactionary but a liberal who cloaked his proposals for reform in traditional garments to make them more acceptable to his contemporaries. Despite its endorsement of the right of revolution, Confucianism had been the handmaid of the supporters of the status quo; the reformers hoped to find in it a sanction for social and intellectual change.

Taoism. The most difficult of the *San Chiao* to characterize and to trace is Taoism. It began as a subtle and lofty philosophy, but by a prolonged process of debasement developed into the Taoist religion which appealed to the masses on a plane of popular superstition. At the same time, philosophic Taoism never died out; it continued as a complement to Confucianism in the intellectual lives of the literate. The official who lived his public life by the formulae of orthodox Confucianism found in philosophic Taoism an escape and release, for reasons which the original teachings of Taoism should make apparent. Tradition names, as the founder of Taoism, Lao Tzŭ (literally "the old philosopher") a contemporary of Confucius and author of the principal Taoist book, the *Tao Tê Ching (The Classic of the Way and Its Power)*.[13] Modern critical scholars question the very existence of Lao Tzŭ and tend to regard the *Tao Tê Ching* as a work of the later Warring States Period, composed

[12] On Neo-Confucianism see chap. 16, by Chan Wing-tsit, in H. F. MacNair (ed.), *China* (Berkeley and Los Angeles, 1946).
[13] See Arthur Waley (trans.), *The Way and Its Power: A Study of the Tao Tê Ching and Its Place in Chinese Thought* (London, 1935).

perhaps even after the other great classic of the school, the book of the philosopher Chuang Tzŭ (c. 369-286 B.C.).

Taoist doctrine was a far cry from the earnest gentlemanly code of the Confucians. The *Tao Tê Ching* is one of the great poetic and mystical books of world literature. Its companion piece, the *Book of Chuang Tzŭ*,[14] wears a more comprehensible face for it employs witty parables and dialogues in conveying its teachings, but it too eludes precise exposition. Essentially Taoism was a "wordless doctrine." Nothing can be taught: understanding comes only through introspection and illumination. Confucianism offered an essentially practical *tao,* or way of life. The Lao-Chuang school, by its very use of the term *tao* to mean the absolute or infinite as well as the "way" by which one may lose one's self in it, transferred the scene of discussion from man to the universe—of which man is only a tiny part. The Taoists stressed the flux and relativity of all things and the need for man to put himself in harmony with nature. The Taoist sage, by following the true *tao* of harmony with nature, would build up within himself such tremendous *tê* or spiritual power that by "actionless activity" he could do all things while seeming to do nothing. With hardly a twist of the wrist, the enlightened disciple of *tao* could accomplish far more than the ordinary Confucian activist, who was eager to get things done but had no real understanding of what was worth doing. The Taoists inclined to oppose formal culture on the ground that it was unnatural. As to government, they held that the true sage would govern without seeming to govern, emptying men's minds and filling their bellies, wiping out distinctions between good and evil, restoring natural simplicity.

The poetic mysticism of the early Taoist teachers unfortunately had illegitimate offspring as well as legitimate perpetuation. The Taoist books, with their poetic view of the universe and their startling use of paradox, were meant to challenge men's preconceptions rather than to explain what to the Taoists could not be explained in words. Unfortunately, however, the idea that the sage could use things, not be used by them, was taken only too literally by later pseudo-Taoists, and by the ending of the Warring States Period there were many magicians and alchemists who claimed, in the name of Taoism, to be able to concoct elixirs of life, transmute base metals into gold, and in other ways defy the laws of nature through supernatural power.

A further stage of degeneration came in the Later Han period, with the formation of a Taoist religion[15] which imitated the trappings and

[14] See Lionel Giles (trans.), *Chuang Tzŭ: Mystic, Moralist and Social Reformer* (rev. ed., Shanghai, 1926).
[15] See W. E. Soothill, *The Three Religions of China* (3d ed., London, 1929).

rituals of Buddhism and, through the centuries, became a catchall for Chinese popular superstition. The priests were generally poorly educated, and the temples were full of images of deities, each of whom had his assignment to deal with some human problem, for a price. The Taoist priests had taken on the administration so to speak, of the Chinese belief in *fêng shui* (wind and water), which assumed the existence of powerful natural forces among which man must walk warily or incur bad luck. The Taoist priests would pick a fortunate site for a house, choose a lucky day for a wedding, or read a horoscope. The intellectuals rather scorned religious Taoism but called on the Taoist priests in certain emergencies, just to be on the safe side. At the same time, philosophic Taoism persisted in the intellectual, spiritual, and aesthetic lives of the literati as a necessary antidote to the worldliness and formalism of official Confucianism and as an abiding influence in Chinese poetry and painting. Confucianism was the state cult, but in their essential durability, quietism, and closeness to nature, the Chinese have in many ways been more Taoist than Confucian throughout their history.

Besides Confucianism and Taoism, no native doctrine survived to play an independent role in Chinese history. Mo Ti (Mo Tzŭ, c. 468-382 B.C.) tried to found a religion based on his ideas of utility and universal love,[16] but Mohism eventually died out, though not without leaving its mark on Han Confucianism. The Legalist teachers influential at the court of Ch'in left as their monuments Draconian legal codes and the administrative structures by which a huge state could be held together, but Legalist doctrine was too harsh and totalitarian for Chinese taste, and no distinctive Legalist philosophic school survived.

Buddhism. It was the imported religion of Buddhism [17] which won the allegiance of the Chinese and became the third of the three "teachings." Buddhism had its beginnings in the sixth century B.C. in India. Its founder, Gautama, was an Indian prince who after various spiritual experiences achieved enlightenment and arrived at an interpretation of the meaning of life and the way it should be lived, which he preached during the rest of his long life. The original teachings of the Buddha, which means "the enlightened one," were austere, even forbidding. Life was suffering from which one could escape by extinguishing desire. Buddhism adopted the original Hindu idea of reincarnation and of the unity of life. The Buddha taught that each creature would experience several reincarnations, each new birth bringing it into that status and that form which its spiritual growth or retrogression in the previous reincarnation warranted. Eventu-

[16] See Y. P. Mei (trans.), *The Ethical and Political Works of Motse* (London, 1929).
[17] A very helpful general survey of Buddhism is J. B. Pratt, *The Pilgrimage of Buddhism and a Buddhist Pilgrimage* (New York, 1928).

ally, each creature might attain enlightenment and so escape from the wheel of life and from self into Nirvana, or identity with the Absolute. This combination of predestination and free will, in which conduct at each state determined status in the next, held forth little comfort or solace for erring humans. Here were the rules: obey and be righteous and you would find your way out of the maze; disobey and you would be entangled in it for incarnation after incarnation. However, as one student of Buddhism has pointed out, the Buddha, while stern and rigorous in his teaching, was in conduct a warm, sympathetic, and winning human being, and the sort of Buddhism which swept the Far East and still claims hundreds of millions of believers followed the Buddha's heart rather than the Buddha's head.

Before it reached China, Buddhism spread into northwest India and central Asia. There it came into a very cosmopolitan atmosphere, for that area was the crossroads where Indian, Chinese, Persian, and Hellenistic cultures met. In this atmosphere there evolved the Buddhism of the Mahayana, or the Greater Vehicle, so called in contrast to the Hinayana, or Lesser Vehicle, the earlier and more rigid version of the doctrine. Mahayana Buddhism was a great religion of salvation. It assumed that there had been many Buddhas or Enlightened Ones besides Gautama, and that in due course, there would be many more. A Buddha, by the very nature of things, has escaped from the wheel of life and is not accessible to ordinary humans, but there are spiritual beings, the Bodhisattvas, who, though ready to achieve enlightenment, defer entrance into Nirvana and remain to help those who suffer. Here were the fountainheads of mercy, the saints of this dispensation who would intercede for sinners and bring comfort. Moreover, Buddhism as it came to China from central Asia, brought with it beautiful forms of art, a rich literature, and a subtle metaphysic.

During the Han period, Buddhism was confined chiefly to court circles where scholars labored to put its literature into Chinese and to relate its ideas to Chinese beliefs and attitudes. From the beginning it was apparent that Buddhism contravened certain strongly held Chinese views. Celibacy of the clergy and the existence of monastic orders for men and women obviously would be hard to reconcile with Chinese filial piety and the feeling for the perpetuation of the family line. However, the centuries following the fall of the Han created a situation in which Buddhism won men's hearts, as Christianity did in the West at much the same date and in a comparable state of society. In these times of great troubles, men's minds turned to the kingdoms not of this earth. Confucianism was in many ways spiritually and aesthetically meager and limited. It had no answer to offer to the great enigma of death, and little comfort to offer in suffering. Here the Buddhists could meet a lack in the Chinese spiritual view; they became the experts on the after life, or lives.

Taoism tended to copy many of the popular features of Buddhism, but asserted its superiority as a completely Chinese doctrine. The Confucians were hostile to Buddhism, claiming that it was antisocial in its advocacy of celibacy as the noblest "way" and that by its accumulation of wealth it constituted a danger to the imperial government. On these grounds there were periodic persecutions of Buddhism; monks and nuns were sent back to the world and temples were deprived of their property. Actually Buddhism never played quite the same role in the history of China that the Christian church played in the West. It did not develop a centralized administrative structure or a binding definition of doctrinal orthodoxy. The temples remained relatively independent of each other, and, while Buddhist sects developed, they were simply differing interpretations of Buddhist doctrine not embodied in definite church organization. The Confucian literati preserved for themselves the role of men of learning and skilled administrators, which in the West was filled by clerics. Under these circumstances there was no struggle between church and state corresponding to that in Europe. By the Ch'ing period, although it had greatly influenced Chinese literature, art, and poetry, Buddhism like Taoism appeared rather shabby and frayed. It was viewed askance by the literati, who thought of it as acceptable only for women and the uneducated.

It is impossible (and would seem to the Chinese quite pointless) to say how many Chinese were at any given time Buddhists, Taoists, or Confucians. Chinese subscribed to Confucian teachings as a guide to life; to choose the wedding date, they summoned the Taoist clergy; and to preside over the funeral, the Buddhist. The most widely and deeply held religious belief was that of veneration of ancestors. Being cautious and reasonable, the Chinese thus divided their spiritual investment. This attitude of more than tolerance toward diverse ethical and religious teachings was confounding to Christian missionaries, whose beliefs were based upon the biblical injunction "Thou shalt have no other gods before Me," and so were moved to wonder whether the Chinese would either take Christianity as a "fourth doctrine" without renouncing the others, or not take it at all. If Marxism can achieve the status of revealed truth for the Chinese, one of the most distinctive of Chinese attitudes will have been obliterated.

Art

The feeling for the beauty of the world of nature and the sense of identity with it which inspires the greatest Chinese poetry is revealed in its fullest in Chinese art. For many centuries China was represented in the West by certain luxury goods. Silks, porcelains, wallpapers, furniture, wood carving, and jade all showed a highly sophisticated naturalness, and great refinement of taste. So great was the charm of these Chinese house furnishings for Europeans of the late seventeenth and eighteenth centuries that a veritable passion for Chinoiserie seized people of fashion, and to this day European and American décor owes much to Chinese ideas and designs.[18] In early Manchu days these crafts had passed the height of their creativity; Ch'ing porcelain, for example, represents great technical skill, but is in danger of being pretty-pretty, sentimental and effeminate in design. However, these characteristics of eighteenth-century Chinese art appealed to rather than repelled Europeans of the Age of the Enlightenment, and Europeans and Americans came to think of Chinese art in terms of rich, highly colored embroideries, elaborately carved green jade, delicate porcelains, inlaid screens, painted fans, and the like.

Undoubtedly in the eighteenth and nineteenth centuries Chinese craftsmanship in all these fields was still of a high order, but these were not, in the estimation of the Chinese themselves, the great arts. The great arts were those in which only the literati could participate. Only a scholar who could use the writing brush and was full of the tradition of Chinese literature could be a great calligrapher, could paint (which involved the same writing-brush technique), or could write poetry. In fact, the greatest aesthetic achievement recognized in China in the old days was a so-called triple masterpiece—a poem, the calligraphy in which it was written, and the painting which accompanied it, all being the work of the same artist.

The Chinese scholar, as artist, was the amateur in the true sense of the term. The arts were his great avocation, not his means of livelihood. He did not need to paint portraits or religious subjects in order to get buyers. He did not need to write literature which would please a patron. His themes were subjective and personal. The great Chinese paintings, like the great Chinese poems, deal with mountains, waters, flowers, birds, plants, and man's place among them. Painting and poetry of this sort were animated by the spirit of philosophic Taoism and Buddhism, not of didactic Confucianism. The Chinese scholar of the Ch'ing dynasty, who was also an artist, was something more than an earnest and stuffy and perhaps corrupt bureaucrat. He was also a connoisseur of the arts and a practitioner of the noblest of them, in which latter respect he

[18] On this influence of China upon Europe see A. Reichwein, *China and Europe: Intellectual and Artistic Contacts in the Eighteenth Century*, translated by J. C. Powell (New York, 1925); and Osvald Sirén, *China and Gardens of Europe of the Eighteenth Century* (New York, 1950).

surpassed contemporary European and American officials. This sort of Chinese gentleman in two dimensions—at once Confucian pedant and Taoist mystic—did not understand and was not understood by the Western traders, soldiers, missionaries, and diplomats who nevertheless were forced to cope with him and his like in the nineteenth century.

Lack of Scientific Development

The traditional culture of China was in essence, then, a humanistic one, marked by human relationships in the spirit of *li* and aesthetic expression of man's complete membership and participation in the world of nature. Turn over the medal, and there is a notable lack of scientific development. The Chinese have been ingenious, inventive, and practical. They have great empirical knowledge in agriculture, ceramics, and other fields. Many of their innovations—such as paper, printing, the compass, and gunpowder—have eventually been learned by the West. But there has been no organized body of scientific thought, no regular formulation of scientific laws, and no systematic development of applied science.

Both Westerners and modern Chinese have tried to discover the reasons for the difference between the roles of science in China and the West.[19] One factor undoubtedly was that for centuries intellectually able Chinese went through the examination process, and in their preparation received an education which stressed history, ethics, and aesthetics. Certainly Chinese scholars evolved no real scientific method, except in the limited field of textual criticism. The Chinese intellectual looked down on physical labor and would have been repelled by the necessity of messing around in a laboratory. The Chinese written language was a further deterrent, since it was not well fitted to the precise formulations of scientific thought. Strongly in Chinese literature and the arts runs the idea of adapting one's self to nature, not nature to one's self. In a sense the view of the Chinese literati was unmaterialistic. When the Chinese confronted the barbarians and felt superior to them, it was not because the Chinese had a richer material civilization, which they had, or better techniques of war, which they did not necessarily have; it was because they felt themselves to be on a higher plane of ethical and social relations and of aesthetic experience.

One can describe and generalize about the Chinese culture of the early nineteenth century almost as if it were completed, finished. That was its last hour before the West began to bear in on it with revolutionary transformations resulting. Of course, the China of 150 years ago was not

---

[19] An extensive study, *Science and Civilization in China*, by Joseph Needham is now appearing. Two volumes (Cambridge, England, 1954, 1956) have already been published. See also J. K. Fairbank, *The United States and China* (Cambridge, Mass., 1948), pp. 73-76.

static, but the process of change then occurring was on the whole not one of growth and creation but one of decline and decay. Whether that decline was simply the periodic downswing of the cycle when a dynasty had passed its zenith, or whether it was a much more fundamental decay in the basic fabric of Chinese civilization is a large issue in historical interpretation. But in that Indian Summer, China was still rich, impressive, composed, and assured.

What were the secrets of the maintenance of cultural continuity and unity in a state which dwarfed European states? What made China hold together and go its own way cannot be stated simply, but this brief discussion of the characteristics of Chinese culture has been meant to suggest some of the elements of strength and cohesion in Chinese life. The unique ruling class of scholar-gentry, product of a standardized education, carriers of a common culture, and possessors of unique prestige, did much to hold China together. But old China is not to be understood as a land of a small glittering aristocracy enjoying the good life at the expense of a mass of illiterate, hardly-human laborers. There was class distinction in China, but no rigid caste and actually a fair amount of social mobility; and poor men's sons, through the examinations, could become participators in the higher culture. Farming, the occupation of the great majority, was a respected activity, and the ordinary Chinese was not a mere animal, but a dignified human being who contributed to and shared in the civilization of his country. The family system, the tendency to admire standards of the past rather than to hanker after novelties, and the technique of social relations, were stabilizing factors. Inequalities in wealth and opportunity which periodically developed were remedied, rather drastically, by revolution; yet such upheavals meant not a basic change in the social system, but a change in the personnel operating the system. Such a society seemed self-regulating and almost eternal, until British victory in the War of 1840-41 set off a chain of events which revealed that some of the very elements that had been the strength of China in the old days were now, in new circumstances, to be her weaknesses. Localism, laissez faire, decentralization, individualism, humanism and traditionalism were to be of little service against the superior technology and physical strength of the West.

SUGGESTED READINGS

On the Chinese Language, see: Bernard Karlgren, *The Chinese Language, An Essay on Its Nature and History* (New York, 1949) and *Sound and Symbol in Chinese* (London, 1923); R. A. D. Forrest, *The Chinese Language* (London, 1948). E. R. Hughes, *The Invasion of China by the Western World* (New York, 1938), chap. 4 deals with the language reform movements.

In addition to the translations of the works of individual philosophers mentioned in footnotes in the chapter, the following works on Chinese philosophy and religion are useful: Fung Yu-lan, *Short History of Chinese Philosophy* edited by Derk Bodde (New York, 1948); Lin Mousheng, *Men and Ideas, An Informal History of Chinese Philosophic Thought* (New York, 1942); Arthur Waley, *Three Ways of Thought in Ancient China* (London, 1939); Liang Chi-ch'ao, *History of Chinese Political Thought During the Early Tsin Period,* translated by L. T. Chen (London, 1930); Witter Bynner, *The Way of Life According to Laotzu* (New York, 1944), "an American version"; H. F. MacNair (ed.), *China* (Berkeley and Los Angeles, 1946), Part III: Philosophy and Religion; K. S. Latourette, *A History of Christian Missions in China* (New York, 1929); W. E. Soothill, *The Three Religions of China* (3d ed., London, 1926); Karl L. Reichelt, *Truth and Tradition in Chinese Buddhism,* translated by K. Bugge (rev. ed., Shanghai, 1934).

Among the many translations of Chinese literary works, the following are representative; Arthur Waley (trans.), *A Hundred and Seventy Chinese Poems* (2d ed., New York, 1936) and *The Life and Times of Po Chü-i, with Translations of 100 New Poems* (New York, 1949); Florence Ayscough (trans.), *Tu Fu, The Autobiography of a Chinese Poet, A. D. 712-759* (London, 1929), Vol. I, and *Tu Fu, Guest of Rivers and Lakes, A. D. 759-770* (London and New York, 1934), Vol. II; Witter Bynner and Kiang Kang-hu, *The Jade Mountain* (New York, 1929); Wang Chi-chen (trans.), *Traditional Chinese Tales* (New York, 1944) and *Dream of the Red Chamber* (New York, 1929); Pearl S. Buck (trans.), *All Men Are Brothers (Shui Hu Chuan)* (2 vols., New York, 1933); Arthur Waley (trans.), *Monkey* by Wu Ch'eng-ên (New York, 1943); C. H. Brewitt-Taylor, *San Kuo Chih Yen I; or, Romance of the Three Kingdoms* (2 vols., Shanghai, 1925, 1926).

On Chinese art see: Laurence Binyon, *The Spirit of Man in Asian Art* (Cambridge, Mass., 1935) and *The Flight of the Dragon: An Essay on the Theory and Practice of Art in China and Japan, Based on Original Sources* (London, 1911); Kuo Hsi, *An Essay on Landscape Painting,* translated by Shio Sakanishi (London, 1935), by a famous eleventh-century Chinese painter; Osvald Sirén, *The Chinese on the Art of Painting* (Peiping, 1936), *Gardens of China* (New York, 1949), and numerous other works; Arthur Waley, *An Introduction to the Study of Chinese Painting;* Dagny Carter, *China's Art* (rev., New York, 1951); Lucy Driscoll and Kenji Toda, *Chinese Calligraphy* (Chicago, 1935). Joseph Needham's comprehensive work, *Science and Civilization in China* (Cambridge, England, 1954, 1956, 1959), of which three of four projected volumes have appeared, undertakes to determine what the Chinese have contributed in various periods to the development of science, scientific thought, and technology.

5

JAPAN: LAND AND PEOPLE

Introduction

The Japanese nation throughout its modern history has been more powerful and influential than its area in square miles and the number of its people would indicate. Western rivals consistently underrated the Japanese, an underestimation which was almost fatal in 1941. Because of the enormous losses in man power, resources, and land which Japan suffered as a result of the second World War, it would be a relatively simple matter today to make the same error. The Japan of December, 1941, was composed of three rather distinct parts. Old Japan consisted of the islands of Honshu, Shikoku, and Kyushu, the region in which Japanese culture developed in the past and in which modern Japan still has its center. Japan proper included the three islands just mentioned and the frontier island of Hokkaido (Ezo) to the north. The Japanese Empire of the period before Japan's surrender in 1945 embraced these four main islands plus the southern half of Sakhalin, the Kuriles, Korea, Ryukyus (Loochoos), Formosa, Manchuria, parts of China proper, and the mandated islands of the Pacific—a range of territories which dramatically demonstrated Japan's political and economic expansion in the latter nineteenth and early twentieth centuries. Since the latter regions, now lost, more than quintupled the land area under Japanese control and added immeasurably to the man power and slender natural resources of the nation, the extent of the loss can be understood. The student of Japanese history, then, in looking upon the Japan of today is considering a nation physically similar to that existing in 1603, the beginning of the Tokugawa era.

Even with a drastically reduced area, Japan today, as throughout most of its history, has a favorable geographical location. While Japan must have known invasion in prehistoric times and was forced to submit to foreign occupation in 1945, during the many intervening centuries its insular position protected it from successful conquest either by invaders from the Continent or by Western imperialistic powers. At the same time only Tsushima, the Korea Straits, and the East China Sea separated Japan

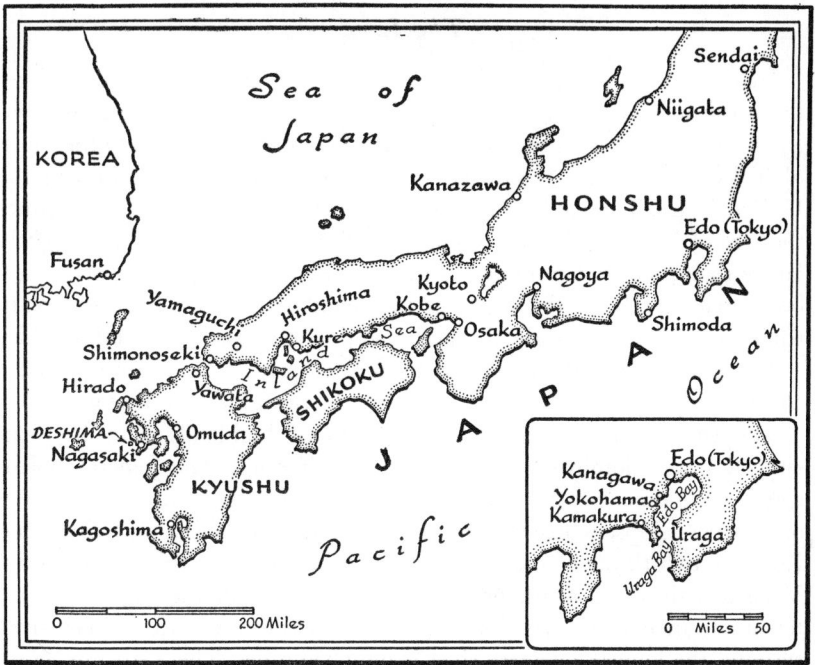

Old Japan

from the mainland of China, a fact which permitted the Japanese people to benefit from contact with the more advanced civilization of China, which came to them for the most part through Korea. In fact, Japan's relation to the continent of Asia was in this respect rather like that of the British Isles to Western Europe: she could acquire and reshape the many aspects of continental culture which came to her, and without being subject even to the equivalent of a Norman conquest. During the nineteenth century, Japan, lying athwart the main trade routes from the United States to the Orient, was one of the principal barriers to the development of American trade with eastern Asia. At the present time Japan is looked upon as one of the main bastions against the spread of Communism from the Asiatic mainland toward the West. Moreover, its long coast line of some 17,150 miles indented liberally with good harbors, such as Yokohama, Nagoya, and Kobe, on the Pacific coast, and Nagasaki and Kanazawa on the western coast, constitutes a permanent asset in international trade.

The Land

Stripped of its former possessions, Japan stretches from Hokkaido on the north to Kyushu on the south. The four islands lie between 30° and 45° north latitude with the main centers of civilization located to the south of Tokyo in a region somewhat similar to that of the Carolinas in the United States. The land area is 147,700 square miles, or about three times the size of New York State, slightly smaller than California, and slightly larger than postwar Germany. To this should be added the area of numerous small islands off the coasts of the main islands, totaling some 9,215 square miles.[1] The latitudinal range extends about 1,000 miles and provides a strategic screen of the mainland from Shanghai on the south to a point considerably north of Vladivostok in the Soviet Maritime Provinces.

The islands are composed of a system of highlands with frequent rugged peaks dominating a mountainous interior. The general north-south development of the terrain is broken on Honshu by the magna fossa, or Japanese Alps, which cut across the island in an east-west direction. Roughly two thirds of the total area is included under this classification. Valleys with short, swift, nonnavigable rivers break the highlands and terminate in narrow coastal plains. In sharp contrast with China's river systems, the longest Japanese river is only 230 miles. These streams, however, do provide Japan with a source for even greater hydroelectric power than has as yet been developed. This region has numerous volcanoes—there are some 500 dotting the landscape, of which sixty have been active in historic times, the most famous being Fujiyama, dormant since 1707. Volcanic activity is especially noticeable during the months of August and September. As many as 1,500 earthquake shocks have been recorded in Japan in a single year. The entire country is quite picturesque and beautiful.

The topography of Japan has had certain definite influences on its history and economic growth. During medieval times the perpetuation of the feudal system was facilitated by the rugged nature of the country. A tendency toward localism was an inevitable result. The loyalties of people naturally were fixed first on the local unit of government or attached to the feudal lord of the area. When a system of communication was developed, unity and cohesion among the people followed easily.

The limited amount of cultivable land sharply restricted agricultural production. Terracing of hillsides advanced Japanese farming toward the mountains. Gains made in this way often were offset by loss of valley

---

[1] G-H. Smith and D. Good, *Japan, A Geographical View* (New York, 1943), p. 5.

land due to excessive deposits of rock and gravel by mountainous streams. As will be seen shortly, the Kwanto Plain near Tokyo and the Mino-Owari or Nobi Plain at the head of Ise Bay have been the two most important agrarian regions. They also are the areas where Japan's largest cities have developed.

Climate

Climatically, Japan may be divided into northern and southern and then eastern and western regions. The northern part of Honshu and all of Hokkaido have a climate similar to that of New England. After one passes through an intermediate zone down to Tokyo, a humid semitropical climate corresponding somewhat to that found in the American cotton belt land is encountered. The western or Japan Sea side of Old Japan has more moisture, especially in winter, and more severe weather than the eastern or Pacific Ocean side. The monsoon winds, ocean currents, surrounding waters, and its latitudinal position help to explain the Japanese climate.

The monsoons generally govern rainfall in Japan. Thus the summer monsoons bring heavy rain to the southeastern slopes of Honshu, Kyushu, and Shikoku. The semitropical seas along the shores of these islands account partly for the relatively heavy precipitation in both winter and summer. The warm Kuroshio (Japanese) Current flows northward along the western coast and modifies seasonal extremes. It ameliorates the effects of the Oyashio (Okhotsk) Current, one branch of which sweeps down the western coast of Japan. This is particularly noticeable in the winter when the monsoon of Asia should bring much colder weather.

In a land, then, where agriculture still ranks first, the rainfall is more than ample. Tokyo, for example, has an average yearly precipitation of 61.8 inches. Some regions on the Inland and Japan seas have more than a hundred inches. This can be compared with the rainfall in New York of 42.2 inches, in Seattle of 33.9 inches, and in London of 25.1 inches. The southeastern monsoon and the Kuroshio Current combine to give the southeastern coast of Old Japan the heaviest rainfall during the period of greatest heat. This explains the flourishing plant growth and the ability to harvest two crops yearly. Unfortunately the path taken by the typhoons so prevalent in late summer also follows that of the Japanese Current. In other areas excessive moisture leads to serious soil erosion and the necessity for carefully planned afforestation projects. In general, however, the net result of the factors influencing Japan's climate is to afford the islands milder climatic conditions than those prevailing in neighboring continental countries in the same latitude. There is less seasonal change both in temperature and rainfall in Kyushu, for example, than in Shanghai.

Resources

Agriculture. In a country one of whose main problems since 1868 has been providing enough food for its people, the agrarian resources rank high in importance. Estimates of the number of people engaged in farming vary from 43 to 48 per cent, according to the sources used and the inclusion or exclusion of those who are only partly dependent on the soil for a living. While this represents a drop of some 20 per cent since 1900, it still shows the important position agriculture has in the Japanese economy. Another way of indicating the seriousness of the pressure of population on food resources is to notice the number of people per square mile of arable land. In 1929 for Japan that figure was 2,774 in comparison with 229.2 for the United States. How well, then, is Japan endowed by nature to meet this problem?

Some indication of the influence of climatic conditions on agriculture already has been given. Adequate or heavy rainfall, a boon to farmers generally, has to be equated with losses these same rains entail. Deposits of silt, sand and gravel, and volcanic ash have ruined some agricultural areas. Leaching of important mineral plant foods from the soil may be attributed to heavy rains. The problem of maintaining the fertility of the soil through use of commercial and native fertilizers thus has been increased. The necessity for forest conservation projects to help prevent excessive soil erosion has decreased the chances for adding to the amount of arable land.

This brings the student to a consideration of one of the main features of Japanese agriculture, the small percentage of cultivable land. This totals 15,000,000 acres or less than 16 per cent of the total land area. The importance of these figures may be shown in several ways. Bergsmark[2] includes three fourths of the land with a 15 per cent-or-less inclination in this estimate. Farming has been pushed far towards the hilly and mountainous regions. Since 1900, efforts of the government through a bounty system to encourage the reclamation of wild explored areas have not been too successful. The average farm in Japan before World War II had only 2.7 acres, a figure quite deceptive when one considers the relatively large agricultural holdings in Hokkaido. Farmers with ten acres or more constituted less than 1 per cent of the total. Moreover, many

[2] D. R. Bergsmark, *Economic Geography of Asia* (New York, 1944), p. 389.

Japanese farms still exist in the form of small strips in different fields. While this at times may cut down crop loss because of drought, flood, etc., the waste involved in the use of boundary ridges between individual holdings is significant. The government before World War II recognized the desirability of changing this system, and was attempting with some success to encourage the combination of these small plots into larger farms.

Intensive Agriculture. Another characteristic of Japanese agriculture is its intensive nature. Just as in China, farming lacks many of the scientific aids quite commonly used in the United States. In both Oriental countries, human labor is expected to compensate for the absence of such assistance. The human factor is particularly significant because of the importance of rice, mulberry trees, and tea in the total agricultural output. All three, as cultivated and harvested in Japan, require intense application of human labor. Another indication of the intensive type of agriculture followed is the resort to multiple cropping wherever possible. With the exception of northern Honshu and Hokkaido, where temperate-zone farming is necessary, various crops which mature at different dates are planted in adjoining rows.

The significance of the human element also is emphasized by the minor position of the Japanese livestock industry. Most frequently the fields are too small to permit the use of draft animals. Then, too, Japan lacks sufficient grazing land to provide the necessary pasture. The people know that many mouths can be fed with the grain necessary to fatten livestock for the market. A final indication of the intensive nature of Japanese agriculture can be gained from the method of fertilization of the soil. The farmer long has appreciated the necessity for liberal use of fertilizer. With little animal manure available, more than half of the fertilizer used consists of night soil and green manure. Over 50 per cent of the commercial fertilizer used before World War II was soybean cake from Manchuria. The heavy expense involved has forced the Japanese to adopt a system of frequent fertilization of individual plants. The extent to which this combination of human and natural resources has met Japan's needs should indicate some of the unsolved problems today.

Several criteria can be used in a quick summary. Even before the war, efforts to increase the yield per acre showed little progress. Japan's forty bushels of rice per acre was the highest in the world. The importance of this can be recognized easily because of the dominant place rice has in the Japanese diet. Fifty per cent or more of the total value of the nation's agricultural production normally consisted of rice and other cereals. All of this was consumed in Japan and represented about 85 per cent of prewar requirements. Rice was imported from Taiwan (Formosa) and Chosen (Korea) when they were parts of the Japanese Empire. Another way of indicating the significance of rice is to notice the very low per-capita production and consumption of meat and milk. In 1939 people in the United States consumed 900 quarts of milk and 360 pounds of meat to each one consumed by the Japanese, who did eat 5 times as much fish as Americans. Although an increase in both has been evident, population growth has generally offset the gain and the Japanese remained largely a nation of vegetarians. If any great success in increasing the yield per acre could be expected, the result would be important. That the record of the 1920's was excellent and has not been appreciably increased since means that Japanese rice culture was efficient. The elimination of certain pests and plant diseases offers some slight hope, but relief for Japan's food problems in general will have to come from other sources.

Under the present Japanese farm economy is expansion of the amount of arable land possible? Here again the farmer seems to have given a good account of himself. The maximum increase possible would be from 16 per cent to 20 per cent of the total land area. Changes in farming methods might increase slightly the amount of land in cultivation and the yield per acre. Even so, most of the expansion must come in the utilization of untilled land in Hokkaido. Some estimates indicate that as much as 50 per cent of the land there remains unused. In the past, certain factors have operated against extensive colonization of this region. The people have been reluctant to migrate there because of love of homes long established in Old Japan. This island's climate is not adaptable generally to rice culture whose importance can be seen again by its introduction into Hokkaido's southern valleys. The rigorous climate obviously necessitates a greater outlay of capital for buildings. If this agricultural frontier is to be used, incentives from the government will be needed.

Lumber. Japan is fortunate in possessing both variety and quantity in its timber resources. Coniferous forests predominate in Hokkaido and northern Honshu. Pine alone accounts for a considerable proportion of the lumber cut annually in Japan and is used primarily for building. Intermingled with the conifers are various species of broadleafed trees, the oak being the principal one. In Shikoku and Kyushu this tree is dominant, but bamboo, camphor, and other tropical timbers are common. In addition to building and furniture making, about 40 per cent of the forest resources are used for charcoal and firewood. Although Japan has 50,000,000 acres of forest land, covering almost half of the country, its timber resources in normal times are inadequate. Imports from the

United States and Canada, largely timber and pulpwood, are required to meet at least one-third of the nation's demands. An intelligent program of afforestation designed to check floods, reduce soil erosion, and conserve hydroelectric power has prevented overcutting of most of the forest land Major lumbering projects are to be found in northern Honshu, Hokkaido, and the more inaccessible regions in the southern islands. Increased demands for building materials for reconstruction in war-damaged cities strained the nation's resources for some time.

Fishing. Possibly of greater importance in Japan's economy than timber are the products of the fishing industry. The people are fortunate because the waters of the Inland Sea and offshore seas abound in all types of marine life. Japanese fishermen have dominated the stretch of water from Hokkaido to the Soviet Maritime Provinces and north to the Kamchatka Peninsula, which constitutes one of the three richest fishing grounds in the world. Before World War II a larger percentage of people in Japan were engaged in fishing than in any other country. Fleets of steam vessels of 100 tons or more and salmon and crab canneries were common.

In a country where fish has supplied most of the protein in the people's diet, and provided income on a part-time or full-time basis for as many as 20 per cent of the population, the importance of the fishing industry cannot be overemphasized. Coastal fishing brought catches of sardines, herring, mackerel, sea bream, etc.; in deep-sea fishing the most important fish in addition to crab and salmon were tuna, shark, and bonito. Moreover, large quantities of shellfish and seaweed were caught, or cultivated, and sold. War losses in shipping and difficulties over the valuable Siberian waters fisheries have increased the significance of efforts to utilize purely Japanese waters more efficiently. Some Japanese authorities have contended that many more people could be employed in this industry. Practically speaking, continued revival of the postwar fishing industry has helped feed Japan.

Mineral Resources. Some help in feeding and providing employment for its people may come from an expansion of fishing, but the solution of these problems most actively advanced before World War II, one which must be considered now, was further industrialization. If this is the only way that Japan can regain its old standard of living, the mineral resources on which such industry must rest assume even greater importance than before the war. Careful consideration must be given to further industrialization because there are about seventeen million more Japanese today than there were in 1940.

A study of the Tokugawa period of Japanese history shows that many of the main mineral deposits now known—coal, copper, and silver—were being worked. Japan also has a wide variety of other mineral products, including gold, lead, tin, zinc, aluminum, sulphur, etc. One of the hard economic facts Japanese have had to face is that of all their mineral resources only coal and copper exist in significant quantities. One estimate made for 1928 disclosed the value of coal and copper production at 67 and 14 per cent respectively of the total value of Japanese mineral output for that year.[3] As the Japanese emphasized heavy industry in the 1930's, these figures represent maximum percentages for the pre-World War II period. Of the other metals more gold, for example, has had to be imported than was mined. Local production was hardly sufficient to meet the needs of industry and art. Silver imports were lighter but still necessary. Although copper was exported, almost as much was imported because of the high cost of mining this metal in Japan. Imports exceeded exports for most other mineral products.

Unless Japan's industrial rehabilitation is to rest again on domination of, or free access to, sources of raw material in other Far Eastern countries, an expansion of its coal, petroleum, and hydroelectric power industries must take place. Although estimates of the country's coal reserves vary from six to eight billion metric tons, with figures from Japanese sources being higher, Japan still ranks far below other Asiatic nations such as China, Soviet Siberia, and India. On the brighter side, it should be noted that Japan was the greatest coal-producing nation in the Orient. It is also true that known Japanese reserves should last the country for decades at the prewar rate of consumption.

The principal coal fields in the islands are to be found in northwestern Kyushu and west-central Hokkaido. Thin seams and faulted structure resulting in seepage and gas make mining operations both dangerous and expensive. The high cost of coal is increased by the expense of shipping to and unloading in the industrial areas. The quality of the coal, moreover, is mediocre; only a small percentage of the bituminous coal produces coke suitable for metallurgical use. Only small amounts of anthracite and natural coke are to be found. Before the war Chinese coal was mixed with the native product for coking purposes.

Pressure on coal as a source of energy has been relieved by the rapid development of hydroelectric power, which in prewar years supplied as much as 22 per cent of the total energy available. Japanese topography with its mountains and numerous swift streams and the Japanese climate

[3] H. G. Moulton and J. Ko, *Japan, An Economic and Financial Appraisal* (Washington, 1944), p. 55.

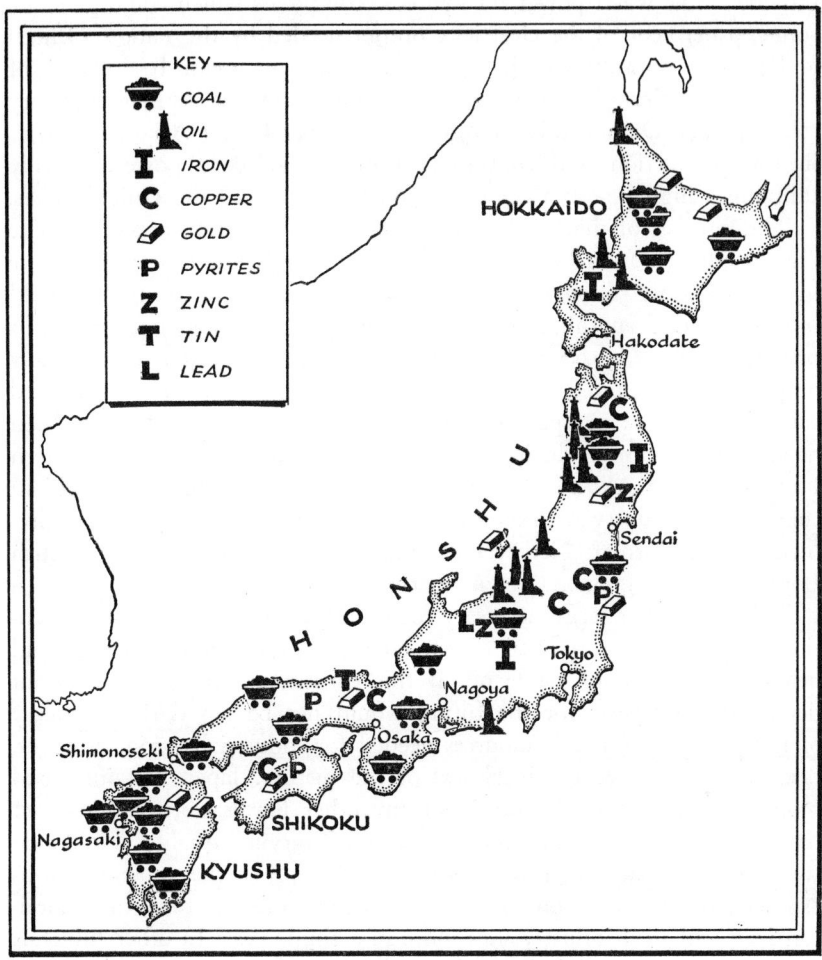

Mineral Resources of Japan

Note concentration of coal in northwestern Kyushu where two thirds of the entire output is mined.

provide ample water power for hydroelectric plants which could generate some 80 per cent of the electricity output needed by the nation. Central and eastern Honshu are the principal producing areas. Irregularity of rainfall and droughts handicap the industry and necessitate auxiliary steam plants. Despite this, in 1940 Japan proper led all Asiatic countries in the production and consumption of hydroelectric power, actually utilizing a higher percentage of its potential than did the United States.

The reserves of the third source of energy, petroleum, are small. The highest estimate found was only 500 million barrels; the estimated reserve in 1924 was only 56,000,000 barrels. Actual production in the 1930's would indicate that, if anything, this was an overestimate. The Japanese wells produced only 2,659,000 barrels in 1941, an amount equal to the daily output of the United States.[4] Although the government has offered subsidies to those prospecting for new oil fields, the results have been meager. The main producing areas are in Hokkaido and in northwestern Honshu in the Akita and Echigo fields. Domestic production seldom supplied the country with as much as 10 per cent of its civilian requirements. The former Netherlands Indies, India, Burma, and British Borneo all have greater known reserves.

To supply the energy necessary for industry will mean further expansion of hydroelectric power, continued maximum coal production, and heavy importation of crude oil. If this constituted the only important deficit, the prospects for the future would not be too dark. A survey of the principal mineral resources needed for industrialization, however, does little to relieve the bleakness of the picture. Japan certainly used more iron ore before the war than any other Far Eastern country, yet iron mines were few and their product of varying quality. Hokkaido was the principal center of production. Accepting the most generous estimates of Japanese iron-ore reserves, 80,000,000 metric tons, the American iron and steel industry uses more in a single year. In other minerals used by and in connection with heavy industry, Japan is somewhat more fortunate. Before the war it was self-sufficient in sulphur and limestone, but had to import some manganese, chromium, and copper. Japanese industry was dependent almost entirely on foreign sources for other minerals (nickel, tungsten, platinum, etc.).

It is evident then that neither in power nor in mineral resources does Japan rank first among Asiatic countries. Cressey estimates that the United States produces 7 times as much copper, 10 times as much coal, 40 times as much iron, and 432 times as much oil as does Japan.[5] Little evidence exists of a sufficient mineral base for heavy industry in Japan.

[4] G. B. Cressey, *Asia's Lands and Peoples* (New York, 1944), p. 182.
[5] *Ibid.*, p. 186.

The People

Japan's rapidly increasing population, accustomed to governmental control, long has constituted one of its major assets and has offset, in part, weaknesses resulting from deficiencies of essential raw materials. Although a spectacular increase in population has been characteristic of the nation in modern times, this was not true during the Tokugawa period. According to the seventeen official censuses taken from 1721 to 1852 during the Tokugawa Shogunate, the population rose only from 26,065,000 in the former year to 27,201,000 just before Commodore Perry helped to end Japan's isolation. Social, economic, and political conditions of the times combined to restrict the size of the population, and to render natural disasters, famines, and plagues particularly destructive. Only subsistence agriculture and very simple handicrafts were permitted under this feudalistic system which also limited drastically the movement of people from one estate and region to another. It is evident that as many people lived in Japan during this period as could be supported by the country.

From this static situation the population of Japan increased rapidly from 34,806,000 in 1872 to 73,114,308 in 1940. In the ten-year period from 1925 to 1935 more than 800,000 were added yearly to the total population. Not only did the total number of people increase dramatically, but the distribution of the population changed drastically. From 32 per cent of the total population in 1920, Japanese living in cities of 10,000 or more increased to 49 per cent in 1940. With an estimate of more than 90,000,000 persons living in Japan in 1956, the pressure of population on means of subsistence has become extreme. The problem of finding occupations for approximately a million new Japanese workers a year is one which no Japanese government prior to World War II had been able to solve by peaceful means. Further complexities arise because of the heavy concentration of people in the few plains areas, the density of population (close to 600 persons per square mile in Japan proper), and the restricted amount of cultivable land available.

Scholars still disagree on the question of the origins of the Japanese people. All are agreed, however, that there are several racial strains in the mixture which constitutes the present Japanese race. In the mountainous regions of Hokkaido can still be found a few thousand of the Ainus. Whether the Ainu is the direct descendant of neolithic man in Japan is open to debate. It seems certain, however, that these people originally came from northern Asia through Sakhalin or Korea into the Japanese islands; at one time they occupied most of the area of Japan proper. When their expansion carried them into Kyushu, the Ainus were confronted by a warlike people, the ancestors of the modern Japanese people. That these inhabitants had come there by sea is a certainty. Existing evidence indicates points of origin for them in Korea and Manchuria, which was one of the main avenues of migration to Japan. This does not account for certain physical characteristics and ways of living which more closely resemble Malayan and Polynesian peoples. Sansom offers a possible solution for the controversy over the origin of the Japanese race. His idea that the islands of the South Pacific and the southern islands of Japan were peopled from a common center of civilization on the mainland, possibly in southern China or Indo-China, is both interesting and plausible.[6] The point of importance here is that at a very early time the diverse strains had been blended into a remarkably homogeneous race, the Japanese.

This people, as are the Chinese, are of the Mongoloid type, more hirsute than their neighbors, possibly because of the admixture of Ainu blood. They generally are small, a little more than five feet in height, but tall men of six feet are not exceptional, especially in the North. Their hair usually is black although albinos are known. Black eyes predominate, though they are frequently light brown. The eyes are quite small and inclined to puffy eyelids and veiled corners. To all of these common characteristics there are exceptions, as many an Occidental found to his surprise during the last war.

To the inhabitants of these tight little islands, all of the above description meant little. The various racial elements which contributed to the physical composition of the Japanese race had to fuse or perish. The process of amalgamation had been completed at an early date, possibly during the tenth century. The Tokugawa era, with its seclusion from contact with the rest of the world and its rigid and minute governmental control of all aspects of life, merely permitted the government to perfect a political, social, and economic pattern for the Japanese people.

SUGGESTED READINGS

Among the most useful and reliable general works are Daniel R. Bergsmark, *Economic Geography of Asia* (New York, 1944); Clayton D. Carus and Charles L. McNichols, *Japan: Its Resources and Industries* (New York, 1944); George B. Cressey, *Asia's Lands and Peoples* (New York, 1944); Harold G. Moulton and Junichi Ko, *Japan, An Economic and Financial Appraisal* (Washington, 1944); John E. Orchard, *Japan's Economic Position, The Progress of Industrialization* (New York, 1930); Edwin O. Reischauer, *Japan, Past and Present* (New York, 1947); George B. Sansom, *Japan, A Short Cultural History* (New York, 1943); Guy-Harold Smith and Dorothy Good, *Japan, A Geographical View* (New York, 1943); and Glenn T. Trewartha, *Japan, A Physical, Cultural, and Regional Geography* (Madison, Wis., 1945).

[6] G. B. Sansom, *Japan, A Short Cultural History* (New York, 1943), p. 9.

6

JAPANESE HISTORY AND GOVERNMENT TO 1867

Prehistoric Japan

Early Japanese history presents a variety of problems to the Western historian and student. The combination of mythology and fact which compose this part of the record depends for authenticity on the ability of the scholar. He must be able to compare successfully dates given in the well-authenticated Chinese dynastic histories and the Korean court annals with those events and personages which Japanese legendary history presents as contemporary in Japan. Not until the art of writing was practiced widely in Japan, sometime between 378 and 405 A.D., can Japanese accounts be taken seriously. Even then it must be remembered that the *Kojiki* (*Records of Ancient Things*), the first history of Japan, was not written until 712. The *Kojiki* was a frank attempt to transcribe for posterity the facts and folklore of the Japanese nation. The *Kojiki* authors failed to achieve the literary quality of Chinese counterparts, a feature which was remedied six years later with the publication of the *Nihon Shoki* (*Written Chronicles of Japan*).

Value of Early Chronicles. Of how much value for the student are these first attempts of Japanese historians? To what extent are the phrases and accounts the recording of native legends? How important was the influence of China and the desire of these court historians to supply a foundation for the existing political, social, and economic system? All these and other questions might be asked and still miss the main point which is "What did the Japanese people believe?"

Even the casual observer learns much of Japan's religious background from these accounts. The existence of *kami*,[1] not only in the form of human beings but in rocks, trees, streams, and such natural phenomena, will help to explain the love and appreciation of the beautiful, so characteristic of the Japanese people. Certainly in the *Kojiki* one can find many stories passed down from generation to generation by word of mouth and from them learn much of Japan's early economic and social

---

[1] Very difficult to translate into English—"superior beings," "gods."

life. Obvious evidence of Chinese influence can be found in the *Nihon Shoki* in the literary style followed and in speeches borrowed from Chinese classics and put in the mouths of Japanese heroes. When the attempt of the reformers of the seventh century to model Japan's government after China's is considered, the effort to support this venture with material from Chinese history and philosophy is understandable. And yet in these historical accounts there is an obvious desire to reduce to writing what the Japanese knew of their country and its traditions.

Mythological Background. After several generations of invisible beings, Japanese mythology records that Izanagi and Izanami, two of the *kami*, were charged with the responsibility of creating "the drifting land" which became Japan. From Izanagi the legend traces the creation of the Sun Goddess who in turn commissioned her grandson, Ninigi, to descend from heaven to become the ruler of the islands. Jimmu Tenno, with whose accession to the throne February 11, 660 B.C., officially accepted Japanese history begins, is the direct descendant of Ninigi. Through him Jimmu Tenno received the three sacred objects, a mirror, chaplet of jewels, and a sword, originally given to Ninigi by the Sun Goddess. From Jimmu Tenno the Japanese trace their line of sovereigns unbroken to the present emperor, Hirohito. This very incomplete account of the origin of the Japanese land and people is given because of its hold on the minds of a majority of the Japanese people. They believed in the divine origin of their nation, their ruling house, and their race. Revivified under the Shinto priests in modern times, these beliefs can be transferred into a "divine" or "manifest" destiny governing Japan's relations with other peoples and other lands. The reader might speculate further as to the influence these strongly held traditions might have on the question of revolution in modern times.

The Yamato Clan

After the forefathers of the Japanese had established themselves in Yamato near the eastern end of the Inland Sea and had gained control of all but southern Kyushu, an account of the political life of the country in the early fifth century can be given. With the exception of the province of Izumo on the western coast, the Ainus remained as a solid block in northern Honshu opposing further political consolidation of Japan. Constant military action against them was required through succeeding centuries. In addition to this hostile group, the topography of the country itself retarded the centralization of authority. Japan at this time was governed by a number of clans, a type of government ideally suited to a country made up of small, self-contained communities. While the clan located in Yamato was recognized by others as the imperial clan from which the present emperor can trace his descent, Chinese accounts show clearly that the sovereignty of the country was divided among many such ruling groups.

The clans were ruled by an hereditary chieftain whose ancestor won the position by force. His main duties were religious and centered around his position as high priest. Consequently his power increased or ebbed in proportion to the strength of the people's faith in their clan deity. Below the clan was the *be,* or hereditary corporation, which constituted the economic basis of the society. There were *be*s for all types of occupations, the most important being those connected with agriculture. As the members of the *be* need not be, and often were not, of the same blood as the clan chieftain, they ranked below him in the social scale. At the bottom of the ladder were the slaves, almost always captives taken in war, but generally few in number. If the population outstripped the means of subsistence, segments broke off from the parent community and moved to new places. Once arrived, they generally took new names, but retained the deity of the original clan, thereby preserving a certain continuity.

Early Contact with China

Another feature of Japanese life in the fifth and six centuries was the early and continued contact with China, generally through Korea. The records of all three countries provide evidence of early Japanese interest in Korean politics. Japan at one time before the fifth century attempted to influence Korean affairs by supporting the western kingdom of Pakche against other Korean states. Chinese probably reached Japan by way of Pakche at an even earlier date. After the fall of the Han dynasty in China in the third century, and as a result of the pressure on China from the nomads of the steppes in the succeeding two centuries, Chinese fled their homeland and reached Japan through Korea.

Influence Upon Japanese Culture. The influence of these emigrants was out of all proportion to their numbers. During the fifth century both a written language and a system of ethics, Confucianism, reached Japan. The latter did much to strengthen the Japanese family; the idea of ancestor worship fitted naturally into the Japanese mythology and could be used to support the position of the emperor as divine head of the entire Japanese people.

In the economic realm, a knowledge of some of the industrial arts was brought in by the Chinese. *Bes* for weavers and sericulturists were established at an early date. Similarly, the type of utensils and implements used in the home and by workmen improved noticeably after the acquisition of Chinese models. The foreigners also brought with them a more advanced knowledge of the construction trades, with the result soon evident in better and more permanent homes for the people, and in temples for their Gods. In order to facilitate trade with Korea and China, the Japanese expanded their shipbuilding industry and for the first time apparently constructed highways along the coast to supplement ocean-borne traffic. The importation of precious metals stimulated the Japanese to prospect for and discover gold, silver, and copper, and to start mining operations. The importance of the Chinese contribution can be seen in all these changes, and others in art, literature, medicine, the adoption of a system of weights and measures, etc. Needless to say this transformation took time, with some Japanese adaptations not occurring until the eighth century. It is equally clear that the speed of the change was increased among those clans that espoused Chinese ways of life.

Buddhism Reaches Japan. The Buddhist religion and the Soga family provided the stimulus and the leadership for the period during which Chinese influence was dominant in Japanese life. Buddhism was brought to Japan by a Chinese monk in 552. Very little is known about it until three decades later when a debate was held over its adoption by the court. Although no decision was reached then, the Soga family were made the custodians of the image of the Buddha. As the head of this powerful clan was the most important civil servant at the court, the new religion gained powerful support with the conversion of his family. The size and influence of the Soga Buddhist group increased with the addition of missionaries, artists, and scholars from Korea in the next century. It became the liberal party, the sponsor of art and learning, and the chief opponent of the conservative party leaders who placed their faith in the native religion and gods, Shintoism. The supplanting of the latter by Buddhism about the middle of the seventh century is one of the most significant events of this early period. The degree to which Buddhism owed its spectacular success to its patron family, the Soga, or vice versa, is a moot point.

Leadership of the Soga Clan

The rise of Soga to power, and the means by which it achieved that power, are important in their own right, but equally so because all other successful noble families followed essentially the same plan.² Soga Inami, the first champion of Buddhism, planned well and used marriage as a means of securing power. Two of his daughters were married to the Emperor Kimmei, which meant that his son, Soga Amako, was the uncle of three successive emperors. Soga Amako also married his daughter to Prince Shotoku who later became the regent for his aunt, the Empress Suiko. In this way the Soga family consolidated its control over the Japanese throne. During the long period of Soga dominance several mechanisms were used to prolong and extend their power. Contenders either for the throne or to replace Soga chieftains were exterminated ruthlessly, and the leaders of rival factions who suggested or supported such rivals were killed.

In this process the complete triumph of the civilian official, personified by the Soga leader, destroyed any semblance of independent power the military clan chieftain once had held. To accomplish this, Soga brought about the greatest unification of the state of Yamato yet accomplished. The imperial office was made completely supreme, a fundamental change from that of a feudal sovereign, for only in that way could the Soga clan enjoy absolute dominance. At the same time great care was taken to see that the emperor was only a puppet ruler whose every move was sanctioned by Soga. Buddhism actively assisted this centralization of authority in the hands of the emperor and his civilian officials. Buddhist monks denied Shintoist claims that every clan leader had certain independent powers upon which no infringement could be made. Of interest here, as in later periods, was the complete agreement of all leaders that only descendants from the Sun Goddess could occupy the throne.

Prince Shotoku's Regime. Shotoku Taishi, a prince whose wife was a member of the Soga clan, certainly must rank among the greatest of Japan's statesmen. During the twenty-eight years when he actually governed Japan he did everything within his power to further the aims mentioned above. His principal concern was to increase the power of the central authorities at the expense of the clans and to substitute morality and religion for force as a foundation for the state.

In 604 he caused the emperor to issue an edict known as the Seventeen Articles Constitution, often referred to as Japan's first written constitution. Three articles in particular deserve attention. In one, Buddhism is substituted for Shintoism by the simple process of telling the people to revere the teachings of the Buddha. No mention is made of observing

---

² Space will not permit a detailed account of the various clans which dominated Japanese political history to the Restoration in 1868.

Shinto rites. The most important innovation is contained in the third and twelfth articles which flatly state that the emperor is the supreme governor of the state. All nobles and officials were told they were the emperor's vassals and as such held only those powers delegated to them by him. Throughout this entire document, emphasis is placed on ruling justly and wisely. Positive support is given to a set of principles which should guide all those in positions of authority. This document clearly shows Shotoku as a Confucian scholar, only one indication of the greatly increased Chinese influence at the court.

It was a natural step, then, for this statesman to send an embassy to the Chinese court at Loyang in 607, and a group of scholars the following year. In this way Shotoku hoped to buttress his administration. Since some of these Japanese remained for years at the time that the T'ang dynasty made China the cultural center of the world, their influence on the reorganization of Japan politically and on its social and economic development was to be great.

With Shotoku's death in 621, the Soga family became more interested in a retention and expansion of their power than in governing the country well. Soga's complete domination of the country with all benefits accruing from that monopoly of power excited bitter jealousy among rival clans. Not until Soga overextended itself by exterminating the Shotoku family and plotting actual seizure of the throne could it be overthrown.

Chinese Political System Adopted

The Soga family was overthrown and their two most powerful leaders were killed in 645 by Prince Naka-no-Oye, who later became the Emperor Tenchi, and Nakatomi-no-Kamatari, the ancestor of the famous Fujiwara family which was to control Japan until 1150. These two very able men had planned carefully the type of government they wanted; essentially they attempted to adapt to Japan the governmental system of T'ang China.

In the reorganization which followed, the old administrative system was abolished, thereby eliminating the existing hereditary officialdom. Centralization of authority in the emperor, one of the chief characteristics of the Chinese government, required that all persons be brought directly under his power. In the implementation of this idea all officers were forced to take an oath of allegiance to the emperor, an oath which obviously took precedence over any allegiance to clan chieftains. As in China at an earlier time, hereditary territorial lords were replaced by governors appointed by the emperor for the eastern provinces where continued opposition by the Ainus made strong military garrisons necessary. In the past, and for the future when this attempt at centralization of political power failed, the military leaders of these areas had been and did become dangerous rivals. Even in more peaceable regions, the emperor appointed the governors. Although they were frequently the old clan chieftains of the district, the throne issued such strict regulations, both for important and less significant matters, that little of the old power remained. Finally the Chinese criminal and civil codes were copied, and the local communities divided into five-household and fifty-household units for the purpose of law enforcement. Collective responsibility of the members of these units for crimes allegedly committed by one of their group thus should have become the heart of Japan's legal system. As this entire procedure developed, however, it proved to be too foreign and never was successful. This attempt to transfer Chinese political institutions to Japan provided that country with too much government, it is true, but the impressive point is that Japanese leaders believed their country was ready for such a government.

One of the most important phases of this thorough reorganization was the annulment of all private land titles. In this way the emperor took over all property from the former owners who now could occupy and cultivate the land, but they were required to pay an annual rent or tax. Thus the economic base of the old order was swept away; at the same time economic centralization was provided to support political reorganization. When Tenchi's reign ended, the reforms were almost complete.

Land Reform Fails. From the beginning, the most difficult of the reforms to enforce was that which abolished private ownership of land. As early as 723, in order to increase the amount of land under cultivation, the emperor was forced to grant titles outright for three generations to those who reclaimed unused land. The next logical step was to make the title to these lands perpetual. Further need for food-producing land made it impossible to limit the size of these holdings and to deny the request that these lands should be tax exempt. As church lands were tax-free also, as were those granted to individuals rendering great service to the state, the tax base shrank even as the demands for revenue increased. In later Fujiwara times governors of provinces often found that as little as 10 per cent of the land was taxable. A few peasants thus came to bear an overwhelming tax burden. Under these conditions evasion ensued. Old estates were abandoned; shortly thereafter they were reclaimed and thus became tax-free. A solid economic base of discontent was created among the peasantry as the Fujiwara period progressed.

The Fujiwara in Control (645-1150)

For almost two centuries the reforms of Tenchi and Kamatari (Fujiwara) prevented the establishment of complete domination by the Fujiwara family. The first leaders of this clan could have chosen either military or civilian positions. As they were completely converted to Chinese philosophy, they quite naturally chose the civilian and tried to control the military.

Fujiwara Domination Established. Politically, the attempted reorganization was challenged by the Fujiwaras whose ancestor, Kamatari, had hoped to end forever the methods used so successfully by the Soga family to obtain and hold power. Under Fujiwara Yoshifusa (842 A.D.) this family achieved complete domination of Japan. Two of this remarkable man's sisters became wives of the emperor. Yoshifusa had the heir apparent to the throne sent into exile and his young nephew so designated. Then this youngster, as the Emperor Montoku, was married to one of Yoshifusa's daughters. In 858, Yoshifusa was the father of the empress dowager, the grandfather of the emperor, chancellor and regent of the empire, and head of the Fujiwara family. His position was more than slightly dictatorial.

From this time until 1150, a constant succession of infants followed one another to the Japanese throne. The emperors frequently cooperated in this process. Often their dual responsibilities as the secular and the religious head of the state were onerous. It was not too difficult to persuade them to retire to a more pleasant life. As each reached his majority, the Fujiwara regent became the Kwampaku ("Mayor of the Palace") and forced the emperor's resignation in favor of an infant son. Fujiwara held all high court and administrative posts and ran the country for their own welfare.

Collapse of the Central Government. If this seemingly foolproof system was to continue to work successfully, a series of capable men must be available. Yoshifusa and his two immediate successors were well qualified. Later Fujiwara leaders became more and more involved in the extravagant, luxurious court life. Corruption and jealousy characterized their rule.

This decline in ability corresponded too closely for the welfare of the Fujiwara with increased administrative burdens placed on the imperial court at Kyoto. During the ninth and tenth centuries the power of

JAPANESE HISTORY AND GOVERNMENT TO 1867

Yamato was extended successfully in Kyushu, Shikoku, and, at the expense of the Ainus, on Honshu. Military campaigns called for greater taxes which Kyoto often was able to meet only by giving military men in the field greater authority to collect them. As many of these leaders had been banished to the outer provinces to keep them from becoming dangerous rivals, their loyalty to the imperial court and to the Fujiwara was unreliable. With the decline in strength of the central government, these military men in the provinces were called to the capital more frequently to strengthen the position of court nobles from whom they held their provincial estates. Over the years these men acquired the political and social experience necessary to succeed their former masters at Kyoto.

Similarly the Buddhists had become more interested in political matters, so much so that the capital had been moved from Nara to Kyoto in 794, as a result of their influence. As potential rivals had been forced into Buddhist monasteries, there was within the cloistered ranks a strong residue of able fighting men. Finally, as has been noted, the burden on agriculture was almost overbearing. Thus the groundwork was prepared for the collapse of the Fujiwara, and with their fall the end of dominant Chinese influence in Japan's government. The climax brought forty years of civil strife (1159-99) between rival military factions before Minamoto Yoritomo restored some semblance of peace and order to the country.

Although it fell from power in 1150, the Fujiwara family was to leave a lasting impression on Japanese history and politics. It continued to have great influence with the emperor, and until recently the imperial consorts have come from this clan; further, the family's domination of court circles has remained intact. Fujiwara support of the emperor helped to establish the imperial office and dynasty in such a firm position in Japanese history that there has never been a serious challenge to either. This influence was to be significant toward the end of the Tokugawa period. Then, because the Fujiwara had recognized the legal supremacy of the emperor, Japanese scholars used this evidence to prove that the emperor rather than the shogun was the real ruler of Japan. Finally the choice of civilian rather than military offices by the Fujiwara provided, to a degree, the historical origins for the struggle between the civilian and military elements for control of the Japanese government. Although the early leaders of this clan failed in their attempts to reorganize Japan's government along Chinese lines into a centralized administration headed by the emperor, the impact of this family clearly establishes it as one of the most important clans in Japanese history.

Incomplete Adoption of Chinese Political System

Japan's imitation of Chinese politics never was complete. There was always an attempt to adapt what they borrowed to Japanese institutions and philosophy. It is of more than passing importance to note that the Japanese never accepted the Chinese theory of revolution: that an imperial line might be replaced by another when "the mandate of heaven" had been withdrawn. Similarly, the Japanese never adopted the Chinese examination system *in toto*. They did establish an imperial university designed to provide the educational training necessary to secure official positions, but the weakness was the failure to appoint graduates to responsible government posts. Admission to this university was open to sons of the nobility alone; from the beginning there was no way for the son of a peasant to break the monopoly of office-holding which the upper classes enjoyed. Inevitably, capable men of other classes turned to Buddhism or the army for careers. Thus the two democratic institutions in Chinese political practice and theory never found acceptance in Japan.

In the last analysis, the attempt to transplant Chinese government in Japanese soil failed because of the essential differences between the two nations. The Japanese were a military and an agrarian people living in a small state which was divided into many principalities under an hereditary ruler. This was indeed alien soil in which to expect Chinese institutions to thrive. With the collapse of Chinese administration, a growth in the power and numbers of the military class attended by the rise of a new kind of feudalism ensued.

The Kamakura Shogunate (1192-1333)

Minamoto Yoritomo's triumph in 1192 introduced the third phase in Japanese history, the acquisition of supreme power by the soldier. Although the Minamoto family could trace its descent from the imperial line, the monopoly of civilian offices held so jealously by the Fujiwara family had forced the Minamoto clan's younger and more ambitious members into the profession of arms. During the twenty-odd years preceding 1192 in which Minamoto's rival, the Taira family, was all-powerful, Yoritomo not only had built well for the struggle to be renewed successfully against his family's arch foe; he also had time to reflect on the reasons underlying the downfall of the Fujiwara and Taira clans.

The Bakufu Established. One of the results of his careful planning immediately was apparent in Yoritomo's establishment of a separate working capital at Kamakura, well-removed from Kyoto, the old capital. It was evident that the ruthless conqueror believed his military leaders and men to be ill-equipped to contend with the intrigues and the luxurious ways of living so characteristic of the imperial city. To his *bakufu* (camp office), Yoritomo transferred the actual government of the country. To give added strength to his administration, Yoritomo placed the management of many governmental affairs in the hands of his father-in-law, Hojo Tokimasa, a Taira, who received the title of *shikken,* or regent. From the beginning the Hojo regents, all men of outstanding ability, attempted with considerable success to attract men of character and ability to administrative positions. Favoritism played a less significant part in the life at Kamakura, with the result that a sound civilian foundation was laid from which the military power of the Minamoto could operate. Internal peace with attendant prosperity consequently characterized the first decades of Minamoto rule.

The Office of Shogun. At the top of the governmental pyramid Yoritomo eventually secured an imperial grant of the title of Sei-i-tai Shogun ("Barbarian-Subduing Great General") which office carried with it complete authority over all the military forces of Japan. This supreme command had been created originally about 800 A.D. to meet extreme emergencies, but the man so honored had always resigned once the critical time had ended. Now Yoritomo had himself appointed shogun for life with the power to designate his successor. Thus began the dualism which was to be one of the most important characteristics of Japanese government until the shogunal system ended in 1867.

Assassination terminated direct Minamoto rule in 1219. Real authority in the hands of the Hojo *shikken* was exercised through puppet shoguns chosen by the *shikken,* first from the Fujiwara family and later from the imperial house. A confused picture of Japanese authority was the natural result. At Kyoto the emperor theoretically reigned supreme. In reality the most important positions at the court remained in the hands of the Fujiwara family which attempted to control the civilian government. The shogun in theory again controlled Japan, but the regents continued their command of civilian and military power.

Kamakura Gradually Loses Power. In the closing years of the thirteenth century, the dominant position of the Kamakura shoguns and their Hojo regents was weakened by their inability to solve successfully many of the same problems which had caused the decline of other ruling groups. Despite the admonitions of the Hojo regents to preserve the old standards of frugality, justice, and loyalty, the followers of Minamoto succumbed more frequently to luxurious ways of life. The physical growth of the city of Kamakura which attracted artists, actors, etc., made it difficult for the clans to maintain their households on a budget which did not increase as rapidly as did the costs of living. More land areas were exempted from taxation with consequent suffering of the peasants through greatly increased feudal exactions. Both nobility and peasantry began to think of a civil war which would permit them to cancel some debts and meet others by acquiring new lands. The Mongol invasions of 1274 and 1281, which ruined many clans financially and forced the Kamakura shogunate to delay settlement of claims arising from them, further weakened the control of the shogun. These attacks also raise a question as to the probable fate of Japan's dualistic government had it been subject to constant foreign pressure.

All these facts were known and the gradual loss of control by Kamakura was observed by the court at Kyoto. After 1319, Emperor Daigo II, who had the naïve idea that an emperor actually should reign, carefully determined the extent to which jealousy and intrigue had undermined the power of the Minamoto. When Daigo II raised the imperial standard against Kamakura in 1333, his forces were swelled by defections of Minamoto nobles dissatisfied with continued Hojo supremacy at Kamakura. Ashikaga Takauji, a *bakufu* deserter and a Minamoto, led the army which destroyed Kamakura in July of that year. In the attempts of the emperor to restore control of the government to the *kuge* (court nobility), the powerful Ashikaga family would not participate. It soon established itself as the leader of the disillusioned *buke,* or military daimyo (feudal lords), who were to have only a minor role under the governmental system proposed by Daigo II.

Kamakura's Legacy. Under the Kamakura shogunate, disciplined feudalism had caused a partial reorganization of society. The prompt and impartial administration of justice based on the Minamoto code of laws had been one of the reasons for the success of the shogun. A careful attention to local government with close periodic checks on constables and stewards, the two classes of officeholders created to supervise this phase of government, gave additional strength. With the decline of the early frugal standards of life at Kamakura had come a progressive weakening of these two supports of Minamoto authority; the constables became daimyo. Although the Ashikaga shoguns never were able to profit completely from the experience of their immediate predecessors, the lessons taught were not to be lost on the later Tokugawa shoguns.

The Ashikaga Shogunate (1336-1603)

What actually transpired during the first years of the Ashikaga period was a redistribution of feudal power, meaning primarily a redivision of land. Until 1392, a sharp struggle between two claimants for the throne disrupted completely the normal life of the country. In the so-called peace which followed, fighting continued in the provinces, preventing the establishment of a permanent and successful base for feudalism. For many years hostilities laid waste many of the most productive regions of Japan. The last decades of the Ashikaga period are known as the "Epoch of the Warring Country" which lasted until Tokugawa Ieyasu overcame the warring clans and re-established the authority of the central government. If to this anarchy are added the disruptive activities of warlike Buddhist sects and the introduction of Christianity with its hostility to both Buddhism and Shintoism, the resulting picture approximately reflects the 245 years of turmoil that took place.

Relations with China. Two factors in particular tended to develop Chinese influence in Japan at this time, Zen Buddhism [3] and trade. It is true that there were years when, through the satiation or exhaustion of the warring clans, an uneasy peace prevailed. Then, and even in the periods of warfare, progress and change occurred. Contrary to Kamakura practice, the Ashikaga shoguns established their capital at Kyoto. There a gradual blending of the warlike civilization so characteristic of the Minamoto shoguns with the more sumptuous ways of life of the imperial capital took place. The luxurious standards of living established at Kyoto necessitated new sources of income, for which foreign trade seemed particularly promising. It was only natural, then, for the Japanese to desire closer relations with the Chinese whose trade was proving very profitable to Japanese merchants. The importance of this group is reflected in the appearance of a mercantile class.

Also turning Japanese interest toward the mainland was the increasing influence held by the Zen Buddhists with the Ashikaga family. Yoshimitsu (1367-1395), the third Ashikaga shogun, exemplified this trend toward closer relations with China. In response to a Chinese demand, he arrested and remanded to the Chinese for punishment a number of Japanese pirates who had been operating along the coast of China. Yoshimitsu established even closer cultural relations with the Chinese court by accepting formal investiture as "King of Japan" from the emperor of China. Chinese influence on Japanese architecture, literature, and religion followed easily.

[3] See Chapter 8.

Increased Importance of the Family. In the turbulent state of affairs which characterized much of the Ashikaga period, the importance of the *han* [4] as the unit of government increased. Within the *han*, each family was forced to rely more on its own resources. Here too the impact of Confucianism with its emphasis on familial relations helped support the social structure which was being molded anew. The growing importance of the family and the necessity of maintaining it intact had certain noteworthy results. No longer was it possible to permit the family's feudal rights to be divided among the several sons and daughters, with consequent loss of those rights when the latter married. This increased the importance of the masculine with corresponding loss of position by the feminine members of the family until they held a definitely subordinate place in Japanese society. It is also under the impetus of troubled times that the Japanese version of primogeniture developed. It should be pointed out that the son showing the greatest ability, rather than the first-born male, was the heir. If all the sons seemed to lack promise, then a boy from a relative's home or a stranger might be adopted to provide strength for the household. Under these circumstances an individual must place the welfare of his household before his own. Virtues such as obedience, patience, and sacrifice were stressed and cultivated.

Feudal Society. A decline in the importance of the clan and a corresponding increase in the power of the family only continued a trend temporarily halted by the reforms of 645 A.D. In some ways this reflected the change in Japan's government from a central, all-powerful authority into a number of self-governing units. Notable in this transformation was the additional emphasis given to common interests based partly on loyalty to a community rather than blood-relationships, as the ground binding together these communities. Equally significant is a rather sharp division of society: soldiers at the top, then farmers, followed by the artisans with the new mercantile class at the base of the social ladder.

Some 260 feudal houses participated in the first stages of the struggle for power. During the Ashikaga wars the number gradually was reduced to twelve from which, in 1603, one was to emerge victorious. A Japanese counterpart of European feudalism, thoroughly decentralized, thus developed. Just as was true under the Kamakura shogunate, the Ashikaga soon lost control of the government whose powers were exercised by the great daimyo.

Reasons for Ashikaga Decline. If the people living at the capital at Kyoto and individual daimyo at times lived a life of ease and luxury, this

---

[4] Neither the early clans nor the *han* had been made up of related groups. *Han* may be roughly translated as manor or fief (the territory of a feudal daimyo).

certainly was not true of the peasants. Despite feudal wars the farmers continued to till the soil. Taxes often taking as much as 70 per cent of the year's crop caused agrarian unrest and frequent open rebellion. From 1428, riots of the peasantry occurred with increasing frequency. The serious nature of these outbursts against authority is shown by the numerous edicts, both local and national, affording relief from debts; these often amounted to complete cancellation. Here was a definite indication of fear which resulted in concessions to popular feeling. Both the central government and the local authorities were too weak, too poorly organized, to withstand this pressure.

To this picture of confusion and turmoil must be added two other factors which increased the anarchy and set the stage for those who were to save Japan. From the beginning of the Ashikaga period, luxurious living and intrigues had placed a heavy pressure on the tax system. As agrarian unrest mounted with a resultant difficulty in tax collection, the shogun's court was forced to seek other sources of revenue to meet its mounting expenses. Temporary relief was gained by supporting the trade with China. The Shoguns found the merchant class in the seaports more numerous and wealthy than ever before in the nation's history. As in Europe, the Japanese rulers found that for political concessions tending toward self-government, especially in judicial matters, money could be borrowed with expected taxes as collateral. Thus, one more element in Japanese society escaped from complete shogunal control.[5]

The other factor which ultimately contributed to the feudal anarchy was the appearance of the first Westerners, the Portuguese,[6] with their new weapons and Christianity. Thus by 1550, all the elements—agrarian unrest, dissatisfaction, the daimyo, a turbulent priesthood, and a complete disintegration of central governmental control over the provinces—necessary for a final struggle against the Ashikaga were present. That Japan was not to be divided into several small feudal states which would have fallen easy prey to the attack of Western nations can be attributed generally to the rise to power of three strong leaders, Oda Nobunaga, Toyotomi Hideyoshi, and Tokugawa Ieyasu.

Internal Disorder

From the time of the Onin War (1467), conflict had spread into every part of the country. Feudal houses rose to power and with equal rapidity declined, in many instances disappearing entirely. Gradually a regionalism appeared with loyalties yielded to the feudal lord, but with no loyalty

[5] See Chapter 7.
[6] See Chapter 9.

from the regions either to shogun or emperor. Under these conditions the five Home Provinces,[7] the Kwanto, the great feudatories of the North, the western provinces including those on the Inland Sea, and the islands of Shikoku and Kyushu represented the political divisions of the country. A final struggle for power took place during the last half of the sixteenth century. This is final proof of the complete failure of the Ashikaga to exercise effective control over the country. From this feudal warfare the Tokugawa was to emerge completely victorious.

As the Japanese scene looked in 1550, however, the principal actors for the future had minor roles. Nobunaga, a mere youth of sixteen and a descendant of the Taira family, held only Owari Province with some influence in adjoining Mikawa. Hideyoshi, the son of a former peasant, and three years younger than Nobunaga, did not enter the latter's service until 1558. Tokugawa Ieyasu, a descendant of the Minamoto clan and therefore the only one of the three eligible for the shogunate, in 1560 was an unimportant daimyo in Mikawa Province and a mere vassal of the powerful Imagawa family. Mikawa was claimed by both Nobunaga and the Imagawa family.

Nobunaga. Actual fighting between these two feudal families began in 1560, and resulted in the complete triumph of Nobunaga, a victory which brought him national recognition. Any attempt to relate in detail the history of the war which followed would take too much time. Between 1562 and 1567, by alliances (one with Tokugawa Ieyasu) and by military victories Nobunaga gained sufficient strength to accept the imperial court's secret invitation to restore order at Kyoto. As part of this process he had Ashikaga Yoshiaki installed as shogun in 1568 and in return was made vice-shogun charged with the responsibility of bringing peace to the empire. During the next decade the task of consolidating the gains of the initial victory was accomplished through a combination of good fortune,[8] force, and diplomacy. The Home Provinces and the Kwanto afforded Nobunaga a secure base from which operations could be conducted.

It is interesting to notice here that some of the most severe and prolonged campaigns were those against the powerful Buddhist Hieizan monasteries near Kyoto and the Ikko sects of Osaka. Before Nobunaga's rise to power armed bands of monks from Hieizan had terrorized Kyoto at various times in order to gain concessions. Both of these militant monastic groups openly had sided with his opponents in the struggle around Kyoto. Ikko forces actually had defeated Nobunaga's army in his home province of Owari. These struggles were climaxed with complete

[7] Yamato, Kawachi, Idzumi, Yamashiro, and Settsu.
[8] Two of Nobunaga's most powerful rivals died.

finality in 1571 when Nobunaga burned Hieizan and killed those of its inhabitants who escaped the flames. Only by treachery, an ambush attached to a projected truce, was he able to lure the Ikko followers from their fortress-like monastery and destroy them. After 1577 Nobunaga entrusted Hideyoshi with the formidable task of pacifying central and western Japan. When Nobunaga was killed by a disgruntled daimyo in 1582 his campaigns had given him control of the most important provinces of Japan.

It should be observed that this attempt, as other previous efforts, of the monks to actively enter the political arena resulted only in their ruthless suppression. The Japanese were very tolerant in matters of religious belief, but would permit no active political interference from any religious group. It is not surprising then to find little objection to the propagation of Christianity as a religion. Once it was suspected that Christianity would have disruptive political consequences, there also should be no surprise at the harsh action taken against this new belief and its followers.

Hideyoshi. Until his appointment as Kwampaku, or regent, in 1584, Hideyoshi's position was insecure. Temporarily the alliance with Ieyasu lapsed: as the supporter of the claims of Nobunaga's infant grandson to his estates and titles, Hideyoshi had to dispose of other claimants, the sons. Although Nobunaga was a brilliant soldier and leader, his uncompromising attitude toward his enemies had forced them to fight to the end. Hideyoshi consequently knew he had powerful foes.

This short, dynamic man already had shown himself to be Nobunaga's equal as a general. He soon proved that he was even more capable as a diplomat. Never averse to fighting, he preferred to win over his enemies by diplomacy. Thus in his campaign against the Shimadzu family of Satsuma on Kyushu, Hideyoshi first mustered a powerful army of 250,000 men. Before attacking he made generous offers to this great feudal house. Once refused, his armed forces easily overpowered Satsuma whose leaders, however, were not put to death. Hideyoshi broke Satsuma's power by taking hostages and dividing Kyushu among the island's lesser daimyo and his own men. The Satsuma leader, expecting the worst, had the major part of his lands restored to him as a fief which forced him to become a loyal vassal of Hideyoshi. Within the short period of six years these tactics enabled him to unite and pacify the empire.

The restoration of order throughout the main islands also confronted Hideyoshi with the problem of disbanding his feudal armies or of finding new employment for them. If he wished to prevent the renewal of civil war and at the same time continue the distribution of spoils to his followers, the only alternative seemed to be a foreign war of conquest. It is difficult to determine the influence which personal ambition had in his decision to attempt the conquest of China, a project first mentioned by him in 1577. Certainly he foresaw no great obstacles which would prevent its success. So it was that the last six years of Hideyoshi's life were passed in unsuccessful attacks on Korea as the first move toward investing China.

Sekigahara. Before his death in 1598, Hideyoshi had attempted to provide for the peaceful accession to power of his five-year old son, Hideyori. Five prominent daimyo, with Ieyasu as chairman, were named to a board of regents, but the country had been pacified too recently for such a transfer of authority to succeed. Tokugawa Ieyasu, himself master of centrally located territory which was about one seventh of the empire, could not long maintain an indifferent attitude. An open break with the forces supporting his ward occurred in the spring of 1600, after which the decisive battle, Sekigahara, was won by Ieyasu on October 21, 1600. In view of the history of the Tokugawa Shogunate, this must rank high among the most important battles in Japanese history. Although his forces were defeated, Hideyori retained control of his family's domains. This necessitated a final struggle ending in the destruction of his castle at Osaka in 1615, and with it the last significant opposition to the Tokugawa. In the interval, in 1603 Ieyasu forced the emperor to name him shogun, thereby securing for himself legal as well as actual supreme military command.

The Tokugawa Shogunate (1603-1867)

Ieyasu. What is known of this man whose descendants were to hold the shogunal office until its abolition in 1867? As an ally of both Nobunaga and Hideyoshi, he had shown only slightly inferior military ability. That he knew the arts of diplomacy is seen from the willingness of both to entrust him with the protection of the home provinces. His diplomatic ability is further shown by his success in achieving the more powerful feudal coalition before the battle of Sekigahara. His outstanding contribution, the mark of genius, is, however, to be found in his administrative reforms, in his recognition that the governmental machine to be constructed must be strong enough to serve the country and his family well even when weak men were its leaders.

The Emperor's Position. Any evaluation of the feudal, political machinery which the first three Tokugawa shoguns established must

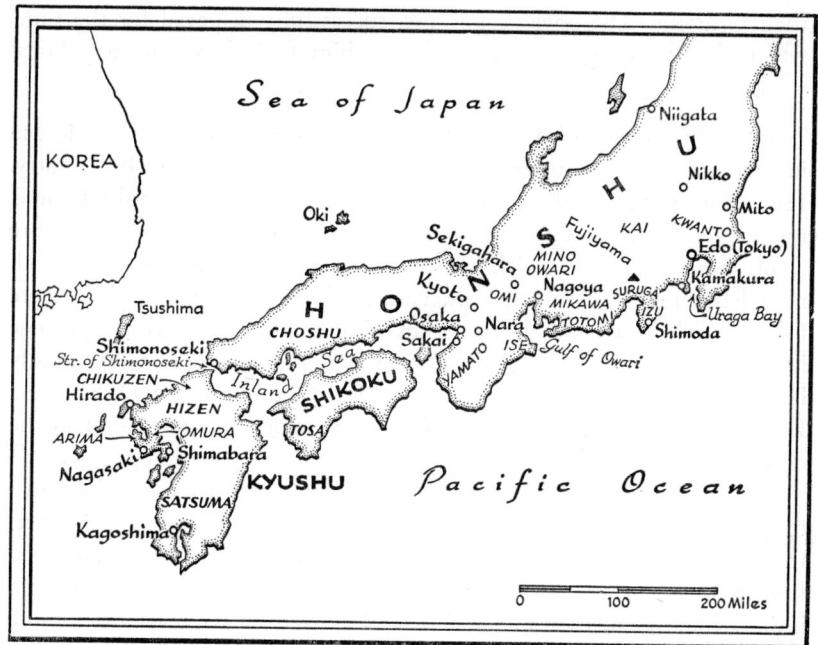

Tokugawa Japan

take into consideration conditions and institutions as they existed after the battle of Sekigahara. Quite in contrast with Europe where national states with monarchical types of government had replaced feudalism, Japan under Ieyasu and his successors was to see feudalism fully developed. Among other things, this meant that the emperor would recede even more into the background, his position becoming almost entirely ceremonial. Although for more than a century after 1600 the shoguns and certain other officers were nominally appointed by the emperor, a more accurate indication of imperial powers than this empty honor can be gained from comparing the amount of rice granted to the court at Kyoto with that allocated to the more powerful daimyo. The latter received a larger allotment, as did many of those of lesser rank. Even with this precaution Tokugawa Ieyasu remembered the occasions in recent Japanese history when court intrigue had acquired political significance. To prevent this, his reforms included the establishment of one of his chief and most trusted retainers in Kyoto as the actual ruler of that city. He insisted that no one should communicate directly with the emperor, that such contact could be made only through the shogun's appointees. Even the high court officials depended on the shogun for their positions. The obvious purpose, successfully achieved for the time, was to isolate the emperor and prevent him from becoming a political rival of the shoguns.

Loyalty to the Shogun Required. In various other ways Ieyasu indicated that he well understood the last century's history of his country. His reforms clearly show, not a desire to improvise completely new methods and machinery to govern the country, but rather to assure a continuation of laws which had proved their effectiveness and to which new legislation was added only where necessary. It was logical then, for the Tokugawa merely to use existing feudal codes whose purpose had been to protect a regional feudal domain. These were essentially house laws of such great families as Mori and Shimadzu of Satsuma. Loyalty to the shogun became the final and most important link in the chain of feudal loyalties.

In 1601, two years before he became shogun, Ieyasu forced all daimyo to pledge loyalty to him, an oath which involved complete obedience, the refusal of asylum, and a promise not to enroll as a samurai [9] any man known to be an assassin or a traitor. As great feudal houses tended to imitate the organization of the shogunal administrative machine, a more uniform governmental and legal system soon appeared. An almost completely new aristocracy, whose power had been acquired by ignoring many rules, now helped to build up a new and stricter ethical code. Absolute compliance with its rules became the supreme test of loyalty.

Position of the People. The obvious intention of these feudal regulations was to strengthen the positions held by the new aristocracy. Consequently the emphasis throughout for the common people is on duties rather than rights. In the field of justice, this meant attention to prompt rather than just punishment. Barbarous penalties, but hardly more so than those imposed in Europe at the same time, were imposed so arbitrarily as to instill fear in the person contemplating a crime. There was little concern about abstract ideas of justice or about permitting discussion or investigation of facts.[10] Considered with the sharp distinction drawn between the warrior class and the rest of the people, to the

---

[9] A samurai ("one who serves") caste had developed during the feudal wars preceding the establishment of the Kamakura Shogunate (1185). Emphasizing loyalty and contempt for death, the samurai, who ranked just below the daimyo, were the vital link in the chain of military feudalism which lasted until 1868.

[10] The emphasis on preservation of order is seen in a proclamation of 1445, stating: "All quarrels and disputes are strictly forbidden. If this is disobeyed, both sides will be put to death, without inquiry into right and wrong." G. B. Sansom, *Japan, A Short Cultural History* (New York, 1930), p. 427. This was typical of feudal edicts in force in the seventeenth century.

former's complete advantage,[11] the result could only be a gradual forcing of all Japanese into a single mold. To this, the minute regulation of every detail of the lives of the people added the finishing touch. Here indeed was sharp contrast with the gradual evolution of democratic insitutions in the Western world. If corresponding political and economic machinery could be devised, here also was a perfect device for the maintenance in power of the Tokugawa shoguns for an indefinite time.

Fudai vs. Tozama Daimyo. The first three Tokugawa rulers were aware of the problems confronting them and took vigorous action to perpetuate their family's power. After the battle of Sekigahara the daimyo were divided into two groups. The *fudai daimyo* either were of the Tokugawa family or had allied themselves with it prior to the battle. To them were given the choice fiefs around Edo, the new capital, and in the Kwanto region extending to the Inland Sea. Geographically Ieyasu's family and friends controlled central and southeastern Honshu. A later decree excluded all but the *fudai daimyo* from holding offices in the newly established *bakufu* and established a complete military and political monopoly in the hands of this group. Furthermore, fiefs of *fudai daimyo* were located throughout the remainder of Honshu and the other islands in such a way as to dominate strategic points or separate powerful rivals.

The latter, the *tozama* (outside) *daimyo* thus held fiefs geographically isolated in northern and western Honshu, or on Shikoku and Kyushu. Their actions were under the constant scrutiny of the *fudai daimyo* who were charged with the responsibility of reporting to the shogun any suspicious activity. Should the *tozama daimyo* succeed in some way in amassing modest wealth, the shogun followed a consistent policy of forcing them to renovate old or build new shrines, roads, etc. Finally the third Tokugawa shogun compelled them to spend equal and alternate periods of time on their fiefs and in Edo. When not at the *bakufu* capital, the *tozama* lords must leave wives and families as hostages. Although these last two regulations applied to all daimyo, the added expense involved in maintaining two costly establishments aided still further in keeping the *tozama daimyo* in an impoverished condition.

It should be observed that this policy of dividing and isolating possible opposition rested upon the continued military predominance and efficiency of the Tokugawa. Its greatest weakness arose from its fostering of a strong clan spirit among the great *tozama* nobility, Satsuma, Choshu, Hizen, and Tosa. Tokugawa decrees preventing intermarriage, intermingling

---

[11] Sansom gives the following quotation from a collection of Tokugawa laws: "All offences are to be punished in accordance with social status." *Ibid.*, p. 463.

of people from one fief with a neighboring fief, or their rise to power in government forced these great feudal families back on their own resources. In order to meet heavy financial demands from Edo, the *tozama daimyo* had to run their lands more efficiently which meant frequently retaining closer contacts with the samurai and peasantry. If the Tokugawa demanded and received the feudal loyalty of the *tozama daimyo,* there was no doubt that this was forced loyalty. These great clans, some with an older family history than the upstart Tokugawa, waited only for signs of weakness at Edo.

"Laws of the Military Houses." Ieyasu and his son and successor, Hidetada, further extended Tokugawa control over the daimyo through the promulgation of "The Laws of the Military Houses" (1615). In essence these dicta established a political code parts of which, i.e., reporting on neighbors, already have been mentioned. Included also was an attempt to formulate a moral code to govern the behavior of the *buke,* or military class. Finally an injunction was given to the feudal soldiers to divide their time between the study of literature and the practices of war. In this way Ieyasu sought an answer to the problem of an unemployed army which Hideyoshi had solved temporarily by the invasion of Korea. Since the study of Confucius was encouraged in particular, it was hoped that the great teacher's emphasis on loyalty would strengthen still further the Tokugawa regime. The only difficulty, overlooked at the time, was the absence in Confucian political thought of any office similar to the shogunate; ultimate loyalty belonged to the emperor. It should be noted in passing that the common people were not supposed to study and learn, merely to be led.

Rules for the Court Nobility. As "The Rules of the Imperial Court and the Court Nobles" attempted to establish similar rules for the *kuge* and other members of the court, Ieyasu hoped to eliminate that group as a danger to Tokugawa absolutism. With his capital at Edo and all appointments to and resignations from high court office requiring the shogun's approval, Ieyasu attempted to avoid and control the intrigues and jealousies of the royal court, factors in the downfall of the Ashikaga shogunate.

Iemitsu Completes the Tokugawa Reforms. If the legal and administrative framework of the Tokugawa regime were built satisfactorily by the first two shoguns, Iemitsu's (1622-51) brilliant tenure of office is responsible for making of the *bakufu* a smoothly running, regimented bureaucracy. It was during Iemitsu's time, also, that the political and economic danger to Japan contained in Christianity was recognized and resolved by the final proscription of that religion and the adoption of the policy of isolation. Of all the shoguns after 1651, only Yoshimune (1716-45) had unusual ability, and many were mediocre men. For this reason, the early establishment of machinery to perpetuate Tokugawa rule is particularly important.

Uniformity in Government Achieved. Without question one of the objectives of the directives which created the governmental administration was the achievement of uniformity from the *bakufu* through to the lowest echelon of the political and economic organization of the country. At the top was the Council of State, composed of four or five elders, with four to six junior elders forming a Junior Council beneath them. The former was almost entirely a policy-making body, while the latter decided upon the rules governing the conduct of the lesser vassals of the shogun. Completing the national governmental machinery were the *bugyo,* or commissioners, including various ministers (finance, state, tax and revenue, etc.) and the chief magistrates of the cities. There seems to have been no logical growth, offices being created in response to conditions as they arose. Within the fiefs and in the field of local government, uniformity gradually appeared as the daimyo created an administration similar to that at Edo. In time even the villages, the religious sects, and the trade guilds lost their autonomy or had their actions rigidly controlled. Within this system, loss of local governing privileges was perhaps inevitable.

Martial Law in Peace. In essence, the Tokugawa imposed in peace a system of martial law. Any tendency on the part of the individual to develop initiative was discouraged, and even regarded with suspicion. All action was group action, which was supposed to prevent any one person from acquiring too much power. To further this end, also, frequent rotation of offices was practiced, with consequent impairment of efficiency often resulting. Throughout all levels of government, officials and daimyo must reckon with the activity of the *metsuke,* or censors, whose business it was to report to the central government what the people and the nobility were doing. If this seems to be a poor training school for wider participation by the people in government, it should be remembered that fear of rebellion was always present; this was true not only in Japan but throughout Oriental countries.

Actually in most instances Tokugawa laws simply reduced to writing what had already become customary law. The Confucian idea that the people should be told what to do, and do it without question, was followed. Similarly, operating on the assumption that man was reasonable, Japanese laws stated only general principles which judges were to interpret. Here was a tradition of government by men, not laws, and the judges quite naturally made the law. This also, it is well to recall, was a government based on force, not consent. The people objected to misgovernment rather than to their own inability to participate in governmental affairs. Finally, the student should remember that the political machinery established was designed primarily to benefit the Tokugawa family and its friends, the country at large only incidentally. Of one result there can be little doubt. When Iemitsu died, he left a bureaucracy almost completely self-perpetuating and so efficient that it could and often did run smoothly without leadership from the shogun.

The Europeans: Arrival and Exclusion

Christianity's Initial Welcome. During the first fifty years of the Tokugawa era, every act of this house was directed toward the twin objectives of restoring peace and maintaining the stability so slowly established. An account of the introduction of Christianity into Japan, of its influence, and of its ultimate expulsion must be written around this central theme. From August, 1549, when the famous Spanish Jesuit, Francis Xavier, landed at Kagoshima in Kyushu until the Shimabara rebellion on that same island in the fall of 1637, the Christian faith could not be considered by Japanese rulers solely on its merits. As a religion, Christianity might have been welcomed, because it did seem to promote good behavior and obedience. Ample evidence exists to prove the liberalism of the Japanese in religious matters; even Buddhist monks invited Jesuit priests to expound their doctrines. The high caliber of the early Christian missionaries won the respect of Japanese leaders, such as Nobunaga who frequently dined and visited with them. Little opposition was offered originally to the conversion of powerful daimyo who forced their subjects to accept the new faith. Although the difference in languages made the translation of Christian concepts difficult, it must be emphasized that there was almost no disapproval of Christianity's doctrines as such.

If the early impact of Christianity on Japan left little impression, reasons other than official opposition to its teachings must be found. The faults with which Christianity was charged, first by Hideyoshi and later by the Tokugawa, arose entirely from the political and economic forces which were associated with the new faith and represented to the leaders a danger to Japan.

Christianity and the Threat of Foreign Intervention. Only so long as Christianity aided the shogun in his fight against his enemies did it receive governmental encouragement and support. Thus Nobunaga welcomed Jesuit aid in his struggle against the Buddhist monks in Kyoto in 1568 and later in other places. Hideyoshi's first anti-Christian edicts (1587) followed closely the active support which he had given them when he thought their assistance might be helpful in dividing the forces of his Kyushu opponents.

There were various reasons for this shift from support to opposition. The latent fears Japan's rulers had of political conquest, which they believed might follow extensive religious conversion, apparently were confirmed by the unwillingness of Spanish Franciscan monks, who arrived after 1592, to obey carefully Hideyoshi's regulations concerning the places where they might preach. The intolerance of Christianity for other religions, the struggle between Jesuit and Franciscan, and after 1600 between Protestant and Catholic, impressed both Hideyoshi and Ieyasu with the possibility that this rivalry might invite the intervention of foreign powers. The first Tokugawa shogun found several thousand Christian converts and four or five foreign priests in Osaka after Ieyasu's forces finally defeated the followers of Hideyori in 1615. The tacit, often open, support given Hideyori by these people was not forgotten by the Tokugawa. Just as soon as Christianity represented a political threat to the stability these Japanese were establishing, its proscription became inevitable.

New Weapons. For almost seventy-five years the dominant faction in Japan hoped that Christianity would strengthen its military and economic position. All Japanese leaders were excited at the possibilities the new weapons—firearms—held for the internal struggle for power in Japan. It is true that the introduction of firearms did not result in Japan, as it had in Europe in the displacing of the warrior class, the samurai, by the soldier drawn from the masses. Nevertheless a revolution in defense, the construction of castles, did follow. Obviously no political faction could afford to permit a rival to obtain a monopoly of the new weapons. Foreign influence which meant greater opportunity to obtain firearms was concentrated in areas controlled by Tokugawa rivals.

Foreign Trade. The struggle for power through the acquisition of wealth gained from trade proved to be more important than the military factor. Despite all efforts of Hideyoshi and Ieyasu to encourage trade between Honshu's ports, particularly Edo, and other Asiatic lands and the West, the trading centers remained in Kyushu. Both the Dutch (1600) and the English (1613) were invited to trade at Edo. Both found that the *fudai daimyo* had little interest in developing trade. The Dutch soon transferred their main activities to Nagasaki, and the English gave up the whole unprofitable venture in disgust in 1623. Both Hideyoshi and Ieyasu followed a liberal trade policy which included encouraging Japanese merchant seamen to develop commerce as far afield as Siam and the Indies. In these ventures, also, only the *tozama daimyo* showed any real interest in building ships and developing trade. Despite their fear that trade with China and India, generally in Portuguese hands, might be cut off, the Japanese feared even more the prospect of intervention from foreign powers under the guise of protecting nationals involved in trade. Of more importance, Hidetada and Iemitsu feared such an addition of wealth to the *tozama daimyo* that the latter might become again serious political rivals.

Christianity Banned. Such is the background which preceded the beginning of the "great persecution" in 1622. All Hideyoshi's and Ieyasu's anti-Christian edicts were enforced and new ones were added. Only after this date were Christian missionaries and their converts hunted down, tortured brutally, and burned at the stake. The complete devotion and simple faith of these early martyrs are attested by the failure of the Japanese authorities to extinguish Christianity for another fifteen years. From the shogun's point of view, it must be admitted that there were ample reasons for the final proscription. Internecine quarrels among the Christians disturbed the peace and always contained in them the possibilities for foreign intervention. Intrigues in Japan, in which Christians as citizens were active partisans, endangered the shogun's position. Finally the Tokugawa rulers were not impressed by reports received from envoys sent to Europe to observe Christianity at work there. The period of European history dominated by the Thirty Years War was not calculated to inspire confidence in the nonpolitical, peaceful aims of Christianity.

In the last analysis, Iemitsu realized that there was an irrevocable connection between Christianity and Western trade and influence. As narrated elsewhere, [12] at the same time that he was eliminating Christian influence, he adopted the policy of exclusion to cut off these dangerous contacts. The decrees forbidding Japanese to leave their country, to construct ships large enough for ocean trade, etc., paralleled the increased intensity of the anti-Christian drive. In 1624 all Spaniards were ordered to leave the country. Thirteen years later the Shimabara Rebellion (near Nagasaki) of about thirty thousand Christians marked the end of Christianity as an organized religion in Japan. As some suspicion of Portuguese aid to the rebels existed, the revolt also gave Iemitsu a reason to order the expulsion of the Portuguese. In 1639 they withdrew to Macao. Only the Dutch remained to carry on a restricted trade on the small island of Deshima in Nagasaki Harbor. Through this small opening, and from equally limited contacts with China, Japan would have to receive all its information concerning the outside world.

[12] See Chapter 9.

By 1641, then, law and order through an efficient, centralized shogunal administration had been achieved in Japan. The Tokugawa knew well their rivals for power, and did not intend to permit them to receive outside assistance. If the *fudai daimyo* had developed Edo as a trading center, then the wealth and power of the *tozama daimyo* would have been decreased proportionately. With continued trade, Christianity, never condemned as a religion, might not have been banned. As events developed, just the opposite was true. Japan closed its doors to the world primarily because of internal political factors. The Tokugawa shoguns believed that their retention of power, dependent as it was on keeping rival feudal nobles weak, demanded the adoption of an isolationist policy. It is now possible to appraise the effects of exclusion on Japanese institutions.

SUGGESTED READINGS

Among the most useful general works are: F. Brinkley and D. Kikuchi, *A History of the Japanese People from the End of the Meiji Era* (New York, 1915); Kenneth S. Latourette, *The History of Japan* (New York, 1947); Edwin O. Reischauer, *Japan, Past and Present* (New York, 1947); Robert K. Reischauer, *Japan, Government—Politics* (New York, 1939); George B. Sansom, *Japan, A Short Cultural History* (New York, 1943); G. Nye Steiger, *The Far East* (New York, 1944).

For additional general works and for studies of specific phases of the political history of Japan, see: E. W. Clement, *A Short History of Japan* (Chicago, 1915); W. Dening, *The Life of Toyotomi Hideyoshi* (Kobe, 1930); H. H. Gowen, *Outline History of Japan* (New York, 1927); W. E. Griffis, *The Mikado's Empire* (2 vols., New York, 1913); K. Hara, *An Introduction to the History of Japan* (New York, 1920); L. Hearn, *Japan: An Attempt at Interpretation* (New York, 1904); E. Kaempfer, *The History of Japan, Together with a Description of the Kingdom of Siam, 1690-1692* (Glasgow, 1906); W. M. McGovern, *Modern Japan, Its Political, Military, and Industrial Organization* (London, 1920); J. A. Murdoch, *A History of Japan* (3 vols., New York, 1926); I. Nitobe, *Japan* (New York, 1931); S. Okuma, *Fifty Years of New Japan* (London, 1909); and H. Saito, *A History of Japan* (London, 1912).

7

JAPANESE ECONOMIC AND SOCIAL INSTITUTIONS

The interest which the Tokugawa shoguns had in maintaining law and order, once established, had an economic as well as a political base. From the records left by the Ashikaga rulers and from personal experience, Ieyasu and his immediate successors recognized clearly the relationship between peace and prosperity. Peasant dissatisfaction from the midfifteenth century to the close of the Ashikaga period could be traced directly to pestilence, natural disasters, and onerous taxation, all of which helped produce famine conditions and widespread starvation. Thousands of peasants had abandoned their farms for the easier life represented by service in the feudal armies. Almost constant warfare, resulting in great confusion and disorder had further upset the nation's economy. Under the impetus of increased internal and foreign trade, later Ashikaga years also had witnessed the growth in numbers, wealth, and power of members of the commercial class. Reference already has been made to the extreme reluctance with which the Tokugawa terminated the very profitable and already well-developed external trade.[1] It is easily demonstrable that Tokugawa Japan's economic problem was not the discovery of sources of wealth and skills to both of which foreign contacts had contributed. Rather it was, as Sansom observes, how to conserve and increase its own resources, a problem complicated by the country's change from an agricultural to a mercantile economy.[2]

During the first half of the Tokugawa period, the true nature and difficulty of this economic problem were somewhat obscured by the progress and prosperity which resulted directly from internal peace. In the seventeenth century, the government at Edo encouraged the improvement of communications between the various sections of the country. The *tozama daimyo* were directed to repair and extend the system of roads, bridges, and related services. All feudal retainers were urged to create conditions within their domains (i.e., equitable taxation) which

[1] See Chapter 6.
[2] G. B. Sansom, *Japan, A Short Cultural History* (New York, 1943), p. 455.

would aid the peasantry. The relative peace and prosperity, based in large part on a better distribution of existing wealth, and especially food, led to a general rise in the standard of living.

Agricultural Conditions

The farmers, about 75 per cent of the population, benefited with the rest of Japanese society. This prosperity, and the actions of the government, were not enough to counteract the basic faults existing within the system of economic feudalism. Agriculture remained essentially at a subsistence level, with the primary concern in each district being an adequate food supply. It was essential that a feudal district be self-sufficient in foods, because little if any help could be expected from other areas in case of famine. Only the Shogun Yoshimune stored rice during the years of abundant crops and thus was able to provide assistance when starvation stalked the land. The necessity for self-sufficiency in itself prevented any kind of regional specialization. Even though the farmer might have made greater profits from tea and mulberry trees, his first concern had to be a rice crop. The fact that 60 to 70 per cent of the trade with the Dutch and Chinese was in silk reveals the extent to which sericulture was neglected in Japan for the food staple.[3]

Roads, despite improvement, remained poor. Inadequate supplementary transportation by sea (vessels were first restricted to 50 tons and later to 100 tons) and a crippling system of internal taxation further increased the division of the country into numerous economic units. A final factor which weakened the nation's economy was the failure to add to the amount of arable land, variously estimated at from 8 to 13 per cent of the total. Only by increasing the food supply in proportion to the increase in population which resulted from better times could Japan have avoided for long a recurrence of the agrarian problem which had plagued the Ashikaga.

Population Pressure

With a population of approximately 30,000,000, the extremely limited amount of arable land meant that each square mile of cultivated land had to support about 2,671 Japanese. Feudal regulations and the mountainous character of the islands had prevented any appreciable expansion of farming land. Other solutions then became imperative. The consequent

[3] J. E. Orchard, *Japan's Economic Position* (New York, 1930), chap. 2.

preoccupation of the people with the daily task of providing food is reflected in many ways.

This problem had been aggravated somewhat when the Tokugawa shoguns insisted that the daimyo and the samurai, who formed their personal guards of honor, spend alternate periods of time at Edo and on their manors. This naturally destroyed any inclination these samurai might have had to continue as part-time tillers of the soil. Severe economic pressure forced other samurai to become artisans and merchants. Since the samurai and their families numbered some 2,000,000 of a total population of from 28,000,000 to 30,000,000 during the last half of the Tokugawa era, a heavy drain on the nation's food supply resulted.

The emphasis on a rice economy was increased further through the regulation in operation during the seventeenth century that taxes must be paid in rice. Even though Ieyasu and his son and grandson set a ratio of 40 per cent for taxes and 60 per cent for the peasants, the natural tendency would be to produce more rice and to avoid otherwise profitable diversification of agriculture. Peasants did form associations with elected officials who were to meet with the shogun's representatives on tax matters. These same associations also established rules governing the cultivation of the land. Any attempted experimentation with crops or methods of cultivation had to be approved by all the villagers. The overwhelming necessity to provide rice for food and taxes precluded much variation from normal routine.

Further evidence of the pressure of population on food supply is found in the birth and death rates in Tokugawa Japan. In particular the death rate was high among the samurai and the birth rate low, yet the same was true to a degree among all classes. Primogeniture, which had become increasingly important as emphasis on family solidarity increased, now came to mean that only the first son had economic security. As in European countries, only he could inherit the estate and titles or privileges. Unless other sons were adopted by childless samurai, their only recourse was to become farmers, artisans, or merchants. Even more important was the food problem and the fact that the samurai and peasantry had fixed incomes in inflationary times which forced men to marry late in life and have small families. Tokugawa records contain numerous decrees aimed at preventing abortion and infanticide, practices which became increasingly prevalent. The equally obnoxious custom of doing away with the aged can be attributed to economic pressure. Farmers preferred to buy children from gangs of kidnapers operating in the cities rather than have large families. Constant worry over food supply accounts largely for these unpleasant aspects of Japanese social life.

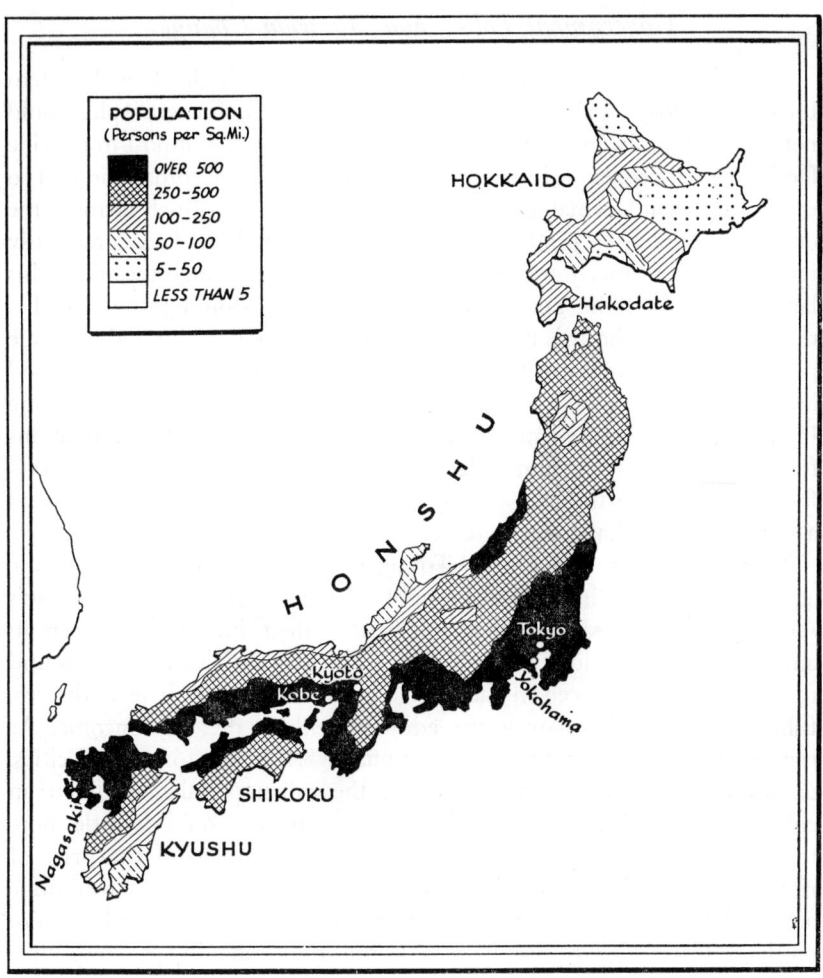

Population Density in Japan

Government Policy and Agrarian Changes

In addition to the restrictions already mentioned, the feudal system further impeded agricultural production. Peasants, for example, could not sell their lands. In a land system already taxed to the utmost to provide food for the people, this could only mean inefficient production. Too much good land remained in the hands of the marginal farmer, the one most unlikely to produce all that the land could yield. As previously indicated, the farmer found it extremely difficult to change the use of his land even though he knew more valuable crops would result. Finally, the custom that the son must follow the occupation of his father made poor farmers of many men who, for example, might have been good leather workers. When, in later Tokugawa times, high taxes became higher and were more capriciously levied and collected, the foundations for peasant uprisings would be laid. When, in addition, various disasters—flood, drought, earthquake—brought famine and death, there followed a series of sharp challenges to the existing regime.[4]

During the last half of the Tokugawa period, failure to solve the agrarian problem inevitably brought changes. Even before Ieyasu's shogunate, the peasants had supplemented their income by a certain amount of home industry. Certainly all ordinary articles needed around the home were produced in the village or on the manor. If near the sea, fishing had provided a welcome addition both to diet and income. As time passed, more peasants found seasonal work in the towns and cities, or left the farm for the easier life of the urban population. Even an enlightened and liberal shogun, Yoshimune (1716-45) could do little more than manipulate the price of rice. Since his adjustment of the price of rice was undertaken primarily to increase his own income, Yoshimune achieved no solution to the farmers' problems. A tax imposed by him on the feudal lords was simply passed on to the people in their respective territories and only added to peasant hardships.[5] After Yoshimune, shoguns repeatedly attempted to control the price of rice, but generally failed to do more than accentuate the already dramatic rise and fall in the price of that commodity.

As taxes came to be collected in money rather than rice, further pressure was exerted on the peasantry whose standard of living remained stationary. This accentuated the movement of people from the farms to the cities and caused a sharp drop in farm production. Many of those

---

[4] Orchard, *op. cit.*, p. 8. There were twenty-two famines recorded in the period 1690-1840 of which half caused extensive loss of life.

[5] Y. Takekoshi, *The Economic Aspects of the History of the Civilization of Japan* (New York, 1930), Vol. 3, p. 134.

who remained lost control of their farms and became tenant farmers. By the end of the Tokugawa period, capitalism was entering the agricultural occupations and a farm labor class was developing.[6] The fact that the tax burden rested heavily on the peasantry but permitted the artisan to remain virtually untaxed added one more grievance to the long list from which the farming class suffered.

In the last century of Tokugawa control, agrarian uprisings became increasingly frequent. It is a sad commentary that the only times the samurai were called to arms after 1641 were when they had to disperse armed rebellions of their own countrymen. In each instance the pattern was the same. The people would organize around a local leader and demand or use force to obtain a solution for their problems. Since combinations of the people for such purposes as relief from exorbitant and inequitable taxes were illegal, the leaders when apprehended were executed. In most instances, however, the demands of the petitioners were met. It was also noticeable that as time passed the samurai were increasingly reluctant to answer the call to arms. Thus, the same agrarian discontent so influential in the downfall of the Ashikaga was present when Japan again opened its doors to the Western world. Only the *tozama daimyo,* forced as they had been to operate more efficiently and maintain closer and better working relationships with their samurai and peasantry, remained in a relatively strong position. The Tokugawa had to retain military supremacy, which rested on the loyalty of their feudal retainers, and they had to gain new allies among the commercial classes. Unless these conditions were met, the discontented peasantry would align themselves with the *tozama daimyo* in a revolution on the first occasion when sufficient pressure from the outside was applied.

The Guild System

It should be evident that the Tokugawa would require the complete support of the merchant-artisan class in order to compensate for a loss of prestige among and assistance from the peasantry. In the closing years of the Ashikaga era, Japan's trade with Portugal, Spain, Holland, and England had increased the numbers and power of a group of wealthy merchants. During the Tokugawa period, however, their loyalty was divided among the several feudal clans. The house of Mitsui, a typical representative of this class, assumed importance from this period.

The Mitsuis had little to learn of the arts of salesmanship and publicity. They provided free umbrellas to customers caught unprepared by

[6] G. C. Allen, *A Short Economic History of Modern Japan* (London, 1946), p. 13.

unexpected showers; each umbrella bore the sign, or trademark, of the House. They paid popular actors to introduce subtle references to the firm in their lines. They had a code in the best tradition of Rotary.[7]

By this time also these merchants had formed associations, or guilds, and had gained certain important privileges. Thus they controlled roads leading to Osaka and Kyoto and had the right to levy taxes at certain collection points along these highways. Members of merchant guilds possessed the right to increase the number and usefulness of ports and markets. The minting of gold coins rested in the hands of some powerful families. That this system was restrictive in nature and hindered free trade is demonstrated by the efforts of Nobunaga and Hideyoshi to destroy the special rights and privileges of these powerful merchants.

Both Ieyasu and his son Hidetada originally preferred the expansion of internal and external commerce under a relatively free-trade system to the controlled trade under the guilds of the later years of the Ashikaga shoguns. Ieyasu, in particular, invited the English to develop trade at Edo and actively encouraged Japanese to trade with other Asiatic peoples. He was well aware of the benefits in terms of revenue from import duties, and he knew that the Japanese wanted the goods brought by the Dutch, Portuguese, and Chinese. He tried to stimulate interest among the *fudai daimyo* in shipbuilding and foreign trade. When these efforts failed, Ieyasu realized that continuance and an expansion of commerce with other nations would remain in the hands of the *tozama daimyo*, his potential rivals for power. Since this would increase their wealth and strength, he had to consider restrictions on trade. The fact that Osaka, long representing a breach in the feudal walls, also had been Hideyori's last stronghold emphasized the dangers of uncontrolled domestic commerce. Even then it was necessary for the third Tokugawa shogun, Iemitsu, to be convinced of the necessary inseparability of foreign trade and the danger of foreign intervention. When the evidence seemed conclusive, the exclusion policy and a return to the guild system were natural results.

Reluctant Support of the Guilds. The revival of the guilds was made easier by the shogun's search for instruments through which his control of the country could be made more effective. Both craft and merchant guilds existed in Japan and were used by the government to control the economy. They may be compared roughly with their European counterparts. In Japan these groups of artisans and merchants either had a *kabu* ("exclusive trade rights")[8] granted by and henceforth recognized

---

[7] *Ibid.*, p. 15.
[8] Takekoshi, *op. cit.*, Vol. II, p. 473.

by the government, or had acquired the same monopolistic privileges through custom. In the former category were those to whom the shogun had granted a monopoly of copper, and the right to control and thus systematize means of measurement (including measures and scales), and the minting of money. *Kabu* also existed for fish dealers, raw-silk merchants, and those who dealt in tobacco, lacquered ware, etc.; in many cases these organizations had been carried over from later Ashikaga times. The Tokugawa ultimately recognized these guilds and the monopoly each had in its particular industry or line of trade. The shoguns taxed the organizations and used them as agencies to enforce administrative policies. Quite in contrast with developments in Europe, neither the executive branch of the government nor the guilds attempted a union against the feudal nobility. The guilds did obtain limited self-governing rights and political privileges in the cities, particularly Osaka. But they never did exercise the pressure through control of wealth and the ability to aid the government so characteristic of the developments in Europe. They remained a distinctly subordinate part of the Japanese feudal system.

The craft guilds exercised the same types of monopolistic control as those which existed in Europe. Membership was both limited and hereditary. The only way for a person outside the system to gain admission was through the purchase of the rights of a retiring member. As the buyer was forced to pay any debts attached to the purchased *kabu*, plus an admission fee and contributions to other members, an originally high price paid became even higher. Despite these obstacles, the goal of every struggling craftsman or merchant was membership in a guild. The Trade Association Decree of 1721, which legalized and formalized existing practices and provided for the registration of the names of members with the government, only increased the desirability of membership for those outside the charmed circles. (It might be noted that the possibility of purchasing membership provided some possibility of change in the economic feudal system.) In addition to controlling membership, the guilds determined the numbers and conditions of apprenticeships as well as regulating prices and setting rates for production. Any member refusing to carry out guild policy was faced with the possibility of exclusion, the threat generally being sufficient to compel compliance.

The guilds for the first time did provide the artisan-merchant classes, through organization, with some protection against the samurai, but there were attendant disadvantages for the economic life of the entire nation. Limits on the number of members imposed by the government, or set by the guilds themselves, denied membership to many who wanted to join. While the guilds resulted in an association of men with similar interests and provided credit facilities and market opportunities to members, the net result for consumers more often than not was an unreasonably high price for the product. Certainly the resultant monopolies eliminated competition and freedom, and resulted in a certain stagnation these stimuli often overcome.[9]

Internal Trade and Industry

The existence of an extensive guild system in itself was an indication of the development of internal commerce and industry. The feudal system required the operation of a system of home industry to supplement its self-sufficient agricultural economy. At an early time certain towns had earned reputations through specialization in the production of swords, armor, furniture, and other articles needed by the daimyo and samurai and their families. Kyoto was known for highly skilled craftsmen who catered to the artistic tastes of the court and its entourage. Osaka and Edo, with about 350,000 and 1,000,000 population respectively in the later Tokugawa period, became important manufacturing centers. Other cities of importance were Hirado, Nagasaki, and Kagoshima, all on Kyushu, and Sakai, Osaka's sister port located at the eastern end of the Inland Sea on Honshu. The size and number of these large towns always were distinct surprises to European merchants.

In addition, then, to the rural areas which provided most of their own necessities, there existed from the beginning of the Tokugawa era commerce between the cities and the country, and among the cities themselves. Throughout most of the seventeenth century, conditions remained relatively stable and, as previously noted, the people were more prosperous. Gradually, certain factors operated to produce a change. The shogun's decree requiring alternate residence by the daimyo in Edo and on their home estates led to a rapid increase in the population of that city. As the new capital grew, its demand for food and manufactured goods increased. Thus, more artisans, merchants, and bankers crowded into Edo. To facilitate this trade, roads were improved and coastal commerce assumed greater importance. Production from home industries simply was unable to meet the new demand. So-called "factories" had been part of Japan's economic life for some time; now they increased in number of plants, in types of goods produced, and in number of workers. The manufacture of textiles, wax, and sake brewing had occurred in plants employing as many as fifty people. The mining trades, gold, silver, and copper, to which coal was added in the seventeenth

[9] *Ibid.*, Vol. II, p. 467.

century, may have employed as many as a hundred workers in a single enterprise. Just as in Western countries, more money and organization were required to develop and operate the mines successfully. Here the serious breach in the feudal economic walls occurred, and a form of capitalism appeared.

The gradual weakening of the feudal economy can be traced in part to the increased commerce between the provinces and the towns and cities. A domestic system, quite outside the guilds, gradually developed to provide goods demanded by the city people. In some instances, merchants distributed raw materials to peasants to be made into finished products in the winter months. Some articles manufactured by farmers and their families were bought by merchants for distribution and sale in the cities.

That these transactions became increasingly difficult with only rice as a medium of exchange can be readily understood. Similarly it was true that the great feudal lords were handicapped by having to store rice at Edo and in their home provinces. The problem of transportation with its attendant costs was serious enough. Thus the use of gold and silver coins, accepted by Nobunaga and Hideyoshi, became more common as trade increased. With the gradual substitution of a money for a rice economy, financiers who arranged credit and carried on other banking operations followed and sometimes preceded the merchants in their business operations through the islands. When merchandising and financing were combined in one family, as was true with Mitsui, the resulting concentration of power posed a challenge for both daimyo and samurai.

The important classes in feudal Japan—the daimyo, samurai, and peasants—were ill-equipped to meet the economic crisis created by the gradual shift to a money economy throughout the country. The incomes of these three groups were fixed in terms of so many acres of land capable of producing so much rice a year.[10] If the daimyo and their feudal retainers were to remain solvent, the price of rice must always correspond to prices of other commodities. If the peasants were to continue, or even increase, the amount of rice produced, then their return after all feudal exactions must be enough to keep body and soul together. That this was not true can be seen from the fluctuation of the price of rice from slightly more than 100 momme (standard unit) of silver per kaku (i. e., 5 bushels) in 1695 to more than 225 in 1713-15 to as low as about 37 in 1718.[11] The hardships involved in this crazy quilt of prices can easily be understood.

[10] G. N. Steiger, *History of the Far East* (New York, 1944), p. 569. For a daimyo, fiefs were granted on the basis of an estimated annual yield of about 50,000 bushels of rice.
[11] Sansom, *op. cit.*, p. 470.

Economic Conditions Undermine Feudalism

The last 150 years of Tokugawa rule demonstrate clearly how little the Japanese from the shogun down understood the economic problems and consequences involved. The feudal aristocracy were caught in a vicious cycle. As they became more accustomed to the pleasures of city life and consequently drifted farther away from the austerity of a martial existence, their demands for goods and services quickly outstripped their incomes. They tried almost every expedient to balance their budgets. The daimyo decreased the amounts of their samurais' rice allowances; this action was the equivalent of requiring forced loans. They further resorted to borrowing large sums from moneylenders or merchants with their expected revenues of rice as collateral. Frequently financial crises were met by the issuance of paper money.[12] Ultimately many became almost hopelessly indebted. The frequency of shogunal decrees which forbade collection of debts incurred by daimyo or samurai before a given year, or ordering payment in such small annual sums as to amount to cancellation, indicated the desperate measures the *Bakufu* took. That none of these measures brought more than temporary relief shows merely that no one understood the problems faced both by the individual and by the government.

Inevitably, the daimyos' attempts to recoup their fortunes at the expense of the samurai led to an acceleration of the latter's impoverishment and to the gradual disintegration of feudalism. Increasing poverty brought a gradual breakdown of the system of personal loyalty and feudal ideals on which the Tokugawa system rested. As the samurai sank more deeply into debt to the merchants, they too tried many ways of escape. Samurai were forced to practice infanticide to cut down expenses. Frequently they adopted the sons of wealthy merchants, a practice which became so common that a customary price was established which the merchants paid to the samurai. Samurai, themselves, with greater frequency entered business and trade. More and more frequently they found it impossible to retain swords, armor, horses, and servants, all marks of their former proud position. The disintegration of the old rigid class system was progressing. It left in its wake an increasing number of disgruntled

---

[12] Metallic currency had replaced rice to an increasing extent from the thirteenth century on. Although gold and silver coins were used, the principal money in Ashikaga times was copper *cash,* much of it imported from China. From that country, too, came the idea of issuing paper money which was used with increasing frequency after 1661. The economic life of the country, and the currency in particular, were further confused by the failure of the shogun to control the issue of paper money. The individual daimyo issued it in large amounts in later Tokugawa times.

samurai who became more vocal in their criticism and hostility to the Tokugawa regime.

Finally, the peasants lost all incentive to produce more rice and to attempt agrarian improvements. A rice crop larger than usual came to mean only heavier taxes, which a poor year might make impossible of payment. The farmer's comparison of his position with that of the artisans in the cities could only be unfavorable to himself. The latter group were virtually tax-free and had a money income which gave them a chance at least to keep up with the abrupt and weird rises and declines in the price level. Attempts on the part of the shogun's government to fix the price of rice generally failed to help the farmer, primarily because they were not intended for that purpose but rather to increase the revenue of the government. The peasantry, as a consequence, although ordinarily conservative, and restricted as were the samurai by the traditions of loyalty inherent in the family system and in feudalism itself, became active opponents of the existing regime. Agrarian unrest, which caused thousands of farmers to migrate to the cities, often led to open peasant revolts and uprisings.

Government Policy: A Failure

What was the government's position in this emergency, and what program did it develop to meet these multiplying signs of collapse? The failure to understand the economic problems which confronted the Tokugawa regime is shown by the measures taken to resolve recurring crises. Instead of attempting to guide and use the power represented by wealth in the hands of the merchant class, the shoguns and their advisers strengthened the features of the feudal system which restricted the production of goods by members of that group. Decrees which banned the wearing of silk by people not of the nobility were scrupulously obeyed externally, but the families of wealthy merchants wore the costliest undergarments. Similar evasions were practiced to nullify an edict limiting the number of presents which might be given on certain occasions. The demand for consumers' goods made foolish government regulations designed to limit production to local markets. After 1641, the exclusion policy crippled foreign trade. The net result of such restrictions was curtailment of the natural growth of manufacturing and the creation of another dissatisfied group within the nation. The *Bakufu* officials also recognized the need for constructive legislation, but their manipulations of the price of rice, revised systems of taxation, and cancellation of debts all failed to produce the desired economic changes throughout the country.

By the beginning of the nineteenth century the financial position of the Tokugawa government was desperate. The administrative costs of the *Bakufu* remained constant or increased. Natural disasters, such as the flood and fire which had destroyed much of Edo in 1657, had depleted the financial reserve acquired and built up by the first three Tokugawa shoguns. The epidemics, famines, and droughts of the last two decades of the eighteenth century forced the shogun into further heavy expenditures. To meet these the Tokugawa could rely only on rice revenues, plus some income from government-owned and -operated mines. As prices soared and the salaries of tax collectors remained low, the difficulty of maintaining a healthy treasury was increased by lax tax administration. Further, even competent officials soon found that there was a limit to the tax load the peasantry would accept peacefully. Under these conditions, the government turned more frequently for a solution to debasing the currency. An inevitable rise in prices followed. The purchasing power of silver and gold coins fell until in 1850 it was only one eighth of what it had been in 1661. Finally, the *Bakufu's* efforts to collect forced taxes from the new merchant and financial class failed to produce enough additional revenue. By 1850 the Tokugawa regime was casting about desperately for new sources of income to support routine services and governmental activities.

Economic Conditions in 1853

From an economic as well as a political viewpoint, then, internal conditions in Japan immediately prior to the visit of Commodore Perry's ships in 1853 had deteriorated to the point where any serious pressure would initiate revolutionary changes. It was quite evident that the basic cause for the weakened position of the Tokugawa shogunate was its utter lack of understanding of the changes involved in the nation's transfer from a rice economy to a money economy. Constantly throughout the last century of this era, the government had used an ethical approach to economic and political problems, the primary idea being the preservation of existing social institutions. The agrarian problem obviously was fundamental to the country's welfare, yet production of more food was impossible within the framework of feudal Japan. Both officials and people failed to recognize the impossibility of stretching the country's available wealth, even with good distribution (which was lacking), to provide an improved standard of living. Finally, as the prosperity of the merchants grew, disaster struck both daimyo and samurai. The former, the feudal aristocracy, could and often did become industrialists, thereby adding to the number of monopolies already in existence. The financial pressure which they felt caused them to cut the allowances of their retainers, the samurai. In the last analysis, this induced over a period of years a gradual weakening of the whole system of personal relationships which in turn resulted in the gradual disintegration of Tokugawa society. In this process, classes lost their sharp distinction, and a fluid state prevailed in which people were finding new positions in the social structure. To a degree this illustrates one characteristic of Japanese life frequently underemphasized. The Japanese never have been blind imitators, but have been willing to try new practices and ideas. The Tokugawa era demonstrates again a capacity for organization and planning which was a continuous process. It is obvious that there was not the sharp break between old and new Japan that some historians have indicated occurred with the Meiji restoration in 1867. This will be further demonstrated in the chapters on cultural history and on the transition period from Perry's first visit in 1853 to 1867.

SUGGESTED READINGS

Among the most useful general works are: George C. Allen, *A Short Economic History of Modern Japan 1867-1937* (London, 1946); John E. Orchard, *Japan's Economic Position; The Progress of Industrialization* (New York, 1930); Edwin O. Reischauer, *Japan, Past and Present* (New York, 1947); George B. Sansom, *Japan, A Short Cultural History* (New York, 1943); G. Nye Steiger, *A History of the Far East* (New York, 1944); and Yosaburo Takekoshi, *The Economic Aspects of the Civilization of Japan* (3 vols. New York, 1930).

For additional general works and for studies of specific phases of the economic and social development of Tokugawa Japan, see: F. Brinkley with D. Kikuchi, *A History of the Japanese People* (New York, 1915); Eijiro Honjo, *The Social and Economic History of Japan* (Kyoto, 1935); Kenneth S. Latourette, *The History of Japan* (New York, 1947); Harold G. Moulton, *Japan, An Economic and Financial Appraisal* (Washington, 1931); James Murdoch, *A History of Japan* (3 vols., London, 1925-26); J. J. Rein, *The Industries of Japan* (New York, 1889); Matsuyo Takizawa, *The Penetration of Money Economy in Japan* (New York, 1927); scholarly studies and other articles of value may be found in such periodicals as *Transactions of the Asiatic Society of Japan* and *The Far Eastern Quarterly*.

8

JAPANESE RELIGION AND CULTURE

The internal peace and relative prosperity of the Tokugawa period gave Japan an unusual opportunity to develop and perfect its own culture. Here again attention must be centered on the fact that the Japanese were not blind imitators. Even a brief survey should convince the Western student that importations from Korea, China, and the Occident in the written language, the arts, and religion were adapted by the Japanese to their own ways of life. The result was a distinctly Japanese civilization. Similarly, even a cursory examination of Japanese religion and philosophy reveals a people willing to accept new thoughts, willing to experiment and to improve on existing methods and ideas, and attempting always to equal and surpass those characteristics which made first Chinese and then Western civilizations more powerful than the Japanese. The student of Japanese history also will become aware of the close association between religion and cultural change.

That the interrelationship between religion and culture is a close one in Western countries is evident, but in Japan it is even more intimate. In politics, in painting, in every aspect of life, the inseparable part religion has played in Japanese civilization is revealed. With these facts in mind it is well to remember Reischauer's statement that a Japanese may be, often is, "...a Shintoist, a Buddhist, and a Confucianist at one and the same time; for religion is something indivisible, a tree whose roots may be Shinto, whose trunk may be Confucianism, and whose fruit and leaves may be Buddhism and Christianity..."[1] What, then, were these religions and their contributions to Japanese life?

Shintoism

Prior to the sixth century A.D., the religion of most Japanese was Shintoism, the only native doctrine among those prominent in Japanese history. It was essentially nature worship, and as such was pantheistic and came to be highly ritualistic. Sacrifices were performed in honor of

[1] R. K. Reischauer, *Japan: Government-Politics* (New York, 1939), p. 23.

the *kami,* the spirits of various natural objects and forces, such as the sun, lightning, rocks, trees, and wells. The very extensive list of *kami* so honored included many things pleasant and beautiful, which indicates that an appreciation of the beauties of nature was an early, rather than an acquired, characteristic of the people. Also present was the idea of propitiation through sacrifice rather than the concept of prayer for assistance in meeting life's dangers and problems. There is in this religion as much emphasis on appreciation, love, and gratitude for gifts granted as there is on fear or on the attempt to pacify angry spirits. If there is in its early history little that is speculative or philosophic, that may be accounted for by the very simple agricultural existence its adherents lived. Shintoism had no body of sacred writings such as those which guided Christianity, Buddhism, or Islam. If there is a religious core in Shintoism, it is found in the ideas of purity and fertility. Death, childbirth, wounds were abhorred because they were looked upon as unclean. Purification ceremonies were demanded of people and priests, and provision was made at each shrine for cleansing one's hands.

Shintoism Formalized. These popular traditional beliefs and practices which had a single ritual based on animism with some elements of magic should be distinguished from the formalized religion of the same name which was openly supported and fostered by the ruling classes during the sixth century. To the early religious observances of Shintoism were then added ancestor worship, imported as a religious observance from China. To the long list of natural objects and forces was added a new hierarchy of *kami,* including household, clan, and imperial ancestors, and legendary heroes. Gradually a fusion between the older and newer gods took place, an amalgamation particularly important in the worship of the Sun Goddess and the emperor. From this compound, Japan's monarchs in modern times were to derive a "divine right" to rule quite similar to the theory practiced by European monarchs from the sixteenth through the eighteenth centuries. The important difference is that Japanese emperors were regarded as being themselves divine, in addition to having a divine right to rule.

Loyalty became the cardinal virtue as seen in the familiar admonition, "Honor the Gods and serve loyally their descendants." This quite easily developed into a religion essentially for a race of warriors. Before the period of great Chinese influence on Japanese government, and again after the Tokugawa era, this religion was to be used by strong, nationalistic parties to justify retention of power or revolution. The closest integration of Shintoism with Japan's political system resulted in each case. It was the highly institutionalized phase of Shintoism which was overwhelmed during the seventh century when Chinese influence dominated the Japanese government. The same thing was true in the first years of the American occupation of Japan after World War II. In both cases the people maintained their simple household Shintoist shrines.

Before commenting on the appearance of foreign religions and philosophies in Japan, it should be noted that Shinto shrines, at Ise and elsewhere, still provide examples of the purest and oldest Japanese architecture. Small, quite simple in construction, with very little ornamentation, these structures typify the thatched, wooden huts of early times. All that is needed is room for an altar and the attending priests: the service does not require a place for the congregation whose members arrive singly or in small groups, make their offerings of food, paper streamers, etc., and depart. The differences between Shinto rites and those of Buddhism became almost as marked as those governing the construction and furnishing of the religious temples of the two faiths.

Religion and Philosophy from China

Chinese and Korean records provide evidence of continuous Japanese contacts with the Asiatic mainland from an early period of history. During and after the third century A.D., refugees and travelers from China had made their way through Korea to Japan. Specifically, in the fifth century, knowledge of sericulture and of silk-weaving was brought to the Land of the Rising Sun by Chinese and Korean emigrants. So too did the first knowledge of a written language and of a new system of ethics, Confucianism, reach Japan. It was natural, then, that in 552 a Chinese Buddhist monk arrived from Korea with copies of Buddhist scriptures and an image of the Buddha.

Origins of Written Language

The political struggle between the conservatives who supported Shintoism and the reform group headed by the Soga family who became proponents of Buddhism has been narrated elsewhere.[2] The fact that this powerful clan adopted Confucianism as a working philosophy on which its leaders based their ideas of government had interesting repercussions in nonpolitical fields. For one thing, until both Buddhism and Confucianism achieved real significance in Japan, a written language had little importance. As a consequence, writing had been monopolized by a small class of official scribes. Its use was limited to a few formal messages such as those addressed to the Chinese emperor; otherwise there seemed

[2] See Chapter 6.

to be little reason for Japanese to master the difficult Chinese ideographic written language. When the Emperor Yōmei late in the sixth century became a Buddhist, even though remaining a Shintoist, the new religion attained respectability. With the triumph of Soga in its struggle to control the government, that family's support of Confucianism made the acquisition of a written Japanese language a necessity. Nothing could have been more natural than the adoption by the Japanese of the Chinese system of writing.

A Japanese Script Developed. Although a mongrel type of native writing, the *manyōgana* which used characters phonetically, persisted, the importance of Chinese as a medium of communication is indicated by the fact that it remained the principal written language of the court and of the arts until the beginning of the tenth century. At this time, as part of a movement emphasizing native institutions, Japanese scholars simplified the *manyōgana* style of writing. Gradually by invention and evolution, syllabaries of abbreviated Chinese characters, each representing a single Japanese sound, were developed. This was a part of a general decline in Chinese influence. The last great embassy from Japan to T'ang China occurred in 838. With an increased interest in things Japanese prevalent, the development of a system of writing the native tongue was a natural result. The Japanese syllabaries, or *kana,* were more clumsy than the English alphabet, but were fairly efficient.[3] The effect of this vastly simplified style of writing on literature will be discussed later. Here it is important to note that it did not displace Chinese, which was still the official language of the professional groups.

Influence on Education. Thus there was created a written Japanese language which was excellent and very simple. Much later this simplicity vanished with the incorporation of Chinese words into the Japanese language. The complexity of the language was increased by the fact that Chinese characters, standing for Chinese words which might have several Japanese equivalents, were used increasingly. The written script thus became a formidable bar to the development of a sound educational system for all the people. It might be observed here that the same arguments, both pro and con, obtained on the question of a romanization of Japan's written language as are mentioned elsewhere for the romanization of Chinese.

With all the difficulty attached to the actual learning of the language, it still remains the primary means of preserving and transmitting the culture of the nation. It is true, of course, that a complete change from

[3] See E. O. Reischauer, *Japan, Past and Present* (New York, 1947), chap. 3, for an excellent discussion of this topic.

the present Japanese script would effect the most abrupt and complete break with the past. At the same time it would permit today an easier influx of a new economic and political philosophy which would counteract to a degree the heritage of the past.

Education and Government Positions

The seventh century reformers did recognize the desirability of establishing a university as a place where candidates for government positions could be trained. The Emperor Tenchi and his Fujiwara ally, in carrying out their reforms after 645, founded a university for that purpose. Appointment to and promotions in the government service were to depend on knowledge and ability rather than on rank. Unfortunately, as noted in an earlier chapter, by limiting admissions to the sons of noble families, the Japanese omitted the democratizing influence within the Chinese system.

Officeholding in Japan thus was limited at a very early date to men of the upper classes and failed to provide an outlet for other gifted men. Thus, although the regents during the later Kamakura period and the early Tokugawa shoguns insisted on having trained men in government jobs, the leavening influence of an educational system which offered opportunity to all was lost. Brilliant commoners, and in Tokugawa times members of the *tozama daimyo,* were forced into the priesthood or into the army, both potentially powerful rivals of the government. Here too is evidence of the high esteem for the scholar such as was found in China, but, by contrast, in Japan the literati seldom achieved high positions and paramountcy over the military or the political leaders.

Such education as existed thus became still another part of the system of privileges enjoyed by the nobility alone. The content was classical, consisting primarily of a study of the most important works of Confucius. With rare exceptions it was limited to the sons of families, as women held an inferior position in Japanese society. Little interest in or necessity for any kind of mass education was to be felt until modern times.[4]

Decline of Shintoism: Shotoku's Opposition

The impact of Buddhism and Confucianism on Japanese life extended far beyond the field of education. The century following the introduction of Buddhism (522) witnessed the arrival in Japan of an increasing number

---

[4] The Shinran sect of Buddhism brought its message to the people partly through discussion groups, or lay congregations, which supplied the lower classes with much of their intellectual life.

of artists, scholars, and priests from Korea. As almost all these were Buddhists, the influence of that religion increased rapidly. The code of Prince Shotoku in 604 ordered the people to revere the "Three Treasures" of Buddhism: the Buddha, the Law, and the Priesthood. Since Shotoku and later reformers were interested in the widespread adoption of the moral and philosophical teachings of Buddhism, it was natural that the number of priests, nuns, and temples should increase.[5] The fact that the Shotoku code fails to refer to Shintoism emphasizes this interest in Buddhism. This omission may be attributed in part to the greater emphasis the native religion had placed on the superstitious, ritualistic side of the faith. The idea of sacrifices or fines as a measure of propitiation had degenerated into a system whose punitive character was indicated by frequent fines for ritualistic offenses.

At the same time the very fact that Shotoku's code—a set of moral laws—had been formulated was revolutionary. Its principles require as great an insistence on the obligations of superiors to inferiors as on the obedience required of inferiors to superiors. Of paramount importance to Shotoku was the fact that Buddhism supported the idea of centralized government with ultimate power held by the emperor. Shintoism contrariwise was closely allied with the clan system which Shotoku was opposing. These facts help to account for one of the remarkable features of Japanese history in the period ending in the twelfth century, the complete submergence of Shintoism.

Confucian Influence

At the same time that Shotoku turned to Buddhism for a moral and philosophical basis for his state, he sought guidance in Confucian ethics for his political theory which was in fact almost completely Confucianist. From this quite naturally arose Shotoku's insistence that both scholars and officials should be thoroughly learned in the Confucian Classics. This, together with the influx of emigrants from China, ushered in the period when Chinese influence thoroughly dominated the Japanese governmental system.

Why Confucianism Was Accepted. It could well be asked why at this and later periods of Japanese history, Confucianism was welcomed by the Japanese? In general, Confucianism certainly was not inimical to Japanese institutions. Only the formal religious aspects of ancestor worship had to be adopted by the Japanese from Confucianism. Most

---

[5] Sansom, *op. cit.*, p. 71: "By the end of 624 there were 46 temples, 816 priests, and 569 nuns." In 572 only one priest could be found in all Japan, and he had become a layman. Buddhism's powerful sponsor did not win its struggle at court until the end of the century.

of its other characteristics were consistent with existing Japanese philosophy and practice. Its rites and ceremonies were associated with acts of life. Further the emphasis on and support of the family system fitted neatly into the Japanese way of life. The five Confucian relationships of ruler and subject, husband and wife, parent and child, elder child and younger child, friend and friend, dominated all phases of Japanese life.

The rulers of Japan, the superior men, found support for their right to dictate to the masses in the Confucian recognition of the inequality of men. Certainly Shotoku knew that in Confucianism the state was closely identified with religion. The teaching of the great Chinese and his disciples emphasized that the affairs of men were governed by the Will of Heaven as expressed and directed by the king in accordance with the command of Heaven. In this philosophy too could be found justification for a government of men rather than a government of laws. The seventh-century attempt to replace loose clan loyalties with an allegiance to the emperor as the supreme ruler was thus buttressed by Confucianism.

Confucianism Not Completely Adopted. Chinese influence, and with it Confucianism, had its greatest influence on Japanese art, philosophy, and politics for the almost five centuries which emcompassed the brilliant reign of the T'ang dynasty in China (618-906) and the dominance of the Fujiwara in Japan. Although its importance fluctuated after 1150, Confucianism was not seriously challenged until Shintoist attacks on this foreign faith occurred in the eighteenth and nineteenth centuries. Earlier Japanese scholars of the works of Confucius and his disciples apparently had not known that the great Chinese had been an advocate of liberalism and had used old forms as a means of infusing new ideas into the society of his day. They either had missed or overlooked that part of the teachings of Mencius, Confucius' most prominent disciple, which stated that a wicked ruler was not the rightful or lawful one and that therefore rebellion against him was permissible. The idea of revolution was completely foreign to Japanese political theory. Once this phase of Confucian philosophy was understood, Confucianism would be placed in the same category as Buddhism and Christianity; it would be condemned as being dangerous to the Japanese state because of some of its doctrines. Even when this developed, the hold of Confucianism on Japanese life remained strong.

The Power of Buddhism

Buddhism became the dominant religion in Japan in the seventh century and retained its paramount influence until the middle of the Tokugawa era. In addition to the close association of this foreign religion with governmental centralization originally and with politics continually, Buddhism's hold on the government and people may be explained in other ways. It had the emotional appeal, the promise of a better existence in the next life, and a rationalization of man's present status which Shintoism lacked. Buddhism, for example, taught that the emperor was a living manifestation of the Buddha's spirit, thereby giving further support to the Shotoku party's insistence on the paramountcy of the emperor over other clan chieftains. This close association of the emperor with the Buddha also served as an additional justification for the regulation by the government of every aspect of a man's life. After all, any action a man took might affect his relations with the supernatural. Buddhism also tended to be conservative in its social philosophy by counseling acceptance of one's status in life as being his just reward or punishment for acts occurring in a previous life.

Evidence of Buddhist Influence. The power Buddhism had in Japan can be demonstrated in many ways. A new capital, Nara, was built in 710, yet within the century (784) the influence of Buddhist monasteries near the city had become so great that still another imperial city, Kyoto, was constructed in 794.[6] Here is evidence of the dangers involved in forcing potential political rivals to become monks. The existence of a large number of able political and military men within the ranks of the monks created at times an unruly group willing to use force to gain their ends. In later days, during the Ashikaga shogunate, the rivalries of Buddhist sects added immeasurably to the confusion and destruction of civil wars. Nobunaga in the 1570's befriended Christian priests because of their hostility toward Buddhists who were among the most inveterate foes that brilliant leader encountered. The intimate connection between Buddhism and politics in Japan frequently led to abuse, and certainly prevented the birth and growth of any tradition of separation of Church from State.

Buddhist Sects. Space will permit only brief mention of the various Buddhist sects which came into Japan during these centuries. Thus the Tendai and Shingon monks established themselves early in the ninth century at the new capital of Kyoto. These sects contended that the Shinto *kami* were nothing more than incarnations of Buddhist *bodhisattvas*. Why the Shinto priests permitted this heresy to remain virtually unchallenged, thereby contributing materially to their loss of a place in Japanese religious life for a thousand years, is a perplexing question for which no completely satisfactory answer is known. Shingon and Tendai both helped the

[6] Buddhist temples, examples of the oldest and most beautiful architecture using wood, still may be seen.

Emperor Go-Daigo in his fight against the first Ashikaga shogun in 1336. The Tendai monasteries were located on Hieisan, a hill northeast of Kyoto. Monks from these monasteries opposed Nobunaga, often successfully, until he destroyed their buildings and their inhabitants in 1574. Together with the Hosso and Kegon sects, Tendai and Shingon dominated the Buddhist religion in Japan for about four centuries (until *ca.* 1200).

This monopoly was broken during the next half century by the appearance of four new sects, Jodo, Shin, Zen, and Nichiren. In general it might be said that these new systems repudiated the extreme emphasis on metaphysics of the earlier sects. Simplicity of doctrine was stressed in the teachings of the monks. Shin became the most popular of all Buddhist sects; even today it is the strongest. Nichiren is known as a nationalistic, fighting sect quite different in its lack of tolerance, universalism, and pacifism from earlier Buddhist sects. In particular, Zen Buddhism became popular with the military classes in Japan. Scorning the sutras and most of the other formalities of the older sects, Zen insisted that only by introspection and self-purification could the truth, the real meaning of the world, be found. Here was a sect almost nonphilosophical, not based on the written word but dependent upon "sudden enlightenment," which could be achieved only by complete mastery of self. The dominant place held by the older Buddhist sects in Kyoto partially explains the decision of the shogun to build a capital at Kamakura rather than remaining at Kyoto. While one of the interesting aspects of the Kamakura shogunate is the widespread acceptance of Buddhism, the popularity of the Zen sect among the military can be ascribed to the reasons just mentioned. The frugality of Zen monks and the obvious necessity for self-discipline, if one is to experience the great enlightenment, fitted well into the code of ethics of the samurai. Patronage of Zen by such powerful Ashikaga shoguns as Takauji and Yoshimitsu helped its followers in their struggle against rival sects. Zen, too, retained its popularity in modern times.

Shintoist Revival

The number of Buddhist sects and their continued close association with China provided Japan with spiritual and intellectual stimulation and leadership. Not until the Tokugawa shoguns destroyed these characteristics of Buddhism by making it more and more of a support for their regime, did this religion lose its dominant position. Although the Tokugawa supported Buddhist churches generously and forced every Japanese to be a member of some Buddhist sect, Buddhism by becoming a tool of the government lost its intellectual and religious drive. First, Confucian scholars attacked it, but the spiritual gap left by the decline of Buddhism was filled not by Confucianism but by a revived Shintoist faith. The native religion repudiated the *bodhisattva* role given by the Buddhists to the *kami* which once again became independent deities to be worshiped by all good citizens. From this step it was natural for Shintoism to turn against Confucianism as being a religion just as foreign as Buddhism. That this religious struggle occurred in the eighteenth century and focused attention on the divine ancestry of the emperor, forces the student to notice some other aspects of Japanese cultural change before considering further political history.

Japanese Civilization

The culture and civilization of Japan prior to 1850 were the products of three successive phases of development. A native foundation in the arts, the influence of which is always present, dates from the pre-Chinese period. This is followed by the period of strong Korean and Chinese ascendancy which began in the fourth century and lasted until the seventeenth. Finally, in Tokugawa Japan, isolation and the changes in the economic and social structure of the country permitted the perfection of a society whose culture resulted from the demand for a more vigorous, natural, and national expression in literature and art, combined with an important residue of things Chinese. In this way, and during these later years of relative calm, the country developed a typically Japanese civilization.

The Native Period. That these periods cannot be distinguished clearly, is evident even during the prehistoric period. Although Japan's civilization at this time was extremely primitive, the division of the country into clans suggests a relatively advanced system of social organization. Both stone and iron implements have been found in sepulchral mounds. That the architecture of this early period was quite primitive is shown by the fact that the rulers had simple, wooden-thatched homes. Although hunting and fishing supplemented the supply of food, rice was the staple product, and society thus was primarily agricultural. From Chinese accounts of Japanese life further support for this is obtained from lists of criminal offenses most of which were concerned with rice fields, water supply, and the violation of the rights of the individual therein. Although spinning and weaving were apparently known to Japanese of the third century, clothing made from hemp and mulberry bark was worn by the common people. An interest in and preference for elaborate costumes featuring jewelry was another characteristic.[7]

The Chinese Period: Architecture. Certainly the material culture of the Japanese through the sixth century was poor and was rapidly altered by Chinese importations. The complete domination of Japanese political institutions by the Chinese political system brought with it the acceptance of other elements of Chinese culture. Thus, when new capitals were built at Nara and Kyoto in the eighth century, architecturally both cities were modeled closely after Ch'angan, the capital of T'ang China. The grace and color of Buddhist architecture provided a vivid contrast to the plain Shinto temples and showed a definite Korean influence. Domestic architecture in Japan continued to reflect a Korean influence until the tenth century. Until the Tokugawa period of Japanese history, religious architecture in Japan changed its styles as those of China varied. The Ashikaga shoguns almost slavishly imitated architectural models provided by Ming China.

Other Chinese Importations. The same imitation and adaptation were followed by the Japanese in other phases of their cultural life. Even the name *Dai Nippon* from which is derived the modern Western word, *Japan,* is of Chinese origin and meant originally "Great Sun-Origin-Kingdom." The Japanese liked this so much that during the Nara period (710-784) the new name displaced the older one, *Yamato.* As Chinese was the official, written language, Chinese literary styles prevailed. Both the early Japanese histories, the *Kojiki* and the *Nihon Shoki* reflect this tendency. Although syllabic *kana* came into increasing use, becoming a national language during the ninth century, Chinese remained the language of polite literature and of the scholar class.

Isolation Aids in Developing a National Culture. It is true that both poetry and prose were being written in *kana,* and in literary forms quite different from the Chinese. The women of the court, who seldom had an opportunity to learn Chinese, wrote the first great Japanese prose. Lady Murasaki's *The Tale of Genji* was an outstanding example of the new romantic narratives and was a part of the first flowering of Japanese literature and the arts in the tenth and eleventh centuries. The luxury of the Fujiwara court at this time and the high esteem accorded to things Chinese encouraged cultural progress. During this period and that of the Kamakura shogunate which followed, isolation from the rest of the world was a powerful factor which affected all phases of the nation's life. Culture borrowed from China was assimilated; native arts were developed. The twelfth century witnessed a crystallization of these trends. With the

[7] Sansom, *op. cit.* The writer is indebted to Professor Sansom for much of this material.

warrior becoming the dominant figure in Japanese life under the Kamakura shoguns, the principal literary form became the heroic tale of feudal warfare, generally some story based on the struggle between the Taira and Minamoto families.

Ashikaga Culture: Chinese Influence. When the Ashikaga shoguns won control of the government in the fourteenth century, the luxury of their court soon surpassed that of the Fujiwara. Even though Japanese porcelain workers had learned the fine points of their art from Chinese potters, this industry did not flourish until the Tokugawa period. Although an earlier attempt to make tea drinking popular had failed, its reintroduction from China early in the thirteenth century had been more successful. Contacts such as these were increased constantly under Ashikaga leaders who actively sought closer commercial, religious, and cultural relations with Ming China. In this period of extravagant living, extremes in art and literature became commonplace. The cultural advancement of the time is all the more extraordinary when the almost constant civil war of the Ashikaga shogunate is considered. Buddhism should receive most of the credit for keeping the arts alive, yet religion as such did not dominate painting, architecture, and literature. All tended to become secular, even though sponsored by Zen monks. In literature, the height of a writer's ambition was attained upon his production of poetry and prose which were mistaken for the work of Chinese authors. There existed a veritable passion for anything Chinese. The Japanese benefited particularly from historical and philosophical studies of Chinese writers.

A New and Frivolous Culture. During these troubled years, a certain nostalgia led the Japanese to look back to more peaceful days for the guidance of ancient rules; particularly was this so in matters of taste and behavior, which were regulated to a minute degree. Other phases of Ashikaga life reflected more truly the restlessness then current, a factor which led to emphasis on the exotic and the frivolous. In poetry this was seen in the development into a popular game of the old Japanese habit of supplying the second half of a previously written verse. Teachers and judges were in as great demand as were acceptable verses. The same extravagance is to be found in landscape gardening, the arrangement of cut flowers, and in incense-judging contests.

The Tea Ceremony. Two aspects of Ashikaga culture require more explanation because of the contribution which they made to Japanese cultural life, and because their influence extended into the Tokugawa period of Japanese history. A new contribution to manners was provided by the tea ceremony, the *cha-no-yu*. Shuko, a Zen monk, is regarded as the founder of the tea cult, and certainly Zen Buddhism sponsored the ceremony in the belief that it would promote courtesy and spiritual color. Sansom describes it "... a Tea Ceremony is a gathering, conducted according to a prescribed etiquette and in simple, quiet surroundings, of friends who have artistic tastes in common." [8]

With the country torn by feudal war, this ceremony encouraged a withdrawal from the responsibilities and ugliness of daily life, and an appreciation of the beautiful as seen in a vase, a painting, or a poem. Regrettably, it soon lost the discipline involved in Zen principles of simplicity and ritual; nevertheless the tea ceremony definitely affected the Japanese cultural scene. Because it became a very costly cult through its passion for beautiful and expensive porcelain, the tea ceremony contributed to the ceramic art by providing wealthy patrons. One room, or alcove, in Japanese homes was used as a "tea room." With all its extravagance, the basic idea was admirable and did much to foster the courtesy which has been such a charming feature of Japanese life.

The *Nō*. The second phase of Ashikaga culture which served as a link with the past and the future was the development of the lyric drama, or *Nō*, a contribution as original as Japan was to make to the arts. From an early time, the Japanese had known dancing and music of a popular type, as well as the solemn rituals. In addition to Chinese and Korean influences, there were performances in which juggling, acrobatics, and humorous gestures played a considerable part. Gradually during the Kamakura period the actors costumed themselves as, and acted the part of, legendary personages. From this developed a more finished performance, staged and rehearsed by specialists, which was called *Nō*.

Certainly by the middle of the fourteenth century groups of competing actors existed; there remained only the necessity for perfecting the plays and the raising of the profession of the actor to one of respectability. Both these advances were achieved by Kwanami (1333-84) and his son Seami (1363-1444). The father, an accomplished actor, together with his son, who was favored by the Shogun Yoshimitsu, made their greatest contribution by the production of a harmonious whole from the poetry, dancing, and music already a part of Japanese culture. From these traditional elements was created a rare and composite work of beauty.

Actually there is little originality in the *Nō* plays; rather an attempt is made to weave together parts of existing verse. There is, of course, the most intimate connection between the beat of the music and the words and movements of the actors. In its finale, emotional tension is shown by an elaborate posture rather than by words. Although definite religious and secular elements are to be found in the *Nō*, Kwanami and

---

[8] *Ibid.*, p. 397.

his followers definitely were its creators. Its originality and difference also can be shown by saying that the *Nō* owed nothing directly to China. Zen Buddhism supported its development as a means of teaching the concepts of Buddhism. It should be noted that all *Nō* performances were in accord with Zen dictates of good taste. After all, the audiences for whom the *Nō* plays were presented had Zen aesthetic standards which insisted upon the importance of form and an emphasis on suggestion or allusion rather than outright mimicry to reproduce any action. If these plays were at times somewhat superficial, they were very popular and served as an active stimulation to the allied arts such as painting.

Tokugawa Civilization

Early Influences. As previously indicated, the Japan of the sixteenth and seventeenth centuries was a nation on which beat conflicting pressures. The last decades of the Ashikaga shogunate were tumultuous ones which saw almost continual feudal warfare. This was also a period during which the population was shifting from the country to the towns and cities as the wealth of the latter increased. During this time, also, the impact of the West was first felt. While it is true that certain material things, such as guns, improvements in shipbuilding and navigation, mosquito nets, and potatoes almost became necessities, the Occidental influence on Japanese culture was not deep and soon lost its significance. It was natural, therefore, that with the virtual end of contact with Western civilization after 1640, the Japanese should turn their attention to the perfection of their own culture. Japan was left then with only casual relations with China whose culture was static. Such a condition may be contrasted sharply with the European nations whose civilization at this same time was being enriched from many and varied sources.

A Culture for the People. By the end of the seventeenth century, the economic and political changes described elsewhere had their effect. Originally, developments in the arts had been conditioned by the fact that patrons generally came from the nobility, particularly the military class. As the people acquired wealth, their ability to patronize the theater, to buy paintings, and to satisfy their artistic desires in other ways, added strength in the development of literature and art which reflected more naturally native genius. Kyoto and the new city of Edo welcomed the new culture which was characterized by its emphasis on colors, bluntness of expression, and general vigor rather than the restrained shading of the older forms of artistic expression. Carving became extremely intricate, and blazing colors were customary. These replaced the exact proportions and sense of gracefulness of the old order. Poetry and prose told their stories with brutal frankness. The delicacy of the brush paintings of landscapes and flowers was overwhelmed by the vivid color prints of artists such as Hokusai and the caricatures of Matahei.

Genroku. The story of these changes and of the waning popularity of the *Nō* plays can be told best by a reference to Genroku, a short period from 1688 to 1703. It effectively represents the new trend in Japanese culture which clearly defined and reached a climax during these years. Some of its characteristics have just been indicated. They were established by the people of the towns who set the standards for the arts, but in this only followed the feverish pattern set for them by the ruling classes. Although the artists of the time were less restricted by convention and expressed a more native spirit, it should not be inferred that the standards of the wealthy city patrons were careless. Their ideas on good literature, plays, or art, while different from the older criteria still popular with the samurai, were nonetheless definite and strict. It is impossible to describe in detail the changes occurring in painting, sculpture, and architecture. Despite the stimulus provided by the building of Edo and its rapid expansion, no outstanding changes in architectural design developed, and religious sculpture was almost second rate. Painters abandoned the old subjects for street scenes and the vivid colors of costumes and color prints.

One of the most interesting phases of Genroku culture concerns the theater. Ieyasu and his immediate successor patronized the *Nō* plays which continued to be popular with the upper classes. About 1700 a Confucian scholar professed to find in the *Nō* a danger to the State, a charge which led to the reluctant withdrawal of official support. Without court patronage, the *Nō* plays survived only because of their aesthetic appeal and as part of the training of many amateur players. This is only a partial indication of the appeal the theater had for the townspeople.

Although the origin of the popular drama is hard to determine, its popularity in the Genroku period was well established. This approval by the people was increased as music for the romances improved. Puppet shows became more popular as the dolls were made more lifelike and their manipulators became more skilful. It was for such a puppet theater that Japan's greatest playwright, Chikamatsu, worked.

In appraising the many plays written about this time, the student should remember that most of them were written for puppets, which would tend to make the plays overly discursive as well as to restrict them with the limitations of their mechanical performers. The popularity of the plays increased, too, as the actors became more polished and capable of portraying well the *aragoto,* or "rough business," which Edo audiences demanded, or *nuregoto,* "moist business," which was favored in Kyoto and Osaka.[9] As most of the plays depicted conflicts in the society of the time, such as a struggle between feudal loyalty and family ties, and were steeped in Confucian ethics and Buddhist sentiment, their social significance was important.[10] For these and other reasons, a study of these popular dramas (metrical romances) is richly rewarding.

Chinese Influence. The patronage of the arts generally owes much to the attempt by the Tokugawa shoguns to encourage scholarly pursuits among their military retainers. Among other things, this resulted in an increase in Chinese influence in Japan. Neo-Confucianism provided a knowledge of a system of ethics which emphasized the position of the civilian at the expense of the military. Gradually, too, the moral code of the warrior class (later known as Bushido, "The Way of the Soldier") which was similar to that of Western chivalry, was modified by new ideas and became the property of all the people. Although the Tokugawa fostered Bushido and Confucianism primarily because of their insistence upon loyalty as the cardinal virtue, it was impossible to prevent some scholars from noticing that the emperor was the legitimate head of the Japanese state. Similarly, as Japan's economic and political problems multiplied, too frequently without solution, it was inevitable that dissatisfied Japanese leaders would look elsewhere for a solution to their difficulties.

Foreign Contacts. It was fortunate that Japan never had been completely isolated from contact with foreign ideas. The Dutch, first at yearly intervals, later quadrennially, had been forced to report to Edo on world events. After 1716, Yoshimune repealed the ban on foreign books and ordered the compilation of a Dutch-Japanese dictionary. Despite efforts to restrict the knowledge of the outside world to government officials, individuals did study such foreign subjects as anatomy, medicine, and geography. Even before the downfall of the shogunate, daring Japanese had defied the edict forbidding travel abroad. Thus, the efforts of the Tokugawa to suppress all new habits and thoughts as being dangerous were challenged. Some Japanese believed the causes of their country's economic weakness could be found in the policy of isolation. With more frequent contacts from China and Russia in the eighteenth and nineteenth centuries, other Japanese feared their nation was being weakened militarily by the exclusion of foreign ideas. In many ways then Japan was being prepared for Commodore Perry's visit to Uraga Bay in 1853.

[9] *Ibid.,* p. 486.
[10] The favorite literary and dramatic theme in modern Japan is based on the tale of the "Forty Seven Ronin."

Individualism in Japanese Culture

In Japanese culture, finally, the student will find little which emphasizes the value of the individual. Even critics of the existing regime approved of existing social stratifications and institutions and adhered to a group or class morality which discouraged individual responsibility. One was first a member of the family which was in turn a part of the *han,* the most important unit of government. Some Japanese were thinking of the nation, with the emperor as the father, as the last step in the chain of loyalties. In this philosophy, there was a strong sense of unity; this in turn was a strong factor in making each person believe that, however lowly his status in life might be, his contribution was essential for the state to function properly. Certainly this was a philosophy, supported by religion, which could supply a strong foundation for the rapid changes in Japanese life soon to become necessary. It is equally true that it provided no base from which democracy might be expected to grow quickly, a fact hardly of importance to the Japanese of 1850.

SUGGESTED READINGS

Among the most useful general works are: Edwin O. Reischauer, *Japan, Past and Present* (New York, 1947), and George B. Sansom, *Japan, A Short Cultural History* (New York, 1943).

For additional general works and for studies of specific phases of the cultural history of Japan, see: Masaharu Anesaki, *History of Japanese Religion* (London, 1930); Charles N. E. Eliot, *Japanese Buddhism* (London, 1935); D. C. Holtom, *The National Faith of Japan: A Study of Modern Shinto* (London, 1938); H. Minamoto, *An Illustrated History of Japanese Art* (Kyoto, 1935); August K. Reischauer, *Studies in Japanese Buddhism* (New York, 1925); Noritake Tsuda, *Handbook of Japanese Art* (Tokyo, 1935); Arthur Waley, *Japanese Poetry, The 'Uta'* (Oxford, 1919); Arthur Waley (trans.), *The Nō Plays of Japan* (New York, 1922); Arthur Waley (trans.), *The Tale of Genji* (London, 1935).

9

SINO-JAPANESE INTERNATIONAL RELATIONS— PRE-TREATY

Early Chinese Foreign Contacts

While it is somewhat difficult to say whether China had knowledge of Europe before Europeans learned about China, it is patent that the Chinese had relations with what would now be called foreign peoples virtually from the dawn of Chinese history. Those with whom the Chinese first came into contact were Mongoloids of central Asia whom the Chinese made subservient to themselves.[1]

The centuries passed and by 115 B.C. China had reached the point of having treaty relations with a number of states. This fact, which was later apparently forgotten when China was rediscovered by the West, would seem to indicate that China, far from being hostile and inhospitable to foreigners, was originally quite willing to have relations with other peoples. Trade developed at a somewhat brisk pace, thereby increasing the need for political relations. The exchange of commodities between China and her Asiatic neighbors to the west by the great desert route led naturally to an interchange of ideas as well as of goods. Not the least of such concepts which thus entered China was Buddhism.

It is entirely possible that Far Eastern merchants had actually reached Rome before the birth of Christ. The arrival of an envoy from Marcus Aurelius in 196 A.D. is duly recorded in Chinese history. Even earlier, a celebrated treatise on astronomy reached China from some part of the Roman Empire.[2] To India, China was indebted for many new ideas and with that country enjoyed fairly close contacts. Another group of foreigners with whom the Chinese early came into contact was the Arabs, who appear to have reached China early in the second century A.D. Excellent relations ensued until the proselytizing activities of the Moham-

---

[1] W. E. Soothill, *China and the West* (London: 1925), p. 3. This little book presents an excellent short summary of China's relations with the West. See also H. G. Creel, *The Birth of China* (New York, 1937); and G. F. Hudson, *Europe and China; a Survey of Their Relations from the Earliest Times to 1800* (New York, 1931).

[2] Soothill, *op. cit.*, p. 16.

medans resulted in bloodshed, as, for example, when the Islamites set fire to Canton in 758 A.D. Arab contacts with China were maintained both by land and sea. It was the former which provided an entree for the Mohammedan religion into western China. China's contacts with the Arabs had lasting effects as far as the Western world was concerned, because it was from the Chinese that the Arabs learned the secret of making paper which, centuries later, the Moors introduced into Europe.[3] It was, it should be noted, the Chinese who also invented printing.[4]

Christianity first made its appearance about 625 A.D. in the form of Nestorianism. Chinese converts to this form of Christianity were many, and its tenets enjoyed wide success. A suppression of foreign dogmas in the ninth century A.D. reduced it to negligible proportions, however, and although a brief revival took place during the Mongol dynasty, it died out with the end of that era.

During the Sung dynasty (960-1280), China was sorely pressed by a nomadic tribe, the Khitans, in the northeast and by the Tibetans in the west. At the same time, the power of Islam was such that it cut off China from any effective contacts with Europe. In the twelfth century both the Sungs and the Khitans began to deteriorate at a time when a new and more formidable force, the Chin or Golden Horde, arose. The Horde drove away the Khitans and invaded and seized all of China north of the Yangtze. Yet as powerful as the Golden Horde was, it proved itself no match for the Mongols, a race originally hailing from the area north of the Amur River and southeast of Lake Baikal.

After a century of struggling with the Golden Horde, the Mongols, whose name means "brave men," in 1234 succeeded in conquering and expelling their rivals from China. Greatest of the Mongol leaders was Jenghiz ("Very Mighty") Khan (1162-1227) who before he died overran great portions of Asia and eastern Europe and who was responsible for the deaths of millions of people. So great was the setback received by Mohammedanism from the ravages of the Mongols that they lost their control over the land route between China and the West which consequently was reopened during the time of Jenghiz' successors. Among the first to avail themselves of this opportunity to reach China were European missionaries. As the Mongols began to grow somewhat more civilized, they saw to it that the land route to Europe was kept open. Meanwhile, under Kublai Khan, they completed their conquest of China in 1279. Kublai sought unsuccessfully to add Japan to his dominions but did include Burma, Siam, and Indo-China among his vassal states.

---

[3] *Ibid.*, pp. 24 ff.

[4] On both paper and printing, see T. F. Carter and L. Carrington Goodrich, *The Invention of Printing in China and Its Spread Westward* (2d ed., New York, 1955).

The Coming of the Europeans. The amazing adventures of an intrepid Venetian by the name of Marco Polo served in Europe to throw considerable light upon the Mongols in general and their Great Khan in particular. Marco's celebrated book of travels was widely read, among its most careful readers being Christopher Columbus who was greatly influenced by it.

Marco Polo's father and uncle were the first Europeans known to have reached Kublai Khan's court, where they were given both a letter and an envoy to the pope requesting the latter to send a number of missionaries to explain Christian doctrine to Kublai's subjects. On their return to Peking, then called Khanbalik or City of the Khan by the Mongols and later by the Europeans Cambaluc, the elder Polos brought with them fifteen-year-old Marco, the son of Nicolo who had become a widower while he was in China. Two Dominicans who set out with them gave up and returned to Europe, and after a trip of some three and a half years of dangerous and exciting travel, the Polos in 1275 reached Peking where they received a warm welcome from the Khan who was enchanted by young Marco's pleasing personality. Marco was placed in Kublai's diplomatic service and was employed on numerous missions, one of which involved his ruling a city for some three years.

In 1292 the nostalgic Polos finally convinced the reluctant Khan, through some Persian envoys, that they should guide the latter and a youthful Mongol princess from Kublai's court, who was betrothed to the Mongol Khan of Persia, to the Persian court. Permission was granted on the grounds that they would return to Cambaluc, which they promised to do. After accomplishing their mission in Persia, the daring Venetians continued westward alone and reached Venice in 1295. Their stories and their evidences of wealth attracted wide attention, and Marco became known as *Messer Millione,* owing to his constant references to China's uncounted millions. While in prison following Genoa's victory over Venice in 1298, Marco dictated his adventures to a fellow prisoner. His account became widely known and won a measure of fame probably never equaled by a travel book.

Meanwhile, as pointed out above, the Church had sent a few missionaries to China.[5] As early as 1245 a Franciscan, John of Plano Carpini, had penetrated as far as the former capital of the Mongols, Karakoram, and succeeded in contacting the then Mongol khan. More successful in his endeavors was another Franciscan, who later became the first Archbishop of Peking, John of Monte Corvino, a diplomat as well as a

---

[5] Through missionaries and diplomats Europe received in the thirteenth and fourteenth centuries its greatest knowledge of China up to that point in history. G. F. Hudson, *Europe and China* (London, 1931), pp. 134-35.

missionary, who was sent by the pope in 1289 to Kublai and who arrived at the Khan's court shortly after the departure of the Polos. John's reception was a most cordial one, and by the time of his death in 1328 there were approximately 100,000 Christian converts in China.

The overthrow of the Mongols in 1368 by the Ming dynasty was a harsh and almost deadly blow to Christianity in China. Missionary activity now diminished. One important factor accounting for this decline was the great distance and the severe dangers involved in trying to reach a China no longer friendly following the conquest of the Mongols.[6]

As the fifteenth century waned, European knowledge of China had largely disappeared owing to the lack of intercourse. The discovery of the sea route to India by the Portuguese navigator Vasco da Gama (1497-99) started a veritable frenzy of rivalry among the European powers seeking to exploit the fabulous riches of the East. Da Gama was interested not only in spices but in the winning of Christian converts as well.[7] In the face of strong opposition by the Arabs who controlled the rich trade of India, the Portuguese made great strides, including the conquest of Goa. Portugal's dominion was then extended into Ceylon and the East Indies.

Meanwhile, China again became a goal of European merchants and traders. The first European known to have reached China by sea was the Portuguese Alvarez in 1514. Since he did not set foot on the mainland, this distinction was won by a relative of Christopher Columbus named Rafael Perestrello who arrived in 1516 in a Malay junk accompanied by some thirty Portuguese. Canton was reached about 1518 by a Portuguese diplomatic mission eager to inaugurate commercial relations. Success crowned this effort, and a commercial treaty was ratified but annulled before it could take effect because of Chinese anger over the depredations of a Portuguese freebooter who preyed upon Chinese shipping. The unfortunate Portuguese mission was later executed by the Chinese in retaliation for their countryman's misdeeds. However, other Portuguese remained undaunted and some time not long afterwards won permission to use the island of Shang Ch'uan as a base to trade with Canton. Then in 1557 Portuguese traders were granted the privilege of occupying a tiny corner of an island (Macao) at the mouth of the Pearl River. The Chinese erected a wall across the narrow strip of land in order to separate their territory from the Portuguese buildings. Ownership of the land remained Chinese, but the Portuguese were permitted to occupy it in return for the payment of an annual tribute. In 1849 owing to a disagreement the

[6] *Ibid.*, pp. 154-55.
[7] C. W. Allan, *Jesuits at the Court of Peking* (Shanghai, 1935), p. 6.

Portuguese ceased paying the annual levy and have held this territory, considerably enlarged, down to the present day.

Other Europeans. Portugal's neighbor on the Iberian Peninsula, Spain, was also interested in China, but the best the Spanish could achieve was a foothold on Formosa, which they secured in 1626 only to lose it to the Dutch a few years later. The latter, in turn, were put to rout in 1661 by the famous Chinese pirate Koxinga. Spain's contribution to the China trade lay in the introduction of the Spanish (later Mexican) dollar which became the principal currency along the China Coast due to the fact that the only money minted by the Chinese was the copper cash.[8]

The Dutch who had established themselves in Java in 1618 almost succeeded in wresting Macao from the Portuguese three years later. They did manage to occupy the Pescadores (between Formosa and the mainland) but had to leave these islands or give up the privilege of trading with China. In general the Dutch did not enjoy much success in China despite their willingness to kotow.

The people destined to be most prominent in the China trade were the English who, for almost two centuries, sought a way to reach China. It was not until the end of the seventeenth century that they ultimately succeeded in opening commercial relations. Even then conditions were far from satisfactory, and after some years the English government decided to send a diplomatic mission to Peking. The first man chosen for this task was drowned when his ship foundered. Accordingly, in 1792, his successor, Lord Macartney, set out. Although granted an interview by the emperor, Macartney and his entourage were regarded as representatives of an inferior power, "bearers of gifts." The emperor was so unimpressed that he refused Macartney's requests.[9]

The French also reached China at the end of the seventeenth century but evinced greater interest in missionary work than in trade and devoted their major endeavors to the task of converting the Chinese.

Work of the Missionaries. The Portuguese interest in winning converts to Christianity led to the reappearance in the Far East of the Catholic missionary. These men endured any hardship for the sake of winning souls in lands newly opened to their activities. Their return to China coincided approximately with the work of the Counter Reformation in Europe. In this movement the greatest accomplishments were achieved by the new preaching and teaching order, the Society of Jesus. Outstand-

---

[8] Soothill, *op. cit.*, p. 84.

[9] The Chinese inscription on all boats and wagons used by Macartney read "Ambassador bearing tribute from the country of England." H. B. Morse, *The International Relations of the Chinese Empire* (Shanghai, 1910), Vol. I, p. 54.

ing among the Jesuits who went to the Far East to toil under incredible hardships was the brilliant St. Francis Xavier who pledged himself to the conversion of China.[10]

Xavier worked long and devotedly in India, Ceylon, and the Moluccas before he began his famous work in Japan. After his achievements there, he turned toward the realization of his dreams, the conversion of China. In 1552, he arrived at the island of Shang Ch'uan, the only place then available to the Portuguese traders. Before he had a chance to risk the dangers of a visit to the mainland, Xavier died. His body was later returned to Goa where, remarkably preserved, it is frequently displayed for the veneration of Catholic pilgrims.

His failure to reach China provided a stimulus for those who followed him. The first of these entered China in 1555, but were not allowed to remain for long. The man who enjoyed the first real success was an Italian Jesuit, Michele de Ruggieri, although the most outstanding of these Catholic pioneers was the Italian Jesuit Matteo Ricci. Both these men were highly cultured individuals who had a considerable knowledge of scientific matters. But it was not until they had demonstrated their familiarity with the Chinese classics, and so won respect for their Oriental culture, that the early Jesuits had an opportunity to impress the Chinese with their scientific knowledge. It was fortunate that they were so accomplished, because the Chinese were thoroughly convinced that all foreigners were barbarians. Based upon contacts which the Chinese had had with Europeans, this view was not far from the truth, for those Westerners had been avaricious merchants and ruthless freebooters who preyed upon all Orientals at every opportunity.

Through his maps and other devices, Ricci began to win a number of prominent converts. Following a long series of vicissitudes, he managed to reach Peking but was unable to secure an audience with the emperor. Some years later he won this important privilege. He and his companion then became persons of prominence in the capital where they won people to their religious beliefs, in no small measure because of their mathematical and scientific knowledge which provided them with opportunities to discuss religion. Clocks which they brought as gifts so delighted the decadent Emperor Wan Li that Father Ricci and his companion were made official keepers of these timepieces, which no Chinese could then understand. Ricci's labors were most fruitful; before his death in 1610 his numerous converts included two imperial princes.

Despite the outstanding accomplishments of men like Ricci, the dislike and distrust of foreigners were so strong that the Chinese were constantly plotting to expel them from the country. Finally, in 1617, the emperor

[10] Allan, *op. cit.*, p. 131.

succumbed to the misrepresentations with which he was being beset and ordered the expulsion of the missionaries. However, some were given secret protection in the homes of prominent native converts, so that the country was not emptied of all who had come to bring Christianity to the Chinese people.

Yet about ten years after their banishment, the Christians were invited to return in the hope that they might give useful advice on how to check the encroachments of the Manchus, who were seriously threatening China's security in the North. Under the last Ming emperor, Ch'ung Cheng, the Jesuits and a number of their most important native converts were given posts of honor in the imperial service. This fine opportunity to win influential Chinese officials to Christianity was carefully developed with encouraging results. Unfortunately for the new religion, a controversy developed over the rites to be observed by the Catholic Church in China. This followed the establishment of the Dominicans and Franciscans in China, along with the Jesuits with whom they were not in complete agreement. The newcomers looked askance at what they considered the wide latitude given the Chinese by the Jesuits in several matters, including Confucianism and ancestor worship, connected with the rituals of the church. The upshot was a split which proved most grievous for the Catholic Church in China.[11]

Meanwhile, the Manchus continued to advance, and rebellions broke out in various parts of the empire, thereby adding to the weakness and confusion of the last decades of the Ming dynasty. Despite these blows the government was able for some years to hold the Manchus at bay and prevent their crossing the Great Wall. The end came in 1640 when a rebellion broke out in Shensi Province. The hapless Ming emperor, faced with the invasion of Peking by the insurrectionist Li Tsu-ch'eng and deserted by his leading officials, committed suicide. So ended almost three hundred years of Ming rule.[12]

The rebels, however, were destroyed by loyal troops assisted by the Manchus, but not before the emperor's palace had been set on fire. With the throne now vacant and the Manchus too powerful to eject, their Khan,

---

[11] This question is exceedingly complicated, and the reader is advised to consult the excellent account in K. S. Latourette, *A History of Christian Missions in China* (New York, 1929), chap. 8.

[12] It was under the Ming, toward the latter part of the sixteenth century, that the Chinese inaugurated their policy of excluding foreigners. As Soothill, *op. cit.*, p. 77, notes: "To an age-long history of Tartar aggression on the north and west was now added the anxiety of a huge coast line, at the mercy of a piratical nation like the Japanese, and of a new influx of men of barbarous breed, with a language no civilized tongue could master; beards black, brown, and even red; eyes not a decent black or brown, but like those of cats, blue and grey; and of a manner ferocious. It was high time that China shut itself in to itself, and excluded foreign wares which it did not need."

a six-year-old boy, was made emperor of China under the name of Shun Chih. Thus began the Ch'ing or Manchu dynasty. When he assumed full power upon the death of his uncle the regent some eight years later, the young emperor chose as his chief adviser a Jesuit named Adam Schaal. In 1662 the death of Shun Chih brought a sharp change in the fortunes of the church and the beginning of Christian persecutions.

There ensued a period of ups and downs which culminated in the issuance of a decree of suppression by the Emperor Yung Cheng in 1724 which prohibited any Chinese from becoming a Christian and resulted in the expulsion of all missionaries except those in the service of the imperial court. The reason for this severe step was the emperor's apprehension that the Christians might eventually be able to harm him politically. His fear was based on the fact that so many previous attempts in Chinese history to overthrow the government had had their origins in religious movements, e.g., the White Lotus sect.[13] From this time forward until 1858, when treaties signed with the victorious English and French brought relief, Christianity in China was subjected to terrible trials, but its persecutors never succeeded in eliminating it. Nonetheless, untold thousands of both Chinese Christians and their European mentors suffered cruel punishments and even death for their faith.

Treaty of Nerchinsk. The Russians, who had been engaged in the conquest of Siberian nomadic tribes, had by 1683 succeeded in extending their holdings to the Sea of Okhotz. Border conflicts ensued between the Russians and the Bannermen (Manchus) which led to the opening of unfruitful negotiations by the Russians who vainly tried to treat with the Manchu emperor. The Chinese, considering the Russian construction of some forts as an invasion of their territory, opened hostilities. The fighting resulted in a stalemate, and finally the Chinese changed their minds and agreed to seek a settlement of their differences.[14]

In 1689, largely through the tact and diplomacy of two Jesuits from Peking who were ordered by the emperor to act as interpreters for the Chinese delegation, an agreement fixing the boundaries between the two powers was signed. There were four official copies of this Treaty of Nerchinsk. Two were in Latin, indicating the important role played at the court of Peking by the missionaries despite the persecutions. The original correspondence of the Chinese with the Russians which had preceded the treaty negotiations also had been in Latin. Nerchinsk proved significant in that it marked the first treaty ever signed by China with a European power.

[13] Allan, *op. cit.*, pp. 265 f.
[14] Mingchien Joshua Bau, *The Foreign Relations of China* (New York, 1921), p. 5.

One of the articles of the treaty provided both for arbitration of disputes and mutual extraterritoriality. Criminals were to be handed over to their own national authorities for punishment, and frontier troubles were made the subject of diplomatic negotiations rather than treated as causes of war.[15]

Earliest Japanese Foreign Contacts

China and Korea. It would be virtually impossible to say exactly when the people of Japan made their earliest foreign contacts, but it is fairly well established that Japan's first official contacts were with Korea and occurred in 33 B.C. Shortly afterwards, in 27 B.C., the Japanese began the practice of having a magistrate in Korea to assist in keeping order.

According to Japanese legend, the Empress Jingo invaded Korea in the year 200 A.D. and succeeded in forcing one of the kings in what is now Korea to pay tribute semiannually and to send annually a number of slaves to Japan. This legend also says that the success of the Japanese under the empress led two other Korean kingdoms to undertake similar arrangements with the Japanese. This legend is now generally believed to have no basis in fact. However, there is evidence that, both before her reign and after it, the Japanese had made inroads upon Korea. On some of these occasions the Japanese captured Korean prisoners; on others they forced Korea to send hostages to Japan.[16]

Between the third and the eighth centuries A.D., new religious and artistic influences were introduced into Japan from the Asiatic Continent. Buddhism, Confucianism, and other schools of Chinese philosophy all played major roles in the modification of Japanese ways.

In the third century A.D., there is evidence that Chinese writing was introduced from Korea and, seemingly, Buddhism also made its appearance at this time. Immigrants and presents from Korea were forthcoming from time to time thereafter. In 552 a number of Korean doctors and scientists, who brought with them Buddhist missionaries, took up residence at the Japanese court. Thus it was in the sixth century that Japan received so much of the foundations for its civilization which came to her from China by way of Korea. Most important in this respect was Buddhism.[17]

In the year 600 A.D., Japan sent an unofficial representative to China to learn what China's attitude was toward Korea. Formal diplomatic intercourse between China and Japan was not established until 607. In that year

---

[15] Min Ch'ien T. Z. Tyau, *The Legal Obligations Arising Out of Treaty Relations Between China and Other States* (Shanghai, 1917), p. 4.

[16] Yoshi S. Kuno, *Japanese Expansion on the Asiatic Continent* (Berkeley, 1937), Vol. I, pp. 3-4.

[17] See chapter 8.

the Japanese emperor sent an emissary to the Chinese court where he was graciously received and accompanied on his return by a Chinese envoy and his suite. They in turn were cordially greeted by the Japanese emperor.

China and Japan first became engaged in war in 663. Appropriately, it was over Korean affairs. Two of the Korean kingdoms, beset by a third which was in alliance with China, sought aid from Japan. The Japanese expeditionary force and its Korean allies were defeated by the combined power of China and its Korean partner. The latter then absorbed one of Japan's defeated partners and, with China, split up the third; thereby resulted the virtual unification of Korea. Strangely enough, the victorious Korean kingdom continued its earlier practice of sending tribute to Japan. The latter, as a result of its defeat inaugurated a hands-off policy toward Korea and China, although within two years after Japan's setback the Chinese had sent a diplomat to Japan, an action which was quickly reciprocated.

The Mongols. From the seventh century, the Japanese had had contacts with various nomadic tribes living in what is now Manchuria. Some of these relations were friendly, others were not. These incidents, however, were extremely minor compared with events of the thirteenth century. At that time the Mongols had successfully invaded Korea in 1261, reducing it to a vassal state. Under the great Kublai Khan, they determined to reduce Japan to a similar status. Various Mongol missions having been either rebuffed or slaughtered in cold blood by the Japanese, the Mongols elected to invade and conquer Japan.

In 1274 a powerful Mongol fleet, equipped with weapons acquired from the Venetians, together with a strong force of Korean vassals, captured Iki and Tsushima islands and was apparently destined to overcome the defenders of Kyushu when a howling typhoon destroyed most of the invading fleet, forcing the survivors to flee.

Kublai again sought to secure Japanese acknowledgment of his suzerainty by sending envoys. Japanese truculence was climaxed by their murder of the ambassador sent in 1280. Therefore, Kublai decided upon another invasion. This time (1281), an armada estimated at some 4,500 vessels and a huge force of Mongols, Chinese, and Koreans was raised. Split into two divisions, the first, consisting of 900 ships and 40,000 men, set sail in May, 1281, for Japan. In July, the second division, some 3,500 ships and 100,000 men, joined the attack. Again the elements aided the doughty Japanese, who were superior mariners anyway, and the carnage among the invaders who reached Japanese soil was frightful. The Mongols were compelled to surrender, and, although some Chinese and Korean vassals were spared, the rest were all put to the sword.

While the fighting was in progress, the Japanese nation prayed to its gods for deliverance. At a crucial moment in the battle, a typhoon struck, wreaking havoc on the Mongol fleet and saving Japan once again. To the Japanese, these winds which had twice saved them from the Mongols were heaven sent. They named them Kamikaze (divine winds) and exulted that their gods had proved superior to those of the Chinese. This incident served as a basis for the formation of units of Japanese suicide fliers in World War II, the Kamikaze Corps, who were supposed to save Japan from invasion and who did manage to inflict serious losses on the American forces, especially at Okinawa.

It was not long after the Mongol failures that Japanese pirates began to make life miserable for some of China's coastal regions, as well as those of Korea. These devastating activities lasted throughout the fourteenth and fifteenth centuries and virtually cut Japan off from outside contact.

Early Success of Christianity. Then in the sixteenth century came the men destined to unify Japan: Nobunaga, Hideyoshi, and Ieyasu. The first of these three military conquerors smashed the power of the Buddhist monks and was disposed in friendly fashion toward Christianity, largely for domestic political reasons. The missionaries had arrived in Japan in the wake of the Portuguese traders. The first port opened to the Portuguese was Kagoshima in 1542. This was followed by the opening of Nagasaki in 1570. The Portuguese were granted exceptional privileges there by the local feudal lord (daimyo), including the right to travel into the interior to carry on their trade, together with exemption from taxes and other duties.

The gentle St. Francis Xavier reached Japan in 1549. Following a rapid success, he left his work in the hands of other Jesuits. Xavier once asked his interpreter, a Japanese who had been converted at Goa, what likelihood there was of the acceptance of Christianity and was told that the Japanese "would not immediately assent to what might be said to them, but they would investigate what I might affirm respecting religion by a multitude of questions, and, above all, by observing whether my conduct agreed with my words. This done, the king, the nobility (daimyo), and adult population would flock to Christ, being a nation which always follows reason as a guide." [18] Within a generation or so after Xavier's

---

[18] Verification of this assertion is found in the following written by Xavier in 1551: "These Japanese are supremely curious,—eager to be instructed to the highest degree.... Their spirit of curiosity is such that they become importunate; they ask questions, and argue without knowing how to make an end of it; eager to have an answer and to communicate what they have learned to others." James Murdoch, *A History of Japan* (New York, 1926), Vol. I, pp. 5-6.

arrival, some 200,000 Japanese had been converted and more than 200 churches, monasteries, and schools had been erected. By 1600, the number of converts had doubled, but the same unfortunate differences which arose in China between the Jesuits and the Franciscans were repeated.

Korean Conquest. Nobunaga was assassinated in 1582 and his mantle of leadership in the struggle to unify Japan was assumed by Hideyoshi. The latter was most successful in his efforts to subordinate the powerful feudal lords. He was almost consumed with ambition to conquer the Continent and did restore the old tributary position of Korea which had grown moribund. However, he was unable to convince the Koreans that they should make common cause with him against China, and as a result diplomatic relations between Japan and Korea were broken in 1591.

In 1592, a formidable Japanese force, armed with firearms to which they had been introduced by the Portuguese, set out to invade Korea. Opposition was easily overcome, and the Korean capital, Seoul, was quickly captured. A Chinese force which came to the assistance of Korea was crushed. In January, 1593, a more imposing Chinese force drove the Japanese invaders back to Seoul. Peace negotiations failed, and a second Japanese invasion in 1598 culminated in victory for the latter who decapitated almost 40,000 Chinese and Koreans. The nose and an ear of each victim were shipped back to Japan where they were formed into the famous Ear Mound at Kyoto.

Contacts with Europe. Although Marco Polo mentions Japan, which he called Cipangu, no European appears to have set foot there until a Portuguese ship was wrecked in 1542 and its survivors reached shore. This led, as mentioned above, to the opening of the first Japanese port for trade with the Portuguese in 1548 and later to the arrival of Catholic missionaries.

The Spanish, who were jealous of Portugal's successes in the East, violated a treaty with their rivals when they entered Portugal's sphere by conquering the Philippines, 1565-71. Their presence there was known to the Japanese who, under Hideyoshi, sought to exact acknowledgment of the vassalage of the Philippines to Japan. However, the Spanish followed their refusal to accede by sending an envoy to Hideyoshi in the hope of weakening Portugal's exclusive position. This mission did result in hurting the Portuguese but it availed Spain little at the moment. Ultimately, the Spanish won trading privileges with the proviso that they introduce no missionaries. Their failure to observe this prohibition resulted in an unfortunate struggle in the Japanese vineyard between rival Portuguese and Spanish missionaries. As in China, the cost of this ill-advised struggle was the loss of a good opportunity to win the nation to

Christianity. From a material standpoint, Spanish commercial gains served to open the doors of Japanese trade to the later European arrivals, the English and the Dutch.

The first Dutch ship to reach Japan arrived in 1600, and two years later the Dutch East India Company was formed to take advantage of this and other opportunities in East Asia. Under the shogunate of Ieyasu, the Dutch were given very generous trading privileges, much to the discomfiture of the Portuguese.

The English were slower in winning trading rights, although since 1600 an English pilot named William Adams had resided at the shogun's court. Adams was the pilot of the first Dutch ship which reached Japan. That same year saw the chartering of the famous "John Company," the English East India Company, but it was not until 1613 that the first English ship reached Japan. Then Adams became a major asset, for his popularity in Ieyasu's court helped the English to win the most liberal trade conditions yet granted by the Japanese.

The Dutch, whose rapaciousness for trade had led them to lie about the English, proved extremely obnoxious. They had even gone so far as to assist in bringing about the deaths of Japanese Christians in the hope of being rewarded with better trading privileges. Even they, finally and fittingly, felt the force of the policy of seclusion adopted by the Tokugawas and in 1641 were restricted to the small island of Deshima around which a high board wall was erected. Furthermore, only two Dutch ships a year were permitted entry thereafter. Thus was Japan shut off from the rest of the world.

SUGGESTED READINGS

China:

C. W. Allan, *Jesuits at the Court of Peking* (Shanghai, 1935); Mingchien Bau, *The Foreign Relations of China* (New York, 1921); T. F. Carter, *The Invention of Printing in China and Its Spread Westward* (New York, 1931); T'ien-tse Chang, *Sino-Portuguese Trade from 1514 to 1644* (Leiden, 1934); M. P. Charlesworth, *Trade Routes and Commerce of the Roman Empire* (Cambridge, 1924); H. G. Creel, *The Birth of China* (London, 1936); J. B. Eames, *The English in China, 1600-1843* (London, 1909); Henry H. Hart, *The Life and Times of Marco Polo* (Stanford University, 1947); G. F. Hudson, *Europe and China: a Survey of Their Relations from the Earliest Times to 1800* (London, 1931); K. S. Latourette, *The Chinese: Their History and Culture* (3d ed. rev., New York, 1946) and *A History of Christian Missions in China* (New York, 1929); Alexander Michie, *China and Christianity* (Boston, 1900); H. B. Morse, *The Trade and Administration of the Chinese Empire* (London, 1908) and *The International Relations of the Chinese Empire* (Vol. I, Shanghai, 1910); A. C. Moule, *Christians in China Before the Year 1550* (New York, 1930); A. C. Moule and Paul Pelliot, *Marco Polo* (London, 1938); E. H.

Parker, *China's Intercourse with Europe* (Shanghai, 1890); Marco Polo, *The Adventures of Marco Polo...*, edited by Richard J. Walsh (New York, 1948); Arnold H. Rowbotham, *Missionary and Mandarin: The Jesuits at the Court of China* (Berkeley, 1942); C. S. See, *The Foreign Trade of China* (New York, 1919); W. E. Soothill, *China and the West* (London, 1925); P. Sykes, *The Quest for Cathay* (New York, 1936); Min Ch'ien T. Z. Tyau, *The Legal Obligations Arising Out of Treaty Relations Between China and Other States* (Shanghai, 1917).

Japan:

Roy H. Akagi, *Japan's Foreign Relations, 1542-1936: A Short History* (Tokyo, 1936); Otis Cary, *A History of Christianity in Japan* (2 vols., New York, 1909); W. E. Griffis, *The Mikado's Empire* (2 vols., 12th ed., New York, 1913); Richard Hildreth, *Japan As It Was and Is* (2 vols., Chicago, 1906); Albert Hyma, *The Dutch in the Far East* (Ann Arbor, 1942); Englebert Kaempfer, *The History of Japan* (3 vols., New York, 1906); Yoshi S. Kuno, *Japanese Expansion on the Asiatic Continent* (2 vols., Berkeley, 1937, 1940); K. S. Latourette, *The History of Japan* (rev. ed., New York, 1947); James A. Murdoch, *History of Japan* (3 vols., Kobe and London, 1903-26); M. Paske-Smith, *Western Barbarians in Japan and Formosa in Tokugawa Days, 1603-1868* (Kobe, 1930); Peter Pratt, *History of Japan, Compiled from the Records of the English East India Company...*, edited by M. Paske-Smith (2 vols., Kobe, 1931); John Saris, *The Voyage of Captain John Saris to Japan 1613*, edited by Sir Ernest Satow (London, 1900); Sir Ernest Satow, *The Jesuit Mission Press in Japan 1591-1610* (Tokyo, 1888) and *The Origin of Spanish and Portuguese Rivalry in Japan* (Yokohama, 1890); James E. Walsh, *Tales of Xavier* (New York, 1948); Harry E. Wildes, *Aliens in the East; a New History of Japan's Foreign Intercourse* (Oxford, 1937).

10

TREATY PATTERN FOR CHINA

China and the World at the Opening of the Nineteenth Century

As the nineteenth century opened, China remained virtually closed to the West except for the Portuguese at Macao, the single unsatisfactory foothold permitted to other foreign traders outside of Canton on the island of Shameen,[1] and the frontier privileges accorded to the Russians. The latter had followed up the Treaty of Nerchinsk with a new agreement, the Treaty of Kiakhta (1727), which defined the boundary, regulated trade along the frontier, and provided for the settlement of disputes by peaceful methods. Further provision was made for a Russian embassy in Peking and permission was granted for four priests of the Russian Orthodox Church to live there as well.[2] The Treaty of Kiakhta proved an enduring one and lasted until 1858 although amended in 1768. In 1792 a protocol was signed whereby the frontier trade was further regulated.[3]

It should be noted that Russia's treaties did not give her citizens any entree into China beyond the privilege of border trade and an embassy at Peking. Any doubts the Russians may have had were removed in 1806 when Russian merchant ships arrived at Canton and were excluded from trade by the Chinese on the grounds that Russia enjoyed sufficient bounty from China in her frontier trade.[4]

Early British Failures. Thus no power had yet succeeded in opening China, a task which ultimately fell to Great Britain. Lord Macartney's mission in 1793 had proven fruitless as the emperor adopted the attitude of a suzerain toward a vassal and sent George III his "mandates." Again in 1804, when George III sent a letter to the Celestial Empire complaining

---

[1] China granted this limited trade out of its great charity. Chinese goods (tea, silk, porcelain, etc.) were a necessity to Europe according to the Emperor Ch'ien Lung in a mandate to George III. E. Backhouse and J. O. P. Bland, *Annals and Memoirs of the Court of Peking* (Boston, 1914), pp. 322 ff.
[2] Bau, *Foreign Relations of China*, p. 5.
[3] Tyau, *Treaty Relations*, p. 4.
[4] Bau, *op. cit.*, p. 5.

against Napoleon in the hope that the Chinese would exclude the French from the country, the emperor adopted a highhanded attitude toward his English "vassal." Despite this and other setbacks, the British persisted. In 1808 the first Protestant missionary arrived at Canton. He was Robert Morrison of the London Missionary Society.[5]

In 1816, a second official British embassy arrived in Peking with Lord Amherst at its head. His Lordship had just completed a fatiguing journey from Tientsin to the Summer Palace in Peking and had arrived early in the morning when, without any opportunity to rest or to change his clothes and gather together his credentials, he was unceremoniously urged to present himself at court. The refusal of this English "tribute bearer" to do so, coupled with the knowledge that he would not perform the kotow, a series of nine prostrations before the throne (sometimes empty), brought about his instant dismissal from China. The letter he bore from George III did find its way to Emperor Chia Ch'ing whose extremely haughty and insulting reply to His Britannic Majesty was most disappointing. Amherst's failure made it evident that the British were left with perhaps three alternatives—the use of force, submission to Chinese arbitrariness, or complete withdrawal from trade.[6]

Restraints on Foreign Traders. At this point, it is advisable to consider the conditions which faced foreigners doing business in the Canton area. For some time the barbarians had been herded together in the Shameen near the gates of Canton. In this tiny and rather unhealthy spot they were penned up and forbidden even to learn the Chinese language. Their homes and places of business were combined and were known as "factories," a name derived from factor or agent. They were forbidden to have any relations with either Chinese officials or other gentlemen, were required to employ the humble "petition" in all their communications, were refused permission to purchase books or other printed forms of information, and were restricted to contacts only with Hong merchants, compradores,[7] and coolies. The foreigners were also prohibited from owning either land or houses and were not supposed to bear firearms. They were likewise denied servants, other than a cook and some coolies who were required to tell the linguists of all that the barbarians did. The linguists (so called, as the wits used to say, because they knew no languages) acted as interpreters. They in turn were required to pass on any information gained from the servants of the barbarians to the Hong merchants who then had to relay the news to the government. Naturally, the various laws restricting the foreigners were sometimes

[5] Soothill, *op. cit.*, pp. 97 f.
[6] *Ibid.*, p. 103.
[7] A sort of native major domo or factotum.

broken, but it was always for a price since any Chinese involved in breaking the law risked his property and perhaps his life as well.[8]

The End of John Company. British trade at Canton was a monopoly in the hands of the English East India Company which had established a factory at Canton in 1715. After 1720 the Chinese end of the trade was conducted by the Co-hong, a small guild of merchants (at the most, thirteen) who possessed special licenses granted by Peking to trade with the barbarians. The Co-hong was held responsible for the actions of the foreign devils. The privilege of being a member of these "security merchants" was expensive. Hence, it is clear that their profits must have been considerable, since in addition to the cost of a license a Hong merchant was subjected to "squeeze" by one official or another. Often the amount of the commission ran as high as $50,000 in the case of important officials such as the viceroy.

Because of a long series of protests from British merchants eager to engage in the China trade, the British government decided in 1833 not to renew the charter of the East India Company, which was due to expire the following year. One of the bitterest complaints against John Company was that American merchants had been able to make great inroads in the trade at Canton while nonmember British merchants, who were their natural competitors, were prohibited by the company. The latter was not interested in the European carrying trade, and Americans were proving too successful in it to suit the average British merchant. Accordingly, late in 1833 Lord Napier was appointed Chief Superintendent of Trade in China. His instructions required him to seek the opening up of China, together with the recognition of Britain's equality with China.

This "barbarian eye," as the Chinese called foreign officials, was rebuked and rebuffed by Chinese officialdom and reminded that any duties collected on British trade by the imperial government were of no consequence. Equally trivial, from the Chinese standpoint, were British goods. Since, however, the British ruler had always in the past adopted the proper attitude of a vassal, Lord Napier's insulting attitude would be forgiven. After all why should a nation be cut off from the very necessities of life supplied to it so graciously by the Celestial Empire simply because of the insolence and stupidity of one of its representatives? In other words, Lord Napier's attitude in daring to suggest that Britain be considered an equal really deserved the annulment of trade, but China would be charitable. Temporarily all trade was suspended. Shortly afterwards, Napier's health deteriorated and he contracted malaria from which he subsequently died at Macao a month later. While he was ill

---
[8] Harley F. MacNair, *Modern Chinese History Selected Readings* (Shanghai, 1927), p. 15.

and absent from Canton, trade with the British was resumed and the suspension lifted. In the light of the hostilities soon to break out between China and Britain, it is interesting to note that Napier had observed that it would not be a very difficult matter to destroy China's coastal fortifications.

The Opium War

Many Vexations Imposed. Following Napier's death, he was succeeded by an experienced member of the English East India Company's staff who in turn gave way to another. Each of these officials was forced to accept the conditions laid down by the Chinese or suffer the loss of the existing trade. It was Napier's third successor as Superintendent of Trade, the youthful Captain Charles Elliot, who brought matters to a head. At first, he, too, followed the rather humiliating procedures forced upon his predecessors. In fact, he seems to have made every effort to satisfy the Chinese. He continually exceeded his instructions from the Foreign Office by employing the degrading petition to address the Co-hong. Not only had his instructions required him not to use this form, but he was also expected to by-pass the Co-hong and address the government directly.[9]

Elliot's difficulties over the proper language to be employed in his correspondence was merely one of his problems. He was considerably disturbed by Chinese methods of jurisprudence, as were his government and the British merchants doing business at Canton. In particular, he abhorred, as did all Westerners for that matter, the Chinese doctrine which held a group responsible for the crimes of one of its individual members.[10] In other words, if some unidentified Englishman murdered a Chinese, the law held any Englishman punishable by death. It was a matter of simple justice as far as the Chinese were concerned—a life for a life. To the foreign element at Canton in general, and to the British in particular, the question of jurisdiction was a most important one. Convinced of their inability to secure justice from the hands of the Chinese and appalled at the horrors of Chinese jails, the British were desirous of winning extraterritorial privileges. Furthermore, the complete lack of treaty relations was most vexing, as was the unwillingness of the Chinese to open ports other than Canton to trade.

Opium Issue Brings Crisis. It was the opium question that brought a crisis in the relations between China and the West which culminated in the first Anglo-Chinese War, and yet which, in itself, was not the

[9] Alexander Michie, *The Englishman in China* (Edinburgh, 1900), Vol. I, pp. 40 f.
[10] W. C. Costin, *Great Britain and China, 1833-60* (Oxford, 1937), p. 40.

cause of the war.¹¹ Although known previously in China, it was not until the seventeenth century that the practice of smoking opium was introduced by the Dutch, close upon the heels of the introduction of tobacco smoking by the Spanish. The early leader in the Chinese opium trade was Portugal, but by the latter part of the eighteenth century the British East India Company was actively engaged in it and ultimately superseded the Portuguese in this lucrative trade. Opium as a drug was looked upon with official Chinese approval, but as early as 1729 the smoking of opium was the subject of an imperial edict banning it and prohibiting opium divans. Nonetheless, within fifty years after this edict the importation of opium had increased fivefold to about a thousand chests a year. At that time, the British East India Company decided to exercise monopolistic control over the production and sale of the drug in India, which was the chief source of opium. For a time, individual British merchants were permitted to purchase it, but in 1780 it was made a company monopoly and within ten years the importation of opium in China had increased another fourfold.¹²

The Chinese government, alarmed at the proportions to which the trade had grown, intensified its earlier edicts; in 1800 it placed a ban on the importation of opium for any purpose and prohibited any domestic cultivation of the poppy. Not only was the government distressed over the spread of the vice among its subjects, but it was also greatly concerned by the resulting drain upon the amount of hard cash in China's possession. By 1838 China's unfavorable balance of trade, due in no small measure to the opium traffic, had reached £2,000,000 sterling. Gold and silver were flowing out of China in steadily increasing amounts, and even copper cash was being hauled away in barbarian ships.¹³ With opium banned by the government, but in great demand, many merchants resorted to smuggling. Owing either to the supineness or corruption of Chinese officialdom, however, no attempts were made to enforce the prohibition, and between 1820 and 1830 the average number of chests imported reached 16,000! ¹⁴

The reason for this farce was due largely to the dishonesty of the officials. Such highly placed personages as the viceroy at Canton and the Hoppo,¹⁵ the Manchu Superintendent of Trade there, were the worst

---

¹¹ For an excellent summary of the causes of the war, see P. C. Kuo, *A Critical Study of the First Anglo-Chinese War* (Shanghai, 1935), pp. 194-99; also David E. Owen, *British Opium Policy in China and India* (New Haven, 1934), pp. 167-75.
¹² Soothill, *op. cit.*, pp. 112 ff.
¹³ Michie, *op. cit.*, pp. 42 f.
¹⁴ MacNair, *op. cit.*, p. 86.
¹⁵ The Chinese name for this latter official was Hai Kwan Pu which the English had corrupted into Hoppo.

offenders. A falling out among various Chinese officials in 1821 resulted in the moving of the opium depots from Macao and Whampoa, where they had been established following the edict of 1800, to such places as Hong Kong and other nearby islands. The trade prospered despite the fact that officially the barbarians were permitted to trade only in the factories outside of Canton. Under the subterfuge that the "Son of Heaven, whose compassion is as boundless as the ocean, cannot deny to those who are in distress from want of food, through adverse seas and currents, the necessary means of continuing their voyage," foreign traders in opium were received by Chinese officials and deals were made for the chests of opium they had aboard.[16]

Trade Alarms Chinese. By 1836 memorials on the subject of opium had begun to pour into the imperial court at Peking. Some sought to have the trade regulated as a necessary evil, while others insisted upon its prohibition. Some were disturbed over the economic dislocation brought by the drain upon Chinese specie. Others were concerned on moral and social grounds. It was pointed out that the army was becoming badly infected by the vice. Meanwhile, the importation of opium increased by leaps and bounds. From an average of about 18,000 chests in 1835, the figure had reached 30,000 by 1839.[17]

By the end of 1838 the emperor decided to stamp out the nefarious traffic. He was thoroughly convinced that it would ultimately reduce his nation to depravity if it remained unchecked. On one occasion before reaching this decision, the emperor wept over the plight of his "dear children," and as one English contemporary noted, "his paternal heart, in the exuberance of its benignity, determined to cut off all their heads, if they would not mend their ways."[18]

Chinese Take Stringent Action. The man chosen by the emperor to wipe out the illicit trade was the energetic and purposeful Lin Tsê-hsü, former Governor-General of the Central Provinces, who was now appointed both Governor-General of the Two Kwang and Imperial Commissioner to handle the opium question. Lin arrived in Canton on March 10, 1839, and began action immediately. All Chinese who had not cured themselves of the opium habit within a year were warned that they would be decapitated. All foreign devils were ordered confined to their factories. Meanwhile, Captain Elliot, who had been residing in Macao, arrived in Canton. His first act was to order all British shipping in the area to assemble at Hong Kong in readiness for any emergency.

[16] Michie, *op. cit.*, p. 47.
[17] Morse, *op. cit.*, Vol. I, p. 191.
[18] MacNair, *op. cit.*, p. 103.

Lin ordered Elliot to instruct the British to turn over to him all the opium in their possession, a quantity of perhaps 20,000 chests worth over £2,000,000 sterling. Having no choice in the matter, Elliot had to obey, and the British merchants were forced to part with their valuable stocks. All other foreigners, including American merchants, were ordered to surrender their opium also, but they convinced the Chinese that their opium was included in that surrendered by the British.

The surrender of the opium stocks did not noticeably lessen the strained atmosphere, and the foreigners remained confined to their factories, outside of which Chinese military and naval forces were stationed. Finally the foreigners, with the exception of the Americans who elected to remain, were permitted to leave Canton, and the confiscated opium was destroyed. Despite this, the trade was clandestinely continued from outside of China as smugglers were willing to run the great risks involved in return for the huge profits which the greatly increased cost of the drug now brought.

Matters grew worse when a Chinese was killed in a scuffle involving some intoxicated British and American seamen at Kowloon near Hong Kong. Commissioner Lin demanded that Captain Elliot turn over to the Chinese authorities, for immediate execution, the murderer of the slain Chinese, whoever he might be. Elliot protested that he was unable to discover who was responsible and pointed out that the culprit was not necessarily an Englishman. For this Elliot was roundly denounced by Lin and presented with an ultimatum giving him ten days in which to surrender the alleged murderer or face the annihilation of all Englishmen in Canton. This truculence prompted the entire British colony to flee to Macao where the Portuguese in violation of the Treaty of 1703 with Great Britain refused the British asylum after having first received them. The English then went to Hong Kong where they remained aboard ship in the harbor. Lin issued proclamations to the Chinese exhorting them to attack the English and take them prisoner. They were told "even when they land to take water from the springs, stop their progress and let them not have it in their power to drink." Proclamations that wells had been poisoned appeared to warn the Chinese people not to use the water themselves.[19] In Hong Kong the British had to use their superior firepower to drive away Chinese boats seeking to prevent their getting supplies from people willing to sell them. In a brush between the British and some Chinese junks at Hong Kong, several Chinese were killed and Superintendent Elliot narrowly escaped death when a shot carried away his hatband. Possibly as a result of this firm stand the desperate position of the British improved in the month of September, 1839.[20]

[19] Michie, *op. cit.*, Vol. I, p. 56.
[20] Costin, *op. cit.*, p. 63.

In October the British began to venture back to Macao, and upon Elliot's promise to confiscate any ship carrying opium, British trade was reopened on the Pearl River at the Boca Tigris (Tiger's Mouth) rather than at the factories. The following month the Chinese renewed their demand that the murderer of the Chinese citizen at Kowloon be surrendered. At this time the first engagement of what is called the "Opium War" took place on November 3, 1839, in the Pearl River. Here H.M.S. "Volage" and H.M.S. "Hyacinth" in an hour's action destroyed three war junks and dispersed and made unusable a number of others, including that of the Chinese admiral commanding this fleet.

Meanwhile, British goods were being offered for trade by Americans and other foreigners. In effect, British manufacturers were able to sell their goods, but the British trading community at Canton was prevented from making its livelihood while matters continued as they were. Naturally, this group complained bitterly as did their associates in England. Most of the protests were raised against the "Yankees." Elliot himself was quite upset over the fact that the Americans had remained in Canton when the British were obliged to vacate. He felt strongly that if they too had departed all would have gone well. He believed that "their submission to the inadmissible pretensions of this government [the Chinese], and to the practical reduction of the foreigners at Canton almost to the condition of the Dutch at Japan, is excessively inconvenient to the interests of the Western nations holding intercourse with China."[21]

First American Traders. American trade with China had commenced in 1784 with the arrival of the first American ship at Canton, the "Empress of China." Within a few years an American consul at Canton was appointed although diplomatic relations of a formal nature were not begun until 1844. Intrepid American sea captains carried to Canton such products as ginseng (a root highly valued by the Chinese as a medicine),[22] textiles from New England, sea-otter skins, sandalwood, and sealskins. Most of the American firms, which had residences in the factory district, also engaged in the opium traffic. In return for their goods they brought home cargoes of tea, rhubarb, silks, chinaware, etc.[23] Not only did the United States send merchants and traders to China, but missionaries as

[21] *Ibid.*, p. 66.

[22] Explanation of its popularity among the Chinese may be found in Mikhail Prishvin, *Jên Sheng: The Root of Life* (New York, 1936); also J. Dyer Ball, *Things Chinese* (5th ed., Shanghai, 1925), pp. 272-74.

[23] From the beginning, the profits from the China trade were great, and in many cases became the foundations of great New England fortunes. These profits were invested in the early years of the Industrial Revolution and helped to account for the many factories which sprang up in New England.

well. The first Protestant missionaries from America reached Canton in 1830, but it was not until after 1844 that there was much opportunity for the work of such men. From that time forward, however, American Protestant missionaries have played a very important role in the history of China.

The Outbreak of War. The actual outbreak of hostilities in the so-called Opium War took place in November, 1839. During the period of quiet that followed, Britain prepared for further fighting. According to Lord Palmerston, British Foreign Secretary, his government had three objectives: to secure an apology for the treatment accorded Elliot and other British subjects; to get an indemnity for the loss of the merchants' property which, of course, was opium; and finally to achieve an improvement of conditions under which the British would trade in the future.

Instructions were sent to Elliot and the British naval commander, Admiral Elliot, his cousin, who were designated plenipotentiaries by the Foreign Secretary. Certain stipulations were to be laid down to the Chinese, and the immediate seizure of one of the Chusan islands, just south of the Yangtze, was ordered. A blockade of the Pearl River was effected by the British, the Chusan Island was seized, and military preparations in India were quickened. The plenipotentiaries, backed by a strong show of force, negotiated with Chinese officials during August, in the course of which Captain Elliot blandly remarked that "extensive smoking of opium was a lesser evil than extensive smuggling." [24] The conversations ended with a British agreement to return to Canton to await further developments. The chief representative of Peking, the Manchu Kishen (Ch'i Shan), appeared conciliatory in the negotiations, but the Cantonese authorities remained adamant.

Before his replacement by Kishen at Canton, Commissioner Lin, who had published a list of bounties for English heads, ships, and guns in June, 1840, dispatched a letter to Queen Victoria which is worth quoting in part:

> You savages of the further seas have waxed so bold, it seems, as to defy and insult our mighty Empire. Of a truth it is high time for you to "flay the face and cleanse the heart," and to amend your ways. If you submit humbly to the Celestial dynasty and tender your allegiance, it may give you a chance to purge yourselves of your past sins. But if you persist and continue in your path of obstinate delusion, your three islands [sic] will be laid waste and your people pounded into mincemeat, so soon as the armies of his Divine Majesty set foot upon your shores.

[24] Costin, *op. cit.*, p. 81.

As expressed by the authors of the book in which this letter appears, this was hardly a sensible policy to adopt for a person "who proposed to destroy the British fleets with stinkpots." [25]

By the end of December, Kishen replied to the demands of the British. While he was unable to agree to indemnify the British for their confiscated opium, he was willing to pay a compensation of $5,000,000 to the British for losses suffered over the previous ten years and to place future official intercourse on a basis of equality. The answer to Britain's demand for the cession of an island was negative, and the British were asked to evacuate Chusan. Future trade would have to be confined to Canton, but conditions would be ameliorated. This was, in effect, a refusal of Britain's demand that four other ports be opened. Negotiations continued, and both sides made concessions although the British continued to press for a place where they might fly their flag as the Portuguese did at Macao. Kishen's refusal, together with the knowledge that an imperial edict against the English had been issued, convinced Elliot of the futility of further conversations, and on January 7, 1841, Elliot ordered the British fleet into action.

In an extremely brief engagement the British easily captured Chuenpee and Tycocktow, the principal forts at the gateway to Canton, and then seized the inner forts in the Bogue beyond the Boca Tigris. This was accomplished without the loss of a single British life, although Chinese casualties were high. Kishen, a very sensible man, arranged for an armistice and on January 20, 1841, signed the Convention of Chuenpee with Elliot. The terms provided for the cession of the island and harbor of Hong Kong, a $6,000,000 indemnity payable in annual instalments, equality of official intercourse, and the reopening of trade at Canton.[26]

Both Elliot and Kishen were severely criticized by their governments for their work, although each was convinced he had accomplished a significant achievement. Kishen was the first to be punished. The emperor denounced and degraded him, and he was taken to Peking in chains. Rewards of $50,000 each for the heads of Elliot and the British naval commander were posted in Canton, and hostilities were reopened in February. It was then Elliot's turn for censure. He was denounced by Palmerston for having failed to carry out his instructions and for having exceeded his authority, and was replaced by Sir Henry Pottinger.

Treaty of Nanking. By May, with the British in a position to capture Canton, the Chinese promised a satisfactory settlement if the troops would withdraw. This being done, the Chinese went back on their word, and fighting was resumed. This time the British attacked with determina-

[25] Backhouse and Bland, *op. cit.*, p. 396.
[26] Maurice Collis, *Foreign Mud* (New York, 1947), p. 287.

tion and captured or blockaded one important place after another, climaxing their drive at Nanking. Unable to resist the British drive, the Chinese capitulated, and the Treaty of Nanking was signed August 29, 1842, and ratified in June, 1843. By its terms Hong Kong was ceded to the British, who were also given an indemnity of $21,000,000, and the ports of Amoy, Foochow, Ningpo, and Shanghai were opened for trade in addition to Canton. The practice of requiring foreigners to trade with the Co-hong was abolished, an equitable tariff was established, and Britain's equality with China was recognized.

No word of the status of opium is to be found in the treaty, since the Manchu negotiators expressed their reluctance to mention the subject to the emperor. The attitude adopted by the British was that opium was illegal and that the British government would accord no protection to its nationals engaged in that trade. The result was that, officially, the trade remained illegal but actually continued to flourish. That opium was not the real cause of the war should be clear. That it proved to be the issue which brought to a climax the whole unsatisfactory question of the China trade should be equally clear. Although general opinion in the United States put the blame on opium and continued to do so for a long time, one distinguished American, John Quincy Adams, held that opium was "a mere incident in the dispute, but no more the cause of the war than the throwing overboard the tea in Boston harbour was the cause of the North American revolution. The cause of the war is the *kotow*!" [27]

The "Unequal Treaties"

The year following the war's end, Great Britain and China signed a new agreement, the Treaty of the Bogue, on October 8, 1843. This new treaty contained a most-favored-nation clause whereby any favors granted by China to another nation would be automatically accorded to Britain. The British insisted upon this clause because the privileges which they had won in the Treaty of Nanking, other than Hong Kong and the indemnity, were accorded to the nationals of all countries which had previously traded at Canton and so were not exclusive with the British.

Following Britain's success, the first nation to avail itself of the opportunity of making a treaty with China was the United States. Caleb Cushing of Massachusetts, appointed Minister Plenipotentiary and Envoy Extraordinary for the negotiations, arrived in Macao under an impressive naval escort in February, 1844. Cushing bore an interesting and rather

---

[27] Tyler Dennett, *Americans in Eastern Asia* (New York, 1922), p. 107. For a good recent account of the war and the treaty following it, see Ssŭ-yü Têng, *Chang Hsi and the Treaty of Nanking* (Chicago, 1944).

naïve letter from President John Tyler to the Chinese emperor. The letter, which included a list of the twenty-six American states, called for peace and friendship between the two countries and was signed by the emperor's "good friend, John Tyler." [28]

The American had a rather trying time but ultimately succeeded in his purpose. One incident in particular resulted in considerable unpleasantness. The erection of a weather vane on the combined American factory and consulate at Canton was considered by the Chinese to be the cause of an epidemic in that city, and its removal at the request of local leaders was misconstrued by a mob as a sign of weakness. This led to anti-American demonstrations culminating in the stoning of several Americans, attacks upon some British subjects, and an assault on the factory district by a mob which was dispersed only when confronted with gunfire. The death of one Chinese on this occasion prompted the Chinese viceroy at Canton to imply that an American life would probably be required to make amends. Caleb Cushing cleverly got around this by having the American consul and a jury of six countrymen try an American for the murder. The verdict of acquittal on the grounds of self-defense was accepted by the viceroy.[29]

The latter now sought out Cushing in Macao and after brief negotiations in suburban Wanghia agreed to sign a treaty of friendship, commerce, and navigation, the Treaty of Wanghia, of July 3, 1844. This agreement included recognition of the principle of extraterritoriality whereby Americans committing crimes in China would be tried by their own nationals and not under Chinese laws and in Chinese courts. The treaty piously prohibited the opium traffic, a statement for the record which proved meaningless in reality. In general, the other terms gave the Americans the same rights of residence and trade at the treaty ports which the British had. Wanghia, however, provided more clearly than did Nanking for the protection of foreigners, and also gave American naval vessels the right to visit any port and be assured of a courteous reception.

The French followed up the British and Americans, and their representative, M. Théodose de Lagréné, signed the Treaty of Whampoa, October 23, 1844, with the same Chinese negotiator who had dealt with Caleb Cushing, Kiying. M. de Lagréné's championship of Christianity, in his case Catholicism, led to the promulgation of an imperial edict ordering toleration for the Christian religion as one which recognized the principles of virtue. Belgium was granted all the privileges accorded

---

[28] S. W. Williams, *The Middle Kingdom* (New York, 1883), Vol. II, pp. 565 f., contains the text of the letter.
[29] Rodney Gilbert, *The Unequal Treaties* (London, 1929), pp. 127 ff.

to the other treaty powers in a vice-regal letter of July 25, 1845, and Sweden and Norway signed the Treaty of Canton, March 20, 1847, virtually a repetition of the American treaty.[30]

Before leaving the subject of the "unequal treaties," it should be noted that the British and Americans who had neglected the subject of religion in their negotiations now quickly had brought to the emperor's attention the fact that his decree on toleration applied only to Roman Catholicism ("the Lord of Heaven Religion"). Whereupon, the emperor granted Protestantism the same privileges in 1845 thus putting "the Jesus Religion" on an equal footing. Rounding out his generous stand, the emperor also restored to the French the various Catholic properties previously confiscated throughout China.

The Taiping Rebellion

Despite China's defeat in the Opium War, her xenophobia grew stronger. Scarcely a year went by in which serious incidents involving foreigners did not occur. Canton proved especially obstreperous. Here the barbarians remained confined to the factory area and, unlike the other treaty ports, were not permitted to reside within the city. The stubborn refusal to allow foreigners this privilege greatly exacerbated matters. The foreigners living just outside Canton were subjected to repeated acts of violence, even to murder. The factories were attacked a number of times, and on one occasion some buildings were burned. Especially annoying to the legitimate foreign traders was the handsome treatment accorded their unscrupulous countrymen engaged in the opium traffic. More and more, the need for real equality of treatment by China became apparent to the foreigners; and more and more it became clear that the only way it could be achieved was through superior force.

In April, 1847, the British decided to teach the truculent Cantonese a lesson. The native forts on the Pearl River were successfully raided but the city was not captured due to a promise that it would be opened in two years. Antiforeign agitation increased, and at the expiration of the agreed time the Chinese officials refused to open the city on the grounds that they were powerless before the popular will. Matters thus went from bad to worse.

While the government was revealing itself to be strongly antiforeign, the people proved to be both antiforeign and hostile to their own government whose weakness in the Opium War manifested that it had lost the Mandate of Heaven and should, therefore, be overthrown. A serious and almost successful effort to accomplish the downfall of the Manchus

[30] Tyau, op. cit., p. 6.

was the Taiping (Great Peace) Rebellion which broke out in 1851; before the rebels were finally crushed in 1865, it brought widespread ruin in about half of China and death to at least 20,000,000 people.[31]

The "Arrow War"

It is now necessary to retrace our steps to events before the Taiping uprising. It will be recalled that, despite Britain's victory in the Opium War, the attitude of the Chinese government and people toward foreigners, especially at Canton, was extremely intransigent. It became increasingly obvious to the British that the principles for which the recent war had been waged were not being realized and that yet another war would have to be fought to remedy conditions. Palmerston sent a strong note to Peking in June, 1850, complaining of the Chinese attitude, only to have it unceremoniously rejected, and instructions were sent out to Chinese officials to ignore the foreigners.[32]

That the Chinese had some justification is clear from the continued smuggling of opium, and from the iniquitous practice of kidnapping coolies and placing them in what often amounted to slavery in parts of Latin America and in California.

About 1850, the British in Hong Kong began the practice of registering Chinese vessels under the British flag. While correct in a strictly legal sense, it was almost certain to lead to incidents in the touchy situation which then existed. It was such a ship, in fact, that provided the spark that touched off the second Anglo-Chinese War. The lorcha[33] "Arrow" was a vessel flying the British flag, owned by a Chinese resident of Hong Kong, and manned by a Chinese crew under a British captain, a twenty-one-year-old Irishman. On October 18, 1856, the "Arrow" was boarded by a Chinese naval force in Canton, its crew was imprisoned, and the British flag was hauled down. Actually, the "Arrow's" registration had expired but it was covered by a technicality in the Hong Kong ordinances.

The refusal of the Chinese authorities to live up to the provision of the Treaties of Nanking (1842) and the Bogue (1843) led the British to bombard Canton, an act which brought Chinese retaliation in the burning of the British factories. France decided to take a hand because a French missionary, the Abbé Chapdelaine, after severe torture, had been executed in a town in Kwangsi in 1856. A French plenipoteniary, Baron Gros, was appointed to cooperate with his English opposite number, Lord Elgin.

---

[31] The Taiping Rebellion is described in chapter 12.
[32] MacNair, *op. cit.*, p. 234.
[33] A foreign hull with Chinese rigging.

On October 23, 1856, the British captured and disarmed some forts near Canton, but the Chinese soon rearmed them and from these forts fired upon an American ship. Its commander, Captain Foote, promptly captured and dismantled the forts with the loss of seven American lives. The Chinese commissioner in Canton was quick to make an apology to the Americans, and the incident was considered closed.

In January, 1857, an attempt was made to poison the whole foreign population of Hong Kong. The baker who supplied the foreigners with their bread put arsenic in his dough, but word of the plot leaked out in time and there were no fatalities. Despite evidence to the contrary, the government denied any implication in the plot in its reply to the American, French, and Portuguese protests.[34]

Treaties of Tientsin. After some months of relative inaction, the British captured Canton on January 5, 1858. Still unable to secure satisfaction from Peking, the British and French plenipotentiaries sailed north. Their forces captured the forts of the Pei Ho which finally brought negotiations culminating in the signing of the Treaties of Tientsin. The British and French negotiators had been joined by American and Russian representatives, who, although they had elected to remain neutral, were nevertheless interested in obtaining improved conditions.

Treaties were signed June 13, 1858, with Russia, June 18, with the United States, June 26, with Great Britain, and June 27, with France. The American treaty granted permission to the American representative in China to reside in Peking should that right be granted any other nation. The treaties, as a whole, provided for an exchange of ministers and allowed foreign ministers residence rights at Peking, arranged for the appointment of consuls, granted toleration to Christianity and promised missionaries the protection of the Chinese government,[35] permitted travel in the interior, opened eleven new ports for trade including the island of Formosa, called for tariff revision, provided for extraterritoriality, reimbursed the British and French for their war expenses, and agreed to prohibit the use of the word barbarian in reference to foreigners. In a supplementary agreement reached with the British, opium was legalized.

The Chinese were provokingly slow in ratifying the treaties and when the British and French went to Tientsin in 1859 for this purpose they were blocked. Fighting ensued, and a setback was administered to the allies at the Pei Ho forts. During the fighting an American, Commodore

[34] MacNair, *op. cit.*, pp. 249 f.
[35] On the status of missionaries, see K. S. Latourette, *A History of Christian Missions in China* (New York, 1929), chaps. 11-21, and W. W. Willoughby, *Foreign Rights and Interests in China* (2d ed., Baltimore, 1927), Vol. II, chaps. 27-28.

Josiah Tatnall, and his men assisted the beleaguered attackers on the reputed grounds that "Blood is thicker than water."

The arrival of strong British and French forces the following year brought about China's capitulation, but not before the Chinese had been guilty of rather treacherous behavior. An English peace negotiator and his party were mistreated and made prisoners, and a French priest was murdered. In retaliation the allies looted the famous Summer Palace at Peking and later put it to the torch. Peking surrendered, and the Treaties of Tientsin were ratified October 24 and 25, 1860, in the Convention of Peking. Indemnities were increased, Chinese subjects were granted permission to emigrate from China if they so desired, Tientsin was added to the ports opened for trade, and Kowloon, adjacent to Hong Kong, was ceded to the British. Shortly afterwards, the British established a legation in Peking, and the old attitude of China's superiority and the vassalage of all foreign devils to the Middle Kingdom came to an end officially, although about a dozen years were required before the *kotow* question was finally settled.

In conclusion, it is necessary to consider briefly the activities of the Russians and the Americans, whose importance in Chinese affairs is reflected by the fact that they, too, secured treaties despite not being forced to fight for them.

In 1857, Admiral Count Putiatin attempted to secure for Russia a commercial treaty similar to the ones China had signed with the West in 1842-44, so that the Russians might supplement their special position at Kiakhta with trade at the treaty ports. However, it was the Russian General Ignatieff who won Russia's greatest prize at China's expense. After spending almost a year in Peking seeking to wheedle the Chinese into parting with their territory east of the Ussuri River, a considerable strip of land with 600 miles of coastline on the Pacific, he acted as an intermediary when the Treaties of Tientsin were ratified and as a reward was granted his wish. Thus by astute diplomacy the Russians were able to gain far more without having fought than were their Western rivals who had gone to war.

Anson Burlingame. In 1861 the American Minister to China, Anson Burlingame, arrived to become the first American to establish a residence at Peking. Burlingame became a staunch advocate of the twin policies which John Hay was later to make famous: the fullest trading rights for the United States and the territorial integrity of China. His work in China won great respect for him and served to make the country of the "Flowery Flag Devils" (the United States) rather popular. Upon his resignation from his post at Peking, the Chinese government prevailed upon him to head a Chinese mission of good will to tour the world. Accompanied by a considerable entourage headed by the Manchu, Chih Kang, and the Chinese, Sun Chia-ku, Burlingame arrived in the United States in 1868 where his mission created a near sensation. President Johnson officially received the mission and was most cordial. Mr. Burlingame's triumph was not so great abroad. Unfortunately, he was taken ill and died in St. Petersburg in 1870.

The principal result of the visit of Burlingame and the Chinese to the United States was, in addition to a renewal of interest in China, the signing of an understanding between the United States and China to supplement the Treaty of Tientsin. Its terms were in general unchanged except for a clause recognizing the right of the citizens of the two countries to trade, travel in, and even become permanent residents of the other country.

Burlingame's views on China were coolly received by many who knew conditions in that country, and actually were not those of the court at Peking which was strongly xenophobe due to the powerful influence of that extremely forceful and interesting personality, the Empress Dowager, Tz'ŭ Hsi. Nonetheless, he had to some extent conveyed the notion that the United States did not covet Chinese territory.

SUGGESTED READINGS

E. Backhouse and J. O. P. Bland, *Annals and Memoirs of the Court of Peking* (Boston, 1914); J. Dyer Ball, *Things Chinese* (5th ed., Shanghai, 1925); Mingchien Bau, *The Foreign Relations of China* (New York, 1921); Exhaustive but still useful is *The Chinese Repository* (20 vols., Canton, 1833-51); Paul H. Clyde, *United States Policy Toward China: Diplomatic and Public Documents, 1839-1939* (Durham, 1940); Maurice Collis, *Foreign Mud* (New York, 1947); W. C. Costin, *Great Britain and China, 1833-1860* (Oxford, 1937); Tyler Dennett, *Americans in Eastern Asia* (New York, 1922); Foster R. Dulles, *The Old China Trade* (Boston, 1930); Claude M. Fuess, *The Life of Caleb Cushing* (2 vols., New York, 1923); Rodney Gilbert, *The Unequal Treaties* (London, 1929); Carl Glick and Hong Sheng-hwa, *Swords of Silence; Chinese Secret Societies Past and Present* (New York, 1947); W. C. Hunter, *The 'Fan-Kwae' in Canton Before Treaty Days, 1825-1844* (Shanghai, 1911); G. W. Keeton, *The Development of Extraterritoriality in China* (2 vols., London, 1928); P. C. Kuo, *A Critical Study of the First Anglo-Chinese War* (Shanghai, 1935); K. S. Latourette, *A History of Christian Missions in China* (New York, 1929) and *History of Early Relations Between the United States and China (1784-1844)* (New Haven, 1917); Harley F. MacNair, *Modern Chinese History—Selected Readings* (Shanghai, 1923); Alexander Michie, *The Englishman in China* (2 vols., Edinburgh, 1900); H. B. Morse, *The International Relations of the Chinese Empire* (Vol. I, Shanghai, 1910); David E. Owen, *British Opium Policy in China and India* (New Haven, 1934); Mikhail Prishvin, *Jên Sheng: the Root of Life* (New York, 1936); Earl H. Pritchard, *Anglo-Chinese Relations During the 17th and 18th Centuries* (Urbana, 1929) and *The Crucial Years of Early Anglo-Chinese Relations, 1750-1800*

(Pullman, Wash., 1936); W. E. Soothill, *China and the West* (London, 1925); Min Ch'ien T. Z. Tyau, *The Legal Obligations Arising Out of Treaty Relations Between China and Other States* (Shanghai, 1917); W. W. Willoughby, *Foreign Rights and Interests in China* (2 vols., rev. ed., Baltimore, 1927); S. Wells Williams, *The Middle Kingdom* (2 vols., New York, 1882).

11

TREATY PATTERN FOR JAPAN

Pre-Perry Foreign Contacts Under the Tokugawas

As has been described, a number of internal factors combined to bring about the decay of the Tokugawa shogunate. These developments would probably have brought about its fall anyway, but the impact of the United States and other Western powers in the 1850's and '60's accelerated matters, and brought about a new era ending the absolutism of the Tokugawas.

To cite but one illustration of the ridiculous extremes to which such control could go, there is the case of the Shogun Tsunayoshi who, because he was born in the "Year of the Dog" prohibited the killing of any animals, birds, or reptiles. Known as the "Dog Shogun," he was most solicitous over the welfare of that animal. During his regime the people referred to the creature as the "Hon. Mr. Dog," and there were Dog Commissioners, Dog Samurai, and Dog Doctors. Even the Grand Council deliberated dog problems and once concluded:

> The Grand Council does not, after consideration, think it seemly that there should be provided in each block a bucket inscribed "Dog-parting water" with an attendant bearing a ladle and wearing a jacket with the character "Dog" on the back of it.[1]

Unable to cope successfully with economic problems, the increasingly reiterated teachings of loyalty to the emperor rather than to the shogun, and the influence of those who stressed the desirability of renewing contacts with the outside world, the Tokugawa shogunate could not prevent the visit of Commodore Matthew C. Perry in 1853 as it had turned back earlier attempts to reopen Japan.

Perhaps the first non-Chinese or non-Dutch to set foot in Japan after the seclusion policy of the Tokugawas took effect in the seventeenth century was an Italian missionary, Father Sidotti, who made his way there from Manila in 1709. Although he was not executed after falling into the hands of the Japanese authorities, he was kept imprisoned until his death six years later. Rather than attempt to list all of the many attempts to

[1] A. L. Sadler, *A Short History of Japan* (Sydney, 1946), p. 231.

penetrate Japan during the pre-Perry period, a few will be examined from the point of view of the nations these attempts represented.[2]

Great Britain. Prior to Father Sidotti's ill-fated attempt, the English East India Company had sent a ship, the "Return," to Nagasaki in 1673 to open trade relations. After a lengthy interval of questioning under strict surveillance, the "Return" was ordered to leave Japanese waters without being permitted to unload its cargo. The reason given for the refusal was that the English ruler, Charles II, was married to a Portuguese, Catherine of Braganza.[3] In such grounds for refusal could be seen the work of the Dutch at Deshima who were, of course, not anxious to acquire any rivals for Japanese commercial favor.

Another English ship arrived, probably at Shimonoseki, in 1683 but was likewise doomed to disappointment. Many years later, in 1791, the "Argonaut," a British vessel engaged in the Pacific Northwest fur trade, made an unsuccessful attempt to sell its cargo to the Japanese. The "Argonaut" was allowed only to take on wood and water and was escorted out to sea with unmistakable instructions not to return. Somewhat more successful was the "Providence" which managed to make a survey of Japanese waters in 1795-97. Some of its crew were enabled to get ashore on Hokkaido, but it was made clear to them that the Japanese did not welcome them, although the Ainus were quite friendly.

Lord Macartney, who headed an unsuccessful embassy to China described in the previous chapter, had instructions to visit Edo upon completion of his Chinese mission. Upon his failure in China, he determined to try Japan, a country which produced tea "as good as and probably cheaper than that of China." The outbreak of war between England and France in 1793 forced him to give up his projected trip.[4]

In 1808 an English frigate, the "Phaeton," under nineteen-year-old Captain Fleetwood Pellew, arrived unheralded in Nagasaki to take on provisions. The superiority of its firepower made it possible for the ship to secure the needed supplies and sail away unscathed. The local governor was so disgraced by this episode that he committed suicide, and a number of the other Nagasaki officials did likewise.

---

[2] For full lists of illegal arrivals in Japan during the Tokugawa era, see Harry Emerson Wildes, *Aliens in the East* (Philadelphia, 1937), pp. 339-41, and Shunzo Sakamaki, "Japan and the United States, 1790-1853," *Transactions of the Asiatic Society of Japan,* 2d Series, Vol. XVIII (December, 1939), pp. 174-90.

[3] The ship's captain asked if he might return after the queen's death and was somewhat unglamorously refused because "the royal word, like the sweat of the human body, when once escaped, re-entered not again." C. W. King, *Notes of the Voyage of the Morrison and the Himmaleh* (New York, 1839), p. 50.

[4] M. Paske-Smith, *Western Barbarians in Japan and Formosa in Tokugawa Days, 1603-1868* (Kobe, 1930), p. 128.

As a result of the Napoleonic Wars, the Dutch in Deshima had been cut off from contact with the outside world for some years. In 1813 two ships appeared off Nagasaki flying the Dutch flag and bearing the news that the Dutch factor, Doeff, was to be replaced by one Cassa. The arrivals included Doeff's predecessor, Waardenar, who acted as a government representative.

When the ships arrived in the harbor, it was discovered that their crews were English-speaking. The Japanese concluded that they were Americans hired by the Dutch at Batavia, since American ships had served the Dutch in the trade at Deshima from 1798-1809. Doeff was handed a letter stating that Waardenar and an Englishman named Dr. Ainslie [5] had been appointed commissioners in Japan with full authority over the Dutch factory at Deshima. The letter was signed "Raffles, Lieutenant Governor of Java and its Dependencies." [6] The Dutch Resident now learned for the first time that Holland was no longer independent and that the British had seized Java, which was now being ruled by Stamford Raffles.

By threatening to expose them to the Japanese, Doeff worked out an arrangement with Ainslie and Waardenar whereby the ships were to be passed off as American in Dutch employ, used to secure the protection of a neutral flag. The business was speedily concluded, Doeff kept his post, and he also made a neat profit for himself. The next year, 1814, Raffles again sent Cassa to replace Doeff. Once more Doeff worked his stratagem with considerable personal profit and kept the Dutch flag flying, the only place in the world where it then flew. After Java had been restored to the Dutch at the Congress of Vienna, the crafty Heer Doeff was replaced and returned to Holland where he was honored for his services.

A few years later, in 1818, an intrepid and extremely clever young English sea captain named Peter Gordon sailed the brig "The Brothers" right into Edo Bay. Despite his charm and tact, he was not allowed to trade. Although he made a fine impression on the Japanese, particularly since he denounced the Russians who were very unpopular with the Japanese, he was dismissed.[7]

[5] Ainslie, upon his return to Java, labored under the mistaken notion that the Japanese "were entirely free from any prejudices that would stand in the way of an unrestricted intercourse with Europeans." King, *Voyage of Morrison*, p. 65. He also reported to Raffles that the Japanese were considerably superior to the Chinese and might easily in time equal Europeans in civilization. Paske-Smith, *op. cit.*, p. 131.

[6] Raffles' opinion of the Dutch at Deshima was rather low: "The Dutch factory was a sink of the most disgraceful corruption that ever existed; the director submitted to every possible degradation to obtain his own ends, and the Batavian government never knew more than it was his interest to tell, of what was going on in Japan." King, *op. cit.*, p. 50.

[7] Wildes, *op. cit.*, pp. 180-86.

France. French interests in Japan did not approach those of the British. However, Japan was not unnoticed in France. When Colbert was Minister of Finance, he gave serious consideration to sending a French embassy to Japan under Francis Caron, a former director of the Dutch factory at Deshima. Colbert agreed that only Protestant subjects of Louis XIV should participate in the projected mission. For some undiscovered reason the project never materialized.[8]

In 1785 France revived interest and sent the Comte de la Perouse to explore the entire Pacific coast of Asia. He was the first European to visit some of the waters he traversed. De la Perouse proved that Sakhalin and Hokkaido were separate islands and has left his name on the straits he discovered.[9]

In 1844, Rear Admiral Cécille arrived at Napa in the Liu Ch'iu Islands and forced the natives to sign a treaty. This action was not countermanded by the Japanese resident and, surprisingly, it was approved at Edo on the grounds that a partial opening of Japan in such a distant and unimportant place might satisfy the foreigners. Nonetheless, the agreement was to be kept secret. Despite this, both France and Britain landed missionaries who did not succeed in converting any of the natives. The French withdrew after a few years. Although the single British missionary remained until 1854, when Perry opened Japan, the treaty lapsed, and nothing came of this modified attempt to throw open the country.

Cécille visited Nagasaki in July, 1846, only to be treated so rudely that he withdrew without accomplishing anything. He reappeared in 1850 but again had to take an unceremonious departure in the face of menacing troop movements.

Russia. The Russians, since they were geographically so close to Japan, were especially interested in the country. They were quite active in the eighteenth century in the neighborhood of the Kuriles. Under a Danish navigator, Martin Spanberg, a Russian expedition did succeed in making a landing on Japanese soil, when men from a ship which had become separated from the squadron touched at Kochi in 1739. Although their reception was friendly, they departed hastily because of the presence of so many armed guards in the harbor. Spanberg's was but one of five such Russian expeditions. After each of these was reported in Japanese waters, uprisings had taken place on the part of the people against the government. The fact that these events bore no relation to one another did not cross the minds of the Japanese officials, who equated the arrival of

---

[8] For a copy of the letter to the emperor of Japan from Louis XIV, see Ernest W. Clement, ed., *Hildreth's Japan as It Was and Is* (Chicago, 1906), Vol. II, pp. 364-67.

[9] Wildes, *op. cit.*, pp. 13 f.

foreigners with domestic troubles and consequently became even more hostile toward foreigners.[10]

Lieutenant Adam Laxman landed on the northern coast of Hokkaido in 1792 in the small ship "Catherine" and spent the winter there. In the spring he went to Hakodate on the southern coast. He brought back to their homeland some Japanese sailors who had been shipwrecked about ten years earlier and in the meantime had been the guests of the Russian government. The Japanese received their countrymen, but these unfortunates were imprisoned for life on the grounds that it was against the law for Japanese subjects to visit foreign countries. The Russians were informed that as foreigners they were liable to life imprisonment for having landed anywhere except Nagasaki, where one Dutch ship a year was permitted and where Chinese junks occasionally traded, but because of their ignorance they would be excused if they sailed away and never returned. Laxman had no alternative but to comply.

The "Red Hairs" were decidely unpopular in Japan, but this did not deter them. Their unpopularity stemmed from their suspected plots against Nippon and from aggressions committed on Sakhalin. Regardless, in 1804, Nicolai de Rezánov of the monopolistic Russian-American Company, a very colorful figure who later became a leader among the Russian pioneers in Alaska, arrived in Nagasaki aboard the "Nadezhda."[11] His mission was subjected to a most humiliating experience. Allowed to land only part of his party, and that after a very lengthy delay and and in what amounted virtually to a prison, Rezánov was rebuffed by the Japanese, and his mission failed.

Rezánov, upon his return to Russian soil, ordered two hotblooded young Russian naval officers, Lieutenants Chvostov and Davidov, to destroy some Japanese settlements on Sakhalin which they proceeded to do with gusto in 1806 and 1807, thereby adding to Japan's fear and dislike of the Russians. These onslaughts "having no object but sheer mischief, and hatched in the true spirit of revenge by an angry and insulted ambassador" were quite senseless.

Especially active on behalf of Russia was Admiral Count Putiatin, whose activities will be discussed below.

The United States. By a circuitous route, news reached Japan in 1777 that Russia and Britain were planning to attack her. This fantastic story had been originated by a notorious Polish liar and adventurer, Graf von Beniowski, who had traveled widely in the Far East. The news produced tremendous excitement in Japanese official circles and aroused a feeling

[10] *Ibid.*, pp. 81 ff.
[11] See Gertrude Atherton, "Rezánov," in *Encyclopaedia Britannica*, 11th ed., Vol. XXIII.

of friendship toward any enemies of either the British or the Russians. As the Americans were then engaged in their War of Independence, their cause became popular among the Japanese. Knowledge of this war was gained from the Dutch who were, of course, quite well disposed toward the American cause and were soon to enter the war against the British because of their trade with the American states.[12] George Washington's picture, which the Dutch had later introduced, was widely circulated. Had any American ships put into a Japanese port at this time, there is little doubt that they would have been handsomely received.[13]

Unfortunately, the first American ship, the "Lady Washington" out of Boston, to reach Japan came when this friendly feeling had given way to a strong xenophobia based on a false report spread by the Dutch that the "Red Hairs" (Russians) were planning to attack Japan. For a variety of reasons, the efforts of Captain John Kendrick to trade his cargo of sealskins with the Japanese ended in failure.[14]

The development of whaling in the North Pacific to the point where, by 1820, it had become an extremely important business brought many foreign ships into close proximity with Japan. The steady disappearance of the crews of wrecked whalers last known to be in Japanese waters led to the conviction that the Japanese were, at best, guilty of inhospitable treatment of the castaways and, at worst, of executing them. Since American whalers were prominent among those so treated, it was no wonder that President John Quincy Adams, who as Secretary of State had become intimately associated with the problem, asserted that "it was the duty of Christian nations to open Japan, and that it was the duty of Japan to respond, on the ground that no nation had a right to withdraw its private contribution to the welfare of the whole human race."[15]

As early as 1815, Commodore Porter, assigned to the protection of American whalers from the depredations of the British in the North Pacific, had written to the then Secretary of State, James Monroe, to urge the opening of Japan. It was proposed to send Porter with a small naval squadron to Japan for that purpose, but the project was defeated.[16]

---

[12] Ishii Kendo, "Ikoku Hyoryu Kidanshu" (Tokyo, 1927), pp. 429-47, quoted in Shunzo Sakamaki, "Japan and the United States, 1790-1853," *Transactions of the Asiatic Society of Japan*, 2d Series, Vol. XVIII (1939), p. 148. [The Dutch helped to increase the popularity of the Americans, whose land was not well known to the Japanese. The first Japanese book to contain a description of America had been printed in 1708. This was the five-volume *Zoho Kai Tsûshô Kô* (*A Study of the Commerce of Chinese and Barbarians, Revised and Augmented*).]

[13] Wildes, *op. cit.*, pp. 87-92, contains full details of this interesting episode.

[14] Wildes, *op. cit.*, pp. 101-4.

[15] Inazo Nitobe, *The Intercourse Between the United States and Japan* (Baltimore, 1891), p. 32.

[16] *Loc. cit.*

Because of the landing of so many foreigners on Japanese soil and their continued presence in Japanese waters, the *Bakufu* (the Shogun's military government) issued a new edict of expulsion in 1825 aimed at all foreigners except the Dutch and the Chinese:

> Therefore, if in [the] future foreign vessels should come near any port whatsoever, the local inhabitants shall conjointly drive them away; but should they depart peaceably it is not necessary to pursue them. Should any foreigners land, they must be arrested or killed, and if the ship approaches the shore it must be destroyed.[17]

During the Jackson administration, a Portsmouth sea captain, Edmund Roberts, made the first American treaties ever signed with Orientals. These treaties were with Muscat and Siam. Sent on a second mission to seek the opening of trade relations with the Japanese, Roberts died in Macao without reaching his objective.

Despite the prohibition of Japanese citizens from going abroad, many did so involuntarily. The powerful Japan Current, the Kuroshio, carried unknown numbers of Japanese wrecks across the Pacific to the Aleutians and the Pacific Northwest.[18] In 1837 some of these survivors, together with others picked up elsewhere, provided the subjects of a plan for securing commercial relations with Japan and for reopening the country to missionaries. The "Morrison," an American brig under Captain David Ingersoll, set off from Macao on July 4, 1837, bound for Japan. To prove that its mission was peaceful and merely designed to return the shipwrecked Japanese, all guns and armament were removed. The ship's complement of thirty-nine included the Reverend Dr. Peter Parker, a medical missionary, Dr. S. Wells Williams, head of the American Board Mission Press at Canton, the Reverend Dr. Karl Gutzlaff, chief interpreter for the Superintendent of British Trade at Macao, a young American merchant, Charles W. King, and his wife, and the seven Japanese who were to be repatriated.

On the day of departure, Independence Day, not having any cannon and being unable, therefore, "to make the loudest of noises," the Americans contented themselves "with thanking the God of Nations for all the liberty, prosperity, and honor of our happy country." The "Morrison" put in first at Napa Bay in the Liu Ch'ius and then left directly for Edo, whose environs were reached July 30, marking the first time that an American ship had ever entered Edo Bay.

King had four letters in Chinese to be delivered to the proper officials: one introduced the repatriated Japanese and recounted their history of

---

[17] Sakamaki, *op. cit.,* p. 184.
[18] For details *cf.* Harry Emerson Wildes, "The Kuroshiwo's Toll," *Transactions of the Asiatic Society of Japan,* 2d Series, Vol. XVII (December, 1938), pp. 209-34.

shipwreck and rescue by people who respected the words of Mencius that "he who does not rescue the shipwrecked, is worse than a wolf"; the second described America; the third contained a list of presents; and the fourth listed the ship's cargo. The second letter is worth reproducing:

> America lies to the east of your honorable country, distant two months' voyage. Its western parts are not yet cleared, but are still inhabited by savage tribes. On its eastern side, where the people are civilised, and from which we come, it is separated from England and Holland by a wide ocean. Hence it appears that America stands alone, and does not border upon any of the nations known to the Japanese. The population of America is not great, though the country is extensive. Two hundred years ago it was entirely inhabited by savages; but at that time, English, Dutch, and other nations went there and established colonies. Their descendants increased gradually, and sixty-two years ago they chose their first President named Washington. That high office is now filled by the eighth President. Within the space of sixty-two years America has been twice invaded, but its people have never attacked other countries, nor possessed themselves of foreign territory. The American vessels sail faster than those of other nations, traversing every sea, and informing themselves of whatever passes in every country. If permitted to have intercourse with Japan, they will communicate always the latest intelligence.
>
> The laws of America are just and equitable, and punishment is inflicted only on the guilty. God is worshipped by every man according to his own conscience, and there is perfect toleration of all religions. We ourselves worship the God of Peace, respect our superiors, and live in harmony with one another. Our countrymen have not yet visited your honorable country, but only know that in old times the merchants of all nations were admitted to your harbors. Afterwards, having transgressed the laws, they were restricted or expelled. Now, we coming for the first time, and not having done wrong, request permission to carry on a friendly intercourse on the ancient footing.[19]

The list of presents included a portrait of Washington, a telescope, a pair of globes, an encyclopedia, a collection of American treaties, and an American history. Along with the list of presents was appended the promise that one member of the party would be pleased to remain in Japan to teach the language of the American people if the Japanese so desired.

Despite the precautions to assure the Japanese of the friendly nature of the visit, the "Morrison" was fired upon as it entered Edo Bay. No damage resulted, and after the firing ceased, the ship was boarded and searched. The following day the firing was resumed without warning,

[19] King, *op. cit.*, pp. 117 f.

and the ship was forced to flee for safety. Undiscouraged, the "Morrison" attempted to put in at Kagoshima, but the result was the same.

The ship had no alternative but to return to Macao where it arrived in August, 1837. King concluded: "Still I do not insist on the reception given to the "Morrison" as proving anything more than this—that the policy of Japan remains unrelaxed, and that on it mere private proposals, however often repeated, can be expected to have no effect." S. Wells Williams, who was later to be a member of Perry's expedition on both its visits, summed it up this way: "Commercially speaking, the voyage cost about $2,000 without any return; and the immediate effects in a mercenary or scientific way, were nil. But not finally, the seven men brought back were employed in one way or another, and most of them usefully." They were used largely to teach the Japanese language and were ultimately responsible for the interpreters who were supplied to Perry.[20]

King took umbrage at the fact that "the only flag fired on in the harbors of Japan should be that of the only nation which maintains no church establishment; forms no offensive leagues; holds no foreign colonies; grasps at no Asiatic territory; and whose citizens present themselves, for the first time, at the gates of the capital, unarmed, and with every pledge of peaceful, humane, and generous intentions; that the American flag should be dealt with without warning . . . calls for acknowledgement in the name of the country." He even hoped that "the time is near when my own country will be prepared to cast the first stone at Japan, unless she will sin no more against the dearest human interests." King did not seek revenge but merely redress of grievances, he asserted.[21]

Specifically, he proposed stationing a small naval squadron on the coasts of Japan throughout the summer of 1839. The commander should submit an ultimatum calling for friendly reception of the ships and crews of both Japan and the United States in the other's ports; admission of an American minister to the court at Edo; and "the necessary exequatur for such consuls as may be appointed to care for our seamen, and some other like provisions." He did not doubt that such an ultimatum would be refused, but it should be "pressed again, along with a free exposition of the injustice of such a policy as respects America, and an exhibition of the defencelessness of Japan, its immense coast line, its exposed capitals, its feudal weaknesses, its entire dependence, in fact, on the very moderation and good will in our own and other foreign nations." [22]

---

[20] *Life and Letters of S. W. Williams* (New York, 1889), p. 99, quoted in Nitobe, *op. cit.*, p. 32n.
[21] King, *op. cit.*, pp. 171 ff.
[22] *Ibid*.

Should the ultimatum again be refused, he advocated the emancipation of the insular dependencies of Japan from Satsuma southward to Formosa, beginning with a blockade of the port of Kagoshima. The result could not fail to produce the "ruins of feudalism," and the Japanese people would then be enabled to call their "despotic chiefs, and their liege lord too, to better manners." This, of course, all depended upon American action. Would there be any, was the question King asked as his patience began to grow exhausted.

> Oh! when will she [America] be sensible of her advantages?[23] When will she make her waiting honors her own? Besides I confess I am tired of hearing every allusion to American influence in behalf of E. Asia answered every day, as it now is, by men of all nations—"O, your government will never do anything here." I would silence the taunt, I would disappoint the sneer.[24]

King's ideas were destined ultimately to bear fruit, since Commodore Perry's mission was considerably influenced by them. But for the time being nothing concrete resulted although, in 1842 the Japanese mitigated somewhat the rigors of their expulsion edict of 1825 as a result of their having learned the full truth of the "Morrison" expedition.[25]

The next private American attempt after that of the "Morrison" was made by Captain Mercator Cooper in his Sag Harbor whaler, "Manhattan." Cooper landed twenty-two shipwrecked Japanese at Edo in 1845 but, although extended some unusual courtesies, was likewise forced to withdraw.

Far from discouraged, American interest in opening Japan was intensified. The navy, merchants, and missionaries were all very actively interested in the subject. Early in 1845 the Honorable Zadoc Pratt, congressman from Prattsville, New York, placed before the House of Representatives a resolution advocating speedy action in the sending of an American embassy to Japan and Korea. The resolution predicted that "another year will not elapse before the American people will be able to rejoice in the knowledge that the Star Spangled Banner is recognized as an ample passport and protection for all who, of our enterprising countrymen, may be engaged in extending American commerce into the

---

[23] He predicted that "It is not improbable that G. Britain will interfere *in China* ere long. But for what? For the preservation of the revenue on opium in Bengal; for the protection of an article which it is a shame even to the Chinese pagan to consume. Thus far, and no farther, will she interfere. I rejoice that America can approach this empire [Japan] for better purposes and with cleaner hands; that she can place herself as much above the charge of mercenary turpitude in China, as above the dread of colonial designs on the Archipelago, or the suspicion of ecclesiastical connexions in Japan."

[24] *Ibid.,* p. 197.

[25] Sakamaki, *op. cit.,* p. 186.

countries into which it is now proposed to dispatch suitable diplomatic and commercial agents on behalf of our government." [26]

Action followed quickly. Commodore James Biddle led an expedition consisting of the "Columbus" and the "Vincennes" and bearing Alexander H. Everett with instructions from the State Department to secure a commercial treaty with Japan as soon as he had completed the necessary ratifications of Caleb Cushing's treaty of 1844 with China. Biddle had to take over the job himself, as Everett became ill and was forced to leave the expedition in Rio de Janeiro. Commodore Biddle, following calls in China, arrived in Edo Bay, July 20, 1846. After a stay of ten days in the harbor, Biddle left following the receipt of an anonymous communication stating that Japan regarded Americans as no different from any other foreigners and denying the requests made by the Americans who were told that they would be wise to "consult your own safety by not appearing again upon our coast." [27]

Just before Biddle's arrival, the "Lawrence," an American whaler, from Poughkeepsie, was wrecked on the rocky coast of one of the Kuriles. Seven of the crew survived and reached shore where they were well treated by the natives until they were discoverd by officials who imprisoned them. One managed to escape but was killed while being recaptured. Following almost a year and a half of incarceration and terrible privation, they were sent to Batavia aboard a Dutch ship.

In 1848, five boatloads of deserters from the New Bedford whaler, "Lagoda," attempted to land at what is now Fukuyama. Two of the small boats foundered, and only fifteen men reached shore safely. Nine of these were Hawaiians. The men were jailed as spies and later removed to Nagasaki where their numerous attempts at escape resulted in more severe treatment by their captors who, among other things, forced them to trample upon the crucifix. One of the Hawaiians, a man named Mauri, committed suicide, and one of the Americans died of the effects of their ill-treatment. The threats uttered by the surviving Americans failed to impress the Japanese who reminded them that Commodore Biddle had been struck by a common Japanese guard with impunity. What they neglected to state was that the Commodore had received ample promises that the man would be punished and was content to let it go at that.

The crew of the "Lagoda" was finally rescued when news of their plight reached the American Commissioner to China, John W. Davis, through the Dutch. Commander James Glynn of the U.S.S. "Preble" arrived in Nagasaki on April 17, 1849, and after a prolonged conference

[26] Charles Lanman, *Leading Men of Japan* (Boston, 1886), p. 399.
[27] Nitobe, *op. cit.,* p. 34.

arranged to repatriate the men of the "Lagoda." The captives were released to the Dutch and turned over by them to Glynn. This indirect release was achieved only after Glynn had threatened to bombard Nagasaki. Also rescued was the famous Ranald MacDonald, son of a Hudson Bay Company factor and a Chinook princess, who in his childhood had seen three shipwrecked Japanese captured by Indians of his mother's tribe. These Japanese were among the seven whom the "Morrison" had attempted to repatriate.

MacDonald had arranged to be put afloat alone in a little boat just off Hokkaido by the captain of a whaler of whose crew he had been a member. His experiences with the Japanese, and his entire life for that matter, make delightful reading.[28] In Nagasaki he trained native Japanese interpreters in the English language. In this work he discovered his charges could not pronounce the letter "l" which they always made into an "r" sound, e.g., they pronounced his name "Ranardo MacDonardo." His students were among those present when Perry was negotiating his treaty. They passed along to their superiors the remarks made by Perry and his men who did not suspect that their English could be translated by other than the official interpreters. One of the Japanese with a good knowledge of English who was kept from the presence of the Americans but who nevertheless was in a position to eavesdrop had attended school in Fairhaven, Massachusetts, after having been rescued by an American whaling captain.

The Perry Mission

Despite the fact that the Japanese had surrendered the crew of the "Lagoda," the lot of a sailor shipwrecked in Japanese waters was extremely hazardous. These unfortunates were frequently attacked and abused. Often they were caged like wild animals and put on display for the common people to stare at and vilify.

The increasing number of whalers shipwrecked off Japan, pressure by businessmen,[29] missionaries, and the navy, coupled with the general expansionist air which then prevailed finally led the United States government to take the steps recommended by Charles King of the "Morrison." Commander Glynn made an unsuccessful effort to secure command of a naval expedition to Japan on the basis of his recent experiences there. He believed that the securing of a coaling station there

---

[28] Ranald MacDonald, *Autobiography*, William S. Lewis and Naojiro Murakami, eds. (Spokane, 1923).

[29] Especially active was Aaron Haight Palmer, Director of the American and Foreign Agency of New York. *Cf.* Aaron Haight Palmer, *Documents and Facts Illustrating the Origin of the Mission to Japan* (Washington, 1857).

might serve as an entering wedge for the eventual opening of the whole country.

It remained, however, for Commodore John H. Aulick to win the coveted assignment. He convinced Secretary of State Daniel Webster of the wisdom of returning to their homeland some shipwrecked Japanese who had recently been landed in San Francisco. This would serve as a pretext for an official mission to seek the beginning of diplomatic and commercial relations with Japan.[30] Both Webster and President Fillmore were quite enthusiastic over the idea, and Aulick was given the assignment.

Perry Heads Mission. Due to a misunderstanding, Aulick was relieved of his command when he arrived at Macao in 1852. His replacement was Commodore Matthew Calbraith Perry, USN, who set sail on November 24, 1852, from Norfolk, Virginia, after having made a very careful personal preparation for the task. He was not given a squadron of the promised strength and set off in a single ship, the "Mississippi." Once arrived in China, he made Aulick's "Susquehanna" his flagship and sailed for Japan with a squadron of four ships.

There was no secret about the mission, even to the Japanese who were informed in advance by the Dutch. The press, both in the United States and abroad, was full of news and comments about it. Numerous applications were received from all kinds of people, Europeans as well as Americans, seeking to join the expedition. All were refused, Perry's view being that the mission called for the strictest kind of naval discipline which he felt would be difficult for civilians to accept. Scientists were rejected on the grounds that the mission was strictly naval and diplomatic. An exception was Dr. James Morrow who was appointed agriculturist for the expedition by Secretary of State Everett.[31]

The first stop made by Perry after leaving China was in the Liu Ch'iu Islands where considerable fencing took place with the local authorities over protocol. Following this visit, Perry went to the Bonins ("No Man" or "Uninhabited Islands"). Although discovered in 1593 by a Japanese, these islands were claimed by the British. To complicate matters further, an American whaler, Captain Reuben Coffin of the "Transit" out of Nantucket, also claimed them in the name of the United States. The British, however, had actually sent a rather motley group of colonists

---

[30] Of the seventeen Japanese landed in San Francisco by Captain Jennings of the "Auckland," the only one who finally went to Japan with the naval expedition then under Perry was a man called by the sailors "Sam Patch," and he refused repatriation, preferring to settle down in the United States.

[31] Cf. *A Scientist in Japan: the Journal of Dr. James Morrow,* Allan B. Cole, ed. (Chapel Hill, 1947).

to establish a British colony which Perry refused to recognize. Rounding out the list of countries interested in the islands was Russia. Perry liked the favorable location of the Bonins and felt that the United States should plant a colony of its own there. He purchased some land on the islands for a coaling station in 1853, and the following year one of his officers formally took possession of the Bonins, an action never officially ratified by the United States government.

Perry Delivers Letter. Returning to the Liu Ch'ius, Perry set sail for Japan on July 2, 1853. En route, he and his men celebrated the Fourth of July as had the "Morrison" before them and entered Edo Bay, anchoring off the city of Uraga in their "black ships of the evil mien," late on the afternoon of July 8. The arrival created pandemonium in Edo, where the people were badly frightened. Perry maintained an attitude of aloofness and dignity and refused to treat with lesser officials. The Japanese were forced to send officials of an acceptable rank, and, when this was done, arrangements were made to present the letter from President Fillmore addressed to the emperor. This letter, addressed to Fillmore's "Great and Good Friend," explained that Perry's objects were solely "friendship, commerce, a supply of coal, and protection for our shipwrecked people." In closing the emperor's "good friend" expressed the wish "May the Almighty have your imperial majesty in His great and holy keeping." [32]

This letter was presented at a town not far from Edo in a specially constructed pavilion. Perry was accompanied by a landing force of several hundred fully armed men and covered by the guns of his ships. Perry, aware of the difficulties with which they were faced by his proposals, sensibly offered to give the Japanese time to deliberate his suggestions and informed the negotiators that he would return in the spring with a larger force to receive their answer. Edo Bay was left on July 17 as the "black ships" sailed to Napa in the Liu Ch'ius and then to Hong Kong.

Perry achieved official acknowledgment of the receipt of the President's letter together with the promise of the Japanese to deliver it to the emperor. The Americans were told, however, that foreign business could be transacted only at Nagasaki, but because Perry "would feel himself insulted by a refusal to receive the letter," it was accepted "in opposition to the Japanese law." [33]

In a quandary over what course of action to follow, the *Bakufu* addressed copies of Fillmore's letter to the daimyos for their recommen-

[32] Francis L. Hawks, *Narrative of the Expedition of an American Squadron to the China Seas and Japan under the Command of Commodore M. C. Perry, USN* (Washington, 1856), Vol. I, pp. 42 f.

[33] *Ibid.*, Vol. I, pp. 256 f.

dations, an unprecedented step. In general, the replies were not in favor of the American requests, a view cordially shared by the government. Accordingly, elaborate military preparations were begun to repulse the Americans when they returned.

Russian Cooperation Rejected. Shortly after Perry's departure, the Russian Admiral Count Putiatin arrived in Nagasaki with a fleet of four warships burning coal obtained, during Perry's absence and against his orders, from American supplies at Hong Kong. The Russian request for the opening of ports for trade, for improved Russo-Japanese relations, and for a border agreement relative to Sakhalin were rejected by the Japanese on the grounds that no foreign negotiations could be carried on for at least a year due to the recent death of Shogun Ieyoshi. The Russians had to accept this decision, although they made an unsuccessful attempt to get the Dutch to join them in a show of force. They then returned to China where they sought to join forces with Perry and also requested more coal. Both requests were rejected by Perry who was quite suspicious of the Russians; with great prescience he later prophesied that the day would inevitably come when there would be a clash between Russia and the United States on whose outcome the fate of the world would hinge.[34] Not only did the Russians cause Perry concern, but so did the French who appeared also to harbor designs upon Japan.

Perry arrived in China during the Taiping Rebellion and was importuned by American merchants to stay on for the protection of their property. He completely disregarded their pleas, as he was determined to complete his mission in Japan. Disturbed not only by the Russians and the French, he was concerned also about the British. Not knowing that war in Europe was imminent between the British and the French, on the one hand, and the Russians on the other, he erroneously concluded that their objective was Japan. Accordingly, he advanced his return date for the departure to Japan and set sail for the Liu Ch'ius in early January, 1854. There he assembled a considerably stronger fleet consisting this time of three steam warships, three frigates, and three supply ships. In the Liu Ch'ius, news was received from the Dutch that the Japanese had asked them to inform the Americans that no business could be conducted owing to the period of mourning for the late shogun. Perry elected to disregard this and sailed into the Bay of Edo on a raw unpleasant day in February. He was again subjected to a treatment of evasion and delay, but his mission had arrived at a time when, despite the desire of the daimyos to resist, almost every other force in Japan outside of the *Bakufu* itself

---

[34] Arthur Walworth, *Black Ships Off Japan: the Story of Commodore Perry's Expedition* (New York, 1946), p. 129.

was anxious for change. The especially weak financial condition of the government was most helpful to Perry's objective.

Japan Informed About the United States. During the earlier negotiations, the Americans had been astonished at the knowledge of the United States, and even its most recent history, displayed by the Japanese who knew the names and locations of not only important American cities but even some extremely remote places in the prairies and mountains.[35] Much of this knowledge stemmed from Nakahama Manjiro who had attended school in Fairhaven, Massachusetts, had spent many years on American whaling vessels, and had even prospected in California during the gold-rush days. Although he did not publish any account himself, stories of his travels were written by various individuals who had heard his tales of adventure after he returned to Japan in 1851. Some of his impressions were quaint, to put it mildly. Speaking of government, he observed that:

> The government of America is, in general, similar to that of Japan. There is a written law of twelve articles, and there are no troublesome affairs. Seven persons act as rulers.
>
> North America is divided into thirty-six counties. Wise men of the country are chosen to serve as rulers. The term of office is four years, but very sagacious men serve for eight years, it is said. When they go out in public, they are accompanied by only one servant or so.
>
> The residences of the rulers of America are built upon flat ground, and not one of them is constructed like a *daimyō's* castle in Japan. When a ruler retires, he receives a pension and spends the rest of his life without want or worry. The officials do not parade their authority in public.
>
> Distinctions of rank are noted by the color of the clothes. Even farmers are chosen to office, according to the amount of education possessed by them. Well-educated persons, even though they may not be officials, are permitted to wear high-class clothes.
>
> America is now in the midst of development, and its culture is becoming more and more refined every year.[36]

As to what kind of people the Americans were—a question frequently put to him, Manjiro remarked:

> The people of America are upright and generous, and do no evil. Among them there are neither homicides nor robberies, as a rule. If such things occur, there are laws covering them, and the offenders are promptly seized.

---

[35] *With Perry in Japan: The Diary of Edward Yorke McCaulay.* Edited by Allan B. Cole (Princeton, 1942), p. 27.

[36] Ishii Kendo, "Ikoku Hyoryu Kidanshu," p. 447, quoted in Sakamaki, *op. cit.*, p. 148.

TREATY PATTERN FOR JAPAN 197

> For their wedding ceremony, the Americans merely make a proclamation to the gods, and become married, after which they usually go on a sightseeing trip to the mountains. They are lewd by nature, but are otherwise well-behaved.
>
> Refined people do not drink intoxicants; and only a small quantity, if they do. Vulgar people drink like the Japanese. Drunkards are despised and detested. Their intoxicants are worse in quality than the Japanese drinks.
>
> Husband and wife are exceedingly affectionate to each other, and the happiness of the home is unparalleled in other countries. The women do not use rouge, powder, and the like.[37]

Although the first book to contain a description of America had appeared in 1708, it was not until 1847 that the first detailed Japanese description of the United States was published. This was in an eleven-volume world atlas brought out by Mitsukuri Seigo. The section on the United States was entitled "A General Account of the Republican Government States." Referring to the American Revolution, the author wrote that the Americans

> resented their [the English] abusive language and scorned their cheap wages, and refused to obey their orders. They even seized and threw into the sea some 342 boxes of tea that had been brought from India by the English . . . A military official named Washington, and a civil official named Franklin promptly . . . declared "We must not lose this heaven-given opportunity. We must sever relations with the English forever" . . . In 1780, a certain official of this land reached an agreement with the English that this should forever be a free and independent nation. Since then, the nation's strength has steadily increased, and its territory has expanded tremendously.[38]

The first book devoted exclusively to the subject of America was a five-volume work entitled *Meriken Shinshi* (*New Account of America*) which appeared in 1853. It contained over fifty pages of maps and drawings. Among the illustrations were included "Koronbus," "Queen Isabirla," "Wasinkton," and "Amerikus." A double-page drawing depicted the Battle of Saratoga and contained the inscription "JOCKTOWN" and made the further mistake of showing Washington with the legend "Washington greatly defeats the soldiers of England at Saratoga."[39]

Still another book on the United States appeared in 1854. This was the *Amerika Sôki* (*General Account of America*) produced "from a desire

[37] *Ibid.*, p. 149.
[38] *Ibid.*, pp. 133 f.
[39] *Ibid.*, pp. 142 f.

that the [Japanese] people should know about them and make preparations with respect but not fear."[40]

Negotiations Difficult. Returning to Perry, the negotiations carried on between him and the Japanese were far from smooth until the arrival of a friendly interpreter, Einosuke Moriyama, who had been trained by Ranald MacDonald, with whom he was very cordial. Unknown to the Americans, Nakahama Manjiro, the onetime Fairhaven schoolboy and California prospector, was hidden nearby during the conversations. Here he could make speedy translations and also overhear some of the side comments of the Americans which were frequently far from complimentary.[41]

On March 13, following a series of preliminary negotiations, the Japanese were given numerous presents which included arms and ammunition, books, perfumery, considerable quantities of whiskey, wine, cordials, and champagne, a telescope, two telegraph instruments, a miniature "locomotive and tender, passenger car and rails complete," eight baskets of "Irish potatoes," etc. The presents created a sensation. The telegraph wires were strung over a distance of a mile, and every day crowds of dignitaries and people came to watch the sending and receiving of messages. The spectacle of the Japanese riding atop the Lilliputian train was "not a little ludicrous to behold," especially if he happened to be "a dignified mandarin whirling around the circular road at the rate of twenty miles an hour, with his loose robes flying in the wind."[42]

A few days later the Japanese returned the compliment by delivering to their guests numerous presents including "four small dogs of rare breed" and the other ceremonial presents of rice and dried fish given by the emperor. These, together with the dogs, were customarily part of an imperial Japanese gift.

On another occasion, the commodore gave a state banquet aboard the "Powhatan." The Japanese are described on this occasion as having become "quite uproarious under the influence of overflowing supplies of champaigne, [sic] Madeira, and punch, which they seemed greatly to relish." Among the toasts offered were "Japan and California—may they be united by steam and commerce" and "The ladies of Japan—may we become better acquainted with them." The Japanese ate as heartily as they drank, and the party was such a huge success that "the jovial Matsusaki threw his arms about the Commodore's neck, crushing, in his tipsy embrace, a pair of new epaulettes, and repeating, in Japanese, with maudlin

[40] *Ibid.*, pp. 145 f.
[41] Walworth, *op. cit.*, p. 174.
[42] Hawks, *op. cit.*, Vol. I, pp. 357 f.

affection, these words, as interpreted into English: 'Nippon and America, all the same heart.' "[43] One of the high lights of the proceedings was a minstrel show put on by the sailors. Midshipman Sproston confided to his diary that he thought "the Commissioners would have died with their suppressed laughter [for they never laughed out as we do]. The dancing rather surpassed all, and during this part of the performance, I looked, and to my astonishment, saw an arm placed affectionately around the Commodore's neck. That arm appertained to the Chief Commissioner. What will not champagne do!"[44]

The Treaty Signed and Ratified. The Treaty of Kanagawa [now Yokohama] was signed March 31, 1854. Its main points included: the opening of the ports of Shimoda and Hakodate where American ships could take on wood, water, coal, and provisions; humane treatment of the shipwrecked, a most-favored-nation clause; and permission to station an American consul at Shimoda. The treaty was immediately rushed to the United States by Commander H. A. Adams where it was promptly and unanimously ratified by the Senate.

On the return to China, a stop was made at Naha on Okinawa where the commodore made the Compact of Naha, the terms of which virtually duplicated those of the main agreement. Despite the criticism raised in some quarters that he had secured a most inadequate treaty, Perry had successfully achieved his purpose of "opening the gates of Japan." He had fulfilled his instructions to the letter, and the task of implementing and improving upon his work was rightly left to his successors.

Townsend Harris

American Tourists Welcomed. Within fifteen days of Perry's departure from Shimoda, the "Lady Pierce" entered the Bay of Edo with some American tourists. This ship had set out from San Francisco with the express intention of being the first American vessel to enter Japan after its reopening. It was well received by the Japanese who approved its peaceful intent, which contrasted with Perry's guns and force. The ship's owner was, nonetheless, informed that henceforth no foreign intercourse whatsoever would be permitted at Edo, only in Shimoda or Hakodate, despite Japan's pleasure that the "Lady Pierce" had come "without any money-making business of trade, and only to see Japan, to become acquainted with us, and bring home one of our shipwrecked people, the

---

[43] *Ibid.*, Vol. I, p. 376.
[44] *A Private Journal of John Glendy Sproston, USN*, edited by Shio Sakanishi (Tokyo, 1940), p. 16.

first that has returned to his country from America or [any other] foreign land." [45] This latter statement was, of course, patently untrue.

The "Powhatan" returned to Shimoda, February 21, 1855, to complete the exchange of ratifications, which was accomplished without much difficulty. Shimoda was found in ruins from the effects of a severe earthquake which had taken place in December, 1854.

Harris Becomes Consul. To follow up Perry's auspicious beginning, Townsend Harris, a New York merchant, was appointed the first American consul in Japan. He arrived at Shimoda in August, 1856. The difficulties which he encountered would have disheartened a less determined individual. Despite all the petty inconveniences put in his way, Harris concluded the Shimoda Convention, June 18, 1857, granting American citizens, including missionaries, residence rights at Shimoda and Hakodate and trading privileges at Nagasaki, together with the right to station a vice consul at Hakodate. Extraterritoriality was also conceded, and the exchange rate between American and Japanese money was improved to the former's advantage. After more than a year in Japan, Harris was permitted to visit Edo in November, 1857, although its distance from Shimoda is not great.

Townsend Harris' greatest achievement was the Treaty of Edo, signed July 29, 1858, which permitted the United States to maintain an official diplomatic resident at Edo and consuls in every port open for trade. Although Shimoda was now closed, Edo and four other ports were opened. Religious freedom was granted, a promise made not to excite religious animosity, and permission accorded to the American fleet to use Yokohama, Hakodate, and Nagasaki as supply depots. This treaty was concluded against the stiffest kind of opposition which taxed Harris' diplomacy to the utmost. He stressed both the power of the United States and the danger to Japan from the designs of Britain and Russia in winning his treaty.

Although his opinion of the Japanese was sometimes not too high, e.g., "they are great liars, consequently you do not know when to believe them," [46] he ultimately came to be very popular in Japan, and after his death his memory was deeply honored.[47] He remained at his post until

---

[45] *Hildreth's Japan as It Was and Is*, edited by Ernest W. Clement (Chicago, 1906), Vol. II, pp. 313 f.

[46] *The Complete Journal of Townsend Harris*, edited by M. E. Cosenza (Garden City, N. Y., 1930), p. 310.

[47] For a sympathetic account of the controversial case of Harris and the tragic Okichi San, see Herbert H. Gowen, *Five Foreigners in Japan* (New York, 1936), pp. 245-60.

For an example of the high esteem in which he was ultimately held by the Japanese, see Alfred Stead, ed., *Japan by the Japanese* (London, 1904), pp. 153-54.

A writer in *Frank Leslie's Illustrated Newspaper*, June 30, 1860, reflecting the popularity

1862 and watched the arrival of British, French, Russian, Prussian, and Dutch diplomats, together with businessmen from these countries. He was a witness also to the growth of international rivalries in these few years time.

Other Foreign Treaties

Just as the United States had hastened to secure a treaty with China following Britain's victory in 1842, so other nations hurried to capitalize on the pioneer work of the Americans in Japan. Great Britain was first; her agreement was signed October 14, 1854, by Admiral Sir James Sterling. Owing to its lack of a commercial understanding, it proved unsatisfactory to the British government. This defect was remedied by the signing of the first Anglo-Japanese Treaty of Commerce and Friendship, August 26, 1858, by Lord Elgin. To bind the bargain, the British turned over to the Japanese the steam yacht, the "Emperor," which the Japanese renamed the "Dragon."

Russia secured her treaty on January 26, 1855, after Putiatin and his men had survived the sinking of their ship, the "Diana," in Shimoda. France was granted an agreement on October 7, 1858; followed by Portugal, August 3, 1860; and the German *Zollverein,* January 25, 1861. Other nations, in order of the signing of their treaties, included Italy, Spain, Denmark, Belgium, Switzerland, Austria-Hungary, Sweden and Norway, Peru, China, Korea, Siam, and Mexico.

Antiforeign Reaction

Their country opened against the wishes of many powerful clans, the feeling of disaffection spread to the Japanese masses who became increasingly hostile to foreigners. One reason for this growing antagonism was the fact that several disasters had visited the country since Perry's departure. Another was that the nation was in the throes of great domestic upheaval. Incidents began to pile up alarmingly. A Russian officer and two sailors were cut to pieces in Yokohama in August, 1859. Shortly afterwards, a Chinese servant of the French consul was slashed to death for wearing European clothes on the streets of Yokohama. In 1860 Dankichi, a Japanese interpreter in the employ of the British legation, was murdered in broad daylight. He, incidentally, was one of the Japanese sailors rescued in 1851 by the "Auckland." Shortly afterwards, the French

---

Harris then enjoyed in the United States, noted that the only reason he could think of for not "cordially" recommending Harris as a candidate for the presidency was that he was a bachelor.

legation was set on fire. A month later, two Dutch sea captains were butchered in Yokohama.

The Regent Assassinated. On March 23, 1860, the regent of the shogun, Ii, the man responsible for permitting Japan's reopening, was slaughtered on his way to court and many of his retainers murdered, in what is known as the Sakurada Affair. His head was sent to Kyoto for public exposure with a placard reading: "This is the head of a traitor who has violated the most sacred law of Japan, that which forbids the admission of foreigners into the country." His death was followed by a lull which was broken by the cruel murder of C. J. Heusken, Townsend Harris' devoted young Dutch interpreter, in January, 1861, by a group of Japanese swordsmen. For this act, Harris demanded and received an indemnity of $10,000 which was forwarded to Heusken's mother in the Netherlands. Twice during that year and the next, the British legation was attacked by *ronin* with the resulting loss of British lives. An English merchant from Shanghai, Charles Lenox Richardson, en route home to England, was murdered and two of his companions were wounded (an English woman being the only one of the party to escape unhurt) by a retinue of the Satsuma clan in Yokohama in September, 1862, in what is known as the Namamugi Affair.

Matters were rapidly reaching a crisis in the struggle between the *Bakufu* and the Imperialists who sought to restore the power of the Mikado. In 1863, in an unprecedented move, the shogun was called to Kyoto to give an account of his government. This marked the first time since 1634 that a shogun had visited this city. In Kyoto the emperor's advisers ordered the immediate expulsion of all foreigners who then were told to leave. All the foreign diplomats except General Robert H. Pruyn, the American Minister, had already moved to Yokohama. Pruyn remained in Edo until the legation was burned to the ground. Then convinced that his life was in danger, he left for Yokohama.

Meanwhile, the British had made strong representations over the Richardson murder and the deaths of two sentries in the fires at their legation. Their ultimatum having been apparently rejected, Mr. Neale, the British charge d'affaires, ordered the British fleet to prepare for action. This move quickly produced results, and the required indemnity of £110,000 was paid by the shogunate on June 24, 1863. Nothing was done about the punishment of Richardson's murderers nor was an additional £25,000, asked for his relatives and those in his party, forthcoming.

Closing of Ports Ordered. On June 25 an order from the emperor to the shogun instructed him to close all ports and expel all foreigners. The shogun at Edo did nothing, but the Choshu daimyo, whose guns controlled the Straits of Shimonoseki, fired upon an American merchant vessel, the "Pembroke." The ship was fortunate to escape as it was attacked by two naval vessels as well as by the shore batteries. General Pruyn immediately ordered the U.S.S. "Wyoming" to retaliate, which it did quite successfully, although suffering the loss of five men killed and six wounded. An indemnity of $12,000 was later paid to the owners of the "Pembroke." The action of the "Wyoming" was well received in the United States where Congress passed an act directing the Treasury to pay a sum of money to the officers and men for their "specially meritorious and perilous services in the destruction of hostile vessels in the Straits of Shimonoseki." [48]

The French had a similar experience with Choshu a few days later, and the Dutch were also attacked. The French blasted the forts on the north side of the straits into submission, routed an army four times their number, and burned the local Choshu barracks.

The British, disgusted with Satsuma's failure to apologize for Richardson's murder, confiscated three Satsuma ships shortly after the above incidents in 1863 and were fired upon by shore batteries. The British silenced these, burned the captured ships, and reduced the city of Kagoshima to ashes. Four months later the indemnity was paid, and a promise was made to find and punish Richardson's assassins.

Throughout 1863 and into the next year the Japanese made painfully clear their strong desire that foreigners should abide by the emperor's decree of expulsion. Complicating the Japanese situation further, there was bitter internecine fighting going on between the Imperialists and the adherents of the *Bakufu*. Finally, on September 5, 1864, a fleet composed of French, British, and Dutch ships, together with a small American vessel, attacked and destroyed the Choshu forts guarding the Straits of Shimonoseki.

Japan Capitulates. The result was the Convention of Shimonoseki, signed October 22, whereby the Japanese agreed to pay an indemnity of $3,000,000 in six quarterly installments to be divided equally among the four powers. The foreigners agreed to waive the indemnity if Shimonoseki or some other port in the Inland Sea were opened for trade, a suggestion which the Japanese rejected. The first three payments were made on time, but the Japanese asked for postponement of the fourth until 1872, which was granted. When that time came, the Powers voluntarily agreed to consider the entire matter closed. The United States received over $500,000, or one fourth of the sum paid. With interest the

---

[48] Quoted in Frank E. Ross, "The American Naval Attack on Shimonoseki in 1863," *Chinese Social and Political Science Review*, Vol. XVIII (No. 1, April, 1934), p. 154.

fund grew until it was finally returned to Japan by act of Congress on February 22, 1883 in the sum of $785,000.

The four powers engaged in the Shimonoseki affair signed a tariff convention with Japan on June 25, 1866, which divided all imports into four classes: (1) low duties; (2) free goods; (3) prohibited goods, e.g., opium; and (4) goods subject to an ad valorem duty of 5 per cent on original value.

Antiforeign incidents did not cease,[49] but under the Meiji Restoration a decree was issued, March 26, 1868, which placed all foreigners officially under the protection of the law. Thus Japan settled down to the acceptance of the Westerners on her soil.[50]

In the meantime, the first official Japanese missions to go abroad had visited Europe and the United States. One of the terms of the treaty made by Harris in 1858 was that a Japanese mission should go to the United States to exchange ratifications of the agreement. A party of more than seventy Japanese was brought to the United States on an American warship in 1860 and handsomely entertained by the American government and people. The erroneous impressions which they formed about life in the United States make humorous reading.[51]

The British took a delegation of three principals and thirty-four assistants to Europe in 1862. A third mission went to France in 1864 to apologize for the murder of a young French officer. It was followed by a fourth in 1871 which went both to Europe and the United States and comprised more than fifty members. This mission sought unsuccessfully to end extraterritoriality, which the Japanese were finding irksome, so that "Japan might stand on an equality with the most enlightened nations."[52] This failure led to a constant agitation for treaty revision by Japan until they finally succeeded in 1899.

SUGGESTED READINGS

Ernest Clement (ed.), *Hildreth's Japan As It Was and Is* (Chicago, 1906); Allan B. Cole (ed.), *With Perry in Japan: The Diary of Edward Yorke McCaulay* (Princeton, 1942) and *A Scientist in Japan: the Journal of Dr. James Morrow* (Chapel Hill, 1947); M. E. Cosenza (ed.), *The Complete Journal of Townsend Harris* (Garden City, New York, 1930); Captain Golownin, *Japan and the Japanese* (2 vols., London,

---

[49] Nitobe, *op. cit.,* p. 90. The last and most serious was the decapitation of eleven Frenchmen at Sakai by some samurai. France obtained full redress.

[50] For the decree, see Paske-Smith, *op. cit.,* pp. 182 f.

[51] Cf. *The First Japanese Embassy to the United States of America* (Toyko, 1920) and *The First Japanese Mission to American (1860): Being a Diary Kept by a Member of the Embassy,* translated into English by Junichi Fukyama and Roderick H. Jackson, edited with an Introduction by M. G. Mori (New York, 1938).

[52] J. H. Gubbins, *The Making of Modern Japan* (Philadelphia, 1922), p. 110.

1818); Herbert H. Gowen, *Five Foreigners in Japan* (New York, 1936); J. H. Gubbins, *The Making of Modern Japan* (Philadelphia, 1922); Francis L. Hawks, *Narrative of the Expedition of an American Squadron to the China Seas and Japan Under the Command of Commodore M. C. Perry, USN* (Vol. I, Washington, 1856); C. W. King, *Notes of the Voyage of the Morrison and the Himmaleh* (New York, 1839); Charles Lanman, *Leading Men of Japan* (Boston, 1886); Ranald MacDonald, *Autobiography*, ed. by Wm. S. Lewis and Naojiro Murakami (Spokane, 1923); M. G. Mori (ed.), *The First Japanese Mission to America (1860): Being a Diary Kept by a Member of the Embassy*, trans. by Junichi Fukyama and Roderick H. Jackson (New York, 1938); Inazo Nitobe, *The Intercourse Between the United States and Japan* (Baltimore, 1891); A. H. Palmer, *Documents and Facts Illustrating the Origin of the Mission to Japan* (Washington, 1857); C. O. Paullin, *Diplomatic Negotiations of American Naval Officers, 1778-1883* (Baltimore, 1912); A. L. Sadler, *A Short History of Japan* (Sydney, 1946); Shio Sakamishi (ed.), *A Private Journal of John Glendon Sproston, USN* (Tokyo, 1940); Shunzo Sakamaki, "Japan and the United States, 1790-1853," in *Transactions of the Asiatic Society of Japan*, 2d series, XVIII (December, 1939); Payson J. Treat, *Diplomatic Relations Between the United States and Japan, 1853-1895* (2 vols., Stanford University, 1932); Arthur Walworth, *Black Ships Off Japan: the Story of Commodore Perry's Expedition* (New York, 1946); Harry E. Wildes, *Aliens in the East* (Oxford, 1937).

12

CHINA IN REBELLION, 1844-1878

The Background of Rebellion

During the first decades of the nineteenth century there were many indications that China was growing ripe for major rebellion. The economic situation bred widespread dissatisfaction. Overtaxation and exploitation of the peasantry increased constantly. Population continued to grow and to make ever heavier demands upon the means of subsistence. In consequence of these difficulties and the drainage of specie to pay for smuggled opium, commodity prices rose, to the further misery of the mass of the population. In fact, with the retirement of the Ch'ien Lung Emperor, in 1796, "China entered on her normal course of rebellion."[1] At the turn of the century, spurred on by the greed and corruption of officials, there was a big rising of the White Lotus Society in north central China. In 1813 the revolt of another secret society actually threatened the capital, Peking. A list of the sizable risings which took place in the 1820's and 1830's is impressive testimony to the declining capacities of the Manchus. The Ch'ing dynasty was unable to deal with the increasing agitation against it, of which the feebleness of the regime was both cause and effect. The notorious Ho Shên, court favorite of the later Ch'ien Lung period, had left an evil legacy of corruption in government service. At best the officials were conventional and unimaginative, typical products of the examination mill; at worst they were sticky-fingered and greedy. The two emperors of the first part of the century, the Chia Ch'ing Emperor (r. 1796-1820), and the Tao Kuang Emperor (r. 1820-50) were exceedingly frugal and full of hortatory maxims for officials, but such efforts fell short of the constructive activity needed and did little to disabuse the people of the idea that Heaven was growing weary of the dynasty, both because it was incompetent and because it was non-Chinese. Lacking vision and positive policy to arrest and reverse the general social and economic decline, the dynasty also lacked the military strength to suppress rebellion. The Manchu bannermen lived on their pensions and kept up their

[1] H. B. Morse, *International Relations of the Chinese Empire* (London, 1910-18), Vol. I, p. 439.

pretense of being a hereditary fighting force, but as soldiers they were useless. The Chinese Green Standards matched them in ineffectiveness: indeed in large part they were "paper soldiers" who existed only on review day and as names for whom the officers could draw pay to put in their own pockets. The result was that in cases of active rebellion, the Manchus found it necessary to fall back on the use of locally recruited militia, which served to suppress the rising but did not contribute to the strength of the central government.[2]

Besides these general portents of serious upheaval, there were particular circumstances in southeast China which were to make it the breeding place for the great mid-nineteenth century rebellion, the Taiping movement. The border area of the provinces of Kwangsi, Kwangtung, and Hunan was a spawning ground of lawlessness. By the 1840's there were in these provinces social elements which, if they could be fused, would produce a rebellion strong enough to shake the Manchu throne to its foundations. The region was full of disbanded soldiers who had been gathered to fight the British and had seen the weakness of the imperial government. Secret societies, such as the White Lotus and the Triad Society, were active. Bad crops, landlord pressure, and the development of large estates near the cities as a result of wealth made in foreign trade turned many poor farmers into bandits. The shores were thick with pirates. During the Anglo-Chinese War, the prohibition on possession of firearms by the people had broken down, and rebellious groups had acquired some modern weapons. The minority groups, the Hakka and Miao, played a special role because of their feeling of being in, but not of, Chinese culture. Even the gentry were restless, and in the 1830's and 1840's rose against the exactions of local officials.

The Origins of the Taiping Rebellion

In this confused state of affairs, as regular government proved ineffective, local groups organized their own defense corps to protect themselves from other local groups; it was such local forces of the Hakka and the Miao which formed the nucleus of the Taiping armies, just as some of the other local defense forces were the beginnings of the militia which eventually opposed the Taipings. By 1850 this anti-Manchu, religious, and socioeconomic movement emerged as a rival of the Ch'ing dynasty itself. Its origins make a strange tale.

Hung, Visionary and Leader. The founder of the movement and the first and only Heavenly King (T'ien Wang) of the Taiping (Great

[2] F. Michael, "Military Organization and Power Structure of China During the Taiping Rebellion," in *Pacific Historical Review*, Vol. XVIII, No. 4 (November, 1949), pp. 469-83.

Peace) dynasty was Hung Hsiu-ch'üan (1814-64), son of a poor Hakka family in Kwantung.[3] His family, by great sacrifice, gave him an education in the hope that he could pass the examinations and become an official, but he was chronically unsuccessful in the examination halls. In 1836, at the provincial examinations, Hung got some Protestant tracts, which he probably glanced at but saved. After another failure in the examinations in 1837, Hung not too surprisingly fell ill and began to see visions. According to the official Taiping version of these visions, which was probably an elaboration of them for politico-religious purposes, Hung went up to Heaven, where he was washed clean and given a new heart and other organs. God, a venerable old man, told him that the human race, which He had created, was ungrateful and unregenerate. Hung was given a sword with which to kill demons and a seal against evil spirits. He also met a middle-aged man, the Elder Brother, who instructed him in the art of demon slaying. For the following six years Hung, like most rejected examination candidates, was a schoolteacher. In 1843 he failed the examinations again, and thereafter read more carefully the Christian booklets which he had received in 1836. These tracts, the work of an early Chinese convert to Christianity, contained translations and paraphrases of scriptural passages and some sermons and essays. Here at last Hung found the explanation of his dreams. The old man was God, the Elder Brother was Christ, and he, Hung, was the Heavenly Younger Brother. Hung now began to preach this extraordinary doctrine and gradually gathered a group of converts, mostly Hakka and Miao in Kwangtung and Kwangsi, who were organized into an Association for the Worship of God and were taught the necessity of baptism and of the breaking of "idols." In 1847 he studied for two months with I. J. Roberts, a Presbyterian missionary in Canton, but was not baptized, a circumstance for which Mr. Roberts later had reason to be grateful.

At first Hung's movement was chiefly religious, but in the late 1840's it began to become something more, thanks to the economic and social conditions of South China. Converts to the new religion were mostly poor people who were thereby expressing their feeling of dispossession from Chinese culture. The Associations for the Worship of God developed a combination of religious, economic, and political goals which could rally all the discontented. Many of the local armed groups which had been formed came over to the Taiping movement. The leaders of these units expected to receive important positions in Hung's enterprise, and there were stormy scenes as Hung and the other men prominent in the

---

[3] In preparing this account of the Taiping rising, the author has found very useful the biographies of Taiping and government leaders in *Eminent Chinese of the Ch'ing Period (1644-1912)*, edited by Arthur W. Hummel (Washington, 1943-44).

movement tried to draw up plans for a real revolutionary organization. Revelations and visions were so abundant in the inner circles that, according to Taiping records, Jesus came to earth several times in 1848, and even God himself found it necessary to visit the Taiping camp in 1851 to straighten out the tangled affairs of the leadership.

Taiping Victories

In 1850 the rebellion had its real beginning. The God-Worshippers, their homes destroyed and their movable property turned into the common store, opposed the government troops in Kwangsi knowing that they had nothing to lose and everything to gain. The prospect of sharing in communal property attracted many poverty-stricken recruits: a noted pirate joined with all his followers. As the movement snowballed, imperial troops were powerless. These first successes justified the open organization, in January, 1851, of Hung's movement as a kingdom, the rightful substitute for the decadent Manchu regime. The *T'ai P'ing T'ien Kuo* (Great Peaceful Heavenly Kingdom) was proclaimed, with Hung as T'ien Wang, or Heavenly King. Five other chiefs also bore the title of King. Of these, the most notable was the Tung Wang (Eastern King), Yang Hsiu-ch'ing, who until his death in 1856 was commander in chief and the most forceful person in the movement. He had been a Kwangsi charcoal worker. His knowledge of military strategy, which proved to be considerable, came to him by divine revelation, which he was certainly in a good position to receive since he regarded himself as the incarnation of the Holy Ghost. Also worthy of individual mention is the Assistant King, Shih Ta-k'ai. He was a well-to-do farmer, somewhat better educated than most of the Taiping generals, but joined the movement because he resented discrimination against the Hakka group to which he belonged. He was one of the most successful of the Taiping commanders in the years 1850-55, but left the court after the murders of 1856 and wandered off to southwest China.[4]

In 1852, Fêng Yün-shan, one of Hung's earliest converts and in many ways the real founder and organizer of the God-Worshippers, was killed in battle. However, despite some reverses, the Taipings moved north toward the Yangtze River and in January and February, 1853, occupied Wuchang for the first of several times. The Taiping forces, a tremendous crowd of 500,000 men, women, and children, then moved down the

[4] It may be that in the early stages of the movement there was another king, Hung Ta-ch'üan, who bore the title of T'ien Tê Wang (Heavenly Virtuous King) and was equal in status to the T'ien Wang, but if so he was captured and executed by the imperialists in 1852 and the surviving Taiping leaders obliterated most records of his activity.

Yangtze capturing cities as they went and in March, Nanking, so often in past centuries the seat of Chinese dynasties, was proclaimed the capital of the new regime. This was really the high point of the rebellion. It lasted eleven years longer and the rebels won some later military victories, but it owed its length of life as much to the feebleness and confusion of the opposition and the uncertainties of foreigners about it as to its own merits and strength.

Rebel Successes Explained. There are several factors which account for the tremendous success of the Taiping Rebellion in its first years. Hung's religious teachings, eccentric though they were, had a strong attraction. This "homemade Christianity," as one historian of the Taiping movement has called it,[5] was simple, powerful stuff, capable of inspiring a mass movement. Hung had at hand not a complete Bible but passages from both the New Testament and the Old Testament. From these, plus ideas and practices from Confucianism, Buddhism, Taoism, and Judaism, he fashioned his creed. He preached a God who was the God of all mankind, the Heavenly Father, who had sent his son, Jesus Christ, into the world to redeem men by his suffering. Hung himself was also a son of God; he was the Heavenly Younger Brother, whose duty it was to establish the kingdom of heaven on earth. God was a jealous God, who would not countenance worship of idols. Satan existed, and the world was full of demons and evil spirits whom the God-Worshippers must combat. The chanting of hymns, baptism, and Saturday as a day of rest were features of Taiping religion. Hung accepted and incorporated into his teaching many Confucian ideas, but he bitterly criticized Confucius for having failed to hold the Chinese to the monotheism which Hung believed had been their original religious belief. Hung's religion was anthropomorphic, naïve, and crude, but it was infused with great evangelical zeal, and under its inspiration the early Taiping armies were formidable idol-smashing "Ironsides." Hung preached strict moral laws by which the God-Worshippers were bound and which helped the convinced members of the new faith to hold a strong sense of purpose and righteousness. The rank and file had to memorize the Ten Commandments and attend religious services. Prostitution, foot-binding, the sale of slaves, adultery, gambling, and the use of wine, opium, and tobacco were forbidden. Women enjoyed equal rights; they served under the command of Hung's sister in the army and in the administration. Marriage was compulsory for all women, but at Nanking there was a great camp of women whose husbands had died in battle or were absent, or who had not yet married. Commoners were

[5] Ssu-yü Teng, *New Light on the History of the Taiping Rebellion* (Cambridge, Mass., 1950), p. 49.

to observe monogamy, which however was certainly not practiced by the higher ranks. The Tung Wang was the greatest enforcer of these regulations and, until his death, did much to maintain the discipline of the movement.[6]

The economic and social program of the Taipings, which Hung derived from one of the Confucian classics, the *Chou Li,* was radical and appealing. Hung declared that land should be owned by those who cultivated it, and that there must be no discrimination against minority groups. The Taipings advocated a general redistribution of land, which was to be divided into nine grades by quality, and given to peasants according to need. In Nanking a sort of state socialism was in effect, with each person getting his share from the common stock. In the beginning, the Taiping armies paid for their supplies instead of looting, taxes were lower in the Taiping regions than in the rest of the empire, and trade was flourishing. The economic doctrines and practices of the Taipings were to be of decisive importance in the history of the movement. Chinese rebellion is traditionally agrarian rising, and in the competition to win the support of the mass of the peasantry the Taipings and the imperialists were offering rival cures for poverty and oppression. It is therefore of considerable importance that though Taiping economic doctrine was tremendously attractive, Taiping achievements in land redistribution were inconsiderable.

As a political movement against the existing dynasty, the Taiping rebellion was also in the Chinese revolutionary tradition. In fact, the outward and visible sign of the Taipings came from their anti-Manchu belief, for they refused to wear the queue and were called "the long-haired rebels." Taiping administration at first was fair enough, but the military always took precedence over the civil, chiefly because the Taipings never achieved peaceful government over a large area. In the early stages, the kings combined military command and administrative control. At Nanking the T'ien Wang was both a civil and religious ruler. The civil institutions of the Taiping realm were supposedly based on those of the golden age of the early Chou when God was still receiving his due of worship. There was a civil service examination system, including questions on religion, and six boards, one of which was for foreign affairs. Titles abounded: kings came in four grades, with five of the first grade in the early period and a few more created before 1856. Going down the line there were marquises, state ministers, supervisors, and commanders, with groups of twenty-five families as the basic political and social unit. Most of the Taiping edicts on military, land, ceremonial, and calendar

[6] H. F. MacNair, *Modern Chinese History, Selected Readings* (Shanghai, 1923, 1927), chap. 9, gives interesting samples of Taiping literature.

reform were issued during 1852-53 when the Tung Wang had become the chief figure in the movement. From 1853 to 1856 he served as prime minister. Hung retired to the pleasures of a harem of eighty-eight concubines, and until his murder in 1856 the Tung Wang as the Holy Ghost incarnate ran the Great Peaceful Heavenly Kingdom.

The Taiping rising was in many ways a standard Chinese antidynastic movement, born of economic discontent and rationalized by the "Mandate of Heaven" theory. Such movements regularly combined political and economic purposes: a new dynasty was to replace the old and the have-nots were to become the haves. It was the religious aspect of the movement, the Associations for the Worship of God, which gave it distinctive character. The strange tincture of Christianity makes it appear as the first large-scale indication of Chinese receptivity to Western ideology. Admittedly Christian doctrine was refracted almost beyond recognition by its involvement with Hung's visions. Nevertheless it is significant that the Taiping movement, made up chiefly of peasants, accepted a modified foreign ideology, while the gentry and officials were to continue to oppose any compromise with Western philosophy long after they had reconciled themselves to the adoption of Western mechanical methods. The Taiping movement was not of course a real movement for westernization, open to Occidental influence on a broad front. It was essentially an old-fashioned Chinese revolution, but with an interesting and conspicuous tinge of foreign doctrine. Hung's version of Christianity was an asset to the rebellion at first, since it won followers and gave them a sense of devotion and dedication. In the long run, however, it was a liability, for it shocked respectable Chinese and even not very pious foreigners.

Decline of the Taiping Movement

Nanking a Turning Point. Almost from the moment of the capture of Nanking, the Taiping movement went into decline. True, a northern expedition was launched, but it was unsuccessful. The expedition got near to K'aifêng and then Tientsin, but not to Peking. The southerners who made up the Taiping armies were not used to the severe northern winters and were short of provisions. The Mongol troops under Seng-ko-lin-ch'in which were sent against them were effective, and in May, 1854, the remnants of the expedition were decimated in Kiangsu. Two leaders of this northern foray held out until 1855 when they were captured and executed. After the failure of the northern expedition, the area under Taiping control was confined virtually to the provinces of the lower Yangtze, and its extent in that area fluctuated with the fortunes of the civil war. In 1853 the three chief cities held by the Taipings were Yangchow, Chinkiang, and Nanking. Near each of them was a large encampment of imperial troops, which however were not able to enforce an effective siege. Tsêng Kuo-fan (1811-72), scholar-official turned soldier, had by order of the throne organized a militia in Hunan, which in 1854 began to win occasional victories. In 1855 and 1856, in battles between these Hunan Braves and Taiping armies under Shih Ta-k'ai, the Taipings seemed to be coming out ahead. In August, 1856, they administered a crushing defeat to the imperial forces, which broke up the encampment around Nanking.

Hung Purges Potential Rivals. These military triumphs, however, had appalling consequences for the political leadership of the Taiping movement. The Tung Wang, made arrogant by success, liked to be called Wan Sui ("Ten Thousand Years"), a designation reserved for the emperor, and plainly had designs on the throne occupied by the indolent and debauched T'ien Wang. Hung, fearing the Tung Wang's ambition, told the Pei Wang (Northern King) to work out with Shih Ta-k'ai, the chief commander in the field, a plan for disposing of the Tung Wang. The Pei Wang enthusiastically exceeded his instructions and saw to the murder not only of the Tung Wang, but also of several thousand of his relatives and supporters. Hung then arranged the murder of the Pei Wang and, fearing that Shih Ta-k'ai also might become too powerful, relieved him of military power. Shih, with a large following, thereupon withdrew from the cannibal atmosphere of the Taiping court and moved through South and southwest China, seeking the basis for a separate kingdom. His anabasis finally carried him into the frontier areas of Szechwan near Tibet, where in 1863 he surrendered to government forces and was executed. Hung, having managed to deprive the Taiping movement of two of its most able leaders, proceeded to fill high posts with his own corrupt and incompetent relatives.

As a consequence of this crisis in the capital, the Taipings were unable to follow up their victories of 1856 and through 1857 and 1858 the rival armies fought up and down the lower Yangtze, looting and destroying. However, a new general came forward to replace Shih Ta-k'ai and gave the Taipings a few more years. He was Li Hsiu-ch'êng, who was made Chung Wang (Loyal King), in the course of a wholesale elevation of Taipings to kingly rank. The Chung Wang, most knightly and admirable figure in the Taiping movement, came of a very humble family. He gained the rudiments of an education and read the Confucian classics while serving as a common soldier in the Taiping forces during the campaigns preceding the capture of Nanking. The soldiers whom the Chung Wang commanded in the early 1860's were no longer the disciplined and efficient zealots of early days, and they had only a devastated area on which to forage. Despite these handicaps, this considerate and statesmanlike conqueror began in 1860 a revival of Taiping military activity which lasted into 1862. He first defeated imperial forces near Nanking and then went on to victories in the comparatively undamaged provinces of Kiangsu and Chekiang.

Frederick Townsend Ward. In these years the Chung Wang repeatedly threatened Shanghai, wherefore the foreign and Chinese business community undertook to organize its own defense forces. Frederick Townsend Ward, an adventurer from Salem, Massachusetts, was employed as a mercenary by a firm of Shanghai merchants, and with a tiny force, the nucleus of which consisted of one hundred Filipinos trained Western style, won a notable victory at Sungkiang in July, 1860. The American government disapproved of Ward's activity and accused him of encouraging desertion from American ships and endangering American neutrality, but Ward claimed Chinese citizenship and built his little force into what came to be called the "Ever-Victorious Army."

Despite Ward's local successes in defending Shanghai, the Manchus were in a very bad way in 1860 and the first part of 1861. The war of 1857-58 with the British and French had a very unpleasant aftermath when the Allies resumed military action in 1860, took Peking itself, and forced China to make further treaty concessions. Had the Taipings been more alert to the significance of the simultaneous existence of civil and foreign war, they might well have staged a successful northern expedition at this point. However, the foreign powers, having secured from the Manchus very advantageous treaty terms, began to regard the Ch'ing regime as the goose which laid golden eggs, and shifted from a policy of neutrality and nonintervention to one of support of the Manchus, in whose survival they now had a considerable stake.

Imperialist Tide Turns. By the fall of 1861 victory began once more to rest on the banners of the government forces. The group of famous Chinese generals who were to save the Manchus had by this time developed fairly effective militia forces and were rallying Chinese popular support. Chief of them were Tsêng Kuo-fan, who in 1860 had been made Viceroy of Anhui and Kiangsi and Imperial Commissioner for the suppression of the Taipings in South China, Tso Tsung-t'ang (1812-85) who was made Viceroy of Chekiang in 1862, and Li Hung-chang (1823-1901), who early in 1862 became acting Viceroy of Kiangsu with headquarters at Shanghai. In September, 1861, Tsêng Kuo-chüan, brother of Tsêng Kuo-fan, captured the key city of Anking, which became an important base for the anti-Taiping forces.

Ward's Ever-Victorious Army was still active around Shanghai, but in September, 1862, he was killed in the fighting near Ningpo. After some unfortunate appointments, the Ever-Victorious Army came under the command of Major Charles Gordon of the British Army, who had the express blessing of the British government in thus entering the Chinese service. Other small foreign-style forces under French and British leadership were in the field against the Taipings. Tsêng Kuo-fan was exceedingly suspicious of these foreign forces, however, fearing that they might become an entering wedge for foreign control of China.

By the end of 1862 the Chung Wang's forces retired to Nanking, hungry and exhausted, while the imperial forces organized a coordinated attack which they hoped would recapture the cities still in Taiping hands and end the rebellion. How certain their eventual victory was by this time is shown by the fact that in the summer of 1863 the Chung Wang urged Hung to leave Nanking with 500,000 men and try to make a fresh start elsewhere. Hung however declared that God would take care of him and refused to go. In the winter of 1863-64 the imperial forces carried on a systematic and successful campaign. One of the dramatic episodes was the surrender of Soochow to Li Hung-ch'ang by eight Taiping officers. Li did not trust their conversion to the Manchu cause and promptly had them killed, and Gordon, horrified at what he considered a barbarous act of betrayal, withdrew in protest. While Li, Tso, and Tsêng Kuo-fan were capturing the lesser Taiping centers, Tsêng Kuo-chüan was engaged in the painful siege of Nanking. At last, in July, 1864, the city fell. When disaster seemed certain, the T"ien Wang committed suicide, and after the imperial troops entered the city, 7,000 of his followers were put to death. The Chung Wang escaped from the city with Hung's son, heir to the Taiping kingdom, and gave the boy his own horse to help him to escape. The Chung Wang was soon captured by government troops, questioned, made to write a deposition which is one of the chief sources of knowledge of the Taiping movement, and was then executed.[7] The young Taiping prince was also seized and killed and the remnants of the Taiping forces were pursued into Fukien by Tso Tsung-t'ang and eliminated. The *T'ai-P'ing T'ien Kuo* had fallen and the Ta Ch'ing dynasty continued on the Dragon Throne.

Reasons for Failure Numerous. The reasons for the failure of the rebellion run much deeper, of course, than any estimate of the relative efficiency of the two fighting forces. The Taiping movement decayed rapidly from within. Even in the beginning it was composed of assorted

---

[7] H. F. MacNair, *Modern Chinese History, Selected Readings* (Shanghai, 1923, 1927). Items 218 and 236 give extracts from the Chung Wang's deposition.

groups: some wanted to advance Hung's new religion, others to achieve a new political order, still others just to loot. After the first successes, the number of undisciplined and opportunist recruits who climbed on the bandwagon soon outnumbered the true God-Worshippers. These divergencies among the rank and file were also present in acute form among the leaders who represented different power groups and had to be kept in line by being given positions of rank, both supernatural and earthly. Failure to put its economic doctrines into practice cost the movement many followers. Since its history was one of incessant battle, it brought to China not the new order of economic justice, but the old scene of devastation and death, while the imperialists, in an intelligent effort to offset the appeal of Taiping promises of prosperity for all, did institute land-tax reforms in some areas. Moreover, the idea of redistributing wealth was of course offensive to the tremendously influential scholar-gentry group. Many of them, by the 1850's, favored economic reform, although they thought of it not as a good in itself but as a way of heading off just such revolution as the Taiping movement threatened, and they were willing to fight hard and long against the revolutionary regime. Disillusionment with Taiping economic doctrine was matched by growing distaste for Taiping political doctrine. The Taiping attack on Confucianism offended many of the scholar-gentry. As to Taiping administration, it was a weird blend of military, theocratic, and traditionalist methods. The defects in the Taiping system of government were made painfully apparent by the weaknesses and savage rivalries of the leaders. In conclusion, little was to be hoped for from a ruler who put his trust in an anthropomorphic deity and a crowd of corrupt relatives.

Had the Taiping leaders, early in their revolt, been willing to negotiate with foreign governments to give the movement their blessing, it might have played a somewhat different role in Chinese history. Many foreigners, especially Protestant missionaries, looked with favor on the movement at the outset, thinking that God, although moving in a somewhat mysterious way, had brought this "Christian" movement into being as the means for the redemption of the Chinese. Foreign diplomats who were not fond of the Manchu regime carefully weighed the chances that the Taipings might become the new recipients of the mandate of Heaven. However, for all their strange semi-Christianity, the Taipings had virtually no understanding of the West or the role that it was playing, and could play, in Chinese history; and those foreigners who visited Nanking were dismayed at the caricature of Christianity there presented. The fact that the Holy Ghost was, until 1856, conducting the foreign relations of the regime was a circumstance which, far from increasing Occidental confidence in the movement, seemed to diminish it rapidly.

The aberrant quality of Taiping religion, and the nature of Taiping economics and politics, both in theory and in practice, meant that as time went on many Chinese turned from the Taipings to the Manchus as the lesser of two evils. The gentry led this reaction, but the mass of the population followed as it became apparent that the Taipings were not providing economic, political, and spiritual blessings in accordance with their doctrine. The best representative of this anti-Taiping reaction of the Chinese scholar-gentry is Tsêng Kuo-fan who, with such other leaders as Tso Tsung-t'ang and Li Hung-chang, defeated the Taiping armies and gave the Manchus a longer tenure of the throne. Tsêng, essentially a neo-Confucian scholar and essayist, was directed in 1852 to organize a Hunan militia. The dynasty frankly recognized that only forces of this type could win, and in 1854 canceled the edict prohibiting the holding of firearms by the common people. Tsêng demonstrated the soundness of the Confucian theory of the versatility of the superior man by becoming a good general. His Hunan Braves, aided by marines and gunboats, became a real army. Tsêng was especially astute in selecting good subordinates; many of the gentry followed his example and became military officers. He recruited substantial peasant farmers, rather than the poverty stricken and outcast who largely made up the Taiping army, and saw that they were well paid. He had great difficulty at first in paying his army, since the local landlords were hostile to levies upon them until they saw the advantages of the new army. Eventually the government authorized the sale of titles and in 1853 the imposition of likin, an internal transit tax, as means of paying for defense, and from these sources Tsêng and his fellow commanders were able to finance their forces.

By the 1860's, the result of these military experiments had materialized in a series of regional armies, with key military leaders given posts as viceroys and governors in the war area. More Chinese and fewer Manchus were placed in high office, and many of these new Chinese dignitaries were men who had come to the fore as gentry officers in the new armies. Fortunately for the Manchus, at this time the new military leaders drawn from the Chinese literati showed loyalty to the throne as the symbol of the Chinese cultural tradition, but in the later decades of the Ch'ing dynasty, the great provincial leaders with their local armies were to play a significant separatist role. In a sense, both the Taipings and the Manchus lost, and it was the Chinese gentry who won.

To what extent the survival of the Manchus should be credited to the attitude of the foreign powers and the activities of the small but efficient foreign-trained armies rather than to the support of the Chinese militia leaders and their forces is a question which is answered somewhat differently in historical works by Westerners than in those by Chinese. The policy of the Western states undoubtedly influenced the course of the rebellion. Despite the enthusiasm of Protestant missionaries, they did not give the Taipings recognition early in the struggle. Later, the reports of foreign visitors to Nanking indicated the degeneration of the Taiping movement, and in the early 1860's the foreign powers shifted from neutrality to defense of their commercial interests and treaty privileges, and finally to outright support of the Manchus. It is true that the Ever-Victorious Army and its analogues were successful out of all proportion to their size and were to set an example for ambitious viceroys for years to come. Nevertheless, it is doubtful that even foreign intervention on a much larger scale could have destroyed the Taipings and restored the Manchus had the Taipings been strong and popular and had there been no widespread Chinese revulsion against them, such as was embodied in the armies of Tsêng Kuo-fan and his colleagues. The Ever-Victorious Army was disbanded in January, 1864, and the coup de grâce was administered by Chinese armies alone.

A Choice of Evils. At the end of the rebellion, China was in a sorry state. Many provinces had been devastated. Nanking was a ruined city which shrank to a tenth of its former population. Fighting, flood, famine, and disease had cost the lives of perhaps 20,000,000 people. The central government was weak, caught between the foreign powers and the great provincial satraps. What was the meaning of all this suffering and disaster for the Chinese people? Sometimes the Taiping Rebellion is treated as a great popular movement for the salvation of China, which looked to the West, and, if it had triumphed, would have saved China much of the anguish of adjustment of the next decades, but which was thwarted by foreign imperialists and reactionary gentry who laid on China again the dead hand of the Manchus. This is a sentimental—or Marxist—version of the rebellion. It was in essence an old-style Chinese revolution, with Western trimmings. Its unhappy religious obscurantism and ineffective economic millennialism were not the answer to China's problems. Neither was the perpetuation of the decadent Manchus, but to both Chinese and foreigners they seemed more tolerable than the Taipings.

Other Rebellions

The Nienfei. The Taiping rising was not the only rebellion of these extremely agitated years, and even after its suppression other agitations continued to spring from economic and religious discontent. Not until the late 1870's was anything resembling internal peace restored. Concurrent with the Taiping revolt, there were many smaller groups up in arms, such as the Small Swords, around Shanghai. In fact in the mid-1850's the whole country was in ferment. One of the most persistent risings was that of the Nienfei, who appeared in North China in the 1850's. Although the Nienfei on occasion collaborated with the Taipings, they were simply large bandit groups, with no broad religious, political, or economic purpose. They were rather less well organized than the Taipings and did not attempt to hold cities or govern territory, but the effort to suppress these marauders turned out to be the graveyard of a number of very substantial military reputations won in struggle against the Taipings. In the early 1860's, Seng-ko-lin-ch'in, who was sent against them with his Mongol followers, won some victories and executed a few of the bandit chiefs, but was himself ambushed and killed in 1865. Tsêng Kuo-fan next inherited the assignment of putting down the Nienfei. Having little success, he was succeeded by Li Hung-ch'ang who, in collaboration with Tso Tsung-t'ang, accomplished so little that they were both temporarily deprived of their ranks. The real conqueror of the Nienfei was Liu Ming-ch'uan, a soldier of fortune and ex-bandit, who achieved high rank fighting the Taipings and who in 1867 and 1868 finally annihilated these troublesome raiders.

Two Moslem Outbreaks. The two great Moslem risings of this period had greater social meaning than the activities of the Nienfei. In both southwest and northwest China were large and self-conscious Mohammedan minorities, ready to resist mistreatment by local officials and stirred by a "new teaching" which had been going on within the Chinese Moslem community since the end of the eighteenth century. In Yünnan, in 1855, one of the most prolonged of the Moslem rebellions broke out in a region which had seen four major Mohammedan outbreaks within forty years. Part of the trouble sprang from conditions in the mines of Yünnan; as a result, Moslems were joined by non-Moslem miners who had economic grievances. The leader of the rebellion, Tu Wên-hsiu, took the title of Sultan Suleiman, calling his government the P'ing-An Kuo (Peaceful Kingdom). At the height of his power he ruled western Yünnan and had adherents in Szechwan and Kansu. The Manchu forces had a long, uphill struggle to eliminate him, partly because his revolt coincided with lesser risings in the southwest. At last, in 1872, Suleiman's capital of Tali was captured and he was executed. Two years later the Imam of Tali, a religious politician who had both stirred up the revolt and continued to draw Manchu pay, was also executed. What these years of warfare meant to Yünnan is clearly shown by the fact that of 8,000,000 inhabitants of the province only 3,000,000 remained at the end of the revolt; the rest had died or fled.

Another Moslem rising was going on in the northwest simultaneously with the one in Yünnan. Tso Tsung-t'ang was chosen to deal with this and in 1866 was appointed Viceroy of Kansu and Shensi, but was delayed by his efforts against the Nienfei and did not take up his new post until November, 1868. By that time the rebellion had been going on for six years. Tso went at his task vigorously. Shensi was pacified in 1869 and Kansu in 1873. Revolt in the outlying area of Sinkiang (Chinese Turkestan) then led to Tso's appointment to restore Manchu authority in central Asia. Tso systemically organized his forces, even securing Russian grain for them, although Russia seemed to be taking advantage of Manchu weakness to detach the region of Ili from Chinese Turkestan. It is interesting that Tso was eager to have the government borrow to finance the central Asian campaign, but ran into opposition from many high officials who wanted to spend money on naval and coastal defense. Tso finally won his point, arguing that China was in no danger of loss of territory along the seacoast, where the Western nations were interested only in commercial privileges; the real danger of shrinkage of China's frontier lay to the west and northwest, where Sinkiang, a buffer guarding Mongolia and therefore Peking, might be handed over to Russia or Britain by the local Moslem leaders.

Tso's strategy was to conquer the territory north of the T'ien Shan first, before moving into Sinkiang against the local ruler, Yakoob Bey. Yakoob had come from Khokand to aid a Moslem rebellion in Sinkiang in 1864 and by 1873 was in control of the region. He had acquired some international standing as an independent ruler: the Sultan of Turkey had conferred a title on him, and the British were inclined to support him against Russia, so that when Russia occupied Ili in 1871 and signed a treaty with Yakoob, Great Britain also established treaty relations with him. In 1876 Tso was ready to attack Yakoob in full force, to the displeasure of the British who suggested that the Chinese government accept him as a vassal. Tso opposed this policy and in 1877 moved south. Turfan fell soon and Yakoob died, probably by suicide. The territory which Tso recovered for the Manchus, and the Ili territory finally returned by Russia, were in 1885 made into a nineteenth province. Thus by 1878 all the major risings which for almost thirty years had rent China had been suppressed. Heaven had not yet withdrawn its mandate from the Ch'ing dynasty, but it had certainly indicated its doubts by tolerating rebellions of unprecedented extent and duration, and the Manchus now sat on the Dragon Throne by sufferance, trying to rule a population which was exhausted, still confronted by major problems, and dubious of their virtue as monarchs.

SUGGESTED READINGS

Useful scholarly studies of the Taipîng Rebellion are: W. J. Hail, *Tsêng Kuo-fan and the Taiping Rebellion* (New Haven, 1927); Têng Ssŭ-yü, *New Light on the History of the Taiping Rebellion* (Cambridge, Mass., 1950); and G. E. Taylor, "The Taiping Rebellion: Its Economic Background and Social Theory," in *The Chinese Social and Political Science Review*, Vol. XVI (January, 1933), pp. 545-64. H. F. MacNair, *Modern Chinese History, Selected Readings* (Shanghai, 1927), chap. 9, gives useful material. The biographies of Taiping and government leaders in *Eminent Chinese of the Ch'ing Period*, edited by Arthur W. Hummel (2 vols., Washington, 1943, 1944), are of great interest and importance. Information about the general condition of the empire, the Taiping Rebellion itself, and the other risings of the period will be found in the first two volumes of H. B. Morse, *The International Relations of the Chinese Empire* (3 vols., London, 1910-18). For interesting survey and interpretation see K. S. Latourette, *The Chinese, Their History and Culture* (2 vols., 3d ed., New York, 1946), Vol. I, chap. 10, and E. R. Hughes, *The Invasion of China by the Western World* (New York, 1938), chap. 1. H. Cahill, *Yankee Adventurer* (New York, 1930) is a biography of Frederick Ward. *The Last Stand of Chinese Conservatism: The T'ung-Chih Restoration, 1862-1874*, by Mary C. Wright (Stanford, Calif., 1957) gives an effective account of the suppression of the rebellions of the 1860's and 1870's.

Among the many contemporary works which deal with the Taiping Rebellion, some of the more important are: T. T. Meadows, *The Chinese and Their Rebellions* (London, 1856); S. Wells Williams, *The Middle Kingdom* (rev. ed., 2 vols., New York, 1907); C. C. Gordon, *General Gordon's Private Diary of His Exploits in China* (London, 1885); A. E. Hake, *Events in the Taiping Rebellion* (London, 1891).

13

REACTION AND REFORM IN CHINA, 1861-1894

Tz'ŭ Hsi as Regent

Chinese history in the second half of the nineteenth century shows clearly the decline and degeneration of the ruling house. The years from 1850 to 1894 saw three feeble emperors, two long regencies, some fortuitous deaths in the imperial family, and a number of other circumstances very inauspicious for the perpetuation of Ch'ing rule or the good government of China. In 1850 a new ruler, the Hsien Fêng Emperor,[1] mounted the throne. These were bad years to be at the head of the state, and the young emperor retired to the pleasures of the palace, leaving political affairs largely in the hands of the powerful Manchu official, Su Shun. In 1860, when the British and French troops took Peking, the imperial family fled to the hunting lodge at Jehol. Humiliated by this forced exodus from the capital, the emperor refused to return to Peking when the British and French withdrew; remaining in Jehol, he engaged in excesses which caused his death on August 22, 1861.

Beginning of the Regency. The emperor had only one son, born to him in 1856 by the ambitious and unscrupulous woman who is usually called in Western literature the Empress Dowager Tz'ŭ Hsi, although her proper designation was Hsiao Ch'in (1835-1908). She had entered the palace in 1851 as a concubine of low rank, but as mother of the heir to the throne, she achieved higher status and gained great personal influence over the emperor. When it became apparent that the emperor was dying, Su Shun, the three other adjutants-general, and members of the Grand Council got his consent to the creation of a Council of Regency made up of the eight members of these two groups. Edicts issued by the regents were to have the approval of the two prospective dowager empresses, the Empress Hsiao Chên, usually referred to in the West as Tz'ŭ An, and Tz'ŭ Hsi. Neither the empresses nor the regents cared to share power, and each began to plot against the other, a game in which

---

[1] As in the preceding chapter, the author has made extensive use of the biographies in *Eminent Chinese of the Ch'ing Period*, edited by A. W. Hummel (Washington, 1943, 1944).

Tz'ŭ Hsi was to become very formidable indeed. Early in September, Prince Kung, who had been left in Peking to negotiate with the Allies, came to Jehol to persuade the court to return to Peking. Subsequent events were to reveal that he had struck a political bargain with the empresses at the expense of the Council of Regency. On October 26, the court began its five day journey to Peking. Su Shun followed at a slower pace, escorting the imperial funeral cortege. Immediately upon arrival in Peking, the empresses issued an edict denouncing the regents. The seven regents already in Peking and Su Shun en route, were arrested. Su Shun was beheaded, two other regents were allowed to commit suicide, and the others were degraded and punished. The long period of regency by Tz'ŭ Hsi had begun.

It was announced that during the miniority of the T'ung Chih Emperor the two empresses were to be joint regents, with Prince Kung as Prince Counselor. A regency of women was relatively unusual, but the presence of Prince Kung might make the arrangement acceptable. Prince Kung in fact was a sort of Pooh Bah, in charge of foreign affairs, the Grand Council, and the education of the young emperor. The Taiping Rebellion was still going on and the future of the Manchus was in the balance. However, the reaction of many Chinese to the new regime was favorable. It had achieved peace with the foreigners, and Occidentals as well as many Chinese were inclined to think that the new government might be preferable to that of the Taipings. Tz'ŭ An was indifferent to politics, but Tz'ŭ Hsi was not. By 1865 she had so consolidated her position that, on a pretext, she was able to deprive Prince Kung of his offices. He was later reinstated in some of them, but did not regain the title of Prince Counselor. Tz'ŭ Hsi did not use her new influence very wisely, however. She tended to rule through eunuchs in the palace to an extent that was in no way customary, and the execution of her favorite eunuch, An Tê-hai, in 1869, was a distinct setback to her. She had sent An, whom she had used as a spy on officials at court, on a mission outside the palace. He behaved arrogantly and unreasonably, and was arrested and executed, probably at the instance of Tz'ŭ An and Prince Kung. Tz'ŭ Hsi was less assertive and less reliant on eunuchs for a time thereafter.

Death of T'ung Chih. As the young emperor grew older, the end of the regency approached. On October 16, 1872, he married, taking a bride who was not his mother's choice. He formally ascended the throne on February 23, 1873, but Tz'ŭ Hsi continued to try to dominate him and the policies of state in the name of filial piety. The T'ung Chih Emperor does not seem to have been of the material of which great rulers are made. He had little judgment, he disliked governmental routine, he readily yielded to the importunities of certain eunuchs and officials, and he spent much of his time on incognito expeditions of debauchery outside the palace. When Prince Kung memorialized criticizing his behavior, he was enraged and did not change his habits. In November, 1874, the emperor contracted smallpox, probably in the course of one of his extramural journeys. His illness was so serious that on December 18 the regency of the empresses was restored. He subsequently showed signs of recovery, but relapsed and died on January 12, 1875, possibly of smallpox or some other disease, although rumors of unnatural death were prevalent.

Before the emperor's death, Tz'ŭ Hsi had already laid plans for a succession to the throne which would involve another long regency. Having garrisoned the palace with troops under her faithful henchman, Jung Lu, she called a council of princes and high officials. To this group she presented the name of Tsai T'ien (1871-1908), first cousin of the T'ung Chih Emperor. This choice would violate dynastic precedent and Chinese custom: only a member of a younger generation could act as a son toward the deceased emperor and render the proper rites to his spirit. It was reported that the widow of the T'ung Chih Emperor was pregnant, but Tz'ŭ Hsi argued that to hold the throne open until her child was born might cause disorder. She promised that Tsai T'ien's first son would, in due course, be made the adopted son of the late ruler, and thus won approval for the enthronement of Tsai T'ien, who had, to Tz'ŭ Hsi, the very great merits of being both a young child and her nephew.

The Regency Resumed. As soon as agreement was reached, Jung Lu brought the new emperor to the palace. He was given the reign title of Kuang Hsü, the empresses resumed the regency, and it appeared that the general pattern of palace politics was about to repeat itself. There was not universal satisfaction, however. Realizing the hopelessness of her position, the widow of the T'ung Chih Emperor committed suicide; there followed the usual and almost inevitable rumors that she had been assisted out of this world. And the dismay and disapproval of many old-line officials were summed up in the valedictory memorial of the minor official Wu K'o-tu, who committed suicide in 1878. Wu, already known for his denunciation of corrupt officials, volunteered to be one of the group which escorted the coffin of the T'ung Chih Emperor to the imperial mausoleum. He then composed a memorial asking the regents to give further reassurance that the spirit of the late emperor would not continue to go untended, and, to give weight to his memorial, took poison. Tz'ŭ Hsi once more declared that the first-born son of the Kuang Hsü Emperor (who, as it proved, was to have no children) would act as the son of the

T'ung Chih Emperor and would inherit the throne, and graciously raised Wu K'o-tu posthumously to the fifth official rank, but criticism of the manipulation of the succession continued. Many Chinese, both officials and commoners, were inclined to feel that Heaven could not be expected to look favorably upon a monarch whose very presence on the throne was an offense against the cult of veneration of ancestors.

Whether for this reason or for others, the Kuang Hsü Emperor was certainly the most unhappy of all the Manchu rulers. Tz'ŭ Hsi had chosen him simply as a convenient puppet. In 1880, Tz'ŭ Hsi was ill and Tz'ŭ An for a time was sole regent. Upon Tz'ŭ Hsi's recovery however, Tz'ŭ An's life ended abruptly, ostensibly from acute indigestion, but with other causes suggested by rumor-mongers. As sole regent, Tz'ŭ Hsi then arranged matters to suit herself. She removed Prince Kung from office, and advanced the young emperor's father and the corrupt Prince Ch'ing to high position; foreign affairs she left in the hands of Li Hung-chang, now viceroy of Chihli. She once more began to make extensive use of eunuchs as spies and agents, the chief of them being the notorious Li Lien-ying. In 1887 the young emperor became technically of age, but Tz'ŭ Hsi yielded very quickly to inspired requests that she continue as regent and instruct him in state affairs.

In 1889 the emperor was married to a niece of Tz'ŭ Hsi; thereupon, the Empress Dowager at last brought the regency to an end. She retired to the new Summer Palace, the I Ho Yüan, built to replace the Yuan Ming Yüan which had been destroyed by the Allies in 1860, but she did not relinquish political activity. She continued to accept little presents from officials eager for promotion, to get her followers into government posts, and to read important state papers. The emperor's tutor, Wêng T'ung-ho (1830-1904) saw to it that he received an excellent education, including the study of English and Western civilization. There are many indications that he was an intelligent, imaginative, and sensitive man, genuinely concerned for the welfare of his subjects. Nevertheless he was not a free agent. The Empress Dowager, whom he feared, continued to dominate him; his consort was her spy; and many officials regarded him as a mere figurehead and still looked at Tz'ŭ Hsi as the possessor of power and patronage.

A Period of Distress. The China over which Tz'ŭ Hsi exercised her long regency was in an unhappy state. Rebellion had cost dearly in lives and in wealth. In the mid-seventies natural disasters came in force. South of the Yangtze there were great floods; north of it, drought and locusts. The land tax was remitted in those provinces where suffering was the greatest, and titles and honors were sold to gain funds for relief; but the famine, which cost perhaps 7,000,000 lives in North China strained the resources of an empire which was just emerging from more than a quarter of a century of major rebellion.[2] The central government, greatly weakened, was even less competent to deal with major issues than it had been at the beginning of the century. The great provincial officials with their local armies and their schemes for strengthening their provincial preserves could not be commanded by Peking. The Empress Dowager was a shrewd, energetic, and skilful politician, eager to restore the power of the Manchu house, but the tide was flowing strongly the other way.

Chinese Reactions to Western Culture

Westernization Divides Leaders. The great problem of the late nineteenth century was that of adjustment to the West. China had of necessity come to terms with the Occidental powers in the matter of granting them treaty rights. However, the question of accommodation to Western culture was a deeper and broader one than that of mere diplomatic relations and trade agreements. The West had shown itself stronger in war and possessed of certain skills and techniques which gave it the decided edge in any power struggle. Must China therefore adopt Western ways, and if so which ways? Or, if the Chinese tried to shut their minds and doors against westernization, would Occidental tastes, techniques, and ideas seep in anyway? Was a synthesis of desirable elements from both cultures possible and desirable? Or had Western culture such persuasive and pervasive power that it was bound eventually to undermine the foundation of the old Chinese way?

Chinese leaders of the late nineteenth century were aware of these problems and were trying to find answers. That their answers were not effective or final is no reproach, for the whole process of acculturation was in a relatively early stage and they could hardly be expected to comprehend all its possibilities and ramifications. In the 1860's, the leading officials, having rallied round the throne, were engaged in an attempt to restore the Confucian social and political order after the ordeal of mid-century.[3] Some sorts of westernization were ruled out as inconsistent with restoration, while many Western-style changes of the T'ung Chih period faded out later in the century as their implications for change in the traditional structure became apparent. There were some Conservatives in high office who felt that a revival of Chinese morality and learning would serve China without recourse to westernization of any sort. This

---

[2] H. B. Morse, *International Relations of the Chinese Empire* (London, 1910), Vol. II, pp. 307 ff.

[3] *The Last Stand of Chinese Conservatism: The T'ung-Chih Restoration* by Mary C. Wright (Stanford, Cal., 1957) gives a scholarly and detailed account of the policies and activities of the Chinese government during this period.

view is well exemplified by Wo Jên, Manchu chancellor of the Hanlin Academy: when in 1866 the T'ung Wên Kuan, the new school for interpreters, added mathematics and astronomy to its curriculum, he declared in a memorial to the throne that the nation was better established on rites and ethics than on schemes and contrivances and that what China needed was not technical skill but moral cultivation.

Most of the prominent officials were less far to the right than Wo Jên, however. They realized that Westerners could not be assimilated to the extent that China's less civilized neighbors had been brought into Chinese culture. They were not inclined to admire Western culture as they understood it. It seemed to them to be a matter of military and industrial techniques, since these were the aspects encountered in the wars of 1840-41 and 1857-60. They cherished a strong feeling of cultural superiority: Chinese civilization was fundamental—a matter of ethical and social relations which provided the very basis of organized human life and for which Westerners seemed to have nothing comparable. However, it was true that Western weapons had been effective against China and against the Taiping rebels, and it was possible that to protect the inner essence of Chinese culture from Westerners it might be necessary to put on Western armor. This attitude accounts for the seeming paradox of thorough Neo-Confucianists advocating westernization. Tsêng Kuo-fan, in his essays, urged a return to the traditional principles and protection of China's ethical system, but at the same time he took the lead in the introduction of new-style armies, arsenals, and factories. He and others like him found justification for this position in Neo-Confucian philosophy. Sung Confucianism was dualistic, and distinguished between substance and functions, root and branches. Chinese knowledge and standards undoubtedly constituted the root, but Western techniques could be regarded as the branches. Thus the one could be used to defend the other without impinging on it. The most famous statement of this "division of labor" between Chinese essentials and Western accessories was made in *Learn,*[4] which Chang Chih-tung published in the midst of the reform movement of 1898. It was a theory doomed to failure. Western culture could not be used as a moat surrounding Chinese civilization; it was more like a sea in full tide, eating away at the very substance of China. Nevertheless this dyarchical theory was held by many sensitive and intelligent Chinese of the late nineteenth century and was in many ways a very natural reaction in that stage of Sino-Occidental relations.

There were Chinese intellectuals who, by the end of the century, wanted to go much farther than merely to shore up the traditional culture behind a bulwark of Western-style defense works. The leaders of this school of

[4] Available in English translation as *China's Only Hope,* translated by S. I. Woodbridge (New York, 1900).

advocates of social change to meet changing conditions were K'ang Yu-wei (1853-1927) and his disciple Liang Ch'i-ch'ao (1873-1929). Their ideas will be discussed more fully in connection with the reforms of 1898, in which they played leading parts. In general they represented one of the two main camps into which Chinese scholars were divided. Basically the two groups differed as to the authenticity of certain classical texts. The *ku-wên,* or ancient text school of historical criticism (which K'ang opposed but which included most older Chinese scholars of this period) believed the classics to be valid historical documents of antiquity, which Confucius had edited and preserved. The *ch'in-wên,* or modern text school, regarded Confucius as the author of many of the classics and as a teacher who had used them to support and justify his ideas of social reform. In the name of their Confucius, who was a prophet rather than a traditionalist, K'ang and his followers "urged antiquity for purposes of reform" and declared that Confucius had been an advocate of an ameliorative social philosophy and that such institutions as constitutional government had actually existed in the good old days of the Chou dynasty. It is significant that even the liberals felt it necessary to have Confucius on their side; neither group was yet ready to throw overboard Confucian sanctions. The *ch'in-wên* group led by K'ang Yu-wei did not have great influence until the 1890's. Before that time, and also thereafter, responsible officials were either thorough reactionaries, Neo-Confucians in the manner of Tsêng Kuo-fan, or practical advocates of technical progress like Li Hung-chang and Liu Ming-ch'uan. There was noticeable rivalry between the court and the provincial officials in the employment of Western skills and materials. The great provincial satraps, in the name of strengthening the country, took the lead in innovation, but obviously the new factories, schools, and arsenals in their bailiwicks redounded more directly to their advantage than to that of the central government which, although conservative in its leadership, occasionally experimented with Western gadgets in the hope of strengthening itself against growing provincial separatism as well as foreign incursion.

How Penetration Occurred. Western ideas reached China in many different ways. The treaty ports furnished many examples of Western ways, and Chinese who lived in them began to acquire foreign tastes. Foreign experts in the employ of the Chinese government or of provincial administrators spread knowledge of Western methods. Two eminent examples are Sir Robert Hart, the Britisher who served for many years as Inspector-General of the Imperial Maritime Customs and came to be a respected adviser to the throne, and Sir Halliday Macartney, who assisted Li Hung-Chang in many of his schemes for modernization.

Missionaries were particularly important in helping China to adapt to the West. Although the number of converts to Christianity did not increase rapidly, their indirect contributions were significant. Missionary schools such as St. John's University in Shanghai were important as introducers of new methods and ideas which were to bring about great changes in education.

Protestant missionaries in particular began consciously to present the merits of Western civilization as a whole, rather than of Christianity alone, in the hope of influencing the scholar-gentry group, and their publications reached a wide audience. The *Wang Kwoh Kung Pao* or *Review of the Times,* a monthly magazine founded in 1889, was the most influential missionary periodical. The center of much Protestant activity in the translation of Western works into Chinese and in the publication of textbooks in Chinese was the Society for the Diffusion of Christian and General Knowledge (S.D.K.). Dr. Timothy Richard, who became head of the S.D.K. in 1891, was perhaps the most energetic and effective of all missionaries in getting the ear of prominent Chinese and suggesting reforms, and was in touch with such dignitaries as Li Hung-chang, Chang Chih-tung, and Wêng Tung-ho. Since they knew no Western language and were dependent for knowledge of the West on translations into Japanese, many Chinese who had no liking for Christianity nevertheless made use of the products of the S.D.K., the London Missionary Society, and other similar enterprises. In fact the Chinese scholars who collaborated with Westerners on translations of literature were among the first Chinese to have any substantial knowledge and appreciation of Western culture. A Chinese scholar who worked with James Legge on the great translation of the Chinese Classics into English, went to Britain with Legge in the 1870's and eventually returned to China to become a pioneer in modern journalism and an advocate of reform. A Chinese mathematician who had assisted in the translation of Euclid into Chinese served as head of the department of mathematics and astronomy in the T'ung Wên Kuan from 1869 to 1882.

Members of the first Chinese diplomatic missions to Western countries saw the actualities of Western civilization and, in some cases, became vigorous advocates of westernization. The first experiment in sending Chinese students abroad in any numbers was the famous Chinese educational mission to the United States (1872-81), headed by Yung Wing.[5] After receiving his elementary education in mission schools in Canton and Macao, Yung Wing was taken to the United States by a missionary, attended Monson Academy, in Monson, Massachusetts, and in 1854 received a Bachelor of Arts degree from Yale. After his return to China,

[5] Yung Wing, *My Life in China and America* (New York, 1909).

he interested Tsêng Kuo-fan in a project to send other young Chinese to America to study, and in 1870 the educational mission received imperial approval. The first group of students came to Hartford, Connecticut, in 1872. As a sop to conservatives, Yung Wing shared the headship of the mission with old-fashioned Chinese scholars uninterested in Western learning. Their reports that the young Chinese were being weaned away from sound Confucian principles and behavior led to the termination of the mission in 1881. The returned students were at first viewed with some suspicion and were not given posts of importance, but in time a number of them made their mark and became prominent advocates of reform.

Beginnings of Westernization

The Arts of War. In general, the sort of westernization which developed through such channels as the above was eminently practical and relatively peripheral to Chinese culture, at least in immediate seeming and effect. There were some ventures in industrialization, in military reform, and to a lesser extent in education, but there was as yet no reaching out to understand Western ideology.[6] The first symptoms of serious interest in the West go back to the 1840's when several geographic works about Western countries were prepared, one under the direction of Lin Tse-hsü, of opium suppression fame, which was based on materials translated from Western sources. Western victories in the wars of the 1840's and the 1850's and the effectiveness of Western-trained forces against the Taiping Rebellion stimulated a much keener desire to learn about and adopt Western secrets and strength. The special patrons of these first attempts to supplement Chinese doctrine with Western skills were the great provincial officials Tsêng Kuo-fan, Tso Tsung-t'ang, Li Hung-ch'ang (for twenty-five years Viceroy of the metropolitan province of Chihli), and Chang Chih-tung (Viceroy at Canton and later at Wuchang). One of the first enterprises of a reforming official in the years between 1860 and 1894 was sure to be the drilling of troops in Western style. The central government, aware of the desperate weakness of the Manchu bannermen and the Green Standards, made some efforts in this direction. The Peking Field Force, a division of musketeers equipped with Russian firearms, was organized in 1862, with Jung Lu, Tz'ŭ Hsi's faithful follower, as one of its commanders. The victory of Germany over France in the war of 1870-71 accounted for the fact that both Li Hung-chang and Chang Chih-tung organized provincial forces drilled by German officers.

The effort to provide China with a modern national navy consumed time, effort, and money, and brought little result. In connection with the

[6] M. E. Cameron, *The Reform Movement in China, 1898-1912* (Stanford, 1931), chap. 1.

suppression of the Taipings, Horatio Nelson Lay, the English head of the Imperial Maritime Customs, was asked in 1862 to secure a small fleet for China. Lay got some light craft and a British officer to command them but wanted the enterprise to be directly under the imperial government, whereas it was to be placed, like other forces fighting the Taipings, under the control of Tsêng Kuo-fan and Li Hung-chang. On this issue of status the project foundered, and the fleet was disbanded. Not much more was done about naval armament until China's difficulties with France in 1884-85 emphasized the value of naval defense. The government then set up a Board of Admiralty, and secured some European warships and British instructors. The diversion of funds from the navy to the construction of the new Summer Palace and to the celebration of Tz'ŭ Hsi's birthday handicapped the growth of the navy, and in 1890 Captain Lang, the chief British instructor, resigned. The navy failed to develop any real national loyalty or esprit de corps, and when the Sino-Japanese conflict came in 1894-95 the Northern Squadron showed up poorly against the Japanese and the Southern Squadron simply sat out the war.

Arsenals were among the more important Western-style institutions launched in China in this period. The first arsenals were established during the later stages of the suppression of the Taipings as enterprises attached to the provincial militia forces. The Kiangnan Arsenal, set up near Shanghai in 1867, grew out of a suggestion made in 1863 by Yung Wing who, after winning the support of Tsêng and Li, bought machinery from abroad. The first steamboat built by Chinese was produced at the Kiangnan Arsenal in 1868. Another notable arsenal was that at Foochow, started in 1866 by Tso Tsung-t'ang. Between 1867 and 1874, it turned out fifteen ships. There were important schools in connection with both these arsenals. The Kiangnan Arsenal included a school of foreign languages and a translation department which in the seventies and eighties issued over two hundred translations of Western works on engineering, science, and history. At the Foochow Navy Yard there was a Naval Academy which taught French, English, shipbuilding and navigation, and from which a few able students went to England and France for further training. The best known of them, Yên Fu, was graduated from Greenwich Academy in Britain in 1879 and became one of the outstanding Chinese translators of works on Western science and social thought. There followed a slackening of interest in army and navy reform and in the maintenance of arsenals; a sharp and very understandable revival of interest developed after 1895.

Communications. Some modernization of communications took place before the Sino-Japanese War. The telegraph appealed particularly to a central government eager to exercise more rapid control over distant provinces. On the recommendation of Li Hung-chang, the first line, built in 1881, connected Tientsin and Shanghai. It was later extended to Peking and then to other cities. In the sixties the Imperial Maritime Customs started a postal system to care for the mails of the legations and of the customs service. It grew to such an extent that in 1878 China was asked to join the Postal Union. In 1896 an Imperial Post for all China was established under the direction of Sir Robert Hart, who thereafter served as Inspector General of both Customs and Posts. Li Hung-chang was the patron saint of the first modern steamship line in China. He took up Yung Wing's suggestion of a government-subsidized line to carry rice from the South, out of which developed the China Merchants' Steam Navigation Company, with Li as chief stockholder. Railways were of great potential importance to China but made their way only with considerable difficulty. Some officials were aware of their great strategic and economic value but soon discovered that there was lively popular opposition to them. The construction of a railroad line was almost bound to disturb family graveyards unless the track was laid in serpentine fashion, and the carters and boatmen were quick to see in the iron horse the means to their own technological unemployment. The first railway line in China was built by a British firm in 1876 to connect Shanghai and Woosung. When a Chinese committed suicide by flinging himself under the wheels, popular indignation was roused against this foreign device. The line was then sold to the imperial government, which transported rails and rolling stock to Formosa. There Liu Ming-ch'uan, its very enterprising governor, used these materials to build a line from the capital to the coast.

In 1880 Li Hung-chang, chief proponent of practical innovation, memorialized the emperor advocating four trunk lines of railways, to be built with loans. In his own province of Chihli he sponsored a railway from the Kaiping coalfields to Tientsin which, by 1888, was extended to Peking. Liu Ming-ch'uan, Liu K'un-i, and Tso Tsung-t'ang also memorialized, urging the construction of railways as a defense measure; the best soldiers in China were considered to be those from Hunan, and they could be brought quickly to the defense of the capital if there were adequate railway connections. In 1889, Chang Chih-tung came forth as a vigorous proponent of railway building. Chang, one of the chief props of the Manchus in the later years of the dynasty, was an enigmatic person. He was a Confucian scholar of the old type, famous for a literary style so graceful and well turned that it could easily conceal great lack of substance. Personally frugal and benevolent, he was also ambitious for recognition and leadership, unstable in policy, something of a trimmer, and known as "a scholarly bungler." He was one of the most eminent advocates of the sort of cultural dualism which involved the preservation of the Confucian heritage by the use of Western weapons. He urged a trunk line from Hankow to Peking with such vigor and persuasiveness that he was elected to carry out his own plan and was shifted from the viceroyalty at Canton to that at Wuchang to facilitate the progress of the scheme. Chang, however, soon discovered one of the great difficulties in the way of the materialization of railways in China. To rely on local money was to achieve nothing, for it was not forthcoming; to accept foreign loans for railway building was to put China still further under the economic domination of the West. With no real answer to this dilemma, no major railways were built in China before the Sino-Japanese War.

Industry. The most attractive aspect of westernization in this period was the construction of modern factories. They were built under official patronage and often with considerable investment by officials, which is indicative of the important discovery by the scholar-gentry of a new source of wealth besides landholding. Chang Chih-tung was especially active in this field. While viceroy at Canton, he launched a number of industrial enterprises. During his long tenure of office as viceroy of Hupeh and Hunan he established the great Hanyehping iron and steel works, cotton mills, silk mills, tanneries and other factories to such an extent that the Wuhan cities (Hankow, Hanyang, and Wuchang) became known as the Chicago of China. Two other patrons of industrialization were Li Hung-chang, and Liu Ming-ch'uan, who during his term as governor of Formosa (1885-91) put in a comprehensive, well-planned, and quite effective reform program, which, however, was allowed to lapse after he was forced out of office by reactionaries.

Education. Any moves to westernize education seemed, to conservative officials, to cut much more closely at the heart of Chinese civilization than did modernization of the armed forces or the introduction of transportation facilities and factories, although in the long run these seemingly external changes were just as full of revolutionary import as were new-style schools. In the period before 1894, modernization of education made little progress. Not till after the 1898 reforms and the Boxer rising were there radical changes. This slowness to introduce Western learning in a formal sense is not surprising, since most officials considered it as a matter of tricks and skills with nothing real to offer on the great central theme of human relationships. The mission schools naturally took the lead in introducing foreign curricula and educational methods, but at first they were scorned by substantial or ambitious Chinese. What would it profit a boy to go to one of these alien institutions, which would not and could not prepare him for success in the civil service examinations?

The first government-sponsored schools of Western learning were set up for the very practical purpose of training interpreters to facilitate communication with the Western powers. In 1862, the Chinese government opened such institutions in three cities, Canton, Shanghai, and Peking. The Peking school, the T'ung Wên Kuan (School of Combined Learning) was eventually to grow into the Imperial University. It began very modestly, however, as a set of classes in French, Russian, and English. Soon W. A. P. Martin, a missionary educator who was to have a long career in the Chinese government service, joined its staff. Prince Kung's proposal to add mathematics and astronomy to its course of study aroused the wrath of such reactionaries as Wo Jên but was carried out. In 1887, the inclusion in civil service examinations of questions on mathematics was authorized, but had little effect, since few papers were submitted. Most Chinese students concentrated on that sure road to advancement, the meticulous study of the classics and the Neo-Confucian commentaries, and were hesitant to take their chances with "new" subjects. When one graduate of the T'ung Wêng Kuan passed the examinations and emerged as a member of the Hanlin Academy, the institution gained in prestige, and Tung Wên graduates were chosen to teach the Emperor English in 1893. In the 1890's, K'ang Yu-wei and his group came forward as advocates of more extensive study of the West and reform along Occidental lines, but on the whole the old educational program remained intact, and was apt to be as long as it was the highway to that most desired of all careers, public office.

Missionary Activity

Why did not Christian missionary activity prove to be a more effective means of bringing the Chinese an understanding and appreciation of the ethical and spiritual values of the West? [7] As has been pointed out, some Protestant missionaries consciously acted as protagonists of Western secular learning, hoping by that means to attract the interest of the Chinese educated class, but they were more successful in this program than they were as purely religious propagandists. In fact, there was bitter anti-Christian feeling in China, among both the classes and the masses, which periodically flared out in violence against missionaries and their converts.[8] The Chinese were traditionally a tolerant people, capable of

[7] E. R. Hughes, *The Invasion of China by the Western World* (New York, 1938), chap. 2.
[8] H. B. Morse, *International Relations of the Chinese Empire* (London, 1910), Vol. II, chap. 11.

believing in several major religions simultaneously, and Christianity in itself might well have been entirely acceptable to them as worthy to be added to the Three Doctrines as an additional form of spiritual insurance. The exclusiveness of Christianity, its refusal to settle down with the old Chinese faiths, was an intellectual and social obstacle to its wide acceptance. Christian converts renounced many of the practices which the Chinese considered hallmarks of the civilized man. If a Chinese Christian refused to contribute to the upkeep of temples and perform the rites, he plainly was an antisocial person who had seceded from Chinese culture. What was still worse, he seemed to have become a "secondary foreigner," for back of the converts stood the foreign missionaries and back of the foreign missionaries stood the foreign governments.

The treaties of 1858 had provided for toleration of Christianity, and persecution of Christians thus became a violation of China's agreements and an international matter. It was probably very unfortunate for the natural and spontaneous acceptance of Christianity by the Chinese that treaty toleration was instituted. Christian converts were often from the poorer and less well-behaved groups in Chinese society who had the least to lose by "going foreign" and adopting the new faith. A magistrate might haul a Christian into court on the ground that he, like many other converts, was a habitual lawbreaker who had been converted to get foreign backing and protection; but the missionary was almost certain to cry persecution and might threaten the magistrate with a demonstration of Western power to teach him toleration of the faith and respect for treaties. Christian missionaries were especially quick to take advantage of freedom of travel in the interior and often settled down in inland cities. The missionary was thus the most widely distributed variety of foreigner in China. Add to this the fact that he was an extraterritorial person and was disposed, because of the toleration clause, to extend extraterritoriality somewhat illegally to his converts, and there were the makings of serious trouble.

To many Chinese, Christianity appeared as an ominous manifestation of foreign imperialism, not as a gospel of salvation. Resentment, suspicion, and the willingness to believe any sort of slanderous tale about the foreign religious workers were widespread. Catholic institutions were accused of kidnapping children, killing them, and making them into medicines; tales of this sort inflamed the mob and perpetrated the Tientsin Massacre of 1870. There were similar rumors about Protestant missionaries. When Anson Burlingame, serving as China's representative to the Occident in 1868-69, spoke of China's eagerness to have missionaries plant the shining cross on every hill and in every valley, he was carried far from the facts by the delights of his own rhetoric. Had Christianity been a private movement in China, making its way freely without special privileges and special status, it might have won many more adherents and might have acted as a real bridge of understanding between China and the West. As it was, some Chinese joined the church to fill their rice bowls, and others to get access to foreign learning, but most Chinese regarded Christianity as a threat to the preservation of Chinese civilization, resented its special treaty status, and disliked its pretensions to a monopoly of truth.

Years of Decadence

The three decades before 1894 were a time of false calm, between the revolutionary convulsions of the middle of the century and the disastrous war with Japan. The main themes in the internal history of China in these years are the gradual decline of the central government and the first moves toward reform in imitation of the West. While few would have gone as far as Burlingame in proclaiming China's receptivity to Western inventions, learning, trade, and religion, there were a considerable number of optimists, both Chinese and foreign, who believed that China had awakened and would steadily progress into secure and prosperous life in the modern world. However, a few modern troops and ships, a smattering of factories, and some Western-style schools which commanded little prestige did not constitute a reformation root and branch, nor was there any such thorough program in the minds of the reforming officials of this period. They had no desire to have westernization cut deep. Neither, however, did they realize that the few Western institutions which they had transplanted to China were to act like drops of acid on the already badly worn fabric of Chinese civilization. Had Chinese culture not already been decadent, it would not have been vulnerable to attack by Western ideas and arms. It could not be preserved by calling for revived Neo-Confucianism for the inner man and Occidental railways for the outer.

The contrast between the Chinese reaction to the challenge of Western culture before 1894 and that of Japan is striking and enlightening. In these years, when a few Chinese officials were carrying on random experiments with miscellaneous Western devices, Japan was undergoing a deliberate, programmed westernization, carried on by the Japanese government. There were a number of reasons for Japan's greater willingness to westernize, which will be developed at length later in this book. Certainly the circumstances of the two countries differed in ways very significant to the successful adoption and carrying through of a reform program. The Japanese were accustomed to borrow from other cultures, the Chinese to being borrowed from. The Japanese ruling class, the samurai, was a very different group from the Chinese scholar-gentry; their intense pride, their hatred of being looked down upon by the West, and their determination to shake off the unequal treaties with the Western powers moved them to fight fire with fire, to westernize on the grand scale in order to escape western control. The new government of the restored emperor in Japan served as a focus of loyalty and devotion such as the decaying Manchu dynasty could not command. Japanese society was tightly organized and disciplined, Chinese society was loose and individualistic—a "rope of sand" as Sun Yat-sen was to call it. Japan was a group of smaller islands, comparatively accessible; China was a huge land mass into which novelties penetrated slowly. Thus Japan won the first round of the new competition for leadership of Asia by demonstrating efficiency, educability, and adaptability, while China muddled along under a weak and unpopular regime and with a ruling class on the whole willing to make no more changes than necessity dictated.

SUGGESTED READINGS

On court affairs, see two books by J. O. P. Bland and E. Backhouse, *China under the Empress Dowager* (Philadelphia, 1910) and *Annals and Memoirs of the Court of Peking* (Boston, 1914). As in the previous chapter, the biographical studies in *Eminent Chinese of the Ch'ing Period*, edited by Arthur W. Hummel (2 vols., Washington, 1943, 1944), are very valuable. See also H. B. Morse, *International Relations of the Chinese Empire* (3 vols., London, 1910-18), Vol. II. Probably the most substantial and valuable work in English on any part of this period is Mary C. Wright, *The Last Stand of Chinese Conservatism: The T'ung-Chih Restoration, 1864-1874* (Stanford, Calif., 1957).

Meribeth E. Cameron, *The Reform Movement in China, 1898-1912* (Stanford, 1931) chap. 1; E. R. Hughes, *The Invasion of China by the Western World* (New York, 1938), chap. 1, and K. S. Latourette, *The Chinese, Their History and Culture* (2 vols., New York, 1934), Vol. I, chap. 11 survey the beginnings of reform; Yung Wing, *My Life in China and America* (New York, 1909), gives the story of the first educational mission to the United States. Gideon Ch'en has done studies of the interest of three Chinese officials in Western techniques: *Tso Tsung-t'ang* (Peiping, 1938); *Lin Tse-hsü* (Peiping, 1934); and *Tsêng Kuo-fan* (Peiping, 1935).

K. S. Latourette, *A History of Christian Missions in China* (New York, 1929) is the standard work on the activities and influence of missionaries. See also E. R. Hughes, *op. cit.*, chap. 2.

14

JAPAN: THE END OF AN ERA

If the enforcement of the seclusion policy followed after 1638 by the Tokugawa shoguns had not been completely airtight, it had been sufficiently effective to insure that the Western world generally would know little about Japan and its people. There was no foreign appreciation of the fear that the Japanese had held in the early seventeenth century that civil war and pressure from foreign powers might cause the disintegration of the country. As a consequence there was little understanding of the beneficial results of isolation and good government which had checked disruptive tendencies and given Japan an unparalleled 250 years of peace. In 1853 foreigners could not know that during these long decades of peace the nation had established and perfected its own way of life. It was difficult for them to realize that the Tokugawa family had devoted its entire effort to the maintenance of peace for the primary purpose of retaining the power to govern in its hands. All that the West knew was that Japan should be opened to contact with the outside world.

When Commodore Perry's squadron anchored near Uraga in Edo Bay on July 8, 1853, he supplied the impact on Japanese life which marked the beginning of the end of the Tokugawa era in Japanese history.

It was soon apparent that forces within Japan were working toward a revolutionary change. It was only gradually that acute foreign observers discerned some of the main features of Japanese civilization. Before considering the actual record of the years immediately prior to the Meiji Restoration of 1867, a brief summary of some of the more significant aspects of Japanese life in 1853 will help the student in his evaluation of these turbulent fourteen years.

Characteristics of "Old" Japan

If an impartial and well-informed observer had been asked to point out some of the more important features of Japanese culture at this time, his topics would have included the preferred position of the military class, feudalism, family solidarity, Bushido, strict government control, the

JAPAN: THE END OF AN ERA 239

imperial institution, and the development of an essentially Japanese culture. In a previous chapter [1] changes in the cultural pattern of Japan were noted. The Japanese never had been blind imitators, but had chosen those phases of Chinese civilization which could be adapted to their own use. The natural beauty of their island home, together with their religious heritage, had developed in them a rare appreciation of the beautiful. During the leisurely years of the Tokugawa rule they found ample time to perfect their manners into an almost flawless courtesy. It would take time for Western traders, soldiers, and businessmen to know well this side of Japanese life. Hasty, often inaccurate judgments of other aspects of things Japanese only added to the lack of understanding of this new Oriental people and their way of life.

The Family

Possibly because of contacts with Chinese, Indian, and southeast Asian cultures, the West did understand the importance of the family as the basic unit of Japanese life. This aspect of Japanese life reflects both a natural development from early native custom and the influence of Confucianism. Here, too, Chinese ideas had been adapted, in this instance by making loyalty the cardinal virtue and ranking it above the filial piety in the five Confucian classical relationships which formed the heart of the Japanese moral code. It is also true that Japanese family life tended to be less institutionalized and more sentimental than Chinese family relations under Confucianism. With the family as the foundation for society, it was natural for the lowest echelon of government to be the *kumi,* or group of five peasant families, the basic unit of rural organization. One of the difficulties experienced by the Tokugawa and one that was to continue to trouble the rulers of a reformed Japan was the effective transfer of much of this loyalty from the family and the han to the state.

Changing Feudalism Its Influence

An obvious feature of Japan at the time Perry arrived was the hold feudalism had on the country. The very existence of feudalism at this time contrasts sharply with China where feudal institutions had largely vanished before the Christian Era. An even sharper contrast with Chinese history is evident in the dominant position held by the Japanese military class. They had controlled the government since 1192 and obviously had no intention of relinquishing that power. There were resulting benefits: the military provided a group of leaders whom the people would follow,

[1] Chapter 8.

and a military tradition made easier the adoption of measures necessary to defend Japan after 1853. Western militarism with its power potential and its possible threat to Japan made a strong and lasting impression on the Japanese. At the same time, the dominance of the military over the civilian element in the government posed a real obstacle to the development of liberalism in Japan.

What was not immediately apparent to the Westerners who opened Japan was the degree to which the feudal relationships had changed. From the beginning of the Tokugawa period (1603) the military retainers, the samurai, had been urged to devote as much time to literary as to military pursuits. Gradually, the emphasis on learning at the expense of the older military habits increased. Only Yoshimune, the eighth shogun (1716), had attempted to reverse this trend, much to the discomfort of the military men who were by then accustomed to a far less rigorous life. With the exception of occasional (later more frequent) armed peasant uprisings, the samurai had no reason or opportunity to practice their profession, fighting. Thus, in effect, their reason for being ceased to exist, and they tended to become a parasite class—a large one—totaling with their families some 2,000,000 people out of a total population of about 30,000,000.

With the very existence of the Tokugawa dependent upon continued military dominance, this change in status might not have been catastrophic had the old personal loyalty and close relationship of the samurai to his feudal lord remained the same. As Japan's economy changed gradually from rice and barter to money, a new and fatal stress was placed on this fundamental aspect of feudalistic Tokugawa life. The samurai were paid a fixed sum (in rice) based on their station in life. As part of a military group attached to a daimyo, they perforce lived in the cities or on the manorial fief. They were completely unable to change their income as prices increased. With a higher cost of living, the daimyo often resorted to forced loans by withholding part of the revenue ordinarily paid their feudal retainers.

For the samurai, certain avenues of escape seemed available. Late marriages and infanticide kept down the size of a samurai's family. Frequently by adoption or outright sale, commoners and their sons became part of the family of a samurai. Often they entered the business world. Any of these expedients would weaken the rigid class system considered so essential by the Tokugawa, but none of them kept other samurai from becoming almost hopelessly indebted to merchants and rice brokers. Since appeals to his daimyo too frequently brought no relief, the samurai's loyalty to his master weakened. The discontent of the samurai was to provide one of the reasons for the success of the anti-Tokugawa group after 1853. Added to this was the fact that both the shogun and the leading daimyo had acquiesced in the transfer of the real governing power to samurai in subordinate positions in their official households. Many of these samurai were concerned about Japan's weakness; most of them knew that only by a revolutionary change could they obtain the power necessary to give them an opportunity to test their new economic and political ideas. From the ranks of these disgruntled men were to come the leaders of the restoration in 1867. This situation also introduced the first serious break with feudal ties, for from it developed the idea of loyalty to the state whose head was the emperor. An easier transition to nationalism was possible for all the people once these samurai had made that change.

Government Regimentation

Another phase of feudalism in Japan, strict government regulation of every aspect of a citizen's daily life, was to prove very helpful to the reformers. During Tokugawa times, shogunal decrees had covered every act in a man's life: what he could and should wear; how many presents he might give on certain occasions; what kind of food he might serve; the religion (Buddhism) which he must support; when and if he might collect his honest debts from the samurai; the price of rice, etc. Philosophically, there was an excellent reason for this close supervision. The rulers of Japan were supposed to be superior men who would give the country good government. The people were to be told what to do and were expected to obey. Buddhism with its insistence that every daily act would affect a person's existence after reincarnation lent support to the government's policy. Actually the Tokugawa rulers found it easier to maintain their rigid controls by this exacting supervision of the most minute functions of daily life. The people accepted bureaucracy and governmental regimentation as necessary to their daily living. Obedience to law was deeply ingrained in the average Japanese who seldom thought for himself politically and came to expect the government to guide, interfere, control, and provide. It was not unnatural, then, for the new Japan after 1867 to have a well-disciplined people who would follow their leaders willingly, often blindly. Similarly, in later years a system of free enterprise would have difficulty developing in soil more accustomed to government assistance and regulation.

Individualism De-Emphasized

This government-regulation supplies further evidence of the Japanese emphasis on society as a whole rather than on the individual. There was little room for individualism in a social system which stressed the importance of man's membership in a family first, and that the family in turn was a part of the larger unit, the clan, and ultimately of the state. The Japanese political theory in 1853 rested on the assumptions that men by nature were unequal and that government by man was superior to a government by laws. Quite contrary to the Western idea that laws should protect the rights of the individual was Japanese insistence that laws served to bind society together. Laws, it was believed, should list the duties of the individual to the whole group rather than offer to the individual the protection of a bill of rights. A man's personality, ability, and knowledge of the law were more important than the form or theory of the law. With this background, Reischauer's statement that "... the state is simply a gigantic patriarchal family" [2] assumes added significance. One of the characteristics of Japanese life which was easily missed was the national unity which resulted from the feeling by the individual of being a member of one big family. Every man felt that his contribution to society was important because without it the whole organism, the state, could not function properly. This same sense of unity made it possible for the nation to be divided into social classes without danger of rebellion destroying the Japanese state and its culture.

In theory, these ideas sound plausible enough. In practice some of the weaknesses appeared as the years passed under the Tokugawa shogunate. The rulers of Japan often were not superior men blessed with unusual ability. The very fact that government positions were open only to the aristocracy, actually only to members of the Tokugawa family and their loyal retainers, excluded many people and caused unrest and dissatisfaction. As offices came to be hereditary, men of inferior talents, sometimes corrupt men, often held important posts with the government, which consequently became weaker and more perverted. To the political, economic, and social confusion which existed in Japan when Perry arrived, an inadequate government and its leaders offered little hope for a solution of the nations' domestic and foreign problems.

Under these conditions it is not surprising that the teaching and writing of such eighteenth-century scholars as Motoori Norinaga should attract increasing attention. It had been Motoori who had published the *Kojiki* with full notes, thereby calling attention to the fact that the emperor, not the shogun, was the ruler of the Japanese. Motoori had

---

[2] R. K. Reischauer, *Japan, Government-Politics* (New York, 1939), p. 33.

opposed foreign, i.e., Chinese and Buddhist, influence in Japan and had urged a return to the native religion, Shintoism. Impending political changes were preceded then by an intellectual reformation which re-established many of the old myths, including that of the divine ancestry of the emperor.

Importance of the Emperor

Even without this re-emphasis on the position held by the emperor, one of the outstanding characteristics of Japan in 1853 was the prominent place the imperial institution had in Japanese life and thinking. Here, too, the Japanese had changed Chinese political theory by omitting the right of revolution against an incompetent ruler. The Chinese belief that the emperor held his position because of his supreme virtue and only so long as he possessed that attribute never was adopted by the Japanese. Other aspects of rule by the emperor now proved to be extremely convenient. For centuries the emperor had retained only his religious position and power. All temporal duties had been performed in his name by the *bakufu,* the shogun's government. Even before that, under the Fujiwara family, a civilian bureaucracy had run the government. The theory that the emperor should reign but not rule thus was firmly established in Japanese practice. When the Tokugawa shogunate was unable to retain its hold on Japanese politics, it was simple to transfer shogunal powers to a council of state and later to a cabinet. It could have made quite easy the establishment of a constitutional monarchy similar to that existing in England. As Tokugawa leadership wavered and the emperor was re-established as the central figure in Japanese political life, the imperial institution became the rallying point for the ardent spirit of patriotism in modern Japan.

Bushido

To the emperor also could be transferred the intense loyalty which Bushido emphasized as the cardinal virtue. This feature of Japanese life, with its stress on personal honor, was noticed by foreigners immediately after the opening of Japan. Since then it has been rather incorrectly translated as "the way of the warrior." Actually, only the name was new, and the reason for its association with martial ways was a quite natural development. Some of the ideas common to Bushido can be traced to the code defining a soldier's duties which was observed by military families in the Fujiwara period of Japanese history. During these confused years of feudal warfare, society demanded some rules which would govern the relationship of men, some pattern of loyalties to which all must subscribe. Chinese philosophy further emphasized the virtue of a systematic arrangement of loyalties, and Zen Buddhism stressed the value of self-discipline. However, it was not until the Tokugawa shogunate had brought peace to the nation that Bushido became a major concern of those outside the soldier caste. During the long peaceful years, the Tokugawa shoguns deliberately used Bushido as an instrument of policy. It became a system of practical ethics rather than a code exclusively for the military in times of war. Now the goal of Bushido was to set high ideals for all members of society, and it tended to become one more way to buttress Tokugawa rule. It proved to be a two-edged sword, however, for as that great ruling family lost its control the reformers saw in Bushido a tool which could be used to support the new regime. All that was needed was the transfer of loyalty from feudal leaders to the emperor, and hence to the state.[3] Thus was added one more prop supporting and emphasizing the paramount importance of the imperial institution.

Tokugawa Economic Disaster

Intellectual and economic unrest was undermining the foundations of Tokugawa Japan. It is clearly evident that the intellectual ferment so helpful in producing reforms had been present in Japan for some time. It is also patent that philosophical challenge to existing political and economic institutions took on added strength as the Tokugawa failed to solve Japan's problems. While it is true that many of the leading critics of the Tokugawa exclusion policy were to be found among the *tozama daimyo* and their samurai who formerly had controlled and profited most from foreign trade, there also were leaders within the ranks of the Tokugawa who believed that the isolationist policy was responsible for Japan's weakness. One of the most serious difficulties confronting the shogun when Perry arrived was his complete inability to find a solution of the economic crisis in which the nation and people found themselves. Major elements contributing to this crisis were certain fundamental weaknesses which the static, moralistic policy of the shogun's government failed to alleviate.

Position of the Peasants. The plight of the peasantry has been mentioned previously.[4] The importance of this class in Japan is obvious, as it numbered about three fourths of the population and provided the major

---

[3] Bushido often is compared with chivalry in feudal Europe. Both emphasized loyalty, frugality, courage, and the generous treatment of a fallen foe. Bushido stressed, more than feudalism, filial piety and family unity. Both were alike in the great importance attached to personal honor and in the fact that seldom were the great ideals achieved.

[4] See Chapter 7.

share of the revenue. Also, as the foot soldier armed with Western weapons displaced feudal levies, the significance of the farmers as a source of military manpower increased. Important as the peasants were, their condition became progressively worse. Feudalistic practices prevented regional agricultural specialization and thus blocked the full development of the country's agrarian resources. Under the best circumstances the size of the average Japanese farm was only about one fifth that of the most densely populated countries in the West. To the disadvantage of inadequate acreage must be added the excessively high rents and taxes which varied from 40 to 60 per cent of the yearly rice crop. As the nation's economy gradually changed from a rice to a monetary basis, prices rose and the farmer was pinched even more severely. Although the payments made by the peasants at this time to their Tokugawa lords closely resembled taxation, they still meant ruinous poverty to the farming class. In brief summary, natural disasters (floods, famine, and disease), the system of feudalism, and changing economic conditions had reduced the mass of peasants to a condition of poverty.

The amazing thing was that under all this economic pressure the majority of the peasantry owned their own minute farms. It was inevitable that some became tenant farmers and farm laborers. Despite all their efforts to supplement meager incomes from their farms by fishing or off-season work in the towns, the peasant masses still were left out of any general economic progress which came to the nation. Under these conditions, many peasants lost title to their land through mortgages to a new landowner class composed of wealthy peasants and bourgeoisie. Without any understanding of its meaning, capitalism thus came to agrarian Japan during the closing years of the Tokugawa period.

The ceaseless fight to eke out a bare existence and retain ownership of his land made the Japanese farmer an industrious, well-disciplined person. He had no time to become interested in or obtain the training necessary to participate in national affairs and government. Accustomed to following orders, the peasant needed only to have his loyalty shifted from a feudal lord to the emperor as the head of the state to become a good citizen of the new Japan.

Growth of a Middle Class. Certain other economic facts must be considered in an evaluation of the last years of Tokugawa rule. If the farmers suffered economic hardship as a result of changing economic conditions, the merchant-financier group profited. There is ample evidence that Japan's economy during the isolation period was neither primitive nor stagnant. Both feudalism and the restrictive practices of the craft guilds forced the nation's economy toward a goal of self-sufficiency. Despite this pressure considerable internal trade developed, and with it a merchant and financial class. Towns and cities increased in size and importance. As the financial position of the daimyo and the samurai deteriorated, they came more and more under the influence and control of the merchants and rice brokers who extended credit to them. This alliance of the merchants and their guild organizations with the feudal barons was to blind the former to the opportunity presented to them by the reformers. With a few exceptions, such as the Mitsui family, the leaders of the middle class failed to ally themselves with those who, after 1853, were to be the leaders of modern Japan. The samurai of lesser rank, especially the followers of the *tozama daimyo,* thus were free to play the major role in establishing a new economic and political pattern for Japan.

Government Policy

At the time of Perry's arrival, the desperate economic and financial straits in which the Tokugawa found themselves were mirrored in their rapidly shifting policy. As recently as 1841, shogunal decrees had abolished the guild system in an attempt to stimulate production. The chaos resulting from the abrupt abolition of this tightly knit system of special privileges caused the shogun to rescind this action in 1851, but by that time the number of journeymen had increased so greatly that a return to the status quo of 1840 was impossible. The drastic effects of another major factor, the change from a barter to a money economy, are reflected by the estimate that by 1850 more than 90 per cent of all the property of the daimyo and samurai had been mortgaged to the merchant-financier class. Together with the misery of the peasants and the failure to tax proportionately the wealth of the townspeople, this meant that Tokugawa Japan was almost bankrupt. While the shogun's government still attempted to keep its rivals weak, the entire feudal system was collapsing. Until Perry forced open the doors of Japan, the Tokugawa rulers failed completely to comprehend the economic collapse which was occurring.

Fortunately for Japan, economic changes were taking place which made the break between old and new Japan much less abrupt. Furthermore, after an initial period of hesitation, the last Tokugawa shogun initiated a series of radical reforms which were carried on by the leaders of the Meiji restoration. Among these changes was the lifting of restrictions on the construction of shipping. Japanese also were urged to acquire Western scientific, industrial, and military knowledge. It was most fortunate that some preliminary steps had been taken, because the opening of the country to Western trade completed the disruption of the nation's economy. Many commodities were affected. There was an immediate rise in the price of such items as raw silk and tea, caused by foreign purchases. Similarly, the price of such consumer goods as cotton textiles, which could be produced cheaply by the machine industry of the West, fell sharply. As foreign capital became available to supplement native funds, the number of factories increased and the domestic system expanded rapidly, a result which further disturbed the Japanese economic system. Without the initial reforms of the Tokugawa and the increasingly harsh measures that were to follow under the new rulers of Japan, the nation's economy would have lapsed into complete chaos. Confronted with economic disaster, Japan needed all its devotion to the emperor, buttressed by feudal discipline and a capacity to organize effectively to meet the desperate problems of a new world.

Political Factors

In addition to the economic difficulties, sufficient in themselves to demand the full attention of its leaders, Japan faced serious political problems incident to the death of the dual system of government. The internal political and economic pressure which arose from unsolved questions already threatened the very life of the Tokugawa shogunate. The appearance of Perry on July 8, 1853 simply supplied the overt act needed to push the tottering rulers to their downfall. Previous attempts at intervention by foreigners had failed. Events elsewhere in the world, lack of sufficient Western interest, occasional determined resistance by Japanese, and, after 1815, Western concentration upon the opening of China had saved Japan until the middle of the nineteenth century. Now, in 1853, to an older American interest in the whaling trade was added a desire to expedite commerce with Canton by establishing ports in Japan at which fresh provisions and water might be obtained. The desirability of coaling stations in Japanese harbors only added to existing American needs and interests in having Japan opened to Western trade.

The Shogun's Dilemma

Although it was fortunate for the Japanese that the United States, which had no territorial ambitions in the Far East, took the lead in forcing Japan to open its doors, the political impact of the series of treaties started by Perry in 1854 was violent. Shogun Iesada's position became even more untenable. Neither he nor his advisers had the courage or imagination to develop and adopt a new policy, such as exclusion had been in 1641. Well aware of the tenuous hold he had on the country, the Tokugawa shogun, as its de facto ruler, had not indicated any such change in his real authority. He also had led the Western powers to believe that the emperor was only the nation's spiritual leader. Had Iesada followed a consistent course of action, and boldly thrown open Japan's doors, he might have carried the country with him. Since the Japanese never had been completely cut off from foreign ideas, there was a small faction of daimyo and samurai already convinced of the superior force of the West. Another group, which included the shogun, favored opening the door only as far as was necessary. A third large section of Japanese opinion, including the leaders at the imperial court, supported the continued exclusion of Westerners and their ways. By temporizing, the shogun lost his chance to lead and found himself caught between the emperor and the West.

Iesada's downfall started in 1853 when he sent to Kyoto a copy of the letter from the President of the United States requesting a treaty of commerce and friendship. At the same time that he was persuading Emperor Komei to approve the American treaty, he called a council of the great daimyo to consider its implications for the country. It is true that many of the *tozama daimyo* had urged the resumption of trade with the outside world. These same men also had waited for the time when Tokugawa control of the country would become so weak that the shogun could be overthrown. In securing the emperor's approval of the treaties of 1854-55, the shogun had provided his enemies with their opportunity. All they had to do was to persuade the emperor to change his mind. The very fact that the shogun had presented the question to the emperor also strengthened the contention that the latter, not the shogun, was the rightful ruler of Japan.

Opposition to the Treaties

For political reasons, then, the *tozama daimyo* assumed the leadership of those who opposed the opening of the country. With the assistance of the court nobles, they induced the emperor to change his mind. Emperor Komei forbade further concessions to the Western powers and ordered the shogun to impose such restrictions on the carrying out of the provisions of the treaties as to nullify them. With continued pressure for further concessions, from the foreign powers, the shogun in 1857-58 was forced to make a decision. By concluding new treaties with Townsend Harris, first American consul to Japan, and other foreign representatives, the shogun's government chose to follow a policy of closer relations with the West. An immediate reprimand from the emperor for concluding the Harris treaty marked the outbreak of a direct clash between the opposing political factions in Japan. A casualty of this political turmoil was Japanese foreign policy, which became a football in the game of domestic politics.

After 1859, when foreign legations were opened in Edo, opposition to the shogun's policy erupted in violent forms. In the next two years attacks on foreigners and on leaders favoring the shogun's policy were carried out by fanatical bands of samurai. At the same time, under the able leadership of Iemochi (who became the shogun in 1858), the Tokugawa suppressed all opposition within its own ranks. Unfortunately for the shogun, his opponents also resolved their differences and formed a solid antiforeign party. The increase of Western commerce—and with it the presence of more foreigners and the reappearance of Christianity—only added to the turmoil.

Events now moved rapidly. In May of 1862 the leaders of the Satsuma and Choshu clans, having reached an understanding, arrived in Kyoto and joined the court forces. A showdown between these powerful daimyo and the West followed shortly. The Richardson incident in September resulted in the death of this British subject and the wounding of two others. Under English pressure the shogun's government agreed to pay an indemnity, but showed its weakness by admitting its inability to punish the guilty Satsuma samurai. After futile negotiations a British squadron, in August, 1863, shelled and destroyed a large part of the Satsuma town of Kagoshima. Choshu, in carrying out a direct imperial order of 1863 to the daimyo to expel the foreigners by force, bombarded any and all foreign shipping in the Shimonoseki Strait. In retaliation an allied squadron systematically destroyed the Choshu shore batteries in September of 1864.

With the arrival of the Hizen and Tosa leaders in Kyoto in the fall of 1863, all the great clans of the Southwest were arraigned against the Tokugawa at Edo. The superior force shown by the West at Kagoshima and Shimonoseki convinced this group of the futility of open resistance to the West. They now sought to convince the representatives of the foreign powers that the Tokugawa regime did not represent the will of the Japanese people, who were reputed to be pro-Western and angry because the Tokugawa were not cooperating more completely with the West. This argument, so dangerous to the shogun's government, was made more plausible by his inability to secure the emperor's consent to the ratification of the treaties of 1858-59. Only after the foreign diplomats had assembled an international fleet off Hyogo near Osaka in November, 1865, and had threatened to negotiate separately with individual daimyo did the shogun promise and secure the emperor's approval for ratification. The inability of the shogun to control the daimyo and the emperor had shown the Western powers the weakness of his position. Without their continued and complete support, his cause was hopeless.

The Restoration

The death of Shogun Iemochi in September, 1866, followed by that of Emperor Komei in February of the following year provided the opportunity for radical change. In October of 1867 Yoshinobu (Keiki), the fifteenth and last Tokugawa shogun, received a memorial from the leader of the Tosa clan. In this petition Keiki was urged to resign his shogunal commission as a means of ending the disastrous division of political authority within the country. With his authority completely undermined Keiki, on November 3, 1867, sent his resignation to the emperor whose new authority was reflected by the curt note of acceptance sent to the shogun. Thus after more than two hundred and fifty years, the Tokugawa rule ended. All that remained was more than a year, 1868-69, of sporadic fighting between imperial and clan forces brought on by the order of the new emperor, Mutsuhito, which stripped Keiki of his vast landholdings. With the disintegration of Tokugawa power, the western clans led by a Satsuma-Choshu combination were in complete control of the court of Kyoto.[5]

In the political conflict prior to and after the fall of the Tokugawa, new and younger forces led by the samurai of lesser rank and certain court nobles were gathering reins of authority in their hands. This did not mean, however, that this revolution was a people's movement. Here was no complete break with the past. A bureaucracy as an instrument of state direction was taken over intact. The spirit of Tokugawa government, careful and minute control of all phases of the nation's life and human activity, remained as a basis for united activity. It was natural for the new Japan to emphasize from the beginning governmental participation in many fields of activity. Japan as a nation had the advantage of excellent organization and a unified front in its new competitive race with the West. In this manner was the Meiji Restoration launched in Japan.

SUGGESTED READINGS

Among the most useful general works are: K. S. Latourette, *The History of Japan* (New York, 1947); E. O. Reischauer, *Japan, Past and Present* (New York, 1947); R. K. Reischauer, *Japan, Government-Politics* (New York, 1939); G. B. Sansom, *Japan, A Short Cultural History* (New York, 1943) and *The Western World and Japan* (New York, 1950); G. Nye Steiger, *A History of the Far East* (New York, 1944); Chitoshi Yanaga, *Japan Since Perry* (New York, 1949).

[5] These clans never intended to transfer real power from the Tokugawa shogun to the emperor.

For additional general works and for studies of special phases of the period 1853-94 in Japanese history, see: T. Baba, *The Political Condition of Japan* (Philadelphia, 1888); F. Brinkley and D. Kikuchi, *A History of the Japanese People* (New York, 1915); E. W. Clement, *Constitutional Imperialism in Japan* (New York, 1916); M. E. Cosenza (ed.), *The Complete Journal of Townsend Harris* (New York, 1930); J. H. Gubbins, *The Progress of Japan, 1853-1871* (Oxford, 1911); K. Hamada, *Prince Ito* (Tokyo, 1936); H. Ito, *Commentaries on the Constitution of the Empire of Japan* (Tokyo, 1889); U. Iwasaki, *The Working Forces in Japanese Politics, 1867-1920* (New York, 1921); T. Iyenaga, *The Constitutional Development of Japan, 1853-1881* (New York, 1921); D. Kikuchi, *Japanese Education* (London, 1909); W. W. McLaren, *A Political History of Japan During the Meiji Era, 1867-1912* (New York, 1916); W. W. McLaren, "Japanese Government Documents," *Transactions of the Asiatic Society of Japan*, Vol. XLIII (Tokyo, 1914); J. A. Murdoch, *A History of Japan* (3 vols., New York, 1926); E. H. Norman, *Japan's Emergence as a Modern State* (New York, 1940); and H. S. Quigley, *Japanese Government and Politics* (New York, 1932).

15

JAPAN: REFORM BY THE FEW, 1867-1894

Among the more apparent problems confronting the new Japan and its leaders as the Tokugawa era ended, were the danger of increased foreign intervention, the rivalry among feudal leaders for control of the government, inflation, and near economic chaos. Each of the four southern clans, Satsuma, Choshu, Hizen, and Tosa, had hoped to replace the Tokugawa as the chief adviser to the emperor. Since not one of the four proved to be powerful enough to dominate as had the Tokugawa, one of the major elements of Japanese politics in the next three decades was the struggle to retain control of the new government by this Sat-cho-hi-to combination or parts of it.

Support for the New Regime

The reader should note that a relatively small group of men was responsible for the reforms of this time. Kido and Ito of Choshu, Saigo and Okubo of Satsuma, Itagaki of Tosa, Okuma of Hizen, and Iwakura and Sanjo of the court nobility (*kuge*) were the most influential leaders. They knew that any reorganization of Japan's government and society must contain new Western ideas, yet they based many acts on the institutions and practices of the past. Quite deliberately they sought popular support for the new governmental system they were building by centering attention and respect on the emperor. Shintoism was revived and modified somewhat to become the vehicle for this system of emperor-worship. In 1869 Buddhism was still further discouraged by having its rival, Shintoism, designated as the official cult of the nation. By placing emphasis on the achievements of the imperial ancestors, Shinto identified itself closely with patriotism and thus established itself as a fundamental part of the new state structure being created. Japan's new leaders supported a revival of Shinto and thus deliberately sought strength for their plans by fostering worship of the emperor.

Pressure From Foreign Powers

In addition to their desire to get and retain power, these southern clan leaders had to contend constantly with the Western powers. Pressure and friction with the West worked constantly to force change in Japan. No Japanese politician could accept the humiliation caused by foreigners' enjoyment of extraterritorial rights and privileges in his country. A further indignity, and a crippling factor economically, was Japan's inability to control its own tariff. The desire and demand for judicial and financial independence from the West were used by the government to justify and support both the speed and the radical nature of new legislation. In fact, only through sweeping internal reforms would it be possible to obtain treaty revision from the Powers.

In 1871, for example, Prince Iwakura headed a mission to the West to attempt treaty revision. Even then he could point to the progress being made on new civil and criminal codes. These codes and an entirely revamped judicial system patterned in general after that of France and Prussia were to be ready by 1890. Similarly, part of the motive for establishing parliamentary government and a constitution arose from the well-founded Japanese belief that such political change would bring more quickly and more completely Japan's acceptance as an equal by the West. With foreign pressure a constant consideration, Japan's leaders knew that the government must be quickly centralized; that progressive social and economic programs must be developed. Without quick action the fruits of their victory over the Tokugawa might be taken away from the new leaders. Whatever the motivation behind the changes, the reader should notice the systematic and careful planning involved. Another feature common to the entire Meiji reform program was the lead taken by the government, another indication that Japan's needs as a nation were to be dominant over those of individuals or groups.

Feudalism Formally Ends

Pacification of the country hardly had been accomplished before the leaders of the southern clans and of the court nobility began those changes in government necessary to retain and strengthen their position. Of particular importance is the fact that the real leaders of the clans were the lesser samurai rather than the daimyo. The first step taken was the appointment of an imperial official for and in each fief. The following year, 1869, the younger leaders persuaded the Sat-cho-hi-to daimyo to restore to the emperor the registers of their lands and peoples (official records of the feudal manors). Many of the remaining feudal chieftains voluntarily relinquished their registers; an imperial order forced others to do so. Since no clan or combination of clans could hope to defeat the southern coalition, resistance would have been futile. In 1871, by imperial decree, feudalism was abolished. It was to prove, however, more difficult to change feudal habits of thought and action.

The Daimyo and Samurai Divided. The end of feudalism was an absolute necessity for the plans of the reform group to be successful, but why did the daimyo and other feudal leaders acquiesce in their own demise? Initially, the transformation was made easier and more attractive by permission granted to the feudal lords to retain their former domains. All that was different was the new title, "Governor," and the quite evident addition to the authority of the central government. Shortly after feudalism ended, the blow was further softened by putting into effect a plausible system of pensions for the daimyo and the samurai. The daimyo were guaranteed one tenth of their nominal incomes which always had been higher than the real incomes of the feudal nobility and the pensions therefore were quite generous. They benefited also from the fact that their income no longer was tied to rice production. The last financial argument needed to gain the support of this group was the shifting of the costs of local or provincial governments from them to the national government. If a daimyo were not completely won over by self-interest, he could be appealed to for cooperation in advancing the welfare of the state.

Both self-interest and patriotism help to explain the cooperation of the clan chieftains and their retainers, the samurai. The latter's support in this rapid destruction of the feudal system often was grudgingly given; certainly the implications for the samurai were not clear. Although many professed little concern about financial problems, most of the samurai already were living on restricted budgets; many were almost hopelessly in debt. For this class, with an insufficient income except under the best of conditions, with much less difference between nominal and real income than was true for the daimyo, the government's guarantee of one half their nominal income represented ruin in many cases. It is true that the government also relieved them of some of their special privileges and responsibilities. First, the samurai were told they would not be required to wear two swords; by 1877 they were forbidden to do so. If some samurai welcomed the increasing opportunities to enter business or the new governmental service, others were extremely bitter as they witnessed the gradual dissolution of feudal Japan's elite warrior class. Loyalty and the easy acceptance by the public of the reform legislation confused the issue for many samurai. Lack of effective leadership among those who

JAPAN: REFORM BY THE FEW, 1867-1894

opposed reform during the critical years (1868-73) prevented successful opposition. Even then, the overwhelming military power of the four southern clans was necessary to prevent sharp opposition to the establishment of a national conscript army, the formerly exclusive reservation of the samurai. Later, when dissident elements led by Saigo did rebel in 1877, this new army's power was demonstrated conclusively. Whether intentional or not, the division of daimyo and samurai, which the reformers accomplished by 1871, deprived the latter of their principal source of leadership. After that year the daimyo were not responsible for the samurai and other feudal retainers. (The reader should recall the gradual loss of power by the daimyo as they relinquished administrative positions to the samurai.) As the old personal ties which had bound the two groups together had been weakened previously, their failure to unite in a common defense of a privileged position is more easily understood.

The Government Commutes the Pension Plan. Both the daimyo and the samurai seemed to accept without question the ability of the state to assume such a heavy financial burden as their pension plan represented. With the government's general expenses increasing, the cost of paying the daimyo and samurai would have been difficult under ideal conditions, but conditions were far from ideal. Tariff revenues were fixed by treaties that Japan had made with Western powers, and they were not interested in raising tariff rates to help Japan meet a financial crisis. Increases in direct taxes, the only other way to add to the government's income, met popular resistance, both because of lack of understanding and the inability to pay. By 1873 Count Okuma, then Finance Minister, was faced with a financial crisis. He offered the daimyo and samurai a chance to commute their pensions, one half in cash and one half in government bonds bearing 8 per cent interest, which for lesser daimyo and samurai meant a reduction of income by 50 per cent. This was so satisfactory from the government's point of view that the plan was made compulsory in 1876. It may have been a financially necessary expedient for the state, but it amounted to a partial repudiation of the original obligation. Once more, with little knowledge of financial matters, many daimyo and samurai accepted the new settlement and spent the cash quickly. Others used the money to enter or enlarge business ventures; thus the rise of a capitalist class was expedited, with many former samurai as charter members. As some samurai and daimyo were confronted with hard economic facts, they joined those who were opposed to parts of or all the new government's policies and plans.

Middle Class and Peasant Reaction. The support of the new bourgeois class and at least passive acceptance by the peasants were necessary in this critical period in Japanese history when the formerly dominant feudal leaders, the daimyo and the samurai, were divided in their attitude toward the new regime. The new middle class was won over by permitting them to enter any business or profession, or the field of politics. Furthermore, when feudalism was abolished, with it went the regulation which prevented a peasant from alienating his land. Japan's new leaders thus honored mortgages which under feudalism had been illegal. In this way many small businessmen could and did become absentee landlords, for them an important gain both economically and socially.

One might ask then why the peasants supported a reform group which allowed them to lose control of their land. As will be shown, the new leaders, while permitting changes in land titles, helped in many ways to make possible the existence of a large class of small landowners. Of more importance to the peasant, he now was free to go anywhere and to leave his farm and become a cityworker. Finally, under the reorganized military system the Japanese peasant became the heart of the conscript, national army. The reader should remember that ever since 1600, when the peasants had been disarmed, armed rebellion on their part had been a capital offense. The recognition of equality and freedom which service in the armed forces carried with it, however, was offset by bitter opposition to conscription. It was none the less an army of peasants which was to crush the remnants of Japanese feudalism in 1877. Mass acceptance, if not mass support, thus was gained by this small group for their reforms.

War or Internal Reorganization

From the beginning of the Meiji era, many Japanese wished to embark on a policy of expansionism. Extreme nationalists among the Meiji Restoration leaders who favored this course were so powerful that the government was faced with a crisis as early as 1873. Two years earlier the controversy over the killing by Formosans of Liu Ch'iu (Ryuku) Islanders had exposed this division within the ranks of those who had supported the restoration of the Emperor Meiji. Those who opposed sending an ultimatum to China, which was Formosa's protector, were not opponents of an aggressive foreign policy. They believed that the issue resolved itself into a question of timing alone. War, it was feared, might interfere with their reorganization plans. The fact that Japan through diplomacy was winning its struggle for control over the Liu Ch'iu Islands from China failed to satisfy the exponents of expansionism; neither did the dispatch of a small but completely successful punitive expedition to Formosa in 1874 convince them that Japan's honor had been satisfactorily upheld.

Korea and Domestic Reform. It was unfortunate for Iwakura, Ito, Okubo, and the other reform leaders that the Liu Ch'iu Island controversy could not have been concluded before relations with Korea reached a critical point. In some ways the Korean question was the most important domestic issue of the first decade of the Meiji era. As early as 1857 proposals for the extension of Japanese rule over Korea, Manchuria, and eastern Siberia had been made. Now, after Korea's haughty and poorly conceived refusal on three occasions to negotiate with Japanese envoys, this diplomatic problem was seized upon by the extreme nationalists in 1873 as offering the occasion for a show of force. So heated became the debate that only the return of Iwakura and his mission from abroad prevented the sending of Saigo to Korea to demand satisfaction. Only after a Japanese warship had been fired on by the Koreans in 1875 and actual hostilities threatened, did Korea sign a treaty. By the terms of this agreement, obtained in 1876 in a manner reminiscent of Perry's negotiations with Japan, it recognized the "Hermit Kingdom" as a completely independent state. Japan did, however, insist upon the inclusion of articles granting its subjects the same extraterritorial rights and privileges which Japan was seeking to obliterate from its treaties with Western states. Although the treaty of 1876 represented complete victory, the extremists [1] were incensed at the seemingly pusillanimous approach of the government. Consequently in 1873 Saigo and Kido left the government.

The Satsuma Rebellion. Saigo retired to his Satsuma fief and watched with interest the increasing evidence of discontent with central government policies. Four rather small armed rebellions occurred in 1874 and 1876. After commutation of their pensions became compulsory in 1876, more disgruntled samurai flocked to the southwest to join the ranks of those opposed to the Tokyo government. Saigo [2] in 1877 assumed the leadership of some 150,000 rebels, possibly 40,000 of whom were actual fighting men, who represented the elite of Japan's old feudal forces. Against them the government sent a force much larger than probably would have been necessary, yet the rebellion lasted eight months. Superior leadership, better discipline, and more modern equipment led to the complete overwhelming of the most serious rebellion in modern Japanese history. Saigo was critically wounded in the final stand at Kagoshima and was killed by a faithful servant. Other leaders either were killed or committed suicide rather than surrender. Thus it was demonstrated

---

[1] Extreme nationalists, or extremists, were reactionary in their belief that Japan's expansion should take precedence over internal reforms which should be delayed or occur more slowly.

[2] Authorities still disagree on the reasons for this move by Saigo.

beyond doubt that sons of peasants and merchants could and would fight well.

Saigo and his followers were honest in their assertion that they were not opposed to the restoration of powers to the emperor; they merely wanted to become his advisers. The rebels also were correct in their contention that the emperor never had assumed personal power. What they finally fought against, the retention of control by the southern clan leaders and their friends, indicated very clearly that not even all the aristocracy, let alone all the people, were to share political power. Thus the rebellion of 1877 removed one of the most prominent of the early leaders of the restoration movement. It also solidified the hold that a small group had on the government and its policy. In addition it should be noted that the ultimate goal of all Japanese leaders—expansion—was begun through the addition, between 1876 and 1878, of the Ryukyu (Liu Ch'iu), Kurile, and Bonin islands.

Early Japanese Political Parties

Itagaki's Patriotic Public Party. At the time (1873) when Saigo and Kido left the government in disgust over what they termed a cautious policy toward Korea, Itagaki, another of the original reformers, also was considering withdrawal. In his case the reason was essentially the same, a desire for greater influence in the government. The fact that several reform policies, and acts implementing them, were rather arbitrary in nature gave Itagaki his reason for withdrawing from the government in 1874. For some time he attempted to dissuade Saigo from resorting to force and instead to depend upon political agitation. Failing in this, Itagaki convinced his followers of the wisdom of an appeal to public opinion. The Patriotic Public Party, a national organization, was created for that purpose. Increasing government action to liquidate all political opposition, undoubtedly spurred on by an attack on Iwakura by some of Itagaki's hotheaded partisans, caused the latter to disband the party in 1874.

Itagaki then retired to Tosa which rapidly became the center of Japanese liberalism. An interesting question is suggested by the use of the word "liberalism." In what sense were Itagaki and his cohorts liberals? Their political bible might be said to have been Rousseau's *Social Contract*. They professed belief in the political ideology of the French Revolution, and they certainly espoused the cause of constitutional government. On the other hand, these men almost completely lacked the cultural and political background which is essential to understand and interpret the teachings of Locke, Rousseau, and other Western political philosophers.

This expressed belief in liberalism was mixed with a strong desire for prestige in the political field. Itagaki disliked his exclusion from power and sought to recoup his political fortunes by leading a vocal opposition to the government's policy. There were many examples of similar political leadership in Western states for him to observe; the blindness with which men followed Itagaki also had its parallel elsewhere. The sense of loyalty to a leader, so natural in Japan which had just formally abolished feudalism, is another factor to be considered.

Whatever the motives may have been, the publication of the imperial rescript of October 12, 1881, which promised the establishment of a Diet, made increasingly evident the necessity for political parties. Itagaki's original party had served as a vehicle to compel the government to establish a popular assembly. Now three parties were quickly born with the avowed purpose of educating the people to their new responsibilities under a constitutional government. Specifically, the leaders of two of these parties hoped to use them to carry out their own policies, as opposed to those of the government. On the surface, at least, they professed varying degrees of interest in popular rights and liberties.

The *Jiyuto*, the *Kaishinto*, and the *Teiseito*. Before the end of October Itagaki and his followers had founded the *Jiyuto* or Liberal Party, the forerunner of the *Seiyukai* Party. Okuma, who had been forced to resign from the government in 1881, established the *Kaishinto* or Liberal Conservative Party,[3] the forerunner of the *Minseito* Party, in March, 1882. By this time the government had become convinced by the popular reception accorded the two opposition parties that the only way to fight fire was with fire. As a result the government sponsored a party of its own, the *Teiseito* or Constitutional Imperialist Party.[4] This in itself was a concession to the growing strength of the factions led by Itagaki and Okuma.

Fundamentally there was little difference in the party platforms of the *Jiyuto* and the *Kaishinto*. Both advocated the establishment of constitutional government and the gradual extension of popular rights as cardinal objectives. They subscribed to a limitation of the powers of the national government and an expansion of authority on the local government level. (Both the Liberal and Liberal Conservative parties believed firmly that internal reorganization must precede imperialism.) The membership of Itagaki's party was drawn more from the nonpropertied and small landowner group. The Liberal Conservatives included more wealthy businessmen and members of the professions. On a political pendulum the *Jiyuto*

---

[3] Sometimes known as the Reform Party.
[4] Sometimes known as the Imperial Party.

would have been on the left, the *Kaishinto* more toward the center, and the *Teiseito* on the right. Actually the principal differences between the first two were to be found in the organization and methods and ideas which were used to achieve their goals. Emphasizing once more the importance of personalities in Japanese politics was the hard fact that temperamentally Itagaki and Okuma were poles apart. Not only was the hope for a merger, held by many of their followers, doomed to disappointment, but the gap separating the two parties was to widen.

If the constant support of the government is forgotten, the *Teiseito* might be underestimated. With the other parties it favored a constitution, but one which reserved all powers to the emperor. This meant, among other things, an absolute imperial veto. Its program generally included those policies which the government had decided to adopt. Its relatively small but influential membership was drawn largely from the bureaucracy on all levels of government, as well as from Shinto and Buddhist priests and from businessmen who had been awarded government contracts or hoped to get them. In its attempt to counteract the propaganda of the *Jiyuto* and *Kaishinto* parties, it used newspapers such as the Tokyo *Nichi Nichi* to defend its policies and smear those of the opposition.

The *Teiseito* argued that sovereignty resided exclusively with the emperor; the *Jiyuto* held that sovereignty belonged to the people, and the *Kaishinto* maintained that sovereignty was divided between the two. At least some of the ideas and terminology pertinent to democracy had been adopted by Japan's leaders in the 1880's. Whether political parties would serve to further liberalism in Japan as they had in Western states remained to be seen. Could they destroy the cliquishness of the bureaucracy and liberalize it? Could they win a struggle to make the ministers of the state responsible to a popularly elected assembly?

A Japanese Constitution: First Steps

The Charter Oath. In the first rush of reforms after the restoration of 1868 the most significant event was the taking of the Charter Oath by the Emperor Meiji before the court nobility, the daimyo, and the samurai. Three parts of this oath constitute imperial approval for the study of political and social problems by all citizens. Japanese were urged to "seek wisdom abroad," an attitude at sharp variance with Chinese governmental policy throughout most of the last half of the nineteenth century. Another section of the oath seemed to sanction the calling of a deliberative assembly. Certainly sanction was given to discussion, or argument and debate, on questions of national importance. Were decisions to be reached by this method? Those who advocated popular government interpreted this part of the Charter Oath somewhat as follows: "An Assembly widely convoked shall be established, and thus great stress shall be laid upon public opinion." [5] Undoubtedly this is an extreme view, but it does indicate the general terms used which could mean various things to different Japanese leaders and groups. It is very difficult to find in this document a promise for the establishment of a parliamentary type of government. Whether any Western political institution was intended is, indeed, questionable. Certainly the assembly of daimyo and samurai called in 1869 was not revolutionary.

Initial Governmental Reforms. Of this original effort at the establishment of a national legislature, nothing remained after 1873. Its conservative, nonrepresentative nature, and the limitation of its power to consultation, had shown it to be an empty and futile body. During these same years, an official mission headed by Iwakura was abroad studying foreign institutions. At home, as previously noted, the reformers moved ahead in such an arbitrary fashion as to drive Itagaki from the government. Popular agitation in 1874-75 led by Itagaki did force the next steps toward a constitution. In 1874 a Senate was established as a distinct legislative chamber. Membership in this body was by appointment and was restricted to the noble and official classes in a rather obvious effort to solidify their support behind the government. Even with these precautions, the Senate was granted only deliberative powers. An assembly of prefectural governors also was authorized. Obviously intended as another step on the long road of political education, its close association with the central government and its lack of authority caused it to be of little value. Far more important to the agitators was the imperial rescript of 1875 which promised the establishment of constitutional government by gradual stages. In government administration those who desired the reform of the Japanese government to follow the examples set by the Western democracies were encouraged by a reorganization of departments which took place at this time. In this process, a high court of justice was created which might presage the separation of the judicial from the executive and legislative branches of the government.

Agitation for the speedy implementation of the emperor's promise of constitutional government in 1878 culminated in the assassination of Okubo, Minister of Home Affairs. Although the government did increase repressive measures against its opponents, it also ordered the immediate organization of local assemblies. One of these "legislative" bodies, which could only advise the governor, was established in each prefecture; their

---

[5] McLaren, "Japanese Government Documents," *Transactions of the Asiatic Society of Japan*, Vol. XLIII, Pt. 1 (Tokyo, May, 1914), p. 8.

members were to be elected by a strictly limited electorate. Furthermore, they were to meet for one month each year to discuss primarily taxation and the supervision of the prefectural accounts. Establishment of these assemblies provided a genuine opportunity to learn about government on the local level and might have led to control of the purse strings. As similar assemblies were set up in villages, towns, and cities, a vast governmental training school came into existence.

The Imperial Rescript. One of the goals of Itagaki and his followers was achieved with the promulgation of the imperial rescript of 1881 promising the convocation of a national assembly in 1890 and the granting of a constitution. They now knew the "when" and could turn their attention to the all-important question of the content of the document. The government also devoted its entire attention to the creation of a constitution which would mirror its ideas. In this struggle Itagaki and Okuma first used their political parties as media through which public attention could be focused on various issues. Okuma's *Kaishinto* died naturally in 1883 through its failure to successfully establish local branches. The government order of 1884 abolishing political groups opposed to its policies brought about the demise of Itagaki's *Jiyuto*. Thereafter these two leaders, through pamphleteering, public meetings, and similar activities, did their best to arouse the public to support their concept of a constitution.

A Japanese Constitution: Last Steps

Repression of the Opposition. The weapons which Iwakura, Ito, and other government leaders possessed in this struggle were formidable. The development of journalism, which owed little to the government and consequently could be and often was hostile to it, early attracted the attention of those in power. A Newspaper Press Ordinance of 1876 provided for jail sentences and fines for all critics of the government. With this edict the press was muzzled. Fines and jail sentences became so common that many papers paid employees whose primary duty was to serve time in jail for infractions of the press law. In 1881 Iwakura purged the government of all liberally inclined bureaucrats. Okuma was dropped from the Council of State, the executive branch, for challenging certain government policies, particularly the cheap sale of government holdings on the island of Hokkaido. As a last resort, Japan's powerful ruling clique secured the issuance of a Peace Preservation Ordinance. In 1887, as an aftermath of the suppression of political parties, secret societies and public assemblies were banned. Prison sentences were given disturbers of the peace; and troublemakers, as defined by the courts, were forced to move at least seven and a half miles from the Imperial Palace. This was tantamount to forcing antiadministration leaders out of the capital.

Constitutional Development Controlled. After 1881 the most powerful weapon in the hands of the government was its complete control of the immediate steps which had to be taken prior to the promulgation of the constitution and the convening of the first national assembly. Iwakura's purge had assured the country that the architects of the new order would be conservative and nationalistic. The significance of this power became apparent in 1882 when Ito was sent abroad to study constitutions. It is evident now that he was looking for certain characteristics in a government administration and constitution; these must be the gift of the sovereign to the people and must protect the emperor's position. They should also, to the greatest degree possible, guarantee the continuance in power of those then in control of the government. In view of the agitation at home and the trends in government abroad, there must be provision for a representative assembly. The constitutions of some of the German states and the government which Bismarck had established for a united Germany fitted this description far better than their more liberal French counterparts. Ito was visibly influenced by the great Prussian leader to the point of mimicking his personal habits, such as the Bismarckian manner of smoking a cigar. Between 1883 and 1888 Ito laid down the broad principles which were to be used as a guide by a constitutional bureau headed by Inoue Ki, a brilliant bureaucrat, in drafting a suitable document. It is interesting to notice that this group worked in secret. The public and press were permitted no part in their deliberations.

Creation of Supplementary Governmental Machinery. While this work was progressing, Ito made sure that the machinery necessary to launch the new constitution was available. In 1884 the aristocracy was reconstructed along Prussian lines. About five hundred of Japan's leaders were incorporated within its ranks (prince, marquis, count, viscount, and baron). Members of the old court nobility and former daimyo, and the samurai who had served the government were well rewarded. For obvious reasons the Sat-cho group was dominant; Itagaki and Okuma of the Tosa and Hizen clans were not included. The following year a cabinet replaced the Council of State. Its first members were young (Ito was forty-five) and failed to include a single one of the old court nobility. This was a blow to the old clan-dominated oligarchy, and made possible a new bureaucracy thoroughly loyal to the government. Ito built up a loyal, personal following by giving preference in appointments to graduates of Tokyo Imperial University, on the staff of which were several professors of his own selection. Unfortunately for the university, it almost became a training school for bureaucrats. The results for Japan were more fortunate because the new bureaucracy was more efficient than its predecessor.

No Popular Voice in the Constitution. To increase further the effectiveness of the governmental machinery, Ito in 1887-88 revamped the system of local government. In the process the mayors were to be chosen by the emperor from the three men who received the most votes in local elections. Here was a compromise with democracy, yet one which permitted control of local affairs by the central authorities. As the time approached for the promulgation of the constitution, the Privy Council, composed of members of the nobility and distinguished statesmen, was created for the explicit purpose of deliberating on the final draft of the constitution and such other pertinent documents as the Imperial Household Ordinance and the Law of Elections. There was to be no constitutional convention, no consultation with party leaders or the people. Preparations for the imperial announcement were made in the same spirit; for instance, all radical papers were suppressed, and all others were ordered to print no unfavorable criticism.

The Constitution: The Emperor

One of the most outstanding characteristics of the new constitution was that it was granted by the emperor, not won by the people. Even among opposition groups, no one ever had advocated the abolition of the monarchy. It is very important to realize that sovereignty resided in the emperor who remained the source of all power and favors. Of almost equal significance is the fact that there was no distinct break with Japan's feudal past; other agencies, the Council of Ministers (cabinet), Privy Council, and a group of elder statesmen later known as the Genro were to exercise these powers for the emperor. Even laws were made by him "with the consent of the Imperial Diet" (through legislation), and automatic imperial approval was not assured. Furthermore, wide ordinance powers were reserved to the emperor during the time when the Diet was not in session.

Ito followed the German example closely in making the cabinet responsible solely to the emperor. Its members were appointed and dismissed by him. The Privy Council, also, was given real authority through its power to draft constitutional amendments and its right of direct access to the emperor. Finally, a distinctly Japanese feature, the Genro, with no authority from the constitution, exercised unusual power after 1900. Based squarely on feudal Japan, as were many other features of the government, the Genro came to include the restoration leaders of 1868 who remained in favor. Few important decisions were made without their advice and approval.

The Diet

The representative assembly or Diet, the principal Western contribution to Japan's constitution and government, was bicameral. The upper chamber, the House of Peers, was from the beginning one of the most powerful legislative bodies of its kind in the world. It included members of the royal family and the nobility, and in addition permitted the fifteen largest taxpayers in each prefecture and in the three most populous cities to elect one additional member. It was conservative and was intended to act as a brake on any radical moves made by the lower chamber, the House of Representatives. The latter was to be a body of three hundred members elected for a four-year term by all adult males in the empire who paid fifteen yen yearly in taxes. This meant that in the elections of 1890 only 460,000 could vote in a population of about 40,000,000. House members were to have freedom of debate and were not subject to arrest for remarks made on the floor of the houses. The Diet did have the right of interpellation, questioning members of the Ministry in the House. Some of the machinery which had proved useful to Western legislatures in their struggle with powerful executives was present.

Powers Withheld from the Diet. A description of the restrictions placed on the Diet and the powers withheld from its members will complete the picture. Although the legislature must meet yearly for a period of three months, the emperor retained control through his power of summoning, proroguing, and dissolving the House of Representatives. In 1890 the main function of the Diet was to give or refuse its approval on matters submitted to it. Legislation could originate in either house, but the majority of the bills would be sponsored by the Cabinet. Of utmost importance, the control of the purse was not vested distinctly in the lower house. Under Article 57 of the constitution, certain expenditures based on imperial powers or legal obligations of the government could not be reduced or rejected. If the lower house refused to pass the new budget, the budget from the preceding year remained in effect. Here was the one loophole; the House of Representatives could prevent increases in expenditure. As will be seen, the leaders of the opposition were to capitalize on this weakness of the government in the first legislature; their demand for complete legislative control of the budget was to remain constant through the years. To gain their objectives they were supported by public opinion which was to be the principal strength of the lower house.

A Bill of Rights

Almost as an addendum, the new constitution did contain a satisfactory bill of rights and duties of the people. Democracies in the West were prone to take this at face value without paying too much attention to the restrictive clause that such rights "always were subject to law." It seemed to the Japanese that all good constitutions had bills of rights, so they too included one.

A Strong Central Government

In summary it was the intent of the framers that the constitution should aid in the establishment of a strong centralized government, in which the executive branch of the government naturally should be more powerful than the legislative. If this were true, the Japanese saw no reason to weaken the structure by providing for judicial review, a function which was to be performed by the Privy Council rather than by a supreme court. It is true that the Japanese were influenced in their desire and planning for a constitution by a belief that treaty revision would be hastened. The new constitution, government, and codes of law, together with the successful war with China in 1894, were to achieve that desired result.[6]

Possible Future Progress

Constructively, it should be noticed that the very acquisition of a constitution, even a conservative one, by an Oriental state was a tremendous step forward. The document was elastic enough for changes to be made as time made them necessary. It did provide a way for the liberal, democratic ideas of the West to penetrate a Far East which had an autocratic tradition. As has been true with all constitutions, its success in achieving these ends would depend entirely on those into whose hands its implementation was entrusted.

How the Constitution Worked

Political Parties Reappear. Both Itagaki's *Jiyuto* (Liberal) Party and Okuma's *Kaishinto* (Liberal Conservative) Party reappeared as active groups seeking to gain control of the lower house in the 1890 elections for the first Diet. The Japanese electorate evinced general interest in the campaign, which had few incidents. Although Ito's plans resulted in the return of a conservative upper house, much to his annoyance the opposition

---

[6] Great Britain had revised its treaties with Japan before the Sino-Japanese War.

parties won a large majority in the House of Representatives. As soon as it became apparent that an immediate result of the new constitution would be the retention of control of the government by Ito and his associates, Itagaki and Okuma resolved to do all in their power to prevent the smooth functioning of the new governmental machinery. They wanted control of the Cabinet, and they demanded that it be made responsible to the lower house.

Party Opposition to Government Policy. Just as soon as the Diet met, a pattern of attack developed which was to be typical of procedure in the three Diets elected during this period. Itagaki and Okuma saw in the partial control of the purse vested in the lower house the only weapon that might be used to embarrass the Ministry. In both the first and second Diets, concessions were won from the government by the opposition parties, but on the main point of argument, a ministry responsible to the lower house of the Diet, the government remained unyielding. Continued disagreement over this issue caused the dissolution of the first Diet. With the need for control of the House of Representatives thus made clear, the government by threats, bribery, and active campaigning tried to win enough seats to control the lower house. Once again the *Jiyuto* and *Kaishinto* won a clear-cut victory; their prestige was further enhanced by the "face" lost by the government's supporters through their election methods.

Ito Assumes the Premiership. The struggle between the executive and legislative branches of the government became so intense this time that Ito attempted to halt it by assuming the premiership. In effect this was a concession to the parties which could take credit for forcing out the incumbent Ministry. Actually, Itagaki and Okuma continued the fight because they had not been consulted prior to Ito's selection and had not agreed to it. In despair, the latter introduced a new weapon in his fight with the lower house. On his request, the emperor sent a message in which he announced a contribution to the defense budget from the imperial household funds. He asked that all officials make similar sacrifices and specifically requested that the Diet show some cooperation with the government. To a Western student, the interesting item here is that immediately, out of deference to the expressed wish of the sovereign, the parties dropped their attack on the budget. Their opposition to other government policies, however, was so sustained that once again the Diet was dissolved. It should also be noted that Ito carried through a well-planned curtailment in general government spending. Ito then tried to divide the opposition by making arrangements for the support of the *Jiyuto* in the lower house.

These conciliatory moves failed to give the government control of the House of Representatives in the third election in 1894. Ito's concessions to Itagaki's party cost him the support only of his former followers. The almost constant bickering, culminating in a bitter attack on the foreign policy of the government, led to the dissolution of the Diet for the third time. The Sino-Japanese War of 1894 broke out before new elections could be held. As in Occidental countries, the parties then vied with one another in demonstrations of loyalty. By this means, war, the government finally obtained the solid support it had failed to gain by any other method. Japan's first phase of party struggle under the new constitution thus ended inconclusively.

There were, however, certain portents for the future. It was quite clear that a sharp conflict existed between the legislature and the executive. In this fight the upper chamber consistently supported the Ministry. This was not unusual in view of clan domination of the Cabinet and the heavy representation of property, wealth, and rank in the House of Peers. In this struggle it was apparent that too little legislative power had been vested in the House of Representatives. Without ministerial responsibility to that body, a sense of political responsibility among party leaders would develop slowly. Itagaki and Okuma, always leaders of the opposition with too little chance of becoming the leaders of the government, were more likely to obstruct the plans of the ruling oligarchy than to offer constructive criticism. The fundamental problem throughout this period, differences between the Cabinet and the House of Representatives, remained unsolved. The weapons each side was to use in the coming struggle for power already had been indicated and simply required further development. Whether this prelude constituted a sound foundation on which liberal, democratic government could be built in Japan was a moot question.

SUGGESTED READINGS

See bibliography at end of Chapter 14.

16

JAPAN'S EMERGENCE AS A MODERN STATE

Unpopularity of the Unequal Treaties

With the resignation of the shogun in November, 1867, Japan entered a new period in its history, the Era of Meiji, under which the emperor became the nominal head of the government rather than the shogun. Almost immediately Japan exhibited a foreign policy which was based upon the twin forces of imperialism and the desire for equality with the West. Imperialists insisted that Japanese sovereignty be established over such places as Hokkaido, the Liu Ch'ius, the Bonins, the Kuriles, and Sakhalin. Some also felt that Korea, which had ceased paying tribute to Japan, should be required to resume its former status.

Hokkaido, northernmost island of the Japanese archipelago, was so clearly within Japanese jurisdiction that no difficulties were encountered from any quarter when the government proceeded to colonize and develop the island. Nor was there any trouble over the dreary Bonin Islands, which were occupied in 1878. The story of the Liu Ch'ius has already been told, and that of the settlement with Russia over the Kuriles and Sakhalin will be related below. In brief summary, the Liu Ch'ius and Kuriles became Japanese holdings whereas Sakhalin went to the Russians. Finally, the question of Korea has already been treated and will be referred to again later in this chapter.

Prior to the Restoration, Japan had, of course, already entered into diplomatic and commercial relations with the West. These treaties placed such limitations upon Japan's independence of action that they were bitterly resented. Especially angry against the shogunate for having made them were the powerful Satsuma and Choshu clans which attempted to overthrow the shogun and tear up the unequal treaties. The impetuous clansmen were cooled somewhat by such incidents as the British bombardment and destruction of Kagoshima on August 11, 1863, and the destruction of the batteries and fortifications at Shimonoseki by an allied naval force on September 5-6, 1864.

Privileges Transferred by the Treaties. Some indication of how much the Japanese, a very sensitive people, resented these treaties can be judged from the extensive rights granted to the treaty powers and their citizens in the civil and criminal courts. In civil matters, jurisdiction was granted to the courts of the powers in every case in which a treaty-power citizen was sued by a Japanese, in any action between citizens of the same treaty power, and in any action involving citizens of different treaty powers. Similarly, in criminal cases the foreign courts had jurisdiction over crimes committed by treaty-power citizens against either Japanese or foreigners, whether the latter were treaty-power citizens or not. Even cases involving the violation of treaty provisions or trade regulations by citizens of treaty powers were assigned to the consular courts of the powers affected.[1]

The Japanese unsuccessfully maintained that it was within their jurisdiction to try all civil actions brought by foreigners against Japanese, or actions brought by citizens of treaty powers against those of non-treaty powers, or by the Japanese government against any foreigner. Furthermore, Japan held that in criminal matters she had the right of jurisdiction over cases involving all crimes committed by foreigners against the Japanese government, and all offenses committed by foreigners in matters not covered by the treaties.[2]

In 1866, as a result of coercion, the Powers had won from the reluctant *Bakufu* a tariff maximum of 5 per cent, even for luxury items, and the free admission of foodstuffs. With such a low rate, it was apparent that Japan could not secure much tariff revenue and, to make matters worse, the foreigners resorted to such manipulations that in actual practice Japan received only about half of this rate. Furthermore, this low import duty exposed infant native industries to superior foreign competition.

Early Revision Efforts Fail. It is hardly surprising that soon after the Restoration Japan began the long struggle to remove these restrictions. The Japanese case was based upon the infringement of her sovereign rights as an independent nation. Her feeling of humiliation was nationwide. Because of Japanese indignation at their nation's thus being forced into an inferior status, extraterritoriality continued as a major issue in Japanese foreign affairs for more than twenty years, until it was finally ended in 1899. It was an issue that caused the fall of cabinets, and it nearly cost the life of one of Japan's leading statesmen. In 1871 a mission was sent to Europe and the United States to negotiate a revision of the treaties. Headed by the Vice-Prime Minister, Prince Iwakura, it included such leaders of the new Japan as Okubo, Kido, Ito, and Yamaguchi, but this

---

[1] F. C. Jones, *Extraterritoriality in Japan and the Diplomatic Relations Resulting in Its Abolition* (New Haven, 1931), pp. 29 f.

[2] *Ibid.*, p. 30.

distinguished group failed in their task. Although the mission was unsuccessful, its recommendations for needed legal and judicial reforms within the Japanese system brought important changes. Unfortunately, it was a case where haste needed to be made slowly, and the effect upon Japanese life was somewhat confusing.

One power over foreigners, however, was still held by the Japanese government—that of restricting their movements within Japan. This became the means to make the first (although temporary) breach in the hated extraterritoriality when in 1873 Italy signed a treaty partially recognizing Japan's judicial autonomy in return for permission for Italian merchants to travel freely anywhere in Japan. The protests of the other powers nullified this agreement, and Japan then sought unsuccessfully to achieve revision through a conference of the Powers in Tokyo.

The United States, then very friendly toward Japan, granted the Japanese a commercial convention in 1878 which conceded Japan's right to regulate her tariff and taxes and to fix regulations in her open ports in return for the opening of two more ports and the abolition of export duties. Japan was not, however, accorded any modification of extraterritoriality at this time. The last article of the convention declared that it would become effective only when similar agreements were concluded with all the treaty powers. Since not even one of these states was disposed to alter the existing state of affairs, this American convention never took effect.

The one success won by Japan in the early years of her fight to secure equality was the abolition of foreign post offices within her borders. The various treaty powers had set up their own post offices in the different open ports. Since Japan had become a member of the Universal Postal Union on a footing of complete equality, the Powers, except England, consented to the closing of their post offices in Japan. Britain fell in line at the end of 1879; postal administration throughout Japan thence remained firmly in the hands of the Japanese government.[3]

Mexican Pact Breaks the Ice. The decade of 1880-90 saw Japan's drive for equality greatly accelerated. Domestic judicial reforms had been progressing satisfactorily, and so between 1882-87 a number of sessions with the Powers in Tokyo were initiated by the Japanese in their effort to end extraterritoriality and to secure tariff autonomy. As a compromise, Japanese diplomats were prepared to permit the establishment of the mixed court system (composed of Japanese and foreigners), although the idea was obnoxious to popular opinion throughout the country. These efforts, like those that had preceded, resulted in failure, and so Japan

[3] *Ibid.*, pp. 90 f.

changed its tack and sought once more to achieve its goal through individual, rather than group, negotiations. The first success attained by this policy, although relatively slight, was the signing of a Treaty of Amity and Commerce with Mexico in 1888 at Washington. This treaty placed Japan on a basis of complete equality with Mexico, recognized Japan's powers over her own customs, and conceded her jurisdictional autonomy. This treaty was made purposely by Japan in order to have a precedent for similar treatment by other Western nations. It acted in part as a boomerang, since Great Britain, under its most-favored-nation status, claimed the privileges granted to Mexican citizens to travel, trade, and reside virtually at will in Japan.

Nevertheless, this initial success was followed by the negotiation of some really significant treaties with the United States, Russia, and Germany in 1889 which greatly improved Japan's position vis-à-vis these states. Treaties with France and Great Britain were in the process of negotiation and important gains appeared imminent when an attempt was made upon the life of Count Okuma, the Minister of Foreign Affairs, in protest over the news which had leaked out that the projected British treaty called for the appointment of foreign judges to serve in Japanese courts under certain circumstances. The government fell a few days later, and treaty revision efforts came to a halt.

End of Extraterritoriality. The work was resumed a few years later in 1893 when Japan sought to win Britain over to treaty revision, in the knowledge that Britain was the chief stumbling block to fruition of her plans and also possessed the heaviest interests in Japan. Although the negotiations were at times troubled, the result was highly gratifying as Britain agreed to give up her extraterritorial privileges after five years (in 1899). The question of tariff agreement was settled by a compromise which made the duration of the concessions Japan was prepared to offer twelve years instead of the twenty England sought and the ten Japan was willing to offer.

The Aoki-Kimberley Treaty of 1894 was shortly followed by new agreements with the various other powers, which also became effective in 1899. The American treaty provided for the abolition of extraterritoriality, as did the others, and contained a most-favored-nation clause which, however, had some qualifications. It was concluded as a result of negotiations between the Japanese representative, Kurino, and Secretary of State Gresham. While engaged in winning equality with the West, Japan was not disposed to be equally generous with her neighbors, China and Siam, and at about this same time reached agreements with them which provided extraterritorial privileges for Japanese citizens. By August 4,

1899, Japan had won the recognition of equality for which she had been forced to work so long and ardently. Tariff autonomy was not fully achieved until 1911 when the tariff conventions were all terminated.

The Sino-Japanese War, 1894-1895

In the midst of her efforts to be recognized as an equal by the Western powers, Japan engaged in her first modern war. Her difficulties with China over Korea finally culminated in hostilities, which have been previously described. Briefly, Japan, out of her fear of Russian expansion, kept a close watch on events in Korea. To the Japanese, that country in the hands of a powerful state was a weapon aimed at her very heart. Accordingly, Japan pursued a policy in Korea which aimed at bolstering the Korean reform group, then seeking to reshape the weak and corrupt government in order to maintain the nation's independence. China's insistent support of Korean conservative elements eventually touched off the spark that brought on the Sino-Japanese War, 1894-95.

Japanese Resent Interference. Japan's smashing and unexpected victory produced numerous repercussions. For one thing, the interference of Russia, backed by France and Germany, forced Japan to return the Liaotung Peninsula to China for an added indemnity. This action incensed Japanese public opinion and increased the likelihood of an ultimate clash with Russia and possibly also with Germany and France. The sensitiveness of the Japanese, their great pride, and their strong national spirit had already been demonstrated in their attempts to throw off the unequal treaties. Certainly they would not stand for this humiliation but would secure revenge as soon as it became feasible.

Weak China Becomes Prey of Powers. Secondly, there was the effect on the world. Japan's victory revealed what tremendous progress she had made in the few years since the end of her long period of seclusion. Beyond that, the ease and thoroughness of Japan's victory demonstrated how hopelessly inept China actually was. This realization accelerated the great scramble for leaseholds and concessions which almost cost China her independence. Among the Powers which participated in the establishment of spheres of influence in China was Japan. Having been awarded Formosa and the Pescadores in the Treaty of Shimonoseki, Japan advised China that any leasehold to any power on the mainland opposite these island possessions would constitute a danger. Whereupon, she secured a promise from China in the spring of 1898 not to alienate Fukien, the province opposite Japan's insular holdings. It was in this very province that Secretary of State Hay later made the anomalous and embarrassing move of seeking to obtain an American naval coaling station, only to be refused by Japan.

Militarists Gain Control in Japan. Finally, the Japanese victory gave the military a place of dominance in domestic affairs which became increasingly important as time went by. This ascendancy was to make possible an imperialistic policy that plunged Japan into a series of wars and culminated in one of the most crushing defeats in modern history.

The Anglo-Japanese Alliance

In the next episode involving China, the Boxer Rising, the Japanese comported themselves with such efficiency and discipline that they won the openly expressed admiration of most of the Powers. Furthermore, in the negotiations which took place after the incident and led to its settlement, the policy of Japan left little to be desired.

Using the Boxer Rising as a pretext, Russia had acted very aggressively in Manchuria and along the borders of Mongolia. At Newchang, the only treaty port in Manchuria, at Mukden, and along all the Russian railroads in Manchuria, the Russians gave a very pronounced impression of a desire to annex Manchuria. Both Japan and the United States entered strong protests, and it appeared that Russia bowed to their stand. Behind this façade of seeming acceptance, the Russians negotiated the secret Alexieff-Tseng convention which would have reduced Manchuria to a Russian protectorate and enhanced her whole North China position. The concerted and vigorous protests of the Powers forced the abandonment of this agreement, and it was never ratified.

Japan Seeks Tie with Britain. Worried by the persistence of the Russians in their designs on Manchuria and by their attempts to secure a lease over a Korean bay for a naval base, the Japanese Foreign Office decided to seek an agreement with Great Britain. The English were chosen for two reasons. Generally, Anglo-Japanese relations had been sound and friendly. Britain, for example, had not been one of the states forcing the retrocession of Liaotung in 1895. More important, Britain's relations with Russia, Japan's potential future opponent, were quite strained; the two nations had disagreements over such lands as Persia, Afghanistan, and Tibet, and it was known that England looked with disfavor on Russia's aggressive Far Eastern policy.

Yet at the same time that Japan was negotiating with England she was carefully exploring with Russia the possibilities of an understanding which would give Japan a free hand in Korea. This news naturally distressed the British, but their fears were put at rest since nothing concrete came of the Russo-Japanese conversations.

The Treaty. On January 30, 1902, Britain emerged from her splendid isolation, which the Boer War had revealed was certainly isolation but hardly splendid, and signed the Anglo-Japanese Treaty of Alliance at London. The signatories pledged themselves to uphold "the status quo and the general peace in the extreme East" together with "the independence and territorial integrity of the Empire of China and Korea" where they promised that there would be equality of opportunity for "the commerce and industry of all nations." The political interests of each in China and those of Japan in Korea were also guaranteed. Should either country go to war with a single power as the result of a violation of the agreed principles, the other signatory promised to maintain an attitude of strict neutrality and to do its best to prevent a third power from going to war against its ally. In the event that two or more nations went to war with one of the members of the alliance, the other was bound to come to its partner's assistance. The duration of the agreement was to be five years, but it was revised and extended in 1905, again in 1911, and finally terminated after the Washington Conference in 1922.

Pact Enhances Japanese Prestige. The value to Japan of such an alliance was tremendous. It meant that if her difficulties with Russia should ever deteriorate into war, she was secure in the knowledge that Russia could have no ally or Great Britain would come to Japan's assistance. Important as this feeling of security undoubtedly was, the fact that the Japanese, an Oriental people, had achieved the status of complete equality and partnership with the most influential world power was of immeasurable significance. The success thus achieved by Japanese diplomacy served as an inspiration to the colonial peoples of southeast Asia who were greatly heartened over this accomplishment by their fellow Asiatics. Coupled with Japan's success in the impending war with Russia and her recent victory over moribund China, it catapulted the Japanese into the foremost ranks of the Powers.

The Russo-Japanese War

Russia naturally became more cautious as a result of the new union between Japan and Britain and, as if to signify how impressed she was by it, announced a plan of staggered withdrawal of her troops from Manchuria. Unfortunately, she failed to hold completely to this plan, and was guilty of renewed aggressiveness, not only in Manchuria but also in Korea.

In the midst of strong talk of war with Russia in Japan in 1903, the two states began negotiations to settle their differences, but protracted, these talks proved fruitless. Finally, on February 6, 1904, the Japanese minister to Russia broke off negotiations and requested his passports.

The War. At noon on February 8, Japanese naval forces attacked Port Arthur. Japanese torpedoes quickly crippled the main Russian fleet based on Port Arthur. The next day another Japanese detachment destroyed the two Russian ships at Chemulpo. Thus Japan secured command of the seas at the very outset and never relinquished it during the remainder of the war. On February 10, the Japanese emperor issued the declaration of war which under the circumstances came somewhat late.

While the Russians generally were opposed to the war, it was enthusiastically supported by the Japanese people. In her public relations abroad, a very good job was performed which secured Western sympathy for a gallant little Japan fighting for its life against a disgusting, brutal, and corrupt Russian colossus. American and British bankers invested heavily in the Japanese war effort.

On land the fighting was heavy and sanguinary. The Japanese easily overran Korea and on May 1 invaded Manchuria. Port Arthur was besieged toward the end of August and finally captured on January 2, 1905. The remaining units of the Russian fleet, which were located there, were either captured or destroyed. At Mukden a bitter battle lasting two weeks ended in a Japanese victory on March 10, 1905.

Through their naval victories, the Japanese controlled Far Eastern waters, but the Russians sent their Baltic fleet all the way to the Orient in an effort to gain supremacy on the sea. Despite the remarkable achievement involved in this able piece of navigation, the Russian ships were easily trapped by the Japanese in the Battle of Tsushima and almost completely annihilated, May 27-28.

The Peace Treaty. Both sides were now disposed to negotiate, but it was the Japanese who took the initiative. The Japanese minister to the United States requested President Roosevelt to offer his services to mediate the conflict. Roosevelt accepted and on June 8, 1905, requested the belligerents to meet with him to discuss peace. Both accepted, and on August 10 negotiations commenced at Portsmouth, New Hampshire, which resulted in a settlement on September 5.

Although Japan gained no indemnity from Russia in the peace terms, she secured title to South Sakhalin, which she renamed Karafuto, and won Russian recognition of her paramount position in Korea. Subject to the approval of China, she also was awarded the Russian leasehold in the Liaotung Peninsula, which included Port Arthur and Dairen, together with the Chinese Eastern Railway and the various economic rights held by Russia in connection with the railroad.

Japan's success in the war had profound reverberations on world affairs. All over the Far East, including China, Japan achieved respect and in some quarters was considered a natural leader and a model for what others might accomplish if only they had the will. Not only had her prestige increased due to her becoming the first non-Caucasian race in modern history to triumph in a major war over one of the recognized powers, but her territorial and strategic position had been considerably enhanced. She had gained an undisputed foothold on the Asiatic Continent in Korea and in southern Manchuria, gains she was quick to exploit.

Japan and the Powers After the Russo-Japanese War

As a result of her victory, Japan's position in world politics was enhanced as spectacularly as it was among Oriental peoples. Events in the years immediately following 1905 reflected her acceptance by the Powers as a factor of importance in world affairs. Even as peace negotiations were opening at Portsmouth, Japan and Great Britain concluded a new treaty revising and extending their 1902 alliance. By this agreement, signed in London August 12, 1905, the signatories reaffirmed their adherence to the open door in China. Japan's paramount position in Korea was acknowledged by Britain, and promises were made by each country to aid the other should it be attacked by any single power. In this alteration, the British were guarding themselves against a possible future Russian attack on India, as "the extreme East" phrase of the original treaty was now broadened to read "the Far East and India."

As described more fully in Chapter 20, a rapprochement took place between Russia and Japan beginning in 1907. While such an alignment might appear quite strange, it actually had a great deal to recommend it to both parties.

June 10, 1907, Japan secured an agreement with France whereby promises were made to respect the open door in China and one another's possessions on the Continent. The following year some unpleasant situations which had arisen in reference to Japanese-American relations were settled for the time being by the Root-Takahira Agreement of 1908.

Relations with and Relating to China

Japan Strengthens Hold on Manchuria. In December, 1905, Japan and China concluded treaties in Peking which ratified those portions of the Treaty of Portsmouth which applied to China and gave Japan certain other privileges, such as railway rights and the opening of additional ports in Manchuria. Thus, the Peking treaties had the effect of establishing Japan quite strongly in South Manchuria, although the Japanese government publicly announced its adherence to the idea of the open door there.

The proposals of the Harriman interests in the United States for internationalizing the South Manchurian Railway as a link in their proposed around-the-world system were rejected by the Japanese on the grounds that this road had become Japanese property through a heavy sacrifice of their blood and money, and it would not be fair to the Japanese people should international control replace that of the Japanese. Following up their acquisition of this line, the Japanese in 1906 announced the creation of a private corporation, the South Manchuria Railway Company, which took over control from the Japanese military and launched what was destined to become one of the biggest commercial ventures in the entire Far East. The South Manchurian did far more than railroading; its manifold activities included mining, shipping, lumbering, and farming, to mention only the most important.

Japan's political control in Manchuria extended only over the province of Kwantung at the base of the Liaotung Peninsula. This area was officially named the Kwantung Leased Territory by the Japanese, who renamed the former Talien-wan (under the Chinese) and Dalny (under the Russians) Dairen which they declared to be a free port.

China became seriously disturbed as evidence accumulated that Japan meant to extend her position in Manchuria. So it was no wonder that within a short time after the conclusion of the Russo-Japanese War, China and Japan were involved in disputes over Manchuria. These disagreements were confined largely to railway questions but also included a dispute over the Korean boundary. Although dangerous at times, the matter was finally amicably settled in 1909.

The efforts of Secretary of State Philander C. Knox of the United States to secure the internationalization of all existing and future railways in Manchuria proved very distasteful to Japan, a point of view shared by Russia. This opposition, together with the support which Great Britain and France now gave to their respective allies, left only Germany supporting Knox's proposals, with the result that the plan failed.

The Two Consortiums. This setback did not deter the Americans, and in 1911 American bankers took the lead in the formation of the so-called Four Power Consortium. The Powers—the United States, Great Britain, France, and Germany—agreed to loan the Chinese government some £10,000,000 for reforming the national currency and for industrial developments the government planned in Manchuria. This new interference in Manchuria brought protests from Japan and Russia, who had achieved their rapprochement. The following year the American State Department elected to invite Japan and Russia to join the Consortium. The Japanese and Russians both agreed but made certain reservations concerning their special positions in Manchuria and Mongolia. Their reservations were accepted and the two became members, but in March, 1913, the American originators of the idea withdrew because their new President, Woodrow Wilson, felt that the financial operations of the Consortium threatened China's independence. The Consortium was then reorganized by the five remaining Powers only to collapse with the approach of the war in 1914.

Annexation of Korea

Having fought two wars over Korea within a decade, "a dagger pointed straight at the heart of Japan," the Japanese were actively interested in the future of the peninsula country. Before the end of 1905 Japan obtained the reluctant consent of the Koreans to a treaty which gave Japan complete control of Korea's foreign relations and provided that a Japanese official, the Resident-General, should supervise its government. When the news of this capitulation became known in Korea, there was great excitement. To show their disapproval in the strongest manner possible, various patriotic officials committed suicide.

Powers Accept Japanese Action. Although this arrangement placed the treaty rights of the Powers in jeopardy, it was accepted by them rather complacently. The United States was the first to close its legation at Seoul and agree to deal through Japan on matters relating to Korea, an example which was followed sooner or later by all the Powers. Willard Straight, a brilliant young American diplomatist, characterized this action by his government in strong but rather apt language when he said it was like rats deserting a sinking ship. This abandonment of Korea by the United States was in large measure a reflection of the views of President Theodore Roosevelt who felt that Korea had to be written off to the Japanese, and was also a direct consequence of the Taft-Katsura Memorandum of a few months earlier. In this arrangement, the United States agreed to recognize Japanese control of Korea's foreign affairs.

Japan Tightens Its Grip. Japan dignified her establishment of a protectorate over Korea by the appointment of one of her greatest statesmen as Resident-General, Marquis Ito, who soon found himself confronted with the extremely difficult task of making what amounted to a dyarchy operate smoothly. Neither he nor the Japanese as a whole were well received by the Koreans who naturally desired to be free. In 1907 the Korean emperor managed to send a secret mission, including an American adviser, Homer B. Hulbert, to the Hague Peace Conference. It was the hope of the Koreans that they would be permitted to make a plea for the termination of the Japanese protectorate, but they were refused recognition by both the Conference and the government of The Netherlands. This action by the Korean emperor violated the agreement not to engage in any act of an international character except through the medium of Japan and so incensed the Japanese that they soon forced the emperor to abdicate in favor of the crown prince, a youth known to be incapacitated mentally.

There then followed a new agreement which made the Japanese Resident-General the real ruler of Korea. However, conditions from the Japanese point of view did not materially improve, as a wave of plots enveloped the country that caused Japan to embark upon a policy of brutal retaliation. One of the points in the new agreement called for the disbanding of the Korean army whose soldiers proceeded to mutiny. They managed to kill a few Japanese before they were overwhelmed and the army firmly disbanded. In reality, Korean independence was now a thing of the past although formal annexation still lay three years in the future.

Korea Annexed. Ito, sensing the failure of his efforts at a conciliatory policy, resigned his post in 1909 amid a wave of terrorism which shortly afterwards claimed his own life. He was assassinated in Harbin, Manchuria, by a Korean. Although the ostensibly dual system continued a few months longer, it was obviously doomed. On August 29, 1910, a treaty annexing Korea to Japan was officially promulgated. The country was given its old name of Chosen and was made an integral part of Japan. To the Japanese, their action was more justifiable than that of the United States when it acquired the Canal Zone.

As Japanese propaganda put it, President Roosevelt took the Canal Zone because it was considered essential for American national defense. For the same reason Japan took over Korea. The difference between the two cases, however, was that Colombia was not menacing the existence of the United States but Korea threatened Japan's very existence owing to the intrigues she (Korea) was carrying on with Russia.

Now began the thorough and highly systematic work of making over the country to suit Japan's wishes. A tough policy was put into effect. The Japanese attempted to wipe out the cultural life of their subjects by destroying their language and literature, together with their social customs and habits. The Koreans were treated, not as partners in a new union, but rather as conquered people. The Japanese Resident-General following the annexation was the hardheaded old militarist, General Count Terauchi, who lost little time in transforming the country into an armed camp.

Koreans Harshly Ruled. The Koreans were denied freedom of press, speech, and assembly. Japanese was made the official language in all matters, even in the schools where the new teachers all wore swords. Very few Koreans were allowed to go abroad; those who had done so before the annexation were not permitted to return. Religious assemblies of more than five persons were forced to secure a permit from the police in order to hold services. Such hymns as "Onward, Christian Soldiers" were proscribed on the grounds that they tended to develop a militaristic spirit among the people. A native pastor was arrested for having mentioned the kingdom of heaven in his speech. Upon being released he was warned that the only kingdom in which Koreans should be interested was that of Japan. Another pastor was arrested for warning boys against the habit of smoking cigarettes. This was construed by the Japanese as an act of treason since tobacco was a government monopoly and to preach against it was in effect preaching against the government.[4] Making Korean existence even more unpleasant were the economic and social discriminations practiced by the Japanese.

On the credit side, something has to be said for the material achievements of the Japanese who accomplished much in a matter of only a few years. Sanitary measures were widely introduced, improved public health services, a considerable increase in railroad mileage and efficiency, new roads and waterworks, new industries, schools of all types, and vast agricultural improvements were all part of the Japanese accomplishments.

The Koreans resisted as best they could by forming various patriotic societies such as the Wipyung and the Chung Yun Hoi. They also made wide use of some of the Protestant missionary activities to cover their underground activities. Despite the outbursts of terrorism and assassinations, the Korean cause continued hopeless for more than a generation.

SUGGESTED READINGS

For discussions of Unequal Treaties: F. C. Jones, *Extraterritoriality in Japan and the Diplomatic Relations Resulting in Its Abolition, 1853-1899* (New Haven, 1931); E. Herbert Norman, *Japan's Emergence as a Modern State, Political and Economic Problems of the Meiji Period* (New York, 1940); and George E. Uyehara, *The Political Development of Japan, 1867-1909* (London, 1910).

For the Sino-Japanese War: A. J. Brown, *The Mastery of the Far East* (New York, 1919); Edwin A. Falk, *Togo and the Rise of Japanese Sea Power* (New York,

---

[4] E. A. Powell, "Japan's Policy in Korea," *Atlantic Monthly* (March, 1922), pp. 399 ff.

1936); J. H. Longford, *Story of Korea* (London, 1911); W. W. McLaren, *A Political History of Japan During the Meiji Era* (London, 1916); M. F. Nelson, *Korea and the Old Order in Eastern Asia* (Baton Rouge, 1945); and Tatsuji Takeuchi, *War and Diplomacy in the Japanese Empire* (Garden City, New York, 1935).

For the Anglo-Japanese Alliance: A. L. P. Dennis, *The Anglo-Japanese Alliance* (Berkeley, 1923) continues to be most acceptable. An excellent recent account is in Chitoshi Yanaga, *Japan Since Perry* (New York, 1950), pp. 290-304, 332-35. This highly competent text covers all topics listed in these suggested readings.

For the Russo-Japanese War: Roy H. Agaki, *Japan's Foreign Relations, 1542-1936: A Short History* (Tokyo, 1936) is useful despite pro-Japanese overtones; K. Asakawa, *The Russo-Japanese Conflict, Its Causes and Issues* (Boston, 1904); Paul H. Clyde, *International Rivalries in Manchuria* (rev. ed., Columbus, 1928); Tyler Dennett, *Roosevelt and the Russo-Japanese War* (Garden City, New York, 1925), and *John Hay—From Poetry to Politics* (New York, 1933); A. S. Hershey, *The International Law and Diplomacy of the Russo-Japanese War* (New York, 1906); H. F. Pringle, *Theodore Roosevelt* (London, 1932); C. F. Remer, *Foreign Investments in China* (New York, 1933); Payson J. Treat, *Diplomatic Relations Between the United States and Japan, 1895-1905* (Stanford University, 1938); W. W. Willoughby, *Foreign Rights and Interests in China* (Baltimore, 1920).

For Japan and the Powers after the Russo-Japanese War: George Kennan, *E. H. Harriman* (2 vols., Boston, 1922); A. Iswolsky, *Recollections of a Foreign Minister* (London, 1920); Herbert Croly, *Willard Straight* (New York, 1924); E. B. Price, *The Russo-Japanese Treaties of 1907-1916 Concerning Manchuria and Mongolia* (Baltimore, 1933); Pauline Tompkins, *American-Russian Relations in the Far East* (New York, 1949); Yanaga, *op. cit.;* and E. H. Zabriskie, *American-Russian Rivalry in the Far East* (Philadelphia, 1946).

For Sino-Japanese Relations: Agaki, *op. cit.;* H. B. Morse, *The International Relations of the Chinese Empire* (3 vols., London, 1910-18); and Yanaga, *op. cit.*

For the Annexation of Korea: In addition to titles listed under the Sino-Japanese War, see: H. N. Allen, *Things Korean* (New York, 1908); Andrew J. Grajdanzev, *Modern Korea* (New York, 1944); F. H. Harrington, *God, Mammon, and the Japanese* (Madison, 1944); Homer C. Hulbert, *The Passing of Korea* (London, 1906); F. A. McKenzie, *Korea's Fight for Freedom* (London, 1920).

17

THE ATTACK RENEWED BY THE WEST

The Deteriorating Chinese Position

During the remaining years of the nineteenth century (1860-1900), Chinese foreign relations underwent a number of changes. In 1877 its first Western embassy was opened in London, which provided a glimpse of the West at home. Within China, control over the Maritime Customs fell more and more into the hands of foreigners. The work of the missionaries, both Protestant and Catholic, helped the spread of foreign ideas and also served to create many serious problems. The foreign concessions became firmly established at China's expense. Defeats were administered the Chinese by such countries as France and Japan in actual warfare. Territorial possessions were lost to Japan, Russia, France, and Great Britain, and China's hold on others was weakened. Following the disastrous Sino-Japanese War, "spheres of interest" were staked out by the Powers, and China seemed in a fair way to lose even its independence if the process continued. Favorable treaties of friendship, commerce, and navigation were secured by a number of countries. Finally came the unfortunate Boxer Rising on the heels of the abortive reform movement of 1898. So decadent were the Manchus that only the combination of the strong personality of the Empress Dowager and Britain's policy of propping up the Manchus kept the dynasty from utter collapse.

Establishment of the Chinese Maritime Customs. One important result of the Taiping Rebellion was the establishment in China of the Imperial Maritime Customs.[1] This came about through an arrangement made in Shanghai during the uprising to put the collection of foreign duties in the hands of a commission until the revolt was quelled. The British, American, and French consuls each nominated one of their countrymen to constitute a board of inspectors. This arrangement was later defended by the foreigners on the grounds that the traditional system employed by the Chinese was incompatible with the prescribed tariff

---

[1] For details on the founding of the service see Juliet Bredon, *Sir Robert Hart* (New York, 1909), chap. 3.

system which had been fixed on China by the foreigners. It was further held that the new system was Chinese, not foreign; each foreigner was in China's employ and bound to remember that! The constantly reiterated charge that most of the foreigners in the service did not know any Chinese was lightly turned aside on the grounds that knowledge of the language was not indispensable. An able man who understood his duties thoroughly could perform more satisfactory service than one whose only qualification was his knowledge of Chinese.

Thus the service, begun as a temporary expedient, became permanent under the direction of an Inspector-General, always a British subject, who had full charge of employing and paying the staff, collecting all duties, and then turning over to the ranking Chinese official of the service what remained after the deduction of all expenses. It came to be the practice to make the Customs the chief security for foreign loans to China. This brief description of the service indicates what an extensive inroad foreign powers were able to make upon China's independence. It must further be remembered that this was but one of such infringements upon Chinese sovereignty.

The Tientsin Massacre. That the "foreign devils" so violated Chinese sovereignty did not contribute to their popularity with the Chinese. Especially difficult was the lot of the missionary. As a result of the treaties made by France with China in 1844 and 1846, missionaries were allowed to carry on their work in the country. The Treaties of Tientsin in 1858 contained a clause tolerating Christianity. In each case, this clause stressed the moral character of Christianity. How unimportant this clause appeared to at least one of the Powers is reflected in the confession of the English negotiator that it was "an after-thought 'shoved in' at the last moment." [2] Nor were the other Powers much more energetic on the subject. An exception was France. In negotiating the French Convention of Peking in 1860 a French missionary, who served as the French interpreter, interpolated a clause in the Chinese text, which was not in the French text, that granted France's missionary societies the right to buy land and build upon it anywhere in the empire. It further stated that all churches, schools, cemeteries, lands, and buildings previously owned by persecuted Chinese Christians at any time in the past and which had meantime been seized or destroyed by the Chinese were to be paid for by the Chinese government. The French representative in Peking would then turn the money over to the Christian community concerned.

The French government made full use of the clause, which proved to be an increasing irritant to the Chinese. All other Christian sects, from

---

[2] Michie, *Englishman in China*, Vol. II, p. 227.

whatever country its missionaries hailed, benefited from this arrangement if they so desired, just as their countries would from a commercial treaty granted another nation if they had most-favored-nation status. For a long time, nearly all attacks on missionaries stemmed from land disputes, and the missionary question became the principal irritant in China's relations with foreigners. As Michie says:

> Whatever the merits of the dispute, the foreigner is *prima facie* in the wrong; for he is an alien, an intruder, and he erects buildings which are outlandish, offensive to taste, and of sinister influence; and whosoever, albeit the most disreputable member of a family of three or four generations, proclaims a grievance by which he has lost his birthright, is sure of a sympathetic following. Thus without taking into account individual indiscretions, or infirmities of temper, open attacks on time-honoured customs, and so forth, there is a perennial root of bitterness in missionary enterprise in the interior of China, which throws out shoots culminating in murder and fiendish ferocity; and all this without even a distant approach to the kernel of Christianity which lies behind the outworks.[3]

There was a widespread popular belief in China that the Christians resorted to kidnaping and such vile practices as the extraction of children's eyes, the severance of their members, and the use of their blood for their rites. Thus it did not take much to stir up a mob and turn it loose on foreigners, particularly since the mandarins had an annoying habit of arriving too late to help the victims and contented themselves with expressing their willingness to see to it that an indemnity was paid and the requisite number of heads chopped off in reparation.

One of the worst antiforeign, anti-Christian outbreaks was the Tientsin Massacre of June 21, 1870. It was preceded by the murder near the city of a lone English missionary named Williamson and by an abortive antiforeign uprising in Nanking. That something was in the wind was indicated by the warning, delivered to Peking by the Imperial Commissioner at Tientsin, that the French mission was in danger.

There was a French orphanage at Tientsin rumored to be in the business of kidnaping Chinese children. A mob appeared before its gates on the day of the massacre and murdered the French consul who, in the excitement, had fired at a local magistrate. The mob then burned the French cathedral and the mission and murdered ten French nuns, an Irish girl, two French priests, five other French men and women, and a Russian merchant and his wife. Far from being spontaneous or accidental, the onslaught was the work of an organized group led by the city's fire brigade and was under the direction of several of the local authorities.

[3] *Ibid.,* Vol. II, p. 235.

Involved as it was in the Franco-Prussian War of 1870, the French government refrained from the use of force but extracted a heavy indemnity and had two of the local officials banished for life. Some twenty members of the mob were executed by the Chinese authorities as well, and an official was sent to Paris to make an official apology.

Somewhat shaken by this narrow escape from war, the Chinese government in 1871 attempted to gain the assistance of the foreigners in the solution of the missionary question. Its control scheme embraced some eight points and was communicated to the French government, to be sent by it to the other Powers. France refused to accept the proposals, and, while the other Powers gave their approval to the circular in general, they tended to be critical of some details, with the result that no constructive advance resulted.

The Margary Affair. In 1875 Augustus Margary, an interpreter in the British Consular Service, was murdered near the border of Burma.[4] The British demanded an apology and an indemnity, but China demurred. The case then became involved with a number of other matters in dispute between the two governments. It was finally settled, after talk of war was rumored, by the Chefoo Convention, September 13, 1876. China made an official apology, paid an indemnity, recognized the British Supreme Court for China and the Chinese Mixed Court at Shanghai, agreed to a definition of judicial proceedings in criminal and mixed cases, and opened four more ports for trade, together with six ports of call on the Yangtze.

Loss of Dependencies

The Liu Ch'iu Islands. The first modern treaty signed by Japan and China was the Treaty of Tientsin, September 13, 1871. It recognized in effect the equality of Japan, provided for consular relations, and established trade regulations. No most-favored-nation status was granted, nor was there any provision made for extraterritoriality.

In 1871 some Liu Ch'iu sailors, shipwrecked on Formosa, were murdered. The Liu Ch'ius had been a tributary of China's since 1372, and of Japan's since 1451. The latter conquered the islands in 1609, and thereafter the Liu Ch'iu prince was invested not only by the Chinese but by the Japanese as well. Japan immediately sought redress from China for the murders. China adopted the attitude that she had no jurisdiction over eastern Formosa, the half of the island inhabited by savage tribes. The Japanese took advantage of this stupid position by sending troops to punish the savages. China awoke to her error and likewise rushed forces

[4] S. T. Wang, *The Margary Affair and the Chefoo Agreement* (London, 1940) contains a full account of this episode.

to the island. War appeared imminent, but the offer by the British Minister to China of his good offices as mediator effected a peaceful solution of the dispute. In the agreement, Japan's right to act as it had was recognized, China paid an indemnity, and the Japanese forces were withdrawn. While on a tour of the world in 1879 former President Grant of the United States recommended a division of the islands between China and Japan. However, a rapidly deteriorating Chinese government recognized Japanese sovereignty over the Liu Ch'ius in 1881.[5]

Loss of Ili. Russia, which had received fantastic grants of territory from China in 1858 and 1860,[6] took advantage of a rebellion against the Manchus in Ili and Kashgar, to occupy the Ili (Kuldja) region of Sinkiang in 1871. Twenty years earlier, Russia and China had reached an agreement which gave Russia trading rights along the Sinkiang border. Subsequent agreements between the two countries granted extraterritorial rights to the Russians, extended their trade privileges, and allowed the opening of a consulate at Kashgar in southwestern Sinkiang.

The Russian occupation of Ili followed by a few years the creation of Russian Turkestan. Now in Ili, the Russians promised the Chinese Foreign Office that, as soon as order was restored in the region, it would be returned. Much to Russia's surprise, the Chinese under General Tso Tsung-tang annihilated the rebel forces, reconquered all the lost territory, and restored order themselves. Naturally, China demanded the evacuation of Ili, and negotiations were opened for this purpose.

A stupid and thoroughly homesick Chinese diplomat, Ch'ung Hou, who had gone to France to apologize for the Tientsin Massacre and who was the first Manchu envoy to go to Europe, signed the Treaty of Livadia on September 15, 1879, which gave Russia a compensation of 5,000,000 rubles for the expenses of the occupation and "rectified" the frontier in Russia's favor. The latter gained about seven tenths of the province, including its most important strategic points. Ch'ung Hou was sentenced to death, and only the personal intervention of Queen Victoria of England saved his life. The astute Li Hung-chang then took over direction of the affair. Through his diplomacy the case was reopened, and on February 12, 1881, Marquis Tsêng signed the Treaty of St. Petersburg which restored most of Ili to China. Russia's net territorial gain was western Ili, but it won the right to trade anywhere in Ili and in Mongolia without payment of any duties. An additional indemnity of 4,000,000 rubles was paid also. The net result of this episode was to leave Sinkiang a sphere of Russian interest.

[5] M. J. Bau, *Open Door Doctrine* (New York, 1923), p. 23 f.
[6] See below, Chapter 20.

France and Annam. Formerly a Chinese vassal, Annam had been conquered and annexed to China in 1407 but soon reverted to its former status of vassalage. Ever since the beginning of the eighteenth century, the French had been interested in it and had enjoyed some success in converting the Annamese to Christianity. In 1858 French power was extended over the country by the exploits of a joint Franco-Spanish military expedition which waged a war lasting about four years. In the resulting treaty (1862) France was ceded Saigon, three provinces of Cochin China, the island of Poulo Condore, and was given an indemnity to share with Spain. The Annamese king transferred his allegiance from the Chinese emperor to France in 1874, but nonetheless continued to send China its quadrennial tribute.

Fighting broke out in 1883 in Annam between the French and a combination of Imperial Chinese forces and some mercenary troops who were remnants of the Taipings known as the Black Flags. The Chinese gave a rather good account of themselves but were ultimately defeated and such important places as Hanoi were captured by the enemy. An agreement was reached at Tientsin, May 11, 1884, whereby France agreed to protect the borders between China and Tongking (northern Annam), and the Chinese were pledged to withdraw their forces from Tonking. China further promised to respect any future treaties between France and Annam. However, a border misunderstanding shortly afterwards caused the reopening of hostilities which were concluded by the Treaty of Tientsin, June 9, 1885. This understanding was virtually a reaffirmation of that of 1884. No indemnity was exacted from China, but French suzerainty over Annam was recognized.

Loss of Burma. Next to be withdrawn from Chinese sovereignty was Burma, which had been conquered in Kublai Khan's time and had since paid tribute to China decennially. In 1862, the year that the French took Cochin China, the British annexed Lower Burma to their Indian holdings. British influence in Upper Burma, which had been paramount, could conceivably have been jeopardized by France's gains in Indo-China, so the British decided to annex Upper Burma. This action was recognized by a convention signed for Great Britain at Peking on July 24, 1886, by a British diplomat named O'Conor. In return, the British agreed to permit the continuance of Burmese tribute missions to China. The question of Tibet, which had come up at this time, was left in statu quo for the time being. A subsequent convention signed March 17, 1890, saw China recognize a British protectorate over Sikkim.

Korea. Korea, according to legend, was founded by an ancestor of Confucius in 1122 B.C. He named the country Chosen, translated as "Land

THE ATTACK RENEWED BY THE WEST

of the Morning Calm," "Dawnland," or "Morning Radiance." Out of the struggles which took place in subsequent years there emerged three kingdoms. Mention has already been made of Japanese contacts with Korea during the Era of the Three Kingdoms which came to an end in 918 A.D. This was followed by the second period of Korean history, that of the Koryo dynasty, 918-1392. The last period of Korean independence was that of the Yi dynasty, which commenced in 1392 and ended in 1910.

Korea is a rather mountainous country with an area of approximately 85,000 square miles, which makes it a little larger than Minnesota. In length it extends 463 miles and has a maximum width of 170 miles. The land slopes toward the south, which makes the southeastern section of the country reasonably level, whereas the north tends to be mountainous. Korea's granary, consequently, is in the south where most of its people are also to be found.[7]

The people are of Mongoloid origin and possess their own language which, although influenced by the Chinese, is neither Chinese nor Japanese. At the time of Korea's annexation by Japan its population was about thirteen millions. At present this figure has increased to about thirty millions.

Although China took little active interest in Korea until about 1870, the Koreans had paid tribute to China for centuries, the country having been conquered by the Manchus in 1637. Japan, on the other hand, used Korea as the funnel through which she siphoned Chinese culture. In 1592 and in 1598 Hideyoshi's forces invaded Korea with results that have already been described. So devastating were the effects of these Japanese invasions that Korea was perfectly content thereafter to have as little to do with foreigners as possible and became known as the "Hermit Kingdom." Korea long paid tribute to Japan but following the Manchu conquest paid less and less attention to Dai Nippon until finally it ceased payment of tribute after 1811.

In 1866 the Russians appeared in Korea seeking unsuccessfully to establish trade relations; some French missionaries were massacred and their native converts persecuted;[8] and an American schooner, the "General Sherman," was destroyed on the Tadong and its crew murdered. The French sent an expedition to avenge the slain missionaries, but it retired from the country without accomplishing much. The United States sent an expedition in 1871 under Admiral John Rogers to open relations between the two countries, but Rogers was officially told that Korea "was

---

[7] A. J. Grajdanzev, *Modern Korea* (New York, 1944), pp. 8 f.

[8] It is estimated that some 20,000 were slain from 1866-70. H. C. Hulbert, *The Passing of Korea* (London, 1906), p. 119.

satisfied with her four thousand years of her civilization and had no need of any external assistance." [9] This event took place after two vessels of the American squadron had been fired upon by guns from a nearby fort. A landing party was sent against the fort, whose defenders fought to the last man. Although the Americans lost only a single officer, they sailed away shortly afterwards, an act which the Koreans construed as cowardice and acknowledgement of defeat.

In 1876 Korea signed its first foreign treaty, as a result of a skirmish with Japan. A Japanese warship was fired upon by a Korean fort near Chemulpo; a Japanese landing party then captured the fort. Out of this episode came a treaty of friendship and peace between the two countries wherein Japan recognized the independence of Korea and legations were opened in the two countries. Three Korean ports were thrown open for trade.[10]

There then developed in Korea a radical group, influenced by the Japanese who had become very active in Korea. Merchants were quick to utilize opportunities for trade, Korean youths were sent to Japan to be educated, and the Korean court took many Japanese into its employ. The radicals came into conflict with the Korean ruling faction, the Min, which now turned to China for assistance. An anti-Min military riot broke out in 1882; several members of the family were killed, the palace was invaded, and the queen narrowly escaped with her life. Then somewhat inconsistently it was Japan's turn. The Japanese were attacked and driven from the country.

Japan immediately sought to negotiate the difficulties, but the Korean regent then temporarily in power would have nothing to do with them. China now sent three thousand troops under Yüan Shih-k'ai and two other generals to assist Korea in the maintenance of order. Korea was put under the Chinese customs service. The Chinese cooperated with the Min party, and the leaders of the military uprising were executed, the regent taken to China, and the queen restored to her role of assisting the king in ruling. The difficulties with Japan were settled by the payment of an indemnity and an apology.

China, in concluding a commercial treaty with Korea in 1882 inserted into the treaty the phrase "Korea having been, from ancient times, a tributary state, the canons of her intercourse in all matters with the government of China are fixed and need not be changed." [11]

[9] W. E. Griffis, "Japan's Absorption of Korea," *North American Review*, (October, 1910), p. 517.
[10] There were some similarities between the Japanese treaty-making procedures in Korea and the Perry mission to Japan.
[11] S. G. Hishida, "The International Position of Japan as a Great Power," *Columbia Studies in History, Economics and Public Law*, Vol. XXIV, No. 3 (1905), p. 166.

The United States reappeared on the scene in 1882 when Commodore R. W. Shufeldt negotiated and signed the Treaty of Jenchuan with Korea on May 22. This agreement, ratified one year later, contained an extraterritorial article, established trade relations, and provided for diplomatic relations. In a letter to President Arthur of the United States, the Korean king acknowledged Korea's tributary position with China but stated that "in regard to both internal administration and foreign intercourse it enjoys complete independence." [12] Nonetheless when Korea sent a mission to Washington to ratify the treaty, the Chinese attempted to prevent its departure and even kidnaped one of the envoys. However, the U.S.S. "Trenton" carried the mission to the United States and brought it back successfully. Treaties with Great Britain and Germany followed quickly as did others with Russia, Austria, and Italy. This meant that Korea was now recognized as a full-fledged member of the family of nations.

Following the return of the mission to America, the Japanese and the native radical faction were driven out of Korea; the real power became Yüan Shih-k'ai. The ten years preceding 1894 saw the Chinese gradually extend their domination. During this decade several American Protestant missionary societies extended their activities to Korea, various treaty ports were opened, and a number of government institutions built, but Korea fell more and more into its old role of vassal to the Chinese suzerain.[13]

In 1894 a rebellion broke out against the government by a religious organization known as the Tong Hak. The members were extremely antiforeign and anti-Christian and, in particular, had a grudge against Catholicism. Their leader had been executed in 1865 during the persecution of the Catholics. They now demanded that he be declared innocent by the King and honored in death, or they would drive all foreigners out of the country. The rejection of their demands led to their rising in force. Government forces sent against them were defeated. Korea then sought aid from China, which quickly responded. Japan, although not asked for assistance, sent a force many times that of China's. The Japanese justified their action on the grounds that they had never recognized Korea as a tributary state of China's. The latter's insistence that Korea was its vassal, coupled with its refusal to cooperate with Japan in the introduction of reforms the Japanese requested that the Korean government adopt, resulted in both sides declaring war in August, 1894.[14] China confidently

[12] For details of the treaty see "Treaties, Regulations, etc., between Corea and Other Powers, 1876-1879," *China, Imperial Maritime Customs,* Vol. III, Miscellaneous Series: No. 19 (Shanghai, 1891), pp. 41-52.

[13] Hulbert, *Passing of Korea,* pp. 126 f.

[14] Before the actual declarations, however, the Japanese had launched naval action against the Chinese without warning, thus setting a precedent for many of their future wars.

expected to "root the Wo-jên (Japanese dwarfs) out of their lairs," but to the surprise of the whole world was subjected to a thorough beating on both land and sea.

By the terms of the Treaty of Shimonoseki, April 17, 1895, China recognized Korea's complete independence and autonomy. Japan was awarded the Liaotung Peninsula, including Port Arthur and Talien-wan (Dairen), Formosa, the Pescadores (between Formosa and the mainland), and an indemnity. Japan was also accorded extraterritoriality and given most-favored-nation status by the terms of a new commercial treaty signed the following year at Peking.

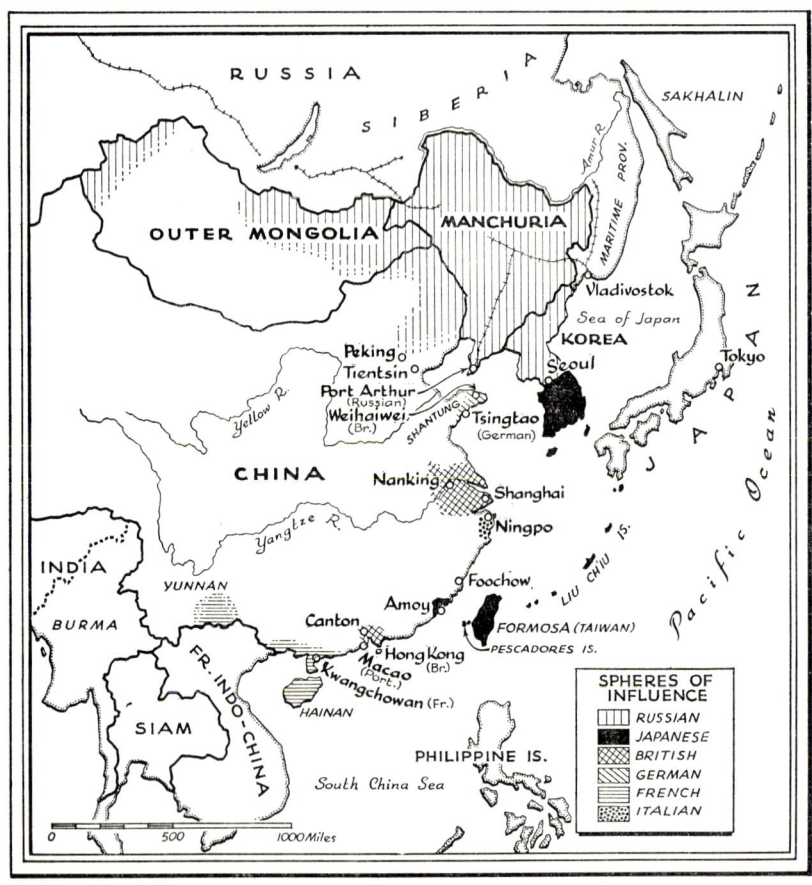

Foreign Possessions, Leases, and Spheres of Influence About 1900

Adapted from *Modern Far Eastern International Relations* by McNair and Lach, copyright 1950, D. Van Nostrand Company, Inc.

Thus concluded a period in the diplomatic history of China which saw China further opened to the West as new ports were thrown open and more nations entered into treaty relations with it. These years also witnessed the loss of numerous Chinese dependencies. China struck back against this forcing open of its ports and trade and the loss of its vassals in the only way in which she could express herself, which was to increase her xenophobia culminating in the great Boxer Rising of 1900.[15]

The Struggle for Concessions

China's defeat by Japan had great and widespread repercussions. Despite its previous setbacks, there had been a healthy respect throughout the West for China's potential might. The feeling had been strong that if China became armed, it would be a most formidable foe. The thoroughness of its defeat by Japan wiped out this notion completely. China was corrupt, decadent, and helpless. Its riches waited only to be plucked.

In the actual cutting up of the "Chinese melon" which ensued, the Powers followed a set pattern. First, a base was obtained from which the influence of that particular Power then emanated. Next a railroad was usually built to carry this influence from the base far into the interior. A foreign bank was usually established to finance the railroad and any mining and other economic enterprises which were started. Finally, in order to prevent clashes among themselves, the Powers reached mutual understandings to respect one another's spheres of influence.[16]

Russia Steps In. First to avail itself of what appeared to be the impending breakup of China was Russia. Li Hung-chang, China's leading diplomat, was sent to Russia in 1896 to represent his country at the coronation of Tsar Nicholas II. Russia had been so alarmed over Japan's victory over China that, with the assistance of France and Germany, it had made successful representations to Japan to restore the Liaotung Peninsula to China in return for an additional indemnity. Russia's supposed reason for this action was its desire to support "the unity and territorial integrity of the Chinese Empire."

While Li was in St. Petersburg for the coronation ceremonies, the Russian Finance Minister and top Far Eastern expert, Count Sergei Witte, conceived the idea of winning his permission to build the concluding sections of the Trans-Siberian Railway directly across Chinese territory through Mongolia and Manchuria to Vladivostok thereby avoiding the great curve of the Amur River. This would mean a tremendous saving of distance and would provide a somewhat better climate through which

[15] Bau, *op. cit.*, p. 34.
[16] *Ibid.*, pp. 38 f.

to pass. Witte argued to Li that, in order to maintain China's territorial integrity, such a line was necessary. A secret pact was concluded permitting Russia to build a railroad through Chinese territory along a straight line from Chita to Vladivostok. This line is the famous Chinese Eastern Railway. Both countries agreed to go to war if Japan should attack the other. The alliance was signed, June 3, 1896, and is known as the Li-Lobanov Treaty. A supplementary agreement provided that the railroad was to be run by a corporation, the Chinese Eastern Railroad Corporation, supposedly a private firm but actually an agent of the Russian government. A strip of land wide enough for the road and a right of way was ceded to the corporation. On this strip the corporation was permitted to maintain its own armed guard and to exercise complete authority. It is perhaps worth noting that Li Hung-chang and some lesser members of his entourage were the recipients of rather expensive "gifts" from the Russians during the negotiations. By these agreements, Russia was enabled to establish its sphere of influence in northern Manchuria and Outer Mongolia.

Germany's Mailed Fist. The Russian success was followed up by the Germans who established themselves on the Shantung Peninsula. At a time when a German naval expedition was in Chinese waters carrying out a survey for the possible establishment of a coaling station, two German missionaries were murdered in Shantung on November 1, 1897. Immediately, the Germans seized Tsingtao on Kiaochow Bay. On March 6, 1898, an agreement was signed between China and Germany known as the Kiaochow Convention. Germany was given a ninety-nine-year lease over Kiaochow and certain railway and mining rights. The German kaiser's notorious bombast was exercised during the period when negotiations were being carried on. He boasted:

> May everyone in those distant regions be aware that the German Michael has firmly planted his shield, with the device of the German eagle, upon the soil of China, in order once [and] for all to give his protection to all who ask for it.... Should anyone essay to detract from our just rights or to injure us, then up and at him with your mailed fist.[17]

One week after the Germans had seized Tsingtao, Russian warships anchored at Port Arthur and Talien-wan, at the base of the same Liaotung Peninsula which they had denied to Japan. On March 28, 1898, the ports were occupied by Russian forces as the result of their winning a twenty-five-year leasehold from China. Some nearby islands and the adjacent territories were included.

[17] Soothill, *op. cit.*, p. 169.

France Expands Its Sphere. About two weeks after the Russians had made their move, the French announced that they had secured a ninety-nine-year lease on Kwangchow-wan and its dependencies. The murder of two French naval officers forced China to ratify this lease reluctantly. Earlier (1895) the French had secured a new boundary arrangement between Tongking and China at the latter's expense. The opening of several new ports, together with certain mining and railroad rights, had also been secured by the French. Their sphere of influence came to embrace Kwangsi, Kwangtung, and Yünnan.

Britain Gains Important Areas. Not to be outdone by their rivals in China, the British secured a lease over Weihaiwei, July 1, 1898, "for so long a period as Port Arthur shall remain in the occupation of Russia." As British influence extended, it became paramount in the rich Yangtze Valley and in Szechwan and Tibet. Just before leasing Weihaiwei, Britain secured a ninety-nine-year lease over the entire Kowloon Peninsula, thereby increasing the size of the original Hong Kong cession about fourteen fold.

Italy Tries and Fails. A newcomer appeared in the field when Italy sought to obtain the lease of a naval base on Sanmen Bay, but the Chinese government had finally stiffened its backbone under the leadership of the Empress Dowager, the "Old Buddha." Faced with the certainty that China would resist, the Italians gave up their project.

Railways and Treaty Ports. The next step in the assault upon China's integrity was the race for railway concessions. In this struggle, the European Powers were joined by little Belgium and by various private American railway interests. So many railway concessions were granted that, combined with the leases, they gravely threatened China's independence.

These steps coincided with or were followed by demands from the Powers that treaty port concessions be granted in some cases, or, in others, enlarged. Such demands included those of the Russians in Newchang; the Germans in Tientsin; the Japanese in Amoy and Foochow; the French, Russians, Germans, Japanese, and Belgians in Hankow; and the French, British, and Americans in Shanghai.[18]

In general, these concessions were located upon land rented to the various foreign governments, usually under terms of perpetual lease. The governments were accustomed to sublease the lands to their own nationals on a ninety-nine-year arrangement. Shanghai was the scene of two great foreign holdings, the International Settlement (founded September 21,

---

[18] For details of some of these cases, see En-sai Tai, *Treaty Ports in China: a Study in Diplomacy* (New York, 1918), pp. 103-22.

1863) and the French Concession (acquired in 1849). To govern the International Settlement there was evolved the Shanghai Municipal Council, largely British dominated.

Reform

In the midst of all this foreign aggression, a belated attempt was made to bring about reforms in China which its long series of humiliating experiences at the hands of the foreigners revealed to be so necessary.[19]

The Boxer Rising [20]

Tz'ŭ Hsi was strongly antiforeign, a feeling shared by many of her subjects. Following the failure of the reform movement in 1898, demonstrations against the "foreign devils" became commonplace. Particularly distasteful to the Chinese were such foreign inventions as railroads and telegraph lines. The railroads, especially, incurred resentment because they frequently disturbed the tombs of respected ancestors. Each Chinese family has its own little burial ground within the land it owns. With tombs all over the countryside, the railroads inevitably interfered with them.

Typical of the feeling against the railroads was this incident which took place during the Boxer Rising. When the Boxers destroyed the railroad station in Peking, the first thing they did was to tear up all tickets in the belief that if there were no tickets the people would be unable to travel on the good-for-nothing railroad.[21]

Boxer Origins. An old, formerly anti-Manchu, secret society was revived at the end of the century. It took the name of the I Ho Ch'üan or "Fists of Righteous Harmony." These "Patriotic Harmony Train-bands" became known as the Boxers. They had their beginnings in various villages in Shantung where small bands of gymnasts were formed. Each group was led by a "demonized" leader. This person, either through hypnotism or more usually by choosing an epileptic as his subject, would cause the latter to display wild, unnatural symptoms and to utter weird incomprehensible sounds. This demonstration was supposed to prove to the gullible mass of the Boxers that their society possessed supernatural power. Every member was promised immunity not only from death but even from physical injury. Especially did they claim to be immune from

---

[19] See Chapter 13. For a fuller account see M. E. Cameron, *The Reform Movement in China* (Stanford University, 1931), chap. 2.

[20] Excellent accounts may be found in G. N. Steiger, *China and the Occident* (New Haven, 1927), and in Paul H. Clements, *The Boxer Rebellion* (New York, 1915).

[21] H. C. Thomson, *China and the Powers* (London, 1902), p. 3.

THE ATTACK RENEWED BY THE WEST

foreign bullets, a security supposed to result from placing their faith in the Jade Emperor, the chief Taoist deity. Taoist and Buddhist priests were very active in the society. From Shantung the movement spread to the province of Chihli. Boxer drills were taking place over a widespread area, and numerous incidents took place against the foreigners beginning with the mutilation and decapitation of a British Protestant missionary on December 30, 1899.

The Boxers cleverly misrepresented to the masses that the government was with them. A favorite motto was "Exalt the Dynasty and Extirpate the Foreigners!" One of their placards read:

> The Universal Boxer Society:
> You are personally invited to meet on the seventh day of the ninth moon.
> > Elevate the Manchus
> > Kill the Foreigners
> > Unless this summons is obeyed you will lose your heads.[22]

Recruits were won over by such promises and threats as the following:

> Hasten, then, to spread this doctrine far and wide; for, if you gain one adherent to the faith, your own person will be absolved from all future misfortunes. If you gain five adherents to the faith, your whole family will be absolved from all evils; and, if you gain ten adherents to the faith, your whole village will be absolved from all calamities. Those who gain no adherents to the cause shall be decapitated; for until all foreigners have been exterminated, the rain can never visit us.[23]

Foreigners Besieged. Prince Tuan, father of the man chosen by Tz'ŭ Hsi to replace the hapless puppet Emperor Kuang Hsü, was won over to the movement and gave it his active support. Finally, the Empress Dowager showed herself sympathetic with the Boxers, and North China became very unhealthy for foreigners. By June 8, 1900, the foreign legations in Peking were seriously threatened. A relief column under a British admiral, Sir Edward H. Seymour, and an American, Captain McCalla, was defeated and turned back with heavy losses. June 11, the chancellor of the Japanese legation, Sugiyama, was murdered. Two days later the Boxers began to destroy the legations and the missions. The foreigners were now forced to take refuge either in the British legation or in the Catholic Cathedral. With them were as many "Secondary Devils" (Chinese Christians) as could be accommodated. On the fourteenth, hundreds of native converts were burned to death in the city. On the twentieth, the German Ambassador, Baron von Ketteler, was shot to

---

[22] *The Boxer Rising* (2d ed., Shanghai, 1901), p. 2.
[23] *Ibid.*, p. 24.

death on the streets of Peking by a Manchu soldier. Three days later an Englishman, Professor Huberty James, was savagely tortured, decapitated, and his severed head placed on exhibition in a cage. A siege of the British legation and the Cathedral was begun on June 20 which was to last for almost two months.

China Declares War. Meanwhile, the "foreign devils" had enraged the Empress Dowager who, up to this point, had been loath to support the Boxers with imperial forces. On June 17, foreign warships, excepting those of the United States which refused to participate, destroyed the Taku forts guarding the entrance to the Pai Ho leading to Peking. This act led to a declaration of war by the Chinese government against all foreigners. The ultimatum which called for the surrender of the forts by their commander prior to their destruction had allegedly called also for the replacement of Tz'ü Hsi by the deposed emperor. This charge, which was untrue, so enraged her that she declared, quoting from the Chinese *Book of Odes,* "Let us exterminate them [the foreigners] before we eat our morning meal" and added that "it were better to go down in one desperate encounter than to surrender our just rights at the bidding of the foreigner."[24] Murder, pillage, and arson abounded in Peking and other places in the north. Thousands of native Christians were slaughtered together with a number of foreign missionaries. A price was put on the head of every foreigner.

Relief of Peking. The long siege of the British legation came to an end on August 14, 1900, when an international force of Japanese, Russian, American, English, French, German, Italian, and Austrian troops arrived. The Cathedral, which had been defended by thirty French and ten Italian marines and which had sheltered more than four thousand natives, was relieved two days later. Although the Americans were the first to fly their flag on the walls of the city, it was the Japanese who had spearheaded the drive to Peking. The "Old Buddha" fled with her court a thousand miles into the west where she remained about a year before returning to the capital.

The victorious foreign troops now indulged in an orgy of savagery and looting in Peking which gathered no laurels for the reputation of the "foreign devils." The leader of a German expedition which arrived after the city's capture, Count Waldersee,[25] was recognized by most of the Westerners as commander of the international forces. He was guilty of

[24] J. O. P. Bland and E. Backhouse, *China Under the Empress Dowager* (London, 1910), p. 265.

[25] As Field-Marshal Count von Waldersee's forces were leaving Bremerhaven for China, the Kaiser exhorted them: "When you meet the foe you will defeat him. No quarter will be given, no prisoners will be taken. Let all who fall into your hands be at your mercy!"

rather brutal behavior, including the sending of a punitive expedition to Paotingfu which was destroyed in revenge for the murder of missionaries there.

China Pays a Heavy Bill. The Allies found it rather difficult to agree among themselves on what terms should be exacted from China. Due in no small measure to the temperate attitude of the United States, which consistently acted to restrain extreme demands and keep down the indemnity, an agreement was finally reached on September 7, 1901, permitting China to escape with its territorial and political independence intact. An indemnity of more than $330,000,000 in gold was decided upon, to be paid in thirty-nine annual installments and bearing an interest rate of 4 per cent on the unpaid principal.[26] The treaty also called upon China to send an embassy of regret to Germany and Japan, to erect a memorial to Baron von Ketteler in Peking, to execute eleven princes and mandarins, including Prince Tuan, to suspend official examinations for five years in all places "where foreigners were murdered or were subjected to harsh treatment," to raze the Taku forts, to prohibit the importation of arms and matériel of war, to recognize the right of foreigners to retain permanent forces to defend their legations, and to replace the Chinese Office of Foreign Affairs (the Tsungli Yamen) by a Ministry of Foreign Affairs (the Wai-wu-pu) which would rank ahead of the other Ministries of State. In addition to the nations involved in the fighting, the treaty was signed by Belgium, Spain, and The Netherlands.

The terms extorted by the victors were so harsh that several of the American Protestant missionary societies refused even to apply for damages, much less to accept any. The Boxer episode may have made few friends in China for the "foreign devils," but it did appear to improve the position of the Manchus, at least temporarily. Actually it tended to hasten their downfall by revealing China's restiveness, its desire for change, and the continued helplessness of the Manchus in the face of foreign power. The Manchus had been allowed to reclaim the throne because the allies chose to act on the "rebellion theory," a useful fiction since there was nothing in sight which could be substituted for the Manchus.

The Open Door

During 1898 and much of 1899, when it appeared as if the breakup of China were imminent, the United States had played a very quiescent role. It was then preoccupied first with the Spanish-American War and

[26] The American share was $24,168,357. In 1907 and again in 1924 a considerable portion of this sum was returned to a grateful China which instituted a fund with it for the education of Chinese students in the United States.

immediately afterward with the Philippine Insurrection. By September, 1899, however, the United States felt impelled to take action, or be relegated to the sidelines while the Chinese melon was sliced into delectable morsels by the voracious European Powers and Japan.

Until the Powers began to establish spheres of influence following China's defeat in the Sino-Japanese War, the American position in China had been satisfactory to the State Department. Through its most-favored-nation position, the United States secured whatever advantages accrued to the other nations trading in China. Now, however, the situation began to alter radically.

Hay Defines Policy. In the fall of 1899, John Hay, the American Secretary of State, sent out to the chancelleries of Great Britain, Germany, Russia, France, Japan, and Italy notes which contained the formulation of a general policy to be followed in China. The notes realistically recognized the existence of spheres of influence or interest and sought only to have the doctrine of equality of commercial opportunity recognized in each sphere.[27]

Three requests were made of each Power in its respective sphere of interest or influence, that it:

> (1) Will in no wise interfere with any treaty port or any vested interest within any so-called "sphere of interest" or leased territory it may have in China.
> (2) That the Chinese treaty tariff of the time being shall apply to all merchandise landed or shipped to all such ports as are within said "spheres of interest" (unless they be "free ports"), no matter to what nationality it may belong, and that duties so leviable shall be collected by the Chinese Government.
> (3) That it will levy no higher harbor dues on vessels of another nationality frequenting any port in such "sphere" than shall be levied on vessels of its own nationality, and no higher railroad charges over lines built, controlled, or operated within its "sphere" on merchandise belonging to citizens or subjects of other nationalities transported through such "sphere" than shall be levied on similar merchandise belonging to its own nationals transported over equal distances.[28]

In their replies to Hay's note, the Powers, with the exception of Russia, substantially agreed to the American proposals. Even the Russian reply closed with the expressed conviction that the answer was "such as to

---

[27] For the role played by an English expert on the Far East, Alfred E. Hippisley, in the writing of the open door notes, thereby making it virtually an Anglo-American project, see A. W. Griswold, *The Far Eastern Policy of the United States* (New York, 1938), pp. 63-67, 71-73, 78, 82, 85.

[28] *Ibid.*, pp. 497-98.

satisfy the inquiry made in the aforementioned [American] note," and that "the Imperial Government is happy to have complied with the wishes of the American Government." [29]

The Policy Expanded. Hay chose to adopt the position that all the Powers had given unqualified acceptance to the proposal of the United States and so notified them of this on March 20, 1900. During the Boxer Rising, on July 3, 1900, Hay sent out a circular telegram to all the Powers having treaty relations with China. This document stated that:

> The policy of the Government of the United States is to seek a solution which may bring about permanent safety and peace to China, preserve Chinese territorial and administrative entity, protect all rights guaranteed to friendly powers by treaty and international law, and safeguard for the world the principle of equal and impartial trade with all parts of the Chinese Empire.[30]

Thus as a sequel to the principle of the open door (equality of commercial opportunity) were added the principles of respect for China's territorial integrity and administrative entity. Yet there really was nothing new or revolutionary about these principles. It had been American policy in China, almost from the beginning, to adhere to these principles, but now they were given a powerful and unequivocal expression. The circular telegram was accompanied by an invitation to the Powers to join in a collective guarantee of the open-door principles. Hay, in sending this cable, was in effect revealing his feeling that there could be no equality of commercial opportunity without adding to this principle the promise of respect for China's sovereignty and territorial integrity. The only government which replied to Hay's invitation was Great Britain, but the effect was nonetheless achieved, if we may judge from the results. The accomplishment, however, was more a result of the mutual fear of the Powers for each other rather than of American policy. Thus the partitioning of China was halted until resumed by Japan many years later. Britain and Germany even included a declaration in effect subscribing to the open door and the maintenance of China's territorial integrity in their treaty of October 16, 1900, which defined their respective positions in China.

Although it was not made public for many years, Hay was guilty of reducing the United States to the role it criticized in others when, in December, 1900, he submitted to pressure from the American Navy and endeavored to secure a lease for a coaling station at Samsah Bay in Fukien. This province was within Japan's sphere, so Hay first consulted Tokyo

---
[29] W. W. Willoughby, *Foreign Rights and Interests in China* (Baltimore, 1920), p. 250.
[30] *Ibid.*, p. 251.

but was rebuffed. That the Japanese made political capital out of this anomalous position is patent.

The Russian Threat

Once the Boxer Rising had been quelled by the Allies, Russia assumed the role of China's friend in the hope of securing all Manchuria as its sphere. The Alexieff-Tseng Agreement (November, 1900), which would have put the important province of Fengtien in Russia's hands was blocked by the protests of the United States, Great Britain, Japan, and Germany. Likewise unratified was the Lamsdorff-Yangyu Convention. This would have limited China's sovereignty as far as its armament in Manchuria was concerned, would have prevented the employment of foreigners other than Russians to act as drillmasters in North China, granted to Russia important mining and railroad rights in many places, and even permitted it a railroad concession from a point on the Chinese Eastern to the Great Wall in the direction of Peking. The Chinese emperor himself was used to appeal successfully to the four Powers which had prevented ratification of the earlier agreement.

When Russia came forward with a proposal that full power over the industrial development of Manchuria be granted to the Russian-controlled Russo-Chinese Bank, Secretary of State Hay entered a protest, as did Britain and Japan. The determined Russians continued their negotiations, but a new factor was injected with the signing of the Anglo-Japanese Alliance, January 30, 1902. This caused Russia to do a temporary *volte face*. Its changed tactics were exemplified by its promise to withdraw all its troops from Manchuria within a specified time agreed to by China in the Russo-Chinese Convention of April 8, 1902. Its failure to do so led to negotiations with Japan, instituted by the latter, which culminated in the Russo-Japanese War of 1904-5, a war fought almost exclusively on Chinese territory.

During this war, China had to play the different role of neutral. The normal difficulties of China's position were increased as its soil was the scene of hostilities, its conception of international law was at best only rudimentary, and its geographical proximity to the two belligerents was so extensive. On February 10, 1904, John Hay issued a circular note calling upon the belligerents to respect China's neutrality and its integrity. Again on January 13, 1905, Hay sent out another circular note, at the suggestion of the German kaiser, requesting the belligerents not to exact territorial gains at China's expense in the peace treaty ending the war. China gave its assent to the terms of the Treaty of Portsmouth, which ended hostilities, since it involved certain transfers of rights granted by it to Russia which now went to Japan. What this war meant to China will be discussed elsewhere.[31]

The Hunt for Concessions Resumed

The Boxer Affair and the Russo-Japanese War temporarily checked the imperialistic rivalry in China, but it was not long before it was strongly revived. Instead of a territorial scramble, the rivalry among the Powers now took the form of a financial struggle.

As early as 1895, the leading British and German banking firms in the Far East reached an agreement whereby each was to share equally any Chinese business obtained by the other. In 1900 they reaffirmed this arrangement. In the interim, the American China Development Company secured a contract to finish construction of the Canton-Hankow Railway. Despite a supplementary agreement of 1900 which prohibited transfer of its rights to any other foreign government or company, the Americans allowed Belgian interests to acquire control of the line's stock. The Chinese government protested, and in 1905 the concession was canceled upon the payment by China of $6,750,000 in gold, which it had to borrow from the government of the British Crown Colony of Hong Kong, thereby adding further to China's already heavy burden of indebtedness.[32]

To attempt to follow the maze of railroad concessions and the financial transactions involved would be pointless. However, the Canton-Hankow case serves as a useful illustration. An agreement was reached in 1905 between various British and French interests to share their business in China. This arrangement aimed at obtaining a monopoly in the Yangtze Valley. In 1908 the Chinese government approached this combination for a loan to complete the Canton-Hankow line and also to build another line from Hankow to Chengtu. Learning of the Chinese application, the German interests demanded and received permission to share in the business.

Nor were the Germans alone in their desire; a group of American banks, formed at the suggestion of President Taft and the State Department, sought to participate. The Europeans, however, refused. Taft thereupon wired a Chinese official, Prince Ch'ing, insisting upon the right of the Americans to participate and calling attention to a promise made by China in 1903 to allow American capital to participate on equal footing in such enterprises. The Chinese government accepted Taft's protest and informed the Europeans that the Americans must be admitted to the loan

[31] See Chapter 20.
[32] Bau, *op. cit.*, pp. 54 f.

group. The consortium thus formed negotiated two loans with China in 1911, one for railroads, the other for currency reform.

By the time the contracts were signed considerable opposition to the railroads had developed in some of the provinces through which the lines were to pass. The local leaders said that they would build the railways within their own provinces, thus precipitating a conflict of authority between the imperial government and the local governments. Gradually, the whole of South China became inflamed over the struggle, which coupled with other issues helped pave the way for the revolution which broke out soon after.[33]

While this reaction to the international battle for concessions was to have a part in bringing about the successful overthrow of the Manchus, another reaction was unsuccessful. This was the plan advanced by Secretary of State Philander C. Knox to neutralize all the railroads of Manchuria. He proposed the grant of an international loan to China whereby China could redeem both the Chinese Eastern and the South Manchurian. China would then own the lines, but they would be under the supervision of the Powers making the loan. This plan applied the open-door principle to the Manchurian railroads and aimed at strengthening China's integrity, since the Chinese government would own the lines. That China favored the plan goes without saying. It failed because of Russian and Japanese opposition.[34]

The outbreak of the Chinese Revolution, October 10, 1911, marked the end of a period which had witnessed the utter humiliation of once-proud China, a period which seemed to threaten its very disappearance and which did produce great territorial losses, the virtual extinction of its influence in the Orient, and its financial enslavement to the West.

SUGGESTED READINGS

For China and Japan: Roy H. Agaki, *Japan's Foreign Relations, 1542-1936: A Short History* (Tokyo, 1936); A. J. Barry, *Railway Expansion in China and the Influence of Foreign Powers on Its Development* (London, 1910); Mingchien Bau, *The Open Door Doctrine in Relation to China* (New York, 1923); J. O. P. Bland and E. Backhouse, *China Under the Empress Dowager* (London, 1910); Juliet Bredon, *Sir Robert Hart* (New York, 1909); Charles S. Campbell, Jr., *Special Business Interests and the Open Door Policy* (New Haven, 1951); Paul H. Clements, *The Boxer Rebellion* (New York, 1915); Paul H. Clyde, *International Rivalries in Manchuria* (rev. ed., Columbus, 1928) and *The United States Policy Toward China; Diplomatic and Public Documents* (Durham, 1940); Herbert Croly, *Willard Straight* (New York, 1924); Tyler Dennett, *Americans in Eastern Asia* (New York, 1922) and *John Hay; From Poetry to Politics* (New York, 1933); A. L. P. Dennis, *The Anglo-Japanese*

[33] MacNair, *op. cit.*, pp. 698 f.
[34] Bau, *op. cit.*, p. 57.

Alliance (Berkeley, 1923); Peter Fleming, *The Siege at Peking* (New York, 1959); W. L. Godshall, *The International Aspects of the Shantung Question* (Philadelphia, 1923); A. W. Griswold, *The Far Eastern Policy of the United States* (New York, 1938); F. H. Harrington, *God, Mammon, and the Japanese* (Madison, 1944); H. B. Morse, *The International Relations of the Chinese Empire* (3 vols., London, 1910-18); David E. Owen, *Imperialism and Nationalism in the Far East* (New York, 1929); C. F. Remer, *Foreign Investments in China* (New York, 1933); G. Nye Steiger, *China and the Occident* (New Haven, 1927); Willard Straight, *China's Loan Negotiations* (New York, 1913); Tai En-sai, *Treaty Ports in China: A Study in Diplomacy* (New York, 1918); Tatsuji Takeuchi, *War and Diplomacy in the Japanese Empire* (Garden City, New York, 1935); Payson J. Treat, *Diplomatic Relations Between the United States and Japan, 1895-1905* (Stanford University, 1938); S. T. Wang, *The Margary Affair and the Chefoo Agreement* (London, 1940); W. W. Willoughby, *Foreign Rights and Interests in China* (Baltimore, 1920).

For Korea: H. N. Allen, *Things Korean* (New York, 1908); A. J. Brown, *The Mastery of the Far East* (New York, 1919); J. S. Gale, *Korea in Transition* (New York, 1909); Andrew J. Grajdanzev, *Modern Korea* (New York, 1944); J. H. Gubbins, *The Making of Modern Korea* (London, 1922); Homer C. Hulbert, *The Passing of Korea* (London, 1906); George M. McCune and Arthur L. Grey, Jr., *Korea Today* (Cambridge, 1950); George M. McCune and John A. Harrison (eds.), *Korean-American Relations: The Initial Period, 1883-1886* (Berkeley and Los Angeles, 1951); M. F. Nelson, *Korea and the Old Orders in Eastern Asia* (Baton Rouge, 1945); Cornelius Osgood, *The Koreans and Their Culture* (New York, 1951).

For Russia: Pauline Tompkins, *American-Russian Relations in the Far East* (New York, 1949); A. Yarmolinsky (ed.), *The Memoirs of Count Witte* (New York, 1921); E. H. Zabriskie, *American-Russian Rivalry in the Far East* (Philadelphia, 1946).

18

CHINA: THE FAILURE OF REFORM, 1894-1911

Reform Movement of 1898

China's defeat by Japan in 1894 and 1895 was the first event which impressed on any considerable number of the Chinese scholar-gentry the urgency of westernization.[1] Defeat by Japan was particularly galling, for the Chinese had long been accustomed to looking down on the Japanese as a people who owed whatever civilization they possessed to the Middle Kingdom. However, the fact that Japan could master Western techniques and use them against China with such effect gave zealous Chinese a sort of hope. What the Japanese could do the Chinese could, but it had better be done soon. The younger literati, especially those who were still taking the examinations or had recently qualified for office, were greatly stirred. Many memorials urging reform were sent in. Among the memorialists was Sun Yat-sen, one of a group of Cantonese who favored constitutional government. The time was not yet ripe, however, so that his proposal was considered much too radical and was denounced as treasonable. Sun then took part in a decidedly premature attempt to launch a revolution in Canton, and was forced to flee from China with a price on his head.

K'ang Yu-wei. Far more conspicuous among the advocates of reform in 1895 was K'ang Yu-wei, "the Modern Sage."[2] Like Sun, K'ang was a Cantonese. In fact, South China, which had had longer and closer contact with the West than any other section, had become a breeding ground for reformers and revolutionaries. K'ang had received an excellent classical education and in 1895 was to win the *chin shih* or highest degree in the examination system. Even before attaining that crown of formal scholarship, he had made a reputation as a textual critic and radical interpreter of Confucianism. In 1891 he produced a study of *The Forged Classics of the Wang Mang Period,* in which he set out to demonstrate that many of the texts on which *ku-wên* scholars placed reliance had been fabricated

[1] In this chapter the author has drawn heavily upon M. E. Cameron, *The Reform Movement in China, 1898-1912* (Stanford, 1931).

[2] See E. R. Hughes, *The Invasion of China by the Western World* (New York, 1938), chap. 3.

under the sponsorship of the usurper Wang Mang (r. 9-23 A.D.) to give sanction for his social and economic program. K'ang hoped, by striking at the authenticity of certain works, to rob conservatism of its intellectual foundations, and thus to open the way for a progressive-reformist interpretation of Confucianism. His second notable work, *Confucius as a Reformer,* published in 1897, portrayed the sage as a creative social thinker and prophet who had hoped to advance the world toward an age of universal brotherhood. K'ang insisted that Confucius' repeated assertions of respect for the good old days were simply a wise use of the end to justify the means. To win popular acceptance for radical ideas, Confucius had had to drape them decorously in the garments of antiquity. The presumption was that if Confucius were to return to life in the 1890's he would confound the orthodox by being a reformer with K'ang Yu-wei.

These views caused a great furore, K'ang's works were condemned by the government in 1897 and again in 1900, but he attracted many followers, of whom the most able and best known was Liang Ch'i-ch'ao. K'ang was not only a conspicuous if radical Confucian scholar but an energetic interpreter of the West to China. Using missionary literature and Japanese works, he secured a remarkably broad although necessarily somewhat shallow view of the development of the West. These ideas he then purveyed to Chinese readers in a series of works which presented certain object lessons drawn from the history of Europe and America. His writings stressed the history of European colonization in America and Africa, the decline of the Ottoman Empire, the growth of English constitutionalism, the career of Peter the Great, and of course, the reform of Japan. China, in danger of becoming like Turkey, should evolve a political system like that of Britain and urgently needed a ruler like Peter the Great to set the course toward fundamental reform, such as Japan was undergoing.

Reform Spirit Grows. Upon publication of the unfavorable terms of the Treaty of Shimonoseki, K'ang was in a favorable position to press his views, since he was one of the crowd of candidates assembled in Peking to take the examinations for the *chin shih* degree. He was already well known through his writings and through a school of Chinese and Western learning which he had opened in Canton in 1891, and he was the natural choice of the examination candidates as their spokesman to protest the treaty with Japan and propose reforms.

The Grand Memorial which K'ang drafted, and which was presented to the throne in December, 1895, was an ambitious proposal for all sorts of westernization to be effected forthwith by imperial decree. It ran the gamut from the establishment of reformatories to the setting up of a popularly elected advisory council to the throne. It is especially noteworthy that the Grand Memorial, emanating from a group trained under the old educational system, urged westernization of education, stress on technical subjects, and new examinations to fit the new curriculum. Only two Chinese institutions were strongly endorsed: Confucianism, which K'ang thought of as a progressive doctrine, and monarchy, since he expected to make his program effective through imperial backing. The Memorial was naïve in its grandiose scope and its faith in the efficacy of imperial edicts; but the young men who proposed it saw much to be done and little time to do it, and felt that events would not wait for some sort of gradual process to produce a new China. The higher officials did not share this sense of emergency and pigeonholed the Grand Memorial.

In the fall of 1895, K'ang organized the *Ch'iang Hsüeh Hui,* or Society for National Rejuvenation, with headquarters in Peking and branches in other cities. For a time, talk of reform was fashionable in some circles. Thus favored, the *Ch'iang Hsüeh Hui* had as members some young men of prominent families, was in touch with Timothy Richard,[3] and had the blessing of a few prominent officials. In 1896 it was denounced by conservatives and the Peking headquarters was closed. Hunan Province then became the center of reform activity. Chang Chih-tung, Viceroy of Hunan and Hupeh, seemed to favor westernization, and the Governor of Hunan, Ch'ên Pao-chên, was especially encouraging. A number of young scholars, intellectual disciples of K'ang, were already active there on behalf of the new learning; notable among them was Tan Ssŭ-t'ung, who was to be one of the martyrs of 1898. A South China Reform Association was established, for which Tan made many speeches, and Liang Ch'i-ch'ao was made chief lecturer in an Academy of Current Events.

The Hundred Days. While this sort of agitation and activity was going on among some of the younger scholars, leading officials were concentrating on what appeared to them to be the more immediately necessary activity of military reform. Japan's victory had revealed China's weakness and the "Battle of Concessions" was under way. With the major powers asking for railroad and mining concessions, boundary rectifications, leasehold, nonalienation agreements, and the right to make loans, the breakup of China seemed imminent.

What could save China from dismemberment? Army reform, or a broader program of westernization such as Japan had undergone? Who would initiate it and carry it out? Answers to these questions came in June, 1898, when the emperor himself came forward to lead what was subsequently known as "The Hundred Days of Reform." The emperor,

---

[3] See page 229.

though now fully of man's estate, was not completely free of the influence of his "August Aunt." He was eager to rule in actuality as well as name and had gathered about him a group of younger officials, who were colloquially referred to as the "Small Lad's Set" to distinguish them from the "Old Mother's Set," the established officeholders who still regarded the Empress Dowager as the center of power. The Empress Dowager was well aware of the emperor's desire for independence and continued to maneuver members of her coterie into key positions in which they could thwart and restrict any dangerous self-assertion by the emperor. For example on June 14, 1898, after the issuing of the first reform decree, T'zŭ Hsi was able to get Jung Lu named Viceroy of Chihli, with the best troops in China under his command.

By 1898 the emperor was so aroused by the plight of China that he resolved to make a great effort to fling off the restraints upon him and sponsor a program of change to save the empire from foreign domination. His tutor, Wêng T'ung-ho, had encouraged the emperor in a study of the West and had done a great deal to make him aware of the pressure of the foreign powers on China and the part which foreign techniques and methods might play in strengthening China against that pressure. The Empress Dowager disliked Wêng's influence and had seen to the abolition of the tutorship in 1896, but Wêng continued to have contact with and influence over his former pupil. Wêng had been greatly impressed by the ideas of K'ang Yu-wei, and had called his writing to the attention of the emperor. In 1898 the emperor asked K'ang to state his views on reform in the form of a memorial. The Empress Dowager, a thorough conservative, then arranged Wêng's dismissal from office, but Wêng had already brought the emperor and K'ang together, and these two reformers, the ruler of China and the outstanding radical intellectual of the day, were ready to act together in a frantic, hasty but altogether sincere effort to regenerate the country.

The Edict of June 11, 1898, which inaugurated the new program, is worthy of quotation in part, as the best indication of the emperor's earnestness and zeal.

> . . . The methods of government inaugurated by the Sung and Ming dynasties, upon investigation, reveal nothing that is of any practical use or that may be of advantage to us. In China, for instance, we have the ethics and doctrines of the sects of Taoism and Buddhism; do they at all agree with the tenets compounded by our five ancient Imperial Sages and three Kings? They are like summer to winter, at opposite extremes to one another. Changes must be made to accord with the necessities of the times. It is apparent that we must issue a plain and unvarnished decree on the subject so that all may understand our wishes.

Let this therefore be made known to one and all in the four corners of this Empire, from Prince to Duke, from highest to lowest among the officials of the capital and the provinces, from Court Minister to the most humble of our subjects—let them know that it is our earnest and sincere desire that one and all bend energetically to the duty of striving for higher things, to show all that they are men ambitious to succeed and to advance their country; let us, keeping in mind the morals of our sages and wise men, make them the basis on which to build on newer and more advantageous foundations. We must also select such subjects of Western knowledge as will keep us in touch with the times and diligently study them and practice them in order to place our country abreast with other countries. Let us cast off from us the empty, unpractical, and deceiving things which obstruct our forward progress, and strive with one-heartedness and energy to improve upon all things that we have learned; let us eliminate the crust of neglect that has accumulated on our system, and cast away the shackles which bind us. In a word, let us evolve useful things out of those which hitherto have been useless, and let us seek by able instructors to fashion the materials in our possession. With these objects in view let us strive toward advancement and progress.[4]

From June 11 until the coup d'état which ended the reform movement on September 22, the *Imperial Gazette* was full of appointments of new men to office. The emperor very naturally was turning to advisers who were in sympathy with his purposes and had some knowledge of the West. K'ang Yu-wei and Liang Ch'i-ch'ao were joined by a group of younger men led by Tan Ssŭ-t'ung. A number of more experienced officials also seemed to give the new course of action their blessing. When the reform movement was in full swing, Chang Chih-tung's celebrated tract, *Learn*,[5] appeared, and the reformers adopted it as a sort of party platform. In *Learn*, Chang stated his Neo-Confucian formula of combining Confucian morality and Western techniques, proclaimed his loyalty to the dynasty, and called for more honesty and more enlightenment on the part of officials. Chang, who was no radical at heart and moved with almost indecent haste to dissociate himself from the reform movement after the coup d'état, may well have meant *Learn* as argument for a more gradual and less drastic reform than that which K'ang and his associates were trying to carry through. Nevertheless *Learn* had tremendous influence and was a revelation to many of its readers of the arguments for adopting certain features of Western civilization.

[4] Quoted in M. E. Cameron, *The Reform Movement in China, 1898-1912* (Stanford, 1931), pp. 36-37.
[5] Available in English translation as *China's Only Hope*, translated by Samuel I. Woodbridge (New York, 1900).

CHINA: FAILURE OF REFORM, 1894-1911

The reforms which the emperor decreed under the guidance of the reform party covered a tremendous range. An imperial university was created with W.A.P. Martin of the T'ung Wên Kuan as head of the faculty. An elaborate hierarchy of schools was proposed. The civil service examinations were to be revised to include essays on "modern practical subjects." *The Chinese Progress,* a newspaper which Liang had been editing in Shanghai, became an official organ of the government, and Liang himself was put in charge of translating Occidental literature and preparing textbooks for the new schools. A Bureau of Agriculture, Arts and Commerce was created, to encourage scientific methods of farming and the use of laborsaving machinery. Technical education was to be expanded. A national militia was authorized. Provision for an annual budget and the abolition of sinecure posts were two projects which proved peculiarly offensive to many old-fashioned mandarins. Action against certain obstructionist officials, and the proposal that Manchus should enter useful employment were the last straws. The conservative opposition which rallied around Tz'ŭ Hsi began to importune her to render the emperor powerless and resume control of the state.

Tz'ŭ Hsi Triumphs. The emperor and his advisers were aware of their danger and resolved to put the Empress Dowager out of the way before she could dispose of them. They therefore decided to call on Yüan Shih-k'ai (1859-1916), who had trained a modern army corps in Chihli, to provide them with the military force necessary to carry out their plan. (Yüan, who at this time was provincial judge of Chihli, had risen from humble beginnings. He had secured official rank by purchase, not by examination, and had been a protégé of Li Hung-chang, representing China in Korea before the Sino-Japanese War. Since the war, Yüan had won the backing of Jung Lu, who was certain to be on Tz'ŭ Hsi's side. It was believed, however, that Yüan, as a careerist and an upstart, might serve the reformers' purpose if offered substantial rewards.) Yüan was afterwards accused of betraying the emperor, but denied the charge. Whatever the story behind the known facts may be, the following events occurred. Jung Lu took the railroad (a Western innovation which in this case greatly facilitated action against the Westernizers) to the capital to see Tz'ŭ Hsi, gathered his troops, and on September 22 supported with military force the dramatic scene in which Tz'ŭ Hsi made the emperor a state prisoner and resumed the regency. K'ang Yu-wei and Liang Ch'i-ch'ao had escaped, the former to Hong Kong and the latter to Japan, but T'an Ssŭ-t'ung calmly awaited arrest, saying that blood must flow before China could be rejuvenated. He and five other young reformers were summarily executed. Reports of the emperor's ill health in the *Imperial*

Gazette suggested that he too might be liquidated, but formal inquiries by foreign diplomats and rumblings of discontent in South China apparently led Tz'ŭ Hsi to think better of this project. A number of officials who had supported the emperor's program or recommended new officials to the emperor were dismissed or demoted. Chang Chih-tung washed his hands of responsibility for the young Hunan reformers and kept his post, and Jung Lu and Yüan Shih-k'ai were greatly rewarded for their roles in thwarting the plot against the Empress Dowager.

Most of the reforms decreed by the young emperor were rescinded. Almost the only enactment of the reform period in which the Empress Dowager showed any interest was the recruiting of a militia; she continued to urge provincial officials to pardon bandits and urge them to turn their talents to the defense of the country. The rank and file of Chinese officials, who had been confounded and harassed by the barrage of reform edicts, now settled back in relieved anticipation of the years of comfortable conservatism which the return to power of Tz'ŭ Hsi seemed to foretell.

There had been no widespread popular understanding of the need for such reform and therefore no public sentiment to support the program and animate officials in putting it into effect. Most officeholders, who had been called on for such unlikely and unprecedented action as the founding of modern schools, the purchase of machinery, or the keeping of accounts, did nothing in particular and did it very well indeed. Ignorance, inertia, and unenlightened self-interest nullified even the most important and urgent proposals. The Hundred Days, as the period of imperial reform is called, nevertheless constituted a major portent despite its apparent failure. The emperor and his advisers were aware that China was in a state of emergency, her very existence threatened by the Western powers. As K'ang Yu-wei later said of the attitude of the emperor in 1898 "... he saw his country about to sink in the earth, about to be buried in ruins, about to burst like an egg, about to be divided up, about to mortify, about to be torn in shreds, about to become like India or Anam (sic), or Burmah —a dependent of another Power!" [6]

Japan by prompt and conscious westernization had escaped this fate; China must hasten to do likewise or be taken captive. Hence the valiant effort of the young emperor and his advisers to do what they thought necessary to save China in the face of opposition, the extent and character of which they well understood. As events developed, China was not partitioned at the end of the nineteenth century. The "Battle of Concessions" rolled to a stop in 1899, chiefly because there were too many would-be partitioners. In 1900 the Chinese were to turn to another and

---

[6] Kang Yeu Wei, "The Reform of China and the Revolution of 1898," in *Contemporary Review*, August, 1899.

very different technique of opposition to foreign influence, the crude and violent antiforeignism manifested in the Boxer Rising. But after the Boxer episode the pendulum swung back again, and the Manchu government under the leadership of Tz'ŭ Hsi herself undertook a program of reform which, despite face-saving denials, was virtually a resurrection of the plans of 1898.

The Empress Dowager's Conversion to Reform

The Boxer Rising, discussed in detail elsewhere,[7] was a bitter fiasco for the Chinese government. The attempt to "drive the foreigners into the sea" was a form of midsummer madness, as the wiser Chinese officials had realized. However the Empress Dowager, hostile to the West, superstitious, and fearful of the growing influence of Prince Tuan, leader of the Boxers and father of the newly chosen Heir Apparent, decided to risk the future of the dynasty on this popular but ignorant and ill-directed antiforeign movement. It was a bad risk, but after it was over the Manchus were still on the Dragon Throne, though through no merit or wisdom of their own. The great Chinese viceroys, Chang Chih-tung and Liu K'un-i had treated Boxerism as a rebellion against the dynasty rather than a government-sponsored movement and had suppressed it in their jurisdictions. The foreign powers, realizing that there was nothing to substitute for the Manchus, had also accepted the "rebellion" thesis as politically convenient, if not precisely accurate. However, when the Empress Dowager and the court fled from Peking in August, 1900, as the foreign troops entered the city, they must have felt that they had misplayed the game and that all was lost. In 1901, while waiting the verdict of the Occidental states upon the Manchu dynasty, the Empress Dowager performed a *volte-face* and announced her intention of adopting a new line of policy, "radical reform."

Clearly the Manchu ruling house was in a bad way. With its mandate nearly exhausted, the Empress Dowager was now ready to resort to the drastic procedure of following a program strangely like the reform of 1898 which she had publicly repudiated, but which she was to carry on with more vigor and with comparatively effective support from officials and some influential groups of opinion. During the next decade the Manchu reforms and the criticisms and promises of the revolutionaries competed for Chinese support. In the end, outright revolution swept the dynasty away, but not until it had at least formulated and in some cases gone some distance with reform projects in most of the areas of Chinese life in which organized, formal westernization seemed an obvious course of action.

[7] See p. 296 f.

After the Boxer Rising, the dynasty sadly lacked competent officials. Older Chinese viceroys and Manchu advisers such as Li Hung-chang and Jung Lu died in the early 1900's. Chang Chih-tung lasted the longest of any of the old guard, outliving the Empress Dowager herself by a year. As the older leadership disappeared, the dynasty was in no position to find younger, more useful partisans. The Empress Dowager was unwilling to call on the exiled K'ang Yu-wei and his followers, while many still younger Chinese had imbibed the revolutionary doctrine that China could not revive as long as the Manchus occupied the throne. The most energetic reforming official of the period was the careerist Yüan Shih-k'ai, and he was dismissed by the Regent after Tz'ŭ Hsi's death. He returned to office in 1911 only to preside over the demise of the Manchu house. The Empress Dowager's formula for saving the dynasty from collapse was imitation of the procedures by which, in the latter part of the nineteenth century, Japan had earned release from international inferiority. This copying of the Japanese copying of the West was unlikely to be carried on with any profound understanding of the significance and effects of such a policy. The Empress Dowager and some of her advisers seem at times to have regarded Western learning and Western methods as a body of magic the practice of which might strengthen China and prolong the life of the dynasty. The first tentative moves toward westernization by government edict came between 1901 and 1905, but Japan's victory over Russia gave the Chinese reform movement a new impetus which lasted until Tz'ŭ Hsi's death in 1908. The period from 1901 to 1911 may therefore be conveniently divided into three stages. Before 1904 the new policy was announced and a few changes decreed; between 1904 and 1908 reform was carried on with greater vigor and on a broader front; and after Tz'ŭ Hsi's death in November, 1908, came rapid decline, with stupid Manchu princelings trying to rule the state, with mounting dissatisfaction, and with a rapidly growing revolutionary movement.

Manchu Reforms

Education. The emphasis on changes in education during the Manchu reform period is indicative of the new seriousness with which the leaders of China took the related problems of contacts with the West and national revival. It was clearly not enough to appropriate certain Western tricks and gadgets; an effort to penetrate more deeply to the secrets of Western knowledge must be made, and this meant a change in the Chinese educational system. To lay hands on the traditional content and methods of learning and transform them in the name of imitation of Japanese and Western example was to attack that very core of Chinese culture which earlier Chinese reformers, such as Tsêng Kuo-fan, had been concerned to protect. Education had been primarily a preparation for public office. The government had not maintained any system of public schools, but it had sponsored a system of examinations to test Confucian learning. Those who passed the examinations were "superior men" who became members of the ruling class.

The examination system had been one of the most durable and most remarkable of human institutions, but at the beginning of the twentieth century it was corrupt and, what was more significant, outmoded. The government desperately needed a new sort of official to meet new problems and therefore it needed a new sort of education to produce the new sort of official. It was also ready to go farther and follow the Japanese example of general schooling to produce a whole population with book learning. In 1901, modifications in the examination system were decreed, the outlines of a public school system were drawn up, and a few new-style schools which taught Western as well as Chinese knowledge were established. Students began to go abroad, moved as much by curiosity as by obedience to governmental exhortation. In the meantime, Chang Chih-tung was at work on a set of full-scale regulations for education, based upon Japan's educational regulations. This new educational system, proclaimed in 1904, was grandiose and comprehensive on paper, although exceedingly difficult to transform into reality. The plans called for a national Board of Education and a Commissioner of Education in each province, and for a hierarchy of schools from kindergartens through the imperial university. The most important and dramatic change was the abolition of the civil service examinations, which were to cease in 1906.

In practice, real progress in educational change was made only in Chihli Province under Yüan Shih-k'ai and the Hu provinces under Chang Chih-tung. The lack of finances and of teachers, the obstructionism or indifference of officials, the intransigence of students, and the vacillations of official policy proved to be the chief obstacles. The Board of Education exercised little control, thus allowing local officials to make or break the new schools. Many of them dealt with the issue by rechristening existing schools and installing indigent and unqualified relatives as teachers. Others built new buildings but put them to no real use. High schools were established much more readily than elementary schools, since they seemed to confer more prestige on their sponsors and on those who taught in them. Teachers prepared to offer the new subjects of study were exceedingly rare. A few who had been educated in mission schools were employed. Some Japanese were imported, their brains were picked, and after a year or two, their lectures were recited by their former students who were now "qualified" instructors. There was no national provision for financing and the local officials, who regarded themselves as having no free funds for this or any other reform, usually charged tuition. Education for women, neglected in the original program, made some headway with missionary support, and in 1907 regulations for primary and normal schools for women were promulgated. It is very hard to judge the results of these educational reforms, either qualitatively or quantitatively. By 1910, perhaps something over 1,500,000 children were in school, though what they were being taught was a very uncertain matter. Probably most schools were poor, and gave adequate training in neither Chinese learning nor Western subjects—but whatever else they learned, the students became politically conscious and inclined to agitation. To the Manchus, a little modern learning began to look like a dangerous thing.

Obviously this new and unformed educational program would not for many years be able to produce the new type of candidates for public office which the dynasty so sorely needed. It therefore urged education abroad. Thousands of young Chinese went to Japan, especially after 1905, since it was the nearest and easiest spot in which one could get the "new learning." Most of the Chinese students in Japan learned more about the desirability of revolution against the Manchus than they did about modern science or anything else. They returned to China converts to the reformist ideas of K'ang Yu-wei, or, in more cases, to the republican program of Sun Yat-sen, both of whom had their headquarters in Japan. Hoping to find a safer environment for foreign study than Japan, the Manchu government in 1908 worked out a plan with the American government for the use of the surplus Boxer indemnity collected by the United States to defray the cost of educating Chinese students in the United States, but the numbers of Chinese students who went to the United States or to Europe in the closing years of Manchu rule were small. The government found returned students very hard to handle. They were given examinations and awarded degrees, but they were discontented with the positions open to them, such as opportunities to teach in the new schools. The dynasty had sent abroad prospective mandarins; it got back vindictive critics and/or convinced revolutionaries, who had great influence over the students in the new schools in China who had not been abroad but who had already begun to learn distaste for the dynasty and desire for change.

Army and Navy. The Manchus were eager to build Western-style defense forces, not only to repulse Western pressure but also to suppress rebellion. Here Yüan Shih-k'ai took the lead. Since he was not a product of the Confucian scholarly tradition, he did not have its prejudice against the military career. In 1896 he had organized a force trained by German officers; this force he took with him to Shantung and later to Chihli, when he became viceroy there in 1901 and succeeded Li Hung-chang in charge of China's foreign affairs. Until 1906, army reform continued in the hands of viceroys and governors as it had been ever since the suppression of the Taiping Rebellion, and Yüan and Chang Chih-tung were particularly active in developing modern provincial armies. Yüan formed a very competent force, the Peiyang army, which was well disciplined and well paid. He even showed his personal interest in this enterprise by appearing in public in Western-style army uniform, in which most Chinese officials would not have wanted to be caught dead or alive!

The year 1907 introduced a trend toward reaction at the capital, the most conspicuous feature of which was the move to deify Confucius, as a sort of counterblast to westernization and cultural compromise. A part of this reactionary movement was an attempt by conservatives to curb the independence of the reforming officials in the provinces, most particularly of Yüan Shih-k'ai. In 1907 Yüan, Chang and other provincial leaders were required to surrender control of their armies to the Board of War. These armies were not likely to be effective against foreign attack, and in 1911-12 they certainly proved unable to save the Manchus. Some of them went over to the revolutionaries while the Peiyang force, still loyal to Yüan, underwrote his skilful political maneuvering which resulted in his selection as Provisional President. After 1905 the dynasty contemplated the development of a modern fleet but accomplished little. Altogether no real national defense forces were shaped in these years, but there was a significant growth of military spirit and a change in the old attitude of scorn toward soldiers.

Beginnings of Political Reform. From the mid-nineteenth century on, increasing numbers of influential Chinese had advocated westernization in industry, defense, and education. The question now was raised: What about Western political institutions? Could they, and should they, also be adapted to Chinese use? No matter what variety of Western political structure is examined, whether republic or constitutional monarchy, it was markedly different from the Confucian bureaucratic regime which the Chinese had evolved. The Chinese formula had been government by superior men, chosen by examination, and appointed by the emperor who was responsible to Heaven for giving good governance to "all under Heaven." Could popular participation in government, in the Western manner, be reconciled with Chinese political ideas? There was evidence to suggest that constitutionalism was one of the devices which especially gave Western states their peculiar strength. All the great powers of the West had constitutional governments, with the exception of Russia which made its first and very slight testimonial to the necessity of constitutionalism in 1906 after it had lost the war with Japan. The Empress Dowager therefore became an advocate of constitutionalism, although with a very limited idea of what it implied. She was seeking "a despotism strict combined with absolute equality," a regime in which the throne could authorize popular participation without surrendering its prerogative. This sleight-of-hand trick the Japanese seemed to have performed in the Constitution of 1889, and in this area of reform, as in others, Japan became the model.

Although the government of Japan was sufficiently conservative, Japan's triumph in 1905 aroused a spirit of nationalistic liberalism all over Asia, and not the least in China. The dynasty therefore hastened to forestall agitation for popular government by moves toward the granting of a parliament of sorts. In 1906 a commission was sent abroad to study foreign governments. It preferred the British and German governments which, though they certainly bore little resemblance to each other, both combined hereditary monarchy with elective institutions; but the commission found in Japan the example most near to hand and most susceptible of imitation. In a notable edict,[8] issued on September 1, 1906, the Empress Dowager expressed approval of "a constitutional polity in which the supreme authority shall be vested in the crown, but all questions of government shall be considered by a popular assembly." The edict went on to point out, however, that "the constitution is not prepared, and the people, too, are not properly equipped with the necessary knowledge." The first move, therefore, was to be a reorganization of the official system. After a few years, when popular education and the study of other governments had advanced further, a form of constitutional government would be introduced.

The reform of the official system, which this edict promised, was an important phase of the drive for centralization which was one of the chief objectives of the Manchu reform program. The Peking boards were reorganized first, and the central government emerged with ten ministries. This change was followed by a grand reshuffling of posts in Peking and great agitation among metropolitan officials, about 1,400 of whom lost their positions. The new appointments included too many Manchus and too many conservatives to be regarded as a blow struck for progress. Provincial government was also to be overhauled, but it was ticklish and difficult business to interfere in the autonomy of the provincial units, and the few changes that were brought about failed to increase the relative power and prestige of the central government.

[8] Quoted in Cameron, *op. cit.*, pp. 103-4.

Preparations for a Parliament. The government also began experimentation with advisory legislative bodies as preparation for constitutionalism, following the example of Japan where various assemblies of assorted composition had been formed to train in parliamentary methods the men who later took their part in the Diet proper. As the plans for China took shape, there were first to be consultative provincial assemblies; later members of these assemblies were to serve in a consultative National Assembly. The scheme was reasonable and realistic in a sense, but was to prove extremely difficult to carry out on schedule in a country where the dynasty was weak and unpopular and the opposition increasingly bold and vociferous. In fact the Manchus were neatly caught: paper promises with no substantial reform to confirm them gave the revolutionaries justification for asserting the insincerity and inefficiency of the dynasty; actual experimentation with popular assemblies gave the opponents of the dynasty a new and most effective sounding board for their criticisms. Reform too fast or reform to slow—either was apt to be fatal to the Manchus.

However, the Manchus went ahead with plans for the introduction of their version of constitutional government. The "Principles of the Constitution" were proclaimed in August, 1908. They were very much in the spirit of Ito's Japanese Constitution of 1889. Their conservative, monarchical tone made it clear that the Empress Dowager had no intention of transforming China into a democracy. Her purpose was "to conserve the power of the sovereign and protect the officials and people." The constitution was to be a magnanimous grant by the throne, not a concession wrung from it. At the time of the announcement of the "Principles," the government adopted a nine-year schedule of reforms to make the country ready for constitutional government by 1917—a year which, for the Manchus, never came. The death of the emperor and the Empress Dowager in 1908 threatened to interrupt these developments, but the new Regent, Prince Ch'un, though weak and biased, carried on with the pre-parliamentary schemes more punctiliously than he did with some other types of reform.

Detailed regulations for provincial assemblies and the announcement that they would convene within a year had been issued before Tz'ŭ Hsi's death. The rules provided for a silk-gowned, conservative franchise, and the assemblies were to have debate as their only real function. This was wise enough, since almost no one in China knew anything about elections and parliaments. However, despite the dynasty's precautions, the assemblies turned out to be intransigent and critical, perhaps because many of the members were returned students. The assemblies at one and the same time were defenders of provincial rights against the central government and advocates of the immediate granting of a full-fledged national parliament.

To swell the importunate chorus, the National Assembly met in Peking in October, 1910. It consisted of 100 members chosen by the throne and 100 selected by the provincial assemblies. Although it had no power of decision and was debarred from discussing the adoption of a constitution, it urged the telescoping of the nine-year program, which was already in arrears. In November the government yielded, advanced the date for parliament to 1913, and set up a three-year program of reforms. The government dissolved the Assembly in January, 1911, but its members, having tasted the delights of setting policy, were loath to remain inactive. The government had to reassemble it in the fall of 1911, so that it was on hand at the fall of the dynasty.

In general, the effort at gradual governmental reform failed. The dynasty was not enthusiastic about real liberalization and was willing to try "popular" government only if it contributed to the strengthening of the dynasty. Desperation rather than understanding and conviction inspired the movement toward constitutionalism. The opponents of the Manchus were quick to accuse them of duplicity and of uttering liberal sentiments to deceive, but there is little evidence that the dynasty ever proclaimed its intention to do more than provide some machinery through which it could more readily ascertain and evaluate public opinion. The new nationalism which developed so rapidly in the years just preceding 1911 was strongly anti-Manchu; and there was probably no way in which the Manchus, ever more feeble, inept, and unpopular, could have come to terms with the spreading desire for rapid political change, especially since it involved, for many Chinese, desire for a change of rulers.

Opium Program. The most successful of the Manchu reforms was the antiopium program, because here governmental purpose and public opinion were united. Most Chinese knew little of constitutions or juries or modern schools, but they did know the effects of the habitual use of opium. The habit had spread rapidly in China in the later Manchu period. The high point of importation of opium was reached in 1888, but the subsequent falling off simply reflected the extent to which Chinese opium was replacing foreign opium. The Chinese government was disinclined to check the growth of opium in China, since that would only mean that more Indian opium would be imported. Since the Indian trade was secured by treaty (opium had been legalized in 1858), China could not stop it. As a final difficulty, opium, both foreign and domestic, was eminently taxable and brought in vitally needed revenue.

The whole situation seemed to be in an impasse until early in the twentieth century, when a real public opinion against opium developed. Missionaries and returned students especially attacked the habit, and British sentiment against it became more effective with the coming into power of a Liberal government in Britain in 1906. In May, 1906, the Chinese government decided to try a consolidated tax as a means of choking off the production of opium, but this procedure was overshadowed a few months later by a prohibition scheme. The new regulations owed something to the program of regulation looking to ultimate suppression, which the Japanese had put into force in Formosa, but China had one problem which Formosa did not—the widespread cultivation of the opium poppy. A ten-year license period for poppy growers was set up, with reduction each year. To stop smoking, a licensing system on the Formosan model was instituted, no new licenses were to be granted and there was to be gradual reduction of the amount allowed to habitual and licensed smokers, with the exception that those over sixty years old could continue to have the same amount. Antiopium pills were to be issued. Opium dens were banned, but retail shops were to be allowed to remain open for ten years. The provincial authorities were made responsible for the enforcement of these regulations, while the central government undertook to negotiate with Great Britain about the foreign supply of opium.

British opposition to the opium habit notwithstanding, the British government felt no disposition to impoverish the Indian opium farmers by reducing export to China unless the Manchu government actually reduced the cultivation of opium by the Chinese. To find out whether the antiopium program was more than a set of paper regulations, the British government made a series of surveys in China from 1907 to 1911, the reports of which constitute the most impressive evidence of the surprising degree of success which this particular reform achieved.[9] The report of the first British tour of inspection in 1907 was so favorable that the British government agreed to a three-year trial of a plan of reduction of British opium traffic proportionate to the annual reduction in the cultivation of the poppy in China. If successful, this arrangement might be renewed for seven years more. The progress of opium suppression in China continued to be impressive, although there was variation between provinces, depending on the nature of the local problem, the strength of local opinion, the economic interests involved, and the zeal of the officials. By 1911 in provinces where the fields had formerly been white with blossoms, the poppies had been cut down, and bonfires of opium equipment testified to the state of sentiment in many parts of the country. In May of that year, Great Britain showed confidence in the success of the program by

[9] See Sir Alexander Hosie, *On the Trail of the Opium Poppy* (London, 1914).

renewing the Anglo-Chinese agreement for proportionate reduction until 1917.

However, the antiopium crusade created many problems for the dynasty, which in a sense was sacrificing economic advantage to moral principles. The elimination of opium meant loss of government revenue. It also brought about serious economic dislocation in the many areas of China where farmers had grown opium; the resulting crop had large value and small bulk, and was thus transportable under the poor conditions of communication that prevailed. Many of the popular opium "cures" created another major problem, since they killed the taste for opium only by substituting cocaine and morphia.

After the fall of the Manchus, the campaign against opium faded out as transient regimes and greedy officials encouraged the growing of the poppy as an eminently taxable crop, but the great achievements of the five-year period of 1906-11 demonstrated what could be accomplished in China when the throne and the people were of one mind, as they were on almost no other issue of these years.

Currency. The Manchus sponsored a number of miscellaneous changes, many of which got no further than the pages of the *Imperial Gazette.* An effort was made to bring order out of the chaos of currencies. In the latter part of the nineteenth century, money included copper cash, new-style coins from provincial mints, such as those opened by Chang Chih-tung, paper bank notes, bar silver, and the *tael,* an uncoined unit of value, which had variable forms. The whole question of Chinese currency was involved with the international value of silver in relation to gold. Various proposals for a currency standard were advanced, among them a project for a gold exchange standard worked out by Professor Jenks of Cornell. In April, 1911, the Manchus signed a contract with the four-power consortium for a currency reform loan, but no solution to the currency problem had been reached by the time of the dynasty's collapse.

Law and Justice. Reforms in China's legal and judicial system were attempted, with the purpose of getting rid of extraterritoriality. As China was westernized—even superficially—the traditional legal system became inadequate, but the real pressure for legal reform came not so much from Chinese desire for Western-style law as from the declaration of the United States, Great Britain, and Japan in the commercial treaties of 1902 and 1903 that they would surrender their extraterritorial rights when the state of Chinese laws and courts satisfied them. Whatever sort of law was desirable for the Chinese themselves, the Chinese government was going to have to produce a reasonable facsimile of Western justice before it could hope to revise the key provision of the "unequal treaties." The old Chinese system was certainly open to criticism, and the Chinese themselves traditionally avoided courts and tried to settle their disputes by private compromise. Officials took bribes, witnesses were detained, torture was used to extort testimony, and punishments were very harsh. In 1905 a mitigation of punishment was decreed. Chinese officials were assigned to study Western law, both criminal and civil. A code concerning merchants and company law, which showed the influence of English commercial law, was approved. In 1906 a draft code of criminal procedure, including the use of juries and lawyers, was presented. It was rejected by the government, perhaps wisely, since this sort of promiscuous borrowing was apt to produce a court system in which Occidentals would feel more at home, but Chinese less. Later moves toward legal reform under the Manchus reflected less British influence and more inclination to copy Japan's version of Western law and the systems of Continental Europe. In 1907 judicial functions were separated from other governmental activities and a separate system of courts was established. A new criminal code based on Japanese law was issued in 1911 and was continued in force by Yüan Shih-k'ai after the revolution.

Discrimination. The popularity of the dynasty might well have been increased by the elimination of the distinction between Manchus and Chinese. The privileged position of the Manchus was irritating to the Chinese, and the value of the Manchu banners as hereditary fighting forces had become virtually nil. The Empress Dowager removed the prohibition on intermarriage between Manchus and Chinese and, in 1907, at the instance of the liberal Manchu official, Tuan Fang, decreed that the pensions to the bannermen were to cease and that they were to receive individual farms. No aspect of Prince Ch'un's rule as regent was more unwise than his reversal of this policy. He hastened to assure his fellow Manchus that their pensions would continue and showed marked favoritism to Manchus in appointments to high posts at a time when the Manchus needed to take on protective coloring and identify themselves with the Chinese in every way possible.

Finance. One vitally necessary reform, which the Manchus were unable to carry through, was financial reorganization. The financial system of the Chinese government was the marvel of any Westerner who got a close view of it. Corruption, of course, was not unknown in the West, but at least Occidental governments had developed practices of budgeting, accurate accounting, and fixed salaries. In China an obligation to one's family greater than to one's country, approximate rather than precise methods of handling revenue, and token salaries supplemented by squeeze added up to a financial system which was no system at all. Only the

Imperial Maritime Customs, staffed with foreign administrators, was run on a Western "business basis"; but its good example did not, Confucian theory to the contrary, have any noticeable effect on Chinese officials. Since the middle of the nineteenth century the financial demands on the central government had increased far more than its income. Costs of suppressing rebellions, indemnities for lost wars, and expenses of reform all called for additional revenue. The Manchus were not sufficiently beloved to dare to impose new taxes. That way lay mass rebellion. To attempt to stop corruption and corral for the central government some of the funds which officials pocketed would turn the official class against the dynasty, and that it could not afford.

A Summing Up

If many reforms were stillborn or feeble, it was in part because the government lacked the money to do more than issue edifying regulations in the *Imperial Gazette*. Somehow the Manchus had to reform the empire without cost, or fall. The financial problem was an essential test of the strength of the dynasty, which here ran head-on into provincialism, long-established corrupt practice, and general anti-Manchu sentiment. The total result of the Manchu reform program is at first view not too impressive, but the modifications which were projected have an importance beyond their immediate effectiveness or ineffectiveness. They were indications of a great psychological change in China, a greater receptivity to Western ideas and a belief in Western methods as a necessary therapy. However, the throne's hope that westernization would result in a centralized, peaceful Manchu empire was vain. China did not become another "new Japan." Instead of controlled, deliberate reform from the top, there came revolution from below which overturned the Manchus and led to a prolonged period of chaotic change.

SUGGESTED READINGS

The most detailed study of this period is Meribeth E. Cameron, *The Reform Movement in China, 1898-1912* (Stanford, 1931). Other works which deal with the period in general terms are: E. T. Williams, *China Yesterday and Today* (New York, 1929); Paul H. Reinsch, *Intellectual and Political Currents in the Far East* (Boston, 1911); George H. Blakeslee (ed.), *China and the Far East* (New York, 1910); J. O. P. Bland and E. Backhouse, *China Under the Empress Dowager* (Philadelphia, 1910); E. R. Hughes, *The Invasion of China by the Western World* (New York, 1938); K. S. Latourette, *The Chinese, Their History and Culture* (2 vols., 3d ed., New York, 1946), Vol. I, chap. 12.

Chang Chih-tung's *Learn* has been translated into English by Samuel I. Woodbridge under the title *China's Only Hope* (New York, 1900); Wen Ching (Lim

Boon-king), *The Chinese Crisis from Within* (London, 1901) is a work by a disciple of K'ang Yu-wei. Information on various aspects of the period will be found in W. A. P. Martin, *A Cycle of Cathay* (New York, 1897); Timothy Richard, *Forty-five Years in China* (New York, 1916); Sir A. Hosie, *On the Trail of the Opium Poppy* (2 vols., London, 1914); H. B. Morse, *The Trade and Administration of the Chinese Empire* (London, 1908); Lin Yutang, *A History of the Press and Public Opinion in China* (Shanghai, 1937). Arthur W. Hummel (ed.), *Eminent Chinese of the Ch'ing Period* (2 vols., Washington, 1943, 1944) provides valuable biographical sketches of the chief persons of this period.

19

THE UNITED STATES AS A PACIFIC POWER

The Growth of a Basic Policy

In the late years of the eighteenth century, following the winning of American independence, traders and merchants from the United States began to trade at Canton, the only Chinese port then open to foreign commerce. Furs from the Pacific Coast were traded with great profit for native teas and silks. Later the furs were superseded in importance by such items as hides and tallow from California together with ginseng and sandalwood—to mention but a few of the staples. From the very beginning, American merchants in Canton had sought equality of commercial opportunity. In other words, the fundamental policy of the United States in the Far East was commercial in character. By 1898 that policy had all but achieved a fixed and definite form. Its aims included, besides the commercial, such points as the following: (1) no acquisition of Far Eastern territory for the United States; (2) the development of an East Asia sufficiently strong of itself to resist European aggression; and (3) the restriction of Oriental immigration into the United States. Summed up, American policy was one of trade, friendship, and peace, "but you fellows stay at home, we don't want you here." [1]

Early Relations with China

For many years following the establishment of the American-China trade, the main objective pursued by the Americans was the securing of conditions as favorable as those enjoyed by their competitors, at that time chiefly British. From 1840 on, the Asiatic policy of the United States was directed toward winning the lion's share of the apparently insatiable markets of the East, especially China. Already American products had made substantial strides but, until their superiority was clearly established, it was paramount that the doors to this great market be kept open and free from political domination by other powers.

[1] A. W. Griswold, *The Far Eastern Policy of the United States* (New York, 1938), p. 8.

First Treaty Sets Policy. The first successful treaty negotiated in eastern Asia by the United States was concluded with Siam in 1833 by Edmund Roberts, a New Hampshire seafaring and mercantile man. The treaty is significant because it struck the keynote of future American commercial policy in the East; that is, it sought to put the United States on a most-favored-nation basis thereby insuring equality of commercial opportunity for American nationals.

The position of American traders in China in those early days was neither happy nor secure. Seeking to improve their lot, these pioneers of commerce appealed to their government for more efficient consular service, but Washington turned a deaf ear. Undismayed, they sought the appointment of a commissioner who could negotiate a treaty with China that would improve the unsatisfactory conditions of their position.

Revived American Interest in China

The actual outbreak of hostilities between Great Britain and China in 1839 finally directed the attention of the American people to China, toward which they had been for long most apathetic. There were several reasons for this new attitude. For one thing, it was popularly believed that Great Britain was the aggressor, that it was trying to force opium upon an unwilling China. Anglophobia was still strong; many Americans vividly remembered the War of 1812. Furthermore, the interest of groups other than those previously active in China, viz., the mercantile and shipping interests of New England and the Middle Atlantic states, was aroused. Cotton growers of the South began to see great potentialities in the Chinese market. Then, too, American Protestant missionaries had been laboring in China since 1830 on an increasingly active scale. Their reports attracted notice, especially since they attacked the evils of the opium traffic.[2]

Finally in 1840-41, Congress took cognizance of a request from the Americans at Canton for naval assistance and the appointment of a commissioner to negotiate a treaty with China by studying the whole question of American relations with the Chinese. The first part of the request was granted when the American East Indian squadron under Commodore Lawrence Kearny was sent to Chinese waters.

China Adopts Policy of Equal Treatment of Foreigners. Following the completion of the Treaty of Nanking between Great Britain and

---

[2] T. Dennett, *Americans in Eastern Asia* (New York, 1922), p. 102. This standard work was relied upon heavily in the preparation of this chapter.

China in 1842, Commodore Kearny expressed the hope in a letter to the governor of Canton that American commercial interests would be placed on a most-favored-nation basis. The governor's reply was most encouraging. Not long thereafter the Chinese voluntarily opened Canton to all foreigners on an equal basis. This was the commencement of a policy to which China long adhered, i.e., most-favored-nation treatment. It was based upon China's practice of considering all foreigners equal in that all were barbarian rascals and, secondly, was grounded on the very sensible assumption that such a practice would prevent any one power from getting the upper hand on China. The most-favored-nation clause in relation to China made its first formal appearance in the British Supplementary Treaty of 1843.

Meanwhile, President John Tyler in response to a strong popular opinion requested Congress, in a message dated December 30, 1842, to appropriate funds for a special commissioner to China. $40,000 was voted, and the man chosen for this important task was Caleb Cushing, a congressman from Massachusetts. An account of his mission and its successful culmination in the Treaty of Wanghia, July 3, 1844, which contained most-favored-nation and extraterritorial clauses, has already been given.[3]

China Trade Prospers. With the improvement of their position in China thus accomplished, Americans began increasingly to develop the opportunities of the China trade. Missionaries became quite active and performed a number of worth-while services. Unfortunately, not all the Americans who descended upon China in growing numbers after 1844 were of such excellent character as the missionaries and the better class of merchants. Indeed many were rascally adventurers who seriously injured the reputation of the United States among the Chinese. Another deterrent to good Sino-American relations occurred after the Civil War when Congress adopted restrictive immigration policies toward the Chinese which culminated in Chinese exclusion.

The appearance of the swift American clipper ships in the fifties and sixties captured for the United States an impressive share of the China trade and did much to found American fortunes which were invested in the growing industrial revolution then occurring in the United States.

The increasing interest and activity of Americans in China led inevitably to the involvement of the United States in related questions of international politics.[4] The American government was under pressure from both commercial and religious interests to bring about a wider opening up of China than then existed. The other powers interested in China

---

[3] See Chapter 10.
[4] Dennett, *op. cit.*, p. 181.

were also anxious to win greater opportunities, but the danger from the American point of view was that in so doing they might tend to win exclusive privileges. Therefore, the United States had to take precautions that no other power should secure such an ascendancy that the American position would be jeopardized. Thus, the territorial integrity of China became a matter of paramount importance to the United States. It should be noted in this connection that Caleb Cushing had foreseen the importance to the United States of the continued independence of China and that the able Humphrey Marshall, who served as American Commissioner to China for a year beginning in 1853, was also of this opinion.

Early Relations with Japan

Although the American Civil War was to check seriously all activities of the United States in the Far East, the decade beginning in 1850 was one of intense American activity in this region. Not only did American ties with China become closer as a result of the activities of the commercial and religious groups, but interest was also manifested in annexation of the Hawaiian Islands, and Commodore Perry succeeded in reopening Japan. The American people at this time were in an expansionist frame of mind. The successful acquisition of California, to which thousands of Americans flocked, and the equally happy settlement of the Oregon question had combined to place the American people securely on the shores of the Pacific. It was only natural that they should direct their gaze across the vast waters of the Pacific toward the Far East.

Some Protagonists of American Leadership in the Pacific

Perry and Seward. Two men, above all others, were particularly inspired by the prospect of American leadership in the Pacific. They were Commodore Matthew C. Perry, and the man who was soon to consider himself the real leader of the new Republican party, William H. Seward. The latter was the spokesman for those who envisaged an American empire in the Pacific. Seward felt that the best interests of the United States required a positive Far Eastern policy if the commercial foothold already acquired by the United States was not to be engulfed by its great commercial rival, Great Britain. Seward's view was that ultimately Asia would dwarf Europe in importance and in opportunities for trade and investment.

The activities of Perry have already been recounted.[5] It will be recalled that in addition to his work in securing a treaty with Japan, which re-

[5] See Chapter 11.

sulted in the reopening of these islands to the world, Perry had purchased land for a coaling station in the Bonins and later had one of his officers formally take possession of these islands. Formosa also appealed greatly to Perry, and he felt that the United States would be well advised to establish a protectorate there. His very strong views on the subject of Pacific expansion fell upon deaf ears in official Washington and nothing came of his suggestions, so he concentrated upon the main objective of his mission, the securing of a treaty with Japan, which he accomplished successfully.

Acquisition of Formosa Urged. That he was not alone in his thinking, however, may be seen from the unrewarded efforts of Dr. Peter Parker [6] to secure possession of Formosa for the American government. Parker felt that American seizure of the island was justified due to the treatment which China accorded American interests in that country. He felt that it might teach China a lesson. Furthermore, it could serve as a preventive measure, since it would foil any designs Britain might have upon the strategic island. That the latter power entertained any such project was disavowed by the British governor of Hong Kong, Sir John Bowring, who told Parker that he would be quite happy to see the United States acquire Formosa if it so desired.[7]

Seeking to advance the cause of annexation, two partners in a private business venture in Formosa had in 1856 raised the American flag over their holdings on the island. These American citizens offered to help in colonizing the island should their government decide to annex it. Washington, however, showed no disposition to do anything about annexing Formosa, so the American flag had to be removed and the plans jettisoned.[8]

When Townsend Harris went to Japan to follow so ably the trailblazing work of Perry, he, too, was infected with the fever for annexing Formosa. Once again the American government took its stand against acquiring territory in the western Pacific.

The reiterated proposals to annex Formosa are significant because they reveal that there was American sentiment for the annexation of Asiatic territory, even in official circles, despite the prevalence of the Cushing-Marshall thesis that the United States not only should refrain from acquiring territory belonging to China but should let it be known that such actions by any power would be considered inimical to America's best interests. This latter view was to form the second plank in American

---

[6] Dr. Parker, a medical missionary with a long record of service in China, was appointed American commissioner in China in 1855.

[7] F. R. Dulles, *America in the Pacific* (Boston and New York, 1938), pp. 77 f.

[8] *Ibid.*, p. 78.

Far Eastern policy for years to come, complementing the point of equality of commercial opportunity.

Early American Interest in Hawaii

Astride the sea lanes to the Orient lay the Hawaiian or, as they were then called, Sandwich Islands. First visited by American commercial interests, they attracted American missionaries as early as 1820. American whalers also found the islands an attractive and convenient base in the years prior to the Civil War. Their ideal location made them desirable to the British and French as well, so much so that in 1842 the United States government announced through both the President and the Secretary of State that, although America did not contemplate annexing the islands, it could not view their acquisition by any other power with equanimity.

A British naval officer did actually seize Hawaii in 1843. His action was not only disavowed by his government, but Britain and France reached a joint agreement that same year not to annex the islands.

Renewed American interest in Hawaii was manifested, and Secretary of State Marcy went so far as to negotiate a treaty of annexation with the Hawaiian monarchy in 1854, only to have it turned down by those in Congress opposed to such a step. An effort to ratify a treaty of reciprocity was also defeated the following year, so nothing concrete materialized in the relations between the United States and Hawaii until after the Civil War.

Acquisition of Alaska

William H. Seward has already been identified as one of the chief advocates of a vigorous, expansionist American policy in the Pacific. As Secretary of State under Lincoln and Johnson, Seward did succeed in expanding the American domain. This addition was Russian America, or Alaska as it was later known, which was purchased from the Russian government in 1867. To Seward it represented an important steppingstone to Asia and its acquisition was a stride in the direction of ultimate control of the Pacific, which he predicted was destined to be "the chief theatre of events in the world's great hereafter." [9]

The derision which greeted Seward's treaty purchasing Russian America for the sum of $7,200,000 is well known; that time proved Seward right is also accepted. The acquisition of noncontiguous territory by the United States was thus commenced and paved the way for ultimately acquiring such more distant possessions as Hawaii and the Philippines.

[9] *Ibid.*, p. 81.

As Tyler Dennett has said: "If the United States were again to set out by isolated action to protect its interests in Eastern Asia, it is probable that the line of advance would be over the bridge to which 'Seward's folly' points." [10]

China Again

The Work of Anson Burlingame. During the Civil War the attention of the United States was necessarily withdrawn from the Orient. However, in 1861, President Lincoln appointed as American Minister to China the remarkable Anson Burlingame. The first American representative to take up official residence in Peking, he was a firm believer in the Cushing-Marshall thesis of preserving China's territorial integrity. He was charged with the task of promoting among the Powers a cooperative attitude toward China and sought in his conversations with the diplomats in Peking to maintain the principle of equality of commercial opportunity, the abolition of force and its replacement by diplomacy in the dealings of the Powers with China, and, of course, the maintenance of China's territorial integrity.

His work was so painstakingly sincere that he won the respect and admiration of the Chinese. Upon his resignation in 1867, he was prevailed upon by the Chinese to lead a Chinese mission on a goodwill tour of the Western nations. The Manchus, mindful that they were to be faced with the revision of their treaty with Great Britain in 1868, were hopeful that Burlingame's mission might help them secure more favorable terms.

Although he seems to have considered himself the leader of the Chinese party, later research has revealed that Burlingame was actually equaled in authority by a Manchu and a Chinese who accompanied him.[11] Nevertheless, he was well received wherever he went and treated as if actually the chief of the mission. He was stricken ill and died in St. Petersburg before he was able to return to China where he has since been honored for having given his life in the service of China.

In Washington the Burlingame Mission reached an agreement supplementing the earlier Treaty of Tientsin. A significant addition to the earlier agreement was a clause which gave citizens of the two countries extensive trade, travel, and residence rights in the country of the other.

The visit of Burlingame and his Chinese colleagues did much to renew American interest in China, but the picture of the progressive attitude of

---

[10] Dennett, "Seward's Far Eastern Policy," *American Historical Review*, Vol. XXVIII (October, 1932), p. 45.

[11] K. Biggerstaff, "The Burlingame Mission," *American Historical Review*, Vol. XLI (July, 1936), pp. 652-82.

China painted by Burlingame was greatly overdrawn and was destined to be a source of ultimate disappointment to Americans. The truth was that the court at Peking remained staunchly antiforeign under the influence of the strong-minded Empress Dowager, Tz'ŭ Hsi.

Anti-Chinese Feeling in the United States. By 1880 Chinese had taken such advantage of this opportunity to emigrate to the United States that they constituted 9 per cent of the population of California. Their alien speech and customs, together with their remarkable industriousness, made them so unpopular on the Pacific Coast and in the western mining towns that the cry was raised "The Chinese must go!"

Because of this growing antagonism the American Congress sought in 1879 to repudiate, in effect, the terms of the Burlingame Agreement which permitted unrestricted immigration by passing the Fifteen-Passenger Bill which prohibited any vessel bringing in more than fifteen Chinese passengers. President Hayes vetoed the measure on the ground that it was in reality an exclusion act in violation of the pledged word of the United States. Realizing the need for action, however, Hayes sent a special three-man commission to Peking to arbitrate the question with the Chinese. This commission concluded the Treaty of 1880 which gave the United States the right to regulate, limit, or suspend Chinese immigration, but not to prohibit it. Such regulation, limitation, or suspension was to apply only to Chinese laborers and not to students, merchants, travelers, or officials. At the same time an agreement was reached between the two nations which forbade the further importation of opium into China by American citizens. This understanding had the value, from the Chinese standpoint, of helping to save face as a result of the concessions granted the United States in the matter of immigration.[12]

Congress quickly passed a bill suspending Chinese immigration for twenty years. It was, however, vetoed by President Arthur in 1882 on the grounds that it was not a suspension but rather an unreasonable restriction and so in defiance of the treaty. Congress then passed another measure, the Act of 1882, suspending Chinese immigration for ten years. This met the President's approval and became law. It was replaced in 1888 by a new agreement which suspended immigration for a twenty-year period but which also provided that the United States pay an indemnity for damages to Chinese lives and property which had occurred in various anti-Chinese outbreaks in the United States, such as the Rock Springs, Wyoming, incident in 1885 during which almost thirty innocent Chinese miners were slaughtered. China's slowness in ratifying this agreement resulted in the passage of a bill to put into immediate effect the provisions

[12] F. R. Dulles, *China and America* (Princeton, 1946), p. 87.

relating to Chinese exclusion without waiting for China's ratification. This bill passed without a presidential veto, since President Cleveland adopted the subterfuge that China had failed to cooperate with the United States.[13]

Diplomatic Ties Seriously Strained. Diplomatic relations between the two countries were practically suspended for the next few years as China was very bitter over this cavalier treatment. Congress took advantage of this situation to extend the provisions of the Act of 1882 for a ten-year period, and in general tightened the terms permitting entry of the non-coolie Chinese as well as the re-entry of Chinese residing in the United States prior to the passage of the legislation.

Another treaty was negotiated in 1894 as a result of which the United States adopted a somewhat less rigid attitude toward those Chinese who were permitted entry. For its part, China gave its consent to the exclusion of the laborers for the ten-year period stipulated in the 1892 legislation. The failure of the United States to live up to its part of the agreement soon resulted in China's abrogating the treaty and resorting, in 1904 and 1905, to boycotts against American goods. Whatever the reason, the United States then pursued a fairer policy but adhered rigidly to the exclusion of all laborers, as well as the denial of citizenship to those already in the country.[14]

The ironical part of this series of episodes was that the United States had reversed the earlier roles being played by itself and China. Formerly it was the United States which resented China's indifference to her pledged word. Now China was irked by the refusal of the United States to honor its commitments. The whole business represents a somewhat less than glorious page in American history and has only recently been remedied to a modest extent.

Improved Sino-American Trade Relations. From the time of the passage of the 1882 legislation until the beginning of the Sino-Japanese War in 1894, trade between the United States and China slumped. But war brought a critical need for American goods, and China had to pocket its pride. The treaty which marked the end of the war further improved American commercial opportunities in China since the trade privileges won by Japan as a result of the war were automatically accorded to the United States in its most-favored-nation role. American imports and exports now jumped sharply. Actually, Japan proved to be a much better customer than China, but American business interests were greatly heartened by the improvement which took place.

[13] *Ibid.*, p. 91.
[14] *Ibid.*, p. 94.

Annexation of Hawaii

In the years following the Civil War, the United States again became actively interested in the Hawaiian (Sandwich) Islands. In 1875 a reciprocity treaty between the United States and the Hawaiian monarchy was signed, despite the fact that similar treaties had been rejected by the United States Senate in 1855 (which followed the defeat of a treaty of annexation in 1854) and in 1867. The successful reciprocity treaty provided that each country would admit the principal products of the other duty-free.

The agreement was renewed in 1887 at which time the United States was granted the privilege of using the Pearl River Harbor (Pearl Harbor), both for a coaling station and for naval purposes. In the years between the first treaty and its renewal, the production of sugar increased greatly, with the result that American planters became increasingly influential in the islands' economy and politics. These people became dissatisfied and put pressure on the king to adopt a constitution which provided a parliamentary form of government and enhanced the power of the Americans.

When the famous Queen Liliuokalani began her reign in 1891, she revealed her dislike for the Americans and planned to replace the constitution of 1887 with one of her own which the Americans felt would be prejudicial to their interests. They proceeded to launch a revolution and established a provisional government which requested military assistance from the American minister. Their plea was heeded, and there then followed a request that the provisional government be accorded recognition by the United States. Owing to the fact that the queen surrendered to the American Minister, not to the provisional government, and because of the close connection between this official and the provisional government, he took it upon himself to announce that Hawaii had now become an American protectorate. The American flag was raised on all public buildings, and it appeared as if a *fait accompli* had been achieved. In February, 1893, a formal treaty of annexation was concluded, but before it could be passed by the Senate the congressional session ended.

In the meantime the Democrats under President Cleveland came back into office. Cleveland elected to send a personal representative to the islands to study the situation before his administration took any action. As a result of the recommendations of his emissary, the President decided to aid the deposed Queen Liliuokalani if she would grant an amnesty to the revolutionaries. Her refusal to make this pledge prompted Cleveland to turn the matter over to the Congress for action. The Senate decided against the restoration of the queen, and agreed that the provisional government should continue in control for the time being.

With the return of the Republicans under McKinley in 1897, a treaty of annexation was defeated in the Senate; but in 1898, owing to the turn of events in the Spanish-American War which put Dewey in Manila, Hawaii was formally annexed through the passage of a congressional joint resolution. Thus, the United States had gained another important Pacific outpost, one which eventually gained recognition as the fiftieth state of the Union.

The Acquisition of the Philippines

The period of the 1890's was one of feverish nationalism in the United States. The long moribund spirit of Manifest Destiny, so strong in the 1840's and 1850's, came to vigorous life. It differed somewhat from its earlier phase because to the old emotionalism had been added a large dose of rationalization. Both history and science were enrolled in the cause. The Anglo-Saxon was pictured as superior in all respects to other peoples and was actually said to have been divinely commissioned to be his brother's keeper. Prominent apologists for Manifest Destiny from all walks of life professed firm belief that the United States had a world mission to perform.

War With Spain. Against such a backdrop, war with Spain over the latter's mistreatment of her subjects in Cuba became increasingly probable. The sinking of the American battleship "Maine" in Havana Harbor, February 15, 1898, with the loss of over 250 American lives brought frenzied demands that Spain be punished. The result was that the United States declared war on Spain.

The story of this conflict is too well known to require retelling here. What is of interest is the Philippine aspect of the conflict. For more than a century the United States had engaged in commercial relations with the Philippines, but the trade had never been particularly important and, as a matter of fact, had fallen off in the later period. One American in high place not only knew where the islands were located, a piece of knowledge that distinguished him from the vast majority of his countrymen including President McKinley, but had ambitions that they might become an American possession. He was Assistant Secretary of the Navy, Theodore Roosevelt. Warmly backing him was Senator Henry Cabot Lodge. Although some doubt exists as to when Roosevelt first came to favor acquiring the Philippines, he was without question the first to take action in the matter. As early as September, 1897, Roosevelt was busily engaged in urging that the American Navy attack the Philippines as soon as war with Spain should commence.

Taking advantage of the absence of Secretary Long from the Naval Department, on February 25, 1898, Roosevelt, as Acting Secretary, cabled

Commodore Dewey, in charge of American naval forces in the Far East, to have his squadron get up steam at Hong Kong and be prepared for immediate action in the event of war with Spain. Should war break out Dewey was instructed to "see that the Spanish squadron does not leave the Asiatic coast, and then [to commence] offensive operations in [the] Philippine Islands."

Victory Spurs Annexation Spirit. On May 1 at 5:41 A.M., Dewey went into action against the Spanish squadron and the shore batteries in Manila Bay. By 12:30 P.M. the fighting was over, and the Spanish ships had been destroyed or incapacitated without the loss of a single American life. This dramatic and sudden victory brought a quick transformation in the attitude of American business interests which up to this point had been either hostile or apathetic toward the war. The markets of the Far East now became more attractive than ever, and the President, the Congress, and the State Department were subjected to a flood of petitions urging that the United States secure possession of the islands as a valuable link in the trade with the Far East, especially since events in China seemed to emphasize the need for an American base from which the commercial rights of Americans could be protected.[15]

Added to the pleas of business was the voice of many American missionaries who welcomed an opportunity to carry on their work in new fields. Then, too, there was a widely shared view in official Washington that, if the United States did not take the islands, some other power would with results that would be damaging to the strategic and commercial interests of the United States.

Annexation and Insurrection. Following a long period of indecision, the McKinley administration decided to pursue an annexationist policy. The Treaty of Paris, concluding the war, was ratified on February 6, 1899, and provided that the Philippines and Guam [16] should become American in return for the sum of $20,000,000. The battle against ratification in the United States was a bitter one, based on the twin forces of constitutional and humanitarian arguments, and was lost by a margin of only two votes.

America's "little brown brothers," the Filipinos, were even more stubborn to convince. They launched the sanguinary Philippine Insurrection on February 4, 1899, and continued a bitter resistance until the spring of 1901.

---

[15] J. W. Pratt, *Expansionists of 1898* (Baltimore, 1936), chap. 8.
[16] The failure of the United States to acquire Spain's remaining Pacific possessions, the Marshalls, Carolines, and Marianas was to prove very costly in the light of the future.

As Griswold points out, chance supplied a little group of American expansionists with the Philippines. United States interests in the Far East were definitely an afterthought used to rationalize the acquisition of colonies in the China Sea.[17] But whatever the background, the United States had broken with her traditional policy and had acquired territory, thousands of miles way, inhabited by people who did not wish to be ruled by the United States. The significance of this action in precipitating the United States into the ranks of the colonial powers and placing under her rule Asiatic people cannot be underestimated. For good or for ill, the United States was now a major force in the ranks of world powers and would have to take a livelier interest in the Far East whether it wished to or not.

American Far Eastern Policy Restated

With such important Pacific outposts as Alaska, Hawaii, and now the Philippines in American hands,[18] it will be useful to take stock at this point by briefly reviewing the situation in China. In China the great European Powers and Japan were engaged in a sharp battle for concessions and spheres of influence, a struggle which appeared to doom China to the loss of its territorial integrity. Yet there were other factors which indicated that all was not yet lost. Great Britain, for example, forced to reassess its world position as the result of discovering that its policy of "splendid isolation" had become dangerously tarnished, was anxious to preserve the open door. Furthermore, its overtures to the United States had borne fruit in that the new American Secretary of State, the Anglophile John Hay, leaned strongly toward cooperative action to maintain the open door.

Hay favored this course, but others were open to him. He might, for instance, have recommended acceptance of the gains made by the powers bent on the destruction of China and allowed American interests to go by default. Or, on the other hand, he might have suggested that the United States actively (although belatedly) join the scramble for concessions and thereby take part in the division of China. As has already been shown,[19] he elected to seek the establishment of international cooperation in China, a course of action which would preserve America's historic policy of equality of commercial opportunity. This was done through

---

[17] A. W. Griswold, *The Far Eastern Policy of the United States* (New York, 1938), pp. 16 f.

[18] In addition to these key spots, such less vital ones as American Samoa, Wake, Midway, Guam, and the Guano Islands had also been obtained by the United States.

[19] See Chapter 17.

the medium of the Open Door Notes of 1899 and 1900 which, thanks to the open mistrust of the Powers for one another in China, helped to put a stop to the slicing of the Chinese "melon."

American participation in the defeat of the Boxers was followed in 1900 by the Powers' acceptance of the open door principle. The moderate role played by the United States in the Boxer episode revealed that this nation's role in the Far East was again dictated by commercial rather than imperialistic tactics. It was a return to established policy rather than a resort to the "large policy" of the acquisition of the Philippines. In his 1900 notes to the Powers, Hay extended his position of 1899, which called for the recognition of equality of commercial opportunity, by taking the position that China's territorial and administrative integrity must be respected. It is quite obvious, however, that the United States was not prepared to defend this position by force. What the United States was ready to do was to use its influence to help check, by diplomatic means, any Power bent upon harming its interests in China. It was not prepared to oppose such privileges as exclusive railway and mining rights which the Powers might utilize to harm legitimate American interests. When Russia appeared determined to secure a monopoly in the North by its advances in Manchuria and Korea, the United States backed Japan in the Russo-Japanese War of 1904-5. The setback dealt Russia in this conflict, and the emergence of Japan as a threat to the open door prompted a shift in Japanese-American relations which directed American energies against the new Japanese policy of exclusive rights and finally culminated in war in December, 1941.

The Struggle for Economic Control of China

The defeat of the one country willing to resort to force to upset the balance of power in China, coupled with the close watch the Powers kept on each other, resulted in a new approach to affairs in China. This was the rivalry to secure power in China, not by gaining territorial cessions but rather by domination of China's finances through loans, investments, and concessions of an economic nature, such as exclusive railway, mining, and other rights.

Although the United States participated to some extent, it finally withdrew from a big international venture, the consortium, which was a cooperative effort on the part of the Powers to win economic advantages of a mutual rather than an exclusive nature. The United States pulled out of the consortium because President Wilson in 1913 expressed the opinion that the venture came too close to threatening China's administrative independence to suit his country's policy.

Deterioration of Relations with Japan

For fifty years before the Russo-Japanese War, the relations which existed between the United States and Japan had been extremely cordial. An exception was the strong Japanese protest lodged against the proposed American annexation of Hawaii in 1897. The Japanese felt that such a step was a violation of the status quo in the Pacific and was also inimical to the interests of the thousands of Japanese living in the islands.[20] When annexation did take place in 1898 Japan put as good a face on the matter as possible, and its earlier protest left no visible scars. In the case of the Philippines, Japan's position was quite different; it welcomed American annexation apparently on the grounds that if some foreign power other than itself must acquire these islands in the China Sea the United States was the least obnoxious to Japan.

Portsmouth Treaty Opens Breach. It remained for the Russo-Japanese War to bring about a change for the worse in Japanese-American relations. The reader will recall that the United States, through President Theodore Roosevelt, extended its good offices at the conflict's end. On May 31, 1905, Roosevelt was requested by the Japanese government of his "own initiative to invite the two belligerents to come together for the purpose of direct negotiations."[21] Although at first unenthusiastic, Roosevelt plunged into the task and arranged the meetings which produced for the combatants the Treaty of Portsmouth, and for himself the 1906 Nobel Peace Prize.

Japan's failure to secure an indemnity produced such repercussions among its people that the government used the United States as a scapegoat to cover its own inability to gain a more favorable treaty. The situation became so serious in Japan that martial law had to be proclaimed. From this time forward relations between the United States and Japan became more strained, culminating finally in the outbreak of war in December, 1941.

United States Alarmed. The United States grew alarmed over the consequences of the Japanese victory. Japan now became a potential threat to the open door in China and Manchuria and to the Philippines. Roosevelt admitted in 1906 that he would now like to be rid of the Philippines and in 1907 referred to them as an "Achilles' heel." Fears for their safety would now influence the United States to make concessions to Japan's imperialistic tendencies in both Korea and Manchuria.[22]

[20] T. A. Bailey, "Japan's Protest Against the Annexation of Hawaii," *Journal of Modern History*, Vol. III (1931), pp. 51 ff.
[21] A. L. P. Dennis, *Adventures in American Diplomacy* (New York, 1928), pp. 401 f.
[22] Griswold, *op. cit.*, p. 123.

Two wars had seriously altered relationships in the Pacific area. The first, the Spanish-American War, coupled with the annexation of Hawaii, had made the United States one of the two most important Pacific Powers. The other, the Russo-Japanese, had made Japan the second leading Power in this area. The two now stood face to face, each recognizing the other as the potential enemy.[23]

Korea, an Exception to the Rule. The principal exception to this record of constantly deteriorating relations was American willingness to give Japan a free hand in Korea. In 1905, the same year that the Portsmouth Treaty was signed, the Taft-Katsura "agreed memorandum" was signed in Tokyo whereby the United States agreed to recognize Japanese suzerainty over Korea in exchange for Japan's promise not to harbor aggressive designs toward the Philippines. A few months later the United States was informed that henceforward Korea's foreign affairs would be cared for by Japan. The very next day the United States announced the withdrawal of its mission from Korea and declared that it was prepared to deal with Japan from then on in matters relating to Korea. The practical advantages of such an attitude on the part of the United States are clear enough, but it should be noted that such a procedure involved violence to the principle of the open door. Nonetheless, their conflicting interests and ambitions in Asia seemed bound to bring a clash between Japan and the United States.

Immigration Question. Following closely in the wake of the bitter feelings engendered toward the United States in Japan as a result of the Treaty of Portsmouth, the immigration policy of the American government helped to make matters worse. For some years after the reopening of Japan in 1854, the Japanese were slow to go abroad. Beginning in 1868 some Japanese contract laborers went to Hawaii, but the Japanese government was not cordial toward the practice, and emigration to Hawaii was soon suspended. This emigration was resumed in 1885, and by 1900 there were more than 61,000 Japanese in Hawaii.[24]

Japanese emigration to the United States was also slow to develop. There were only fifty-five Japanese in the United States in 1870, and the total reached only 148 ten years later. Another decade saw the number grow to 2,039, a minuscule figure compared to the 132,000 Chinese then in the United States.[25] Owing to the discriminatory legislation against the Chinese, the Japanese began to be employed in their place. By 1900 there were 24,236 in the United States, and ten years later the figure had

---

[23] E. O. Reischauer, *The United States and Japan* (Cambridge, Mass., 1950), p. 20.
[24] C. Yanaga, *Japan Since Perry* (New York, 1949), p. 429.
[25] *Ibid.*

swollen to 72,157.[26] As their numbers increased on the West Coast, the same discrimination that had been shown to the Chinese was practiced against them. As early as 1900, the San Francisco Labor Council passed a resolution demanding that the Chinese Exclusion Laws be extended to include the Japanese. The American Federation of Labor, in convention at San Francisco in 1904, added its voice to the cry, and the following year the California Senate went unanimously on record as opposed to unrestricted Japanese immigration and requested protective action from the federal government.[27]

In 1906 the San Francisco Board of Education required Chinese, Japanese, and Korean children to be segregated from other public school children. Although there were only 93 children of Japanese ancestry attending the schools, the measure was aimed principally against the Japanese, and was so interpreted by the Japanese government which entered a strong protest in Washington. The Roosevelt administration had to point out that this was a matter over which the federal government had no jurisdiction. However, it took steps in 1907 and 1908 to remedy the situation which finally proved acceptable to both the Japanese government and the San Franciscans. In the former year the Immigration Act of 1907 was amended in such a way that Japanese laborers were prevented from entering the United States by way of Hawaii, Mexico, and Canada, as many had been doing. This prompted the San Francisco School Board to remove the restrictions which they had placed on Japanese children (although Chinese and Koreans continued to be excluded from the regular schools). In 1907-8 the so-called "Gentlemen's Agreement" was worked out between the Japanese and American governments. Under this arrangement the Japanese authorities promised not to issue any more passports to Japanese laborers desiring to come to the United States. In other words, Japan itself would do the restricting, thereby saving face.

The disproportion between males and females among the Japanese in the United States led the former to select "picture brides" from Japan who were admitted to the United States to join their mates whom they had married by proxy. Admission of these women came under the terms of the "Gentlemen's Agreement" but remained for long a source of friction among West Coast Americans. The practice was finally curtailed in 1920 by the Japanese government following a request from President Woodrow Wilson.

That anti-Japanese feeling was growing rather than diminishing on the American Pacific Coast may be seen from the passage by the California legislature in 1913 of an antialien land law which discriminated against

[26] Reischauer, *The United States and Japan*, p. 17.
[27] Yanaga, pp. 431 ff.

the Japanese. The Wilson administration considered this measure to be of such importance that the Secretary of State was sent to California to persuade the legislators to kill the measure.

A slight break in the steady retrogression of Japanese-American relations occurred in 1908 when the American fleet, on a round-the-world trip (designed primarily to impress Japan), was cordially received in Japan where the officers and men were elaborately entertained. Also in 1908, the Root-Takahira Agreement was signed. This executive agreement, undertaken by the Roosevelt administration, pledged both countries to respect the status quo in the Pacific, to respect each other's possessions in that area, to uphold the open door in China, and to support China's independence and integrity.

Thus the years from 1905 until the outbreak of the first World War in 1914 had been, on the whole, rather unpleasant ones in the history of Japanese-American relations, with only a few events, like the Root-Takahira Agreement, to break the continuity of bad feelings and mutual fears and suspicions.

Summary

At the outset of this chapter, it was stated that American policy in the Far East up to 1898 was based upon three major points. The first was that the United States would refrain from acquiring any Far Eastern territory. This principle was shattered in 1898 when the United States annexed the Philippines and put itself, at least temporarily, within the ranks of imperialistic Powers. It also meant that the United States was now forced to play a leading role in Far Eastern affairs, with consequences that ultimately led to war.

Secondly, the United States wished to see the development of an East Asia sufficiently strong in itself to resist European aggression, but it had to recognize the impossibility of forcing others to hold rigidly to our policy and so had to play along for the time being. In 1914 this was still true, but Japan's new position had become a source of grave concern to the United States and had brought the two countries face to face as the two leading Pacific forces. It still remained the policy of the United States to work for the strengthening of China, whose territorial integrity and administrative independence were thought to be of great importance to America.

Finally, the restriction of immigration from the Orient into the United States was a policy being pursued with considerable vigor and increasing diplomatic problems, especially as concerned Japan.

In short, the United States still hoped to maintain the open door in China (although its withdrawal from Korea before Japan's had weakened the universality of the principle throughout the Far East) and to preserve China's independence and territorial integrity. And in addition it was not anxious to have Orientals enter its own doors.

SUGGESTED READINGS

Indispensable to the student of American Far Eastern policy is Tyler Dennett's *Americans in Eastern Asia* (New York, 1922). The period from 1898 on is covered splendidly by A. Whitney Griswold, *The Far Eastern Policy of the United States* (New York, 1938). A brief but important era, 1896-1906, is well covered by Alfred L. P. Dennis, *Adventures in American Diplomacy*, chaps. 1, 3, 4, 8, 9, 13 and 14. An interesting account of the first century of American expansion and policies in the Pacific area is Foster Rhea Dulles, *America in the Pacific* (2d ed., Boston and New York, 1938). Also useful are Owen Lattimore, *America and Asia* (Claremont Colleges, 1943); James Morton Callahan, *American Relations in the Pacific and the Far East, 1784-1900* (Johns Hopkins University Studies in History and Political Science, Series 19, Baltimore, 1901); Charles O. Paullin, *Diplomatic Negotiations of American Naval Officers, 1778-1883* (Baltimore, 1912); T. A. Bisson, *America's Far Eastern Policy* (New York, 1945), chaps. 1-3.

For American relations with China, the following are recommended: K. S. Latourette, *The History of Early Relations between the United States and China, 1784-1844* (New Haven, 1917); Paul H. Clyde, *United States Policy Toward China* (Durham N. C., 1940); Foster Rhea Dulles, *The Old China Trade* (Boston, 1930) and the same author's *China and America* (Princeton, 1946); and Arthur H. Clark, *The Clipper Ship Era* (New York, 1910).

The open door is discussed in Griswold, *op. cit.*, chap. 2; Dennett, *op. cit.*, chaps. 31-33; and Dennis, *op cit.*, chaps. 8, 9; and much more fully in M. J. Bau, *The Open Door Doctrine in Relation to China* (New York, 1923); and Yen En-tsung, *The Open Door Policy* (Boston, 1932).

Helpful on the financial side of American relations with China are C. F. Remer, *Foreign Investments in China* (New York, 1933); and T. W Overlach, *Foreign Financial Control in China* (New York, 1919).

For relations with Japan in addition to the general works cited above, one should use the standard accounts of Payson J. Treat. These are: *Japan and the United States, 1853-1921, Revised and Continued to 1928* (Stanford University Press, 1928); *Diplomatic Relations between the United States and Japan, 1853-1895* (2 vols., Stanford University Press, 1932); and *Diplomatic Relations between the United States and Japan, 1895-1905* (Stanford University Press, 1938). The first three chapters of Edwin O. Reischauer's authoritative *The United States and Japan* (Cambridge, Mass., 1950) are pertinent to this chapter. Well-written, factual, and informative is Chitoshi Yanaga, *Japan Since Perry* (New York, 1949).

The acquisition of the Philippines is covered by Dennis, *op. cit.*, chap. 3; Griswold, *op. cit.*, chap. 1; Julius W. Pratt, *Expansionists of 1898* (Baltimore, 1936); and Walter Millis, *The Martial Spirit* (Boston, 1931). For Hawaii, see Pratt, *op. cit.*, and Dulles, *America in the Pacific*, chaps. 9-11.

20

RUSSIA'S ASIATIC INTEREST AND POLICY

Russian Expansion in Siberia

A people, chiefly of Russian stock who lived at a considerable distance from Moscow and tended to be rather lawless, was destined to play a great role in the history of Russian expansion in Asia. These were called Cossacks to distinguish them from the more settled Russian peoples. The most famous of these daring people lived along the Dnieper in Little Russia. Here they won great reputations for their expert horsemanship. Theirs was the role of buffer between the savage tribes of Asia and the more civilized Europeans. Placed in such a position they responded readily and produced a tough hardy race, not unlike the frontiersmen and pioneers of American history. From the Dnieper, the Cossacks advanced to the Don, the Volga, and the Urals.

Strogonov's Pioneer Expansion. Seeking trade and adventure, the Cossacks, many of whom were employed by the great commercial firm of Strogonov,[1] crossed the "girdle," the Russian name for the Urals, separating Europe from Asia, and pushed into Siberia. In a series of expeditions the Cossacks acquired for Russia a great empire in Siberia. The barrier of the Urals was crossed and an expedition sent out to conquer at the end of the fifteenth century when western Europe was deeply interested in the great voyages of discovery and exploration.

In 1581 the famous Cossack adventurer Yermak[2] was brought into the employ of the Strogonovs. He and his men brought the savage tribes dwelling in Siberia under the rule of the Tsars. One of Yermak's accomplishments was the seizure of Sibir, then the capital of the principal tribal chieftain of western Siberia. Shortly afterwards, the city of Tobolsk was erected on the site. During a surprise attack on his forces on the Irtish,

---

[1] In securing a charter in 1558 the Strogonovs were granted numerous privileges, including that of raising troops and administering justice, as the British East India Company was later to do in India. In return for these privileges the merchants agreed to build, to develop the resources of the region, and to defend it against the wild uncivilized tribes.

[2] "The Millstone" so called because he ground the corn for his party. His real name was Vassil, son of Timothy, a trader of the Volga. P. Leroy-Beaulieu, *The Awakening of the East* (New York, 1900), p. 2n.

Yermak was drowned, and his men overwhelmed. But his work was carried forward with even greater vigor by his successors.

Yermak's career approximately marks the commencement of an organized effort by the Russian government to drive to the east. For the next hundred years, bands of intrepid traders and adventurers plunged farther and farther into Siberia. Due to the fierceness of the tribes dwelling in the south, the Russians avoided them as much as possible and continued eastward. The numerous rivers of Siberia proved a boon to the Cossacks whose skill on the water enabled them to skim along in their swift canoes. Progress in the terrible winters was impossible so they were spent in blockhouses (*ostrogs*) surrounded by stockades. As these hardy adventurers advanced, they were drawn ever forward by the almost incredible tales of the natives about the fabulous mineral resources said to be lying to the east. Everywhere they heard stories of a wondrous river which was supposed to originate in the very heart of China and wend its way through immensely rich lands into the great ocean at the extreme eastern end of the Continent.[3]

Pacific Reached in 1639. In 1636 the Yenisei River was reached, where the Russians came into contact with the Tunguses and soon afterwards the Buriats, who proved quite formidable. A year later the Lena was crossed, and in 1639 they were on the Sea of Okhotsk. Their problems increased greatly, and the distances to the nearest outposts were now measured in terms of days. In some instances, provisions had to be transported a thousand miles or more. Despite these difficulties, it took the Cossacks only a little over fifty years to traverse from the Urals to the Pacific. Everywhere they went, they collected tribute in the form of furs. The garrisons of the *ostrogs* often acted as mediators in tribal disputes and so proved of some value to the natives. On the other hand, the Cossack, never a gentle soul, was frequently guilty of excesses committed at the expense of the subjugated peoples, "God being too high, and the Tsar too far."

Thus, with amazing rapidity, the Cossacks made their way from western to eastern Siberia. Having covered the inhospitable wastes of the north and the center, they now began to interest themselves in the warmer lands of the south where rumor told of the great river whose basin abounded in cattle and where the people cultivated the soil. Anxious to verify these tales, the governor of Yakutsk Province sent out an expedition under Vasily Poyarkov which, in 1646, reached the Amur River, the subject of these many stories. The natives were surprised at the tall stature, thick beards, and long hair of the Cossacks and were terrified by their

[3] L. Pasvolsky, *Russia in the Far East* (New York, 1922), pp. 10 f.

guns. Poyarkov sailed down to the junction of the Amur and the Sungari and then on past the junction of the Ussuri to its mouth where the party wintered. They made their way by sea to Okhotsk in the spring. Although Poyarkov reported the conquest of the Amur to be easy, nothing was done about it by the government for some time.

The Manchus Encountered. In 1650 Khabarov, a man who had raised himself from the peasantry to become a successful trader and had learned to write, sailed down the Amur, captured several towns, and soon found himself faced by the Manchus for the first time. He built a fort at the mouth of the Ussuri which the Manchus besieged. After a successful defense, Khabarov and his band retreated in 1652, leaving the fort to the Manchus. He was subjected to a trial in Moscow for this, was acquitted, and later became governor of one of the Siberian districts. He has left his name on the city of Khabarovsk. Two years before his expedition, two Cossack adventurers, Alexiev and Dezhniev, had reached Kamchatka.

Other expeditions took up the work begun by Khabarov, and clashes with the Manchus occurred which led ultimately to the Treaty of Nerchinsk (1689) between Russia and China whereby the Amur territory was conceded to belong to China. The relinquishing by Russia of any claims to the Amur confined the efforts of Siberian settlers for a century and a half to the region lying west of the Amur.

Then came the appointment in 1847 of thirty-eight-year-old Nicolai Muraviev as Governor-General of eastern Siberia. Muraviev decided to conduct some surveys and sent an expedition to the Amur under Captain (later Admiral) Nevelskoy. Among other things, it was discovered that Sakhalin was an island and not a peninsula, a fact which later enabled the Russians, who kept this information secret, to save a squadron of theirs which the British thought they had bottled up during the Crimean War. In August, 1850, Nevelskoy established a fort near the mouth of the Amur which was later to become the city of Nikolaevsk. The Russian Foreign Minister, Nesselrode, was quite upset over this action as he did not wish to give the Chinese any cause for the opening of hostilities. Nesselrode's caution was based largely on the delicacy of the European situation. The tsar, however, felt differently, declaring that "when Russia's flag has been raised anywhere it should not be taken down." A compromise was ultimately worked out, and Nikolaevsk was construed to be the property of the Russian-American Company, a private trading company engaged in the exploitation of the Alaskan coast.

Muraviev now reorganized the Siberian military system and sent Nevelskoy on other explorations. In 1852 De Kastri Bay on the Gulf of Tartary was occupied, and the Russian-American Company established a trading post at Mariinsk. The permission of the tsar himself was received to occupy Sakhalin, which was declared annexed in 1853.

With the outbreak of the Crimean War, Muraviev made the Amur his line of communication with the coast, after having first explained to the Chinese what he was doing. As China then had its hands full with the Taiping Rebellion, no objections were offered. Muraviev made a successful defense of Petropavlovsk against the British and French, established four settlements on the right bank of the Amur, and settled a colony of Cossacks on an island opposite Mariinsk.

China Recognizes Russian Expansion. Negotiations between Russia and China culminated in 1858 in the Treaty of Aigun which transferred all the territory on the left bank of the Amur to Russia. The land between the Ussuri and the Pacific was to be held jointly by both countries.[4] The first settlers in the newly acquired territory were Cossacks who were ordered there in 1858. Colonization, however, proved slow, as the first peasants did not arrive until about ten years later. By the end of the century there were less than a million people in the Russian Far East.

In 1859 the Russian General Ignatiev was sent to Peking to complete the ratification of the Russian Treaty of Tientsin (1858). He attempted also to secure the cession of China's interests in the region across the Ussuri jointly occupied by Russia and China. Ignatiev offered to intervene on China's behalf and promised to save Peking from the victorious Allies who had defeated China in the "Arrow" War. His price was the cession of Trans-Ussuri. Having no other apparent recourse, China agreed and on November 14, 1860, turned the territory over to Russia. That very year, Vladivostok ("Ruler of the East") was occupied, thus beginning the colonization of the Maritime Province. Through the agreements reached with China in 1858 and 1860, Russia added some 400,000 square miles to her empire. But it was almost completely uninhabited land. The populating of the region was to be an important task for the Russian government which began this assignment in a manner somewhat less than wholesome by shipping in criminals and prostitutes.

Sakhalin and the Kuriles

In 1853 the Russian-American Company took over Sakhalin then peopled by a handful of Ainus, and the island became a bone of contention between Russia and Japan. The latter was willing to cede the northern

[4] T. C. Lin, "The Amur Frontier Question Between China and Russia, 1850-1860," *Pacific Historical Review,* Vol. III (1934), pp. 1-27.

portion of the island, but Russia wanted it all. On March 18, 1867, an agreement was reached providing for joint occupation with complete freedom of travel and settlement on the island accorded to both Russians and Japanese. Then in April, 1875, an earlier Russian offer to exchange the Kurile Islands for Sakhalin was accepted by Japan which was already recognized as the owner of Iterup, the most southerly island of the Kurile group. Little progress was made by the Russians on Sakhalin as the government's policy was to people it largely with convicts serving sentences in forced labor.

The Trans-Siberian Railway

Tsar Alexander III in 1891 named his son and heir, Crown Prince Nicholas, to be head of a great governmental project aimed at linking Russia more closely with the Far East. This was the famous Trans-Siberian Railway. Curiously enough an Englishman named Dull had first suggested the idea many years earlier. He had proposed a horse tramway which, to say the least, was somewhat impractical. At any rate, the official beginning of the Trans-Siberian soon produced widespread repercussions. The able Russian statesman, Count Sergei Witte, observed that the Sino-Japanese War of 1894-95 was a result of the building of the Trans-Siberian, a view shared by the British minister to Japan.[5]

The physical difficulties to be overcome in constructing the railway were enormous. To them was added no small amount of graft and corruption. As a consequence, the finished line was both grossly inefficient and even dangerous. A Japanese officer who traversed the road soon after its completion remarked that riding over it was "like being on board a vessel in a lively sea." The St. Petersburg correspondent of the *Etoile Belge* wrote:

> ". . . the works have been constructed in a manner which shows very little conscience. Everything, or nearly everything, will have to be done over again before the authorities can think of opening this gigantic line to regular working. In very many places the road gives way on the passage of a train a little heavier than usual or travelling at a speed of twenty miles an hour, and accidents more or less grave are continually happening. More than usual courage is demanded of anyone undertaking a journey on this railway. This construction *a la Russe* has already swallowed up hundreds of millions of roubles, or to speak more truthfully, the constructors, and not the construction, have absorbed the millions."[6]

International Politics and the Chinese Eastern Railway. Japan's success in the Sino-Japanese War was most distasteful to the Russians, just

---

[5] D. Dallin, *The Rise of Russia in Asia* (New Haven, 1949), p. 36.
[6] *The Story of Russia and the Far East, Being a Series of Papers Contributed to the Shanghai Mercury* (Shanghai, 1902), pp. 37 f.

as the latter's actions in setting up a stronghold in the East and in making numerous surveys of Korean waters had been to Japan. Russia, however, was not alone in actively opposing any resulting gains for Japan. Supported by France and Germany, Russia's demand that Japan return the Liaotung Peninsula to China and accept in lieu an added indemnity from China was too strong for the Japanese to resist. Twice before the signing of the Treaty of Tokyo, May 8, 1895, wherein Japan yielded to the tripartite demand, the Russian fleet had threatened to go into action against the Japanese navy.

The stage was now set for a bitter rivalry between Japan and Russia. The latter's aggressiveness swung both British and American policy and sympathy to Japan. Russia now began to pose before China as its only genuine friend among the Powers, but for this proffered friendship exacted a high price. In 1895, the Russo-Chinese Bank, recently established in St. Petersburg, made an advantageous loan to the Chinese government. The following year a secret alliance, the Li-Lobanov Treaty, was signed on June 3. To run for fifteen years, it provided a pledge for mutual assistance against any Japanese aggression. While helpful to China, the price for this aid was China's permission for the building of a branch line of the Trans-Siberian across Manchuria by the Russian-dominated Chinese Eastern Railway Company. Permission to develop mines in the regions through which the line passed was also granted. Furthermore, the line was allowed to develop other enterprises. Russian troops were given permission to protect the railroad. In the event of war, Russia was empowered to use Chinese ports.

Korea Becomes a Factor. Following China's defeat by Japan in the Sino-Japanese War, China was excluded from Korea, where Japanese influence quickly became paramount. Native opposition to Japanese predominance was swiftly suppressed, and the anti-Japanese queen and several of her advisers were assassinated. The king fled for his life and took refuge in the Russian legation where he remained for an entire year until February, 1897. While there, he requested the Russian government to establish a protectorate over the country, but nothing officially came of this suggestion, as the Russian Foreign Office was loath to antagonize Japan further at this time. Instead Russia and Japan reached an understanding on Korea which permitted each country to station a token force of troops there, an agreement which the Russians violated by sending a number of their army officers to train and rebuild the Korean army. In addition, the Russians established under their influence a Russian-Korean Bank.

Port Arthur and the South Manchurian Railroad. Then, on March 27, 1898, came a new agreement between Russia and China which leased to Russia for twenty-five years the two ports of Port Arthur and Talienwan, together with their adjacent areas at the base of the Liaotung Peninsula; a supplementary agreement permitted Russia to extend the Chinese Eastern Railway southward to Port Arthur. This line became the South Manchurian Railroad. This action of Russia in leasing the Liaotung ports was in direct contradiction of her announced reasoning for dislodging Japan from those very ports three years earlier. It was so barefaced that even such ardent Russian imperialists as Count Witte protested it in the deliberations of the Russian policymakers.

Japan was, of course, dismayed and resentful. Realizing that the blow was a very bitter one, Russia moved swiftly to soften it. The result was the signing of a Russo-Japanese agreement, the Nishi-Rosen Protocol, on April 25, 1898, wherein both parties recognized Korean independence, but also agreed that Japan should have predominant rights, amounting virtually to a monopoly, in the Korean economic sphere. Russia did not quite leave Korea by default as the Russian government proceeded in 1899 to acquire from private Russian interests the vast Korean timber concessions which Korea had previously granted, and even added to them in 1901.

Imperialism Threatens China's Existence

The significance of Russia's actions in seizing Port Arthur and Talienwan cannot be overestimated. Preceded by Germany's occupation of Kiaochow, the acquisitions precipitated a race which threatened the virtual extinction of Chinese independence and was checked largely by the mutual rivalries of the Powers. They occasioned the timely announcement of the open door policy by the United States. Certainly rivalry was far more effective in moderating this imperialistic race than was the American statement which, however, had a certain convenience value that proved quite useful.

Russia's aggressiveness in Manchuria, as mentioned above, tended to antagonize the United States and Great Britain. It helped ultimately to draw the latter and Japan together into the Anglo-Japanese Alliance of 1902 and also served to alienate the United States, which had long been rather well disposed toward Russia. From 1898 on, the Americans and the British began to draw closer together for a variety of reasons.

Russia and Britain Agree on Spheres. Somewhat earlier, the British sought an understanding with Russia delimiting their respective spheres in China. This was achieved after lengthy negotiations on April 29, 1899. Theoretically, it was restricted to recognizing spheres of economic activity only, but areas of political preponderance were tacitly understood as well. Britain's sphere of influence was recognized to be the Yangtze area, whereas Russia's was placed north of the Great Wall, which meant that Manchuria was being written off as far as Britain was concerned. This also meant that the province of Chihli, south of the Great Wall, where the Russians had harbored designs, was being abandoned by them.

Although Britain conceded Russian pre-eminence in Manchuria, the United States did not. It held that Hay's open door applied there as elsewhere in China, thereby complicating things from a Russian standpoint. Russia was not in accord with Hay's thesis but for appearance sake replied to Hay's proposals as ambiguously as possible. Hay clearly understood that Russia's attitude was unsatisfactory, but pretended that all the Powers, including Russia, had accepted his proposal.

The outbreak of the Boxer Rising gave Russia a chance to move toward the consolidation of its position in Manchuria, although it professed to the Chinese that it was their only true friend. Its reasons for this subterfuge are patent. It hoped to be rewarded by China for its "friendship" as it had been previously in the days of 1858 and 1860 when it had gained several hundred thousands of square miles of territory by adopting this pose. When the other Powers evacuated their main forces from China after the Boxer settlement, Russia alone remained. It even tried to force on China a treaty which would have extended Russian influence not only in Manchuria, but in Mongolia and western China as well. This was so brazen that British, Japanese, and German opposition finally forced the Russians to withdraw the proposed treaty, although it kept its troops in Manchuria and intensified its efforts to secure what amounted to an economic monopoly over this region.

The Anglo-Japanese Alliance and Other Treaties. Japan, backed by Great Britain, now emerged as China's principal defender. The Japanese, however, continued to seek a strong understanding with Russia which would guarantee Russia's position in Manchuria in return for recognition of Japanese hegemony in Korea. Even as Japan and Britain approached their historic alliance in 1902, Japan made one last attempt to come to terms with Russia. Marquis Ito made a trip to Moscow to suggest that, if Russia would give up its designs on Korea, Japan would have no objections to Russia's claiming Manchuria.[7] Russia refused, and the Anglo-Japanese Alliance was then signed (January 30, 1902) giving Japan a free hand should it go to war against Russia alone and assuring

---

[7] D. Dallin, *Russia's Rise in Asia*, p. 73.

it of British assistance should France or Germany fight on Russia's side. Both signatories emphasized their desire to see the status quo in the Far East maintained.

Shortly afterwards, on March 16, Russia and France reached an understanding which stressed the status quo in Manchuria. This apparently was meant to show that Russia harbored no aggressive designs upon Manchuria and was just as interested in keeping the situation unchanged as were its rivals, Britain and Japan.

As a further manifestation of its peaceful intentions, Russia then concluded an agreement with China (April 8, 1902) which pledged it to withdraw its troops from Manchuria within two years in three successive withdrawals to occur at six-month intervals. Unfortunately, Russia did not live up to its word, and the danger of a Far Eastern conflict, which had seemed to recede, now grew threatening.

A Final Peace Effort. Japan, however, determined upon yet another attempt to negotiate with Russia on the same proposals as earlier. This time, June, 1903, Russia appeared willing to accept. Unhappily, changes took place within Russia's Far Eastern policy personnel. The moderates Witte and Kuropatkin were bypassed as new posts were created giving to extremists vast powers which made them practically independent of the Cabinet. The rest of the year was spent in a fruitless exchange of notes between the two states. This period saw Russia return to its earlier intransigence. By late December Japan was losing hope of a satisfactory settlement and so began preparations for any emergency, including war.

Since Russia was also making military preparations, the Japanese let it be known in January, 1904, that war would ensue if Russia did not answer Japan's latest set of proposals. Hostilities commenced on February 10 when the Japanese attacked the Russian Far Eastern fleet at Port Arthur without warning other than their earlier one that there would be war if Russia did not reply to the Japanese proposals.

The Russo-Japanese War and Its Aftermath

Japan had made great progress since 1895 when it had defeated China. It had invested the indemnity received from China in improving its material strength. As a result, its army had been increased tenfold and its navy had become superior to Russia's. It had made a strong ally in England whose benevolent neutrality was most useful, and it had America's complete sympathy. Finally, it received considerable financial assistance from both British and American bankers.

Overwhelmed on land in the bloody fighting in Manchuria and Korea, its Far Eastern fleet decimated, Russia's last hope, the Baltic fleet, was destroyed by Admiral Togo at Tsushima in June, 1905, after having made an epic trip to the Far East. Despite its unbroken series of victories, Japan was badly spent, whereas Russia was reorganizing and rebuilding its shattered forces and might have been able to continue the war and thereby change the results. Since the war was extremely unpopular in Russia and involved almost fantastic problems of supply over the single-track Trans-Siberian Railway, and the revolutionaries were strengthened by these military reverses and the stories of official graft and corruption in connection with war supplies, Russia was willing to consider peace terms although it knew Japan was virtually exhausted. Their near state of collapse made the Japanese very anxious to discuss a settlement.

Through the good offices of President Roosevelt, the rivals came together at Portsmouth, New Hampshire. The conference opened August 5, 1905, and the treaty was signed September 5 after Japan had been forced to reduce its early demands by the refusal of Witte, head of the Russian delegation, to accept them because he felt that Russia was in a better position to resume fighting than was Japan.

By the terms of the treaty the Liaotung Peninsula was transferred to Japan, provided that China approved, which it of course had to do, and it became known as the Kwantung Leased Territory; Russian-built railroads in southern Manchuria were turned over to Japan, along with certain mining rights there; some fishing rights were acquired by Japan from Russia; and the southern half of the island of Sakhalin was ceded by Russia and given the name Karafuto by the Japanese. Japan's "paramount political, military, and economic interests" in Korea were also recognized by Russia, but no indemnity was paid to the victors, although they had earlier insisted on it. As President Roosevelt foresaw during the progress of the war, a new balance of power was created in the Far East. In the future, relations between Japan and the United States were to show a marked worsening. Portsmouth clearly marked a turning point.

Russo-Japanese Rapprochement

Almost worn out from their expensive and sanguinary triumph, the Japanese had to consider the future of their relations with their late enemy. The success of the tsar's government in crushing the revolution of 1905 seemed to indicate that the Russians were free to turn once again to their interrupted imperialistic ambitions in the Far East. Should a second war be fought in the near future between Russia and Japan, it was quite possible, perhaps even probable, that Japan could not win. It was also well known that certain influential Russians considered Portsmouth merely as a truce.[8] Furthermore, the Russians had been dislodged only from Korea and southern Manchuria. They still exercised paramount influence over much of Manchuria and already had begun to push an ambitious project aimed ultimately at putting North China under their sway by making a protectorate out of all of Mongolia. Moreover, in order to make its newly acquired Manchurian railroads a success, Japan needed the effective cooperation of Russia. With all these factors to consider, it was logical for the Japanese to seek a rapprochement with their recent adversary.

Agreements on China and Fisheries. Since the question of Japan's fishing rights in Siberian waters had not been completely clarified in the Treaty of Portsmouth, the Japanese used this issue as an opening wedge toward an entente with Russia. The result was the Russo-Japanese Fisheries Convention, July 28, 1907, which was to last for twelve years, after which it might be renewed or modified if both sides desired to continue it.

The fisheries agreement was followed two days later by a political convention containing two articles. Article One pledged the signatories to respect each other's territorial integrity, together with "all the rights accruing to one and the other party from treaties, conventions, and contracts in force between them and China." The second article pledged them "to recognize the independence and the territorial integrity of China and the principles of equal opportunity in whatever concerned the commerce and industry of all nations in that empire"—in other words, the open door —and also "to undertake to preserve and defend the status quo and the above-mentioned principle by all peaceful means at their disposal."

Division of Manchuria Planned. This was the convention as it was made public. However, a secret agreement provided for the division of Manchuria between them, the special position of Japan in Korea, and a Russian sphere in what now became known as Outer Mongolia.

Having prevented an attempt by the Harriman interests of the United States to develop a railroad to compete with the South Manchurian, and having witnessed the failure of the proposal of Secretary of State Knox for international control of the Manchurian lines, the Japanese, despite several earlier serious disagreements with the Russians, again turned toward Russia. A new convention was signed July 4, 1910. The public portion of it declared that, should the status quo be threatened, the two Powers would decide what steps should be taken to maintain the status

---

[8] Evidence of this feeling on Russia's part was the construction of the Amur Railroad, begun in 1908. This line was built around Manchuria from Chita to Vladivostok and was intended as insurance against the possible loss of the Chinese Eastern to Japan in the event of war.

quo. The secret portion was directed basically against the United States and went so far as to provide for agreement on common action should their interests in the Far East be threatened.

Korea Annexed. Japan immediately proceeded to annex Korea, and it appeared likely that Russia would move shortly to take over Outer Mongolia. Russia had by now apparently regained full confidence after having been thrown off stride by Japan in their war, and Russian advocates of an imperialistic Far Eastern policy were again pressing their aspirations. However, early in 1911 the Russian government presented China with an ultimatum relating to economic matters which did not call for territorial concessions. This hesitancy was due to two considerations: that official Russian opinion was still divided over what course of action to pursue in the East, and that Russia was being driven more and more to devote its principal attention to European affairs.

Outer and Inner Mongolia

China's failure to answer this ultimatum prompted Russia to repeat its demands and to make menacing military moves which forced China to capitulate to the Russian proposals. These demands having been granted, Russia devoted itself to the establishment of what was virtually a protectorate over Outer Mongolia, an achievement which was fulfilled by 1913.

Russia took its next step in 1912 when it became a member, along with Japan, of the international consortium formed for the purpose of making loans to China. These loans were guaranteed by Chinese state revenues, which in some cases were to be administered by the foreigners. This consortium consisted of American, British, German, and French bankers and was conceived by the United States. Shortly after becoming President, however, Wilson reversed American policy toward the consortium, withdrawing the United States from membership because he disapproved of its control measures which he felt were a distinct threat to China's political integrity. The failure of the consortium to function very effectively was welcomed by St. Petersburg which always feared that its sphere might be jeopardized by this collective action of the Powers.

The outbreak of the Chinese Revolution in 1911, coupled with the financial activities of 1912, led Russia and Japan to sign yet another convention, which was completely secret this time, on July 8, 1912. The new agreement divided Inner Mongolia as a sphere of interest to the mutual satisfaction of the contracting parties.

This was the last agreement Russia reached in the Far East before the outbreak of the first World War. From the date of its signing down to 1914 Russian relations with Japan, which served as the cornerstone of her Far Eastern policy from 1907 to 1917, underwent some deterioration.

SUGGESTED READINGS

Except for such studies as David Dallin's excellent *The Rise of Russia in Asia* (New Haven, 1949); the very useful study by Pauline Tompkins, *American-Russian Relations in the Far East* (New York, 1949); and E. H. Zabriskie, *American-Russian Rivalry in the Far East* (Philadelphia, 1946) the suggested readings for this chapter are not, for the most part, of very recent origin. They include such standard works as those by Tyler Dennett, *John Hay: From Poetry to Politics* (New York, 1933); *Roosevelt and the Russo-Japanese War* (New York, 1925), and *Americans in Eastern Asia* (New York, 1922); and A. Whitney Griswold, *The Far Eastern Policy of the United States* (New York, 1938).

The following are also valuable: K. Asakawa, *The Russo-Japanese Conflict* (Boston, 1904); J. F. Baddeley, *Russia, Mongolia, China: Being Some Record of the Relations Between Them* ... (London, 1919); H. Chevigny, *Lost Empire: The Life and Adventures of Nikolai Petrovich Rezanov* (New York, 1937); Frank A. Golder, *Russian Expansion on the Pacific, 1641-1850* (Cleveland, 1914); Andrew J. Grajdanzev, *Modern Korea* (New York, 1944); George Kennan, *Siberia* (New York, 1891); Robert J. Kerner, *Northeast Asia* (Berkeley, 1939); A. Krausse, *Russia in Asia* (New York, 1899); Owen Lattimore, *High Tartary* (Boston, 1930) and *Inner Asian Frontiers of China* (New York, 1940); Paul Leroy-Beaulieu, *The Awakening of the East* (New York, 1900); Prince A. Lobanov-Rostovsky, *Russia and Asia* (New York, 1933); Leo Pasvolsky, *Russia in the Far East* (New York, 1922); E. B. Price, *The Russo-Japanese Treaties of 1907-1916 Concerning Manchuria and Mongolia* (Baltimore, 1933); Baron Rosen, *Forty Years of Diplomacy* (London, 1922); M. Stanoyevich, *Russian Foreign Policy in the East* (Oakland, 1916); *The Story of Russia and the Far East, Being a Series of Papers Contributed to the Shanghai Mercury* (Shanghai, 1902); Vladimir, *Russia on the Pacific and the Siberian Railway* (London, 1899); Victor A. Yakhontoff, *Russia and the Soviet Union in the Far East* (New York, 1931); and Abraham Yarmolinsky (ed.) and (trans.), *The Memoirs of Count Witte* (London, 1921).

21

THE FAR EAST IN WORLD WAR I

Introduction

Although soon affected by the outbreak of the first World War, China continued neutral for some two and a half years. As the war began, China was in the throes of a very tense political situation. Less than three years had elapsed since the Chinese Revolution had broken out, and the new government was far from being a success. President Yüan Shih-k'ai, who had taken the extreme step of expelling a number of representatives from the Parliament, was very unpopular with many of his countrymen, especially those from the south. A new constitution, known as the Constitutional Compact, was promulgated May 1, 1914. It was most unacceptable to liberal elements within the country since it made Yüan Shih-k'ai a virtual dictator.

Under these circumstances, China's only course when the war started was an immediate declaration of neutrality. Prior to Japan's declaration of war on Germany, August 23, 1914, the Germans had evinced some disposition to return Kiaochow, their leasehold in Shantung, to the Chinese. The latter, however, were promptly given to understand by Japan that it would not permit such an arrangement.[1] A little later China pondered declaring war on Germany and cooperating with Japan and Great Britain to drive the Germans out of China, but once again Japan would have none of it.[2]

Japan Goes to War Against Germany

Japan entered the war after an exchange of views with its ally, Great Britain, which indicated that it was entering the war in support of its alliance commitments.[3] The British did nothing to encourage Japan's

[1] T. F. Millard, *Democracy and the Far Eastern Question* (New York, 1919), p. 95.
[2] *Ibid.*, pp. 97-100.
[3] This agreement stated that: "If by reason of unprovoked attack or aggressive action, wherever arising, either of the High Contracting Powers should be involved in war in defence of its territorial rights or special interests, ... the other High Contracting Party will at once come to the assistance of its ally and will conduct the war in common and will make peace in mutual agreement with it." Quoted in W. R. Wheeler, *China and the World War* (New York, 1919), p. 8.

action, showing no great desire to have Japan come into the war unless the Germans should attack India or some British holding in the Far East.

Britain later revised its attitude, requesting Japanese assistance within circumscribed limits; the proposal was that the Japanese confine themselves to attacking German naval units and armed merchantmen preying on British commerce in the Far East. This suggestion was repugnant to Japan which was bent upon making war against the Germans in China, and so advancing its own imperialistic ambitions. Failure of the Japanese to agree to Britain's repeated proposals resulted in the latter's reluctant approval of Japan's intentions, with the reservation that Japan should limit its maritime activities to a specified area. This was done in order to avoid giving offense to Australia and New Zealand. Again Japan refused to limit itself and so worded its ultimatum to Germany as to indicate that Japan had made no promises to Britain to restore Kiaochow to China after the war or to circumscribe its belligerent activities in any respect.[4]

As there was a growing apprehension throughout the Orient regarding Japan's ultimate objectives, the Japanese Premier, on August 15, 1914, wired the American press that Japan's geographical proximity to China was the cause of many silly rumors which prompted him to declare unequivocably that Japan's actions were just and its conscience was clear. He disavowed any territorial ambitions on the part of his country and claimed that Japan was acting merely to preserve peace in the Orient.

Japan's War Objectives. Japan's real reason for going to war was to improve its position on the Asiatic Continent, especially in Manchuria. For the ten years following the Russo-Japanese War, many Japanese were increasingly anxious to bring about a revision of the settlement in China and Manchuria that would be more advantageous to Japan. Furthermore, economic conditions in Japan, particularly in the agrarian regions, were growing acute. War offered the government the hope of improving its domestic situation.[5]

On November 10 the Germans finally surrendered the besieged city of Tsingtao, thereby marking the end of their resistance in the Far East. Their naval squadron had left Far Eastern waters once it became known that the Japanese were determined on war.

Sino-Japanese Relations Strained. The hostilities in China, brief though they had been, produced violations of Chinese neutrality by both belligerents. With the end of organized German resistance, the thing that most disturbed the Chinese authorities was that Japanese troops remained

---
[4] T. E. LaFargue, *China and the World War* (Stanford University, 1937), pp. 8-15.
[5] M. Royama, *Foreign Policy of Japan, 1914-1939* (Toyko, 1941), p. 18.

in possession of the Tsingtao-Tsinan Railway, which extended beyond the German leased territory. Japan defended its action on the grounds of military necessity.

This question aggravated Sino-Japanese relations which were worsened by China's note of January 7, 1915, informing the Japanese and British governments of its cancellation of the war zone which it had previously attempted to delimit. The Japanese were extremely angry, and in a formal reply to the Chinese note on January 9 they refused to recognize the cancellation. In his rejoinder one week later, the Chinese Minister of Foreign Affairs stated that, as military action in the special area had ceased, there was no further need for it.

The Twenty-One Demands

The whole question of Sino-Japanese relations was then brought to a head when Japan, on January 18, suddenly confronted China with a dictate, known as the Twenty-One Demands, aimed at achieving the fulfilment of various Japanese economic and territorial ambitions. These "proposals," as the Japanese referred to them, were rather subtly written on Japanese War Office paper which contained dreadnought and machine-gun watermarks.

While Germany's defeat left the question of the future disposition of Kiaochow and the German economic rights in Shantung at issue, the Shantung question, as these matters were commonly referred to, was not the only point over which China and Japan were divided and which called for settlement, at least as far as the Japanese were concerned. Two other important problems were the question of Japan's position in South Manchuria and the Japanese position in China vis-à-vis the various European Powers and the United States.[6]

Rivals' Gains Spur Japan. Japan was not extending its influence in Manchuria as it had hoped, due to the efforts of her competitors to extend to this rich region the theory of equality of opportunity which was supposed to characterize competition in China proper. In this latter economic rivalry, Japan was being outstripped by its more wealthy rivals who were grabbing off the cream of the railway, mining, and other concessions being granted by China. What was happening in reality was that despite the open door, China, economically at least, was being divided by the Powers into virtually exclusive spheres, except for Manchuria where the Japanese were getting rather stiff competition.[7]

---

[6] LaFargue, *op. cit.*, p. 28.
[7] For the extent of this economic penetration of China, see *ibid.*, pp. 30-31n.

Losing out in this race for economic concessions, finding itself increasingly ignored by the government of China after 1911, and fearing that it would be inundated in South Manchuria, Japan felt constrained to take steps to protect its interests. That this involved political, and possibly military, action seemed clear to Japan's policymakers. The preoccupation of the Powers, seemingly bent on mutual destruction in the war, indicated that Japan's golden opportunity for action had come. The one possible fly in the ointment was the United States, but action by that country alone seemed improbable; in any case it had to be risked if Japan were to solidify its leasehold and economic position in Manchuria and strengthen its subordinate economic and political position in China proper.

The Demands Analyzed. The Twenty-One Demands, which were presented in five groups,[8] may be broken down into the following basic Japanese policies in China: paramount influence, economic exploitation, political control, and territorial expansion. The policy of economic exploitation may be seen in Group II, Article 4, which reads:

> The Chinese Government agrees to grant to Japanese subjects the right of opening the mines in South Manchuria and Eastern Inner Mongolia. As regards what mines are to be opened, they shall be decided upon jointly.

Group III, Articles 1 and 2, also covers this area:

> The Japanese Government and the Chinese Government, seeing that Japanese financiers and the Han-Yeh-ping Company have close relations with each other at present and desiring that the common interests of the two nations shall be advanced, agree to the following articles:
> Article 1. The two Contracting Parties mutually agree that when the opportune moment arrives the Han-Yeh-ping Company shall be made a joint concern of the two nations and they further agree that, without the previous consent of Japan, China shall not by her own act dispose of the rights and property of whatsoever nature of the said Company nor cause the said Company to dispose freely of the same.
> Article 2. The Chinese Government agrees that all mines in the neighborhood of those owned by the Han-Yeh-ping Company shall not be permitted, without the consent of the said Company, to be worked by other persons outside the said Company; and further agrees that if it is desired to carry out any undertaking which, it is apprehended, may directly or indirectly affect the interests of the said Company, the consent of the said Company shall be first obtained.

---

[8] These are conveniently listed in *United States, Foreign Relations, 1915*, pp. 99-103.

Also by Group V, Article 5, which reads:

China agrees to grant Japan the right of constructing a railway connecting Wuchang and Kiukiang and Nanchang, another line between Nanchang and Hangchow, and another between Nanchang and Chaochow.

The policy of paramount influence is exhibited in Group I, Articles 1, 2, 3, and 4 which read:

Article 1. The Chinese Government engages to give full assent to all matters upon which the Japanese Government may hereafter agree with the German Government relating to the disposition of all rights, interests, and concessions, which Germany, by virtue of treaties or otherwise, possesses in relation to the Province of Shantung.

Article 2. The Chinese Government engages that within the Province of Shantung and along its coast no territory or island will be ceded or leased to a third Power under any pretext.

Article 3. The Chinese Government consents to Japan's building a railway from Chefoo or Lungkow to join [the] Kiaochow-Tsinanfu railway.

Article 4. The Chinese Government engages, in the interest of trade and for the residence of foreigners, to open by herself as soon as possible certain cities and towns in the Province of Shantung as Commercial Ports. What places shall be opened are to be jointly decided upon in a separate agreement.

Also by Group II, Articles 1, 5, 6, and 7:

The Japanese Government and the Chinese Government, since the Chinese has always acknowledged the special position enjoyed by Japan in South Manchuria and Eastern Inner Mongolia, agree to the following articles:

Article 1. The two Contracting Parties mutually agree that the term of lease of Port Arthur and Dalny and the term of lease of the South Manchurian Railway and the Antung-Mukden Railway shall be extended to the period of 99 years....

Article 5. The Chinese Government agrees that, in respect of the cases mentioned herein below, the Japanese Government's consent shall be first obtained before action is taken:

(a) Whenever permission is granted to the subject of a third Power to build a railway or make a loan with a third Power for the purpose of building a railway in South Manchuria and Eastern Inner Mongolia.

(b) Whenever a loan is to be made with a third Power pledging the local taxes of South Manchuria and Eastern Inner Mongolia as security.

Article 6. The Chinese Government agrees that if the Chinese Government employs political, financial, or military advisers in South Manchuria or Eastern Inner Mongolia, the Japanese Government shall first be consulted.

Article 7. The Chinese Government agrees that the control and management of the Kirin-Changchun Railway shall be handed over to the Japanese Government for a term of 99 years dating from the signing of this agreement.

Also by Group IV:

The Japanese Government and the Chinese Government with the object of effectively preserving the territorial integrity of China agree to the following special articles:

The Chinese Government engages not to cede or lease to a third Power any harbour or bay or island along the coast of China.

Finally by Group V, Articles 2, 5, 6, and 7:

Article 2. Japanese hospitals, churches and schools in the interior of China shall be granted the right of owning land....

Article 5. [cited above.]

Article 6. If China needs foreign capital to work mines, build railways and construct harbour-works (including dock-yards) in the Provinces of Fukien, Japan shall be consulted.

Article 7. China agrees that Japanese subjects shall have the right of missionary propaganda in China.

The policy of political control is the motive in Group V, Articles 1, 3, and 4:

Article 1. The Chinese Central Government shall employ influential Japanese advisers in political, financial, and military affairs....

Article 3. Inasmuch as the Japanese Government and the Chinese Government have had many cases of dispute between Japanese and Chinese police to settle, cases which caused no little misunderstanding, it is for this reason necessary that the police departments of these places shall employ numerous Japanese, so that they may at the same time help to plan for the improvement of the Chinese Police Service.

Article 4. China shall purchase from Japan a fixed amount of munitions of war (say 50% or more of what is needed by the Chinese Government) or that there shall be established in China a Sino-Japanese jointly-worked arsenal. Japanese technical experts to be employed and Japanese material to be purchased.

The policy of territorial expansion is laid down in Group II, Articles 2 and 3:

Article 2. Japanese subjects in South Manchuria and Eastern Inner Mongolia shall have the right to lease or own land required either for erecting suitable buildings for trade and manufacture or for farming.

Article 3. Japanese subjects shall be free to reside and travel in South Manchuria and Eastern Inner Mongolia and to engage in business and in manufacture of any kind whatsoever.

Finally in Group V, Article 5, which is quoted above.

In presenting the demands to China, the Japanese Minister was instructed to intimate that, if the Chinese accepted the Japanese "proposals," Japan might "well consider the question [of Kiaochow] with a view to restoring the said territory to China, in the event of Japan's being given [a] free hand in the disposition thereof as the result of the coming peace conference between Japan and Germany." This was not the only *douceur* offered by the Japanese, for it seems that the Japanese Minister hinted broadly to President Yüan Shih-k'ai that Japan might be willing to help him become emperor of China.[9]

Attempt at Secrecy Fails. Yüan Shih-k'ai was cautioned under the threat of even more stringent "proposals" to keep secret the fact that Japan had presented China any demands. China did its part, but the news leaked out through an Osaka newspaper, following which the demands appeared in a Tokyo paper. The Japanese government then sought to adopt the position that only eleven demands, and these of an innocuous nature, had been made, not twenty-one.

Ultimately, the truth had to be admitted. There were Twenty-One Demands, but the Fifth Group, the Japanese claimed, were only "wishes" or "requests for friendly consideration," a position which the Chinese emphatically denied. Meanwhile, negotiations between the Chinese Foreign Minister and Hioki, Japanese Minister in Peking, had lasted from February 2 until April 17, when they became temporarily deadlocked. Then, on April 26, the Japanese presented an amended series of "proposals." If China accepted these,[10] Japan promised under certain conditions, which included a Japanese settlement in the area under discussion, to return Kiaochow to China at the war's end, if the peace settlement left it in Japan's hands.

Ultimatum Brings Capitulation. China made a counterproposal on May 1 which proved unacceptable to Japan. The latter then presented the Chinese with an ultimatum May 7, 1915, allowing approximately forty-eight hours after which the Japanese threatened to take "such inde-

[9] G. Z. Wood, *The Twenty-One Demands* (New York, 1921), p. 24n.
[10] For the official texts see Carnegie Endowment for International Peace, Division of International Law, Pamphlet 45, *The Sino-Japanese Negotiations of 1915* (Washington, 1921), pp. 10-19.

pendent actions as they may deem necessary to meet the situation" should China fail to make an acceptable reply.[11]

The following day China capitulated and accepted the demands as revised by the Japanese on April 26. Treaties were signed and notes exchanged on May 25, 1915. By the terms thus agreed upon, China yielded on most, but not all, of the Twenty-One Demands. China's principal stand all along, realizing the weakness of its position in the face of Japan's superior force, was against Group V, the acceptance of which would have reduced China to the role of a Japanese colony. The virtual elimination of this section was a source of gratification to China.

The chief gains registered by Japan as a result of forcing these "proposals" on China were in South Manchuria, where its leasehold (the Kwantung Leased Territory) and railway agreements were extended greatly, and in Eastern Inner Mongolia.

The Powers and the Twenty-One Demands. The European Powers, involved as they were in a fight for their very existence, took little notice of the whole episode. For example, Lloyd George admitted at Versailles in 1919 that he had not previously heard of the Twenty-One Demands. Among the Occidental Powers, only the United States followed these developments at all closely. Yet its help to China and protection of its own interests were confined to ineffectual protests.

While negotiations were in progress between China and Japan, Secretary of State Bryan informed the Japanese on March 13, 1915, that:

> While on principle and under the treaties of 1844, 1858, 1868, and 1903 with China the United States has ground upon which to base objections to the Japanese "demands" relative to Shantung, South Manchuria, and East Mongolia, nevertheless the United States frankly recognizes that territorial contiguity creates special relations between Japan and these districts....
>
> [Nonetheless] the United States... could not regard with indifference the assumption of political, military, or economic domination over China by a foreign Power,... [which would] exclude Americans from equal participation in the economic and independent development of China and would limit the political independence of that country.[12]

On May 11, 1915, the Department of State sent identical notes to both China and Japan to the effect that the United States could not recognize "any agreement or undertaking which has been entered into or which may be entered into between the Governments of China and Japan

---

[11] *Ibid.*, pp. 19-31, contains the memorandum from the Chinese Foreign Minister to the Japanese Minister and the texts, both Chinese and Japanese, of the new Chinese proposals.

[12] *United States, Foreign Relations, 1915*, pp. 108-111.

impairing the treaty rights of the United States and its citizens in China, the political or territorial integrity of the Republic of China, or the international policy relative to China commonly known as the open-door policy." [13]

It was in China, itself, that the resentment was strongest. Although the government had been powerless to resist Japan, popular anger was not directed against it but against Japan. Yüan Shih-k'ai had played his difficult role with such skill that he avoided becoming an object of resentment by forcing Japan to deliver its ultimatum before he accepted any of its terms.

In Japan, the Okuma government was widely criticized on a variety of grounds, all deriving from the Twenty-One Demands. The chief criticism was that the government had blundered badly.

China Enters the War

Chinese National Spirit Grows. In the wake of China's humiliation through the forced acceptance of the Twenty-One Demands, many things happened. Probably the most significant in the long run was the appearance of a nascent nationalism which expressed itself in such ways as the boycott of Japanese merchants and goods, the raising of a National Salvation Fund to fight any future aggression, and the marking of May 25 as a symbol of national humiliation.[14]

Yüan Seeks Imperial Title. Following his successes in crushing the Nanking rebellion and dissolving Parliament in 1913, Yüan Shih-k'ai headed toward complete dictatorship. The Provisional Constitution of 1913 had been scrapped and replaced by the Constitutional Compact of May 1, 1914, which made the chief executive's position extremely powerful. Now in the late spring and summer of 1915 it became increasingly obvious that Yüan was bent upon overthrowing the republic and establishing himself as emperor. Various interested groups, like the Chou An Hui (Society for the Preservation of Peace), began to propagandize actively for the revival of monarchical government in China. The examples of Japan and Germany were held up as ideals which China would do well to emulate. The movement gained considerable momentum but failed to receive genuine popular support.

Then, on October 28, 1915, Japan, Great Britain, and Russia made representations to the Chinese government that the projected change in

---

[13] Conference on the Limitation of Armament Senate Document No. 126, 67th Congress, 2d Session (Washington, 1922), p. 779, quoted in H. F. MacNair, *Modern Chinese History Selected Readings* (Shanghai, 1933), p. 817.

[14] LaFargue, *op. cit.,* p. 78.

China's form of government would be unwise and dangerous alike to China and the Powers. The French and Italians soon followed suit. On the other hand, the United States, in reply to the requests of Japan and Great Britain for its support, took the position that China was the best judge of its own institutions and any interference on the part of the United States would amount to an infringement of China's sovereignty.

Yüan's Failure and Death. Despite the opposition of these Powers, the champions of the proposed change went ahead, and on December 11, 1915, Yüan was unanimously nominated Emperor of China by the Council of State. For his part, Yüan announced his acceptance of the nomination. Rebellions in such places as Yünnan, however, caused him to postpone the enthronement ceremonies. Finally, following a rising in Kwangsi, Yüan issued a mandate on March 23, 1916, canceling the idea of the monarchy, but he continued in the presidency. Because he clung to his position, a revolt broke out in the south and spread so rapidly throughout the country that Yüan soon held but ten loyal provinces. On May 29 he issued a statement that he was anxious to retire, and that he always respected the will of the people. One week later, on June 6, 1916, Yüan died suddenly. The presidency was assumed by Vice-President Li Yuan-hung, a man who had won some measure of fame in the Revolution of 1911. Li proved acceptable to most of those who rebelled against Yüan Shih-k'ai. Parliament was reconvened on August 1, 1916, and the Provisional Constitution of 1912 was declared in force until a definitive one could be drafted.

While various domestic problems continued to trouble the restored republic, progress was sufficiently orderly to enable China to direct attention once more to foreign affairs. The major international question was raised by American severance of diplomatic relation with Germany on February 3, 1917. Believing that other neutrals should do the same, the American diplomatic representatives were instructed to invite neutral governments to which they were accredited to break with Germany and its allies.

China Severs Relations with Germany. The Chinese responded by sending a note of protest to Germany (February 9, 1917) over the latter's declaration of unlimited submarine warfare. The Allies then expressed their satisfaction over this action [15] and announced that they were prepared to give favorable consideration to the question of suspending China's indemnity payments arising from the Boxer Rebellion, and

---

[15] In the interim, the United States moved to restrain China rather than urge her to enter the war actively. *Ibid.,* p. 93.

also of revising China's customs tariffs. Events moved swiftly, and on March 14, 1917, China severed diplomatic relations with both Germany and Austria-Hungary.

With China drawing closer to a declaration of war against Germany, the Japanese government became seriously concerned. Since the early months of the war, a major Japanese objective had been to prevent China's being represented at the conference table when the Shantung question came up for settlement. Should China become a belligerent, this would be impossible. Accordingly, taking the bull by the horns the Japanese approached Great Britain (January 27, 1917) with a request that the British pledge their support of Japan's claims to Shantung and to the former German islands north of the equator which the Japanese had seized in 1914. Britain assented to the Japanese requests and received the latter's assurance that they would back Britain's right to retain the former German islands south of the equator. On February 19, Japan sought similar promises from France and Russia. Both agreed, provided that Japan do whatever it could to get China to break with Germany, a request which the Japanese honored.

Chinese Oppose the War Policy. As for China itself, the news that relations had been broken with Germany was not very well received by the public at large. In the first place, of all Europeans doing business in China, the Germans were by far the most popular. There is no question where the sympathies of most Chinese lay in the matter of the European war, even after the declaration of war by their government. Secondly, there was a widespread conviction that German military expertness would ultimately triumph, and it was feared that China would be punished for having opposed her. Thirdly, Japan was one of the Allies, and resentment against Japan over the Twenty-One Demands continued strong. Fourthly, liberals in China were apprehensive that the reactionaries and conservatives would use the war as a pretext to entrench themselves in power. Fifthly, the danger of inflation would be heightened. Finally, China simply had not a strong enough military force to get involved in anything as dangerous as the first World War.

The principal supporters of continued neutrality were the southerners from whose ranks came most of the Kuomintang. On the other hand, the chief advocates of entering the war were the followers of Premier Tuan and the northern military governors. Basically, Tuan and his supporters hoped to strengthen themselves politically by adopting such a course. Publicly they advanced such appealing arguments as the need for China to have a seat at the peace table (should the Allies emerge victorious), the fact that the Allies were supposedly fighting unselfishly in the interests of humanity, and thirdly, that China's great friend, the United States, had declared war in April.[16]

The issue became so involved with questions of domestic politics that the situation became quite confused. On May 23 Premier Tuan was dismissed without warning by President Li, who in turn was forced to accede to the wishes of the military governors and dissolve Parliament, which was done on June 11. At this point, an abortive coup d'état took place whereby the Manchu boy emperor, Hsüan T'ung (the later Henry Pu-yi and Emperor Kang Teh of Manchukuo fame), was placed on the throne during the night of June 30 by the old militarist Chang Hsün. Peking was then attacked by a group of military governors under the leadership of former Premier Tuan and captured on July 14.

Farcical as the episode was, it brought about the resignation of President Li and paved the way for Tuan's return to the premiership. Since most of the radical Kuomintang members of the dissolved Parliament had fled to Canton where they set up a government of their own, the northern militarists had things pretty much their own way at this stage. Vice-President Fêng Kuo-chang became Acting President, and on August 14 the Tuan government declared war on Germany and Austria, a step which was received by the Chinese nation as a whole with remarkable indifference.

China in World War I

Once at war, China seized all German and Austrian shipping in its waters and sequestered various properties belonging to or controlled by enemy nationals. All Germans and Austrians in the service of the Chinese government were required to resign their posts, but in general enemy nationals were rather mildly treated, those in nonpolitical posts being required only to register and continuing to hold their jobs although deprived of their extraterritorial rights. Control over the German concessions at Hankow and Tientsin, as well as over the Austro-Hungarian Concession at Tientsin, was resumed by Peking.

China Wins Concessions. In recognition of China's entrance into the war, the Powers in a collective note of September 8, 1917, made several concessions to it. In the first place, they agreed to postpone for five years payment of the Boxer Indemnities [17] and stated that Germany and Austria-Hungary should permanently forfeit any payments remaining due. Secondly, an increase of 5 per cent *ad valorem* was allowed in Chinese customs duties, a level at which they already were in theory but not in

[16] Wheeler, *op. cit.*, pp. 76-84.
[17] The Socialist government in Russia, then briefly in power, agreed to yield only one third of its share.

practice. Thirdly, Chinese troops, long barred from Tientsin by the Powers were now granted limited entry there. In so acting, the Powers indicated that there were a few things, such as interning certain enemy aliens and turning over to the Allies the enemy shipping which had been seized, which they would like done in return. To some of these, China agreed, but not all. In general, however, relationships were reasonably satisfactory, although from an Allied point of view China was irritatingly slow in fulfilling her part of the bargain.

China's military contributions to the Allied cause were negligible, as the civil war raging between Peking and Canton absorbed every such resource.[18] China sent no troops whatsoever to the European or other war theaters except a special military commission to France. Her chief contribution was the dispatch of more than 175,000 laborers for behind-the-lines work in Europe and the Middle East.

Factionalism Brings Civil War. As far as the domestic situation in China was concerned, once it was in the war control over the government was exercised by Premier Tuan Ch'i-jui and a group of northern military governors, most prominent among whom were Acting President Fêng Kuo-chang and Chang Tso-lin. In opposition to the central government, South China established its own government at Canton. While theoretically under Dr. Sun Yat-sen and the Kuomintang, it was actually dominated by the militarist Lu Yung-t'ing who gained control when Sun was forced to resign in May, 1918. This division of the country resulted in civil war between North and South. The former was largely conservative and reactionary while the latter possessed most of China's leading liberals and radicals, although it had its militarists as well.

The dilatoriness of both the United States and the Allies in providing China any substantial financial assistance helped to throw the central government into the arms of the Japanese, who made war loans to China in 1917 and 1918 known collectively as the Nishihara Loans. Furthermore, on March 25, 1918, a secret Sino-Japanese military agreement was reached, which was followed on May 19 by a naval agreement. The net effect of these agreements, coupled with the financial arrangements, was to put China under the control of Japan at least as long as the war lasted.[19]

Russia's Collapse Brings Complications

The outbreak of the Bolshevist Revolution in November, 1917, brought about the collapse of Russian authority in the Chinese Eastern Railway

---

[18] The military expeditions against Canton by the Republic of China were financed largely by Japanese loans.

[19] LaFargue, *op. cit.*, p. 112.

zone. This famous line provided a short cut across Manchuria, saving passengers on the Trans-Siberian bound for Vladivostok some six hundred miles of travel. Russia's one-sided interpretation of the terms of the Chinese Eastern Railway Agreement of 1898 had given Tsarist officials virtual sovereignty in the railway zone, including control over such cities as Harbin and Changchun.

With the Bolsheviks gaining the upper hand in Russia, General Horvat, an anti-Bolshevik who was both Russian governor of the railway zone and manager of the railway, was in doubt as to what course he should follow. The Allied diplomatic corps in Peking urged China to send troops to his assistance in order to maintain order. The Allies' interest stemmed from their fear of a Bolshevik-German partnership which might dangerously upset things in the Far East. The resulting intervention of the Chinese troops temporarily saved the day. Horvat's authority was reestablished, and the Chinese forces settled down to protect the line as the year 1917 came to a close. Where China made a mistake, however, was in its failure to exercise its treaty rights by declaring the situation an emergency and taking control of the railway.

There now commenced an anti-Bolshevik movement led by a Captain Semenov in Manchuria which used Chinese soil for its headquarters. The United States, Great Britain, France, and Japan all became involved. Ultimately, northern Manchuria was occupied by Japanese forces, and there was some talk of Sino-Japanese cooperation in Manchuria which led to the signing of the Sino-Japanese Military and Naval Agreements of 1918 alluded to above.

The question of occupying the Trans-Baikal section of the Trans-Siberian Railway came up for discussion among the Allies, and there seemed to be a feeling that Japan should be permitted to be the occupying power. However, the United States objected on the ground that such an undertaking should be a joint enterprise. Meanwhile, the fighting in the East between the Bolsheviks and the Whites produced a serious defeat for Captain Semenov and his forces who were driven from Russian territory into Manchuria in June, 1918. This action opened the possibility of a Bolshevik invasion of Chinese territory. To forestall such a move, the Japanese prepared to move troops into northern Manchuria, only to find the United States opposed to such a step. American distaste to the contrary, the Japanese moved forces from South to North Manchuria in the vicinity of the Siberian border. This action was defended on the grounds of its consonance with Sino-Japanese Agreements of 1918.

Another anti-Bolshevik leader in Siberia, and a person of considerable importance, was Admiral Kolchak who cooperated with Semenov for a time. The Japanese, however, played off these two men against each other, with the result that they had a falling out and pursued their separate ways. Kolchak, although he had the backing of both the English and the French for a time, suffered a disastrous defeat in the Urals in the summer of 1919 and his capital of Omsk was taken by Soviet forces in November of that year. He himself was executed by the Bolsheviks early in February, 1920.

General Horvat's invasion of Siberia in July, 1918, prompted China to seek control over the Chinese Eastern only to find that the United States was not sympathetic with such a plan at that particular time. What the Americans proposed was that their Russian Railway Corps [20] should work jointly with Russian railway officials, presumably some of Horvat's men, and take over the line maintaining close cooperation with the Allies. Ultimately, this plan proved acceptable as both the British and the Japanese consented to it, and early in 1919 an Inter-Allied Commission was empowered to control the railways wherever the Allies should be operating in Siberia.

The Siberian Intervention.[21] As early as December, 1917, Japan had sent a war vessel to Vladivostok under the pretense of protecting Japanese nationals there. Suspicious of Japan's motives, the United States, Great Britain, and France each sent ships there in January, 1918. Ultimately, the United States and Japan reached an agreement on the question of Siberia. Signed August 3, 1918, it declared that Russia's sovereignty there would not be interfered with. Her territorial integrity was pledged, and both signatories promised not to interfere in internal Russian politics. Each nation was to send 7,500 soldiers to Siberia for the protection of Allied war matériel and to assist the 50,000 Czechs who had fought for Russia during the war but who had now become involved in clashes with the Bolsheviks.

These men were attempting to fight their way home. Other troops (British and French included) likewise participated in the intervention. The principal forces, however, were Japanese and American.

These two groups failed to get along, and there was considerable ill will engendered on both sides. Japan broke her promise and sent in over 70,000 men. Although the United States had withdrawn its troops by April, 1920, and was shortly followed by all others having troops, the Japanese stayed on in the face of adverse world opinion. The Japanese

---

[20] A group of several hundred American railway experts whom the Kerensky government had invited to Russia in 1917 to help rebuild Russia's railways but who had reached Russian waters after the Bolshevik Revolution and, without landing, turned back to Japan to await developments.

[21] For an excellent account of this question, see Pauline Tompkins, *American-Russian Relations in the Far East* (New York, 1949), chaps. 5 and 6.

were not withdrawn until the subject of their removal was taken up in the Washington Conference of 1921-22, at which time they had to yield in the face of determined American opposition.

The Far Eastern Republic. An interesting buffer in this whole question of Siberia was the abortive Far Eastern Republic which was formed in 1920 as a sort of compromise between the Bolsheviks and the Japanese. The leading personality in this briefly enduring state was Alexander M. Krasnoschekoff, its Foreign Minister. The leaders of the Far Eastern Republic made enough progress in the first few months following the creation of their government to gain control of Chita by jettisoning Semenov who controlled this city for a time. Chita then became the capital of the Far Eastern Republic.

Following a series of negotiations with the Japanese, the Bolsheviks, and the United States, the Far Eastern Republic ultimately passed out of the picture and was absorbed by Moscow, toward which it leaned increasingly as time went by.

Effects of the War upon China

The war had had profound and extensive effects on China, but disillusionment was the strongest. For one thing, the Republic had been swept away and had left in its wake a host of military adventurers seeking self-aggrandizement at the nation's expense.

Secondly, the Japanese had used the war with considerable success to undermine China's independence and had acquired not only treaties granting special privileges wrung from China during the war years, but also secret agreements with the Allies which directly affected China.

Thirdly, China had, on the whole, been subjected to humiliation and degradation by her supposed partners, rather than accorded the equality which she had hoped entrance into the war would bring.

Fourthly, there seemed to be something sordid about a war which made China drive out German traders and missionaries six months after the war was over in order to satisfy the greed of its imperialistic European allies.

Yet there were hopeful elements in the situation. The war years had shown the impossibility of returning to the old ways. Too much had happened for this to be possible, even if it were desirable which, of course, it was not. There had been a spread of leavening ideas which had stimulated, among other things, a feeling of national consciousness. This was destined to strengthen following the shabby treatment China received at Versailles—a conference which failed to produce the kind of international order upon which many Chinese intellectuals had placed their hopes.

The Lansing-Ishii Agreement

The war, having removed the attention of the European powers from China, left the field clear to Japan and the United States. These two maneuvered to prevent each other from securing too favorable a position in China. While the United States strove from 1914 to 1917 to expand its commercial activities in China, particularly in Manchuria, the Japanese became apprehensive. They were alarmed over American financial penetration of China, and so redoubled their own efforts to stay in the race.

The entrance of the United States into the war brought about a changed attitude on the part of the American government toward China. Far Eastern matters were sidetracked as Americans concentrated virtually all their energies upon the defeat of Germany. Seizing this golden opportunity, Japan swiftly gained an ascendancy in Chinese affairs which lasted until the war's end. This change in the attitude of the United States is clearly illustrated by the Lansing-Ishii Agreement.

In reply to questions asked by the Japanese Ambassador in Washington, Secretary of State Robert Lansing, on January 25, 1917, replied that "the American Government recognized that Japan had special interests in Manchuria" and that "although no declaration to that effect had been made by the United States, yet this Government had repeatedly shown a practical recognition of the fact that it did not desire to do anything there to interfere with Japan's interests."

That very day Lansing explained to Dr. Paul Reinsch, American Minister in Peking, that what he meant by "special interests" referred "only to such specific concessions as the lease of the Kwantung Peninsula and the lease of the South Manchuria Railway and other railways with [the] right to maintain railway guards, et cetera..."

Nonetheless, Lansing used a phrase charged with dynamite, and the Japanese were determined to turn it to their advantage. Having secured recognition from the other Allies of their interests in China,[22] the Japanese were naturally anxious to take advantage of the fact that they and the Americans were now on the same side by securing a similar understanding with the United States.

The way was opened when Great Britain and France sent Balfour and Viviani on special missions to express their gratitude over America's joining in the war. Japan appointed Viscount Ishii to join the two Euro-

---

[22] The London Declaration of September 4, 1914, pledged Great Britain, France, and Russia not to make a separate peace and also to consult one another upon peace plans before the peace conference should be called.

Japan became a signatory in 1915, as did Italy. By subsequent secret agreements in 1917 in accordance with the London Declaration, Japan was promised Shantung and the German possessions north of the equator.

pean statesmen. Ishii was instructed to seek an agreement to govern Japanese-American relations in the Far East. The result was the Lansing-Ishii Agreement of November 2, 1917. This was merely an exchange of notes. In the first place: "The Governments of Japan and the United States recognize that territorial propinquity creates special relations between countries, and, consequently the Government of the United States recognizes that Japan has special interests in China, particularly in the part to which her possessions are contiguous."

For its part, Japan declared that "while geographical position gives Japan such special interests, they have no desire to discriminate against the trade of other nations or to disregard the commercial rights heretofore granted by China in treaties with other Powers." The "independence or territorial integrity of China" was reaffirmed as was the principle of the so-called "open door" or equal opportunity for commerce and industry in China.

A difference of opinion arose over the meaning of Japan's "special interests." Lansing held that the phrase referred only to economic matters and lacked any political or other significance whatever. Ishii, on the other hand, argued that Japan's political as well as economic "special interests" were recognized. Otherwise, he maintained, there was no point in making the agreement, since Japan was already on record in the Root-Takahira Agreement as recognizing China's political independence and territorial integrity, as well as the open door. The Japanese position, however, was the one which was most widely accepted. It was almost universally believed that the United States had accorded to Japan a recognition of the latter's paramount influence in China and accordingly was guilty of selling China down the river. Nevertheless, in spite of the Lansing-Ishii Agreement and the embarrassing position in which it put her, the United States continued to block Japan's efforts to secure paramount influence in China right down to the end of the war, even though China and the Far East continued to be of secondary importance to the United States until the war ended.

What was not known at the time, however, was that the Japanese had agreed in a secret protocol, not made public until 1938, that neither signatory should take advantage of the present situation to seek special rights or privileges in China which would be discriminatory to the interests of other friendly states.

The Shantung Question at Versailles

Chinese Objectives. With the conclusion of World War I, despite the prevailing air of disillusionment, hopes ran high among Chinese that many past injustices would be rectified at the peace conference. The speeches of Woodrow Wilson, replete as they were with lofty idealism, did much to raise Chinese hopes.[23]

Among the many wrongs which China hoped would be righted were the financial strictures imposed by the Powers. The Chinese especially desired that the Boxer Indemnity would be totally canceled and that the right of China to fix her own tariff rates would be fully recognized. They also hoped that extraterritoriality would be abolished, along with all other special rights held by foreign powers. In other words, many Chinese hoped to see the end of the "unequal treaties."

The achievement of these goals, along with the return of Shantung and the abrogation of as many of the Twenty-One Demands as possible, was the objective of the Chinese delegation at the Paris Peace Conference. The Chinese group consisted of more than fifty members, including a number of foreign advisers and technical experts. Lu Cheng-hsiang, Minister of Foreign Affairs for the central government, headed the emissaries who included the American-trained Dr. V. K. Wellington Koo, Minister to Washington, and two representatives of Canton, Dr. C. T. (Cheng-t'ing Thomas) Wang, American representative of the Canton government, and Dr. C. C. Wu. Present in an official capacity during some of the time was Wang Ch'ing-wei, one of the luminaries of the Revolution of 1911 who was destined toward the end of his life to become a Japanese puppet. The Chinese at Paris looked to the United States for guidance in a number of matters and received from the Americans the warmest kind of cooperation; the sole exception came when the Americans yielded on Shantung.

Japanese Objectives. The Japanese delegation included Marquis Saionji, Baron Makino, and Viscount Chinda. Their program embraced three major points: first, the transfer to Japan of Kiaochow, German leasehold in Shantung, and the other German interests there; second, acquisition of the former German possessions north of the equator, the Marshall, Mariana, and Caroline islands; and third, the inclusion of a statement of racial equality in the Covenant of the League of Nations. The Japanese anticipated little trouble in gaining the first two points, as the European Powers had already approved them in the secret agreements of 1917. Furthermore, in regard to Shantung, China had agreed in the 1915 treaties and agreements to transfer the former German rights in Shantung to Japan who would then return Kiaochow to China, although

---

[23] A collection of Wilson's speeches had been translated into Chinese and became widely known. That everyone did not know them may be glimpsed from the story of Duke Kung, seventy-sixth lineal descendant of Confucius, who blurted out to an English friend in late 1918, "Who is President Wilson?" From R. T. Pollard, *China's Foreign Relations, 1917-31* (New York, 1933), pp. 50-51n.

retaining a concession in Tsingtao. To strengthen its case, in the fall of 1918 Japan had negotiated some secret agreements with China which recognized its position in Shantung.

At the very outset of the peace conference, the Chinese, spearheaded by Koo, who was extremely proficient in English and a good speaker, and Wang, argued for the restoration to China of Shantung and of German economic rights there on the grounds that Shantung was Chinese territory and that the "unequal treaties" wrung from China by Japan during the war were invalid since they were agreed to under duress. Koo's argument on the first point was based on the contention that China's declaration of war against Germany abrogated all treaties with that power. Therefore, Germany had nothing in Shantung which could be transferred to Japan. This fact, he contended, made worthless the 1915 and 1918 agreements between China and Japan concerning Shantung.

Japan Rejects Compromises. The United States, to whom the question of Shantung was very important, suggested as a solution that the former German holdings and rights in Shantung be placed under the safeguarding of the Powers with a view toward their eventual return to China. Japan steadfastly refused this proposal and was no less adamant toward Lloyd George's idea of making Shantung a League mandate, which was of course substantially the same idea.

Japan began to get angry and threatened to refuse to sign the Treaty of Versailles. Such an action would have involved boycotting the League of Nations, since the Covenant of the League was an integral part of the treaty. As Japan had already been defeated on its proposal that the Covenant of the League recognize racial equality, and, secondly, as Italy had just left the conference in a huff, these Japanese demands were reluctantly met in April, 1919.

By the terms of Articles 156, 157, and 158 of the Treaty of Versailles, Japan came into possession of all former German rights in Shantung. Japan then announced that its policy would be "to hand back the Shantung Peninsula in full sovereignty to China, retaining only the economic privileges granted to Germany and the right to establish a settlement under the usual conditions in Tsingtao."

Defeat Stimulates Chinese Nationalism. This concession to Japan represented a defeat for President Wilson and has been considered by some to have been his greatest setback at Versailles, both because of his support of China and because this arrangement was a patent violation of one of the most important of his Fourteen Points, the self-determination clause. As embarrassing and humiliating as this defeat was to Wilson, it was worse for those Chinese who were informed and articulate. There can be no doubt that the central government itself had little hope, but the really excellent performances by Koo and Wang had raised hopes in other quarters. As a result there were numerous protest meetings of Chinese students, especially in Peking, Shanghai, and Tientsin. These meetings received the support of numerous merchant associations and even many of the coolies in Shanghai. So successful were these demonstrations that there was a cabinet shakeup in June. This was an event of unparalleled significance, for it revealed that China at last had developed a public opinion, and one that had strength and vitality. Out of this, the nascent nationalistic spirit which had perhaps first manifested itself in the Revolution of 1911, and again in 1915 at the time of the Twenty-One Demands, grew stronger. The hope persisted that China, itself, might ultimately be able to do the job of putting its house in order.

Islands Mandated to Japan. From the Japanese point of view, its ambition to secure outright the German possessions north of the equator had fallen short. Put another way, they had been realized but not in the manner desired by Japan. Lloyd George, backed by Wilson, came up with a plan to make all of Germany's Pacific possessions the property of the League of Nations. They would be administered as League mandates and not outright annexations. Japan was accordingly granted a mandate over the Marshall, Mariana, and Caroline islands. They were styled Class C mandates, a classification which gave the mandatory power almost unlimited authority. Although Japan was keenly disappointed, it was eventually able to do with the islands approximately what it wanted despite the fact that title to them was technically vested in the League. Hence, this arrangement in the long run proved to be about as dangerous as if the islands had been given outright to Japan. The guiding spirits in the decision to do things this way were the Australian and New Zealand premiers, especially the former, William Morris Hughes. Hughes felt that Australia and New Zealand should have a correspondingly free hand with Germany's possessions south of the equator, which were mandated to these two commonwealths. The small island of Yap, which the Japanese felt now belonged to them, was temporarily withheld and declared internationalized because of its importance as a cable station.

Failure to Win Equality Rankles. While this settlement did not represent an actual defeat for Japanese diplomacy, it was a compromise. On the other hand, the refusal of the Powers to recognize racial equality in the League Covenant was bitterly resented by Japan, a nation of intensely proud people laboring under the feeling that they were considered inferior by the white Powers. To prevent any misapprehensions about its motives, Japan made it quite clear that it did not infer that racial equality should be construed to mean that Japanese workers could freely emigrate to other countries.

Japan reopened the question in April, proposing that there be included in the preamble of the Covenant a declaration that the signatories approved of "the principle of the equality of nations and the just treatment of their nationals." China was among those supporting the Japanese proposal, as were France and Italy, but both the United States and Great Britain were opposed. The British took the position that such a proposal was an infringement of the sovereignty of the various states, maintaining that the question was basically an internal or domestic one. In other words, within its empire it would continue to draw the color line if it suited its purposes. Wilson's view was that the question was too controversial.

The Japanese spokesman, Baron Makino, pressed his point and insisted upon a vote of the commission hearing the question. Japan won eleven out of a possible seventeen votes. Wilson, as chairman, had not voted, but he ruled that a unanimous vote was necessary to carry. The American President's action was most distasteful to Japan, whose representative declared that his government and people felt "poignant regret" over the failure to adjust a "longstanding grievance, a demand based upon a deep-rooted national conviction."

Thus Japan won one victory, Shantung, suffered one humiliating defeat, racial equality, and secured a favorable compromise on the other objective of its diplomacy at the peace table. In time to come that defeat was to assume very large proportions and the consequent resentment was to spur Japan down the road to war. Its victory, however, was a sweet one and seemed to promise ultimate achievement of Japan's goal on the Continent, which was unilateral domination of China.

SUGGESTED READINGS

For China during this period the most useful study is the excellent monograph by Thomas E. LaFargue, *China and the World War* (Stanford University, Calif., 1937). Also very good, but not so scholarly, is W. Reginald Wheeler, *China and the World War* (New York, 1919). Thomas F. Millard, *Democracy and the Eastern Question* (New York 1919), while rather anti-Japanese, is extremely knowledgeable. Useful, too, are Robert T. Pollard's *China's Foreign Relations, 1917-1931* (New York, 1933) and Putnam Weale, *The Fight for the Republic in China* (New York, 1917). Dr. Paul S. Reinsch's memoirs, *An American Diplomat in China* (New York, 1927), must be used carefully. Reinsch was partisan toward China.

For Japan at this time Roy H. Akagi, *Japan's Foreign Relations, 1542-1936* (Tokyo, 1936), pro-Japanese and reduced to the briefest coverage, Viscount Kikujiro Ishii, *Diplomatic Commentaries,* trans. and ed. by William R. Langdon (Baltimore, 1936), Masamichi Royama *Foreign Policy of Japan: 1914-1939* (Tokyo, 1941), and Tatsuji Takeuchi, *War and Diplomacy in the Japanese Empire* (Chicago, 1935) are all very helpful. Attention is again called to Chitoshi Yanaga, *Japan Since Perry* (New York, 1949). Also not to be overlooked is A. Morgan Young, *Japan in Recent Times, 1912-1926* (New York, 1929).

On the international side or dealing with special topics, the following are all recommended: Paul Birdsall, *Versailles Twenty Years After* (New York, 1941); Thomas A. Bailey, *Woodrow Wilson and the Lost Peace* (New York, 1944); Paul Clyde, *International Rivalries in Manchuria, 1689-1922* (Columbus, Ohio 1926), and *Japan's Pacific Mandate* (New York, 1935); W. L. Godshall, *The International Aspects of the Shantung Question* (Philadelphia, 1933); William S. Graves, *America's Siberian Adventure, 1918-1920* (New York, 1931); A. Whitney Griswold, *The Far Eastern Policy of the United States* (New York, 1938); Robert Lansing, *War Memoirs* (Indianapolis, 1935); Eleanor Tupper and George E. McReynolds, *Japan in American Public Opinion* (New York, 1937); G. Zay Wood, *The Shantung Question* (New York, 1922); Carl W. Young, *The International Relations of Manchuria* (Chicago, 1929), and *Japan's Special Position in Manchuria* (Baltimore, 1931); Pauline Tompkins, *American-Russian Relations in the Far East* (New York, 1949); John A. White, *Siberian Intervention* (Princeton, 1950).

22

CHINA, 1911-1926: REPUBLIC, MILITARISM, AND RENAISSANCE

The Revolution of 1911

For some years before 1911 it had been evident that the Manchus had nearly exhausted their mandate. Even the Empress Dowager could only delay, rather than prevent, the collapse of the dynasty, and what she was able to do was in great part undone during Prince Ch'un's regency. Did the Manchus in 1911 still have the vitality or had the National Assembly the leverage to prod them to carry out a peaceful change rapidly enough to head off violent outbreak? That seemed doubtful. Granted that revolution was on its way, the great question was, what sort of revolution. The traditional variety of Chinese revolution had many times down the centuries swept away dynasties without destroying the foundations of Chinese political, economic, and social institutions. In the unsuccessful Taiping Rebellion, a new portent had appeared; that was a strong and strange tincture of Christianity which was one of the first effects resulting from the impact of the West on Chinese culture. The revolution of 1911 very naturally surpassed the Taiping movement as a manifestation of Western influence, for it was promoted and led by an active group of professional revolutionaries who admired and wished to adapt many aspects of the culture of the West. It destroyed not only the dynasty, but the whole basis of the old type of monarchical bureaucratic rule in China. No new dynasty could mount the Dragon Throne; instead there emerged something new under the Chinese sun, a republic.

However, although the movement that overthrew the Ch'ing dynasty was in some ways a new phenomenon which brought unexpected results, it was also in many of its phases a traditional antidynastic rising. Most of the Chinese were not in touch with Western thought, and their reasons for rejection of the Manchus were essentially the ones which had repeatedly produced antidynastic risings in Chinese history. Overpopulation, poverty, epidemics, flood and drought, official corruption, and the dynasty's failure to provide internal order and security against foreign pressure were all present in the closing years of Manchu rule, and were taken as significant signs of Heaven's declining interest in the dynasty. The Manchus tried to save their heritage, but the Taiping Rebellion had sapped the strength of their administration, their inability to resist Western domination cost them face, and they were unable to carry through their policies of centralization and reform. Also, they were non-Chinese, and their foreignness was increasingly remembered against them in a day when a new patriotism was beginning to take form in China. The revolutionaries made the alien Manchus the villains of the story, with the corollary that once the hated dynasty was out, the Chinese, ruling themselves, would have no difficulty in making rapid progress. However, it would be an obviously naïve or politically colored judgment to lay at the Manchus' door all the blame for the failure of China to achieve a sound modern national life by peaceful evolution. Even Japan's apparent success in adapting Western culture was demonstrated somewhat later to be in many ways a tragic failure. The mass of the Chinese were not yet ready to follow extreme reformers, whether they were Manchu aristocrats or Chinese revolutionaries, while the bulk of the official class remained conservative and largely corrupt.

Regency of Prince Ch'un. On November 14, 1908, the Kuang Hsü Emperor died, and T'zŭ Hsi herself departed this life the next day, a coincidence which invites speculation. The Empress Dowager had already decided that the imperial title should go next to Pu-yi, nephew of the Kuang Hsü Emperor and grandson of Jung Lu. At the time of his elevation to the throne this last of the Manchu emperors, who ruled under the title of Hsüan T'ung, was only two. He was to be heir to both of the preceding emperors, thus settling the long agitated question of the rites to the spirit of the T'ung Chih Emperor. Prince Ch'un, father of the new ruler and brother of the Kuang Hsü Emperor, became regent, although with the death of T'zŭ Hsi, the widow of the Kuang Hsü Emperor became Empress Dowager and her desire to be another T'zŭ Hsi caused complications. With the inauguration of the new reign it was clear that the twilight of the dynasty had arrived. Prince Ch'un was young, inexperienced, and tactlessly pro-Manchu. One of his first moves was to thrust Yüan Shih-k'ai out of public life. Yüan was instructed to retire to his native place for treatment of a "leg disease" and there he sulked in his tent until the events of 1911 put the Manchus at his mercy. Some of Yüan's young Western-trained protégés also went out of office. Court intrigue resulted in the dismissal of the able Manchu official Tuan Fang, ostensibly for taking photographs of the Empress Dowager's funeral cortege. The death on October 5, 1909, of that enigmatic, variable, and energetic servant of the state, Chang Chih-tung, removed virtually the last of the loyal and competent old-line Chinese officials. What the throne had left to rely on were nondescript and not too ethical Chinese officials and untrained Manchu princelings, to whom Prince Ch'un unwisely showed favoritism.

As the Manchus weakened, their organized opponents gained in strength. The reformist group, led by the exiled K'ang Yu-wei, were at a disadvantage since they had pinned their hopes on the Kuang Hsü Emperor's outliving the Empress Dowager and re-establishing the program of constitutional monarchy and general reform which had been launched in 1898. Prince Ch'un did not pardon the surviving reformers. In any case, the allegiance of young and restless Chinese was being won, not by K'ang Yu-wei and Liang Ch'i-ch'ao, but by the advocates of an antidynastic revolution. In Tokyo, where many Chinese went to study after Japan's victory over Russia, several revolutionary organizations had been formed. The chief of these societies came together in 1905 to form the T'ung-mêng Hui (forerunner of the Kuomintang) in which Sun Yat-sen was the chief figure. The principal doctrine of the revolutionary group was that the Manchus, who were to blame for China's weakness, must go before China could experience any real renovation. Revolutionary sentiment among Chinese students and residents overseas was matched by an increasingly organized opposition to the Manchus at home in China. During the last decade of Manchu rule there was a renaissance of secret societies, those traditional agencies of antidynastic agitation, and there were many local risings, some the result of extortion or famine, others more consciously revolutionary. Chinese newspapers flourished in the treaty ports. Inflammatory sheets, they were full of the spirit of the new nationalism and played up every Manchu failure in foreign or domestic policy.

Railway Nationalization. The particular issue which became the focus for many of the sentiments and problems of the time was the nationalization of railways. In this case the feeble Manchus, after taking unpopular foreign loans, tried to enforce a strong policy of centralization in the face of hysterical opposition. The use of foreign advice and foreign money in railway enterprise in China was bound to provoke general Chinese nationalism and to irritate those Chinese who themselves wanted to make railway profits. Provincial feeling was also involved: each province desired a local railway program without central government interference. Yet by their very nature, trunk railways had to be national enterprises, and China lacked the capital necessary to finance these large undertakings. The *cause célèbre* was the contract for the Canton-Hankow-Chengtu line.

In 1898 a concession for the Canton-Hankow Railway had been given to American interests but was not carried through. Local gentry then professed their desire to build the line, but did not produce the necessary funds. Chang Chih-tung, who was in charge of railway negotiations, next sought European capital, and in June, 1909, negotiations with British, German, and French capitalists were initiated. A telegram of protest from President Taft brought American capitalists into this group. Finally in May, 1911, the Chinese government acceded to the four-power loan, after considerable delay because of the state of public feeling, and followed the loan contract with a declaration of the nationalization of all trunk lines.

The Manchus thus managed to combine in one policy submission to foreign imperialism and a move for centralization. There was already agitation for the earlier summoning of the promised parliament, rumor of the impending partition of China by foreign powers, a crop of revolutionary risings, and plague and flood. The foreign loan for railways and the edict of nationalization were last straws. There were great flutterings among disgruntled provincials who themselves wanted to build railways (or perhaps more precisely, to collect and control money meant for railway building). The worst situation developed in Szechwan Province where Chinese investors lost heavily in a promotion scheme which never got beyond the planning stage. Although 11,000,000 taels had been subscribed, after the bursting of this bubble the government proposed to return only 4,000,000 taels when nationalization went into effect; the balance had been lost by the president of the local railway company through speculation in rubber. The gentry of Szechwan broke out in "states' rights" agitation and the mass of the population joined them as a demonstration against heavy taxation. After a mob stormed the viceroy's yamen on September 7, revolt spread quickly through the province. Tuan Fang was sent to restore order, only to be murdered by his own troops in November.

Fall of the Manchus. While the Szechwan rising was growing, the "official" revolution, the one planned by Sun Yat-sen and his group, broke out somewhat impromptu in the Wuhan cities after a chance bomb explosion in the Russian concession on October 10; the date is observed as Nationalist China's national holiday. Some of the troops at Wuchang went over to the rebellion, literally dragging one of their officers, Liu Yüan-hung, with them; shortly after, a new government was proclaimed with Liu as president. In South and Central China, one province after another repudiated the Manchus, and the National Assembly which met in Peking on October 22 took advantage of the dynasty's dire plight to press for more concessions. The Manchus yielded, a constitutional monarchy was promised, and on October 30, 1911, in a document redolent with traditional Chinese political thinking, the five-year old emperor was made to take upon himself the blame for everything which had gone wrong.

It was the surest indication of the bankruptcy of the Manchus that, in the face of this crisis, they could think of no more promising course of action than to recall Yüan Shih-k'ai. Yüan could hardly be expected to be loyal to the dynasty which had dropped him so summarily three years before, but the core of the northern army was Yüan's old Peiyang force which would follow only him in full confidence. To gain an effective military force, the Manchus were forced to accept the great risks involved in trying to use Yüan. Yüan was coy and several times raised his price, but by October 27 the dynasty had virtually put itself in his hands and he then left for the front. Yüan was next urged to become premier in the new government, and after pleading continued ill health—his leg disease was difficult to cure—he finally accepted the position and on November 16 announced a cabinet which even included the now pardoned Liang Ch'i-ch'ao. However, these changes were plainly not enough to end the revolt, so on December 6 the regent resigned.

Sun Yat-sen, who had been abroad at the outbreak of the revolution, returned to China and in late December was chosen provisional president by an assembly at Nanking. As Yüan held the Manchus in the hollow of his hand, it was with him that republican representatives negotiated in January, 1912. Military action had resulted in a stalemate, and it was clear that unless reconciliation could be effected, there might for some time be two Chinas, a northern government headed by Yüan and based on his loyal forces, and a republican regime with its capital at Nanking having at least potential control over central and southern China. The answer was found; the republicans, hoping to control the new government, decided to accept Yüan, who was plainly no republican, as president of a united China. The Manchu dynasty, already a mere shadow, then did what it must. In an edict of February 12, 1912, the Ch'ing house gave up its power and designated Yüan to work out with the republicans the future form of government. The revolution seemed to be over and China apparently had achieved in one great leap the noblest form of Western political organization, a republic, from which peace and progress would inevitably flow.

Presidency of Yüan Shih-k'ai

Subsequent events nullified the fine optimism of the early months of 1912. It is not easy to diagnose what really happened in the Chinese body politic in 1911 and 1912. As a destructive force, the revolution had been almost too successful. More had fallen than the Manchus; the rule of the scholar-gentry was also at end, although it took the literati themselves and other social groups some years to recognize the fact. But though the old order had lost its sanction, no new order was ready to take its place. The Republic proved abortive, and China wallowed in social confusion as the revolutionary leaven continued to work. Many early Westernizers came to feel in the years after 1912 that they had ploughed the sea, and that China was being swept along on a deep running tide of revolutionary change toward some goal which none could see. "Down with the Manchus" had been an effective slogan, but the fall of the dynasty, while virtually inevitable and quite desirable, brought no magic cure of China's ills. The unresolved conflict between the old and the new which continued unabated after 1912 meant very hard years for the "new China" which had been hailed with such enthusiasm. China's modernization was not to be orderly and guided as the Manchus and both Yüan and his republican opponents hoped, but violent and tempestuous.

Sources of Yüan's Strength. The partnership of Yüan Shih-k'ai and the republicans, by which the new Chinese regime was created, was no more than a marriage of convenience. The republicans had accepted a president who, they realized, was no believer in republicanism; and Yüan had acquired political associates who, in his opinion, were egregiously ignorant of the art of government. Each hoped in due course to dispense with, or render innocuous, the other party to the bargain.

In the struggle for power which followed, the advantage, at least in the short view, was on Yüan's side. To most Chinese and to most foreigners with knowledge of China, his record looked very good. He was an experienced official with a reputation for vigor, efficiency, and progressiveness. He had been the most conspicuous reforming official in the last years of T'zŭ Hsi's control. He was also an opportunist and a realist of sorts, but these qualities, which eventually betrayed him, served him well at the outset. Adding to his strength was the fact that the mass of the Chinese people knew little of republic and something of Yüan Shih-k'ai; their chief concern was to shake off the old government with its burden of heavy taxation and official corruption. Yüan thus had on his side the forces of old-style Chinese antidynastic rebellion which had been an essential element of the 1911 revolution.

In addition to the advantages which Yüan derived from this quite general personal support, Yüan had two immediate assets of great importance. First he had an army. The Peiyang force was his personal tool. In addition many military leaders of the time were graduates of Yüan's Military Academy at Paotingfu and were his protégés in somewhat the same way as, in later years, the graduates of the Whampoa Military Academy were supporters of Chiang Kai-shek. Yüan had a shrewd appreciation of the decisive importance of military power in the new political situation and sought to draw to him the local militarists who had popped up everywhere in China during the confused winter of 1911-12. It was soon evident that Yüan, rejecting the Chinese tradition of the superiority of the writing brush over the sword, was building a military machine by installing as provincial governors soldiers favorable to him. While elimination of provincial armies was highly desirable, it would have been difficult to accomplish inasmuch as no individual general wished to part with his troops, and severance pay would mean tremendous expense. Yüan therefore accepted and sought to use the provincial militarism which now showed itself even more openly than in the days of the Manchus. While recognizing the dangers, he hoped to be able to suppress any individual militarist who would not play the game his way. That Yüan was sowing the whirlwind became only too clear after his death, but in 1912 and 1913 his control of armed force gave him a great edge over the republicans.

Yüan's other immediate asset was money, or at least, the means of getting it. The foreign powers, although in earlier crises they had sought to influence the nature of China's government, had made no real effort to save the Manchus.[1] In Yüan they thought they saw a "strong man" capable of giving China a more competent and more stable government. If Yüan would accept and carry through China's obligations to the Powers, they would provide him with a "reorganization loan." In July, 1912, the consortium was extended to six powers by the inclusion of Japan and Russia. It then proposed terms for a reorganization loan which involved the placing of the gabelle under foreign direction as a source of revenue from which loans could be repaid, and the close supervision by foreigners of the expenditure of the loan. These provisions were of course very distasteful to politically aware Chinese, including Yüan, who tried to get money elsewhere, but failed. The consortium shrank to five Powers in March, 1913, after President Wilson's sharp criticism of the terms of the loan, and the withdrawal of the American group, but in April, 1913, a reorganization loan of £25,000,000 was signed and sealed. Yüan now had the wherewithal not only to function as chief executive but also to dispose of his political opponents.

Yüan Shih-k'ai versus the Republicans. The republicans, lacking general popularity, military strength, or ready cash, found the contest with Yüan an uneven one. To Yüan they appeared to be rank amateurs

[1] J. G. Reid, *The Manchu Abdication and the Powers* (Berkeley, 1935), is a careful study of the attitude of the powers toward the 1911 revolution.

in politics, ideologues denationalized by foreign study. Unfortunately Yüan's estimate contained considerable truth: the republicans did not show up well in 1912 and 1913. Too many were uncritically enthusiastic about Western political ideas and failed to realize the difficulty of transplanting them to China. They had been a group of conspirators who were unready to become a government. They were so eager to curb Yüan and make of him a French president in the manner of the Third Republic that they appeared merely factional, offering no constructive policy for the reorganization of the country. Their naïve belief that overturn of the Manchus was the cure of all ills was quickly replaced by the equally innocent conviction that elimination of Yüan would make everything right with the republic. Yüan was certainly no asset to the republic, but more was wrong with the new regime than his presence as president.

Under these circumstances, it is not surprising that the first rounds in the contest for power went to Yüan. In March, 1912, Yüan was due to be inaugurated at Nanking as provisional president under a provisional constitution drawn up by the republicans there. A suspiciously opportune mutiny made it impossible for Yüan to leave his stronghold of Peking. The mountain had to come to Mohammed; Yüan was inaugurated in the former capital of the Manchus, and there, too, the temporary legislative body, the National Council, met in April. The provisional constitution was somewhat on the French model, with a weak executive and a strong legislature. It was a carefully done piece of constitutional drafting but bore no noticeable relation to China's own political development. Indeed, this constitutional document and the many other constitutional drafts which followed in the teens and early twenties were revelations of an imported faith in passing laws which ignored the old Chinese conviction of the superiority of *li*—moral standards and customs—to *fa*—legislation.

The new Cabinet had to be approved by the National Council, an arrangement that touched off a sharp political wrangle. Although settled by compromise, it widened and embittered the differences between Yüan and the parliamentarians. The republicans therefore in the summer of 1912 organized a political party, the Kuomintang, in preparation for the elections for a National Assembly. These were to be held on the basis of suffrage for all males over 21 who paid a small tax or had a certain amount of property or education. The Kuomintang was very successful in its campaigning and won majorities in both houses, but Yüan offset its victory at the polls by drastic action.

In August, 1912, two republicans had been arrested on charges of treason and embezzlement and had been summarily condemned to death by a military tribunal. In early April, 1913, an eminent leader of the Kuomintang, the prospective premier in the new government, was assassinated. Both these events were charged to Yüan. Then, capping the climax, while many Kuomintang politicians were out electioneering, Yüan, by devious means, secured the assent of the remaining members of the National Council to the reorganization loan. He proceeded to sign it in April, 1913, without submitting it to the new National Assembly which met that month in an atmosphere of extreme tension between the president and the legislators. The result was the attempted "Second Revolution" of July, 1913, in which some of the Kuomintang leaders tried to rouse a national movement to "punish Yüan Shih-k'ai." Unfortunately for them, most Chinese did not know what offenses Yüan had committed for which he should be punished. He easily suppressed the rising; Sun Yat-sen, leader of the Kuomintang, once more became an exile in Japan, and many members of the National Assembly became refugees.

What was left of the Assembly then went to work on a permanent constitution, and a combination of some of the Kuomintang members who had not rebelled plus some of the members of the Progressive Party led by Liang Ch'i-ch'ao produced what is known as the "Temple of Heaven Draft." Yüan urged that they first complete and put into effect those portions of the constitution which would relate to the executive, so that he could become a full-fledged president instead of continuing in a provisional capacity. With the necessary constitutional provisions completed, Yüan was elected president on October 6, 1913, by an Assembly terrorized by an organized "mob" outside its doors. Thus on October 10, 1913, the second anniversary of the outbreak of the republican revolution, the most notable opponent of republicanism in China became president of the Chinese republic. Once installed as president, Yüan quickly showed his hand. On November 4 he suppressed the Kuomintang as a treasonable organization and in January suspended what was left of the Assembly. A council which met in its place produced the Constitutional Compact, a governmental system very much to Yüan's taste since it gave the president great powers and thus threw a cloak of constitutionality over Yüan's thoroughly dictatorial regime. Yüan now bore down with great harshness on all opposition, apparent or suspected. He also undertook the formulation of a new system of provincial government with civilian governors appointed by the president to replace military governors, a move obviously intended to reduce his dependence on provincial militarists.

Yüan Plans to Restore the Monarchy. There were many indications in 1915 that Yüan was preparing to carry the traditional Chinese historical cycle to its usual conclusion. A dynasty had been overthrown; now the new man of virtue, Yüan Shih-k'ai, was ready to receive the mandate of heaven and mount the Dragon Throne. Yüan sacrificed at the Altar of Heaven, and stressed veneration of ancestors and old-style Confucianism. Professor Goodnow of Johns Hopkins, formerly adviser to Yüan, expressed an opinion that constitutional monarchy might be better for the Chinese, if they wanted it, than the mere appearance of republicanism. Yüan cynically seized on this opinion, which was a reasonable view, and also welcomed old-fashioned monarchical sentiment as grist to his mill. Actually what he intended to establish was neither the traditional rule of scholar-bureaucrats nor a constitutional monarchy, Western style, but absolutism based on physical force and general political inertia. The stage setting for the new regime was carefully prepared: "public opinion" was organized, a rigged convention met and begged for monarchy, and Yüan, after appropriate gestures of unworthiness, agreed to hear the voice of the people and assume the throne.

But events soon demonstrated that if the republicans had misjudged the general temper of the Chinese people and the political possibilities in this stage of their revolution, so had Yüan. It was impossible to set up a real republic, but it was also impossible to re-establish even the appearance of the old monarchy. Strong opposition came from various quarters. Liang Ch'i-ch'ao, certainly no radical, advised against upsetting the country by changing the type of government. The old National Assembly of 1913 met in Shanghai and asked Yüan to give up the project for the restoration of the monarchy and to resign from the presidency of the republic. Most significant, Ts'ao Ao, military governor of Szechwan, launched what proved to be a widespread rising against the proposed monarchy. Even the foreign powers were hostile. Great Britain, Russia, France, and Italy were clearly opposed to Yüan's scheme and advised delay; Japan, which Yüan had thought might approve, seems not to have given too strong encouragement to the monarchical movement. The enthronement was postponed and finally canceled, and Yüan's timely death in June, 1916, provided a way out of an extremely difficult situation.

The War Lords

With Yüan eliminated, the next stage in China's evolution was the period of the war lords, the outward and visible symbols of the breakup of the old pattern before the shaping of the new.[2] An effort was made to revive the republic, but in many ways the general history of 1912 to 1914 repeated itself. After Yüan's death, Li Yuan-hung, who had been vice president, assumed the presidency and summoned to Peking the Parlia-

---

[2] H. F. MacNair, *China in Revolution* (Chicago, 1931), contains the most helpful account of the complicated politics of the war-lord period.

ment which Yüan had turned out in 1914. Like the Bourbons, the Parliament members had learned nothing and forgotten nothing during their exile. They were soon engaged in acrimonious dispute with Premier Tuan Chi-jui, who was the leader of the Anfu faction of the Peiyang military group. The Parliament returned to the Sisyphean task of composing a "permanent" constitution. It still favored decentralization and a weak executive, which Tuan disliked as much as had Yüan. Tuan tended to rely on the *tuchuns,* or military governors, who were left over from Yüan's regime, and felt a healthy scorn for the parliamentarians. The air was full of factional opposition to Tuan, threats of impeachment, and adjournments for lack of a quorum.

The question of entry into World War I brought to a head the disagreement between Tuan and the Assembly, which was the contemporary manifestation of the continuing struggle between military and civil power. Tuan was eager to go into the war and obtain foreign loans; the Parliament feared that he would use any money he could get and any connections he could establish with foreign governments to strengthen his position in the internal political quarrel. Tuan then attempted to put pressure on the Assembly, which in turn called upon him to resign. President Li tried to calm the troubled waters by dismissing Tuan. Instead the storm grew worse. The military governors marched on Peking. Parliament refused to dissolve, although most of the individual members departed. Li then called in the most astonishing of mediators, General Chang Hsun of Kiangsu, who was so thoroughly unreconstructed that on the strength of his pig-tailed army he forthwith proclaimed the restoration of the Manchus! For a fortnight the dynasty was restored with K'ang Yu-wei in attendance. Then the *tuchuns* heroically marched on Peking to save the republic (although they were generally its chief danger) and the Manchus once more retired into the shadows of the Forbidden City. Li Yuan-hung, who had lost face in layers, understandably chose this moment to give up his office. Feng Kuo-chang, head of one faction of Peiyang militarists, became president; Tuan Chi-jui, head of the other, became premier.

Recurrent Civil War

The members of the Assembly adjourned to the South, and a government was set up in Canton with Sun Yat-sen as its chief figure. There were now two Chinese governments. While they were able to combine to send a joint delegation to the Paris Peace Conference, they failed to cooperate in any other respect. But to treat China as divided into only two parts in the years after 1917 would be to indulge in grievous over-simplification. Actually China was a political kaleidoscope, with each piece of colored glass a militarist; as the kaleidoscope turned, the combinations and permutations of the war lords, great and small, would have taxed the skill of an expert mathematician.

The war-lord armies were accumulated from peasants who decided that it was better to loot than be looted. Each war lord viewed his army as his most precious asset, one not to be dissipated in bloody combat, and most contests were settled by "silver bullets" which brought changes of allegiance before matters came to the point of actual fighting. Foreign correspondents sometimes found the civil war amusing in a comic-opera way, but for the Chinese people it was no laughing matter. The rival armies plundered the land like locusts, and the country was far gone in chaos and misery. Warlordism lasted at least until 1928, when the Nationalist Government was established, and continued in practice in some parts of the country for years after that date. It was soon clear that the contests of the war lords would never produce a unified Chinese government, even a military dictatorship. Each of the major war lords had imperial ambitions, but centrifugal forces were too strong.

The Principal War Lords. At Peking the nominal republican government lingered on, but it was obviously for sale to the highest bidder. In the later stages of World War I the Anfu clique was dominant, with plenty of Japanese money at its command. However the terms of the Versailles Treaty brought a sharp revulsion against this state of affairs and showed that at least one segment of the population—the student group—was thoroughly alert. The first great student demonstration, that of May, 1919, forced out three members of Tuan's Cabinet and kept his government from signing the Versailles Treaty. Chang Tso-lin then began to emerge as a formidable opponent of the Anfu group. Starting as a bandit in the tall kaoliang of Manchuria, he had become respectable by cooperating with the Japanese in the Russo-Japanese War, and in 1911 had become military governor of Fengtien. Chang came to an understanding with Ts'ao Kun, *tuchun* of Chihli, who was also annoyed by the Anfu clique's monopoly of spoils. As a result, in the summer of 1920, Wu Pei-fu, subordinate of Ts'ao Kun, marched on Peking to "save the republic" and to call a constitutional convention. He took the city, Tuan retired to study Buddhism, and Chang and Ts'ao moved in to enjoy the results of Wu's fighting—and did not summon a constituent assembly.

Thereafter military affairs in North China became more muddled. Wu built himself an army in the Yangtze region and in 1922, with the support of Fêng Yü-hsiang of Shensi, took his revenge on Chang by driving him back to Manchuria. Li Yuan-hung now resumed the presidency and reconvened the 1917 Parliament, but there was no magic by which a real republic could be based on the power of a major militarist, and Peking politics were as shabby as ever. Ts'ao Kun got the presidency in 1923 by wholesale bribery. The Parliament returned to its constitution-making labors and brought forth a refurbished version of the Temple of Heaven Draft, but it was stillborn.

Fêng Yü-hsiang now came to the fore as a major figure. One of the most colorful war lords, Fêng was known as "the Christian general" in the earlier stages of his career and had his well-drilled and well-paid army singing "Onward Christian Soldiers." A later visit to Moscow caused him to change the words if not the tune, and disabused Christian missionaries of any idea which they may have had that he was the sword of the Lord. But Fêng kept afloat through the stormy 1920's, came to terms with the Nationalists, and was a hardy perennial in Chinese politics until his death in 1948. In 1924 Fêng betrayed Wu and took Peking for himself. He drove out the boy emperor, forced the parliamentarians to flee, and made a deal with Chang Tso-lin. Tuan Chi-jui then became provisional chief executive. However Fêng and Chang soon eyed each other askance. Fêng retired to the Northwest where he organized an efficient *"kuo min chun"* (National People's Army) with Russian aid, while Chang enjoyed Japanese support as war lord of the Manchurian provinces in which Japan's major economic interests centered. There was more fighting in 1925 and 1926 in which Wu, who had reformed his army with the backing of British commercial interests, joined with Chang against Fêng's group. On this turn of the wheel, Fêng went to Moscow; Tuan fled to Tientsin; Ts'ao Kun, who had been in jail for corruption, was released and resigned the presidency; and Chang and Wu decided on a "Regency Cabinet" as a false front. Finally, Chang thrust aside the corpse of the republic without bothering to give it decent burial and set up a frank military dictatorship which lasted until he was forced out of Peking by the Nationalists in 1928.

In South China in these years Sun's "republican" government was a spectacle scarcely more edifying than the Peking regime. Sun was dependent on local war lords and several times had to withdraw to the International Settlement in Shanghai when he found himself at loggerheads with his erstwhile military supporters. However, Sun became increasingly aware that he must escape from dependence on militarists and must reorganize his party unless his revolutionary movement was to sink into total failure. The result was the triumph of the Nationalist movement, the first great evidence that China might be emerging from the disruptive stage of the revolution into a new period of growth.

Economic Development

The decay of the republic and the maneuvres of the war lords were profoundly discouraging to the Chinese. These conditions also led a number of foreigners to pronounce judgment upon China as another Egypt now sinking into a last long sleep and ready to be taken over and run by those competent to do it, which the Chinese, they said, were not. This "old China hand" estimate of China in the early 1920's was a superficial one. Actually under the surface of political confusion there were creative processes at work. Contact with the West was Janus-faced: it stimulated as well as destroyed.

During the period from the fall of the Manchus to the establishment of the Nationalist government there occurred real though spotty economic progress.[3] Agriculture was relatively unchanged, since any effort to emulate the West and mechanize farming would have required a tremendous agricultural revolution, such as that which in the U.S.S.R. accompanied collectivization. However, modern means of transport as they appeared did something to lessen the traditional self-sufficiency of the village and to break the solidarity of the family unit by making it easier for individuals to draw out and go their own way. Modern factories were increasing in numbers, especially in Shanghai and up the Yangtze, opening the possibility that the guild system might eventually give way, in many lines, to factory methods of production.

Foreign trade was expanding and changing in character. The old days when China was an exporter of luxury goods and felt little need to import anything from the West were gone. A taste and demand for certain sorts of foreign goods were growing: kerosene and matches had gained important roles in the slow but basic transformation of the countryside. China was also importing machinery and raw cotton for the mills. On the other hand, China was represented abroad by a wide range of agricultural products, raw materials, and rare metals. Soybeans, dried eggs, and tungsten had largely replaced silk and tea as China's chief offerings in foreign markets. These economic changes were to have important influence on the politics of the 1920's. The factories were still in an elemental stage, and poor labor conditions naturally led to a labor movement. Since about half of the cotton mills were foreign owned, chiefly Japanese and British, labor trouble had international overtones and became a part of the anti-imperialist movement which the Kuomintang made a prominent part of its program.

---

[3] H. M. Vinacke, *History of the Far East in Modern Times* (New York, 1936), chap. 14, gives a very useful account of Chinese economic and social development.

The Chinese Renaissance

Important intellectual and social changes were occurring in these confused years. By the 1920's a new generation of young people had begun to appear in the new school system, and the "Chinese renaissance" was in full bloom.[4] Toward the end of the Manchu period, students returning from abroad and the young people in Western-style schools had been disposed to pin their faith on the overthrow of the Manchus and the substitution of the best Western political institutions. Many were products of missionary schools and accepted the essentially conservative version of Western culture which was presented there. The early years of the republic brought disillusionment to many young Chinese. The new government was a dismal failure. World War I showed clearly that Western states did not have the answers to their own political, social, and economic problems. The disregard of the old formula of "education equals public office" meant that a career in government was not the inevitable reward of scholarly achievement.

As a result of these and other considerations, many Chinese students by the late teens and early twenties were looking in new directions. They had ceased to believe in reform by constitution-making and had returned to a more validly Chinese conviction of the fundamental importance of education and social standards. In Peking, at the National University (Peita) the ferment was most vigorous. Just as Russian students in the nineteenth century had argued endlessly about the various "isms" which came to them from western Europe, so the Chinese students of thirty years ago reacted in nihilistic fashion against conventional Western doctrines and against their own tradition. Men in the vanguard of Western social thinking found an eager audience in China. John Dewey and Bertrand Russell visited China in the early 1920's and were greeted as the prophets of a new day. Marxist thought also began to exercise a considerable attraction, and a Chinese Communist party, made up chiefly of intellectuals, was organized in 1920 under the leadership of Ch'ên Tu-hsiu of Peita.

As radical Western thought became fashionable, traditional beliefs and institutions were rejected as hampering and outmoded. Confucianism came under bitter criticism as the sanction of filial piety and the family system, against which many young people were in revolt. The Taoist and Buddhism religions, which many Chinese intellectuals had not taken very seriously anyway, were written off as organized superstitions. As to

---

[4] See Hu Shih, *The Chinese Renaissance* (Chicago, 1934); H. M. Vinacke, *A History of The Far East in Modern Times* (New York, 1936), chap. 15; E. R. Hughes, *The Invasion of China by the Western World* (New York, 1938), especially chaps. 4, 6.

Christianity, its doctrines seemed no more tenable intellectually than those of Taoism and Buddhism, and its foreignness made it appear to be a sort of "spiritual imperialism" which was simply one aspect of the attack of Western powers on China's independence.

Writing in the Vernacular. The revolutionary swing from writing in the classical (*wên li*) to writing in the vernacular (*pei hua*) was an especially important feature of this cultural awakening. In 1917 Hu Shih, who had studied at Cornell University and then under John Dewey at Columbia University, announced that he would thereafter write only in the language of everyday speech. For more than two thousand years the classical style had been employed in all serious writing, and mastery of its special intricacies had been the hallmark of scholarship and the passport to public office. Only novels, which were regarded as vulgar stuff, had been written in *pei hua*. Writing in the classical style meant literacy for only a few and a civilization of the elite; writing in the vernacular opened the possibility of a real mass culture. Hu Shih's example won an enthusiastic following, and soon the vernacular had replaced *wên li* much as, only more rapidly than, the European vernaculars had centuries ago supplanted Latin. The "1000 Character Movement" for adult education helped to spread literacy in the vernacular. Dr. Y. C. ("Jimmy") Yen, who had been a YMCA secretary with a group of Chinese coolies in France during World War I, had come to realize how their essential intelligence was thwarted by their inability to read and write. To meet this need he formulated a basic vocabulary of the thousand most commonly used characters as the entering wedge in an attack on mass illiteracy. Newspapers multiplied. A veritable rash of new magazines served as vehicles for the ideas of the student group. The new tide was running fast.

All this questioning of established standards and practices was bound to react upon social institutions, which were also being modified by the economic changes then in process. Young people were resentful of family discipline: they wanted to make their own decisions, plan their own lives, and choose their own husbands and wives. The family had been a sort of cushion protecting the individual from disasters, but the younger generation was willing to surrender some of the security which family membership offered for an increasing amount of the new freedom. The emancipation of women was proceeding, too, to the dismay of older people. In fact many active participants in the student movement were girls. In numerous households the battle of the generations and of the sexes was joined, and although the family system continued as the basic

Chinese institution, it was challenged increasingly to show flexibility and resilience, or to break.

Students and Politics. Much of the new energy and zeal of the students boiled over into politics. Although no longer necessarily potential officials, they continued to think of themselves as having unique competence in political matters and as holding a special responsibility as the voice of public opinion. The student movement, which became open and active in 1919, was keenly antiforeign. Student resentment against the subserviency of the Anfu clique to Japan and the terms of the Versailles Treaty deterred Tuan Chi-jui's government from signing the treaty. The students found in demonstrations and boycotts against foreign goods the means by which they could impress undesirable Chinese politicians and even foreign governments. This vigorous nationalist student movement was first apparent in the North but in time joined hands with Sun Yat-sen's Kuomintang in the South to provide a very powerful expression of the desire of the Chinese to shake off foreign control and achieve national strength.

In the early 1920's it was evident that neither warlordism nor constitutionalism could bring China unity and freedom from Western imperialism. No single war lord could control the whole country; it was too large, too disorganized, too little supplied with modern transport to make unification by force conceivable. Warlordism meant incessant civil war. Also many Chinese had begun to realize that constitutions could not be cure-alls, that they must be products of political and social growth. No matter how skilfully the drafters did their work, any constitution would be meaningless without a new China which could use constitutional government. What was needed for the resurrection of China was a new ideology expressive of the changes in Chinese society, one that could effectively replace the ideology of the old scholar-empire as a means of social integration.

SUGGESTED READINGS

The following works provide helpful analyses of a confused period: H. F. MacNair, *China in Revolution* (New York, 1931); A. N. Holcombe, *The Chinese Revolution* (New York, 1930); H. F. MacNair (ed.), *China* (Berkeley and Los Angeles, 1946), chap. 9, by MacNair, deals with the Chinese Revolution from 1911 to 1928; Ch'ien Tuan-sheng, *The Government and Politics of China* (Cambridge, Mass., 1950), chaps. 4, 5; K. S. Latourette, *The Chinese, Their History and Culture* (2 vols., 3d ed., New York, 1946), Vol. I, chap. 12; Li Chien-nung, *The Political History of China, 1840-1928*, edited and translated by Ssu-yu Teng and Jeremy Ingalls (Princeton, N.J., 1956).

On the revolution of 1911-12 see Reginald Johnston, *Twilight in the Forbidden City* (London, 1934); J. Gilbert Reid, *The Manchu Abdication and the Powers* (Berkeley, 1935); George H. Blakeslee (ed.), *Recent Developments in China* (New York, 1913); P. H. Kent, *The Passing of the Manchus* (London, 1912); Meribeth E. Cameron, *The Reform Movement in China, 1898-1912* (Stanford, 1931).

The constitutional problems and the politics of the period of Yüan Shih-k'ai and the war lords are treated in Wei-tung Pan, *The Chinese Constitution* (Washington, 1945); Ch'ien Tuan-sheng, *op. cit.;* Harold M. Vinacke, *Modern Constitutional Development in China* (Princeton, 1920); W. W. Willoughby, *Constitutional Government in China* (Washington, 1922); two works by S. K. Hornbeck, *Contemporary Politics in the Far East* (New York, 1916), and *China Today: Political* (Boston, 1927).

On economic development, see J. B. Condliffe, *China Today: Economic* (New York, 1932); R. H. Tawney, *Land and Laborer in China* (London, 1932); Marion R. Levy, Jr., and Shih Kuo-heng, *The Rise of the Modern Chinese Business Class* (New York, 1949); Harold M. Vinacke, *A History of the Far East in Modern Times* (New York, 1936), chap. 14.

Various aspects of intellectual change, including the Renaissance, are treated in: Hu Shih, *The Chinese Renaissance* (Chicago, 1932); E. R. Hughes, *The Invasion of China by the Western World* (New York, 1938), especially chaps. 4, 6; Cyrus H. Peake, *Nationalism and Education in Modern China* (New York, 1932); T. C. Wang, *The Youth Movement of China* (New York, 1928); the very interesting self-analysis of a young Chinese intellectual, Ku Chieh-kang, which Arthur H. Hummel has translated as *The Autobiography of a Chinese Historian* (Leiden, 1931); Paul Monroe, *China, A Nation in Evolution* (New York, 1928). Representative examples of the new literature, full of realism and social significance, are to be found in Edgar Snow (ed.), *Living China: Modern Chinese Short Stories* (New York, 1936); two volumes of translations by Wang Chi-chen, *Ah Q and Other Stories* (New York, 1944) and *Contemporary Chinese Stories* (New York, 1944); Lau Shaw, *Rickshaw Boy* (New York, 1945).

23

THE U.S.S.R. IN THE FAR EAST

The Russian Far East After the Revolution

Following the successful Bolshevik revolution in 1917, the Japanese began to show great interest in the Russian Maritime Province. On April 5, 1918, some Japanese troops were landed there, and the Japanese negotiated agreements with the Chinese the same year providing for common action in Siberia.

As has been shown, the Allies decided upon intervention in Siberia in order to assist the Czechs and Slovaks, former prisoners of war of the Russians who were trying to make their way to Vladivostok in order to return home, and to protect war matériel shipped to Russia from falling into the hands of the Germans. The heaviest detachment of Allied troops came from Japan which was a violation of the understanding that their forces would not exceed those of the Americans. The Japanese were not content with remaining along or near the Pacific coast but quickly spread inland as well.

Out of the sanguinary fighting in Siberia between the Bolsheviks and other leftist groups on the one hand, and the Whites on the other, emerged in 1920 the Republic of the Far East, which at that time was not communistic. Its seat of government was located at Chita, near the juncture of the Trans-Siberian and Chinese Eastern Railways.

In theory, the Far Eastern Republic was both independent and democratic. But in actuality, although it professed democratic ideals, its government became, through the process of eliminating its opposition, a communist monolith. The fiction of its independence, however, was maintained, and on May 14, 1920, it was formally recognized by the U.S.S.R., and diplomatic relations were established between the two. Japan, eager to keep Russia as divided as possible, accorded de facto recognition to the Far Eastern Republic on July 15, 1920, and opened prolonged negotiations with it over outstanding issues.

As a result of the Washington Conference, Japan agreed to evacuate Siberia, which she did by October, 1922, although remaining in northern Sakhalin. A conference between the Japanese and representatives of the

Far Eastern Republic held at Changchun failed to produce agreement, and the situation remained in statu quo.

Having strengthened their position greatly by the end of 1922, the Russians were in a position to incorporate the Far Eastern Republic into their own framework, with the result that settlement of the Sakhalin question became an issue with Moscow rather than with the Far Eastern Republic. An understanding between the two Powers was concluded January 20, 1925, whereby, among other things, each promised to refrain from interference in the affairs of the other and Japan agreed to get out of northern Sakhalin by the end of May, 1925. Fishing rights were accorded the Japanese, along with certain oil and coal concessions.

Russia and China [1]

Casting about for allies in their early days in power, the Soviet leaders were quick to reach the conclusion that their two most promising sources were the proletariat of the West and those Eastern peoples now strongly imbued with nationalism.[2] Accordingly, they lost little time in asserting that the Soviet was an arch foe of imperialism, a move certain to attract peoples who had fallen victims to imperialistic forces. To suit their words with appropriate action, the new Russian leaders renounced all treaties of an imperialistic nature made by the tsarist government. As applied to China, this meant terminating the unequal treaties with their provisions for extraterritoriality, tariff concessions, etc. One privilege Russia carefully refrained from returning, however, was its strong position in northern Manchuria and Outer Mongolia. In this area, Soviet Russia pursued a policy of encouraging an autonomous movement until the situation would be ripe for it to assume domination over the region.

Outer Mongolia. China, on the other hand, in 1919 dispatched troops to occupy the capital, Urga (Ulan Bator), in order to forestall Outer Mongolia's hopes of achieving its independence. The troops forced the local ruler to announce reacceptance of Chinese rule over the region. Early

---

[1] The story of the Russian period of the Kuomintang is treated in Chapter 24.

[2] As early as September, 1920, a Congress of the Peoples of the East was held at Baku at which incendiary speeches were hurled against the imperialist Powers, especially the British, who were accused of holding the peoples of the East in bondage. George Creel, *Russia's Race for Asia* (Indianapolis, 1949), pp. 18-19.

Another similar conference was sponsored by the Soviet in 1922 with delegates present from China, Japan, Korea, Mongolia, India, Java, and the Russian Far East. Such meetings were later repeated, and at them great encouragement was given nationalist movements in the hopes that the forces of imperialism would be routed thereby making ready for the intrusion of communist parties into power in those lands.

in 1921, however, the Chinese were driven out of Urga by a force of White Russians who then proclaimed Mongolian independence. This army was in turn routed by soldiers of the Red Army who occupied the Mongolian capital in July, 1921. Ever since that time Outer Mongolia has been securely held within the orbit of Soviet influence.[3]

On November 5, 1921, a treaty, kept secret for some time so as not to aggravate Russia's relations with China, was concluded between the Soviet Union and the puppet government which it set up in Outer Mongolia. This pact provided for mutual recognition and called, among other things, for the cession of whatever land the Russians would require to build railroads in Outer Mongolia. The area to the west, then known as Tannu Tuva and claimed by the Mongolians, was not included in the Russian recognition.[4] Many years later, this nominally independent republic was revealed by the list of electoral districts published in the Soviet press October 17, 1946, to have been incorporated into the U.S.S.R. as the Tuva Autonomous Region.[5]

China naturally was very much upset when it learned of the Mongolian-Russian treaty and protested sharply to the Soviets. The realization of their inability to remedy the situation impelled the Chinese in 1924 to reach a settlement with Russia. The terms of the treaty had little significance, since Russian control over Outer Mongolia was an accomplished fact. On paper, however, Russia permitted it to be stated that Outer Mongolia was a part of China and Russia would recognize it as such. Russia also yielded, formally, all of its unequal treaty rights in China which it had in fact already surrendered.

Manchuria and the Chinese Eastern Railway. The question of Manchuria, which had loomed large in Sino-Russian relations, entered the treaty in clauses relating to the Chinese Eastern Railway. It was agreed that the road's administration, together with the control of the leased territory, should be in the hands of China. This understanding failed to allow for the fact that at the time the real power in Manchuria was the pro-Japanese tuchun, Marshal Chang Tso-lin. This worthy was able to have the treaty altered so that he could have a voice in the line's control. The revised agreement declared that the road would be jointly administered by China and Manchuria on the one side and Russia on the other until 1956 when Russia would drop out of the picture completely.[6]

Another bone of contention between the two countries was Sinkiang,

[3] D. J. Dallin, *The Rise of Russia in Asia* (New Haven, 1949), p. 189.
[4] *Ibid.*, p. 191.
[5] Report of the Committee on Foreign Affairs Pursuant to H. Res. 206, *Background Information on the Soviet Union in International Relations* (Washington, 1950), p. 51.
[6] Dallin, *op. cit.*, pp. 193-97. In 1956, Russia presumably honored the agreement.

or Chinese Turkestan, which sought its independence from China. Russia's influence in this area varied from time to time but remained strong for some time after World War II.

It was, however, the question of the Chinese Eastern Railway which produced an outright clash between China and Russia in 1929. For five years following the conclusion of the Sino-Soviet treaty in 1924, the road had been a source of constant friction. This was a natural development as there were many difficulties in the way of the smooth, efficient, and objective handling of such a joint enterprise. Administration over the road was supposed to be absolutely co-equal, but with both Powers motivated by nationalistic ambitions, trouble was inevitable.

Especially prone to interfere in the affairs of the Chinese Eastern until his death in 1928 was Marshal Chang Tso-lin, dictator of Manchuria. Formerly pro-Japanese, the Marshal had in his last days turned against the Japanese. Always anti-Communist, he grew even more so, with the result that his policies were directly opposed to the interests of both Russia and Japan. His son and successor, Chang Hsueh-liang, was also strongly opposed to the Russians and drew down their bitter denunciation, especially since he had acknowledged the authority of Chiang Kai-shek.[7]

Spurred on by their success in accomplishing the temporary unification of China, and still intoxicated by the heady wine of nationalism, the Chinese Nationalists decided, in cooperation with Chang Hsueh-liang, to seize the Chinese Eastern Railway in 1929. This was done on July 10 through the simple expedient of arresting a number of Russian administrators and closing their offices. A Russian ultimatum demanding the release of these officials not only was ignored, but additional arrests were made. The Soviets retaliated by placing under arrest a considerable number of Chinese, following which all Soviet diplomatic and consular officials were withdrawn from China and the corresponding Chinese officials ordered home, thereby marking the severance of relations. China retaliated on July 20 by ordering the Russians home. Armed clashes followed in the fall of 1929 with Red forces defeating Marshal Chang's Manchurian troops, which on December 3 were forced to accept Russia's terms. Chang's actions were ratified by Chiang Kai-shek and the situation

---

[7] An important factor in impelling the "Young Marshal" to join Chiang was his bitterness toward the Japanese, whom he blamed for his father's death. Although it was widely believed at the time that the Japanese had caused Chang Tso-lin's death, it could not be proved until after Japan's defeat in World War II. In 1945 it was revealed that a Colonel Kawamoto, attached in 1928 to the Kwantung Army, had been responsible. Kawamoto placed a bomb in the Marshal's car, which was part of a special twenty-car train carrying him and his retinue to Mukden. Mori Shozo, "Sempu Nijunen," Vol. I, pp. 18-19, quoted in Chitoshi Yanaga, *Japan Since Perry* (New York, 1949), pp. 456-57.

reverted to the status quo ante, i.e., the Chinese Eastern was once again jointly administered by Russia and China.

Peace Pact Ineffective. American efforts to mediate, although supported by several other Powers, failed because of Japan's opposition, a result highly pleasing to the Soviets since it virtually insured their success in the undeclared war with China.[8] Japan, of course, was not acting in Russia's behalf but strictly in her own. It was a significant lesson quickly absorbed by the fire-eating Japanese militarists, because it revealed the inability of the West to implement the recently concluded Pact of Paris (Kellogg-Briand Treaty) by effectively preventing war which it had so idealistically outlawed on paper. The clash between Russia and China was actual war except for the technicality of a formal declaration by either side.

The Chinese then sought to secure control of the Chinese Eastern Railway by purchase from Russia, but the long and fruitless negotiations were terminated by the Japanese attack on Manchuria nearly two years later. The lack of success of these negotiations was clearly due to Russia's intransigence.

Russia and Japan

For some eight years following the Bolshevik Revolution in 1917, relations between Russia and Japan were somewhat strained, being marked particularly by the Japanese adventure in Siberia which had even extended as far as Lake Baikal. As already mentioned, this affair had terminated with the withdrawal of all Japanese troops from Russian soil except for Japan's retention of northern Sakhalin, an action which continued to draw bitter protests from the Soviet.[9]

Despite these tensions, negotiations to settle their differences had been undertaken by Russia and Japan as early as 1921. Interrupted after nine months, they were soon resumed once more. This fruitless process was continued until May, 1924, when talks were again undertaken. This time they materialized in the Treaty of Peking,[10] signed January 20, 1925. The treaty provided for the resumption of diplomatic relations, revision of the fisheries agreement of 1907, most-favored-nation treatment, mutual prevention of propaganda or other inimical activities, and granted the citizens of each nation certain guarantees, such as those of travel and

---

[8] This question is dealt with more adequately in Chapter 26.

[9] A sore spot from the Japanese point of view was the Nikolaevsk affair wherein some 350 Japanese subjects had been massacred in cold blood by the Russians. It was this slaughter which gave Japan an excuse to occupy northern Sakhalin. Akagi, *op. cit.*, p. 331.

[10] Peking was the scene of this Russo-Japanese agreement because it was negotiated by the Russian and Japanese envoys to China.

residence. Japan promised the withdrawal of its troops from northern Sakhalin by May 15 and received in return certain oil and coal concessions there.[11]

The Manchurian Crisis

With the beginning of Japan's Manchurian adventure on September 18, 1931, tension in the Far East mounted rapidly. Throughout the difficulties arising from the Chinese Eastern Railway affair in 1929 (when Japanese neutrality had proved so valuable to Russia), relations between the Soviet and Japan had been extremely cordial. This friendliness continued even after the Japanese mounted their attack in southern Manchuria,[12] because at this stage in Russian policy Japan's activity was viewed by the Kremlin as a lesser evil than, for example, American interference in this region. Furthermore, Russia's relations with Chiang Kai-shek, who was cordially detested in Moscow, were extremely cool. Then, too, the Japanese had assured Russia that their activities would be confined to southern Manchuria and that they would refrain from interfering in any way with the Chinese Eastern Railway. Finally, Russian concentration on internal development through its Five-Year Plan was another reason for its attitude.

Nevertheless, within a month after the opening of hostilities, Russia protested the massing of Japanese gunboats on the Sungari River. This was not considered of any great significance, and the Japanese ambassador paid a call at the Russian Foreign Office on October 28, during the course of which he expressed great satisfaction over the cordial state of relations between the two countries. But he did go on to say that there were reports that the Soviet Union was aiding an anti-Japanese general in Manchuria. This was quickly denied by a Russian spokesman who hastened to assure Ambassador Hirota that Russia's policy was one of strict neutrality.[13]

Japanese Seize Harbin. Japan's assurances that it would respect the Chinese Eastern Railway soon proved worthless, and by February 5, 1932, not only had the region of the road been violated but the Japanese had even occupied Harbin, the chief seat of Russian influence in northern Manchuria. Still Russian friendliness showed no visible signs of abating as Moscow even went so far as to suggest on December 31, 1931, that the two countries should sign a nonaggression pact. Japan took nearly a year to reject this overture in December, 1932, on the grounds that before

---

[11] Yanaga, *op. cit.,* pp. 459 ff.

[12] For an interesting illustration of Russian feelings just three days after the conflict began see the feature article in *Izvestia* reproduced in H. L. Moore, *Soviet Far Eastern Policy, 1931-1945* (Princeton, 1945), p. 211.

[13] *Ibid.,* pp. 7-8.

such an agreement could be reached various unsettled problems in their mutual relations would have to be solved.[14]

Friendliness Begins to Cool. Meanwhile, the year 1932, while friendly in many respects, did reflect increasing friction in Russo-Japanese relations. The Russians were concerned over what Japan's attitude would be toward the anti-Soviet White Guards in Manchuria and received assurances that Japan would see to it that they were properly restrained. In making these pledges, the Japanese asked for and received permission to transport some troops along the Chinese Eastern Railway to Harbin. Continuing its benevolent attitude toward Japan in international affairs, the U.S.S.R. flatly rejected a proposal from the League of Nations to participate in the work of the Lytton Commission, an invitation which another important non-League member, the United States, saw fit to accept.

Despite incidents in Manchuria which prompted both Russia and Japan to lodge protests with the other in 1932, a new fisheries agreement was reached in August, and a five-year deal calling for Russia to supply Japan with a certain quantity of gasoline was concluded in September.[15] The rest of 1932 did not pass quite so smoothly: the Japanese accused the Russians of removing a quantity of the Chinese Eastern's rolling stock, and Russia turned a deaf ear to Japanese pleas that the forces of General Su, which had fled across the border following their defeat by the Japanese where they were disarmed and interned by the Russians, should be turned over to Japan. The Japanese were further discomfited by the announcement on December 12, 1932, that China and Russia had resumed diplomatic relations, although Russia assured the Japanese that the event was purely routine.

1933 Brings Conflicting Ambitions. The year 1933 saw the beginning in Russia of the Second Five-Year Plan, which placed great emphasis on strengthening the Russian Far East. Ambitious projects for utilizing the region's natural resources, adding to its industrial strength, and improving its transportation facilities were given high priority in the list of accomplishments which Soviet planners hoped to achieve. Many incentives were offered to encourage settlement of the great regions of the Soviet Far East; among these were removal of agricultural taxes and the payment of higher wages to workers and soldiers than prevailed in the European sections of the U.S.S.R.

It was in 1933, also, that Japan determined to oust Russia from Manchuria, once and for all. Japanese activities on the Chinese Eastern Railway indicated that they were prepared to make things difficult for the

---

[14] Dallin, *Soviet Russia and the Far East* (New Haven, 1948), pp. 6-7.
[15] *Ibid.*, p. 11.

Russians. The latter, fully conscious of their relative weakness vis-à-vis their then stronger adversary, elected to avoid hostilities by opening negotiations to sell the Russian share of the Chinese Eastern either to Japan or to its creature, Manchukuo. Talks for this purpose were begun in Tokyo late in June, but proved fruitless. The negotiations were continued intermittently for more than a year and a half, during the course of which the Russians accused the Japanese of trying to reduce the road's value by allowing armed bandit bands to attack it almost at will.[16] At last, an agreement was reached on March 23, 1935, whereby the U.S.S.R. transferred its 50 per cent control of the line to Manchukuo, with Japan agreeing to underwrite the latter's financial commitments. The agreed price was approximately $70,000,000 to be paid one third in cash within three years and the rest in certain specified goods. The line's name was changed to the North Manchuria Railway.

Increasing Soviet-Japanese Friction, 1935-1939

Japanese advances in 1935 in North China, northern Manchuria, and Inner Mongolia resulted in border clashes with both the Russians in Siberia and the Mongols in Outer Mongolia. Russian protests against border depredations increased as months passed. As early as June, representatives of the Russian puppet state of the Mongol People's Republic met with those of the Japanese-sponsored Manchukuo at Manchouli (Manchuria Station) but the situation resulted in an impasse. A resumption of the talks proved equally unrewarding, and they were broken off at the end of November, only to be followed in December by new incidents near Lake Buir Nor.[16a] The main bone of contention was Japan's insistence that the Japanese and Manchukuoan troops were operating on the latter's soil, whereas Russia and the Mongols claimed that the lands in question were Mongolian.

The clashes continued to increase in frequency throughout December, 1935, and January, 1936. Russia then hastened to make it quite clear that the U.S.S.R. stood firmly behind the Mongols, and made its point even stronger by signing a mutual assistance pact with the Mongol People's Republic in March; this provided that if either signatory were attacked the other would come to its assistance. It was, of course, an unmistakable warning to the Japanese to desist. The latter took the hint, and by summer the attacks had been stopped, not to be resumed in this area for a few years.[17]

[16] *Ibid.*, pp. 18-19.
[16a] Moore, *op. cit.*, pp. 56-58.
[17] Dallin, *Soviet Russia and the Far East*, p. 27.

Three Serious Clashes. The next three years (1937-39) saw numerous skirmishes occur between the forces of the Kwantung Army Group and the Special Red Banner Army of the Far East, with each year producing one serious incident.[18] The first, in 1937, took place over the issue of who owned certain islands in the Amur River. The Japanese gained the upper hand in this affair, and the Red forces which had occupied the disputed islands were evacuated. This withdrawal the Japanese interpreted as weakness, coming as it did on the heels of the great Russian purge in June, 1937, in which Marshal Tukhachevsky and a number of other high ranking Red Army officers had been executed.

Between the Amur River incident and that of 1938 at Changkufeng, the situation was altered by Japan's decision to wage an all-out war against China calculated to beat the Chinese "to their knees," to quote the boastful phrase of Prince Konoe. The opening of the full-scale offensive against China was at first a source of worry to the Russians, but, as the Japanese failed to overrun their adversaries, the Reds were considerably heartened.

The second major clash between the Russians and the Japanese took place July, 1938, at Changkufeng, a place where Korean, Manchurian, and Siberian territory converge. Aviation, along with mechanized equipment, played a role in this bitter struggle which both sides represented as a triumph.[19] The matter was settled on August 10 in Moscow between the Japanese ambassador and the Soviet Foreign Commissar, and both sides withdrew their troops.

Border Pact Ends Strife. The third and most serious of these annual encounters resulted from the inability of the two countries to desist from making charges and countercharges at one another. Fighting broke out in May, 1939, along the border between the Mongol People's Republic and Manchukuo in the region called Nomonhan. Increasing in intensity during the following months, by August the fighting reached its peak and was accompanied by considerable aerial activity on both sides. A truce was agreed upon on September 16, followed a few days later by the announcement of an armistice in Moscow. A mixed boundary commission was appointed and worked out a boundary arrangement acceptable to both sides. The Nomonhan Incident marked the last serious clash between Russia and Japan until the waning moments of World War II when the U.S.S.R. declared war against Japan and opened a short but sanguinary campaign against the Kwantung forces in Manchuria. The U.S.S.R. failed to list its losses at Nomonhan, but Japanese casualties were

---

[18] *Ibid.*, pp. 28, 37-41.
[19] *Ibid.*, p. 28, sees the Russians as victors whereas Yanaga, *op. cit.*, p. 576, makes the Japanese out to be winners by a very narrow margin.

announced as being in excess of 18,000. It is generally conceded that the victor in this engagement was Russia.

The Fisheries Question

In addition to the border disputes which exacerbated Russo-Japanese relations so greatly, the question of Japanese fishing in Russian territorial waters was a major source of friction. Virtually ignored in tsarist days, the fisheries came to be appreciated by the Russians as a valuable asset. The Japanese had long been fishing in Russian waters, an activity sanctioned by treaty as early as 1875. The Treaty of Portsmouth provided that further arrangements be made, which was done in a fishery convention signed by the two Powers in 1907. This agreement expired in 1919. but the preoccupation of the Bolsheviks with many more important matters left Japan free to do as it wished for the time being.

Having by 1923 soundly established its regime, the Russian government was in a position to attend to the fisheries. A mixed commission set a figure for back sums owed by Japan, and these were paid. Soviet state fisheries were established and entered the competition, but Japan was able to secure a satisfactory but expensive arrangement in 1924 although it was subject to the fulfilment of various technical stipulations laid down by Russia.

A new agreement was reached in 1928 destined to last eight years, but not long thereafter difficulties began to arise. By 1932 the Soviet Union was becoming more and more active, and the need for a new understanding to implement the basic one of 1928 had likewise increased. This was achieved by the Hirota-Karakhan Agreement of August 13, 1932.

Negotiations were begun in 1935 with an eye toward extending the basic 1928 agreement. Due to the impasse which arose, the existing agreement was continued to the end of 1936, at which time a further extension of one year was arranged. This last extension came at a time when the Soviet was considerably miffed over the Anti-Comintern Pact, just concluded between Germany and Japan. Although relations worsened markedly during 1937, the basic 1928 fisheries convention received another year's prolongation for the year 1938.

That year saw a further worsening of Soviet-Japanese relations so that the fisheries negotiations had to be continued into 1939 before an acceptable compromise could be reached to take care of the rest of the year. Before 1939 expired, however, the Russians had signed a nonaggression pact with Germany on August 23, and a few days thereafter the Germans had started World War II by their attack on Poland. Needless to say, the conclusion of the Russo-German Pact was a serious blow to the Japanese and, conversely, greatly strengthened Russia's position vis-à-vis Japan. Nevertheless, the U.S.S.R. permitted an extension of the fisheries convention through the end of 1940 and also agreed to negotiate a long-term understanding. The *quid pro quo* for these concessions by Russia, now in an improved bargaining position, was the completion of payment by Japan of the sums outstanding on the purchase of the Chinese Eastern Railway.

China Again

Leaving for future discussion the story of Soviet-Japanese relations following the outbreak of World War II, it is now necessary to consider Russian policy toward China. From the very beginnings of the Communist movement in China, the role of Russia has been that of a close and friendly adviser. In August, 1931, the Chinese Communists received instructions from the Comintern to establish a Soviet government in China with a program based on that of Russia. These orders were quickly carried out, and the Chinese Soviet Republic was proclaimed in November of that year. Its policy and tactics were determined for it by Moscow and the Far Eastern Office (Dalburo) of the Comintern.[20]

Despite their successes in the years following their founding, the Chinese Soviets were faced with annihilation at the hands of Chiang Kai-shek in 1934. To save themselves they embarked on the famous "Long March," described in Chapter 24. After a year of incredible hardship, they arrived in northern Shensi, close to the Russians, and bordering Inner Mongolia. There, with their capital at Yenan, they set out to model themselves after Russia in several respects so that an effective coordination of the foreign policies of the two governments was achieved.[21]

Russia Encourages Resistance. It suited Russia's policy to have China resist Japan, especially as Chiang Kai-shek wanted to unify his country by wiping out the Chinese Communists before offering strong opposition to the Japanese. The Communists were determined, with the prompting of Moscow, that China should resist Japan. They consequently modified their tactics to the point of willingness to cooperate with Chiang against Japan in a united front, which was accomplished as a result of the Sian Incident, although no specific agreement was reached until after the Japanese began their war against China on July 7, 1937.

This understanding never did work out well, but Chinese communism's elder brother, the U.S.S.R., did reach an agreement with Chiang in August which proved helpful to China's war effort by supplying the

[20] *Ibid.*, p. 109.
[21] *Ibid.*, chap. 8.

Nationalists with some matériel of war. The fact that Russia was sending him supplies, even though the amount was limited, meant that Chiang had to proceed circumspectly in his dealings with the Chinese Communists. As a matter of fact, both the Kuomintang and the Communists began to indulge in speeches calling for perpetual peace and cooperation with one another. Communists were brought into the new Defense Council and when it was later enlarged and renamed their membership was increased.

Russia Looks Toward Chiang. By the fall of 1939, the honeymoon was over, a circumstance traceable in some measure to the expected improvement in relations between Russia and Japan now that Germany and Russia had signed their nonaggression pact. Chiang Kai-shek was becoming of less importance as far as Russia was concerned, which also meant, of course, as far as the Chinese Communists were concerned. This being the case, the latter now began to insist upon the establishment of a coalition government in China, a step which had the backing of Moscow. Despite these cooperative gestures, skirmishes between the Nationalist and Communist troops began to increase in number and intensity.

Chiang's position, unlike that of his Yenan adversaries with their foreign support, had not improved, so he was forced to reach a new agreement with the Communists in July, 1940, whereby certain areas were given over to the Communist armies as their exclusive areas of operation and additional supplies were promised to them. Even this did not help matters much, and a bloody battle occurred in January, 1941, between the Nationalists and the Communist New Fourth Army, following which the Chiang government declared that the New Fourth Army was disbanded officially, and its commanding general was placed under arrest.

The Soviet-Japanese Neutrality Pact

On September 27, 1940, the axis Tripartite Treaty was signed by Germany, Italy, and Japan. Aimed primarily against the United States, it required the other signatories to take military action against any nation with which one of them should find itself at war. Russia received notification from Germany in advance that the treaty was to be signed. Article V of the treaty specifically declared that the agreement did not "in any way affect the political statutes which exist at present as between each contracting party and Soviet Russia." This fact, plus the advance notice given Russia, led to some talk that the Russians would soon become partners of the signatories, and conversations were actually initiated with the Russians by the Germans with this objective in mind. Refusal by the

Germans to make certain concessions demanded by the Russians caused the project to collapse, although the Russians appear to have maintained a lively interest in such an agreement.

All the while Japan and Russia drew closer together. The fisheries convention was renewed for another year on January 20, 1941 and Russia was fully indemnified for the failure of a Japanese shipbuilding company to build ships after having accepted an initial payment.

Then following a trip to Berlin, Yosuke Matsuoka, Japanese Foreign Minister, stopped in Moscow for a series of conversations with the Russian leaders which resulted in the signing of a neutrality pact. As part of this treaty, the Japanese agreed later to the return of the coal and oil concessions which they had leased from the Russians on northern Sakhalin. In addition, each signatory agreed to respect the territorial integrity of the other's puppet, i.e., Manchukuo and the Mongol People's Republic. On the occasion of the signing (April 13, 1941), Stalin was particularly friendly and demonstrative and remarked to Matsuoka that he too was an Oriental and even went so far as to go to the station to say goodbye to Matsuoka as he was leaving Moscow.

Thus by the spring of 1941, shortly before it was to be attacked by Germany, Russia had put its Far Eastern affairs in relatively good order and could devote its attention more fully to Europe. Its principal problem in the Far East had been satisfactorily settled for the time being by this neutrality pact, and it was also enjoying the situation in China, with whom it had a pact. Finally, its pact of mutual assistance with the Mongols had already paid dividends in that the latter had supplied troops during the border troubles with Japan.

SUGGESTED READINGS

Indispensible are David J. Dallin's *Soviet Russia and the Far East* (New Haven, 1948) and *The Rise of Russia in Asia* (New Haven, 1949). His *Soviet Russia's Foreign Policy, 1939-1942* (New Haven, 1942) and *The Big Three. The United States, Britain, Russia* (New Haven, 1945) are also valuable. Useful for background and its appendices is Harriet L. Moore, *Soviet Far Eastern Policy, 1931-1945* (Princeton, 1945). More specialized but also scholarly is Pauline Tompkins, *American-Russian Relations in the Far East* (New York, 1949).

See also S. S. Balzak and others, *Economic Geography of the USSR* (New York, 1949); Ernest S. Bates, *Soviet Asia* (London, 1942); Max Beloff, *Foreign Policy of Soviet Russia*, Vol. I (London, 1947); Claude A. Buss, *War and Diplomacy in Eastern Asia* (New York, 1941); Paul H. Clyde, *International Rivalries in Manchuria* (Columbus, Ohio, 1926); Violet Conolly, *Soviet Economic Policy in the East* (London, 1933); George Creel, *Russia's Race for Asia* (New York, 1949); George B. Cressey, *The Basis of Soviet Strength* (New York, 1945); Louis Fischer, *The Soviets in World Affairs* (London, 1930); Katsuji Fuse, *Soviet Policy in the Orient* (Peking,

1927); Andrew J. Grajdanzev, *Modern Korea* (New York, 1944); William S. Graves, *America's Siberian Adventure* (New York, 1931); Owen Lattimore, *Inner Asian Frontiers of China* (New York, 1940); Richard Lauterbach, *Through Russia's Back Door* (New York and London, 1947); William Mandel, *The Soviet Far East and Central Asia* (New York, 1944); Henry Norton, *The Far Eastern Republic of Siberia* (London, 1923); Leo Pasvolsky, *Russia in the Far East* (New York, 1922); G. D. R. Phillips, *Russia, Japan, and Mongolia* (London, 1942); Harry Schwartz, *Russia's Postwar Economy* (Syracuse, N. Y., 1947); Lien-en Tsao, *The Chinese Eastern Railway* (Shanghai, 1929); United States Department of State, *Papers Relating to the Foreign Relations of the United States. Russia: 1918 and 1919* (Washington, 1931-32, 1937); Victor Yakontoff, *Russia and the Soviet Union in the Far East* (New York, 1931), and *U.S.S.R. Foreign Policy* (New York, 1945).

24

CHINA, 1923-1937: TRIUMPH OF THE KUOMINTANG

Russian Advisers and the Kuomintang

In January, 1923, Sun Yat-sen, leader of the moribund Kuomintang, and Adolf Joffe, special representative of the victorious Bolsheviks, met in Shanghai. These representatives of two contrasting revolutionary parties issued a joint communiqué defining the terms on which the two organizations could work for the furtherance of the Chinese revolution. The agreement stressed the unsuitability of the Soviet political system for China; instead, the primary objective was established as the achievement of true national independence. But toward the realization of that goal the Russians were willing to make a contribution, which Sun was ready to accept. What had led to this strange bargain? Why was Sun, formerly the great apostle of the adaptation of Western European and American traditions to China's needs, now taking into partnership the Bolsheviks, who were still pariahs beyond the pale of international respectability?

It was the miserable state of the Kuomintang which had led Sun to look for advice and assistance wherever he could find it. After the abortive "Second Revolution" and the proscription of the Kuomintang by Yüan in 1913, the party went underground and once more became a conspiratorial organization. The movement re-emerged into the light in 1917 when the Parliamentarians, who had fled Peking, formed a military government at Canton with Sun as generalissimo. This regime was ridden with factionalism and was extremely liable to control by nearby militarists. In the next few years Sun bounced in and out of Canton, his position at any given moment depending on his relations with the local war lords of South China and with other politicians. Discussions with northern militarists brought no advantage to Sun's movement. The Western Powers turned a cold shoulder; at the Washington Conference, China was represented by the corrupt Peking regime which was the recognized government. After decades of sincere but not always adroit revolutionary activity

Sun had only a handful of personal followers and a precarious toe hold in South China. Either he must take drastic measures or acknowledge defeat.

At this crisis, the Soviet government appeared as the one possible source of aid and comfort. Ever since 1919, Russia had been taking a new line which stressed repudiation of tsarist imperialism and proclaimed friendship toward all peoples struggling against capitalist oppression. This *volte-face* led to negotiation, in 1924, of new agreements between Russia and the Peking government and Chang Tso-lin in Manchuria, but it was Sun Yat-sen's southern regime which offered the greatest opportunity for Bolshevik penetration and development. Both the Soviet government and the Canton regime were international outcasts. They had the same enemies—the great powers of the West. The Russians and Sun's followers differed in doctrine and goals, but for a considerable distance they might be able to travel the same road with mutual advantage. Hence the discussions between Sun and Joffe, and Sun's return in triumph to Canton with new assets for the rebuilding of the Kuomintang.

Each of the parties to this arrangement hoped to use the other without being used. The Russian Communists, seeking an opportunity to spread their propaganda, hoped to make China a key area in the world revolution which was held to be necessary for the survival of the revolution in Russia. Sun, on the other hand, wanted from the Russians the secrets of successful revolution—organizational tricks, propaganda techniques, military strengthening. Doctrine he did not desire; the Bible of the Kuomintang was to consist of the writings of Sun Yat-sen, not those of Marx and Lenin.

Changes in the Kuomintang. The fall of 1923 brought the arrival in Canton of the Russian advisers who were to play a momentous role in the history of the Kuomintang and of modern China. Chief among them was Michael Borodin, a Communist "trouble shooter" of wide experience. He was born in Russia (under the name Grusenberg), was brought to Chicago as a child, later operated a business school there (under the name of Berg), went to Mexico as a Communist agent, and then served as a representative of the Third International in Turkey. Borodin was a remarkably intelligent and adaptable person who played a key role in the reshaping of the Kuomintang. General Galen (or Blücher) was the chief Russian military adviser.

To Borodin's eyes, the Kuomintang was a collection of followers of an individual, not a real revolutionary party. He quickly undertook its reconstruction in the image of the Russian Communist organization, and it is ironical that long after the Kuomintang repudiated the Russian connection and became vigorously anti-Communist its political structure continued to bear a marked family resemblance to the Russian Communist party. The new organization involved local units or cells, definite membership, and party discipline. An annual Party Congress was to select members for a Central Executive Committee which in turn chose a Standing Committee to rule when the Congress was not in session. This Standing Committee of nine members, plus six others, made up the important Central Political Council. In addition to this retailoring of the party, a reorganization of its methods for spreading its ideas seemed indicated. The Kuomintang was, from the Russian point of view, lamentably backward in techniques of agitation and propaganda, and a political training institute was formed to repair this lack. Besides a strong political organization and more effective propaganda, a third element was needed. This was military force, not in the form of precarious loans of troops by war lords but as a basic part of the new Kuomintang. General Galen therefore organized the Whampoa Military Academy, of which Chiang Kai-shek, a young Chinese officer who had just had a short stay in Moscow, was named head, with German and Russian officers as instructors.

Sun still thought of his government as a one-party affair (that party of course being the Kuomintang), but at the first Party Congress in January, 1924, Communists were admitted to the Kuomintang on condition that they would accept its principles. Up to this point the Chinese Communist party had consisted chiefly of young intellectuals who had espoused what they thought to be the latest and most advanced phase of Western thought. With the presence of the Russian advisers and the open interest of the Russian Communists in the development of the Chinese revolution, the Chinese Communist party inevitably acquired a new significance. It was a good deal to hope, as Sun did, that Chinese Communists, once admitted into the Kuomintang, would not attempt to bore from within. As MacNair has said, it was rather like mixing milk and red ink and expecting the milk not to turn pink.[1]

Sun Yat-sen's Doctrines

These measures of reorganization made the Kuomintang a different structure with new techniques and instruments at its command. What was the ideology which this reborn party was now to try to advance?

In the course of his long career as a revolutionary, Sun had had many ideas for a program for China and had worked on a formal presentation of them, but the manuscript had been destroyed at the time of his flight

[1] H. F. MacNair, *China in Revolution* (Chicago, 1931), p. 73.

from Canton in 1922. He once more undertook a definitive statement of his doctrine and, at the time of his death in March, 1925, he had written four major documents which became a sort of scripture for the Kuomintang. This corpus of writings owed its existence in large part to Borodin's urgings, but not its content. The ideas were Sun's own. These works were (1) *General Principles of Reconstruction,* begun in 1918 and never completed, (2) *An Outline of National Reconstruction,* (3) *The Manifesto of the Kuomintang,* issued at the First Party Congress in 1924 and, most important, (4) *The Three Principles of the People (San Min Chu I)*, a series of lectures given in 1924.

The Three Principles of the People [2] is an odd book. It was composed in haste, as lecture notes rather than a considered statement; it is a mélange of conflicting ideas which reflect not only the mixed nature of Sun's own cultural background but the diversities within the Kuomintang; and it is full of naïve exaggerations, inconsistencies, and misstatements. Whether it is an abiding contribution to political thought may be debated, but that it was effective propaganda is unquestionable, for Sun had been able to put his finger on China's chief problems and to set forth three principles which, if carried into practice, would solve those problems.

Sun had come a long way since 1911 when he had been simply anti-Manchu and pro-republic. The *San Min Chu I* show wide if rather uncritical reading in Western books of many different species, and the whole work is a real attempt to fuse Chinese and Occidental ideas. Sun had come to realize that a change in the minds of the Chinese must precede and underwrite any change in their political institutions and he here presented a body of doctrine which was in many ways the result of grafting Western ideas onto traditional Chinese beliefs. He still acknowledged that China must learn from the West how to control the forces of nature, but he recognized that in the governing of men, the West had no monopoly of wisdom. Here the great Chinese tradition of ethics and human relations still had meaning.

The Principle of Nationalism. Sun's idea of three principles was inspired by Lincoln's phrase, "government of the people, by the people, for the people," which Sun interpreted as nationalism, democracy, and livelihood (which seems the best English translation of *min shêng,* people's nourishment). Nationalism was to Sun China's prime desideratum. China was subordinated to the wishes and interests of foreign powers, torn apart by the struggles of war lords, and, at bottom, divided into isolated, spiritually self-sufficient family groups. The necessary prerequisite for the

---

[2] Frank Price (trans.), *San Min Chu I* (Shanghai, 1927). P. M. A. Linebarger, *The Political Doctrines of Sun Yat-sen* (New York, 1937), is a helpful analysis.

creation of a strong national state was an aroused consciousness of nationality and an energetic drive for national unity. The Chinese must learn to enlarge their loyalties, from family and clan, to state and nation. They must beware of internationalism and cosmopolitanism, so much in the air after World War I; only nations which had already achieved nationalism and a strong national state could safely think of internationalism. The Chinese must develop a vigorous racialism and must preserve their race. Sun did not share the nightmare of some modern demographers that there will be more and more and more Chinese; instead he feared race suicide! Though Sun opposed the Marxist idea of class war within China as shattering the national unity he was so eager to achieve, he advocated "the Class War of the Nations": the resistance of the poor, have-not nations to the rich imperialistic states. China was a sort of colony of every country with which she had signed a treaty; she must recover her rights and achieve full independence. The special instrument for the creation of real nationalism was the Kuomintang, which Sun thought of as a new élite comparable to the literati of the old days.

This stress on nationalism and anti-imperialism was to be the most generally accepted and vigorously pushed of the Three Principles; Sun's followers might differ as to the degree of democracy which was expedient or the proper extent and nature of social and economic change, but they were agreed on the campaign for "rights recovery." Chinese national pride was already smarting at the pretensions of foreigners in China and, just as it once had been believed that the exit of the Manchu would mean the well-being of China, so now the elimination of foreign imperialism seemed to be the one prerequisite to united and prosperous national life.

The Principle of Democracy. In the long run, Sun's ideas on democracy were to be honored by his party in breach rather than in observance, but they were perhaps the most genuinely interesting elements of his political thought. Sun looked with a critical eye on those two blessed concepts which are usually linked in public statements about Western democracy—liberty and equality. Of liberty Sun felt that the Chinese had had too much rather than too little: China was like a rope of sand, a loose federation of families, unaccustomed to strong central government and the rule of law. To escape from colonial status and internal disunity, he believed that the Chinese must sacrifice something of their local freedom to achieve the sort of strong state which could be free.

Even more dramatic than Sun's criticism of liberty is his rejection of the idea of equality as a necessary base for democracy. Sun divided human beings into three groups, those who see and perceive first, those who see and perceive later, and those who neither see nor perceive. The great mass of mankind he placed in the third group. It was nonsense, Sun believed, to say that understanding was easier than action: "understanding is difficult, action easy." The mass of the people could not understand and perform the complex operations involved in government, but they could and should have certain rights which would in the last analysis make the government a real democracy. Government was like a powerful automobile. The people should own it, but only those who were skilful and intelligent enough to pass the necessary tests should be the chauffeurs to drive it for the people.

The Four Rights and the Five Powers. Sun's general formula for democratic government assigned to the people as a whole the four rights, which he borrowed from Western democratic practice—initiative, referendum, election, and recall. To insure that the exercise of the right of election would result in the selection of those qualified to govern, he proposed the revival in modern form of that most venerable of all Chinese political institutions, the civil service examination system; only those who passed qualifying examinations might stand as candidates.

The government, operated by individuals drawn from the two more intelligent groups in Sun's listing, was to have the five powers. Three of these were the hardy perennials of classical Western political science: legislative, executive, and judicial. The other two represented the special political achievements of China, examination and control, the latter an amplification of the old censorate, with power to discipline officials and to audit accounts. This ingenious combination of the Chinese tradition of government by superior men with Western belief in rule by the people shows Sun's ability to blend Chinese and Occidental.

In proposing to make China a democracy of this sort, he was not suggesting another attempt to force the Chinese to live in an institutional framework which was altogether alien. In their historical development, the Chinese had been eminent exponents of certain attitudes and practices which in the West are regarded as important aspects of a democratic social order. Chinese belief in government by the consent of the governed had received the testimony of innumerable revolts against rulers who had lost popular support; in fact, the Chinese had formulated and exercised the right of revolution long before John Locke defined it to justify the behavior of the English in 1688. As to equality of opportunity, for many centuries the civil service examination system had been an unusually effective device for opening careers to talents. With these foundations to build on, and Sun's ideas as guides, it was conceivable that the Kuomintang might be able to bring to pass a strong nationalistic China which was also democratic.

The Principle of Livelihood. Livelihood is the most difficult of the three principles to expound and interpret, for two reasons. First, Sun did not finish his lectures on this particular topic, and second he was here dealing with matters about which there was already sharp controversy within the party. Sun's economic and social ideas are notably hybrid and were, in later years, to give interpreters of widely varying outlook justification for claiming to be his true disciples. On the negative side, Sun attacked and proposed to end foreign economic imperialism, which he felt was the primary cause of China's poverty and economic backwardness. On the positive side, the new China must work for prosperity and economic justice. The intellectual progenitors of the livelihood principle obviously include Henry George, Karl Marx, and an otherwise obscure American socialist, Maurice William, who delighted Sun by advocating national socialism without class struggle. From Henry George, Sun took the idea of letting landowners evaluate their land for tax purposes, with the corollary that the government might appropriate the land at that valuation. Sun's criticisms of foreign capitalistic exploitation have a very Marxist ring. Sun was eager to see industrialization in China and was aware of the need for capital to develop China's resources, but wanted foreign capital on nonimperialist terms. In general, Sun seems to have contemplated a mixture of state capitalism, cooperatives, and private property. Agriculture he thought should continue as private enterprise, with redistribution of land and government aid to the farmers to help them raise their standard of living. In establishing economic well-being as a goal, Sun was attacking the greatest of Chinese problems—poverty. Their inability to solve that problem was to cause the eventual downfall of his followers and to allow the Chinese Communists to come into power. Sun's disquisitions on livelihood did not constitute a clear blueprint for economic development, but they were infused with a feeling of concern for the welfare of the mass of the people and a desire to effect economic and social changes more radical than the Kuomintang in later years was willing to contemplate.

The Three Stages. If Sun had once thought of revolution as a single act of political upheaval, he later began to understand it as a gradual process of political, social, and economic transformation. He therefore evolved a program of three stages in which the Chinese revolution was to be realized. The first stage was to be that of military struggle leading to the establishment of order. Then would come the period of political tutelage. During this period the Kuomintang, which theoretically comprised those elements of the populace capable of wielding political power, was to exercise a benevolent dictatorship, carrying on the government and at the same time educating the people in the exercise of the four rights. Sun believed that the development of democratic institutions would proceed locally, from the very lowest level, and that different provinces would be graduated from the period of tutelage at different times. The third stage would be that in which the party dictatorship would liquidate itself, and democracy and full-fledged constitutional government would be set up and all three of Sun's principles would reach the maximum of effectiveness.

Sun's Death. With this new and appealing statement of its doctrines, and its new methods for projecting these doctrines, the Kuomintang was in a position to win mass support. There was not much of a proletariat to listen to simon-pure Marxism, but in China the peasants were the traditional revolutionary class, and in addition there were soldiers in the war-lord armies, student idealists, "modern" young women, and nationalist overseas Chinese, to all of whom the Three Principles of the People had something to offer. Even before Sun's death, the new-style Kuomintang propaganda was directed to the formation of workers' unions and peasant organizations, and to the winning of the student class. Whether all this effective proselyting would in the long run redound to the advantage of Sun Yat-senism rather than Marxism remained to be seen.

While this reorganization of his party was going on, Sun still clung to the hope, which he had entertained for several years, that he might make a deal with some of the northern militarists which would result in the establishment of a real central government. He did not believe that the revitalized Kuomintang could alone create such a government. Accordingly, late in 1924 he went north to negotiate an alliance with Tuan Ch'i-jui, Fêng Yü-hsiang, and Chang Tso-lin against Wu Pei-fu. The effort failed. Sun, desperately ill, died March 12, 1925, in Peking at the home of Wellington Koo. Sun's death was a loss to the revolutionary cause in some ways, but in others a gain. As a revolutionary zealot, Sun had been outstanding; as a practical politician he had had many human weaknesses. Dead, he became a symbol fit to replace the faded image of the Son of Heaven in the hearts of his countrymen. Moreover, Sun could no longer change his mind. His writings became a canon of doctrine in which his followers searched for (and could always find) texts to justify their policy and procedures. Hereafter every Chinese politician, red or white, would be inclined to cite "our beloved leader" as the original advocate of the course of action he was following.

Sun had no sooner become the deceased and sanctified hero of the revolution than there occurred a series of events which greatly intensified nationalist feeling and brought his party many new backers. In May, 1925, police in the International Settlement fired on a labor demonstration. In June, police at Canton fired on demonstrators who were protesting the Shanghai incident. These two episodes brought on an intense outbreak of antiforeign, and specifically anti-British, feeling and did much to align the patriotically-minded students with the Kuomintang. They were followed by a Kuomintang boycott of Hong Kong which brought the trade of that great port to a virtual standstill. "Rights Recovery" slogans were at a premium and foreigners in general were regarded as parasites who were draining the vitality of China and must be shaken off. Even the missionaries were not exempted from the rising antagonism, but were stigmatized as "running dogs of imperialism." Both in its agitation among workers and peasants and in its violent antiforeign character the Nationalist [3] movement was taking a direction very pleasing to the Russians and alarming to the Western powers.

Division in the Kuomintang

However, with Sun gone, the Kuomintang was faced with the probability of a struggle for leadership. A new framework of government was worked out in the later part of 1925 and enacted at the Party Congress of January, 1926. It was very evidently a party dictatorship, in which the government was a mere agent of the Kuomintang, for the members of the Political and Administrative Councils of the government were to be chosen and removed by the Central Executive Committee or the Standing Committee of the party. The great question now was which of the various groups in the party was to be dominant in these key bodies. Could the Communists with the backing of the new peasant and labor groups and Kuomintang leftists now openly seize control, or could the Kuomintang keep the Russians in the status of advisers and hold the Chinese Communists to loyalty to Sun Yat-senism?

Despite the institution of party discipline, the Kuomintang was still a very diverse organization which would have difficulty maintaining a united front. It included very conservative elements, a left wing ready to go along with the Russian alliance, and the group of new militarists who headed the Nationalist army. In December, 1925, the extreme right wing met in the Western Hills near Peking, asked for the dismissal of the Russian advisers, and were read out of the party for their pains; most

---

[3] The literal translation of Kuomintang is "National People's Party." In the West, the party and the government which it set up have customarily been called "Nationalist."

members of the party were not yet ready for that break. Other groups centered around such personalities as Wang Ch'ing-wei, Sun's favorite disciple whose devious political career, impelled by vanity and the desire for recognition, led him ultimately to be Japan's chief puppet; Sun Fo, son of Sun Yat-sen by his first marriage; T. V. Soong, Harvard-trained financier, brother of Sun's second wife, and brother also of the future Madame Chiang Kai-shek;[4] and Hu Han-min, a conservative "Old-Guard" Kuomintang member. Shortly after Sun's death a political upheaval in Canton led to arrests and forced departures of some of the familiar figures; for example, Hu Han-min was sent to Moscow to have his point of view "broadened."

The contest for leadership then shook down to two persons, Borodin and Chiang Kai-shek. Chiang was a Chekiang man, born in 1887, who went to Japan in 1906 as a military student. In 1911 he took part in the revolution. He then went into business in Shanghai but later returned to Nationalist politics. His rise to eminence was the sign of a new dispensation within the party. The middle-of-the-road politicians of the Kuomintang were already beginning to worry about the influence of the neomilitarists, of whom Chiang Kai-shek was the chief. The left wing of the Kuomintang and the Chinese Communists drew their strength from the mass revolutionary movement which they were developing. Into the scales against them, Chiang could throw military power, and the Kuomintang politicians little if anything which carried any weight. In February, 1926, Borodin went north to confer with the astute and important Fêng Yü-hsiang. While he was away, Chiang moved against the left wing and ousted Wang Ching-wei, who then made what was only one of many face-saving trips to Europe. However, neither Borodin nor Chiang was yet ready for a showdown, and at the Central Executive Committee session in May, 1926, a compromise was worked out. The role of the Communists in the Kuomintang was redefined in narrower terms and Chiang became chairman of the Standing Committee, while Borodin retained his position as chief political adviser.

The Northern Expedition. The great project launched by the Kuomintang in 1926 was the northern campaign. Here both the new political wing and the new model army were put to good use. Propagandists preceded the troops, assuring the peasants that these soldiers were heroes

---

[4] The members of the Soong family have played important roles in Chinese affairs, both through marriage with prominent political figures and through their own abilities. T. V. Soong was the chief financial expert of the Nationalists; of his sisters, one married H. H. Kung, a key figure in Kuomintang party politics and finance; another was the second wife of Sun Yat-sen and as his widow came to exercise great political influence; another married Chiang Kai-shek and became well known in the West, especially in the period of the Sino-Japanese War, 1937-45. All four are American educated.

devoted to a cause, not hired looters. Eugene Ch'ên, Trinidad-born and British-educated descendant of coolie laborers, was the foreign minister of the Nationalist government and issued great blasts of extremely effective antiforeign, especially anti-British, propaganda. The Nationalist armies made a triumphal march to the Yangtze; in September and October the Wuhan cities fell. That left outside the Nationalist fold chiefly the northern areas under the control of Fêng Yü-hsiang, Yen Hsi-shan, who had been military governor of Shansi since 1911, and Chang Tso-lin. Fêng seemed inclined to cooperate; back from a trip to Moscow, he drove supporters of Chang Tso-lin from Shensi. Wu Pei-fu, whose seat of strength had been the Yangtze Valley, was ruined. His soldiers deserted in large numbers to the Nationalists, and he himself retired to study Buddhism and write poetry. Even the foreign powers were taken back by the vigor and rapid advance of the Nationalist campaign, and in December, 1926, Great Britain announced a new and more cooperative policy.

Nationalists and Communists Split

These great successes, however, simply presaged a decisive and immensely important split within the Kuomintang. The Wuhan cities, the new center of Nationalist power, were among the most highly industrialized in China. Here at last was a proletariat ready to listen to strong leftist doctrine. The Communists and the radical wing of the Kuomintang, with this new backing, felt ready to try the issue with Chiang Kai-shek and the military group for control of the Kuomintang. The process of organizing peasant and labor organizations was pushed with increasing zeal. Despite Chiang's opposition, Hankow became the capital of the Nationalist government in November. In March, 1927, at the meeting of the C.E.C. in Hankow, Chiang, who had stayed at his Nanchang headquarters, was removed from the posts of chairman of the C.E.C. and commander-in-chief. The left-wing group, which at this point included Eugene Ch'ên, Madame Sun Yat-sen, T. V. Soong, Sun Fo, Wang Ching-wei, and of course Borodin, was riding high.

The Nationalist movement was a house divided against itself, but 1927 was to see the climax and resolution of this internal struggle, the breakdown of the Wuhan regime, the exit of the Russian advisers, and the reconciliation of most elements in the Kuomintang. The domination of the Kuomintang early in 1927 by those most in sympathy with the Russian alliance and with a radical social and economic program was displeasing not only to militarists of the stamp of Chiang Kai-shek, but also to the conservative, propertied, silk-gowned elements in Chinese society. A rapprochement between these two groups was therefore in order.

Almost simultaneously, in March, 1927, left-wing troops from Hunan took Nanking and attacked foreigners there, and Chiang reached the great banking and trading metropolis, Shanghai, which he took almost without a blow. Chiang and his supporters then proceeded in April to a drastic purge of Communists in Shanghai and Canton and to the capture of Nanking from troops loyal to Wuhan. Chiang had now demonstrated that he represented the right wing of the revolution which, while Nationalist, was not red. Business and banking groups and landlords looked on him with favor, and the foreign powers saw in him decidedly the lesser of two evils in comparison with the Hankow regime.

As the two camps in the Kuomintang confronted each other, Fêng Yü-hsiang held the balance of power. In June he decided to line up with Chiang, as did also that most durable of the *tuchuns,* Yen Hsi-shan. After a raid on the Russian embassy in Peking in the spring, Chang Tso-lin, who opposed both Wuhan and Chiang, produced documents which were widely interpreted to indicate that the real purpose of the Russian advisers was to transform the Nationalist movement into a Communist regime. Some of the Nationalist leaders at Hankow, such as Wang Ching-wei and Sun Fo, grew alarmed, wanted to be quit of the Russians, and asked Fêng to call on Borodin to resign. In July, Borodin gave up his position and his mission to China and withdrew to Moscow. With him went Madame Sun Yat-sen, after delivering a parting statement which must have echoed in the ears of Chiang and his group years afterward. In it she accused the right wing of perverting and distorting Sun Yat-sen's revolution by setting their faces against the great economic and social changes which were necessary if the livelihood principle was to be fulfilled. Borodin's withdrawal was in line with his own astute assessment of China's stage of development. He felt that China was not ready for the social revolution, though other Communists in China were eager to go farther and faster. It was also in accordance with the shift in Soviet policy which was going on within the Soviet Union, where Trotsky and world revolution were in decline, Stalin and the development of Russian socialism in the ascendant.

Chiang Kai-shek in the Ascendant. The departure of the Russians opened the way for the reunification of the Kuomintang, but there were still serious rifts. Left wing and right wing were hostile to each other, and Wang Ching-wei was jealous of Chiang and eager to be party leader. In a characteristic move, Chiang withdrew to Japan in August, 1927, a step back from which he later was able to take a long spring forward. Left to their own resources, the Nationalist politicians painfully worked out a government rather rightist in tone, but it was a feeble regime which soon began to fall apart. In December, 1927, Chiang came back to Shanghai to marry Mei-ling Soong, sister of Mme. Sun Yat-sen and of T. V. Soong. He then conferred with Wang Ching-wei and agreed to return to the government.

Chiang was now the indispensable man, both politically, since the party politicians had failed to achieve a viable regime, and militarily, since there was another northern campaign in prospect. In January, 1928, at Nanking, he was chosen commander in chief and chairman of the Central Executive Committee, and remained dominant in the Nationalist party and government for the next twenty and more years. T. V. Soong, his brother-in-law, became minister of finance, to the great satisfaction of bankers and businessmen.

The tug-of-war between civilians and soldiers for ultimate control of the Kuomintang had been settled in favor of the soldiers, but at least Chiang was a militarist of a new style, who fought in the name of the *San Min Chu I* and not simply for personal aggrandizement. The seizure of Canton by the Communists in December, 1927, which was quickly put down, had served to convince the party politicians that Chiang was far preferable to the "rabble rousers" of the left wing. The reunified party thus stood fairly far to the right in its interpretation of Sun's revolutionary program. It was ardently Nationalistic, strongly anti-Communist, dedicated to "eventual" democracy but disposed to envision a long period of tutelage, and not inclined to drastic changes in the name of the livelihood principle. While the structure of the party and the government was still what it had been in Canton in the days of Borodin, the spirit was quite different.

The Nationalists Win North China. This reorganized, narrowed Kuomintang now had the unity and striking power necessary to attack Chang Tso-lin. Its morale was high, and its Nationalist propaganda very effective. Moreover, it had the cooperation of Fêng Yü-hsiang and Yen Hsi-shan. The Nationalist forces moved north in May, 1928, and had some brushes with Japanese troops in Shantung which simply intensified anti-imperialist feeling. On June 3, Chang Tso-lin fled from Peking, and on June 4 he was killed when the train on which he was returning to Mukden was bombed, apparently as a result of Japanese instigation. Yen Hsi-shan's troops entered Peking on June 8. The Japanese warned the Nationalists and their allies to keep out of Manchuria, but in December, 1928, Chang Hsueh-liang, son and successor of Chang Tso-lin, declared his adherence to the Nationalist government. Thus, in theory, China had once more become one. A great testimonial to its new unity and strength was that in response to the Nanking government's request for new treaties of equality, the United States agreed, on July 25, 1928, to give up one of the most bitterly hated treaty rights and grant China tariff autonomy. The other powers followed suit: in 1928 all treaty powers except Japan concluded new tariff agreements. This achievement in "rights recovery" brought the new regime great prestige at home and abroad. When Chiang Kai-shek went to the Pi Yün Ssŭ, the Buddhist temple outside Peking where Sun Yat-sen's body had lain in state, he formally reported to the spirit of the dead leader that victory in the name of his principles had been achieved. This first of Sun's stages, that of military conflict, was supposedly at an end. Now China was to enter the period of tutelage.

The Establishment of the National Government

On October 10, 1928, at Nanking the Organic Law of the new government was proclaimed.[5] The shift of the capital from Peking (now called Peiping, or "Northern Peace," since the term "King," or capital, was no longer appropriate) to Nanking was significant. The Nationalists were repudiating the setting of the false republic and the outworn monarchy, and at the same time were setting their seat of government in a city near the great capitalist metropolis, Shanghai. They were thus recognizing the economic reorientation of China which had gone on in the preceding decades, by which the coastal cities with their foreign trade had replaced the Northwest as China's front door. In Nanking, Sun Yat-sen was embalmed in state, with his writings engraved on the walls of his mausoleum. It was to be hoped that at least some of the ostentatious reverence paid to his memory was inspired by genuine devotion to his ideals and a determination to carry them out.

The New Governmental Structure. The new governmental structure was certainly based on Sun's program and was expressly meant to serve for the period of tutelage which Sun had set as the necessary preliminary to democracy. Frankly a party dictatorship, it was based on the presumption that the Kuomintang embraced those men of talent who were capable of governing and of educating the masses in the exercise of their rights. No elected legislature and no bill of rights were included. These would come only later, in the period of democracy. Instead, the Party Congress was to have ultimate control, which, when it was not in session, would be exercised by the C.E.C. The Central Political Council of the party was to be liaison between party and government. The highest organ of the government was a State Council of from twelve to sixteen members,

[5] For competent discussions of the political institutions and developments of the tutelage period, see P. M. Linebarger, *The China of Chiang Kai-shek* (Boston, 1941), and Ch'ien Tuan-sheng, *The Government and Politics of China* (Cambridge, Mass., 1950).

with the President of the National government as chairman. There was no President of China in the strict use of the title, but the President of the National government was also commander in chief and official representative of the government in diplomatic relations and at public functions; since at the outset Chiang Kai-shek held these concurrent positions, he needed no additional title to indicate that he was "Number One."

The Organic Law provided for a governmental organization in accordance with Sun's idea of five powers, each incarnated in a *Yüan,* or Council. The five Yüan were (1) the Executive Yüan, which included ten ministries and five commissions, initiated measures for submission to the Legislative Yüan, and had the power to fill high offices; (2) the Legislative Yüan, which consisted of appointed members who discussed matters presented by the Executive Yüan and in turn made recommendations to the State Council; (3) the Judicial Yüan which included a Supreme Court, an administrative court, a commission for the punishment of officials, the Ministry of Justice, and a group of legal experts working on new codes and courts against the day when extraterritoriality would end and China recover jurisdiction over foreigners; (4) the Examination Yüan, which was supposed to test the qualifications of candidates for office, but which in the period of tutelage was not a very effective body since party membership was taken as prima facie evidence of competence; (5) the Control Yüan, which could impeach officials and audit accounts.

As might be expected, this government was staffed with party stalwarts. Most offices were held for no fixed term and with no security, but it was surprising how what came to be the Old Guard hung on, and periodic governmental reorganizations meant the same old faces at new windows. Probably no other government in the world changed less in its top personnel between 1928 and 1948, a circumstance which while it insured continuity also tended toward ossification. This failure to bring in new blood was perhaps one of the inevitable consequences of the tutelage system in which the guardians were loath to proclaim their wards of age, and serves to justify A. N. Holcombe's characterization of the Chinese government under the Organic Law as "a system of interlocking directorates dominated by a narrow oligarchy of party politicians and generals." [6] Failure to formulate clearly the relation between the central government and the provinces showed the government's awareness of the delicacy of this perennial Chinese question. The 1928 plan stressed the government of the *hsien* or district, in the hope of bringing this basic unit in direct relation with the central regime and bypassing the provincial authorities. Emphasis on *hsien* institutions was in accordance with Sun's ideas, for he had expected the *hsien* to be the birthplace of democracy, but in practice the

[6] *The Chinese Revolution* (New York, 1930), p. 270.

appointed district magistrates still dominated the district scene and no real development of local self-government took place.

Unification of the country, establishment of the new government, and recovery of tariff autonomy gave rise to high hopes and elaborate plans. However, almost immediately the new government had tremendous problems to face. They were in most instances the same problems which had beset China ever since contact with the West began to have significant effects upon her development. Perhaps the most effective way of stating these problems and showing what the National government was able to do toward solving them before the outbreak of the Sino-Japanese conflict in 1937 is to use Sun Yat-sen's three principles as touchstones. How far did the National government go, in its first decade of power, toward the realization of nationalism, democracy, and people's livelihood?

Nationalism

China's nationalism faced two ways. One face was set toward anti-foreignism and resistance to imperialism. In this direction the Nationalist government encountered serious difficulties—an undeclared war with the Soviet Union in 1929 and the Manchurian crisis of 1931-33—which are discussed elsewhere. Nationalism also looked toward the building of a united national state with a real national government, and here there were problems in abundance. First, the declaration that the period of military struggle had ended was largely bluff. Warlordism and provincialism were still present after 1928. Many local strong men had joined the Nationalist victory march, although they had no intention of welcoming Nationalist officials to their areas or letting local revenues go to Nanking. At the moment of its formal inauguration the new government had political and financial control over only five provinces. As T. V. Soong, Minister of Finance, pointed out, most provinces turned in little information about their tax revenues and less actual cash. To make matters worse, the political and military balance was precarious; more than three fourths of the central government's revenues were required for military expenses. Disarmament was as desirable as it had been in 1912, and as difficult to achieve. It was a very touchy business, involving the issues of supremacy of civilian over military and of the central government over the provinces. A disarmament session in the fall of 1928 served only to make Fêng Yü-hsiang, the Kwangsi generals, and other war lords exceedingly suspicious. All through 1929 there was political-military maneuvering with Wang Ching-wei trying to make capital for himself out of the rift between the central government and some of the generals. After open conflict in 1930, the situation was resolved. Wang and Yen Hsi-shan left for Europe and Fêng withdrew to Shansi. The Kwangsi generals made a settlement with Nanking, but in 1936 broke into resistance again. The central government had also to reckon with the many small militarists whose loyalty to Nanking was limited and who might easily be drawn off into rebellion as supporters of the more powerful war lords. An even more formidable obstacle to national unity and the well-filled treasury was the Communist movement, which, having been forced underground in 1927, popped up in Kiangsi.

The existence of latent warlordism and active communism limited the resistance which the government could offer to the Russians in 1929 and the Japanese in 1931 and 1932. It always feared that the employment of its armies in international conflict would give the war lords or the Communists the chance to take advantage of such involvement. The central government in the 1930's had three enemies—the war lords, the Communists, and the Japanese—and had to decide in what order of priority to act against them. Chiang's general program seems to have been first to suppress the Communists, meanwhile keeping the war lords in hand, and then to face Japan. This policy prevented direct resistance to Japan in 1931. The Nationalist regime in consequence appeared to many alert Chinese, especially the intensely patriotic student group, to be pusillanimous, appeasing, and altogether less than nationalist. The moral union of the Kuomintang and the students began to collapse, and the students became energetic critics of the policy of putting up with Japanese pressure in order to carry on the civil war. The Japanese attack in 1937 evoked a widespread national spirit in support of a government at last willing to bury the hatchet with the Communists and fight the Japanese. But ironically this conflict, while temporarily stimulating a united, nationalistic China, also brought to light and increased serious weaknesses of the Kuomintang regime, thus contributing notably to its later downfall.

Democracy

How did the preparation of the Chinese people for democracy proceed in the years before 1937? What kind of government would China get during the period of tutelage, and how strenuous an effort would be made to shorten that period? The answers to these questions turned largely on the nature of the Kuomintang.

Actually the party was very different from the Russian Communist party from which its formal structure had been borrowed. Linebarger has aptly described the Kuomintang as "a conglomeration of innumerable personal leaderships knit together by a common outlook, a common interest in the maintenance of the National government and formal Party power, and a common loyalty to the Party Chief [a title conferred on Chiang Kai-shek in 1938]."[7] The personal quality of Chinese political organizations had persisted in the Kuomintang despite the Russian overhauling of the party in the mid-1920's. Sun's doctrines should have given the party a strong ideological base, but Sun himself had been for years the leader of a clique rather than the founder of a party, and now that he was dead each of his followers could claim a bit of Sun's mantle and put his own interpretation on Sun's words. The party, in other words, was far more loosely hung than the Russian Communist party and Chiang Kai-shek needed all of his outstanding prestige, military backing, and political skill to hold it together. Within the party were many gradations of opinion and many different types of social and economic interest and background. Certain of these groups were clearly recognizable in the thirties and forties. To cite four examples, the "CC group," headed by the redoubtable brothers Ch'ên Li-fu and Ch'ên Kuo-fu, represented the most conservative interpretation of nationalist ideology; the Ch'en brothers operated particularly in the fields of thought control, education, and party personnel in order to insure what seemed to them to be doctrinal purity for the Kuomintang. The Whampoa Academy consisted of the army officers who had been trained under Chiang Kai-shek in the Canton days, and constituted his most solid following. The Political Scientists were competent administrators with Western training. Another group, made up of bankers and businessmen, centered around H. H. Kung, who was married to one of the Soong sisters.

Developments Pointing Toward Democracy. On one thing the stronger elements of the party agreed: a considerable reluctance to hasten on toward democracy and the end of the one-party system. True, there were some developments in this period that might well have served as foundations for a democratic structure. The educational system was developing rapidly, especially at higher levels; many new universities, colleges, and teacher-training institutions were launched by the government. However, the primary purpose of this development was to increase the supply of trained personnel in such fields as agriculture, engineering, medicine, and law. Elementary education was relatively neglected, though it should have received major attention as the source of a future literate electorate. In extenuation of the government's unbalanced and top-heavy educational structure it must be said that the financial resources available

[7] P. M. A. Linebarger, *The China of Chiang Kai-shek* (Boston, 1941), p. 142.

for a school system were extremely limited and would produce far more if invested in professional, technical, and vocational education.

A second development was the New Life Movement, announced in 1934, which was intended to provide elementary training for citizenship. Sun's doctrines inclined to the political side and hardly constituted a code of personal morality. The New Life Movement therefore provided an everyday formula combining Confucian ethics, personal hygiene, and opposition to defeatism, excessive concern for face, and lack of public spirit. In a sense, it was meant as a counter doctrine to set against Communist teaching, but was not too effective.

More encouraging was Dr. Y. C. (James) Yen's experiment at Tinghsien in Hopei, where an effort was made to apply Western scientific and social knowledge to produce a model district. This illustrated what could be done to reduce illiteracy and broaden the horizons of peasants, but although it was a pilot project and similar reforms were instituted elsewhere, there were too many *hsiens* and too few Dr. Yens to make the movement effective in the short time vouchsafed to the Nationalist regime. Anyway, any project to activate the peasants was apt to eventuate in a strong peasant drive for fundamental social and economic change, and this was a prospect which the ruling group contemplated with little enthusiasm. The party members were the elite; why not let the elite continue for a long time to exercise power on behalf of—and over—the rank and file?

To some Western observers, real democracy seemed far enough away in China to assuage the doubts and apprehensions of even the most self-interested members of the Kuomintang. Neither the old tradition of rule by an aristocracy of book-learning and land or the pseudo democracy of the sham republic had prepared the Chinese people to carry on such Western rituals as the use of the ballot or the activities of multiple political parties. Nevertheless, from the outset the government was under very understandable pressure from intellectuals, professional people, and other politically conscious elements outside the party to indicate how long the period of tutelage would be. Suspicion was strong that the Kuomintang might exploit the role of guardian to maintain its monopoly of political power for many years.

Constitutional Change. The government's first response to its critics was the substitution in 1931 of a provisional constitution (Yüeh Fa) for the Organic Law. Both party doctrine and farsighted commonsense indicated the need for more education and political training at local levels instead of another constitutional document, but a really edifying constitution was still thought of as a hallmark of political progress. The new provisional constitution was supposed to serve for the remainder of the period of tutelage while democracy was in theory developing at the rice-roots level. The Yüeh Fa, which, as it turned out, continued in force all through the war period, was a somewhat more complicated implementation of Sun's political ideas than was the Organic Law. As before, the Kuomintang held essential sovereignty, which it exercised through the Central Political Council, a party agency, which gave orders to the State Council which in turn transmitted them to lower levels. The State Council had under it the Five Yüan, which functioned much as before, except that one of the chief activities of the Legislative Yüan was the preparation of a draft constitution for the period of democracy.

The Draft Constitution of 1936. Late in 1932 Sun Fo proposed the preparation of a permanent constitution which upon adoption would end the period of tutelage, and for three years legal scholars studied Western constitutions and worked on a draft which eventually was known as the "Double Five" Constitutional Draft (from May 5, 1936). The choosing of delegates to consider this constitution was under way in the late summer of 1937 and the Constituent Assembly was due to meet in November of that year, but the outbreak of fighting between Japan and China at Shanghai led to postponement of the assembly and continuation of the period of tutelage. Later, after the Sino-Japanese War, the government attempted to resurrect both the 1936 draft and the delegates who had been chosen in 1937 to approve it, as a way of satisfying Chinese desires and American criticisms. The "Double Five" draft was criticized both in 1936 and 1937, and at its later reappearance, as not being notably democratic, although it provided for an ingeniously constructed political system. Rights carried the limitation "in accordance with law," and law was whatever was passed by the legislative Yüan and promulgated by the president. The National Congress, the body most directly representative of the whole population, was to meet for only one month every three years, and the effective legislative body was to be the Legislative Yüan. The central government was to include the Five Yüan and a strong president with a wide range of powers. The whole plan minimized provincial government and emphasized the *hsien* units in a way which made critics point out that this strongly centralized regime was not subject to proper checks and balances. Whether, if the 1936 draft had been put into effect in 1937, it would have been employed simply as a front behind which the vested interests of the tutelage period could have perpetuated their power, or whether it would have been operated with good will as a training experience for the Chinese people in the arts of self-government it is of course impossible to say.

Livelihood

While the National government was at least making gestures intended to end tutelage and inaugurate democracy, it was doing less to implement the principle of livelihood. Certainly the difficulties in the way of real achievement here were formidable—some of them economic, others political. The Kuomintang had repudiated moves toward social and economic revolution and was to a large extent the party of the status quo. Yet wisdom and its own preservation suggested that it should undertake to kill communism by kindness with all possible dispatch by instituting bedrock social reform.

Most Chinese were peasants, and peasants were the traditional makers and unmakers of government. Although there had been stirrings in the countryside, in all the years since 1911 the peasants had benefited little from the revolution. Nationalist leaders were eager to make China an industrialized, technically up-to-date nation, and had elaborate programs for modernization in many fields—industrial development, flood control, reforestation, improvement of transportation, agricultural education and the establishment of experiment stations, better provision for agriculture credit—but time and money for the execution of these projects were both in short supply.

The most notable Kuomintang testimonial to the plight of the peasants was the Land Law of 1930 intended to alleviate some of the evils of tenancy: rents were not to be higher than 37.5 per cent of the main crop and taxation on farm land was to be sharply reduced. This law, alas, was not well enforced, except later by the Communists, who took particular pleasure in building for themselves a peasant following by putting into effect a piece of legislation which was virtually a dead letter in Kuomintang China. Other parts of the Kuomintang program for improvement of agriculture were the Agricultural Credit Association and the Agricultural Research Bureau, but the benefits which they brought to farmers paled in comparison with the immediate changes which resulted from the Communist program of taking land from the landlords and giving it to the peasants.

The Revival of Communism

The failure to get literally down to earth in agrarian reform was in the long run to be fatal to the Kuomintang, for this failure gave to the Communist party the chance to seize leadership of the peasant movement for livelihood. The Nationalist-Communist split, Chiang's purges, and the departure of the Russian advisers had not killed communism in

China.[8] Quite on its own, without Russian aid, it appeared in Kiangsi Province, in southern China. At first the Communist leaders tried to appeal to proletarian groups, and to that end tried to stage formal battles and capture cities where they would find an audience for denunciations of capitalism. Bitter experience taught them another approach which gave them infinitely greater leverage in Chinese society.

To survive in the Chinese countryside, they had to appeal to and win the support of the peasants. In Marxist theory the peasants were petty bourgeoisie, a drag on the wheels of social revolution; in Chinese history the peasants were the chief revolutionary force. To suit peasant ears, communism had to change from "red" to "green" and stress the struggle against "agrarian feudalism" rather than the struggle against the bourgeoisie. In Kiangsi, tenantry was especially onerous, and the Communist policy of organizing the peasants against the landlords was so successful that in 1931 a Soviet Republic was proclaimed with its capital at Juichin in Kiangsi, a formal rival to the Nanking government.

Communist Leaders. The leaders who came to the top during this period of trial and error, and still today leading figures in Chinese communism, were Marxist in belief but flexible and realistic in adapting Marxist doctrine to Chinese conditions and in pursuing policies which were satisfying to the Chinese masses. The very able political leader of the new Communist regime was Mao Tse-tung, now head of the Chinese People's Republic inaugurated at Peking on October 1, 1949. A Hunanese, born in 1893, Mao came from a family of prosperous farmers. As a student and librarian in Peking in the days of the renaissance, he was caught up in the turbulent intellectual current of that period and became a Marxist. During the period of Nationalist-Communist collaboration he served as head of the All-China Peasants' Union, an experience of major importance in his later activity. Chu Teh, military leader of the Communists, is a son of the gentry. In his youth he was an opium addict and aide to a minor war lord in Yünnan. He eventually reacted against this way of life and went to Europe in 1926, where he came in touch with Chinese student groups in France and Germany who had taken up communism. He returned to China in 1926 ready to put his remarkable abilities at the service of the Communist party.

Communist Doctrine and Practice. In doctrine, the Communist party followed Marxism while still paying tribute to Sun Yat-sen's *San*

---

[8] An effective piece of reporting is Edgar Snow's *Red Star Over China* (New York, 1938, 1944), which tells the story of the early years of the Communist regime in China. See also Benjamin I. Schwartz, *Chinese Communism and the Rise of Mao* (Cambridge, Mass., 1951).

Min Chu I as a suitable formulation of the immediate objectives of social change in China. It was frankly recognized that the triumph of the proletariat (not to mention its very existence in significant quantity) still lay some distance in China's future. In practice the Communist party was quick to capitalize (if this verb is acceptable in this connection) on the Kuomintang's errors of omission and commission in dealing with the peasants. The Nationalists had borne down heavily on peasant and labor organizations in the twenties; the Communists encouraged these groups. The Nationalists tended to support the established agrarian order, subject to gradual reformation; the Communists took land from the rich and gave it to the poor, canceled debts, and stressed opportunities for local self-government through Soviets. To most peasants in Kiangsi it was immaterial whether these social changes were being made in the name of Marxism, predestination, or reincarnation; all that mattered was that here was a regime which took their part against the vested interests of the old order. Moreover, the Communist leaders, despite the internationalism of Marxism, even surpassed the leadership of the Kuomintang in vociferous expression of nationalism. During the Manchurian crisis, while Chiang was carefully husbanding his army and hoping that the League would extract China's chestnuts from the fire, the Communist government declared war against Japan. It was in no danger of having to back up the declaration with action, since the territory it controlled had no contact with Japanese spheres of interest; but this patriotic gesture, coming at a time when the Nationalist government appeared weak-kneed and unheroic, made a strong impression on non-Communist elements in China.

Communist Shift to the Northwest

The experience of the Communists in Kiangsi, which ended in 1934 when they were forced to move to the Northwest, was a sort of series of laboratory experiments out of which they welded their party and evolved a line of policy which, followed with variations to suit changing circumstances, eventually brought practically all of China under their control. The Communist social revolution in South China was accompanied by savage fighting—farmers vs. landlords, White Terror vs. Red Terror. The Nationalist government also entered this struggle with an annual "bandit suppression" campaign—a euphemism, for Chiang knew that he was up against something much more formidable than banditry. The first anti-Communist campaigns in the early 1930's were unsuccessful. The Communists were mastering those techniques of guerrilla warfare based on peasant support which they were later to use so successfully against the Japanese and the Nationalists, and Nationalist victories in formal engagements were soon offset by the impossibility of pacifying the countryside. At last in 1934, with the aid of German advisers who had come to China to study problems of fighting in a vast country with poor communications (knowledge which was to prove valuable to Germany in 1941), Chiang was able to dislodge the Communists, who then undertook the famous "Long March" of over 6,000 miles. They swung across China westward to the Tibetan border and eventually came to a stop in Shensi Province in the Northwest. This exploit, compared to which Hannibal's crossing of the Alps was a pleasure trip, gave the movement heightened morale and unity; thereafter the veterans of the Long March constituted the tested core of the Red Army and the Communist political organization.

The Communists found groups in the Northwest receptive to their doctrine and policy, and in December, 1936, they proclaimed a new Chinese People's Soviet Republic with Yenan as its capital. Here the Chinese Communists put into effect their program of social and economic change, which was actually far short of full-fledged socialism. Their program included the single tax on land, a tax on business operations, and confiscation and redistribution of excessive landholdings. Such ancient evils as foot-binding, opium smoking, slavery, and prostitution were attacked. Local elections took place, and however their results were influenced by the nature of the regime, the very fact that they were held at all contrasted sharply with Nationalist China's failure to encourage local self-government. There was a minority in the Communist areas which was miserably unhappy under the new regime, but the majority liked it and felt a sense of membership in it which led them to refer to it as *our* government," a phrase both novel and portentous.

Tested by the *San Min Chu I*, the Communists were getting results in the small area under their control. They were intensely nationalist and ready to back up that nationalism by fighting the Japanese; they were making more motions that resembled local self-government than were the Nationalists; and they had taken measures in the name of livelihood which were eminently pleasing to their clientele. They were plainly preparing to give the Nationalists formidable competition in the race for the allegiance of the Chinese peasants and intellectuals, on the outcome of which the future of China would depend.

The United Front

In these years non-Communist intellectuals became disillusioned with the Kuomintang, and the siren song of the Communists, that civil war should cease in the name of national unity against the Japanese menace, was music to their ears. The years 1935 and 1936 were the time of decision for the Nanking government. The Manchurian crisis was over, but there were many signs that the Japanese appetite grew by what it fed on, and North China might next be "liberated" by Japan. Would the Kuomintang reverse its order of urgency and face the Japanese, or would it continue to defer and temporize with Tokyo and go on with the civil war?

Chiang continued to put the suppression of the Communists at the head of the list, perhaps in part because he was uncertain that his armies could do anything against the Japanese military machine and was playing for time. Also, it was vitally necessary for the Nationalist government to bring some of the local satraps to heel. To bring them into plans for reorganization, Chiang undertook a series of domiciliary visits by plane to the seats of power of recalcitrant war lords. Measures to strengthen the central government were pushed, such as centralization and equipment of the armed forces, the building of new roads and railways, and the establishment of a new currency. The formula was temporary appeasement of Japan plus preparation to withstand eventual Japanese attack.

But this policy, however one might defend it in terms of political "realism," was costing the Nationalist government the moral support of many patriotic Chinese. There was a growing popular conviction that appeasement of Japan must end lest the Nationalist regime let North China fall into Japanese hands without striking a blow. Many Chinese felt that in the face of Japanese imperialism, the fratricidal struggle of the Chinese Nationalists and Communists was a luxury which China could not afford. An "independence movement" in North China, magnanimously assisted by the Japanese, fizzled out, but led to an explosion of Chinese Nationalist feeling in the winter of 1935 and 1936. Great student demonstrations in favor of ending the civil war, opposition to Japan, and the granting of civil liberties spread like a chain reaction from Peking to other cities.

The National Salvation Movement enrolled many politically conscious Chinese who wanted to see the formation of a united front against Japan. In Kwangsi, Generals Pai Chung-hsi and Li Tsung-jen encouraged discontented students and National Salvationists, and in May, 1936, came out for action against Japan. The Kwangsi revolt was settled by negotiation but was a very significant straw in the wind. The government bore down harshly on student demonstrators and also arrested and imprisoned the "seven gentlemen" (one was a lady) who were the leaders of the National Salvation group. Nevertheless it realized that its popularity was in the balance. Chiang's position was that China was not ready to oppose Japan and hence should not provoke her. The belief of many Chinese was that Japan was preparing to move against China anyhow and that their government should take a courageous and forthright stand. Could the Chinese government achieve a level of technical and military strength adequate for resistance to Japan before it completely lost popular confidence?

Chiang Kai-shek Kidnapped. This situation was auspicious for the Communists. Their professed readiness to fight the Japanese was winning them the sympathy of many Chinese who while disliking their economic views approved their patriotic sentiments. Communist social policy became consciously more moderate at this point; taxation on merchants and industrialists was reduced, and land confiscation was halted. The Communists in fact were trying to create a united front in the territory under their control. Mao Tse-tung also announced that he was personally not opposed to Chiang and that the Chinese Soviet Republic was ready to join with the Nationalist government against Japan.

In this atmosphere occurred what Occidentals at the time were inclined to think of as a peculiarly mysterious Oriental event—the kidnapping of Chiang Kai-shek. The Tungpei (Northeast) Army of the "Young Marshal" Chang Hsueh-liang, driven from Manchuria by the Japanese, had been stationed at Hsianfu (Sian) to carry on "bandit suppression." The soldiers were more interested in fighting Japanese than in suppressing "bandits," and soon some of them were fraternizing with Communists. In fact, in June 1936, Chang Hsueh-liang met Chou En-lai, the European-educated "Number Three" man in the Communist group, who was the Communists' ablest diplomat and negotiator. In December, Chiang made one of his dramatic visits by plane to Hsianfu; unless Chang's forces showed more anti-Communist zeal, he proposed to shift them to the south. This prospect led to the decision by Chang and his staff to kidnap Chiang, which they did on December 12.

Most of the Tungpei officers still considered the Generalissimo their national leader; they simply wanted to get him in a corner, isolated from other influences, so that they could talk him around to their point of view of "unity before resistance." [9] Chou En-lai was one of those who talked with Chiang, and it appears that the Communists were eager for Chiang's release and an agreement with Nanking. When the news of the kidnapping reached Nanking there was great political agitation and some support for hostilities against Hsianfu—which would probably have meant Chiang's death. However, on December 25 Madame Chiang flew to Hsianfu and Chiang soon returned to Nanking with her and with Chang

[9] The text of the manifesto on the seizure of Chiang which his captors issued on December 12, 1936, is given in Department of State, *United States Relations with China with Special Reference to the Period 1944-1949* (Washington, 1949), Annex 34. This important publication of source material from the files of the State Department will hereafter be referred to by its colloquial name of *The White Paper*.

Hsueh-liang. The Young Marshal assumed the responsibility for the seizure of the Generalissimo and has been kept in custody ever since.

Chiang had made no formal pledges to change his policy, but it was soon evident that the kidnapping had served its purpose and a united front of Nationalists and Communists was about to be consummated. At the February, 1937 meeting of the Central Executive Committee there were moves toward the reconciliation of Nationalists and Communists.[10] The Communists had offered to bring their government and their army under the authority of Nanking, to fit in with the impending end of tutelage by establishing democracy in their areas, and to give up their policy of land confiscation. Private negotiations between representatives of the two parties achieved unity along these lines in the earlier part of 1937. The Japanese attack took place in July, 1937, before the united front had been formally announced, but after the Japanese realized that it had come to pass and that, from their point of view, prompt action was called for. The two deadly enemies, Communists and Nationalists, had now come together to face their common foe.

SUGGESTED READINGS

General works which are especially useful for this period are: H. F. MacNair, *China in Revolution* (New York, 1931); A. N. Holcombe, *The Chinese Revolution* (New York, 1930); P. M. A. Linebarger, *The China of Chiang Kai-shek* (Boston, 1941); Ch'ien Tuan-sheng, *The Government and Politics of China* (Cambridge, Mass., 1950); Wei-tung Pan, *The Chinese Constitution* (Washington, 1945).

The most readily available English language editions of Sun Yat-sen's principal works are: *San Min Chu I (The Three Principles of the People)*, translated by Frank W. Price (Shanghai, 1927), reissued by the Chinese Ministry of Information (1945); M. D'Elia, S. J., *The Triple Demism of Sun Yat-sen* (Wuchang, 1931), a translation of *San Min Chu I* with commentary; Sun Yat-sen, *The International Development of China* (New York, 1922), and *Fundamentals of National Reconstruction* (Chinese Ministry of Education, Chungking, 1945); Leonard Shihlien Hsü, *Sun Yat-sen, His Political and Social Ideals* (Los Angeles, 1933), contains texts of Sun's chief writings. Sun's ideas are analyzed effectively in P. M. A. Linebarger, *The Political Doctrines of Sun Yat-sen: An Exposition of the San Min Chu I* (Baltimore, 1937), and A. N. Holcombe, *The Spirit of the Chinese Revolution* (New York, 1930).

Lyon Sharman, *Sun Yat-sen, His Life and Its Meaning* (New York, 1934) is the best life of Sun. Other good biographical studies are: Bernard Martin, *Strange Vigour* (London, 1944) and Stephen Chen and Robert Payne, *Sun Yat-sen, a Portrait* (New York, 1946).

There is no adequate biography of Chiang Kai-shek; those which have appeared are either journalistic or uncritically laudatory. Most acceptable are: Robert Berkov,

[10] For the telegram sent to the C.E.C. by the Central Committee of the Communist Party on February 10, 1937, see *The White Paper*, Annex 35. Other documents relating to the establishment of the united front are given in Annexes 36 and 37.

Strong Man of China (Boston, 1938); H. H. Chang, *Chiang Kai-shek, Asia's Man of Destiny* (New York, 1944); H. K. Tong, *Chiang Kai-shek: Soldier and Statesman* (2 vols., London, 1938). Mayling Soong and Chiang Kai-shek, *Sian: a Coup d'Etat* (Shanghai, 1937) gives Madame Chiang's account of the kidnapping and extracts from the diary which the Generalissimo kept in Sian.

Works which treat one aspect or another of this period are Louis Fischer, *The Soviets in World Affairs* (2 vols., London, 1930), which gives the Russian view of the Communist-Kuomintang alliance; Harold Isaacs, *The Tragedy of the Chinese Revolution* (London, 1938), a Trotskyist analysis; H. F. MacNair, *China's New Nationalism and Other Essays* (Shanghai, 1925); Paul Monroe, *China, A Nation in Evolution* (New York, 1928); two works by a Kuomintang leftist, Tang Leang-li, *The Foundations of Modern China* (London, 1928) and *The Inner History of the Chinese Revolution* (London, 1930); Harold S. Quigley, *Chinese Politics Today* (Minneapolis, 1934); T. C. Woo, *The Kuomintang and the Future of the Chinese Revolution* (London, 1928); Edgar Snow, *Red Star Over China* (New York, 1938, 1944), the pioneer Western reporter's account of the Chinese Communists; H. F. MacNair (ed.), *China* (Berkeley and Los Angeles, 1946), chap. 10 by P. M. A. Linebarger and Robert E. Hosach which deals with the Chinese Revolution 1928-46; Benjamin I. Schwartz, *Chinese Communism and the Rise of Mao* (Cambridge, Mass., 1951).

25

SINO-JAPANESE RELATIONS BETWEEN THE TWO WORLD WARS

With the war concluded and the terms of the principal peace treaties set, it became apparent that two important questions remained to be solved: arms limitation and the situation in the Pacific and the Far East. Reacting favorably to a suggestion of the British that a conference be called to deal with these matters, the United States took the initiative and on August 11, 1921, sent out invitations for a conference to be held in Washington beginning November 11. The countries originally invited were Great Britain, France, Italy, and Japan; China was invited to participate only in discussions relating to the Pacific and the Far East. Due to their interests in the Pacific and the Far East, Belgium, the Netherlands, and Portugal were later invited to attend.[1]

The purpose of the Washington Conference, as far as the Orient was concerned, was to put a brake on Japan's advances in China and to provide for cooperative international relations with the latter country which would help to stabilize the rather chaotic conditions there. The United States had already taken the lead in an effort to bring about cooperative action in the field of Chinese banking and finance.

The New China Consortium

The new China consortium grew out of a suggestion made by Secretary of State Lansing to President Wilson in the late spring of 1918 that American banking firms concerned with China should pool their interests and cooperate with a similar Japanese group to grant a loan to China. The desire of some American firms that British and French bankers also be included led to the organization of the International Banking Consortium at Paris in May, 1919. The Japanese tried unsuccessfully to get South Manchuria and eastern Inner Mongolia, where they had extensive

---

[1] All present were accorded equality. China apparently let it be known that she would attend on no other basis. W. W. Willoughby, *China at the Conference* (Baltimore, 1922), p. 2n.

interests, excepted from the consortium's province. Japan had to be content with a promise that the governments involved would not back their bankers in enterprises which Japan felt were patently against its best interests in these regions.

October 15, 1920, saw the signing at Paris of the consortium which related to "existing and future loan agreements ... to the Chinese Government, or to Chinese Government Departments or to Provinces of China or to companies or corporations owned or controlled by or in behalf of the Chinese Government or any Chinese Provincial Government or to any party if the transaction in question is guaranteed by the Chinese Government or Chinese Provincial Government but does not relate to agreements for loans to be floated in China." Designed to last five years, the consortium made no loans whatsoever to China. Its significance lies in the fact that at least the interested parties did get together, and it was the United States which had taken the initiative, as it did in the Washington Conference.

The Washington Conference

Japan originally was somewhat reluctant about attending the conference as it professed to feel that it had more at stake than any other invited nation. Furthermore, some Japanese felt that the United States, having rejected the League of Nations and by inference having turned its back on Europe, was determined to compensate itself by following a strong Far Eastern policy. The reaction to Japan's hesitancy was not well received by either the United States or Great Britain. However, the conference opened in a rather cordial atmosphere. The Japanese delegation was on the whole a reasonably liberal one.[2] It consisted of Admiral Baron Kato, Minister of Navy, Baron Shidehara, Ambassador at Washington, Prince Tokugawa, President of the House of Peers, and Hanihara, Vice-Minister for Foreign Affairs. This was the beginning of the "liberal decade" (1921-31) when Japan was generally cooperative with the Western powers and pursued a much more wholesome China policy than she had been following.

Naval Limitation. In his address opening the conference, Secretary of State Charles Evans Hughes called for a drastic reduction of naval armaments. His main proposals were as follows: (1) "that all capital ship-building programs, either actual or projected, should be abandoned; (2)

---

[2] A Japanese critic has questioned the ability of the group and held that it was inadequately staffed with civilian statesmen and Far Eastern experts. Masamichi Royama, *Foreign Policy of Japan: 1914-1939* (Tokyo, 1941), pp. 33 f.

that further reduction should be made through the scrapping of certain of the older ships; (3) that, in general, regard should be had to the existing naval strength of the powers concerned; (4) that the capital ship tonnage should be used as the measurement of strength for navies and a proportionate allowance of auxiliary combatant craft prescribed." The first point called for the scrapping of sixty-six battleships either already afloat or being built, displacing some 1,876,000 tons. Replacement should be limited to a ratio of 5:5:3:1.75:1.75 maximum capital ship tonnage for the five great Powers, the United States, Great Britain, Japan, France, and Italy. Furthermore, Hughes called for a ten-year naval holiday in the building of new ships and placed a maximum limit of 35,000 tons displacement on capital ships.

Japan held out for a 10:10:7 ratio but accepted 5:5:3 on two conditions. The first was that no first-class naval bases would be constructed at Hong Kong or in the Philippines, to which the United States and Great Britain both agreed after Hawaii, Australia, New Zealand, and the islands along the American and Canadian Pacific coasts were specifically excluded from such a prohibition. The second condition, which was also accepted, had to do with Japan's wish to keep the battleship "Mutsu" for sentimental reasons and to scrap the "Settsu" in its place. Here both the United States and Great Britain were also allowed to make some shifts in the matter of which ships would be retained and which destroyed.

Rounding out what is called the Five-Power Naval Treaty was an agreement on a ten-year naval holiday, the setting of 35,000 tons as the maximum displacement for capital ships, and the allotting of 525,000 tons each for United States and Great Britain, 315,000 for Japan, and 175,000 each for France and Italy.

Nothing was accomplished in the fields of limiting such auxiliary shipping as submarines, cruisers, and destroyers, nor did the Powers achieve any agreement on the reduction of land armaments.

The Four-Power Treaty. First among the other agreements reached at Washington, and actually preceding the naval treaty, was the Four-Power Treaty signed December 13, 1921, wherein the United States, the British Empire, Japan, and France agreed to respect the status quo of islands in the Pacific (excluding Japan proper) and to confer should any dispute arise over these islands or should the security of any of them be threatened by any other power. This understanding also provided for the termination of the Anglo-Japanese Alliance which had become a source of discomfiture for Great Britain due to the unfavorable attitude of the United States and certain of the Dominions, among them Australia and Canada.

The Nine-Power Treaty. Next came the Nine-Power Treaty, signed February 6, 1922, whereby a pledge was made by all the Powers to respect China's sovereignty, independence, and territorial and administrative integrity. All agreed specifically to respect the open door, including China, herself, for the first time formally. This was a great victory for American diplomacy, on paper at least. China's rights as a neutral in time of war were to be respected, and the Powers promised to do everything within their ability to help China achieve an effective and stable government.

Just as the embarrassing Anglo-Japanese Alliance was terminated at Washington, so too was the distressful Lansing-Ishii Agreement brought to an end. This was done through an exchange of notes between Secretary Hughes and Ambassador Hanihara at Washington on April 14, 1923.

The Nine-Power Customs Convention. A treaty was also reached at Washington on February 6, 1922, known as the Nine-Power Customs Convention which brought about an improvement in China's tariff. China won the promise of other concessions through the adoption of nine resolutions by the Powers. These included promises to abandon the foreign postal agencies in China just as soon as China had an efficient postal system of her own and, even more important, that all foreign troops would be removed from China whenever the latter could assure the protection of the lives and property of foreigners in the country.

Other Settlements

Shantung. Officially not a part of the Washington Conference were the Sino-Japanese talks concerning Shantung. These were begun December 1, 1921, with Secretary Hughes and Britain's Lord Balfour very much interested in a satisfactory result, which finally came about through the signing of the Shantung Treaty on February 4, 1922. By this agreement Japan restored Shantung to China and agreed to give up her special rights there. The Tsinan-Tsingtao Railway was handed over to China for a stipulated sum, and Japanese railway guards were removed. China on its part promised to open the entire area to foreign trade and residence.

Yap. Also accomplished outside the conference proper was the settlement of the Yap issue. Yap was one of the islands in the Japanese mandated area in the Pacific. The United States had refused to recognize its inclusion within the Japanese mandate group on the grounds that President Wilson had made a specific reservation concerning the island. The Yap Treaty was signed February 11, 1922. In it the United States recognized Japan's mandate over all the former German islands north of the equator, including Yap, and won from Japan free access for American citizens to the island in the important matter of the Yap-Guam cable and "of any cable which may hereafter be laid or operated by the United States or by its nationals connecting with the Island of Yap."

Siberia. Japan itself took up the question before the conference of its military expedition in Siberia which was causing adverse comment, particularly in the United States, and claimed that "it is the fixed and settled policy of Japan to respect the territorial integrity of Russia and to observe the principle of non-intervention in the internal affairs of the country, as well as the principle of equal opportunity for commerce and industry of all nations in every part of the Russian possession." While Hughes accepted Japan's position, he made it plain that the "assurances were taken to mean that Japan does not seek, through its military operation in Siberia, to impair the rights of the Russian people in any respect, or to obtain any unfair commercial advantages, or to absorb for her own use the Siberian fisheries, or to set up an exclusive exploitation either of the resources of Sakhalin or of [the] Maritime Province." As far as the conference was concerned, that was all there was to the question. As will be shown below, however, Japan agreed to evacuate its troops from Siberia in 1922.

The Conference Appraised

Japan professed to feel fully satisfied with the results of the Washington Conference, and well it might. For one thing, it was demonstrated that Japan was a first-class power entitled to a position of equality with the two leading Occidental powers. It had won a sense of national security in the promises made by Britain and America to place a prohibition upon the building of certain potential naval bases, and, secondly, in the knowledge that, although Japan was awarded less capital-ship tonnage, it was in a relatively concentrated area whereas that of the Western powers was widely dispersed and lacked Japan's advantage in interior lines of communication. True, it had been virtually forced to return Shantung to China, but it had improved both its business and its international standing by so doing. Furthermore, in the Yap Treaty Japan had gained from the United States recognition of its mandates in the Pacific and in return had had to yield very little. Even the termination of the valuable Anglo-Japanese Alliance had compensations in the form of the Four-Power Treaty.

China, for its part, had achieved great victories at Washington, chief among which was the return of Shantung. The irredentist movement started by the students had forced Japan's hand and revealed a nascent nationalism that seemed to bode well for the future. A more optimistic air prevailed in the country, and it appeared that conditions might be stabilized and an end to the prevailing chaos accomplished.

Internationally, the conference had been productive of a commendable and encouraging degree of cooperation. It had, temporarily at any rate, tied together several very important loose ends left unsettled at Versailles.

In the United States preponderant opinion supported the achievements of the conference, although some observers were less optimistic. As Assistant Secretary of the Navy, Franklin D. Roosevelt made it clear that it was the view of the Navy Department that the conference had made it unnecessary to fortify so strongly in the Pacific as would otherwise have been required.[3]

Japan's Liberal Decade, 1921-1931, and Relations with China

The "Shidehara Policy." Forced by postwar trade readjustments and by a more friendly public opinion, Japan pursued a fairly liberal policy toward China from 1921 to 1931. In Japan this conciliatory attitude became known as the "Shidehara Policy" after the liberal Baron Shidehara who was twice Foreign Minister, in 1924-27 and 1929-31.

The development of a better climate of opinion toward China can be traced to such things as the decline of the Army's influence as a result of the Siberian adventure, the Chinese boycott against Japanese goods (in effect until the settlement of the Shantung question) which brought the merchants to the support of a more conciliatory policy, and the devastating earthquake which struck Japan in 1923. The latter patently required that energies which might ordinarily have been used in other ways, such as building up the military, be diverted into reconstruction and other peaceful channels.

Only in two isolated instances did Shidehara resort to force in China. The first time was occasioned by a serious uprising against Chang Tso-lin in the late months of 1925. Then a Japanese military force was sent to the region (near Mukden) to protect Japanese lives and property. The other time was when a force of Japanese marines was employed to drive out the Chinese mob which on April 3, 1927, had assaulted the Japanese concession at Hankow.

Tanaka's "Positive Policy." If the "Shidehara Policy" was one of nonintervention in Chinese affairs, that of Baron Tanaka was the reverse. Tanaka served both as Premier and Minister for Foreign Affairs

---

[3] Eleanor Tupper and George E. McReynolds, *Japan in American Public Opinion* (New York, 1937), p. 166.

between Shidehara's two terms. For example, in May, 1928, Chiang Kai-shek's Nationalist troops en route to Peking ran into a Japanese force sent to defend Japan's important commercial interests in Shantung, and bitter fighting ensued at Tsinan. This clash brought much loss of life and heavy destruction of property. By superior strength, the Japanese were able to exclude the Chinese troops from a "neutral zone" extending seven miles on both sides of the Tsinan-Tsingtao Railway. Upon the withdrawal of the Nationalists, the Japanese remained for almost a year. Finally, the anti-Japanese boycott which China invoked following the failure of an appeal to the League of Nations by both Peking and Nanking proved effective, and the Tsinan incident was settled on March 28, 1929. Both sides expressed regret over the affair, the Japanese agreed to withdraw within two months and arranged for a joint commission to work out a satisfactory settlement covering the losses sustained by each side.[4]

Under Tanaka and his "positive policy" toward China, Japan was the last of the Powers to recognize the Nationalist triumph in China.[5] By the end of 1928, all other powers had extended formal recognition to Chiang. Japan reluctantly fell in line in January, 1929.

Recognition was followed the next year by the signing of the Sino-Japanese Tariff Agreement of 1930. This accorded China tariff autonomy, provided for mutual most-favored-nation treatment, allowed China to place duties on most of Japan's exports to her, and put a term to a number of reduced customs rates favoring Japan. China's failure to implement its promised abolition of various customs charges proved unfortunate as it provided Japan with grounds for accusing China of bad faith.

Negotiations between the two countries over the question of extraterritorial privileges likewise proved unhappy.[6] Japan was unwilling to agree to an immediate and unconditional end of such rights, whereas China refused to settle for anything else. Lumping all foreign nations together with Japan in this respect, China declared that after January 1, 1932, it would consider extraterritorial privileges at an end. This was a position unacceptable to the Powers, and so matters continued as before.

Manchuria: Background to Conflict

Until 1928 the dominant figure in the three eastern provinces constituting Manchuria was the spectacular Marshal Chang Tso-lin. This

[4] R. H. Akagi, *Japan's Foreign Relations, 1542-1936* (Tokyo, 1936), p. 397.

[5] First to do so was the United States, which acted on July 25, 1928.

[6] By 1930 China had succeeded in negotiating an end of the extraterritorial privileges of nine countries on a contingent basis. These treaties were to become effective when all the Powers had taken similar action.

worthy tended to be rather strongly pro-Japanese and anti-Soviet. Chang, however, was removed from the scene June 3, 1928, as the result of an explosion at the junction of the Peking-Mukden and South Manchurian Railways. To Japan's chagrin, Chang's son and heir, Chang Hsueh-liang, "The Young Marshal," made a deal with Chiang and agreed to recognize the Nationalist regime throughout Manchuria. In return he was accorded various honors by the new rulers of China, including recognition of his power over Manchuria and Jehol.

This development was a little too much for Japan whose ambitions had long been concentrated upon Manchuria; it now saw these interests seriously threatened. In the first place, Manchuria was valuable to Japan as a source of raw materials and food, as a market for Japanese exports, and as a place for both Japanese and Korean immigration. Secondly, Manchuria was vital strategically. Controlled by Japan, it would be a buffer protecting Japanese-held Korea against Soviet attack. Thirdly, there was Japan's by now historic claim to a "special position" in Manchuria. Japan had fought two wars there; the first with China, the second with Russia. The latter had cost Japan a fortune in lives (100,000 men killed) and treasure (at least 2,000,000,000 *yen*). Following these wars, Japan had sunk tremendous sums of money there, particularly since 1909. The great South Manchurian Railway Company, an agency of the Japanese government, was busily engaged in exploiting the territory through which its lines ran and actually exercised complete control over the railway zone.[7]

Japan began to grow increasingly upset over the attitude the Chinese Nationalists were beginning to adopt toward the South Manchurian Railway and some of its subsidiary enterprises. It so happened that China's new nationalism in Manchuria [8] came into existence at a time when the liberal era in Japan was drawing to a close. For one thing, Japan had been

[7] Chatham House Information Papers, No. 21 A., *China and Japan* (3d ed., London, 1941), p. 43.

[8] Two incidents worthy of mention in this respect are the Wanpaoshan incident and the murder of Captain Nakamura.

Wanpaoshan is about twenty miles north of Changchun in Manchuria. Here a tract of land belonging to Japanese capitalists was being worked by Koreans. The latter were constructing a ditch some miles in length. This project irritated the local Chinese farming element which professed to fear that a flood would endanger their farms. Japanese police were unsympathetic, and a fight broke out on July 1, 1931. The Chinese succeeded in destroying the ditch and, although shots were fired, there was no loss of life. The whole business was represented as the culmination of Chinese persecution of the Koreans in Manchuria who were under the protection of Japanese consular officials and police. Cf. A. Morgan Young, *Imperial Japan, 1926-1938* (London, 1938), p. 74.

The Nakamura case involved one Captain Nakamura, who, with a Japanese noncommissioned officer and a Russian and a Chinese guide, was doing some intelligence work on the border between Manchuria and Mongolia, although his passport described him as a student. He and his party were captured by the Chinese in June. 1931, and executed as spies. *Ibid.*, pp. 73-74.

hard hit by the world depression of 1929, especially in its vital silk industry. Then, too, Japanese naval circles were irked by the London Naval Treaty of 1930. Thirdly, financial and industrial groups, already worried by the depression, were further weakened by Japan's monetary policies. They had grown disenchanted over Shidehara's conciliatory policies and had felt keenly the effects of the widespread anti-Japanese boycotts waged by the Chinese. Hence, it was no wonder that a crisis in Sino-Japanese relations was imminent.⁹

The Manchurian Incident

These smoldering tensions blazed forth in the night of September 18, 1931, when a mysterious explosion damaged the South Manchurian Railway at Peitaying near Mukden. The Japanese blamed Chinese Nationalist troops for the bombing and killed three Chinese soldiers from an adjacent Chinese barracks who, it was claimed, were suspiciously close to the scene of the damage.

The explosion had taken place at 10:30 P.M., and by dawn Mukden was completely in the hands of the Japanese, with Colonel Doihara, an intense nationalist, in the role of mayor of the city. The Japanese moved with a lightning-like precision that could only have been the result of a well-considered plan. Marshal Chang Hsueh-liang adopted a policy of nonresistance. Accordingly, his troops were easily captured and disarmed, sometimes with a display of Japanese force which was hardly justified by the circumstances. Baron Shidehara was gravely upset by the news, since the resort to force was without his authorization. On the contrary, the whole affair had been worked out by the firebrand Kwantung Army which had become thoroughly disgusted with what they considered his supineness. Despite such violation of his policies, Shidehara refused to resign and tried to make the best of a very bad situation.

Military operations continued apace,¹⁰ and by the end of the year Japan was in full control of all South Manchuria. Chang's troops had pulled out or were reduced to ineffectual guerrilla warfare. The heaviest fighting had occurred at Changchun, juncture of the South Manchurian and the Chinese Eastern railways.

The League Intervenes. Four days after the bombing incident, the Council of the League of Nations met at Geneva and advised both sides to withdraw their troops,¹¹ a position to which the Japanese objected on

---

⁹ Chatham House, *op. cit.*, pp. 44-45.
¹⁰ One of the worst incidents was the Japanese bombing by air of defenseless Chinchow.
¹¹ This was a stand which seemed to presage ill for China in that China, as the innocent party, was being told to withdraw its forces from its own land.

the grounds, first, that it would prove unsatisfactory to Japanese public opinion and, second, that it was a private dispute which could be worked out by the two nations involved without the intercession of any third party. The Chinese reply to the second objection very logically pointed out the impossibility of negotiations while Japanese soldiers were occupying the disputed areas.

Japan's refusal to withdraw its forces led China to seek a declaration from the League in its favor which prompted the Japanese to reverse their stand and to imply a willingness to withdraw, a development which did not materialize. Meanwhile, Japan sought to deal with the Chinese directly. Marshal Chang was invited to visit Mukden for this purpose but he discreetly refused on the grounds that his superiors at Nanking were the proper authorities with whom to negotiate.

Meanwhile, a boycott, organized in Shanghai, was proving most effective and consequently very damaging to the Japanese merchants in that metropolis. Their protests were received with attentive ears by the Japanese Navy which up to this point had remained quiescent while the Army was gathering laurels.

While these things were going on, the League was devoting considerable time to a discussion of the crisis.[12] It decided at a meeting of the Council in Paris which opened in November, 1931, to send a commission of inquiry to the Far East to conduct a fact-finding investigation, a procedure which greatly angered the Chinese delegate who quite sensibly pointed out that while the League was consuming time with verbiage Japan was overrunning Manchuria and destroying Chinese lives. Despite this protest, the Commission of Inquiry was chosen in January, 1932. Headed by Lord Lytton (and subsequently known as the Lytton Commission), it set sail for the Far East in February.

Japan's continued progress, the rumors that Japan intended to detach Manchuria from China through the device of an independence movement, and the imminence of hostilities around Shanghai (which actually broke out January 28, 1932) led the Chinese to make another appeal to the League on January 24. Failing in this attempt, the Chinese requested that the dispute be transferred from the jurisdiction of the League's Council to its Assembly. China based its appeals strongly on Article Ten of the League Covenant, which provided for the preservation of the territorial integrity of member states.

---

[12] The United States was taking a lively interest in developments and sent a representative to sit with the League Council because of the strong American feeling that Japan had violated the terms of the Treaty of Paris, 1928, by which the signatories renounced war as an instrument of national policy.

As early as January 7, the American Secretary of State, Henry L. Stimson, had sent notes to both Japan and China which held that the United States refused to admit the legality of any situation de facto or to recognize any agreement reached by the two powers which would affect American treaty rights in China, including the open door, or which came about by means contrary to the Pact of Paris.[13]

The Japanese Empire in 1933

Establishment of Manchukuo. The Council, moved by the American position and by the strength of China's argument, sent a strong appeal to Japan on February 16 which called the latter's attention to the language of Article X of the Covenant. That it fell upon deaf ears is clear from the fact that only two days later Japan announced the establishment of the

[13] The American attitude will be dealt with more fully in Chapter 26.

independent state of Manchukuo, consisting of China's three Eastern Provinces and Jehol. Less than a month later China's last Manchu ruler, the former "boy emperor" Henry Pu-yi was installed as regent of the new state.

Shanghai Attacked. Meanwhile, far-reaching events were taking place. A strong Japanese military force, aided by planes and ships, began a sanguinary attack on Shanghai in an effort to break China's effective boycott of Japanese goods. The excuse for this onslaught was provided through the mobbing of five Japanese priests of a rather noisy sect by a crowd of Chinese on a Shanghai street. The priests were severely handled, and one died of injuries the next day. A crowd of Japanese residents then took it upon themselves to secure revenge and in the ensuing melee a Chinese policeman and one of the Japanese were killed.

The Japanese admiral in command of a naval force based on Shanghai announced on January 28 that he was not satisfied with the attitude of the local Chinese authorities and threatened to begin hostilities if a satisfactory response was not forthcoming within twenty-four hours. Shooting began shortly before midnight when a Japanese force attempted to take over the Chapei district from which Chinese Nationalist soldiers had been ordered, but which they had failed to vacate.

Early the next morning, Japanese carrier-based bombers began their destructive work, and the attack on the Greater Municipality of Shanghai was on in earnest. As days passed, much to the surprise and annoyance of the Japanese, the Chinese continued an effective resistance. Especially praiseworthy was the ability demonstrated by the Chinese Nineteenth Route Army. The odds, however, were simply too heavy, and on March 3, 1932, the Chinese were forced to withdraw to an area specified by the Japanese some distance from the International Settlement.

While these events were taking place, the League Assembly continued to busy itself with the dispute and on March 19 created a special body, the Committee of Nineteen. This group consisted of representatives of the twelve neutral nations then holding membership on the League Council, together with seven others elected by the Assembly. Nothing of note was achieved by this body, and it remained for negotiations between the two parties themselves to accomplish agreement. On April 30 the Chinese and Japanese reached a provisional understanding resulting in a truce on May 5 which provided for an end to the hostilities with neutral observers supervising the agreed withdrawals from what then became a demilitarized area. This arrangement applied only to the Shanghai locus of the fighting; as to Manchuria, the creation of Manchukuo had been announced in February and its formal independence celebrated March 1.

On March 9, with appropriate ceremony, Pu-yi was installed as Regent of the new state at Hsinking ("New Capital"), the former Changchun.[14]

Manchukuo vis-à-vis Japan. In the creation of this "independent" state, Japanese policy had gone to great lengths to create the impression that the separatist movement which culminated in "independence" was both spontaneous and purely local in character. It was Japan's position that such action was not in any way contrary to the principles of the Nine-Power Treaty of 1922 which, the Japanese asserted, did not bar separatist movements within China.

Having completed this spade work, Japan proceeded to recognize Manchukuo as an "independent" state by signing of a mutual protocol on September 15, 1932. The new puppet state, for its part, promised to respect all of Japan's rights and interests within its borders, in return for which Japan undertook to protect the fledgling and was accorded the right to station troops in the country.

The Lytton Report. The year 1933 brought further Japanese military operations against China during which its troops crossed the Great Wall into China proper. These fresh acts of aggression typified Japan's reaction to the publication of the Report of the Lytton Commission. The members of this group had arrived in Tokyo in February, 1932, and after spending some time there had proceeded to Shanghai on March 14 in time to see the effects of Japan's attack there. A month of investigation in China proper was followed by six weeks in Manchuria, whence the Commission returned to Peiping.

On October 2 the extremely lengthy report of the commission was published. In brief, the members found that Japan's actions in Manchuria were not self-defense, and that the creation of Manchukuo was not the result of "a genuine and spontaneous independence movement." The report then recommended that an autonomous government be established in Manchuria which, however, should be under the sovereignty of China. This local government should be equipped with a police force competent to maintain order and should also have competent international advisers to assist it. The new administration was then to pledge its recognition of Japan's rights and interests.

Japan strongly dissented from the Lytton Report's two main conclusions, insisting that it had clearly acted in self-defense following the events of the night of September 18, 1931, and that an independent Manchukuo was the logical conclusion of a long effort on the part of the inhabitants of Manchuria to gain their freedom from China. Much diplomatic ma-

---

[14] He was later promoted to be the Emperor Kang Teh.

neuvering ensued, but on February 24, 1933, the Assembly of the League of Nations unanimously approved the Lytton Report and adopted the nonrecognition policy of the United States, whereupon the Japanese delegation took its leave of the Assembly. On March 27, 1933, an Imperial Rescript was issued proclaiming Japan's official resignation from the League. Since the Covenant of the League required that two years must elapse before any resignation could become final, Japan's actual departure did not take place until 1935. Although Japan was no longer a member of the League, the Council of the League made the quixotic ruling in January, 1935, that Japan was still entitled to exercise its mandatory powers over the former German islands north of the equator which it had been holding for the League since 1919. This weird decision coincided exactly with the position that Japan had been belligerently asserting ever since giving notice of withdrawal from the League and certainly smacked of appeasement.

The League's Work Assessed. In its handling of the Manchurian episode, the League of Nations had revealed lamentable weakness. In deciding against Japan it did so at a time when its decision could amount only to an expression of moral indignation because Japan had achieved a *fait accompli* in Manchuria. No sanctions were ever invoked, although England embargoed certain arms shipments to *both* China and Japan for less than a month early in 1933, an action which incidentally was pleasing to Japan where the move was interpreted not as a slight to it but rather a nice gesture! The only thing that can be said in defense of the League was that the whole Manchurian affair came about at a particularly disadvantageous time. The world was in the throes of the great depression which had started in 1929 and had since been growing progressively worse. Furthermore, a new menace was appearing on the horizon in the form of Hitler and the Nazis.

In placing the onus for failure to curb Japan, the United States must properly come in for its share of responsibility. The American government did nothing to indicate that it would use force to back up its announced opposition to Japan's action. The British were well aware of this and were unquestionably influenced in their decision by this knowledge.

Nonrecognition was as far as the League went. On March 15, 1933, its Manchurian Committee appointed subcommittees to explore the matter of an arms embargo and to work out how best nonrecognition could be applied to Manchukuo. Then in June the Far Eastern Advisory Committee of the League sent out a circular letter to all nations, whether members of the League or not, calling for their refusal to accord diplomatic recognition to Manchukuo, asking that the new state be excluded from all international conventions (such as those in communications), and urging a boycott of Manchukuo's currency and postage.

The Tangku Truce. Left to their own devices as far as effective resistance was concerned, and having been defeated in the fighting which took place around Jehol in 1933, the Chinese had no alternative but to seek a truce with Japan. By March they had been driven south of the Great Wall; pursuing Japanese forces were operating in China proper; and Marshal Chang Hsueh-liang's resignation had been accepted by the Chiang Kai-shek government in Nanking. Accordingly, on May 31, a truce was agreed to. Known as the Tangku Truce, it provided for a demilitarized neutral zone south of the Great Wall. No Chinese forces were to be permitted north of this line. Order within the neutral zone was to be preserved by Chinese police, and, once Japan was satisfied that it could be maintained (a very indefinite arrangement), its troops would withdraw north of the Great Wall.

The Post-Manchurian Interlude

On September 14, 1933, Hirota became Foreign Minister of Japan and lost no time in announcing that the Imperial Rescript of March 27 would be the basis of Japan's foreign policy. This document, it will be recalled, had announced Japan's withdrawal from the League, but it had also declared that Japan would continue to cooperate internationally in the hope of maintaining peace. Furthermore, this statement had asserted that Japan would "respect the independence of the New State [Manchukuo] and ... encourage its healthy development in order that the source of evil in the Far East may be eradicated and an enduring peace thereby established." [15]

In January, 1934, Hirota declared in the Japanese Diet that "Japan, serving as the only cornerstone for the edifice of the peace of East Asia, bears the entire burden of responsibility." [16] This was a clear foreshadowing of the revival of plans for the establishment of a Japanese Monroe Doctrine for the Far East.

The Amau Statement. Hirota's sentiments received further emphasis in an interview given to the foreign press in early April, 1934, by Amau, head of the Foreign Office Intelligence Bureau. The significance of these remarks was not grasped at the time, with the result that the Amau Statement was reiterated in a leading Tokyo newspaper on April 17 in such terms as to leave no doubt of what the government had in mind.

[15] Akagi, *op. cit.,* p. 512.
[16] Chatham House, *op. cit.,* p. 57.

In this statement, the world was told that "Japan is so circumstanced that she must do her utmost to fulfil her mission and responsibility in the Far East.... Although Japan's attitude towards China may be at variance with that of other countries in some respects, these divergences cannot be helped, as they arise from Japan's position and mission." Furthermore, the statement continued, China really had no right to conduct foreign relations, except with Japan's approval, and hinted that any time it suited Japan's wishes it might withdraw business privileges held by foreigners in China.[17] Japan's reason for this bold stand stemmed from its fear that China might succeed in setting its house in order. The progress being made by the Nationalists in such ventures as the New Life Movement, which was an attempt to revive and strengthen the best features of Old China's virtues, was, to say the least, very disconcerting to Japan.

Japan's position in China, especially in economic matters, was becoming of increasing importance as other world markets were being closed to her by the building of ever-higher tariff barriers. To meet the world situation, Japan sought to retaliate by passing a Trade Protection Act in March, 1934, which provided the government with power to restrict or even prohibit imports from countries imposing restrictions on Japan's products. Little good, however, was achieved by such a step, and Japan's economic problems continued. As a consequence, the soundness of Japan's economic position tended to depend increasingly upon the success of its China policy.

Japan Renews Military Activity in China

China Must Be "Liberated." Along with Japan's economic difficulties, it became increasingly concerned over the spread of communism in East Asia. As Hirota declared in the Japanese Diet: "The suppression of the communist activities in our part of the globe and the liberation of China from the Red menace is, therefore, a matter of vital importance, not only for China but for the stabilization of East Asia and of the world.... It is the desire of the Japanese Government to cooperate with China in various ways for the eradication of communism."[18]

Japan's efforts to win such cooperation from China proved unsuccessful.[19] However, on November 25, 1936, an agreement directed against the Third (or Communist) International was reached with Germany. This

---

[17] A. M. Young, *op. cit.*, pp. 204-5.
[18] *Contemporary Japan*, Vol. II, 1933-34, p. 765.
[19] As these pages relate elsewhere, the Nationalist government of China was actively opposed to communism but was simply not interested in making common cause with its enemy Japan.

was destined within a few years to blossom into the Rome-Berlin-Tokyo Axis.

Despite China's rebuffs, the Japanese continued to seek its "cooperation," whether the Chinese desired it or not. This insistence was based, publicly at least, upon the professed belief that it was Japan's bounden duty to rescue China in spite of itself. As Matsuoka put it:

> One thing is clear even to a donkey running along an Asian highway: constant and hearty cooperation between the peoples of Japan and China ... alone can work out the destiny of Asia.... China and Japan are two brothers who have inherited a great mansion called Eastern Asia. Adversity sent them both down to the depths of poverty. The ne'er-do-well elder brother turned a dope fiend and a rogue, but the younger, lean but rugged, and ambitious, ever dreamed of bringing back past glories to the old house. He sold newspapers at a street corner, and worked hard to support the house. The elder flimflammed the younger out of his meager savings and sold him out to their common enemy. The younger in a towering rage beat up the elder—trying to beat into him some sense of shame and awaken some pride in the noble tradition of the great house. After many scraps the younger finally made up his mind to stage a show-down fight.[20]

Conflict Renewed. At the beginning of 1935, Japan returned to its "active policy" in China by opening military operations in eastern Ch'ahar and at places along the Great Wall. In justification, the Japanese claimed that the governor of Ch'ahar was guilty of violating the Tangku Truce. By the end of January, 1935, both sides concluded an agreement setting up a demilitarized area near the Great Wall.

Trouble flared again in May when two Chinese in Japan's employ were murdered in Tientsin. This resulted in the presentation of a new batch of Japanese demands to the Chinese government. Dissatisfaction with China's reply brought additional demands to which China was forced to agree.

Although China had again yielded, the Japanese military insisted on written guarantees, which the Chinese were hesitant to give. The news of a new Chinese "outrage" in Ch'ahar at this time (June, 1935) caused the Japanese to increase their demands still further by insisting upon certain Chinese military withdrawals in North China and an additional adjustment of the demilitarized area's border in Japan's favor. China had no alternative but to agree.

Five Provinces Threatened. Japan's activities, wherein the Army and not the government acted as the spokesmen (justified on the grounds that

[20] "Japan Weekly Chronicle," October 21, 1937, p. 548, quoted in H. S. Quigley, *Far Eastern War, 1937-1941* (Boston, 1942), pp. 58-59.

these actions were directly related to the Tangku Truce, a military agreement), made it clear by the summer of 1935 that Japan was aiming at the detachment of five North China provinces from the jurisdiction of the Chinese government at Nanking. These provinces were Hopei, Ch'ahar, Suiyuan, Shansi, and Shantung, a total of some 470,000 square miles of territory. The effort to bring about this separation continued throughout the fall.

The first concrete development along these lines was the announcement of the East Hopei Autonomous Council on November 14 by which a Japanese puppet, Yin Ju-ken, declared 10,000 square miles of Chinese territory to be independent. The rest of Hopei felt the effects of this autonomous movement, as did Ch'ahar. As a result Chiang Kai-shek was reluctantly forced to send instructions to his chief officials in these regions to enter negotiations with the Japanese and try to salvage as much as possible. Chiang's chief representative in the negotiations was Ho Ying-chin who, with his assistants, concluded an agreement establishing the Hopei-Ch'ahar Political Council, an autonomous group including the governors of Ch'ahar and Hopei and the mayors of Peking and Tientsin. The new arrangement took effect December 16, 1935. Bad as it was, it did represent a compromise and for the time being represented a check to Japan's plans for the detachment of the five provinces.

Additional negotiations between China and Japan took place from time to time in 1936, but an increase in anti-Japanese incidents in China served to arm the Japanese with fresh ammunition to push their stringent insistence that the Chinese government must see to it that such affairs ceased. Chiang Kai-shek, himself, now assumed the initiative and made some demands on Japan in the matter of the latter's laxity regarding smuggling in Hopei.

China Stiffens. At this juncture, a combined Japanese-Manchukuoan attack on Suiyuan in October temporarily ended negotiations between China and Japan. The fact that the Chinese proved able to check this invasion of Suiyuan combined with other factors to produce a new appearance of strength on China's part. National unity was beginning to become a pleasing reality.

Then in December came the so-called Sian Incident which produced the realization that a united front between the Nationalists and the Communists was in the offing.[21] As a consequence for the first time since 1931 Chiang held a reasonably strong domestic position and could afford to be much firmer in his negotiations with Japan. While it is true that the

---

[21] This matter is discussed in the chapter on China, 1923-1937, in this book. For a fuller treatment see E. A. Selle, *Donald of China* (New York, 1948).

Japanese struck in July, 1937, before the united front had been formally consummated, its impending realization was plainly visible, especially to Japan.

Governmental changes in Japan early in 1937 seemed to presage a more moderate policy toward China, but the fall of the new Hayashi government on May 31 and its replacement by a Ministry headed by Prince Konoe brought the inauguration of what was clearly a totalitarian regime. The new government had hardly announced its Five-Year Plan in June when, with the Lukouchiao Incident, a full-scale Sino-Japanese War broke out in July.

The Sino-Japanese War [22]

On the night of July 7, 1937 ("Double 7"), an exchange of shots between Japanese and Chinese troops took place at the Marco Polo Bridge at Wanping, a Peiping suburb. Two days later, on the ninth, both sides agreed to withdraw their troops from Lukouchiao but the agreement was not implemented, and skirmishing continued. Then, on July 11, a local agreement was reached which called for the withdrawal of the Chinese forces from Lukouchiao, together with other terms favorable to Japan. Once again an agreement was not carried out, and the battle for North China began in earnest. Chiang made an address to the Chinese nation on July 17 in which he asserted that China had stood all that was humanly possible from Japan and was now determined to resist to the bitter end.

An incident occurred at a Shanghai airfield on August 11 which cost the lives of one Chinese soldier and two Japanese, a naval officer and a seaman. Japan immediately strengthened its forces in Shanghai, and two days later fighting broke out, a battle destined to last for three months and to roll up heavy casualties before the Japanese forces finally proved victorious on November 12.[23]

Communists Support National Government. During the period that the Shanghai fighting was in progress, the "Government of the Soviet Republic of China," which since December, 1936, had had its capital at Yenan, dissolved itself, and the Chinese Communists promised full support of the Nationalist government.

The Nationalist capital at Nanking fell easily to the Japanese on December 13, but the Chinese had already moved their government to

---

[22] Until China declared war on Japan, December 9, 1941, the hostilities were not dignified by the term war. The Japanese usually referred to the fighting as the "China Incident" or "China Affair."

[23] Chiang's decision to throw his best troops into the fight for Shanghai has been criticized in some quarters. Cf. T. H. White and Annalee Jacoby, *Thunder Out of China* (New York, 1946), p. 52.

Chungking in Szechwan Province although Hankow actually served as a temporary capital for almost a year. During the battle for Nanking, Japanese bombers sank the U. S. gunboat "Panay" while it was escorting some oil tankers belonging to the Standard Oil Company. Two Americans were lost, and a number of others were wounded. The same day three American tankers were sunk, and several British gunboats were attacked. The United States government demanded and received a prompt apology for this outrage, as well as a satisfactory indemnity.[24] Climaxing these acts of wantonness, the Japanese conquerors of Nanking indulged in an orgy of looting, murder, and rapine which left the civilized world aghast. The ferocity and viciousness of the sadistic Japanese troops did not become exhausted until several weeks had elapsed.

Major Cities Fall to Japan. Following an initial setback,[25] the Japanese next captured Soochow, May 20, 1938. Kaifeng, capital of Honan Province, fell on June 6, as did Anking, capital of Anhwei, six days later. The great city of Canton capitulated on October 21, followed four days later by the conquest of Hankow. The other Wuhan cities of Wuchang and Hanyang were likewise evacuated by the Chinese the day Hankow was occupied.

With the exception of the capture of Nanning in 1939 and the successful drive in Chekiang in 1942, the taking of the Wuhan cities was the highwater mark of Japan's military operations against China until the big 1944 drive. Nanning's capture put Japan in an excellent position to threaten French Indo-China, should it prove desirable. It appeared that Japan's strategy had left little to be desired. The whole China coast, including the outlets of China's three great rivers, together with all of China's industrial centers were now in Japanese hands. To the Japanese it appeared as if all they had to do now was wait for Chinese resistance to die of economic strangulation. Nevertheless, when the Japanese ultimately surrendered to the United States almost seven years later, the Chinese were still able to put armies in the field and carry out their amazing resistance. The whole process, from the viewpoint of the Japanese, resembled the efforts of a man punching a pillow.

With Pearl Harbor, December 7, 1941, the picture changed, since Japan was no longer able to concentrate her attention so fully on China. Until then, the only distraction had been along the Siberian border where an

[24] The attack on the "Panay" may have been a demonstration by the local Japanese military of their dissatisfaction with the attitude of the United States as revealed by President Roosevelt's famous "quarantine speech" of October 5, 1937.

[25] On April 8 the Chinese had destroyed a Japanese force numbering some 7,000 men at Taierchwang in the vicinity of the strategic Lunghai Railway. This setback marked the first time in modern history that a Japanese army had suffered defeat. It had the effect of exploding the highly propagandized belief that the Japanese were invincible.

uneasy truce with Soviet Russia gave the Japanese no little concern. But Pearl Harbor had another result that, for China, was of inestimable value: as a major element in the world conflict, China clearly must become an integral part of the ultimate world settlement.

SUGGESTED READINGS

An excellent short summary of this topic may be found in Chatham House Information Papers, No. 21A, *China and Japan* (3d ed., London, 1941).

Material dealing with the topic of The New China Consortium will be found in Harley F. MacNair, *China in Revolution* (Chicago, 1931) and Robert F. Pollard, *China's Foreign Relations, 1917-1931* (New York, 1933).

For the Washington Conference see: R. L. Buell's contemporary account, *The Washington Conference* (New York, 1922); A. Whitney Griswold, *The Far Eastern Policy of the United States* (New York, 1938); and Yamato Ichihashi, *The Washington Conference and After* (Stanford University, 1928).

Japan's liberal decade and relations with China is covered by Kenneth W. Colegrove, *Militarism in Japan* (Boston, 1936); Harold S. Quigley, *Japanese Government and Politics* (New York, 1932); R. K. Reischauer, *Japan: Government and Politics* (New York, 1939); Tatsuji Takeuchi, *War and Diplomacy in the Japanese Empire* (Chicago, 1935); A. Morgan Young, *Imperial Japan, 1926-1938* (London, 1938) and *Japan in Recent Times, 1912-1926* (New York, 1929).

The best account of the Manchurian question is The League of Nations *Report of the Commission of Inquiry* (Geneva, 1932) and *Supplementary Documents* (Geneva, 1932). Other useful works are: Paul H. Clyde, *International Rivalries in Manchuria* (rev. ed., Columbus, 1928); Herbert Feis, *The International Trade of Manchuria* (Worcester, 1931); K. K. Kawakami, *Manchukuo: Child of Conflict* (New York, 1933) is sympathetic to Japan; H. L. Kingman, *Effects of Chinese Nationalism upon Manchurian Railway Developments* (Berkeley, 1932); Sara M. Smith, *The Manchurian Crisis, 1931-1932* (New York, 1948); Henry L. Stimson, *The Far Eastern Crisis* (New York, 1936); Henry L. Stimson and McGeorge Bundy, *On Active Service* (New York, 1947); W. W. Willoughby, *The Sino-Japanese Controversy and the League of Nations* (Baltimore, 1935); C. Walter Young, *Japanese Jurisdiction in the South Manchuria Railway Areas* (Baltimore, 1931), *The International Relations of Manchuria* (Chicago, 1929), *The International Legal Status of the Kwantung Leased Territory* (Baltimore, 1931), *Japan's Special Position in Manchuria* (Baltimore, 1931).

On the post-Manchurian interlude and the renewal of Japanese military activity in China see: G. C. Allen, *Japan, the Hungry Guest* (London, 1938); T. A. Bisson, *Japan in China* (New York, 1938); Hugh Borton, *Japan Since 1931: Its Political and Social Developments* (New York, 1941); Lowe Chuan-hua, *Japan's Economic Offensive in China* (London, 1939); John R. Stewart, *Manchuria Since 1931* (New York, 1936); and H. J. Timperley, *What War Means: The Japanese Terror in China* (London, 1938).

The best account of the Sino-Japanese War is Harold S. Quigley, *Far Eastern War, 1937-1941* (Boston, 1942); see also Frank Oliver, *Special Undeclared War* (London, 1939) and George E. Taylor, *The Struggle for North China* (New York, 1940).

26

UNITED STATES FAR EASTERN POLICY, 1919-1941

During the early years of World War I, until the United States itself became a belligerent, it was the United States which alone attempted to block Japan's advances in China. Upon becoming actively involved in the conflict, however, the United States was forced to tone down its opposition to Japan in the interest of expediency and harmony. Then when the war was over, the United States resumed its earlier position and at Versailles sought to champion China's interests against Japan.

In the years immediately following Versailles, the United States turned its back on Europe but found itself forced to maintain a lively interest in the western Pacific and in East Asia. It was in this connection that the United States played host to those nations having a stake in the Far East, except Russia, in the Washington Conference of 1921-22. This proved to be a success in halting the danger of a possible conflict in that area, but it also committed the United States more deeply than ever in Far Eastern affairs.

Immigration Act of 1924. Relations with Japan were somewhat improved following the Washington Conference until the old bugaboo of immigration reasserted itself after having long lain dormant. Legislation then applying to immigration was on the verge of expiring. The proposed new act of 1924 permitted the annual entrance into the United States of a maximum of 2 per cent of the nationals of any country, based on the total of the nationals of that country in the United States in 1890. "Aliens ineligible to citizenship" were to be barred, a provision which nullified the existing arrangement with Japan, the Gentlemen's Agreement of 1907. The measure passed both houses of Congress by huge majorities. Although Secretary of State Hughes opposed it, President Coolidge reluctantly signed it. The statement of the Japanese ambassador to the United States that passage of the measure might be fraught with "grave consequences" unquestionably served to strengthen the measure's adherents and probably swung over to its support some doubtful elements. The reception accorded the news in Japan was extremely bitter; the Japanese people were deeply hurt by such discrimination.

The Russo-Japanese Agreement of 1925

In the years immediately following the Washington Conference, Russia sought to improve its relations with Japan, thereby complicating the problems of American Far Eastern policy. Having made no progress in their efforts to bring about an alliance in the Pacific with the United States, the Russians turned to Japan.[1] The last Japanese troops evacuated Siberia on October 25, 1922, but Japan continued to occupy Sakhalin for over two years more.

On January 20, 1925, Japan and the U.S.S.R. signed an agreement calling for the establishment of diplomatic and consular relations, a complete Japanese evacuation of northern Sakhalin by May 15, and the granting of various concessions to the Japanese by the Russians to take effect following Japanese evacuation of northern Sakhalin. The withdrawal of Japanese forces represented an achievement for American Far Eastern policy; this had been designed to check Japanese expansion which ever since 1905 had been considered a threat to the peace of northeast Asia, an area in which the United States was strongly interested. Although American policy favored Russia in this respect, it vigorously opposed Russian influence in the Nationalist government of China in the years between 1920 and 1929.[2]

The Chinese Revolution During the Twenties [3]

The expanding spirit of Chinese nationalism by 1925 had brought about a marked change in China's attitude toward foreign nations. The Chinese were determined, if it were possible, to end the "unequal treaties" which gave foreigners their distinctly privileged position in China. So intense had this feeling become that not only treaty rights but even the lives and interests of foreigners in China were in jeopardy. This situation naturally raised the question of what the Powers would do to remedy the matter. About as far as they were prepared to go in treaty revision was to hold a Tariff Conference which would make changes in tariff rates and to appoint a Commission on Extraterritoriality to study the question and make recommendations. However, by 1925 no such meetings or studies were yet in progress.

Following an incident at the Louza Police Station on May 30, 1925, when the Shanghai police fired upon a crowd and killed a number of Chinese, the people became insistent that the unequal treaties must go.

---

[1] Pauline Tompkins, *American-Russian Relations in the Far East* (New York, 1949), p. 183.

[2] *Ibid.*, p. 188.

[3] For an excellent study of this material, see Dorothy Borg, *American Policy and the Chinese Revolution, 1925-1928* (New York, 1947), chap. 19.

Believing that a nation like China should not be shackled as it was, Secretary of State Frank B. Kellogg took the initiative in calling together the proposed Tariff Conference and the Commission on Extraterritoriality. In sessions held that summer, he stressed the need for cooperation with China and revealed his opposition to any attempts to continue the old system of foreign domination.

In 1926 the Chinese Nationalist government was strengthened by the growing antiforeign sentiment, thereby complicating matters considerably since this new development was a far greater problem with which to cope. Nevertheless, Secretary Kellogg's views remained fundamentally unaltered. He was opposed to a "strong" United States policy in China, backed by the threat of military or naval pressure, and held firmly to the conviction that the struggle going on in China was a domestic matter for the Chinese to settle themselves. He insisted, on the other hand, that any talk of treaty revision would have to be with a Chinese government which effectively controlled the country as a whole and had the people's allegiance.

Britain Modifies Its Policy. On Christmas Day, 1926, the government of Great Britain issued a memorandum which frankly recognized that conditions had changed in China and that the Powers must let it be clearly understood that they would not seek to force their control on an unwilling China. This action by the British was interpreted in some circles as an effort to steal the role of leadership in the China crisis away from the United States. Kellogg appeared unruffled, since the principles it held were virtually identical with those he had maintained right along. However, on January 27, 1927, he issued an official declaration restating American sympathy with Chinese nationalism and the American policy of noninterference in the internal affairs of China. The Kellogg statement asserted that the United States "has desired that tariff control and extraterritoriality provided by our treaties with China should as early as possible be released.... It [the United States] desires, however, that its citizens be given equal opportunity with the citizens of the other Powers to reside in China and to pursue their legitimate occupations without special privileges, monopolies or spheres of special interest or influence." [4]

United States Offers to Negotiate "Unequal Treaties." The really significant thing about this statement was Kellogg's expression of a willingness to discuss the subjects of tariff and extraterritoriality with any group empowered to speak for both factions in China, even if no other power would be so inclined. This open announcement of American will-

---

[4] *The White Paper*, pp. 11-12.

ingness to proceed alone in negotiating a new treaty with China was a step in a new direction but still was in accord with Kellogg's earlier opinions.

Following the Nanking "incident" of March 24, 1927, when foreigners were subjected to various indignities at the hands of the Chinese Nationalist forces and Western gunboats had been used to bring about the rescue of their nationals, the United States successfully acted to settle the matter so that those who had suffered would be recompensed, but in a manner which precluded the use of force against the Chinese.

In 1928, with the victory of the Kuomintang in China, the Secretary of State, with the approval of President Coolidge, accorded recognition to the Nationalist government of China and on July 25 concluded with the Chinese a treaty restoring tariff autonomy to China. The United States was the first nation to do so.

Although the United States was not then prepared to negotiate on the question of extraterritoriality, Kellogg thought that the time would be propitious in the immediate future and indicated to the Chinese Minister to Washington that he was open-minded on the subject. Formal negotiations relative to the termination of extraterritoriality were later carried on by the United States and China during 1930 and 1931 and had reached a point of widespread agreement by the summer of 1931, when the Manchurian crisis led to a postponement of further negotiations.[5]

Sino-Soviet Dispute of 1929. The northward sweep of Chinese nationalism brought it into conflict with the special rights and privileges of the Russians in Manchuria. China thereupon decided to oust the Russians from the Chinese Eastern Railway. This was in mid-1929. While the United States government quickly moved to bring about a peaceful settlement, the efforts of Secretary of State Stimson failed to prevent clashes along the Manchurian border. Stimson then stressed the obligations of both China and Russia under the terms of the Pact of Paris, according to which each had agreed to outlaw war. In August he offered concrete suggestions for settlement of the dispute, and followed this effort in November with an attempt to get a group of the leading powers to unite in an effort to end the conflict. Britain, France, and Italy cooperated with the United States in sending out identic notes, but Japan and Germany refused to participate. China showed a willingness to arbitrate, but Russia's reply was, in effect, that the United States should mind its own business. Through direct negotiations, however, the U.S.S.R. and China reached a settlement on December 22, 1929, which called for a restoration

---

[5] The history of these negotiations may be found in *Foreign Relations, 1930*, Vol. II, pp. 353-505; 1931, Vol. III, pp. 716-933.

of the status quo ante. By this settlement Russia retained its special privileges in the Chinese Eastern Railway zone.[6]

Some time during the following year the Chinese decided to disavow this agreement on the grounds that the Chinese delegate had acted *ultra vires*. By the year's end the matter was settled substantially along the lines of the 1929 agreement following a Russo-Chinese conference in Moscow.[7]

The Manchurian Crisis

About 10 P.M. on September 18, 1931, Japanese troops began military operations near Mukden which were ultimately destined to expand into an all-out war between Japan and China. For several reasons, including the open door, the United States was interested in developments from the first moment of the Japanese aggression in Manchuria. It became quickly evident to American officials that the Japanese actions were not the result of an accident but had been carefully planned by the military.[8]

On the other hand, it was believed that the Japanese military had acted on its own authority and without consultation with the Foreign Office. Therefore, there was some hope that those civilians in the Foreign Office who believed in a moderate policy might yet gain control. The proper procedure, it was felt, was to watch the situation very carefully and avoid giving offense to Japan. This policy was followed for the first few months but, instead of improving matters, a deterioration of the situation resulted.

The menacing movement of Japanese troops toward Chinchow, in violation of a promise given to the State Department that the Japanese military would refrain from such action, caused Stimson to send a sharp note to the Japanese Foreign Office on November 27. Stimson pointed out to the Japanese Foreign Minister that, relying on Japan's promise, he had urged conciliatory steps upon the Chinese government. The Japanese advance in the face of their pledged word astonished him, said the Secretary, and made him "totally unable to reconcile it with the assurances" given him three days earlier.[9] The following day the Japanese began to withdraw from the vicinity of Chinchow, and it appeared that Stimson's diplomacy had won a victory, but any satisfaction over this development was destined to be short-lived.

[6] For a lengthy account of American efforts, see *Foreign Relations, 1929*, Vol. II, pp. 186-434.
[7] *Foreign Relations, 1930*, Vol. II, pp. 298-302.
[8] See, e.g., telegram from Johnson, the American Minister to China, to Stimson, Secretary of State, on September 21. *Foreign Relations, Japan, 1931-1941*, Vol. I, p. 3. Stimson himself remarked the next day that it was obvious that the Japanese had long planned their moves. Henry L. Stimson and McGeorge Bundy, *On Active Service* (New York, 1947), p. 227.
[9] *Foreign Relations, Japan, 1931-1941*, Vol. 1, p. 51.

Cooperation with the League. It appeared to those charged with framing American foreign policy that the most sensible course to follow on the Manchurian problem was to cooperate with the League of Nations and to work jointly with it in the hope of bringing about an effective solution. Such a course had the advantage of preventing a vigorous unilateral American objection to Japan's action from solidifying Japanese public opinion behind the military.[10]

At a cabinet meeting in October, President Hoover remarked that the events in Manchuria did not "imperil the freedom of the American people" or their economic or moral future and declared that he did not propose "ever to sacrifice American life for anything short of this." He felt that the United States should cooperate with the League in so far as negotiations and conciliation were concerned, but he flatly refused to go along with the League if it decided on war or the imposition of either military or economic sanctions.[11] Stimson was also opposed to sanctions and so instructed Ambassador Dawes, who was temporarily assigned to attend meetings of the League on this matter, when the question came up in the League of Nations. The United States had no objection to sanctions by the League, but the League was not to expect any cooperation from the United States in this matter.

The President's message to Congress on December 10 revealed the deep concern of the United States over the Manchurian affair. As a party to both the Nine-Power Treaty and the Kellogg-Briand Pact, the United States had the responsibility of trying to maintain China's integrity and of upholding, with other nations, the peace there. Hoover declared further that it was a wise course of action to cooperate with the League, which would confront Japan with a united world front rather than individual action. Nevertheless, the United States would maintain freedom to go along with or reject any action by the League.[12]

The Policy of Nonrecognition. Within less than a month after this declaration, the United States came up with its own policy—nonrecognition. This principle possessed several advantages. In the first place, it was a moral sanction designed to let the friends of the United States in China know that, although the United States could not prevent Japan's aggression against China, at least there was no doubt about how it felt on

---

[10] On October 16, over the objections of Japan, the Council of the League of Nations invited the United States to send a representative to sit at the Council table for the purpose of discussing the Manchurian crisis. That same day Prentiss B. Gilbert, American Consul at Geneva, was seated. Walter Lippmann and William O. Scroggs, *The United States in World Affairs, 1931* (New York, 1932), pp. 256 f.

[11] William Starr Myers, *The Foreign Policies of Herbert Hoover, 1929-1933* (New York, 1940), pp. 158 f.

[12] *Ibid.*, p. 150

the subject. Secondly, nonrecognition represented a reinforcing of the international treaty structure, especially the Kellogg-Briand Pact. Finally, the doctrine of nonrecognition expressed the feelings of the people of the United States that Japan's actions in China were wrong.[13]

The nonrecognition doctrine was announced on January 7, 1932, in identical notes sent by Stimson to Japan and China. Both countries were informed that the United States "cannot admit the legality of any situation *de facto* nor does it intend to recognize any treaty or agreement entered into between these Governments, or agents thereof, which may impair the treaty rights of the United States or its citizens in China, including those which relate to the sovereignty, the independence, or the territorial and administrative integrity of the Republic of China, or to the international policy relative to China, commonly known as the open door policy; and that it does not intend to recognize any situation, treaty, or agreement which may be brought about by means contrary to the covenants and obligations of the Pact of Paris of August 27, 1928, to which Treaty both China and Japan, as well as the United States, are parties."[14]

The Hoover-Stimson Doctrine failed to elicit support from the European powers in the League. The British even went so far as to reply to Stimson that they saw no reason to send a formal note to Japan as Stimson had requested.[15] The Dutch, the French, and the Italians likewise refused to follow Stimson's lead.

Shanghai Attacked. A new element was injected into the picture on January 28, 1932, when Japanese marines attacked a district within the Chinese Greater Municipality of Shanghai. The surprisingly formidable Chinese resistance prompted the Japanese commander, Admiral Shiozawa, to order the bombing of the Chapei district of Shanghai, which resulted in widespread death and destruction.

Since Britain had a lively interest in Shanghai in contrast to virtually none in Manchuria, Secretary Stimson decided once again to seek British cooperation despite the recent rebuff. This time support was forthcoming.[16] The Anglo-American opposition, together with China's temporarily improved defense and effective boycott, combined to achieve a Japanese evacuation of Shanghai in May—except, of course, from the International Settlement.

Shortly after the issuance of the nonrecognition notes, Stimson had begun to come around to the position of favoring economic sanctions, a view which Hoover strongly opposed. The President was willing to con-

---

[13] Stimson and Bundy, *op. cit.*, pp. 234 f.
[14] *Foreign Relations, 1932*, Vol. III, p. 8.
[15] Stimson and Bundy, *op. cit.*, pp. 237 f.
[16] *Foreign Relations, 1932*, Vol. III, pp. 124-28.

centrate practically the entire American fleet in Hawaii, which was done in February, but he would go no further. The next step in the program of impressing Japan with American seriousness was the publication on February 23, 1932, of the celebrated letter from Stimson to Senator Borah, Chairman of the Senate Committee on Foreign Relations (an analysis of which follows below). The advantage of this tactic was that it constituted a statement of the American position on the sanctity of treaties. While unofficial, it was good "shirtsleeve diplomacy." (Less than a week before, Japan had taken the far-reaching step of encouraging its puppet regime in Manchuria to declare its independence and to take the name of Manchukuo.)

Stimson next sought to make a new diplomatic protest to Japan on the grounds that it was violating both the Nine-Power Treaty and the Pact of Paris and to get British cooperation in this venture. Despite most strenuous efforts, he failed to secure British backing.[17] The British position was essentially that, as a member of the League, Britain should be bound by what the League decided in this particular matter; furthermore, it tended to be more optimistic about a quick end to the Shanghai fighting than the United States was. During the course of the conversations, Stimson stressed the need for an Anglo-American united front by remarking that, though he very greatly regretted it, "the League does not inspire fear at present in the Japanese. Japan is much more afraid of a union between you and us [Great Britain and the United States] than she is of the whole League." [18]

The Borah Letter. Having failed to secure British cooperation and being forced to circumspection for fear of provoking Japan too far, Stimson called upon his resourcefulness and got his point across by the letter to Borah. In it he traced the development of traditional American policy toward China since the turn of the century and emphasized in particular the Nine-Power Treaty. There then followed remarks on the importance of the Pact of Paris.

He went on to declare that the events in Manchuria which extended themselves into Shanghai "have tended to bring home the vital importance of the faithful observance of the covenants therein to all of the nations interested in the Far East." If other nations would follow the example of the United States' action of January 7, 1932, when it informed both China and Japan that it would not recognize any change in the existing situation brought about by force, "a caveat will be placed upon such action which, we believe, will effectively bar the legality here-

---

[17] *Foreign Relations, 1932*, Vol. III, pp. 280-84, 294-98, 334-40, 341-45.
[18] *Ibid.*, p. 342.

after of any title or right sought to be obtained by pressure or treaty violation, and which, as has been shown by history in the past, will eventually lead to the restoration to China of rights and titles to which she may have been deprived." [19]

Just one day before the letter was released, the Japanese government had replied to an appeal from the League of Nations to cease its attacks on China by contemptuously asserting that China could not be considered an "organized people." Such recognition accorded her in the past constituted a "fiction." China was the real aggressor, not Japan.[20] Coming as it did so closely on the heels of this cavalier attitude, the Stimson letter was the means of stirring up expressions of their views by numerous prominent Americans who favored a strong attitude toward Japan. Bills before both houses of Congress proposed an arms embargo and an economic boycott against Japan but were pigeonholed at the State Department's request.[21]

Other Efforts Fail. A committee headed by President Lowell of Harvard University and former Secretary of War Newton D. Baker, and including over 150 prominent Americans, issued a statement favoring the application of an economic boycott against Japan. In March another committee, headed by President Nicholas Murray Butler of Columbia University, recommended that the United States call a meeting of the Pact of Paris signatories to adopt a provision for determining measures of nonintercourse in order to prevent violations of the Pact. In the event of an actual violation, methods of applying corrective measures and of restoring the status quo should be adopted. Naturally, many were opposed to any steps which could conceivably lead to war.[22]

There was little more that Stimson could do in his remaining days in office except to work for a moral sanction condemning Japan's aggression. Public opinion was his only hope. A speech delivered on August 8, 1932, stressed the power of this weapon and was received with great displeasure in Japan. He worked hard for the adoption by the League of the Lytton Commission's report. It was adopted February 24, 1933, and the following day Stimson issued a statement approving the Commission's findings and stressing the importance of nonrecognition.[23]

---

[19] Thomas H. D. Mahoney and John B. Rae, eds., *Readings on International Order* (Cambridge, 1951), pp. 61 f.

[20] Walter Lippmann, *The United States in World Affairs, 1932* (New York, 1933), p. 215.

[21] On February 24 President Hoover made it clear that his feelings had not changed. In a communication to Stimson on that date Hoover opposed the imposition of any military or economic sanctions against Japan. *Foreign Relations, 1933*, Vol. III, 209 f.

[22] Lippmann, *op. cit.*, p. 215.

[23] Stimson and Bundy, *op. cit.*, pp. 260 f.

Under Stimson the United States had led in the organization of world public opinion against Japan. It is true that this opposition did not deter the aggression, but the record is quite clear; the aggressor was condemned by the moral judgment of the free world. Eventually—in World War II— that moral sanction was to be backed by sufficient force to chasten the aggressor.

Early Years of the Roosevelt Administration

Isolationism Governs Policy. The administration of Franklin D. Roosevelt, which took office in March, 1933, with Cordell Hull as Secretary of State, was in its early years no more prepared to employ force to halt the Japanese than had been its predecessor. Until 1937, this administration gave little sign of being anything but firmly isolationist. Such an attitude was of course understandable, since the American people were still in the depression and had not altered the point of view established during the fight over the League of Nations in Wilson's time. Then, too, popular acceptance of the "merchants of death" concept, i.e., that the United States had been brought into World War I by the munitions interests, was another factor. Not only did isolationism flourish, but pacifism achieved a strong following. Thus it was that United States efforts to halt Japan were limited to continued cooperation with the League of Nations in its efforts to establish collective security, and the recognition of the U.S.S.R. on November 16, 1933.[24] This latter step was widely interpreted abroad as having a direct connection with the Far Eastern situation, and there was some apprehension manifested in Japanese circles as a consequence.

Hull Defines Policy. Although it was clear that the United States was not prepared to use force in defense of its rights, the State Department saw to it that American rights in China were always reaffirmed whenever the situation demanded such a declaration. For example, on the occasion of the Amau Statement of April 17, 1934, when a spokesman for the Japanese Foreign Office asserted to a group of foreign correspondents that

---

[24] The Russians initiated steps the following year for a bilateral nonaggression pact between the United States and the U.S.S.R. The American attitude was that if there should be any nonaggression pact it should include all powers having interests in the Pacific. To this the Russians countered by saying that it would be necessary to leave out China to prevent the question of Manchukuo from arising. The United States made it clear that this was unthinkable, whereupon the Russians said that Japan would never sign any pact involving China unless Manchukuo were recognized. Ambassador Bullitt who discussed these matters with Litvinov stated that he thought his government would never consent to such an arrangement. Nothing came of the proposals, either of a bilateral or a multilateral pact. *Foreign Relations, 1934,* Vol. III, pp. 74, 78, 82-83.

Japan had "special responsibilities in East Asia" and had established a political guardianship of China and warned against any financial, political, or commercial undertakings by other powers which were prejudicial to Japan, the United States reaffirmed its treaty rights in a statement to the Japanese Foreign Office on April 29.[25] In this *aide-memoire* Secretary Hull described American policy toward China in carefully chosen words:

> The relations of the United States with China are governed, as are our relations with Japan and our relations with other countries, by the generally accepted principles of international law and the provisions of treaties to which the United States is a party. In international law, in simple justice, and by virtue of treaties, the United States has with regard to China certain rights and certain obligations. In addition, it is associated with China or with Japan or with both, together with certain other countries, in multilateral treaties relating to rights and obligations in the Far East, and in one great multilateral treaty to which practically all the countries of the world are parties.
>
> Entered into by agreement, for the purpose of regulating relations between and among nations, treaties can lawfully be modified or be terminated—but only by processes prescribed or recognized or agreed upon by the parties to them.
>
> In the international associations and relationships of the United States, the American Government seeks to be duly considerate of the rights, the obligations and the legitimate interests of other countries, and it expects on the part of other governments due consideration of the rights, the obligations and the legitimate interests of the United States.
>
> In the opinion of the American people and the American Government, no nation can, without the assent of the other nations concerned, rightfully endeavor to make conclusive its will in situations where there are involved the rights, the obligations and the legitimate interests of other sovereign states.[26]

This renewal of American protests against Japan's course of action was very annoying to certain groups in Japan. Particularly upset were men like Baron Tanaka, author of the disputed Tanaka "Memorial" which made its first appearance in 1929 and was widely circulated thereafter,[27]

---

[25] The Amau text is in *Foreign Relations, Japan, 1931-1941*, Vol. I, pp. 224 ff. Here also may be found the Foreign Minister's explanation that Amau had spoken without the previous knowledge or approval of the Foreign Office. Hirota then went on to assert that Japan had no intention of seeking special privileges in China or of encroaching upon China's territorial or administrative integrity. *Ibid.*, pp. 227 f. See also *Foreign Relations, 1934*, Vol. III, pp. 117-21, 123, 138, 140.

[26] *The White Paper*, p. 16.

[27] The "Memorial" recommended a strong Japanese policy toward China whose conquest should first be preceded by Japanese absorption of Manchuria and Mongolia. Victory over China would cause the world to recognize Japanese hegemony over all of East Asia. Japan denied the authenticity of this document.

who wrote an article criticizing the actions of the Roosevelt administration as "insolent." This article which appeared originally in the magazine of the Merinkai, an organization of retired Japanese army and navy officers together with other strong nationalists, was translated and appeared in the *Japan Advertiser,* August 5, 1934.[28] The matter was smoothed over satisfactorily but is indicative of Japan's resentment toward the United States at this time.

Another ground for American protest against Japan lay in the attempts of the officials of the puppet state of Manchukuo to close the open door there. The United States continued to uphold the principle of the open door, whereas Japan adopted the view that it could not accept responsibility for the actions of the Manchukuoan government, which they claimed was independent. A series of notes was exchanged between the two governments on the question.[29] Finally, the United States summarized its position in a note dated April 15, 1935:

> The American Government greatly regrets that the Japanese Government has not seen its way clear to use the influence which it possesses through its close and peculiar relations with the present regime in Manchuria to uphold in practice the principle of the Open Door and the fulfillment of the treaty obligations which both the Japanese Government and the authorities in Manchuria have on numerous occasions declared they would maintain.
> ... the American Government is constrained to express its considered view that upon the Japanese Government must rest the ultimate responsibility for injury to American interests resulting from the creation and operation of the petroleum monopoly in Manchuria.[30]

Meanwhile Japan's military machine in China was bent upon deeper penetration. The Japanese effort in late 1935 to turn five northern Chinese provinces—Hopei, Ch'ahar, Suiyuan, Shansi, and Shantung—into an autonomous area brought forth still another American protest. Voiced by Secretary of State Hull, it was a reiteration of the American position and took the form of a press statement:

> ... it seems to this government most important in this period of worldwide political unrest and economic instability that governments and peoples keep faith in principles and pledges.... This country has abiding faith in the fundamental principles of its traditional policy. This Government adheres to the provisions of the treaties to which it is a party and continues to bespeak respect by all nations for the provisions of treaties solemnly entered into for the purpose of facilitating and regulat-

[28] *Foreign Relations, 1934,* Vol. III, pp. 677-79.
[29] *Ibid.,* pp. 699-799.
[30] *The White Paper,* p. 17.

ing, to reciprocal and common advantage, the contracts between and among the countries signatory.[31]

As serious as was the rift between the United States and Japan produced by Japan's aggression against China, it was not the only major irritant in Japanese-American relations. Another very serious problem was the naval question.

Naval Limitation Crumbles

Limitation of Auxiliary Ships. At the London Naval Conference of 1930 Japan revealed its dissatisfaction with the status accorded it at Washington in 1922. This conference was called to consider limitations on cruisers and auxiliary ships. The Japanese delegation requested that a common upper limit be established for the United States, Great Britain, and Japan. This effort to secure complete equality was rejected, but Japan was given parity in submarines and, in the matter of light cruisers and destroyers, was awarded a stronger position than it held in capital ships. The ratio for these two categories was set at 10:10:7. Heavy cruisers were kept at the Washington level, i.e., 10:10:6. It was also agreed in the London Conference that the signatories would meet in 1935 to write a new treaty.

In preparation for the new conference, American and British delegates met in the early summer of 1934. These talks revealed a difference of opinion concerning cruisers. The British expressed a strong desire for greater cruiser strength when the time came to reapportion naval tonnage. The British view more closely approximated Japan's in this respect.

Japan Seeks Equality. The talks were resumed on October 23, 1934, with the Japanese participating. About a month earlier, the American ambassador in Japan had informed the State Department that Japan had decided to give notice before December 31, 1934, of its withdrawal from the Washington Naval Treaty.[32] At the first day's talks in London in October the Japanese delegates presented proposals for a common upper limit of global tonnage which were coupled with suggestions that offensive arms be abolished or reduced in favor of essentially defensive arms. The unwillingness of the British and the Americans to concede upper limit equality caused the Japanese to declare that their government would denounce the Washington Naval Treaty before the end of the year. The conversations ended on December 19 without agreement. The Washington and London treaties still had two years to run, however. That same day

[31] *The White Paper*, pp. 17 f.
[32] *Foreign Relations, Japan, 1931-1941*, Vol. I, pp. 249-53.

the Japanese Privy Council approved its government's decision to abrogate the Washington Naval Treaty. Formal notice of Japan's termination of the agreement came on December 29 and became effective two days later. It was followed by Japanese assurances that they did not intend to practice naval aggrandizement and by a professed willingness to work toward a new agreement to replace the Washington Treaty. Despite these sentiments, Japanese feelings were well exemplified by Ambassador Saito when he said in an earlier interview that the Washington ratio sounded to Japanese ears like "Rolls-Royce-Rolls-Royce-Ford."[33]

If the Roosevelt administration in the years up to 1937 was not noted for its strong views on international affairs, other than the string of protests against Japan's actions which at least kept the record clear, it did take a lively interest in the United States Navy. In May and June of 1935, following the fleet's return to the Pacific in November, 1934, the navy held maneuvers as far north as the Aleutians and as far west as Midway. The force engaged in these war games was the largest ever gathered under the American flag.[34] Earlier in 1934 the Roosevelt administration announced that it would build up the navy to its full treaty strength. Subsequently, it was planned to achieve this status by 1942.

Great Britain, meanwhile, was no longer satisfied with the categories established by the Washington and London treaties, since it desired a larger number of cruisers. The termination of its obligations under the Washington Treaty by Japan, coupled with French and Italian opposition to the ratios assigned to them, led Great Britain on July 22, 1935, to announce that it would no longer support the future limitation of navies by the ratio principle.[35]

Japan and Italy Withdraw. Despite this announcement, the British sent out invitations to a new naval conference to be held in London. All five signatories of the Washington Treaty were invited, and the opening session was held December 7, 1935. Japan continued to adhere stubbornly to its demand that there be a common upper limit for naval armaments and would not discuss qualitative limitation apart from quantitative limitation. Refusal by the United States to accept Japan's stipulations led to the withdrawal of the Japanese delegation on January 15, 1936. A rather unsatisfactory treaty calling for some qualitative limitations and containing several "escape clauses" was signed March 25, 1936, by the United States, Great Britain, and France. Italy, like Japan, refused to adhere.

[33] Whitney H. Shepardson and William O. Scroggs, *The United States in World Affairs, 1934-35* (New York, 1935), p. 186.
[34] *Ibid.*, p. 188.
[35] *Ibid.*, pp. 191 f.

Despite the unsatisfactory outcome of these efforts, further attempts were made to get Japan to agree to place a limitation of 14 inches on the gun caliber of its battleships. This the Japanese refused to do with the result that the United States Department of State issued a press release stating that as a consequence of the failure to achieve qualitative limitation of naval armaments, guns of 16-inch caliber would be mounted on two American battleships then under construction.[36]

Limitation Shattered. Rumors that Japan was building ships exceeding the limits of the London Naval Treaty of 1936 led the British, French, and American governments to present identic notes to the Japanese government on February 3, 1938. This was followed two days later by an announcement of the intention of the United States to exercise its right of escalation under the London Treaty of 1936 unless Japan furnished satisfactory assurances that it would not, prior to January 1, 1943, construct or acquire any vessel exceeding the limits in question without previously informing the United States government of its intentions. The Japanese reply was quickly forthcoming. On February 12, 1938, Hirota, Japanese Minister for Foreign Affairs, informed United States Ambassador Joseph C. Grew that Japan still contended that "qualitative limitation, if not accompanied by quantitative limitation" was useless. The Japanese claimed that they still adhered to their willingness, as expressed at the London Naval Conference of 1936, to bring about "the total abolition of capital ships and aircraft carriers, which are aggressive in their nature" if the other powers would do likewise. Hirota went on to say that in Japan's opinion "the mere communication of information concerning the construction of vessels will, in the absence of quantitative limitation, not contribute to any fair and equitable measure of disarmament" and so refused to comply with the request to participate in a reciprocal exchange of naval construction information.[37]

Japan's Undeclared War Against China

When the Japanese military commenced their undeclared war against China in July, 1937, they had the support and justification of a substantial portion of Japanese public opinion. Conditions were such that expansion seemed to offer the only hope of salvation. The home islands were growing overpopulated; all arable land was being farmed; raw materials were sorely needed for the expansion of old and new industries; Japan was finding it increasingly difficult to dispose of its goods in foreign markets owing to world conditions which raised barriers against Japan's products:

[36] *Foreign Relations, Japan, 1931-1941*, Vol. I, pp. 298-302.
[37] *Ibid.*, pp. 303-6.

and the prospects of Japan's being forced to reduce its standard of living with a resultant loss of prestige among the Powers were serious. The solution to Japan's problems appeared to lie in expansion. Manchukuo was obviously not enough. The adventure in China earlier in the thirties was a mere prelude. Furthermore, if Japan did not move soon, it might be too late. Chinese nationalism was becoming aggressive.

There were some encouraging aspects in the situation. The rise of the Fascist states under Hitler and Mussolini threatened to keep both Britain and France busy. As for the United States, it was hardly in a position to wage a war so far from home; in any case, the prevailing climate of American opinion was isolationist. On and on ran the rationalization, until it reached its climax with the events at the Marco Polo Bridge on the night of July 7, 1937.

The only force which consistently protested Japan's action in China earlier in the thirties was the United States. Time and again the State Department entered protests with the Japanese government. It revealed itself well disposed toward the Chinese Nationalists and refused to recognize Manchukuo and continued to parry Japan's claims that it was seeking only to bring about peace and order in the Far East with the question why did Japan refuse to adhere to the treaty system aimed at that very end. However, all this was for the record and amounted after all merely to talk, or so the Japanese believed. There was no action or any threat of it.[38]

United States Voices Policy Principles. Hence it was no surprise that the United States, through Cordell Hull, Secretary of State, issued a statement on July 16, 1937, on fundamental principles of international policy which were clearly applicable to the Sino-Japanese conflict. Hull's statement listed such principles as maintenance of peace; abstinence from the use of force in relations between states; abstinence from interference in the internal affairs of other nations; adjustment of problems in international relations by processes of peaceful negotiation and agreement; faithful observance of international agreements; modification of provisions of treaties by orderly processes carried out in a spirit of mutual helpfulness and accommodation; respect by all nations for the rights of others and performance by all nations of established obligations; promotion of economic security and stability throughout the world; and effective equality of commercial opportunity and application of the principle of equality of treatment. A later statement, issued by the State Department on August 23, reaffirmed these principles and made it unmistakably clear that the United States considered them applicable to the Far East.[39]

[38] Herbert Feis, *The Road to Pearl Harbor* (Princeton, 1950), pp. 3-7.
[39] *The White Paper*, p. 18.

In the interim between these statements, the United States attempted to bring about a peaceful settlement between China and Japan. Both were urged to seek a peaceful settlement, and the United States informally offered its good offices to Japan to mediate the dispute. The government of Japan made no satisfactory response to this offer.

The question of whether to apply the Neutrality Act of 1937 confronted the administration of President Roosevelt. The latter concluded not to invoke it for several reasons. In the first place, no declaration of war had been made by either Japan or China. Secondly, it was felt that China would suffer more from such a step than would Japan which did not need arms from the United States, whereas China did. Thirdly, the United States might find itself at war with Japan as a result of such an action.

Major Chinese Cities Attacked. Japan began to expand its military operations. Early in August the Japanese Navy took a hand by staging a strong demonstration at Shanghai. Then on September 19 Admiral Hasegawa, the naval commander at Shanghai, informed foreign consular officials that Japanese air attacks against Nanking might begin any time after noon on September 21. His justification for such action was on the grounds that the city was the principal base for China's military operations. The admiral suggested that it would be advisable for all foreigners to move into safe areas farther up the Yangtze, a suggestion which provoked strong protests from the leading nations, including the United States. Secretary Hull used very sharp language in his note to the Japanese Foreign Office. On the very day that the Japanese warning was delivered, Nanking was bombed twice by Japanese naval planes; again, on the twenty-second, it was subjected to two attacks. It was hit four times on the twenty-fifth and once on the twenty-eighth. Canton was raided three times in succession, and Hankow and other inland cities were also bombed with heavy casualties.

In a formal reply to American protests, Hirota defended the bombing of Nanking as "a necessary and unavoidable measure for the attainment of military objectives of the Japanese forces." The rights and interests of "third countries" and the lives and property of their nationals would be respected "as far as possible." There would, of course, be injuries, but the Japanese government would not recognize any responsibility for injuries to Americans as a result.[40]

League Condemns Japan. China's appeal to the League of Nations' Council resulted in the reconstitution of the Far-East Advisory Committee which had not met since 1934. The United States accepted an invitation

---

[40] Shepardson and Scroggs, *op. cit.*, pp. 212-14.

to be represented in the committee's deliberations by its Minister to Switzerland. On October 5 this body placed two reports before the League Assembly which were sharply critical of Japan, whose actions were declared to be in violation of her obligations under both the Nine-Power Treaty and the Pact of Paris. It was decided to call a meeting of the signatories of the Nine-Power Treaty. Furthermore, it was recommended that each League member refrain from any steps which might be at all injurious to China and that each consider how it could best extend aid to China.

Protests, But No Action. On the same day that the League of Nations adopted the reports of its committee, President Roosevelt made his famous "quarantine" speech in Chicago. Although no nations were specifically mentioned in the President's remarks, he clearly condemned Japan's aggression. He cited the spreading "epidemic of world lawlessness" and declared that "when an epidemic of physical disease starts to spread, the community approves and joins in a quarantine of the patients in order to protect the health of the community against the spread of the disease." He asserted that "war is a contagion, whether it be declared or undeclared. It can engulf states and peoples remote from the original scene of hostilities."

Nowhere in the speech, however, did the President recommend any concrete course of action. Near the end of his remarks, he declared that "America hates war. America hopes for peace. Therefore, America actively engages in the search for peace." These were words that seemed to indicate that they might be implemented with action. Unfortunately, Roosevelt's trial balloon failed to attract sufficient following among the American people, with the result that three years were to elapse before the United States took any concrete action against Japan, confining itself in the meantime to a steady stream of protests.[41] About the only visible result of the speech was the beginning of a number of private boycotts against Japanese goods.

Shortly after the proposal by the League Assembly that a conference be held under the Nine-Power Treaty, the British began conversations with the United States in preparation for such a meeting. In all, nineteen nations (interested members of the League and signatories of the Nine-Power Treaty) were present when the conference began its sessions on November 3. From the outset it was apparent that the two most powerful and interested nations, the United States and Great Britain, were both unwilling to employ force to correct the situation and, therefore, little

---

[41] Mahoney and Rae, *op. cit.,* pp. 63-67.

good could come of the meetings. On November 24, 1937, the conference concluded without having achieved anything. Equally discouraging was the fact that three days after the conference had begun, Germany, Italy, and Japan reached their anti-comintern agreement.

The "Panay" Incident. The year 1937 concluded on a tragic note with the "Panay" incident which occurred on December 12. It will be recalled that on this occasion the U.S.S. "Panay" was attacked by Japanese aircraft which succeeded in sinking her with a loss of two American bluejackets. Also attacked were several Standard Oil tankers, three of which were destroyed with the loss of one of the captains. The American protest resulted in satisfactory Japanese apologies which were accepted finally on Christmas Day, 1937.

United States-Japanese Relations, 1938-1939

During the following year it became apparent that the Japanese had underestimated China's ability to absorb punishment and continue to resist. Repeated American protests failed to impress the Japanese with the fact that the United States was slowly becoming deeply angered over Japan's conduct. Partially compensating for these unpleasant aspects of the situation from the Japanese point of view was the growing rapprochement with Berlin and Rome. German military experts who had been helping the Chinese were recalled home and they left for Germany early in the summer of 1938.

The Munich Agreement in September, 1938, encouraged the Japanese, as they felt that Great Britain had revealed her weakness so glaringly that Japan had nothing to fear from that quarter in the Far East. With the United States, however, it was different. The Americans continued to hammer away with their never-ending protests. A new one was issued October 6, 1938. In this note the United States pointed out that Japan had given "categorical assurances" that the open door would be respected in China. The note then recounted the many instances in which Japan had failed to keep its promises in this matter and closed with a request that Japan implement its previous assurances on the open door by taking certain clear and well-defined measures.

Japan Rejects Old "Concepts and Principles." Replying on November 18, the Japanese denied the American claim that Japanese actions in China violated American treaty rights or were discriminatory against American interests in China. The Japanese Foreign Minister then revealed that his interpretation of the open door differed from that of the United States. His reply concluded with the following announcement:

At present Japan, devoting its entire energy to the establishment of a new order based on genuine international justice throughout East Asia, is making rapid strides toward the attainment of this objective. The successful accomplishment of this purpose is not only indispensable to the existence of Japan, but also constitutes the very foundation of the enduring peace and stability of East Asia.

It is the firm conviction of the Japanese Government that now, at a time of the continuing development of new conditions in East Asia, an attempt to apply to present and future conditions without any changes concepts and principles which were applicable to conditions prevailing before the present incident does not in any way contribute to the solution of immediate issues and further does not in the least promote the firm establishment of enduring peace in East Asia.

The Imperial Government, however, does not have any intention of objecting to the participation in the great work of the reconstruction of East Asia by your Excellency's country or by other Powers, in all fields of trade and industry, when such participation is undertaken with an understanding of the purport of the above stated remarks; and further, I believe that the regimes now being formed in China are also prepared to welcome such participation.[42]

This statement was not well received by the State Department. A note of December 30, 1938, challenged the Japanese interpretation of the open door and reasserted the position taken by the United States in the note of October 6. Japan was called upon anew to observe its treaty obligations. The United States denied that Japan could unilaterally abrogate its treaty rights in China but did say that the United States would discuss treaty revision by orderly processes of negotiation and agreement among the parties involved. Until such time, however, the United States reserved all rights as they existed and refused to consent to any impairment of those rights.[43]

Thus ended another year with the situation growing increasingly tense. The opening of 1939 quickly revealed how ominous matters were actually becoming. For one thing Baron Hiranuma, reputedly unfriendly to the United States, replaced Prince Konoe as Premier. Then on February 8 Ambassador Grew reported to the State Department that Japan had begun negotiations with Germany and Italy for a definite political and military alliance. Secretary Hull advised Grew to try to persuade the Japanese against such a step, but to make it seem that he was speaking only for himself and not for his government.[44] For the time being, the Japanese were impressed with this informal warning and indicated to their anti-

[42] *The White Paper*, p. 21.
[43] *Ibid.*, pp. 21-23.
[44] *Foreign Relations, Japan, 1931-1941*, Vol. II, pp. 161-63.

comintern partners that they were not yet in a position to risk offending the democracies.[45]

Japan Seizes Strategic Islands. Despite this temporary setback, the Japanese were acting ominously. On February 10, 1939, the island of Hainan was occupied and in March Japan claimed the region including the Spratly Islands. Both of these steps seemed to presage a southward advance. The same month the Japanese claimed jurisdiction over the Sinnan Islands, a group of coral reefs situated in the South China Sea between French Indo-China and the island of Palawan in the Philippines. A French claim to sovereignty over the islands was rejected by the Japanese and they were incorporated in the territory under the jurisdiction of the Governor-General of Formosa. When the news was delivered to the State Department by the Japanese, Hull answered that their claim over this group would not be recognized by the United States.[46]

In May the Japanese expressed the belief that the United States and Japan should exert their efforts to prevent the outbreak of a war in Europe. The joker in this suggestion that the United States and Japan cooperate to keep the peace was Japan's idea of how true world peace might be established and maintained. This was that all nations have their proper places in the world; a corollary of this was that East Asia was Japan's proper place in the world. Hull's reply, delivered "in a spirit of frankness which I trust will not be misunderstood," was to the effect that it was nice of Japan to wish to prevent war from breaking out in Europe, but that it could make a real contribution to the cause of world peace by putting an end to its invasion of China.[47]

The Road to War

United States Abrogates Treaty. On July 26, 1939, the United States took the strongest step it had yet made against Japan when it notified the Japanese government that the treaty of commerce and navigation, in force since 1911, would be abrogated in six months. The Japanese Foreign Office was quite upset and issued a statement two days later declaring that the reasons given by the United States failed to explain satisfactorily why the notice of abrogation should have been given so hastily and abruptly. The Foreign Office suggested that the American action could easily be interpreted as having political significance. Japan then sought to negotiate a new agreement, but the State Department adroitly evaded a categorical

---

[45] *International Military Tribunal for the Far East Exhibits* (Tokyo, 1946-48), Exhibit No. 502.
[46] *Foreign Relations, Japan, 1931-1941*, Vol. II, pp. 277-81.
[47] *Ibid.*, pp. 6-8.

refusal while appearing to hold the door open. Less than a month later came the dramatic news of the Russo-German Treaty of Nonaggression which stunned the Japanese. Japan, despite this setback, continued its war in China and its efforts to establish the New Order in East Asia, but for the time being the Japanese again found themselves completely alone.

War in Europe. Then came the German attack on Poland followed by the British and French declarations of war against Germany. Japan's announcement of neutrality was well received in Washington.[48]

In October the Foreign Minister told the Japanese Cabinet that upon the expiration of the commercial treaty with the United States on January 26, 1940, relations between the two countries would reach their worst state yet. A few days later Ambassador Grew held a conversation with the Foreign Minister in which he suggested ways in which relations could be improved: (1) cessation of bombings, indignities, and other interferences with American rights and interests in China, and (2) action of a positive type which would concretely demonstrate Japan's good intentions.[49] Within a short time the Japanese again indicated a desire to bring about improved relations, which once again brought the suggestion from the United States that actions spoke louder than words. The first move must come from the Japanese government.

The "Moral Embargo." The big question for the United States, should the Japanese fail to take such steps, was whether to employ sanctions against Japan. With the exception of the "moral embargo," which had been in force since the summer of 1938 and which effectively prevented aircraft, aircraft equipment, and aerial bombs from going to Japan from the United States, Japan could still secure from this country all the oil, copper, scrap iron and steel, automotive equipment, and other materials useful to a military machine that it wished. No decision affecting these exports was reached for the time being, so that when the treaty expired in January, 1940, trade continued pretty much as before but without a treaty and with the ever present possibility that the United States might invoke economic sanctions. In addition there was an extension of the "moral embargo" in response to the President's request of December 2, 1939, that manufacturers and exporters of airplanes, airplane equipment, and materials essential to aircraft manufacture (molybdenum and aluminum, for example) would bear in mind the government's condemnation of unprovoked bombing and machine-gunning of civilian populations from the air before negotiating contracts for exportation of such articles to nations obviously guilty of such unprovoked bombing. A few days

[48] Feis, *Road to Pearl Harbor*, pp. 38-39.
[49] *Foreign Relations, Japan, 1931-1941*, Vol. II, pp. 30-34.

later all plans, plants, manufacturing rights, and technical information required for the production of high-quality aviation gasoline were added to the "moral embargo" list.

Early in January, 1940, the Japanese ambassador protested against these additions to the "moral embargo" and was answered several weeks later with the assertion by Hull that reliable reports indicated that the Japanese in China were guilty of bombing and machine-gunning civilians from the air at places where there were no military objectives and that bombs had damaged clearly-marked American properties. Accordingly, the United States was forced to withhold technical processes for high-quality aviation gasoline. Hull professed inability to see how such action violated the soon-to-expire commercial treaty of 1911.[50]

Thus 1940 opened with the United States and Japan both adhering to their policies: the United States continuing to declare for morality in international dealings and for the preservation of the sanctity of treaties; Japan continuing its war in China and showing no signs of lessening its interest in southward expansion.

Nanking Puppet Protested. The establishment of a Chinese puppet regime at Nanking with Wang Ching-wei at its head was another irritant in Japanese-American relations. Secretary Hull bluntly informed the Japanese ambassador that it was believed in Washington that the new government was nothing but a creature of the Japanese military and would be used by that group for its own purposes, just as the regime in Manchuria was used.[51]

Replying to an interpellation in the Japanese lower house, the Foreign Minister on February 28 stated with regard to Japanese-American relations that even if the United States should insist upon carrying through its demands on Japan, Japan did not fear the future. Unfortunately, the United States simply did not understand the object of Japan's "Holy War" with China and opposed the establishment of the New Order in East Asia. Questions between the United States and Japan which were capable of being settled would be dealt with "appropriately, that is to say, they will be handled in accordance with Japan's 'independent' policy which is, after all, what we mean by 'Imperial way' diplomacy.... We do not know precisely what the American Government has under consideration, but if it is determined to ignore completely the object of Japan's Holy War and to refuse to lift a finger, Japan should display an attitude of resolution."[52] Late in March, the Prime Minister added that he did not

[50] *Ibid.*, pp. 202-11.
[51] *Ibid.*, Vol. II, pp. 53-55.
[52] *Ibid.*, p. 55.

believe that the United States "would risk" applying a general embargo against Japan.[53]

One week later Hull sharply denounced the action of the Japanese in setting up the puppet government of Wang Ching-wei in China, and the next day a spokesman for the Japanese Foreign Office replied in kind.[54]

Dutch East Indies Enters Spotlight. Then, more alarming, the Japanese began to devote attention in their remarks to the Netherlands East Indies. German arms in western Europe had begun to score the first of the several lightning victories they were to win in 1940. Even before Germany invaded the Netherlands, the Japanese had let it be known that they would be deeply concerned if the European War were to have repercussions in the Netherlands East Indies, an announcement which had prompted Secretary Hull to observe publicly that other countries beside Japan would also be interested. Hitler's victories by the end of June opened the eyes of the Japanese military—bogged down in China—to the possibilities of easy and rich conquests to the south: Indo-China, the East Indies, and perhaps Malaya.

Hull's reminder to the Japanese that other countries were interested in any change in the status of the East Indies was one of two actions marking an important development in American Far Eastern policy. The other was his pointing out to Japan that it was bound by two specific agreements directly relating to changes in the Pacific. These were (1) the Root-Takahira Agreement of 1908, by which the United States and Japan promised to respect the status quo in the Pacific, and (2) the Four-Power Treaty which bound the United States, Great Britain, France, and Japan to respect each other's possessions in the Pacific, an agreement later extended to include the Pacific possessions of the Dutch. Together, these statements constituted the recognition by the United States that the Far Eastern problem was but a part of an even larger question, that of the whole Pacific area. Its significance was not lost on Japan. One Japanese newspaper declared that the United States had assumed the role of Great Britain's watchdog and that "the thorns sticking out of the Hull statement show that the Pacific Ocean is not necessarily pacific."[55]

At virtually the same time, Japan demanded greater supplies of essential raw materials from the Netherlands East Indies, freedom of entry for its nationals, and greater opportunities for its economic enterprises there.

[53] *Ibid.*, pp. 57-58.
[54] *Ibid.*, pp. 59, 61.
[55] Shephardson and Scroggs, *op. cit.*, p. 168.

France and Britain Feel Pressure. Pressure was also applied to France and Great Britain. The French in Indo-China were threatened with military action if they did not halt the passage of military supplies to China and on June 20 were forced to sign an agreement prohibiting such traffic. A few days later a portion of the Japanese fleet was sent to Indo-China on the pretext of watching vessels suspected of carrying supplies to China. Late in June Japanese troops surrounded Hong Kong, and Britain was warned to close the Burma Road, which she did reluctantly on July 18, an action criticized by Secretary Hull. Despite Japanese threats that reopening the Burma Road could mean war, it was reopened at the expiration of the three months.

Japan Joins the Axis. Meanwhile, a new government, headed by Prince Konoe with the American-educated Yosuke Matsuoka as Foreign Minister, took office in Japan. The Konoe government announced that it planned to establish a totalitarian regime in Japan which it did and also that it intended to establish a new order in Greater East Asia. The adjective is very revealing as it indicates that Japan was bent on southward expansion. Shortly afterwards, on September 27, 1940, came the signing of a full military alliance with Germany and Italy.

United States Defense Act. While Japan was applying pressure upon France and Britain, the United States passed the National Defense Act, Section VI of which provided for the control of exports and declared in part: "Whenever the President determines that it is necessary in the interest of national defense to prohibit or curtail the exportation of any military equipment or munitions, or component parts thereof, or machinery, tools, or materials or supplies necessary for the manufacture, serving or operation thereof, he may by proclamation prohibit or curtail such exportation, except under such rules or regulations as he shall prescribe."

On July 2, 1940, the President issued the first proclamation under the act. It placed under license all arms, ammunition, and implements of war, certain basic raw materials like aluminum, specified chemicals, and such items as aircraft parts, equipment, and accessories, together with armor plate, glass, plastics, optical instruments, and machine tools. Important as were these items, nothing as yet had been done about oil and scrap iron, both of which the Japanese continued to acquire in the United States in considerable quantities.[56]

The important decision to place scrap iron and petroleum products under license came on July 25. Actually these restrictions did not constitute an embargo but could have the same effect if so desired. For example, on July 31, the Administrator of Export Control announced that the

[56] *Foreign Relations, Japan, 1931-1941*, Vol. II, pp. 211-15.

export of aviation gasoline would be limited to Western Hemisphere nations only. Japan considered this step aimed directly against itself and lodged a protest with the State Department. The American reply was that the United States considered such a measure in the interest of national defense and therefore a protest by any foreign government was deemed unwarranted.

Economic Noose Tightened. The economic strings were drawn even tighter on September 12 with a presidential proclamation putting the exportation of equipment and plans for the production of aviation motor fuel, of tetraethyl lead, and of aircraft engines under the licensing system. This act was followed the next day by a press release from the White House to the effect that the proclamation of September 12, taken with previous proclamations, had the effect of putting under the President's control for export purposes not only aircraft and engines but also the plans and designs for building them. Tighter went the noose a few weeks later with an announcement limiting the shipment of scrap metal to countries of the Western Hemisphere and to Britain. Japan protested these steps as directed against Japan and therefore an unfriendly act.

This protest evoked from Secretary Hull a strongly worded reply in which he declared that it was unheard of for a country engaged in aggression and seizure of another country to turn to a third peacefully disposed nation and seriously insist that it would be guilty of an unfriendly act if it should not cheerfully provide some of the necessary implements of war to aid the aggressor nation in carrying out its policy of invasion.[57]

Japan Gets Indo-China Bases. Despite these severe setbacks, Japan continued to press hard in Southeast Asia. French officials in Indo-China were forced to capitulate to Japanese demands as the United States could promise only moral support should Japan attack. On September 22 an agreement was signed at Hanoi which gave the Japanese the right to establish air bases in Indo-China and to land enough troops to garrison them. The Japanese moved so fast to implement the agreement that they clashed with French troops the very next day. The French government at Vichy ordered the resistance ended and the Japanese were allowed to send in their troops without trouble. Pressure on the Netherlands East Indies resulted in a trade agreement by which the East Indies was to supply Japan with about half the oil which the Japanese had demanded. Even though it fell far short of Japanese hopes, it represented a boon to Japan.[58]

[57] *Ibid.*, pp. 220-28.
[58] For Japan's hopes in this area see e.g., *Military Tribunal for the Far East*, Exhibit Nos. 1314, 1316.

United States Increases Pressure on Japan. Following the presidential election in November, the administration was ready to devote greater attention to foreign problems. For one thing, it was decided to provide Chiang Kai-shek with further financial assistance and to promise him some new planes. Americans who so desired were now allowed to go to China as aviators or aviation instructors. In addition, ships and planes were dispatched to the Philippines. No promises, however, were forthcoming that the United States would undertake to defend either Singapore or the East Indies, as the British and Dutch were hoping.[59]

In December, iron and steel were placed under the licensing system, effective at the end of the month. In addition, certain articles and materials (including bromine, strontium metals and ores, abrasives, specific kinds of machinery, and equipment and plans for the production of aviation lubricating oil) were also put under the system. The Japanese, of course, were quick to protest the restrictions on the export of iron and steel, which they claimed were discriminatory against Japan. Early in 1941, copper, brass and bronze, zinc, nickel, and potash were all added to the list. In February and March of 1941 more and more items were added, including any model, design, photographic negative, document, or any article containing a plan or technical information of any kind, which could be used in connection with any process or operation of any articles or materials already put under the licensing system.[60]

Japan Drives Southeast. Japan meanwhile continued to advance in Southeast Asia. A pact with Thailand was ratified by the Japanese emperor on December 27, 1940. It was a step beyond the usual nonaggression pact and was quite satisfactory to the Japanese. The Japanese then stirred up the Thais to get involved in a skirmish with the French in Indo-China and mediated the conflict. On March 11, 1941, the French were forced to yield portions of Laos and Cambodia to Thailand and also to promise that they would not align themselves with any other country against the interests of Japan.[61]

Pressure was applied to the Netherlands East Indies again and a series of heavy demands made upon its government, but once again the Dutch proved adamant, and the leader of the Japanese mission reported that unless Japan adopted "determined resolutions or measures" little could be hoped for from the negotiations then being held.[62] Nothing came of

---

[59] Feis, *op. cit.*, p. 140.

[60] *Foreign Relations, Japan, 1931-1941*, Vol. II, pp. 232-58.

[61] The fact that the French were given an ultimatum may be seen in *Military Tribunal Far East*, Exhibit No. 633.

[62] For a list of the Japanese demands see *Military Tribunal for the Far East*, Exhibit No. 1309A. See also Exhibit No. 1318.

the talks since the Dutch stood up resolutely against the Japanese, even though their homeland had fallen to Germany and they had no assurances that either Britain or the United States would come to their aid.

While Japan was thus striving to strengthen its position in the south, American and British military men by the end of March 1941 had conferred and agreed on the fundamental aspects of strategy to be followed (1) while the United States remained a nonbelligerent and (2) should the United States become involved in war with Germany, Italy, Japan, or all three.[63]

A Year of Futile Negotiation

The Preliminary Phase (January to May). Late in January, 1941, through the informal medium of private American and Japanese citizens, a suggestion was informally put before the President of the United States and the Secretary of State that the Japanese government would like a chance to change its political alignments and modify its attitude toward China. It was felt in Washington, however, that it would be desirable to await the arrival of the new Japanese ambassador, Admiral Nomura, before taking any action on the proposal. Nomura presented his credentials on February 14 and on March 8 he and the Secretary of State held their first of several lengthy conversations. On April 16 Hull informed Nomura that the United States wanted an unqualified assurance from Japan that the Japanese would give up their present plan of forceful conquest and adopt four principles which the United States regarded as the bedrock on which international relations should rest. These were:

(1) Respect for the territorial integrity and sovereignty of each and all nations;
(2) Support of the principle of non-interference in the internal affairs of other countries;
(3) Support of the principle of equality, including equality of commercial opportunity;
(4) Non-disturbance of the *status quo* in the Pacific except as the *status quo* may be altered by peaceful means.[64]

Ambassador Nomura replied that he believed that his government desired peace but that he would have to consult his superiors concerning the four points raised by Hull.

Japanese Proposal of May 12. On May 12 the ambassador presented the Secretary of State with a Japanese proposal. What it amounted to, basically, was that the United States and Japan should jointly control

---
[63] Feis, *op. cit.*, chap. 21.
[64] *Foreign Relations, Japan, 1931-1941*, Vol. II, p. 658.

the Pacific area. Furthermore, the United States was expected to request the Chinese government to negotiate with Japan a settlement ending hostilities. In this connection, the United States would be expected to discontinue aid to China should the Chinese refuse to negotiate. The United States and Japan would mutually supply the other with commodities which the other needed, in so far as this was possible. Steps should be taken to resume normal trade relations between the two countries, and the United States should assist Japan to acquire such needed natural resources, as oil, rubber, tin, and nickel.

The United States government decided to explore carefully and completely every possible means, starting with these Japanese proposals, of reaching an agreement, although it realized that the prospects were slight. Nevertheless the American government would continue, while exploring these avenues, to oppose the course of aggression which Japan was following.

On June 21, following a series of conversations revolving around the Japanese proposals of May 12, the Secretary of State presented the Japanese ambassador with a draft which brought the discussions up to date as far as the United States attitude was concerned. This draft included, among other points, "A mutual affirmation by the two countries that the basic policy of each was one of peace throughout the Pacific area and a mutual disclaimer of territorial designs there."

Shortly afterward the Japanese called up from one to two million reservists and conscripts, and recalled all Japanese merchant vessels operating in the Atlantic Ocean. Restrictions were placed upon travel in Japan, strict censorship of mails and communications was instituted, and in general every evidence that Japan was preparing for a major war seemed manifest. During this period, also, the Japanese began to insist that they were being pressured unmercifully by the United States and warned that further pressure would bring American-Japanese relations to the point of crisis. Japan claimed that the United States, Britain, China, and the Netherlands were trying to encircle it.

The Conversations Interrupted. In July the United States government received reports that the Japanese were planning a military movement into Indo-China, whereupon it informed the Japanese that such action was hardly consistent with the discussions then being held and asked for information regarding the reports. The Japanese reply was unconvincing and led the United States to adopt the position that under the circumstances further talks would be useless.

The following day the President of the United States proposed to the Japanese ambassador that French Indo-China be regarded as a neutralized country by the United States, Japan, Great Britain, China, and the Netherlands. Solemn promises would be given by each that they had no hostile designs on the country and that Japan would be given the fullest and freest opportunity of assuring itself of food supplies and other raw materials which, according to the Japanese, they were endeavoring to secure. One week later the Japanese ambassador was informed that the President wished to extend his "neutralization" proposal to Thailand as well.

The Japanese went ahead with their plans and moved large forces into southern Indo-China, thereby threatening the Philippines. At the same time there was evidence that a substantial amount of Japanese undercover work and infiltration was occurring in Thailand. As a consequence, the United States decided that a cessation of trade with Japan was now in order and discontinued the talks. On July 26 Roosevelt issued an executive order freezing Japanese assets in the United States, a step tantamount to complete cessation of trade between the United States and Japan.

New protestations of peaceful intent came from the Japanese Prime Minister, Prince Konoe, the new Foreign Minister, Admiral Toyoda who had just replaced Matsuoka, and Admiral Nomura, the Ambassador to the United States. Their words were not matched by Japanese actions, however, as plans for mobilization continued in Japan and more and more troops were sent to Manchuria, Indo-China, and South China. American property was damaged in China, including the American Embassy at Chungking and the U.S.S. "Tutuila," a gunboat there.

The Conversations Resumed. On August 6 the Japanese answered the President's proposal suggesting the neutralization of Indo-China. The Japanese reply suggested among other things that the restrictions which the United States had placed on trade with Japan be removed, that the United States suspend "its military measures in the southwest Pacific area," and that the United States use its good offices to initiate direct negotiations between Japan and China. Japanese troops would withdraw from Indo-China after Japan and China had reached a settlement, but the United States should recognize Japan's special position in Indo-China even after the troops had been withdrawn.

Such a one-sided proposal obviously was not an answer to Roosevelt's proposal, and the Secretary of State so informed Japan on August 8, whereupon the Japanese ambassador inquired whether it would be possible to arrange a meeting between the Japanese Prime Minister and the President to work out an agreement between the two countries. Konoe himself addressed a personal letter to Roosevelt asking for such a meeting.[65] The President hesitated about an answer until on September 3 he

---

[65] The letter is in *Foreign Relations, Japan, 1931-1941*, Vol. II, pp. 572 f.

told Nomura that he would need several points clarified before such a meeting could take place.[66]

Three days later the Secretary of State received a new draft of proposals covering the basic questions specified by President Roosevelt. In this draft Japan reaffirmed its peaceful intentions, but so qualified its proposals that a general basic settlement seemed out of the question as far as the United States was concerned. Nevertheless, on the same day in Tokyo, Prince Konoe informed Ambassador Grew that his government completely and definitely subscribed to the four principles which Hull had set forth at the outset as a basis for reconstruction of relations with Japan. Unfortunately, one month later the Minister for Foreign Affairs told Grew that these points had been accepted in principle but that certain readjustments applying them to actual conditions would have to be made.

The failure of the Japanese leaders to produce convincing evidence of their sincerity toward peace led Roosevelt and his advisers to decide against the idea of a Roosevelt-Konoe meeting until such time as the Japanese would give tentative commitments consonant with both the principles and objectives of American policy and with Japan's professions of a desire for peace. A series of discussions in Tokyo and Washington during September failed to produce results. On the twenty-fifth a new redraft of the Japanese proposals proved to be substantially unchanged from Japan's earlier position. By October it seemed clear to the American government that the most Japan was prepared to offer in return for an agreement with the United States was a promise to move elsewhere the Japanese troops in southern Indo-China and a pledge not to move south of Indo-China militarily. For this Japan expected the United States to remove the restrictions imposed upon the trade of the two countries. As far as China was concerned, Japan made it clear that it intended to keep troops there indefinitely and expected to retain a preferred economic position there. Furthermore, Japan showed no willingness to withdraw from the Axis. Japan continued, however, to press for an agreement, stressing all the while the desirability of swift action.

New Japanese Cabinet Urges Speedy Agreement. On October 17, 1941, a new Japanese government, led by General Tojo with Togo as Foreign Minister, took office. Immediately the new Cabinet began to press for an agreement with the United States along the lines of earlier Japanese proposals. There was no evidence that the new government was prepared to modify Japan's position an iota. On the other hand, new military preparations were being made in both Indo-China and Manchuria, and the Japanese press was calling for positive action.

[66] *Ibid.*, pp. 591 f.

Meanwhile, the exchanges continued between the two governments. On November 15 Secretary Hull gave the Japanese ambassador an outline for a possible joint declaration on economic policy. This, Hull emphasized, was only part of a general settlement which could follow. The draft contained three divisions. (1) The two governments were to cooperate in urging all nations to reduce their trade barriers, put an end to discriminatory practices, and work for the achievement of conditions which would allow all nations to acquire the goods and commodities which they required. (2) The United States and Japan would resume normal commercial relations as soon as practicable and start discussions for the conclusion of a reciprocal trade agreement. Further they were to permit export to the other of desired commodities, subject to necessary restrictions or limitations imposed by security and self-defense during the existing emergency brought on by the war in Europe. (3) Both would agree in the Pacific that complete economic, financial, and monetary control would be restored to China; and that neither would seek preferential or monopolistic rights in China. Both would suggest to China that it commence a long-range program of economic development with most-favored-nation treatment to both Japan and the United States in this program. Finally, both would seek to establish relations with other Pacific nations on the basis of the fundamental principles already set forth, and to urge the other Pacific countries to inaugurate comprehensive programs of economic development in which the United States and Japan would receive most-favored-nation treatment and a full and unfettered opportunity to participate in these programs whenever foreign aid should be desired.

During this conversation with the Japanese ambassador, the Secretary of State failed to receive a satisfactory answer to the important question whether Japan would sever its special treaty connections with Germany and Italy should a Japanese-American agreement be concluded.

The Japanese government then sent Saburo Kurusu to assist Ambassador Nomura in the conversations going on in Washington. The special envoy arrived in Washington on November 15 and made his first call on the Secretary of State two days later. He was also received by President Roosevelt on the same day. The new arrival assured his hosts that General Tojo was very anxious to achieve a peaceful adjustment of the matters at issue between the United States and Japan. He also tried to make light of the Tripartite Pact and endeavored to defend Japan's unwillingness to remove the troops from China. In a talk with Hull the following day, Kurusu said that, although Japan could not break its pact with Germany and Italy, it might well do something to "outshine" it. Hull continued to press for three things: (1) withdrawal of Japanese troops from China;

(2) adoption of a liberal commercial policy; and (3) Japanese withdrawal from the Axis.

Kurusu's Proposal. On November 20 Kurusu's instructions from the Tojo government were revealed when Nomura made the following proposal to Secretary Hull:

(1) Both governments would undertake not to make any armed advance into any of the regions in South-eastern Asia and the Southern Pacific area except that part of French Indo-China where the Japanese had then stationed troops.

(2) Japan would withdraw from Indo-China the troops there either when peace was restored between Japan and China or when an equitable peace had been established in the Pacific area.
In the meantime Japan would remove its troops from southern to northern Indo-China upon the conclusion of the present arrangement which would later be part of the final agreement.

(3) The two governments should cooperate to secure goods and commodities which they needed in the Netherlands East Indies.

(4) Both mutually agree to restore their commercial relations to those prevailing before the freezing of the assets.
The United States should supply Japan a required quantity of oil.

(5) The United States promises to refrain from measures and actions which would be prejudicial to endeavors to restore general peace between Japan and China.[67]

In subsequent conversations the Secretary of State stressed American views on three points in this Japanese proposal. The United States might supply Japan with some oil for civilian purposes but none whatsoever for military uses; Japanese troops in any part of Indo-China were a cause of concern to the neighboring countries; and, finally, that the United States would not discontinue aid to China, which the American people considered on the same basis as aid to England, while Japan was giving assistance to Germany.

Japan Decides on War. One thing which stood out clearly during the conversations was that all Japanese statements professing peaceful intentions were always qualified and restricted. It was obvious that Japan did not intend to desert the Axis, or to yield the preferential position it had forcefully gained in China, or to remove its troops from China. Hence it became quite clear that Japan sought but one goal: to get the United States to accept an agreement which could be beneficial only to Japan.

This being so, one possibility remained: could the United States deter Japan from some new adventure through the conclusion of a *modus*

[67] *International Military Tribunal Far East*, Exhibit No. 3646.

vivendi which would get by the present crisis and buy valuable time. Accordingly, on November 26 Hull presented Nomura with two documents. One was an outline in tentative form of a proposed basis of agreement, and the second was an explanatory statement concerning the first. In effect, the American position was a summary of the now familiar American principles and objectives of American foreign policy. Kurusu said that it was his feeling that the Secretary's proposals were tantamount to ending the conversations. That this was also the feeling in Japan may be seen from Foreign Minister Togo's remark, "Japan was now asked not only to abandon all the gains of her years of sacrifice, but to surrender her international position as a power in the Far East.... The only way to face this challenge and defend ourselves was war." [68]

Hull also thought that the time for action was fast approaching, for he declared that "the matter is now in the hands of the Army and Navy." [69]

On November 28 Germany pledged its support if Japan should become involved in a war with the United States. Two days later the Japanese ambassador in Berlin was ordered to inform the Germans that the conversations between the United States and Japan had been terminated and that war could break out at any minute. Japan planned a southward move and contemplated no moves against the U.S.S.R. [70]

Nonetheless, Kurusu in a telephone call to Yamamoto, American Division chief of the Japanese Foreign Office, indicated that the talks were not quite concluded when he said: "You were very urgent about them [Japanese-American negotiations] before, weren't you; but now you want them to stretch out. We will need your help. Both the Premier and the Foreign Minister will need to change the tone of their speeches!!!! Do you understand? Please all use more discretion." [71]

The decision to make war was reached by the Japanese at an Imperial Conference on the afternoon of December 1, and the work of drawing up a final statement to the American government was begun. [72]

Japan Attacks

Meanwhile, Nomura and Kurusu continued to visit Secretary Hull but had no new proposals to offer; matters were at an impasse. President Roosevelt decided on the sixth of December to address a personal message to the emperor of Japan. Developments were occurring in the Pacific, said the President in his cable, that indicated that the long peace between

[68] *Ibid.*, pp. 755-56.
[69] *Military Tribunal Far East, Transcript*, Vol. XXV, p. 10,954.
[70] *Military Tribunal Far East*, Exhibit No. 802.
[71] *Ibid.*, Exhibit No. 1200.
[72] *Ibid.*, Exhibit Nos. 2954, 2955.

the United States and Japan was being threatened. Events of recent weeks had made the peoples of the Philippines, the Netherlands East Indies, Thailand, and Malaya wonder if Japanese military activities in Indo-China presaged an attack on any one or all of them. The President's fervent hope was that the emperor would attempt to clear things up peacefully. Both the emperor and the President had "a sacred duty to restore traditional amity and prevent further death and destruction in the world."

Nothing came of this dramatic last minute appeal, and on Sunday December 7, around 12 noon, following a telephone request from Nomura, Secretary of State Hull made an appointment to receive him and Kurusu at 1 P.M. Shortly after one o'clock, the ambassador telephoned to request that the appointment be postponed until 1:45. They arrived at the State Department at 2:05 and were received by Secretary Hull at 2:20. The Japanese ambassador informed the Secretary that he had been instructed by his government to deliver a document to the Secretary of State at 1:00 P.M. but owing to difficulty in decoding it, he had been delayed.[73]

The interview started one hour after the opening attack on Pearl Harbor and two and a half hours after the invasion of British Malaya. The Japanese Foreign Office did not know of the exact hour set for the attack at Pearl Harbor and had agreed to deliver at 1:00 P.M. (Washington time) on December 7 the message implying that relations were severed. The Navy had set the time at 1:00 P.M. with their attack to follow twenty minutes later. Nomura's and Kurusu's tardiness thus upset the timing arrangements so that, instead of having notified the United States a few minutes in advance of the actual attack that negotiations were at an end, the news did not come until an hour too late. The Japanese thought that, once the note was delivered implying a rupture in diplomatic relations, treaty procedure was completed and they thereby acquired freedom of action. When deciding how long before the actual attack the note should be delivered, the Chiefs of Staff and the Foreign Office indulged in some argument. All agreed, however, that the timing of the delivery should not interfere with the success of the surprise attack on Pearl Harbor.[74]

The Japanese message given to Hull maintained that Japan had merely sought to bring peace and stability to East Asia and that the United States had not understood Japan's true intentions. Hull's remarks were brief and acid.

> I must say that in all my conversations with you during the last nine months I have never uttered one word of untruth. This is borne out

[73] The United States had broken Japan's code and the contents of the message were known in Washington Saturday evening. See Feis, *op. cit, passim.*

[74] *Military Tribunal for the Far East*, Exhibit No. 3646.

absolutely by the record. In all my fifty years of public service I have never seen a document that was more crowded with infamous falsehoods and distortions—infamous falsehoods and distortions on a scale so huge that I never imagined until today that any government on this planet was capable of uttering them.[75]

Ambassador Grew in Tokyo was informed by the Foreign Minister that the document delivered in Washington was the emperor's reply to President Roosevelt's message. This information was communicated to Grew several hours after the Pearl Harbor attack had begun.

Thus the relations between the United States and Japan were climaxed by war.

SUGGESTED READINGS

Most useful are the volumes of the United States, *Foreign Relations,* covering this period. Good, too, is *United States Relations with China* (Washington, 1949). The White Paper stresses the years 1944-49, but its introduction and some of its appendices apply to the period covered by this chapter. Invaluable but not generally available are the 109-volume series of the International Military Tribunal for the Far East, *Transcript of the Record* (Tokyo, 1946-48) and the International Military Tribunal for the Far East, *Exhibits* (Tokyo, 1946-48) in 60 volumes. Although virtually contemporary, the annual series edited by Walter Lippmann, Whitney H. Shepardson, and William O. Scroggs, *The United States in World Affairs, 1931-40,* is very helpful. So too are *Documents on American Foreign Relations,* a series begun in 1939 under the editorship of S. Shepard Jones, Denys P. Myers, and others. See also: Herbert Feis, *The Road to Pearl Harbor* (Princeton, 1950); Cordell Hull, *The Memoirs of Cordell Hull* (2 vols. New York, 1948); F. C. Jones, *Japan's New Order in East Asia: Its Rise and Fall, 1937-1945* (London, 1954); William L. Langer and S. Everett Gleason, *The Undeclared War, 1940-1941* (New York, 1953); Henry L. Stimson and McGeorge Bundy, *On Active Service in Peace and War* (New York, 1948); Charles C. Tansill, *Back Door to War* (Chicago, 1952); and United States Department of State, *Foreign Relations of the United States, Japan, 1931-1941* (Washington, 1943).

Other studies relating to this chapter are: Knight Biggerstaff, *The Far East and the United States* (Ithaca, New York, 1943); T. A. Bisson, *America's Far Eastern Policy* (rev. and enlarged ed., New York, 1945); Dorothy Borg, *American Policy and the Chinese Revolution, 1925-1928* (New York, 1947); R. L. Buell, *The Washington Conference* (New York, 1922); Arthur E. Christy, *The Asian Legacy and American Life* (New York, 1945); Paul H. Clyde, *United States Policy Toward China: Diplomatic and Public Documents, 1839-1939* (Durham, 1940); David J. Dallin, *Soviet Russia and the Far East* (New Haven, 1948); Foster Rhea Dulles, *The Road to Teheran* (Princeton, 1944) and *The United States and China* (Princeton, 1946); A. W. Griswold, *The Far Eastern Policy of the United States* (New York, 1938); Stanley Hornbeck, *The United States and the Far East* (Boston, 1942);

[75] *Ibid.,* p. 787.

Yamato Ichihashi, *The Washington Conference and After* (Stanford University, 1928); K. S. Latourette, *The United States Moves Across the Pacific* (New York, 1946); Wen Huan Ma, *American Policy toward China as Revealed in the Debates of Congress* (Shanghai, 1934); Harriet L. Moore, *Soviet Far Eastern Policy, 1931-1945* (Princeton, 1945); William Starr Myers, *The Foreign Policies of Herbert Hoover* (New York, 1940); Allan Nevins and Louis M. Hacker, eds., *The United States and Its Place in World Affairs, 1918-1943* (Boston, 1943); George E. Sokolsky, *The Tinder Box of Asia* (New York, 1932); Henry L. Stimson and McGeorge Bundy, *On Active Service* (New York, 1947); George E. Taylor, *America in the New Pacific* (New York, 1942); Pauline Tompkins, *American-Russian Relations in the Far East* (New York, 1949); Quincy Wright *et al., Legal Problems in the Far Eastern Conflict* (New York, 1941).

27

JAPAN: POLITICAL DEVELOPMENT

The political history of Japan from the end of the Sino-Japanese War in 1895 to October, 1940, centers primarily around the struggle to make the Cabinet responsible to the House of Representatives. The political parties made this issue the principal plank in their platforms. The bureaucrats and the representatives of the armed services opposed this movement toward responsible government as an unwarranted infringement upon the sovereign rights of the emperor. Including the war with China in the 1930's, there were five occasions during this forty-five year period when a foreign war vitally influenced the outcome of this internal political battle. This fight for the control of the government had as a background the tension and friction attendant upon Japan's full entry into economic competition with the Western world. As a result of these powerful external influences, the main trends in the political development of Japan often were confused and frequently hardly discernible.

An Initial Failure by Bureaucrats

The political unity which appeared in Japan during the Sino-Japanese War lasted only a few months after the signing of the Treaty of Shimonoseki. The Ito Ministry's alliance with the *Jiyuto* party and with certain conservative elements lasted only until early in 1896. In the Ministries which followed, the necessity of having the support of a large political party in the lower house was clearly indicated. Thus when Matsukata of Satsuma, later one of the Elder Statesmen, took Ito's place in 1896, he found it expedient to win the backing of Okuma's Progressive party, the *Shimpoto*,[1] by offering Okuma the position of Foreign Minister. This arrangement failed when the latter discovered that he had almost no influence on general Cabinet policy. Similarly, the Ito Ministry which succeeded that of Matsukata in December, 1897, lasted less than six

[1] Formed by a union of the old *Kaishinto* (Liberal Conservative) with fifty other members of the Diet.

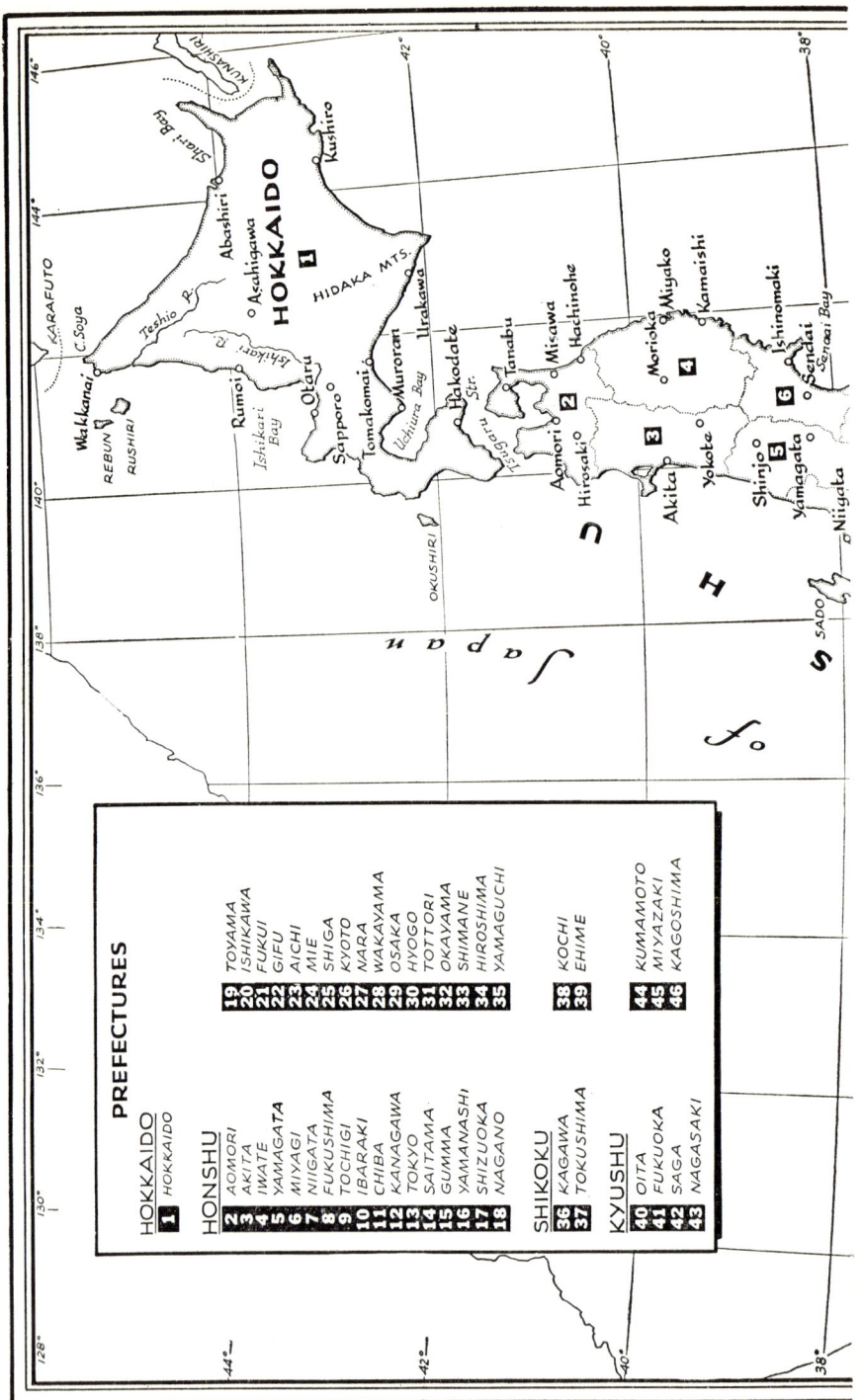

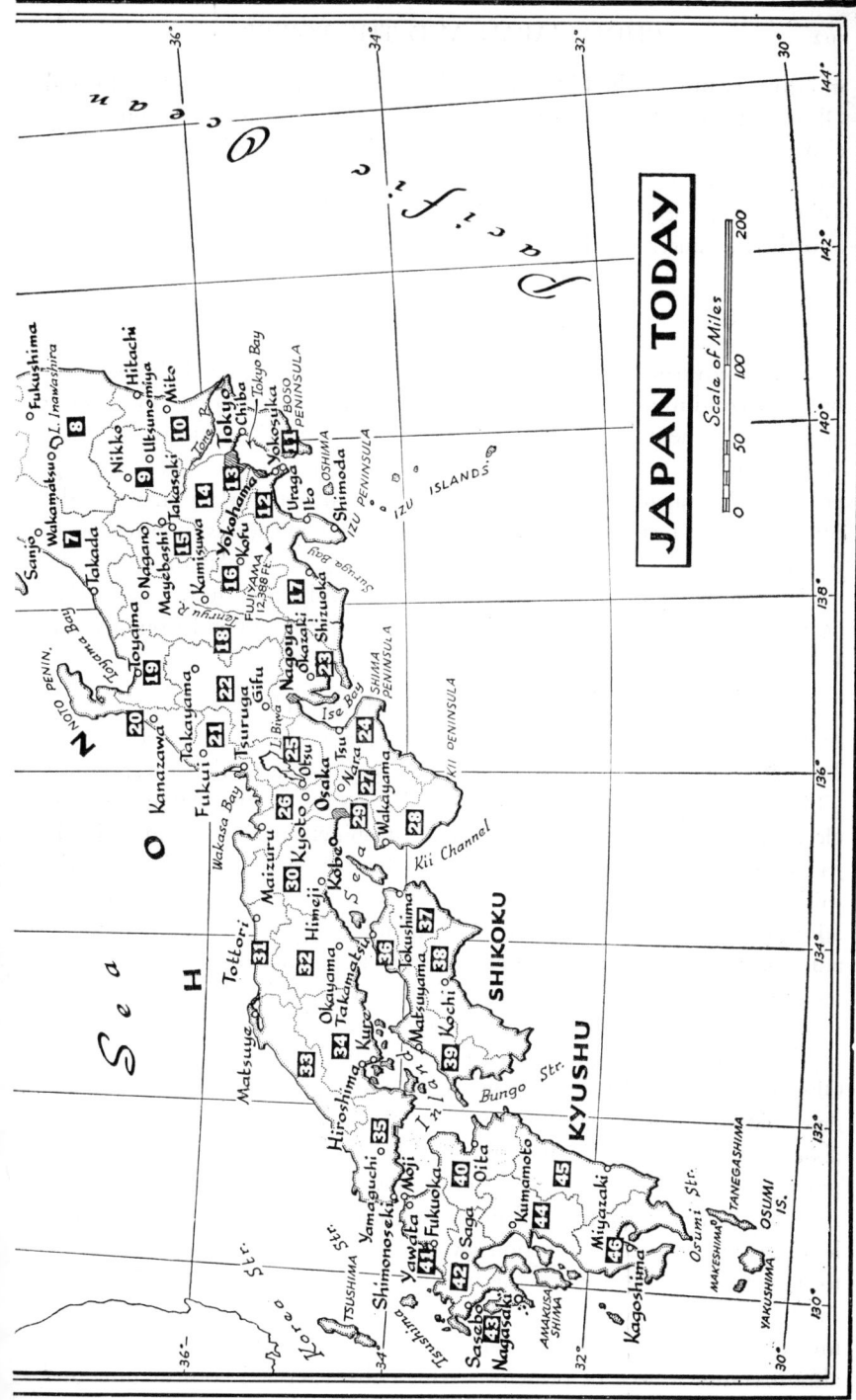

months because of the bitter opposition of the parties led by Itagaki and Okuma. Ito had been unsuccessful in his attempts to gain the support of either of these two men. When the *Kenseito,* the Constitutionalist party, was born June 22, 1898, it represented the union of Itagaki's and Okuma's followers and seemed to spell ruin for those leaders of the Restoration and the bureaucrats who were opposed to party government.

Premature Party Government

In this governmental crisis, Ito seems to have recognized the impossibility of continuing a supra-party government. His proposals to create a large government party which would carry out administration policy, or to request Itagaki and Okuma to form a Cabinet, were violently opposed by Yamagata, a fellow Choshu clansman but a spokesman for the military. Ito's resignation which followed his unsuccessful attempt to convince those in control of the government placed upon the latter the responsibility for finding a successor to Ito. Only after it was clear that none of them would form a Cabinet, was Ito's recommendation that the *Kenseito* party leaders form a government accepted.

The *Kenseito.* It should be observed immediately that the new party, only three days old, was in a position to realize the announced goal of Japanese political parties, a government responsible to the lower house. This possibility was strengthened by the results of the August (1898) election which gave the Okuma-Itagaki Cabinet an absolute majority in the House. This electoral victory more than offset the opposition of the military and bureaucrats to the new government's announced policy of administrative reform and to its plan to fill newly created parliamentary administrative positions by appointing party members. The bureaucrats looked upon the latter move as a first step toward further invasion of government positions by nonbureaucrats.

The *Kenseito,* however, represented an uneasy union from its birth. Okuma and Itagaki had different personalities and had divergent views on affairs of state. Results of the August elections had left the two factions about even in strength in the House of Representatives. Both leaders and party members had been members of the opposition for so many years that they were more interested in the political spoils than in a constructive legislative program. Each faction saw in the existing arrangement a means to achieve complete victory for itself. Consequently, even before facing the test of a Diet session, the alliance collapsed in early November. Too much responsibility had been thrust upon the *Kenseito* too quickly. The almost complete lack of principles which characterized both Okuma and

Itagaki and their followers in intraparty relations made agreement upon government policy most difficult. The resignation of Itagaki December 28, followed immediately by that of Okuma, gave the clan bureaucrats another opportunity to prove their ability to govern the country. Progress toward constitutional government suffered a setback which would require two decades to overcome.

Government by the Few

The extent of the defeat involved in the collapse of the Itagaki-Okuma Cabinet can be measured in part by the fact that only seven men dominated the Ministry in the next twenty years. Of these Yamagata, Katsura, and Terauchi were Choshu clansmen and members of the military, as was Yamamoto of Satsuma. Ito of Choshu and Saionji of the court nobility opposed the military's attempt to gain complete control of the government, yet they were not interested in party government. Only Okuma of Hizen believed more than superficially in the idea of cabinet responsibility to the lower house and the majority party therein. Two of these men, Katsura and Saionji, by extra-party arrangement retained the premiership from 1901 to 1913. All men who held that position had the support of the Elder Statesmen and bureaucrats. A few of the more important events and developments demand more detailed examination because of their relationship to the underlying struggle for control of the Japanese government.

Political Trends

Generally speaking, Cabinets after 1898 found it necessary to have the support of a political party, preferably but not necessarily the majority group, in the lower house to prevent a complete legislative breakdown. This in itself was an important constitutional advance. In some cases, the Yamagata regime of 1898-1900 for example, the Premier resorted to wholesale bribery. To secure passage of a law increasing the land tax in 1899 Yamagata sponsored an increase in the salaries of the presiding officers of both houses, their deputies, and the individual members of the Diet. Another approach was tried by Yamagata in his unsuccessful sponsoring of the Imperial party. Ito, however, was more successful through his assumption in 1900 of the leadership of the Constitutionalist [2] party which generally supported him and Saionji. This did not mean that Ito accepted the principle of party government. He still believed that Cabinet members were responsible solely to the emperor and that they were completely independent of the lower house; the party rather than the leader

[2] Renamed the *Seiyukai*.

changed. Finally, Katsura proved himself to be a master at the manipulation of parties. On one occasion, war (the Russo-Japanese War) gave him the solid backing of all parties. He failed only in 1913 when he attempted to found his own party to support his dictatorial control of the government. All premiers throughout this period counted on the lack of unity among the parties and their leaders. The parties were used, but seldom, if ever, were they consulted when one government fell and a new premier had to be chosen.

The Military Increase Their Power. Another continuous thread which ran through this entire period was the attempt of the military to strengthen its hold on the government. Yamagata, Katsura, and Terauchi are the key figures in this story. At the time of his second premiership in 1898, Yamagata was a field marshal with a large and loyal group of bureaucrats and military behind him. His influence with the bureaucracy began in the 1880's with his efforts to strengthen the clan bureaucracy during his tenure as Home Minister. By 1898 he had also served his country as Chief of the General Staff, Minister of Justice, and Privy Councillor. Further strengthening this governmental alliance, the Civil Service Ordinance of 1899 protected the bureaucrats by establishing regulations covering appointment to the civil service which effectively eliminated party office seekers.

Then Yamagata quietly won for the military a unique power in the government by securing an amendment to an imperial ordinance providing for the organization of the two military departments. This amendment provided that only generals and lieutenant generals on the active list and only admirals and vice-admirals on the active list could hold the positions of Minister of War and Minister of Navy respectively. In effect, this gave the Army and Navy complete control over the life of a Cabinet and the formation of new Cabinets. By ordering the Minister of War to resign or by refusing to name a man for this position, the Army could accomplish these facts. The parties' failure to fight this measure later cost them dearly. In 1912 those leaders who sought greater civilian influence in the government recognized the danger and challenged this provision. Saionji's Cabinet, with the single exception of the War Minister, was opposed to the army demand, supported by the bureaucrats, for the establishment of two new army divisions.

The issue could not have been more clearly drawn. Public confidence in the Saionji Cabinet, as demonstrated by its absolute majority of seats in the House of Representatives gained in the May elections, had been strengthened by a sound administration. Despite this, the military was so strongly entrenched that Saionji was forced to resign December 5, 1912.

His War Minister had resigned three days earlier, and Yamagata, the Army's leader, had refused to sanction the appointment of another general on the active list to the position. From this time party leaders concentrated upon the elimination of this amendment. Only by so doing could the military be held responsible to the civilian Prime Minister and Cabinet, and thus to the lower house. Saionji, incidentally, was commanded to serve the emperor by becoming a member of the Genro,[3] thereby removing him as an active political participant opposed to the plans of the military.

Prelude to Party Government (1913-1918)

Okuma as Premier. The failure in rapid succession of Katsura to establish a personal government and of Yamamoto to maintain in office a Cabinet dominated by the military seemed to have brought the country to an impasse. After a vain attempt to build a Cabinet around Kiyoura, a nonparty man, the Elder Statesmen turned to the aged Okuma. Although Okuma's long opposition to the bureaucracy, the clans, and the Elder Statesmen was due largely to his resentment against the domination of the government by the Satsuma and Choshu clans, he still was a champion of constitutional government. Ushered in with an unusual display of public enthusiasm, the Okuma Cabinet had an absolute majority in the House and a tacit agreement with the opposition party, the *Seiyukai*. This political honeymoon was shattered rudely in the general election of 1915 by Okuma's Home Minister's active campaigning against the *Seiyukai*. There was far too little sense of intraparty discipline to prevent this.

With Hara, a commoner, as the new leader of the opposition party, there were many opportunities for attacking the Okuma government. Navy scandals involving the Mitsui firm, with which Okuma had close connections, were vigorously publicized. Further evidence that the military and Elder Statesmen dominated the Cabinet was provided through the disclosure that the Minister of Home Affairs had bribed Diet members; two additional army divisions had resulted. Hara and the *Seiyukai* criticized bitterly every act of the government.

What had begun then as a promising move toward the establishment of Cabinet responsibility resulted only in cynicism based on a record far short of Okuma's standards and hopes. The attitude of the Elder States-

[3] The Emperor Meiji died in 1912. There is little evidence to prove the part actually played in Japan's government by its emperors. Meiji is given credit by some scholars for much of his country's dramatic progress. His successor Yoshihito became so ill that in 1921 the present emperor, Hirohito, was named regent and became Japan's ruler in 1926. Certainly the influence of Meiji and Hirohito has strengthened the respect the Japanese have had for the imperial institution.

men clearly showed this. When Okuma resigned in October, 1916, his party still controlled the House of Representatives. Consequently, he had recommended as his successor Foreign Minister Kato Takaaki who had just been chosen the head of a new party, the *Kenseikai,* a merger of the groups which had supported Okuma. Yamagata felt perfectly safe in ignoring this recommendation and named his own protégé, General Terauchi. As he passed from the active political arena, Okuma remained true to his lifelong opposition to the Elder Statesmen and refused an imperial invitation to become one of them.

The failure of the Okuma government gave the military another chance to prove their right to govern Japan. The Terauchi Cabinet (October, 1916-September, 1918) demonstrated its inability to do so. Although the government followed a strong China policy and attempted to divert public attention to foreign affairs, it failed completely to provide satisfactory solutions to the internal economic problems which World War I had brought. Strikes and high prices were met by the use of force and the suppression of news unfavorable to the government. An alliance with Hara and the *Seiyukai,* the majority party, disintegrated as the party found itself repeatedly ignored. This complete lack of success of a militarily controlled government paved the way for the only serious attempts to establish party government in Japan.

The Political Picture in 1918

A brief summary of the political picture in September, 1918 will indicate the nature of the problems Hara was to face as he and his nation entered a new era. The past thirty years had been highlighted by two bitter personal feuds. Okuma and Itagaki had been unable to resolve their differences and had wrecked the first attempt at party government. Ito and Yamagata in their struggle for power, ended only by Ito's assassination in 1909, had personified the clash between the military and the civilian groups for control of the government.

Japanese politics revolved so completely around personalities that party leaders had an unusually heavy responsibility. Further evidence of this is seen in the preponderant influence of the Elder Statesmen. R. K. Reischauer points out that the premiership was almost completely controlled by them.[4] Furthermore, all but two of the presidents of the Privy Council, the advisory body closest to the emperor, were Genro. Yamagata of Choshu and Matsukata of Satsuma had almost complete control over the Army and the Navy. In addition, the groups which made the Restoration possible—the Choshu, Satsuma, Hizen and Tosa clans, the court

[4] *Japan, Government-Politics* (New York, 1939), chap. 5.

nobility, and the last shogun—either controlled directly or by marriage such other important posts as President of the House of Peers, Lord Keeper of the Privy Seal, and Minister of the Imperial Household.[5] Until the deaths of Yamagata in 1922 and Matsukata in 1924, the heavy hand of precedent effectively prevented the passing of political power quickly and smoothly to party leaders.

The Weapons of Political Warfare

Finally, the reader needs to know something about how this struggle was fought, about the weapons used by both sides in this contest for political power. Repeatedly the parties embarrassed the government by their refusal to pass a new budget or their attempts to cut the budget. To counter this, the government frequently resorted to dissolution. In 1902, for example, the House refused to approve new land taxes and was dissolved six times. As an election cost each candidate from 2,000 to 6,000 yen, the government felt that enough representatives would ultimately be forced to change their votes in order to remain in office long enough to collect salaries, and to obtain commissions from those to whom their votes were of value.[6] On one occasion the House of Peers restored items in the budget which the lower house had deleted. When a constitutional issue was made of this important aspect of control of the purse, the Privy Council, not the courts, interpreted the constitution and ruled in favor of the upper house.

The notorious use made of the Peace Preservation Ordinance, until its repeal in 1898, unfortunately did not end attempts by the government to prevent adverse criticism. Public meetings were banned, and censorship of the press continued. The manipulation of elections and the use of bribery, both in elections and to secure passage of important legislation, has been mentioned. Against all this, the parties concentrated unceasing criticism of the government. Their cause was helped somewhat by a new election law in 1899 which increased the number of members of the House to 369, provided for a secret ballot, and reduced the tax qualification for voting from 15 yen to 10 yen. By increasing the number of voters and the size of the voting district, bribery of the individual voter was made more difficult and less important.

This sketchy picture should provide sufficient background for the developing situation which the Hara Cabinet entered in the fall of 1918. While it marks the opening of a new era in Japanese politics, the short-

[5] *Ibid.*
[6] The salaries paid representatives were so inadequate that it was common practice for them to receive "gifts" from vested interests, business firms, to help meet expenses.

comings of the past thirty years must be considered if one is to attempt to judge the record of the next fourteen years.

Party Government (1918-1932)

By 1918 the militarists' attempts to govern Japan had been discredited. With the formation of the Hara Cabinet it was easy to assume that Japan had fallen in line with the world-wide swing toward democracy. A careful evaluation of the main events which occurred through May, 1932, will test the validity of this thesis.

The Hara Government

When Hara became premier it was the first time a commoner had held this position. Although he was still responsible directly to the emperor, Hara was also the leader of the largest party, the *Seiyukai,* in the House of Representatives. Only if he was willing to risk a legislative breakdown by ignoring his party could a Premier escape responsibility to that party. Finally, the Premiership now was definitely associated with the Diet and removed from close association with other important governmental bodies, such as the Privy Council. Consequently, it did seem that definite progress toward the goal of responsible government had been made. These generally bright signs were buttressed by the results of the election of 1920 which gave Hara's *Seiyukai* a definite majority in the House of Representatives.

The *Seiyukai* Splits. From a consideration of this last fact one of the differences between Japanese political life and England's, for example, becomes apparent. An intraparty quarrel which found the largest bloc in the party supporting the Army's demand for a free hand in Siberia prevented cooperation between the Premier and his party in the Diet, yet Hara did not resign. Party discipline in Japan was far from an accomplished fact. With little systematic organization of political parties, party leaders held their groups together through ties of personal allegiance. Under these conditions a division between leaders and followers was apt to produce chaos. Hara's assassination in 1921 proved the importance of strong leadership. The *Seiyukai* split into two groups, the *Seiyukai* and the *Seiyu-honto,* and lost its control of the lower house. Takahashi, Hara's Finance Minister, lacking the necessary personal following, could not control the two factions and resigned.

The Hara Cabinet had not held popular support during its three-year tenure, despite its parliamentary majority. Labor problems were only partly ameliorated by wage increases in 1918-19. The failure of the Japanese delegation at Versailles to have the principle of racial equality incorporatd in the Peace Treaty irked the Japanese. Critics of the government contended that the Japanese intervention in Siberia which had continued after World War I had been presented poorly to the Western world. Despite these and other difficulties, Hara retained his personal popularity and his party maintained its control of the House. Internal weakness rather than external pressure caused the downfall of the *Seiyukai*.

Nonparty Interim. That party government did not have a firm hold on the country was demonstrated in the eighteen months that followed. Three successive Cabinets, under Premiers Kato, Yamamoto, and Kiyoura, governed without the support of a parliamentary majority. As Premier each of these men found it possible to work with a party, the *Seiyukai*. By including party leaders in the Cabinet and otherwise dividing the political spoils Kato and Yamamoto prevented the union of their opponents. Only when Kiyoura formed a Cabinet composed entirely of members of the House of Peers did the parties band together against him.

Government by the People

Kato Takaaki, head of the *Kenseikai* party, became the new Premier in June, 1924. In the elections just held, this party had won 146 seats, the *Seiyu-honto* 120, and the *Seiyukai* 101. In this government Baron Shidehara was Foreign Minister, and Wakatsuki, Premier after Kato's death in January, 1926, was the Home Minister. A coalition of the *Kenseikai,* the *Seiyukai,* and other elements kept this group in power until April, 1927.

Universal Manhood Suffrage. This unity among the parties made possible the passage of a Universal Manhood Suffrage Bill in 1925. Opposition to this measure in the lower house by the conservative *Seiyu-honto* was backed by that of the House of Peers and the Privy Council. The strong support given the bill by the general public, however, overwhelmed its opponents. The law, which was promulgated May 5, 1925, increased the electorate from more than 3,000,000 to 14,000,000 and removed completely the tax qualification of 3 yen.[7] Proletarian parties became possible for the first time, but were hampered from their inception by the provisions of the Peace Preservation Law. Another advance had been made toward the goal of a government responsible to the people's elected representatives.

General Progress. Such liberal gains were discounted to a large extent by the passage of the Peace Preservation Law, promulgated on May 12,

[7] A law of 1918 had cut the previous tax of 10 yen to 3 yen.

1925. Mass imprisonment for propounding "dangerous thoughts" could be carried out under this legislation. The formation, or joining, of societies interested in Marxism was sufficient cause for long jail sentences. The law was used in December, 1925, to break up student organizations at Kyoto Imperial University. Later it was to prove a convenient vehicle to silence those opposed to government policy.

With this exception the Kato Ministry made an admirable record. Government expenditures were cut by forcing the Army to eliminate four divisions and by dropping 40,000 employees from the government payroll. The House of Peers was reformed by limiting the number of its hereditary members and including for the first time representatives of the Imperial Academy. Social legislation, including a health insurance law and a labor union law, was enacted. Personnel policies were improved through Kato's insistence that party men without extensive administrative experience and ability should not be appointed to positions demanding those two prerequisites. In these and other ways, Kato demonstrated the soundness of party government as opposed to one dominated by the bureaucracy.

Only in the field of foreign affairs were the Kato and Wakatsuki Cabinets open to wide criticism. Shidehara had insisted on a policy of cooperation with China and the West. Such an attitude was branded by the military elements as "soft" and completely lacking in realism. The *Seiyukai,* particularly after General Tanaka succeeded Takahashi as its president in 1925, concentrated its fire on foreign policy. The exclusion of Japanese as immigrants to the United States, which resulted from the passage of the immigration law in 1924, tended to weaken support for Shidehara's conciliatory policies.

Party Government Discredited. Just at the time when party government seemed to be proving itself, public confidence in parliamentary procedures received a series of rude shocks. The most violent warfare between the *Kenseikai* and the *Seiyukai* marked the year 1926. Scandals and alleged scandals were used to discredit both the government and its opposition. Financial problems made the situation even more difficult. Both the Bank of Taiwan and the Bank of Chosen were threatened with ruin unless the government was authorized to give bonds to cover currency issued to meet reconstruction and rehabilitation expenses necessitated by the earthquake of 1923. The Privy Council realized that the public was critical of the financial measures of the government and used the scandal threatening the Bank of Taiwan as an excuse to force out the Wakatsuki Cabinet. In the handling of these problems, the lack of responsibility shown by party leaders reduced the high esteem which Kato's administration had won from the people.

Tanaka as Premier

For more than two years (April, 1927-July, 1929) General Baron Tanaka's *Seiyukai* Cabinet attempted to run the country. This thoroughly reactionary regime was dominated by the conservative and military groups, yet it did represent a continuation of party government. Only the War and Navy Ministers were not members of the *Seiyukai* which, however, had a minority in the House of Representatives. The *Kenseikai* retained its majority. It worked out a permanent arrangement with the *Seiyu-honto* and became the *Minseito* party. In a constant harassing attack on the government, the *Minseito* exhumed the scandal concerning Tanaka's alleged misuse of funds for the Siberian expedition. The repressive measures taken by the Cabinet against proletarian parties—such as the arrest of all the leaders of the Labor-Farmer Party in March, 1928, and the disbanding of the party a month later—were criticized by the opposition. Failing to strengthen the Peace Preservation Law by action through the Diet, the Tanaka Cabinet set aside responsible parliamentary government by securing enactment of the new law as an emergency imperial ordinance. The Cabinet's financial measures rescued the banks and the big business interests but placed additional burdens on the people.

Ultimately, it was the failure of his foreign policy which wrecked Tanaka's government. By becoming his own Foreign Minister, Tanaka concentrated attacks upon himself. The *Seiyukai* had insisted that Baron Shidehara's conciliatory policy toward China represented bankruptcy for Japan. The Army long had supported Chang Tso-lin, the war-lord governor of Manchuria and frequently much of North China. Consequently, in 1928, when the victorious forces of Chiang Kai-shek approached Tsinan in Shantung Province, Japan's leased territory and economic interests in that peninsula were imperiled. Furthermore, a defeat of Chang Tso-lin might endanger Japan's extensive investments in Manchuria. Japanese troops which had been sent to Shantung presumably to protect the lives and property of Japanese citizens assumed that this involved stopping the Nationalist Chinese armies. Much to Tanaka's embarrassment, the resulting Tsinan incident became more involved; Japanese forces failed to stop the northern advance of the Chinese who bypassed the city. Tanaka was forced to liquidate the affair through direct negotiations with the Chiang Kai-shek government. The ultranationalists and the military blamed Tanaka for this failure and its resultant loss of prestige for themselves.

By this time the Tanaka Cabinet was convinced that whatever it did would be wrong. If the Premier requested that a matter not be discussed, as he did concerning the death of Chang Tso-lin, the lower house debated it. Finally, unable to withstand criticism from all sides (including members of his own party) and seemingly on all issues, Tanaka resigned July 2, 1929.

Last Chance: Hamaguchi

The *Minseito* under its new president Hamaguchi, a commoner, now had a last opportunity to establish party government in Japan. The new Premier's political strength lay in his ability to hold together various factions within his own party. Popular reaction against the failure of Tanaka's "positive policy" toward China gave support to a return to the conciliatory diplomacy of Shidehara. The need for "retrenchment and reform," the two pillars of Hamaguchi's program, was self-evident.

Once again foreign affairs were to prove decisive factors in domestic politics. The success which attended the attempts of Shidehara, who was Hamaguchi's Foreign Minister, to settle diplomatically old questions with China only enraged the militant nationalists who regarded any concession to Japan's giant neighbor as a sign of weakness. The London Naval Treaty of 1930 was attacked because the principle of equality in naval armaments was not won. The extreme "navalists" contended that Japan's security was endangered. Only when Hamaguchi threatened to "pack" the Privy Council was the treaty ratified. By its China policy and its support of naval limitation, the Hamaguchi Cabinet indicated its sympathy with European and American concepts of world peace.

Hamaguchi's Assassination. Under attack constantly by rightist elements supported by the bureaucrats and the military, the government was forced to adopt stringent and unpopular economic measures to meet the world financial crisis of 1929-30. Gold exports were banned early in 1930 and a curtailment of expenditures, including those for the army, was planned and put into execution. For the bureaucrats and the military, the methods used to secure approval of the London Naval Treaty and the proposed cuts in the army's budget raised the dangerous specter of civilian control. Under Hamaguchi's able leadership party government was working; a Cabinet responsible to the majority in the lower house was in office.

On November 14, 1930, this progress received a mortal blow. A fanatical member of a rightist organization interested in continental expansion fatally wounded Premier Hamaguchi. Shidehara, Premier until Hamaguchi's death the following April, was a bureaucrat without an influential following in the *Minseito*. Wakatsuki, who then became president of the party and Premier, lacked decisiveness as a leader and could not hold the party together.

Foreign Policy in Domestic Affairs

The blow which ultimately caused the downfall of the Wakatsuki Cabinet was struck on September 18, 1931, by the Kwantung Army when its overt action brought about the Manchurian Incident. The increasing activity of rightist military and civilian elements in Japan had resulted in March in a plot to blow up the headquarters of the two major parties and to replace the existing Cabinet and Diet by a government headed by General Ugaki. This had failed, in part, because the parties had indicated some favorable interest in Ugaki's becoming Premier. A second reason was the belief in certain army circles that the move was being made too soon. Actually, an important division within the army itself was revealed by the Manchurian Incident, for the officers commanding the Kwantung Army ignored not only the Foreign Office but other army factions as well. It also was apparent that some serious differences between civilian and military extremists existed. Baron Shidehara's earlier moderation in foreign affairs thus was superseded through the direct action taken by the army. By coincidence, a break in the ranks of the Minseito, occasioned by Home Minister Adachi's bid for the premiership, forced the resignation of the Wakatsuki Cabinet on December 11, 1931.

The Last Party Government

Inukai, president of the *Seiyukai* since 1929, became the last leader of a party government. Strengthened by a resounding victory in the general election of January, 1932, Inukai nevertheless found it impossible to resume command of Japan's foreign policy, now firmly in the hands of the military. He was, moreover, unable to effect quick solutions to the problems of acute agrarian unrest, unemployment, and the sharp decline in Japan's foreign trade. In rapid succession Inoue, former Minister of Finance, and Baron Dan, the leader of the Mitsui interests which supported the *Seiyukai,* were assassinated. Then on May 15, 1932, young naval and military officers killed Inukai in cold blood. With the majority party, the *Seiyukai,* torn by internal dissension and its leaders dead, Saionji, the only surviving Genro, had to recommend the formation of a nonparty cabinet. Regarded as a temporary measure at the time, this move was the first step toward the establishment of a permanent nonparty government which was to become completely dominated by the military and the bureaucracy.

Why had the parties failed? A partial explanation lies in the firm grasp gained by the military and the bureaucracy on Japan's government by 1918. Yamagata was a formidable opponent for the parties, but he did maintain discipline within the Army. After his death, splinter groups contended with each other for power, but all army factions were united and increasingly violent in their opposition to the parties' attempts to control the military.

Repeatedly the parties aided their opponents by failing to maintain proper discipline within their own ranks. Thus, the *Seiyukai* attacked Tanaka when his China policy failed, and the *Minseito,* after Hamaguchi's assassination, did not give either Shidehara or Wakatsuki united support. Again, the leaders themselves, with the exception of Hara, Kato Takaaki and Hamaguchi, were unwilling to rely solely on the support of the House of Representatives. Too frequently politicians seeking to remain in power compromised with other governmental agencies. Such bargains became more difficult to make and fulfil as the years passed. In addition, too often the parties demonstrated to the country their own parliamentary irresponsibility; the Diet sessions of 1922 and 1926 are cases in point. Charges of corruption, together with the known alliances of the *Minseito* with the Mitsubishi wealth and the *Seiyukai* with the Mitsui interests, undermined public confidence in party government. The opportunity between 1918 and 1932 may not have been a fair one, but it was gone.

Prelude to One-Party Government

The political scene in Japan from May 15, 1932, until October 12, 1940, is an extremely confusing one. It was a period dominated by such outstanding personalities as Generals Araki and Ugaki, representing respectively the extremists and the moderates in the Army; Admirals Saito, Okada, and Yonai; and Suzuki and Wakatsuki, as leaders of the *Seiyukai* and *Minseito;* and Prince Konoe. These years twice witnessed a repudiation of complete military rule by the people in general elections. At the same time the complete dependence of the voters on their leaders was indicated; the man in the street was too inexperienced politically to organize a party dedicated to stopping the trend toward authoritarian government. As this period began, the parties first attempted to outwit the military by anticipating the moves to be made by the armed services. Ultimately, failing completely in a last-minute regeneration, the parties abdicated their responsibility and acquiesced in the establishing of one-party government.

Transition Cabinets. Opposition to the immediate establishment of one-party government came from several sources, yet the increase in influence of conservative groups including the armed services is easily demonstrable. Only the desperate fight of the *Minseito* and the intervention of Prince Saionji prevented the *Seiyukai* and the Army from coming to mutually beneficial terms after the May 15 murder of Premier Inukai. Although six Cabinet posts were given to the two major parties, this gesture by Premier Saito was unimportant when compared with the appointment of General Mutō to be Commander in Chief of the Kwantung Army, Governor-General of the Kwantung Territory, and Ambassador to Manchukuo. This combination of military and civilian posts indicated clearly the power of the military in domestic affairs. It was used to emphasize further the dissatisfaction which ultraconservative elements felt toward an unsatisfactory economic condition on the home front and rapidly deteriorating relations with the Western powers. The year 1932 also witnessed the formation of three Fascist or semi-Fascist parties, one led by Adachi of the *Minseito,* as an indication of a lack of faith in the existing parties which, according to their enemies, were under the domination of the *Zaibatsu.* Such general political unrest together with the government's failure to secure some relief for agrarian interests and a financial scandal caused the fall of the Saito Cabinet in July, 1934.

The Okada and Hirota Cabinets which lasted to July, 1937, are noteworthy for the opportunity given to the bureaucracy to govern the country. Whatever cooperation had existed between the *Seiyukai* and the *Minseito* disappeared as the latter supported the new Cabinet. The *Seiyukai* ejected from its ranks three of its members who had agreed to accept portfolios in the Okada Ministry. This three-year period also was recognized internationally as a time of crisis because the disarmament provisions of the Washington and London naval treaties came up for review.

The Minobe Case. Further evidence of the division between the two major parties was revealed in the Minobe case. Minobe, a professor of constitutional law at Tokyo University, became a center of controversy. In his teaching and writing he had advanced the theory that the emperor was only an organ of state. Under extreme pressure from the military and the *Seiyukai,* Minobe was forced to resign from the House of Peers. The Cabinet was compelled to issue a statement that sovereignty resided solely in the emperor, not the state. The *Seiyukai*'s use of the Minobe case as an excuse for attacking the Cabinet supported by the *Minseito* led only to an increase of strength for the bureaucratic and military factions.

The entire affair demonstrated clearly the tenuous grounds upon which liberalism rested in Japan. The iniquitous effects of the Peace Preservation Law [8] and constant attacks by the military on any act or phase of life termed un-Japanese had created an atmosphere which forced students, teachers, and moderate politicians and bureaucrats to remain silent.

The Tokyo Mutiny. If Japanese liberalism suffered a defeat in the Minobe case, the Army lost even more "face" in the Tokyo Mutiny of February 26, 1936 which halted temporarily the trend toward military control of the government.

In the general election of January, 1936, the *Minseito* had made significant gains in the House of Representatives; the *Minseito* had asked the voters to choose between fascism and parliamentary government. Shortly after it became known that the Okada Ministry had won a vote of confidence, a regiment en route to Manchuria followed some twenty of its officers in a bloody attempt to overthrow the government. Takahashi, Minister of Finance; Admiral Saito, Keeper of the Privy Seal; and General Watanabe, Inspector of Military Education, were killed. Premier Okada's brother was murdered in the belief that he was the Premier. To the military extremists, Takahashi's supervision of the budget and his association with the financial world had led them to believe that he exercised too much control. Saito and Watanabe had attempted to place themselves above politics and had served their country first rather than the military. Although order was restored quickly, the failure of the insurgents to surrender immediately upon receiving an imperial order to do so was another indication of the serious character of the mutiny. The Army lost more prestige as it became clear that this was a mutiny within its own ranks, directed against itself as well as against the government.

The net result, however, was only a delay in the plans of the military. Apologists for the Army blamed political and economic corruption for the conditions which permitted the mutiny to occur. The resultant recognition of the need for the Army to close its ranks against the parties and for inter-service unity which the incident emphasized ultimately led to an increase in the power of the Army.

---

[8] Passed in 1925 and strengthened three years later, this law provided for heavy penalties, i.e., death or life imprisonment for members of any revolutionary organization or long imprisonment for those found guilty of advocating radical changes in the constitution. Thousands of Japanese were imprisoned for a violation of this so-called "dangerous thoughts law."

Bureaucrats and Militarists

With the authority of the military challenged by factions within the Army and by differences of opinion between the Army and the Navy, the bureaucrats gained their opportunity to form a government. When Hirota became Premier in March, 1936, his inclusion of several party members in the Ministry did not hide the fact that the bureaucrats were dominant. There were three important groups within the bureaucracy at this time. They controlled the Home and Welfare Ministries; the Planning Board which was created to provide some general supervision of national affairs after the China Incident of 1937; the Finance, and the Commerce and Industry Ministries. Each of these groups of bureaucrats maintained liaison between themselves and the military. With the support of the military, the bureaucrats in the Finance, and Commerce and Industry departments had great influence over industrial capital.

The close cooperation between the Japanese bureaucracy and military was clearly evident in the Hirota Cabinet, whose ministers individually had the approval of the military. The Army felt it advisable for the time being to work through the bureaucrats. Its attacks on the parties were supported now by the union of a new capitalist group with vast holdings in Manchukuo and North China with the young-officer element in the Army. A serious challenge to the *Zaibatsu*, Japan's older business and financial giants, thus was offered. The parties had failed them as a means of protecting their interests, and they were forced to align themselves with the military. Very quietly Army and Navy leaders completed the final move in their preparation to assume control of the government. In May, 1936, it was announced that henceforth the War and Navy Ministers again must be chosen from the active list.[9] Any future attempt to instal a civilian in these offices was foredoomed to failure. Political parties and responsible government now could be more easily swept aside.

Konoe: Last Hope

An interim Cabinet headed by General Hayashi, the Army's choice, during the first five months of 1937 was important only because the resounding defeat suffered at the polls by the government caused its resignation. The abrupt collapse of this Ministry gave the parties one last small chance with the naming of Prince Konoe as the new Premier.

---

[9] In 1913 this requirement had been modified to permit reserve officers to hold these portfolios. Since it had been agreed that the War Minister, the Chief of General Staff, and the Inspector General of Military Education must approve all changes affecting general officers, no reservist ever had held the Army portfolio.

Konoe was Saionji's protégé. As the descendant of one of Japan's oldest noble families, the Fujiwara, he knew leaders in all classes; bureaucrats, financiers, service officials, and party men all found him equally acceptable. Despite this wide acceptance, his attempt to force the military to act through the civilian government, not in defiance of it, wrote the epitaph to his Ministry. A purely negative fight to maintain the forms of parliamentary government resulted. The trend of events was shown clearly by the new Premier's consultation with the Army prior to the formation of his Cabinet. There was no serious attempt to restore parliamentary rule. The National General Mobilization Law, passed in the Spring of 1938, further reflected the trend of events and provided the armed services with the vehicle for perfecting a wartime structure in Japan.

One-Party Rule

Between the first and second Konoe Cabinets (February, 1939-July, 1940) Japan's government was headed by three ultraconservative men. By the summer of 1940 everyone was talking about the need for a new party alignment to prepare Japan for its greatest test. Konoe even announced that his government would rest on the people and disregard the old parties. Apparently well aware of the futility of continued resistance, the parties dissolved themselves prior to the formation of the second Konoe Cabinet. The Imperial Rule Assistance Association became Japan's only party in October. As its president, Konoe had absolute authority over the organization which operated through chapters down to the village level of government. Almost symbolically, Prince Saionji, last of the Genro, who had fought so long against complete domination of Japan's government by the military, died in November. A National Economic Cooperative Council paralleled the political machine and rather strongly suggested that the basic structure for a totalitarian state existed. Politically, at last, Japan's military leaders considered the country united and ready for war. Two questions should be asked. Why had the political parties lost this battle? Why had the armed services taken so long to win?

Why It Happened

Party Weaknesses. Little that is new can be added to information previously given on the first question. The parties had consorted too long with the bureaucrats and financiers not to be suspect in the public's eyes. Gradually elements within the parties had sought support from factions within the military. In the critical period following 1932, neither major party, the *Minseito* or the *Seiyukai,* was able to cooperate long with the other. Both resisted too feebly the nationalists' attacks on proletarian parties. Lack of unity among the parties was a fatal weakness. Intraparty feuding further handicapped them in their fight against the military. In 1939 the *Seiyukai* was split three ways, a fact not likely to add to public confidence in parties. Then, too, heavy blows had been struck at party leaders. Assassination and terrorism either had removed strong men from the scene or had forced them into retirement. There were no Haras or Hamaguchis in 1940! Konoe proved himself a weak leader to carry on a tough fight. In the last analysis, the absence of mass support for political parties as an essential part of liberalism or democracy can be seriously questioned. The Japanese people on occasion had supported political parties rather than the military or the bureaucrats. This had been a choice representing the lesser of two evils rather than being based on a strong conviction that the parties espoused wholeheartedly the principles of democracy. Did men, rather than laws, still remain the determining elements in the Japanese government? Adachi of the *Minseito* in 1932 had a personal following in the party; Konoe in 1940 was the last hope for both the people and the parties. Both dealt heavy blows to the ideas of party discipline and responsible government. The confidence of the people in the leadership afforded by the parties was shaken by the demonstrable absence of these two qualities of sound party practices.

Lack of Unity Within the Armed Services. If the parties lacked unity, the military in 1932 were not much better prepared to assume control of the government. The Navy was suspicious of the Army's plans for expansion on the Continent against China or Russia. Glory for the Army would be reflected in a larger share of appropriations. It was the Navy which helped quell the Tokyo Mutiny in 1936. The Navy also had more contacts with the Western world; it was more moderate and was skeptical concerning the Army's desire to align itself with Germany and Italy.

Within the Army itself, various factions struggled for control. The two chief army groups were the *Kodo-ha,* which was extremist and anti-Russian, and the *Tosei-ha,* which was relatively more ready to work with politicians and capitalists and favored expansion at the expense of China.[10] Also, those army chiefs who wished to maintain discipline in the Army had difficulty in coping with the junior officers' groups which had close contacts with the ultranationalist societies and with terrorists. However, inter- and intra-service troubles were resolved between February, 1936, and July, 1937, the date of the resumption of active hostilities with China. The *Tosei-ha* became dominant, and both Army and Navy

[10] See Richard Storry, *The Double Patriots* (Boston, 1957), especially Chapter 6.

worked together to force financiers and politicians to follow their policy. Whether one views the result as fascism European-style or something just as totalitarian but thoroughly Japanese, there can be no doubt that the state had triumphed at the expense of the individual. From the fall of 1940 to the attack on Pearl Harbor on December 7, 1941, all that remained was to fit the nation properly into its new mold, a one-party government completely controlled by the military. After this review, doubt may well exist as to the depth of Japanese understanding of the fundamental concepts of liberalism as conceived and followed in the West.

SUGGESTED READINGS

Among the most useful general works are: H. Borton, *Japan Since 1931—Its Social and Political Development* (New York, 1940); C. B. Fahs, *Government in Japan, Recent Trends in Scope and Operation* (New York, 1940); E. H. Norman, *Japan's Emergence as a Modern State* (New York, 1940); H. S. Quigley, *Japanese Government and Politics* (New York, 1932); R. K. Reischauer, *Japan, Government-Politics* (New York, 1930); and C. Yanaga, *Japan Since Perry* (New York, 1949).

For additional general works and for studies of special phases of the period 1895-1940, see: H. Byas, *Government by Assassination* (New York, 1942); E. E. N. Causton, *Militarism and Foreign Policy in Japan* (London, 1936); K. W. Colegrove, *Militarism in Japan* (Boston, 1936); N. Kitazawa, *The Government of Japan* (Princeton, 1929); K. S. Latourette, *The History of Japan* (New York, 1947); E. and E. Lederer, *Japan in Transition* (New Haven, 1938); H. Lory, *Japan's Military Masters* (New York, 1943); J. M. Maki, *Japanese Militarism* (New York, 1945); E. Okuma, *Fifty Years of New Japan* (London, 1909); B. Omura, *The Last Genro, Prince Saionji* (Philadelphia, 1938); E. O. Reischauer, *Japan, Past and Present* (New York, 1947); and T. Takeuchi, *War and Diplomacy in the Japanese Empire* (New York, 1935); Richard Storry, *The Double Patriots* (Boston, 1957).

28

JAPAN: ECONOMIC AND SOCIAL PROGRESS

Contemporary accounts of Japanese economic and social progress in modern times were often misleading in their effusive praise of noteworthy advances. Too frequently attention was focused upon foreign trade statistics or upon a comparison between certain Japanese industrial and financial concerns and their Western counterparts. Because it became increasingly difficult to obtain reliable statistics from Japan in the years immediately preceding World War II, only accounts written since 1945 have accurately related Japan's success story in its proper setting. Very briefly this chapter will supply the necessary social and economic data to complement the political history.

Pre-Meiji Reforms

Certain changes already had been made or were being made during the last years of the Tokugawa regime. Both external and internal pressure forced the shogun's government to initiate reforms which were to be completed during the Restoration. Thus, Russian efforts, together with those of Great Britain and Holland, forced the Tokugawa to modify their attitude toward trade with the outside world and toward Japanese shipbuilding. An ever-present and seemingly insoluble financial problem compelled the shogun to consider new methods of increasing the government's revenue. Similarly, the gradual breakup of feudal society was having its effect on the daimyo, the samurai, the *chonin* (merchants), and the farmers. Daimyo were going into business; samurai were forced to do likewise. The power of the *chonin* increased. Only the foundation of society, the Japanese peasantry, waited patiently for any change which would improve their lot economically and give them more freedom. In the three decades preceding the Meiji Restoration there were further indications of this social and economic unrest. The lord of Satsuma permitted illicit trading with both the Chinese and the Europeans which provided further contacts necessary for reform. This same clan actively urged some of its young men to leave the country to study abroad. Kagoshima, the Satsuma capital, became a center of the new learning.

Confused Shogunal Policy

The shogun's government not only was unable to prevent these violations of the law, but proved equally indecisive in its official policy. While professing to uphold seclusion, the Tokugawa permitted a Dutch school to be established at Osaka in 1838. More than three thousand students were to graduate from this institution in the next thirty years; all of them learned something of Occidental ways of life. Further recognition that the old order was crumbling was found in shogunal decrees of 1831 and 1843 abolishing the guilds. Evidence of bewilderment can be seen in the government's attempt in 1851 to reinstate the guilds. After having committed itself to cooperation with the Western powers, the Tokugawa encouraged the construction of ocean-going ships and the dockyards necessary for that work. For this and the building of modern factories and iron works, the shogun was willing to borrow from foreign countries.

A Balance Sheet

A Favorable International Situation. When the Meiji reformers first surveyed their position, they found some of the preliminary work already accomplished. Other factors favorable to immediate and ultimate success must be recalled. Although always conscious of the danger of foreign intervention and control, the new rulers of Japan had almost three decades of peace in which to launch their reform program. Further, at the beginning of the period there was little Western interest in imperialism. By the 1890's, when the Powers once again turned their attention to the Far East, Japan was ready. A favorable international scene definitely was an asset for Japan's new government.

Tokugawa Heritage. In these transition years Japan also benefited from its Tokugawa heritage. As most of the reforms were imposed from the top down with little time for the people to understand or be educated, trained leaders and a united people were absolutely essential. Further, a tradition of obedience to a central government was necessary. Japan possessed all three. From a common culture re-enforced by more than two hundred years of seclusion from the world, the Japanese had developed a sense of national unity. The Tokugawa, moreover, had provided the country with a centralized administration which, at least in its early years, had imposed its will successfully on the people. In the emperor, finally, the Japanese had an institution which could be used as a rallying point for all. The fluidity of Japanese society at the time permitted men of ability of all classes to rise to positions of leadership. At the same time, the tradition of cooperative and organized effort which was a part of family, clan, and guild activity proved invaluable to the leaders and the nation. The regimentation of the people by the Tokugawa shoguns prepared the Japanese to accept the dominant role the government continued to play in their lives.

Obstacles to Reform. Many of the conditions which had been and were to be serious handicaps to the Meiji reforms are related directly to inadequate natural resources and have been covered previously in this volume. Like Great Britain, Japan achieved economic progress without many of the basic raw materials, which had to be imported. In addition, the Japanese lacked experience in the managerial field. The Tokugawa policy of isolation precluded the expansion of foreign commerce and thus deprived the nation of badly needed capital. Withdrawal from the world meant also that the people would not have the intellectual and philosophical contacts which would make them more receptive to scientific discoveries. Not only did Japan get a late start in the world race for industrial supremacy, but the foundations necessary for economic development were weak.

The Problem. That the leaders of the Meiji Restoration were aware of these facts seems evident. They knew also that the nation's economy rested on an agricultural base, supplemented by small-scale manufacturing. Their problem, essentially, was to improve the agricultural system to provide food for an expanding population while superimposing on the old economy a big business and industrial machine. To attain this objective successfully would require a master plan which would keep the proper balance among various branches of industry and between industry and agriculture. A modern banking structure, a network of communications, and an educational system had to be provided. To supply the motivation the Japanese had only to look upon China's weakness and their own inability to prevent foreign encroachments on their sovereignty. Defense against Western aggression and a nationalistic demand for equality with these same nations provided strong reasons for the new economic and social structure. After a preliminary survey of general economic progress, a few of the outstanding developments and problems attendant upon Japan's industrialization will be indicated.

First Steps

Need for Financial Reforms. A simple narration of the initial reforms, attempted and accomplished, will indicate the magnitude of the task which confronted Japan's leaders. The country first had to be brought to accept the new program. Sporadic resistance to the new order was continued by the Tokugawa and their allies into the year 1869. Rebellions of varying degrees of severity did not end until Saigo was crushed in 1877. This political unrest, resulting largely from the assumption of control by the southwestern clans, necessitated abnormally heavy expenditures at the beginning of the Restoration period. These burdens, alone, would have made the financial position of the government precarious. The state of chaos in the country made the imposition of new taxes extremely difficult, especially as they had to be new or increased taxes on land. Japan's tariff rates were limited (as were those of China) by its treaties with the foreign powers. Although its financial difficulties were caused by events beyond its control in these early reform years, Japan recognized the urgency of the problem and the need for a sound monetary system as a partial remedy for it.

A Banking System Established. Upon the return of a commission from the United States, banks patterned after those in that country were authorized in 1872 and established a year later. Debasing of the coinage was stopped, and the right of the daimyo and the merchants to issue paper money was withdrawn. In a reorganization and nationalization of the currency system, new coinage was minted and the government reserved to itself all rights to print currency. Both the minting of new coins and the printing of new paper money demonstrated the power of the emperor and the central government.

Too late the Japanese realized that their ratio of gold to silver (4 to 1) was resulting in the purchase by foreigners of Japanese gold. It was then shipped out of the country under the protection given by treaties and sold at a handsome profit. The change to 16 to 1 ratio which existed in Occidental countries was made too late to save Japan's supply of gold. Without it, a bimetallic standard was impossible and Japanese currency consequently had a silver basis. A continuous unfavorable balance of trade down to the 1880's ruined what little chance bimetallism had.

Although failing in this phase of its policy, the new banking system was more helpful in solving Japan's financial problems. A particularly severe inflationary movement between 1878 and 1880 caused a banking crisis. The result of this was the creation of a central national bank (the Bank of Japan) in 1881 and the adoption of a banking structure modeled more along European than American lines. The Yokohama Specie Bank also was founded and charged with the specific task of assisting in foreign trade and with exchange problems. Through its banks the government was able more easily to market its bonds and finance its numerous business ventures. When Count (later Prince) Matsukata became the Minister of Finance the final steps in the establishment of a stable monetary system were taken.

Banking Centralized and Allied with Government. The banking structure of the nation had assumed its permanent form by 1900. The Bank of Japan alone had the power to issue currency. Private joint-stock banks were allied closely with it. After 1894, industrial and agricultural banks were created for the sole purpose of aiding manufacturers and farmers. Many citizens preferred to make their small deposits in postal savings, funds of which were entrusted to the Deposits Bureau (established 1877) of the Ministry of Finance. By 1914 there were some 12 million depositors with 189 million yen in savings accounts. The close connection between this agency and the state is indicated by the ways in which this money was invested. Government bonds were bought, and loans were made to concerns approved by the government. Japan's small investors thus helped finance the nation's colonial enterprises and imperial conquests and so acquired a personal interest in business ventures underwritten by the state.[1] Government supervision, direction, and control were constant elements in the development of Japanese finances.

Governmental Assistance to Japan's Economy

The strain placed upon Japan's financial structure was increased tremendously in the years before the Sino-Japanese War of 1894-95 by the numerous steps taken to provide the country with communications and industrial organizations. In rapid order the government in 1869 sponsored the opening of a steamship line between Osaka and Yokohama and a railroad from the latter city to Tokyo. Two years later the state started a new postal and telegraph system.

The government literally entered, often pioneered in, all economic fields. Japanese were financed so that they might study in foreign countries; at the same time foreign technical experts were employed to advise and direct various projects. Agricultural experiment stations were established to bring new technical knowledge to the peasants. The state, through its ownership of all mineral properties, found itself in the mining business. It owned and ran model mines and leased mining rights. From the start the government encouraged foreign trade in every conceivable way. To finance needed imports it bought rice, tea, and silk in the domestic market and sold these commodities abroad.

It should occasion no surprise, then, to find the state establishing manufacturing concerns or supporting clans and individuals interested in so

[1] G. C. Allen, *A Short Economic History of Modern Japan 1867-1937* (London, 1946), p. 50.

doing. The Satsuma clan as early as 1861 had imported from England textile machinery for a cotton spinning mill. Members of this old Japanese family had made a start in the manufacture of cotton yarn, cannon, and pottery before the Restoration and needed only official encouragement and help. In other cases the state would buy foreign machinery and then sell it to companies or individuals. If, in the process, a financial loss resulted, the government justified this expense with the argument that the industry involved was necessary to make the state strong. One of the first steps taken was the creation of a munitions industry by the state. Japan could not wait for private citizens to organize this essential industry. Where the security of the nation or its future welfare was concerned, the government freely underwrote business ventures which it knew would not pay their way for years. With this encouragement, more than 200 steam factories were in operation by 1890. The government owned directly "... 3 shipbuilding yards, 51 merchant ships, 5 munition works, 52 other factories, 10 mines, 75 miles of railways, and a telegraph system which linked all the chief towns." [2] The industrial revolution was making some impression on the country's handicraft industry.

Textile Trades

In this early period the textile trades experienced complete transformation and spectacular growth. Many factors encouraged this development. Once again governmental policy based upon the drive to increase Japan's exports played a prominent role. An Asiatic market in which Japan's geographic location gave it an initial advantage offered further encouragement. The industry also was one which required relatively light expenditures for capital equipment; many phases of the work could be performed in small workshops scattered throughout the countryside. The presence of a very large supply of cheap labor which either knew or could quickly learn textile production techniques was a major asset in competing with the Western nations whose wage scales were higher.

Paternalism in Japanese Industry

The entire Japanese industrial system was fundamentally influenced in its development by a paternalism deeply rooted in the traditions of Japanese society. The worker felt the impact of this paternalism from two sources, the government and the employer. Both were aided in their relations with the employee by actual working conditions in Japan. If by Western standards the hours were long and the working conditions

[2] *Ibid.*, p. 30.

poor, they still represented an improvement over employment on the farm. For this reason women and girls were a feature of Japanese industrial life from the introduction of the factory system to the present. The barracks and food provided for the women by the manufacturer were better than they would have known at home. The low wages still permitted the worker to send home a good part of her salary while at the same time providing an opportunity for a young woman to amass a small sum for her dowry.

As long as overpopulation remained a Japanese problem, the flow of workers from farm to factory would give Japan a labor advantage over the West. This still was true in the 1930's, but competition had arisen for the Japanese from India and China whose labor standards were substantially lower than those in Japan. Paternalism, the responsibility which Japanese employers had for the complete welfare of their workers, continued strong until World War II and was to cause serious difficulties for the occupation authorities after the war. It was not an easy matter, when efficiency seemed to demand it, to terminate the employment of workers in a Japanese factory or mine.

The government recognized fully the consequences of this paternalistic policy. If, for example, a deliberate buildup of the textile trades meant the importation of foreign-grown cotton and wool and thereby imposed a sacrifice on native agriculture, the government was prepared to pay that price and counted on industry absorbing any displaced agrarian workers. The import of cotton from the United States and India, and of wool from Australia was to be the Achilles' heel of Japanese industry. If imports were stopped or Japan's access to markets blocked, the nation would be in desperate straits. Fortunately for Japan, these conditions did not arise until the 1930's.

Big Business

The Zaibatsu. The first three decades of the Meiji era were characterized by the most active type of governmental supervision and participation in the nation's economic life. In this period the control of private capital by a few families, the second outstanding characteristic of Japan's economic life, was equally apparent. A mutually advantageous relationship was established. The government needed the help of the few great moneyed families to meet various financial emergencies and to supply leaders in all fields of business activity. The *Zaibatsu* (literally "money groups") would have found it difficult to compete with the government and therefore welcomed the opportunity to work with the Restoration leaders. While the term *Zaibatsu* could mean plutocracy, it actually referred to the four giants of Japanese finance and industry—the houses of Mitsui, Mitsubishi, Sumitomo, and Yasuda. The first three groups dominated finance, industry, and commerce; Yasuda was known primarily for its banking interests. In reality each was involved in business activity which encompassed all four fields. Brief descriptions of each, with more specific information about Mitsui, the largest, should give the reader an idea of their importance.

Mitsubishi. Mitsubishi, founded by an ex-samurai, Iwasaka, was second only to Mitsui in size and importance. Its rise can be traced directly to government aid in the shipping industry in the 1870's. In 1874 the government purchased ships from foreign concerns and turned them over to Iwasaka. Both in the Korean expedition and at the time of Saigo's rebellion (1877), troops had to be transported, and the job was given to Mitsubishi. The large profits accruing to that firm are attested to by Okuma's threat to expose them in 1880. Later, as opportunities presented themselves, this firm undertook other businesses. It soon owned copper mines and refineries and had a large interest in the glass trade. The Mitsubishi Shipbuilding and Engineering Company began in 1905 to manufacture marine and mining electrical equipment. As the years passed, it aligned itself with the *Kenseikai,* later the *Minseito,* party. Mitsubishi seemed to agree more with Western concepts of world capitalism (international trade) than did Mitsui, which favored colonial expansion as the means of making the nation more self-sufficient.

Sumitomo and Yasuda. Sumitomo was a large-scale rice trader during Tokugawa days. Capital thus acquired led Sumitomo into banking, shipping, and trust activities. This family concentrated its attention, however, on copper mining and refining in the early Restoration period and later became interested in coal, steel, and the chemical industry. Yasuda, the smallest, got its start as a moneylending family in the Tokugawa period and stepped naturally into the banking field after the Restoration.

The House of Mitsui. Mitsui, largest of the *Zaibatsu,* claimed familial descent from the Fujiwara clan. Their status as commoners had been assumed voluntarily during the Tokugawa period to enable them to enter trade and moneylending. Quietly, they had joined the anti-Tokugawa forces in the 1860's. It was therefore no accident that they became prominent in the management of government finances after 1868. The Meiji reformers rewarded Mitsui generously. Properties formerly belonging to the shogun and his feudal allies were sold to them cheaply. Mitsui in this way became the owner of one of Japan's better coal mines. During the 1870's when the government bought Japanese products to sell abroad,

Mitsui was entrusted with this task and thus acquired an early interest and initial advantage over its competitors in the field of foreign trade.

The wide scope of business and financial enterprises which characterized *Zaibatsu* activity can be judged from that of the Mitsui group. The list is long and diversified and includes banking and insurance activities and the manufacture of wheat flour, rayon, woolen textiles, condensed milk, accounting and tabulating machines, storage batteries, poultry feed, iron and steel, cement, and cotton textiles. It included ownership or interests in mining companies, railways, hydroelectric plants, paper manufacturing companies, oil fields and refineries, and a huge department-store chain. The Osaka *Mainichi*, one of the most influential newspapers, was controlled by Mitsui.

The role the *Zaibatsu* played in Japan's overseas expansion is illustrated by the Taiwan Development and Tea Producing Company, a Mitsui dominated business venture. Literally this was the world's most diversified capitalistic structure. "As bankers, traders, and producers [they could] realistically say: if you don't see what you want, ask for it." [3]

In some cases the Mitsui family controlled directly by owning a majority of stock or by loans or by the placing of Mitsui men in key positions in businesses. Less obvious but equally strong control was exercised over various subsidiary concerns. The complete picture would include heavy Mitsui investments in government-controlled banks (Bank of Japan) and such business and imperialistic ventures as the Japan Steel Manufacturing Company and the South Manchuria Railway. Mitsui supported the *Seiyukai* party and tended to align itself politically with the landowning classes.

The Zaibatsu's Political Power. In general, the *Zaibatsu* provided the managerial and financial genius the government needed to carry out its economic plans. At the time of the Restoration Japan had no large middle class capable of playing a positive role in the economic life of the country. Both capital funds and experience were then concentrated in the hands of a few families. The state could use only the sources available, and in the process the power of these families increased tremendously. The "big four" found their political power growing as their economic strength grew. Originally they probably had little influence on policy-making but were rather the executors of policy. After 1905 they did align themselves rather consistently with the parties and thus, with the seeming triumph of the parties in the 1920's, their influence extended to policy formulation. Mitsubishi, for example, supported the Shidehara policy of

---

[3] Cited by K. S. Latourette, *The History of Japan* (New York, 1947), pp. 207-8, from *Fortune*, September, 1936.

cooperation with China. They opposed the attempts of the military to gain complete control of the government.

Monopoly and Competition

Zaibatsu cooperation among themselves extended to the realm of investment in banks and enterprises controlled by their members. Until the 1930's they successfully opposed the growth of powerful rivals, and actually absorbed many competitors. This was, of course, monopoly in a very high degree. To believe, however, that Japanese economy was not also highly competitive would be a serious error. Even among the *Zaibatsu* the fiercest competition existed, as is indicated by the overlapping interests of each group. It should also be noted that the Japanese retained relative freedom from the international cartels and their restrictive practices.

Further, these giants in the 1920's were invading business fields previously reserved to small businessmen. Mitsui, by loans and by forcing small competitors to accept technical advice, was bringing small business under its control. Competition existed in certain fields of industrial activity (silk, lacquer, pottery, and handicrafts generally), the products of which remained primarily for the Japanese market. Sake manufacture, for example, continued to remain in the hands of the small distillers, but the beer industry rapidly was cornered by four concerns which in turn were controlled by members of the *Zaibatsu*. Even with all its success in industrialization and with *Zaibatsu* monopoly, a surprisingly large percentage of Japan's manufacturing remained in small units.[4]

Before the Depression

Progress: The Government's Contribution. Japan's industrialization and the supporting economic organization by 1929 had made remarkable progress. This could not have been achieved without the assistance of the government and the most careful planning by both the state and big business. It entailed an increasing annual expenditure by the government which was met by higher taxes and, after 1911 when Japan assumed full control over its tariffs, by larger revenue from customs duties. It also involved a staggering growth of the national debt and the importing of foreign capital.

The government had aided industry by using the indemnity paid by China after the war to place Japan's currency on the gold standard (1897).

---

[4] As late as 1934, 59 per cent of Japan's factory workers were employed in plants employing fewer than 200 persons. Forty-seven per cent of the manufactured goods was produced by them. Almost half of the workers in this group were employed in factories with less than 30 people.

This had eased the country's international trade position. The Hypothec Bank of Japan and the Industrial Bank of Japan, both supported by the government and the *Zaibatsu,* were established to make loans available to business concerns which could take as long as fifty years to redeem them. The state encouraged the establishment of heavy industries which in some instances would operate at a loss for years.

Heavy Industries: Liabilities. Here was an example of political necessity rather than economic advantage accounting for the very existence and the ultimate success of a vital part of the nation's economic life. It is true that the Japanese had a long tradition of skill in the metalworking trades, but this was the only asset the Japanese had in attempting a westernization of the industry. Heavy industry had to be built without adequate raw materials. It faced originally the additional liability of producing for a small home market. As the change from old to new methods was made, it was evident that in these industries the Japanese would suffer from a shortage of trained man power; more scientific knowledge was needed by plant and mine managers to make the best use of elaborate technical processes. From the start it was recognized that a greater outlay of capital would be required to establish and carry on a heavy industrial program than had been needed for the textiles trades.

While full recognition was given to these disadvantages, the added strain on Japanese finances had to be assumed. Increased demands for war matériel by the armed services after the Sino-Japanese War (1894-95) and the Russo-Japanese War (1904-5), left the nation with no alternative. The Japanese were finding out that war and imperialistic expansion were expensive and might well endanger the country's financial stability.

Prospects in 1929: Advantages

Government aid helps to explain the nation's economic progress. It was, however, only one of the factors which in 1929 gave the Japanese reason to believe that they could continue to succeed in the highly competitive race for world markets against the more richly endowed Western nations. A most important asset was silk, a commodity in great and increasing demand in Occidental nations, especially the United States. As soon as the Japanese had solved the problem of producing silk of a uniform quality by the introduction of power-driven filiatures, exports increased tremendously. In 1929 Japanese exports of raw silk amounted to 781,000,000 yen; total exports for the year were 2,149,000,000 yen. Here was an industry which supplied more than a third of the foreign exchange so essential if Japan was to maintain the necessary imports for its development program. It is also apparent that any curtailment of this trade would disrupt the lives of the thousands of Japanese farmers who supplemented their meager farm incomes by raising silkworms. Japan's natural advantage in silk production unfortunately had a somewhat precarious base; it depended upon a foreign market which could be limited by the unilateral action of other nations (the United States, for example). Technological advance, as was demonstrated by rayon and nylon, was to prove an even greater danger.

Japan, itself, was responsible for other assets which help to explain its rise in economic fields to world-power status. As industrialization proceeded, the Japanese home market increased. The standard of living by 1929 had improved more than 60 per cent above the pre-World War I period. The removal of all internal trade barriers after the Restoration meant free movement of cheaper goods within the home islands. The Japanese also were developing new and more efficient machinery and business organization. There was no parallel anywhere in the world for the position held by the *Zaibatsu* in Japan's economy. Such concentration of capital and other resources brought superior organization of industry at the top, which was carried on downward through various types of workers' cooperatives. Japanese economy had retained a flexibility which permitted and encouraged innovation at a time when Western nations were beginning to think that they had reached the peak of industrial and financial efficiency and organization.

Depression and War

Effects of the Depression. Although Japan was not as vulnerable to the effects of a prolonged world-wide depression as was imagined, certain of its results taxed her ingenuity and resources severely. The export of silk fell from the high of 1929 to a low of 355,000,000 yen in 1931. The 392,000,000 yen in 1936 marked the peak of recovery for the industry. The resumption of the Sino-Japanese War in 1937 was the main reason for a sharp drop in the value of silk exports—below 75,000,000 yen. While vastly increased exports of cotton goods, the development of the rayon industry, and an increased emphasis on the production of steel, machine tools, and chemicals stimulated a sound industrial growth, they did not prevent extreme hardships for many Japanese farmers. Until Japan abandoned the gold standard in 1931, the nation was at an increasing disadvantage in purchasing raw materials. Even though the economic changes introduced after 1930 were continuations of earlier developments and thereby less disturbing to Japanese society, they resulted in a more uneven distribution of goods among the people than previously had been

JAPAN: ECONOMIC AND SOCIAL PROGRESS

the case. A rather general economic unrest contributed to the political instability so characteristic of the period.

Measures to Counteract the Depression. Japan's reaction to the emergency created by the depression proved the soundness of the planning of its leaders. As exports of silk declined, Japanese industry substituted other products such as cotton and rayon textiles. Japanese cotton goods might not have the quality of Western materials, but they were priced right for the vast Asian market. From a low of 198,700,000 yen in 1931, exports of cotton piece goods increased to 492,400,000 yen in 1934. This significant gain was made despite competition from infant textile industries in India and China. Obviously, it was registered at the expense of Western powers, primarily Great Britain. Japanese exports to the Netherlands Indies grew in volume. Not content with these established markets, Japanese businessmen with government support entered such new areas as Central America. This was one way Japan tried to provide jobs and a higher standard of living for its rapidly increasing population.

A Diversified Economy. In general, the depression forced Japan to diversify and extend its industries. Smaller commercial units did not disappear but grew in numbers. To an increasing degree, reliance was placed on them to produce for the Japanese market. In heavy industry, greater emphasis was placed on the development of the country's mineral wealth. After the Manchurian Incident of 1931-32 and the creation of the puppet state of Manchukuo, the Japanese moved rapidly to build an extensive manufacturing plant there. In the international friction created by this "war" with China, Japan's military leaders found ample reason to insist on the rapid expansion of the armament industry, including chemicals, machine tools, and steel. The nation already was utilizing its coal and copper to the fullest extent possible. Hydroelectric facilities had been developed rapidly to the point where a majority of the power needed by industry would come from this source. Even though there was a general industrial expansion after 1930 emphasis was shifted to heavy industry.

Growth of Heavy Industry. In 1928-29, Japan had imported about 30 per cent of its finished steel requirements and had exported almost none. The production of pig iron was little more than a million tons annually, and that of finished steel only twice that figure. Somehow, Japan had to cut its imports, meet its own requirements, and still have enough steel to export some to its colonies and Manchukuo. By 1936 the production of pig iron had been almost doubled, with steel doing even better. During those years, national imports of steel had been cut by 67 per cent, yet Japan's overseas empire received some 900,000 tons of finished steel from the mother country. Further, imports at the end of the period consisted largely of special steels.

Directly dependent upon the steel industry, the manufacture of machinery made equally rapid progress. The nation's economy still required more machine tools and boilers than could be produced locally, but Japan's exports for that year (1936) included scientific instruments as well as textile, mining, and electrical machinery.

Japan still needed imports of iron ore from Japanese-owned mines in Malaya, from the Philippines, and from China, and scrap iron and steel from the United States. Much of this after 1936 was used for stockpiling against the possibility of war. The nation never could be self-sufficient within the confines of Japan proper, but it had made real progress toward that goal in seven years.

An Increase in Exports: Imperialist Expansion. A general improvement in the nation's international economic position paralleled this growth of the steel industry. Between 1929 and 1937, Japan's share of world trade did not increase dramatically (exports from 2.94 to 3.47 and imports from 2.80 to 3.90),[5] but it was impressive that it showed any gains. During most of this period world trade generally was stagnant. The increases also were made in manufactured goods which competed with similar materials produced in Western countries; this meant that each market had to be captured from the established supplier. With a strong trend toward economic isolation prevalent in the world, such progress is even more remarkable. These years saw tariffs at an all-time high. Every nation seemed to prefer, or was forced to adopt, import and export quotas.

In Japan, one of the first casualties of the depression and the "war" (1931-32) with China was the abondonment of the policy of peaceful economic penetration of the Asiatic continent. To assure access to raw materials and markets, Japan's militarists launched the nation on an imperialistic expansion program. The New Order in Greater East Asia, the blueprint of Japan's economic aggression, envisaged little industrial development outside Japan. With the exception of factory centers in Manchukuo, the main islands were to serve as the industrial heart and the empire as the source of raw materials and markets.

Price of Aggression: The *Zaibatsu*. The acquisition of an empire and the military preparation necessary to protect and expand it levied heavy costs upon the Japanese people and nation. The rise to dominance of the militarists and the bureaucrats (a staggering price in itself) has been explained in the preceding chapter. In this victory over the political parties,

---

[5] H. Wakefield, *New Paths for Japan* (London, 1948), p. 78. See also, Allen, *op. cit.*, p. 151.

the *Zaibatsu* had been attacked for their close alignment with the politicians. The *Shin-Zaibatsu* (new *Zaibatsu*), which were in control of large-scale enterprise in Manchuria and were closely allied with the aggressive Army elements, had been an effective weapon in this struggle. As a consequence, the *Zaibatsu* either had to support the military and share in the spoils of victory, or face the prospect of ruin as the military, with its increasing control over the nation, could throw governmental economic support to the *Shin-Zaibatsu*.

A War Economy

Labor Unions Attacked. If the *Zaibatsu* with all their power had to pay a price, the laboring classes could expect no immunity. Specifically, they found it increasingly difficult to prevent the collapse of labor unions. After 1914 the union movement in Japan had grown in size and importance. Although manhood suffrage (1925) should have led to stronger political influence and greater bargaining power, union members found that membership in a labor organization led to suspicion of one's political loyalty. In the 1930's Japan dropped out of the International Labor Conference. Union activity was replaced generally with cooperatives, through which the government could exercise more control.

Living Costs Mount. The industrial class felt the effects of an increased cost of living. Only in the metal and engineering trades did real wages increase as rapidly as prices. Among other groups of laborers, and among farmers, real wages after 1929 either remained the same or actually declined. The real-wage index for all groups in 1936 showed a drop from preceding highs. The people felt the higher prices and as time passed were able to buy fewer consumer goods. Despite an increasing population, the nation's economy was being geared increasingly to the production of war matériel, of capital goods for an expanding industrial plant, and of manufactures needed in the colonies. After the war with China was renewed in 1937, these trends continued. Takahashi's assassination the preceding year had removed one last effective obstacle to a sharply increased military budget. So it was that government spending mounted, credit was easy to obtain, and inflation followed. With the constant expansion of heavy industry at the expense of industrial plants producing for home consumption, the average Japanese was forced ever closer to austerity. Even before 1941 the people realized the meaning of a war economy.

Agriculture's Contribution. The question of agrarian reform, or relief for the economic plight of the peasant farmer, had not been solved by any government prior to World War II. Higher prices had affected the farmer and added to the difficulty of solving this problem.

The Agrarian Problem. Essentially, Japanese agriculture represented an uneconomic use of man power on too many small farms. By 1920, despite the addition of some new lands, the saturation point had practically been reached: very little untilled land remained which could be farmed economically. However, there had been some advances. The status of the peasants had been improved by granting outright ownership of land and by substituting a money tax for one in rice or labor. The farmer now had a knowledge of different crops, better seeds, and the latest methods of scientific agriculture.

With all this improvement, Japanese agriculture nevertheless remained much the same in 1940 as it had been in 1910. Farmholdings were still small (75 per cent having less than 2.5 acres), with almost no mechanization or suitable crop rotation. Intensive agriculture under these circumstances required too much man power and the frequent, expensive use of fertilizer. Land tenure figures had increased slightly over the 1910 estimate.[6] Before the depression the peasant farmer had supplemented his income by sericulture and various cottage industries. After the depression the future of the silk industry became very doubtful because of production of nylon. The agrarian classes at all times had further supplemented their diets and income by fishing.

The Farmer in a War Economy. Without a proper perspective, the severity of the agrarian problem can be exaggerated. Lighter rents and taxes would have been helpful to Japan's tenant farmers. At the same time the relationship of agriculture to the nation's economy must be considered. The 45 per cent of the population engaged in agriculture was far too high by Western standards, yet this represented a decline of 20 per cent since 1900. Compared with other Asiatic countries, however, this percentage gave Japan a real advantage. These figures on landholdings also fail to show that the largest farms, those exceeding 10 acres, averaged only 70 acres each. A radical redistribution of land, such as was needed in other Asiatic areas, could not produce the desired results and would have disturbed the social life of the entire country.

The student also should remember that the peasants had powerful spokesmen in the Army. Politically, this was a necessity for the military because agrarian Japan furnished much of the man power for the armed services. The peasant-farmer accepted more completely than his city cousin Japanese mythology, the nation's divine mission to lead the world, and the divinity of the emperor. In a final analysis, Japan's leaders also

[6] *Ibid.*, p. 102.

realized that agriculture made an essential contribution to the nation's welfare. However primitive they might be, the farms still produced 80 per cent of the rice and 90 per cent of the wheat and other grains needed to feed the people. With imports of rice from Korea and of sugar from Taiwan (Formosa), the nation could feed itself for a long time during a war.[7] The possibility for improvement and experimentation existed, but this part of the nation's economy was ready for war.

Religion Used by Militarists

Religion, too, was made to serve the state in Japan. Here the instrument was State Shintoism, which must be distinguished sharply from sect Shintoism. Once again the Meiji reformers capitalized on a movement already started during the Tokugawa era. State Shinto became the official cult and was used to add to the respect paid to the emperor. It was identified closely with patriotism and gave a religious tinge to nationalism. Over the years it became a strong instrument for increasing the feeling of national unity.

Shintoism: The State Religion. The revival of this religion was easy, because it merely represented a continuation of religious beliefs and practices whose origin could be traced to the pre-Chinese period in Japanese history. To myths concerning the origin of Japan and its ruling house, part of Sect Shintoism, were added the worship of the nation's heroes and the imperial ancestors. State Shinto was placed under a government department different from that of other religions. It emphasized the building of shrines and supported a large priesthood. At Ise, the people worshiped at the shrine of the Sun Goddess, so intimately associated in legend with the origin of the imperial family. The shrine of the Meiji emperor was located in Tokyo. State Shinto insisted that the reigning emperor and his ancestors were divine. Throughout the entire cult, the superiority of the Japanese as a race, their divine mission in the world, and their supreme devotion to the emperor were stressed. Japan was pictured as an invincible nation.

Shintoism and Education. To accomplish this, Shintoism had its shrines in every school, and its ritual was made a fundamental part of the training of school children. By imperial edict of 1890, Japanese youth were taught that the imperial throne was as ancient as the very origins

[7] As rice was the principal item in the peoples' diet, consumption of rice per capita has significance. In the period 1935-37, despite the highest imports in the nation's history (about 60 million bushels), consumption was only 5.26 bushels per person, the lowest figure since 1900. The highest had been 5.65 bushels per capita in the period between 1925-29. By 1936, only 8.2 per cent of Japan's imports were for food and drink.

of heaven and earth. A portrait of the emperor was provided for each school. Failure to show proper respect for the imperial institution or any attempts to question the factual basis of Japanese mythology indicated a lack of knowledge of the duties and place of the person as a subject of the emperor. The state supported financially this intensely nationalistic cult. Thus was developed an instrument capable of producing the blind loyalty and devotion which Japan's leaders required.

Other Religions. The government, contrary to its attitude toward State Shintoism, at best tolerated and often looked with suspicion upon other religions. Sect Shinto, for instance, attained considerable popularity. In this religion the worship of a divinity often had its foundation deep in the mythology of the people, and it was not unusual to have new cults whose success depended largely upon the founder. On occasion, the number and the enthusiasm of the followers forced the government to attempt their suppression. Buddhism lost official favor as early as 1869 and was discouraged by the state thereafter. While retaining more influence in Japan than it did in China and India, Buddhism ceased to be the positive force in Japanese life it once had been.

Christianity's Influence. Christian converts reappeared in Japan with the return of the foreigner. Although the anti-Christian edicts of the Tokugawa period were not rescinded until 1873, the opening of the treaty ports gave the Christian missionaries their opportunity. In the last years of the old and the first decade of the new regime, Christianity gained ground slowly. A rapid gain in the 1880's was offset by dissatisfaction with Japan's treaties with the Western powers, and a reaction against too rapid change generally. This resulted in a sharp rise in antiforeign sentiment among the people and reverses to Christianity which the granting of complete religious toleration by the emperor in 1889 helped to halt. This made official the fine tradition of religious toleration which was deeply imbedded in Japanese philosophy, a feature of the life of the people still prevalent.

After that time the influence of the Christian churches increased more rapidly than the number of converts. As Japanese nationalism grew, so did the demand by the people that control of the churches be given to native ministers and priests. As the quality of leadership provided by these churchmen improved, this transfer of authority became easier for Western churchmen. The establishing in 1941 of a new group, the Church of Christ in Japan, was the logical culmination of this demand for freedom from outside financial and administrative control. It was an indication, also, of the relatively greater strength of Protestantism, which depended for support on the ex-samurai and professional classes, compared with Catholicism. Never having more than one per cent of the people as its followers, Christianity exerted far more influence than its numbers would indicate.

Education

Educational progress was associated with religion but actually was more closely related to the program of industrialization. Study abroad, illicit before the Meiji Restoration, became legal and was officially encouraged by the new emperor's advisers. In 1872 the first educational code, the basis for a system of universal, compulsory primary education, was promulgated. Within a short time required attendance was increased from four to six years and a complete educational framework appeared. The student progressed from this six-year program to a "higher" elementary school with a two- or three-year curriculum. From this point boys and girls were separated, with the former going on either to an "ordinary" middle school with a five-year course of study, or to special and technical schools with two- to five-year plans of study covering fields such as agriculture and merchant marine. Higher education involved three years of high school which were a preparation for the university, or technical high schools, which qualified the student to begin the study of law, medicine, foreign languages, art, and music, an interesting grouping of "technical skills." There were nineteen universities supported by the government. Twenty-five private universities established by individuals and organizations, some of them foreign missions, practically completed the list of institutions of higher learning.

Purpose of Japanese Education. The specific purpose for which the Japanese educational system was created was "... to instill into the minds of the people, and above all the rising generation, belief in and loyalty to a divine Emperor and devotion to a divine national mission." [8] To achieve the necessary direction and control implied in this quotation, the Department of Education had either direct or indirect supervision over every educational institution in the country. Included in its requirements were the use of uniform and officially approved textbooks and curricula, and the most careful licensing of teachers. The purpose clearly was to use education as another instrument of a national policy intended to unify the people behind a specific philosophy and policy; they were to be trained to think and act, not as individuals, but as a group.

Militarism and "Morals" in the Schools. Other characteristics of the Japanese educational system can be mentioned only briefly. The normal schools were quasi-military in nature, a feature which explains partly the

[8] Wakefield, *op. cit.*, p. 63.

success which organized military training had in the schools. Boys in the middle schools were drilled by officers and, as seniors, instructed in the use of machine guns, bayonets, and hand grenades. The teacher already had received the same training; he had also to become accustomed to the presence of army officers in his classes. One mistake in reading the Imperial Rescript on Education of 1890,[9] or one attempt to inject new ideas into his teaching might cost the instructor his position or cause his imprisonment.

Combined with this military education was a heavy indoctrination in "national morals," with the product usually being an intensely nationalistic, completely law-abiding, and technically well-trained subject of the emperor. The teaching of morals had nothing to do with religion, but emphasized rather the cardinal virtues of loyalty and filial piety which were essential in the creation of a citizen "imbued with the Japanese spirit."

After 1935 the Army openly assumed control of the educational system. The result was that more stress than ever was placed on Japanese mythology, upon heroes whose careers proved that Japan must become the leader of the world.

Education for Women. The difference in educational opportunities available to boys and girls was another important characteristic of the nation's schools. In this field the major influence was the traditional position of women under feudalism. A woman was first subordinate to her father, then to her husband, and after his death to her son. Why educate her? Although the Meiji empress, by her interest in the education of girls, succeeded somewhat in breaking this feudal barrier, progress was painfully slow. Facilities for the higher education of women were inadequate, and standards were lower than in men's schools. The government did not support a single university or college for women, whose higher education had to be provided for by endowments provided by interested private citizens. Christian missions helped here, too, but the opportunities never approached the demand. Woman's position in Japanese society had changed very little in the one hundred years preceding 1940.

Restricted Admission to Universities. The chances that a male student might obtain a university education were better than those of the female student, but were still far from adequate. The worst kind of pressure was experienced by applicants for admission to the colleges and universities, especially to the very exclusive imperial universities. This pressure was increased by the close association between higher education

---

[9] The Rescript had to be read in every school each October.

and appointment to the civil service or employment in business and the professions. There never was enough room in the select universities to accommodate more than a small per cent of those applying for admission, and male students knew that only rarely did the imperial universities accept students who had not graduated from a carefully selected group of schools. Competition was so vigorous that physical or mental illness, frequently suicides, resulted from the intense strain. In pre-1940 Japan, strangely enough under the circumstances, one of the common complaints was the inability of the 30,000 yearly graduates of the universities to find proper positions. The utilitarian approach to education and the existence of a growing class of unemployed university graduates constituted twin social dangers for the nation.

Additional Features of Japanese Education. A very brief enumeration of the other aspects of the Japanese educational system shows items both familiar and unfamiliar to the American educator. Under the stress first of modernizing the country's economic machine and later of the emphasis upon preparations for world conflict, the national budgets never were large enough to pay teachers adequate salaries or to provide enough buildings and supplies. With the Meiji emperor's exhortation in the Charter Oath of 1869 to seek knowledge throughout the world providing the official incentive, Japanese curricula always were too long and involved. There was simply too much new learning to be mastered. The Japanese had an additional handicap in their language. The Chinese characters constituted a serious obstacle, yet once learned they still were far different from the language used daily in the business and professional world. To complicate matters further, various fields of knowledge frequently required an almost entirely new vocabulary.

The student did not change his educational objective lightly or frequently under these conditions. Restricted educational offerings and a tendency toward inflexibility resulted. Once the Japanese had learned his own language, he had to study English as a secondary language to assure himself of success in many business, professional, and government positions.

Educational Progress. Despite these and other handicaps Japan's achievements in the field of education made her the educational center of the Far East. The spirit of scientific inquiry was not completely smothered, a fact attested to by the 59,000 arrests made for "dangerous thoughts" in the years 1933-35. Army control of education was onerous to many university-trained men and women whose abilities might be used in the future. The nation as a whole read widely such newspapers as those published by the *Asahi* and *Mainichi* chains. News of the world also came to the Japanese through books, magazines, and the radio.[10]

A vigorous censorship in times of national emergency made these media of communication useful in molding public opinion. Government control covered, for example, the making and importing of films, because moving picture theaters were very popular. The Domei news agency after 1937 became almost exclusively a government organization for the release of official propaganda.

Certainly, the Japanese educational system had provided the minimum training required for a modern industrial and military machine. Too often the result was mere ability to read and write; without incentive or opportunity adults frequently lapsed into illiteracy. Whether the educational system could be used without radical change to build a new postwar Japan remains to be seen. To the extent that conforming to a pattern rather than originality of thought was a primary objective of Japanese education, this might be doubted. The degree to which rebellion against the system and positive liberal forces existed was promising.

Social Progress?

The externals of Japanese society had changed perceptibly in ways other than those already noticed, but the basic fabric remained relatively unchanged after seventy-two years of technical progress.

Changes in Society. Shortly after the Meiji Restoration many of the old social distinctions were removed or annulled. In the 1880's a new national nobility was created which eliminated the distinction between the court, or civilian, and the military nobility. Theoretically, no difference existed between the warrior and the commoner classes. In the new conscript army of the 1870's all citizens had the privilege—and were forced to accept the opportunity—of defending the state. The next step, the abolition of the *hi-nin* (not human) class among the common people, was completely logical. In theory all subjects of the emperor now were equal before the law, which did not mean at all that the privileged ex-samurai would not dominate the government for years in the future. Nevertheless a peasant could always believe that a gifted son could rise to any position in the State.

The Family. The basic feature of Japanese society—the family—remained largely the same. Attempts were made, with government encouragement, to strengthen the control of the family over its members. The

---

[10] Public loud speakers supplemented privately owned radio sets; probably one out of every four Japanese families owned a radio.

family cared for its members, and expected in return that each member would subordinate himself to the group. This helps to explain the failure of women to improve their status to any marked extent. Education, industrialization with its attendant movement of people from country to city, and contacts with foreign countries had failed to change this foundation of Japanese society. Shintoism, the remnants of Buddhism, and Confucian ethics added support to popular prejudices which were instinctively aristocratic. These forces more than counterbalanced those individuals or groups who sought to liberalize existing Japanese social institutions.

Summary

Japan's extensive accomplishments up to 1940 had been achieved despite a late start from an insecure foundation. The nation's economy possessed a dual character. The base was composed of agriculture and small-scale manufacturing establishments. Superimposed on this was a large-scale business and industrial organization which political decisions had in some instances helped to create and always had encouraged. The Meiji reformers knew that Japan lacked capital resources and a large investing class. This remained true throughout the entire period. The government and a few capitalists had to take the place of the large middle class which in Occidental countries had supplied the money and the brains for the industrial revolution. In the process, more power and wealth came to the *Zaibatsu*. The surprising thing, perhaps, was the increase in the number of small business and industrial units. Japan's economy retained flexibility which constituted one of its principal strengths.

By 1940 Japan's economic progress had been demonstrated in several ways. The nation had the world's third largest merchant marine. Its foreign trade had reached a record high of 2,700,000,000 yen in 1936. If the Japanese in that year had to export a volume of goods much greater than the volume of imports received, that was a price the government was willing to pay to build up imports needed in its preparation for war. By the end of the period, many individuals were making their contributions in the fields of science as well as industry and business.

One good proof of progress lay in the nation's ability to provide a standard of living no lower than that of 1929, despite a rapidly growing population that had reached 73,000,000 in 1940 and was increasing at a rate between 800,000 and 1,000,000 a year. The pressure of finding employment for a million new workers each year was an immediate and lasting reason for Japan's insistence that it must have access to raw materials and markets. To point out that England had faced this problem at a similar period in its economic history, or to prove that China, Java, and India had even more serious population pressures did not provide a solution for Japan.

Before World War II, Japan's economic progress was threatened as much by world events as by internal developments. For continued success, Japan needed world economic conditions which would provide freedom in international exchange. Price competition and sure access to raw materials and markets were essential. While its international competitors were more interested in the preservation of the status quo, Japan's economy demanded greater production and increasing international trade. The Japanese arguments that only by force could they gain security have been discredited, but in 1940 it seemed to Japan that it was being penalized because it had entered the international trade field too late. It was ironic that the Japanese should precipitate the Asiatic phase of World War II in part to break the barriers which were strangling world trade.

SUGGESTED READINGS

Among the most useful general works are George C. Allen, *A Short Economic History of Modern Japan 1867-1937* (London, 1946); Kenneth S. Latourette, *The History of Japan* (New York, 1947); Edwin O. Reischauer, *The United States and Japan* (Cambridge, Mass., 1950); George B. Sansom, *The Western World and Japan* (New York, 1950); Harold Wakefield, *New Paths for Japan* (London, 1948); and Chitoshi Yanaga, *Japan Since Perry* (New York, 1949).

For additional general works and for studies of specific phases of Japan's economic and social progress, see: Ruth Benedict, *The Chrysanthemum and the Sword* (Boston, 1946); Hugh Borton, *Japan Since 1931, Its Political and Social Development* (New York, 1940); Basil H. Chamberlain, *Things Japanese* (Kube, 1939); John F. Embree, *The Japanese Nation* (New York, 1945); Miriam S. Farley, *The Problem of Japanese Trade Expansion in the Post-War Situation* (New York, 1940); Daniel C. Holtom, *Modern Japan and Shinto Nationalism* (Chicago, 1943); Gilbert E. Hubbard, *Eastern Industrialization and Its Effect on the West* (London, 1935); R. Isaii, *Population Pressure and Economic Life in Japan* (London, 1937); U. Kobayashi, *The Basic Industries and Social History of Japan* (New York, 1930); Kate L. Mitchell, *Japan's Industrial Strength* (New York, 1942); Harold G. Moulton, *Japan, An Economic and Financial Appraisal* (Washington, 1931); E. Herbert Norman, *Japan's Emergence as a Modern State: Political and Economic Problems of the Meiji Period* (New York, 1940); S. Okuma, *Fifty Years of New Japan* (2 vols., London, 1912); John E. Orchard, *Japan's Economic Position; The Progress of Industrialization* (New York, 1930); Edwin O. Reischauer, *Japan, Past and Present* (New York, 1947); Elizabeth B. Schumpeter and others, *The Industrialization of Japan and Manchukuo, 1939-1940* (New York, 1940); Yosaburo Takekoshi, *The Economic Aspects of the History of the Civilization of Japan* (3 vols., New York, 1930); and Arthur M. Young, *Imperial Japan, 1926-1938* (New York, 1938).

29

THE FAR EAST IN WORLD WAR II AND A NEW BALANCE OF POWER

In September, 1940, Germany, Italy, and Japan joined together in an out-and-out military alliance, the Tripartite Pact. Japan then followed this up by signing a neutrality pact with the U.S.S.R. in April, 1941, which virtually eliminated threats from the north so that it could push southward toward the possessions of the imperialist nations of the West. That Japan would turn in that direction had been suggested by such preliminary actions as the occupation of the Paracels Islands in 1938, the seizure of Hainan and the Spratly Islands in 1939, the advance into Indo-China in 1940, and the pressure which it was applying to Thailand and the Netherlands East Indies.

Throughout 1941 the United States, the one power at least potentially able to thwart Japan's designs, and Japan engaged in a series of conversations in Washington on the subject of their respective interests and policies in both the Far East and the Pacific. During the course of these talks, Japanese forces moved into southern Indochina, a step sharply protested by the United States. Japan's refusal to agree to the neutralization of Indochina led the United States to freeze all Japanese assets in the United States.

Further negotiations proved unproductive, and one hour before Ambassador Nomura called on Secretary Hull in Washington on Sunday, December 7, to denounce the Far Eastern policy of the United States, Japanese aircraft attacked the American naval base at Pearl Harbor with such devastating force that the Pacific Fleet was knocked out. The following day the United States Congress declared war upon Japan; four days later, Japan's allies, Germany and Italy, declared war on the United States. Japan's lightning blow had caught the United States unprepared and left American forces so crippled that Japan was free for months to come to assault the Pacific strongholds of the various European Powers without fear of American retaliation.

The Japanese Offensive

The day of Pearl Harbor was a busy and successful one for the Japanese military. Clark Field and other important points in the Philippines were bombed, as were Guam and Singapore, and Wake and Midway islands. The International Settlement at Shanghai was seized, and Japanese troops swept into Malaya and Thailand from Indochina. Three days later Japanese planes sent two British battleships, H.M.S. "Prince of Wales" and H.M.S. "Repulse" to the bottom.

The rich port of Hong Kong fell on Christmas Day, 1941. Hong Kong's fall seemed to many symbolic of the disasters in store for the imperialist states. A British possession for almost a century, it represented the pinnacle of Occidental commercial success in the Far East. The same day Sarawak, capital of British North Borneo, also capitulated.

Spectacular as these two victories were, they were overshadowed by the remarkable penetration of the dense Malayan forests by specially trained Japanese jungle fighters who succeeded in overrunning the Malay Peninsula with incredible speed, culminating their progress with the capture of the important British naval base of Singapore on February 15, 1942. Thailand fell after a few days of token resistance, and by June, 1942, Burma was completely in Japanese possession. After the Andaman and Nicobar islands were taken, the invasion of India appeared imminent.

The Solomons, Guam, Wake, and the Netherlands East Indies were all overrun in late 1941 or the early months of 1942, and New Guinea was being set up as a base of operations against Australia. The Philippines also fell following a heroic defense which saw the Filipinos fight shoulder to shoulder with Americans, a fact of great significance since it was the only instance where an Eastern people fought to save their imperialist masters. The story of Bataan and Corregidor have already become an American saga.

Thus, within the short space of six months, Japanese arms by a series of sensational victories had driven Americans, British, and Dutch from the Far East. The French in Indo-China and the Portuguese in Timor and Macao were the only Westerners remaining in the Orient, and they stayed only because they were so permitted by the Japanese. The significance of these smashing victories was immense, and Japanese propaganda was quick to exploit them for all they were worth. Despite the fact that Japan ultimately suffered as complete a defeat as has ever been visited upon a nation in modern times, the memory of its achievements will never be forgotten in the Orient.

Tokyo Bombed; First Allied Successes. The only achievements the United Nations were able to score during this period were modest indeed, but one was portentous for the Japanese. This was the celebrated air raid on Tokyo, April 18, 1942, led by Lieutenant Colonel James H. Doolittle. On this occasion sixteen medium sized B-25 bombers were launched from the carrier "Hornet" some 800 miles off the coast of Japan. Not until November 24, 1944, were American planes able to reach Tokyo again, but the fact that a raid could be carried out on the Japanese capital only four months after Pearl Harbor gave the Japanese something to consider, and provided a real uplift of American morale. The closest the Japanese ever came to bombing the United States itself was a raid on Dutch Harbor, Alaska, on June 3, 1942. Japanese-launched balloons containing explosives did drift to the Pacific Coast where they caused a few deaths, but their value was largely of the nuisance type.

As early as May, 1942, the United States Navy scored a victory over the Japanese in the Battle of the Coral Sea, after which came the great Japanese defeat at Midway, June 5-6, during which four Japanese carriers were sunk by American aircraft.

In the summer of 1942, the United States moved from the defensive to the offensive by launching a bold attack in the Solomons when, on August 7, the First United States Marine Division landed on Guadalcanal and Florida Island. While bitter fighting was taking place on land, the United States Navy inflicted a severe setback to the Japanese in the Battle of the Savo Sea during the night of August 9. Although the cost was great, American marines and doughboys were able to overcome the stubbornly fighting enemy, and effective Japanese resistance in the Solomons came to an end early in February, 1943. While this campaign was going on, the Japanese advance in Papua (southeastern New Guinea) was halted by a combined force of Americans and Australians.

The War in China

China's Difficulties Mount. After four years of undeclared war, China joined the United States and Great Britain with a formal declaration of war on December 9, 1941. Unfortunately, its position instead of improving underwent a change for the worse, and it became increasingly isolated as Japanese forces rolled southward almost unchecked in the six months following Pearl Harbor.

The United States, occupied to the utmost by the war with Japan and that in Europe, nevertheless granted China a loan of some $500,000,000 in 1942, and assigned General Joseph ("Vinegar Joe") Stilwell to the task of military liaison. Stilwell became commander of all ground forces in the CBI (China-Burma-India) theater and also served as Chiang Kai-shek's chief-of-staff.

The only practical route China had open to the outside world following Japan's conquest of Burma was over the "Hump," the flight across the Himalayas from India. This aerial highway was over some of the most difficult terrain in the world, but it was kept open by the heroism of the American pilots who flew it and who succeeded in delivering more supplies every month than had previously been brought in over the Burma Road. Despite this assistance, provided at such a cost, China remained virtually helpless under increasing Japanese pressure and the steadily accelerating inflation which was ruining her economy.

Extraterritoriality Ended. In an effort to bolster China's morale, and to remedy a long-standing grievance still nursed by their sorely beset ally, the United States and Great Britain on January 11, 1943, signed treaties with China calling for the immediate end of extraterritoriality and providing for the satisfactory settlement of outstanding questions.[1]

This was followed by a recommendation, in October, 1943, by President Roosevelt to Congress urging that the laws excluding Chinese from the United States be repealed. This was done on December 17, 1943. The new law set by executive proclamation an annual quota of Chinese immigrants at the modest figure of 105. This act removed an unjust stigma from the Chinese people and in general was well received both in China and the United States, although there was some muttering and grumbling in the latter over the passage of the act.[2]

The Cairo Conference. Between the time of the President's recommendation and its enactment into law by the Congress, the Cairo Conference, November 22-26, 1943, took place. This conference, attended by Roosevelt, Churchill, and Chiang, formally marked China's coming of age as a nation. A public announcement on December 1 declared that Japan was to be stripped of all territories which it had stolen by violence or greed since 1895; such territories "as Manchuria, Formosa, and the Pescadores shall be restored to the Republic of China"; Korea was promised its independence "in due course"; and a pledge was made to fight until Japan surrendered unconditionally.

---

[1] These included such things as the following: The United States agreed to refrain from maintaining troops or gunboats in China, to return the legation quarter in Peiping and the international settlements at Shanghai and Amoy to Chinese control, and to give up all special rights in both inland trade and navigation. Foster Rhea Dulles, *China and America* (Princeton, 1946), p. 237.

[2] For a strong criticism that the measure did not go far enough, see T. A. Bisson, *America's Far Eastern Policy* (New York, 1945), pp. 141-43.

The significance of the Cairo Conference was clear. The Nationalist government of China now had the complete support of both the United States and Great Britain, and the postwar Far East was to rest upon the foundation of a completely sovereign, independent, strong China. Should these goals materialize, it would mean the fruition of American policy of the past hundred years.

Relations with United States. The year 1943 thus ended with relations between the United States and China at the very height of cordiality. Largely responsible for the popular and official enthusiasm with which the United States greeted such steps as the above was the charming Wellesley College alumna, Madame Chiang Kai-shek, who paid a goodwill visit to the United States earlier in the year. She appeared to be the embodiment of China's will to resist the common enemy and captivated the American public with her radiant charm and impressive ability to use the English language. Her basic task was to secure additional American backing for the Nationalists and to promise the American people that they could count upon China to fight to the finish if only it could be given the assistance which was really its due. Following a visit to the White House and an appearance before the Senate and the House, Madame Chiang addressed a capacity throng in Madison Square Garden, New York. So convincing were her words and so charming her manner, the American public accepted her message at full face-value, even the quiet suggestion that the United Nations should do more for China.[3] Unfortunately, her portrayal of the Chinese picture did not quite accord with the actual situation in that severely beleaguered country.[4]

For one thing, the split between the Kuomintang and the Communists had begun to widen. Becoming aware that all was not as advertised, the American public in 1944 began to lose some of the ardor it had shown for China during the previous year, and the American government initiated steps to heal the developing rift in China. Vice-President Wallace and Chairman Donald M. Nelson of the United States War Production Board visited Chiang Kai-shek and pointed out to him the necessity of good relations between the Chinese factions. It was shown that a bigger question, that of United Nations solidarity, was at stake, since an open rupture in China could easily lead to a break between the United States and Soviet Russia. Chiang was assured that it remained American policy to desire a strong, independent, but united China under Nationalist leadership.

Stilwell Recalled. In October General Stilwell was recalled to the United States at Chiang's request. This action was the result of Chiang's

---
[3] Dulles, *op. cit.*, pp. 239-40.
[4] For details see Chapter 30.

refusal to take the steps urgently recommended by the American general, one of which was the unification of all Chinese armies, including the Communist forces, under Stilwell.[5] The American government's attitude in this affair indicated to some Chinese that it took Stilwell's side, and hence Sino-American relations were shaken. Nevertheless, the United States continued to back the Nationalists, who certainly were keeping pinned down large forces of Japanese which, if freed for service against the Allies in the Pacific theater, could have made things even more unpleasant.

Shortly after Stilwell's departure, the United States Ambassador to China, Clarence E. Gauss, resigned. Their places were taken respectively by Major General Albert C. Wedemeyer and Major General Patrick J. Hurley. General Hurley's role has already been described. It is enough to say here that he attempted to discriminate on behalf of the Nationalists as against their Communist opponents. Hurley's attitude was at variance with the State Department's policy which aimed at the unification of China through compromise between the two contending factions. For his efforts Hurley was widely criticized in the American press.

China Near Collapse. The year 1944 brought further Japanese advances in China. As the year closed, it appeared that China was desperately close to defeat, closer than at any other crisis during the long years of the Japanese invasion. Encouraged by their gains, the Japanese mounted a strong offensive aimed at knocking out not only China but the active and dangerously increasing American air power in that country. These American air bases were beginning to pose a serious threat both to the Japanese forces in China and to the Japanese homeland itself. By the end of 1944, it looked as if this Japanese offensive was a success, since the American air bases in East China had been cut off from their sources of supply in the West and in India. Moreover, a number of American bases had to be abandoned as the Japanese advanced. So successful was the great Japanese offensive in China that by the year's end they were able to establish a strong corridor of communications all the way from Manchuria in the north to Indo-China in the south.

The defeat of Germany in the spring of 1945 changed the situation so radically that even in China the Japanese were forced to retreat. The reconquest of Burma reopened land communications between China and India, and with the dropping of the atomic bombs on Hiroshima and Nagasaki and the belated entrance of the U.S.S.R. into the war, Japan

---

[5] A sympathetic account of Stilwell's side of this controversy may be found in Theodore H. White and Annalee Jacoby, *Thunder Out of China* (New York, 1946), pp. 145-65, 214-25.

had no alternative but to surrender. The formal ceremony took place September 2, 1945, aboard the U.S.S. "Missouri" in Tokyo Bay.

Some Other Campaigns

Before proceeding to a consideration of postwar events in the Far East, it is first necessary to glance briefly at military developments in some other Far Eastern and Pacific sections. We have already observed that the spectacular Japanese advances had been halted in 1942 and, by the latter part of that year and in early 1943, the powerful counterattacks of the United Nations forces (very largely American) had begun.

Faced with certain knowledge that United States counterattacks would be soon forthcoming, the Japanese made every effort to solidify their conquests and to organize their defenses to maximum strength. They now began to speak more and more of their Greater East Asia Co-Prosperity Sphere. Late in 1942 a Greater East Asia Ministry was created, and a very thorough and systematic attempt was made to win over their fellow Asiatics, control of whom they had wrested from the imperialist states of the West. Space does not permit a detailed study either of Japan's methods and plans or of the difficulties preventing their fruition. It is enough to note that imperial problems coupled with the mounting intensity of the counterattacks proved too great an assignment for the Japanese.

By mid-1943 the United States Navy, Army, and Marine Corps, under a superb air umbrella, were ready to move forward from the scenes of their first victories at Guadalcanal and in New Guinea. Already the threat to Alaska and the Pacific Northwest had been practically eliminated by the bloody American victory at Attu Island in the Aleutians. Here a force of 2,300 Japanese had to be destroyed almost to the last man, there being exactly fourteen prisoners taken by the victors. To describe the various campaigns which culminated in the Japanese surrender is indeed a temptation, for they represent a series of heroic actions unparalleled in American history. Since this cannot be done, a partial list must suffice: Wake, Makin, Peleliu, Guam, the Marshalls (Roi-Namur, Kwajalein), Saipan, Tinian, Iwojima, and Okinawa.

Japanese Cities Blasted. Meanwhile the Navy and the Air Force were engaged in wiping out the Japanese Navy and in visiting death and destruction upon one Japanese city after another. Some thirty months elapsed after the sensational Doolittle raid on Tokyo before the Japanese capital again felt the sting of American bombs. However, the raid of November 24, 1944, was but the prelude to a savage onslaught that left Japan reeling. In the end 110.8 square miles of Tokyo were burned out and 20.2 square miles of Yokohama suffered the same fate.[6] All other Japanese industrial centers underwent a punishment which tremendously reduced their effectiveness.

By June, 1945, Japan was in a desperate position but refused to quit. While the Potsdam Conference was in session, the United States, Great Britain, and China presented Japan with an ultimatum on July 26 which called for her immediate and unconditional surrender. Four days later Japan announced her refusal, and the slaughter continued. As Japan had asked Russia on July 13 to use its good offices with the United States and Great Britain to bring an end to the war, this continuance of the fighting bordered on the suicidal.

The Atom Bomb. August 6 a new and terrible force burst upon the scene with the dropping of an atomic bomb by an American Superfortress on the city of Hiroshima. Approximately four square miles of the city were reduced to rubble by the terrific blast, and about 78,000 people lost their lives. Russia, which up to this time had ignored Japan's request that it act as peace mediator, now informed Japan that, as a result of Japan's rejection of the Potsdam Declaration and of Russia's adherence to it, the basis for Russian mediation had been destroyed and furthermore that a state of war between Russia and Japan would exist as of August 9.

That same day (August 8) a second atomic bomb was dropped, this time on Nagasaki. The loss of life was even greater than on the first occasion. These bombings, coupled with Russia's entry into the war,[7] accelerated the decision of Japan's leaders to surrender. Although this decision had already been reached, there had been delays due to inability to determine either the exact terms or the specific method whereby they would surrender.

The Emperor Acts; The War Ends. On the evening of August 9 an imperial conference was called by the emperor acting entirely on his own initiative, an unprecedented step. Present were the Premier, the President of the Privy Council, the Ministers of War and Navy, and the Chiefs of General Staff and Naval General Staff. With only the War Minister insisting that the fight be carried on to the bitter end, it was decided to accept the Potsdam Declaration "with the understanding that the said

---

[6] Thomas E. Ennis, *Eastern Asia* (Chicago, 1948), p. 502.

[7] The Russians invaded Manchuria on August 9, seized the Korean ports of Rashin and Yuki, and took over Karafuto (the southern half of Sakhalin). They refused to honor Japan's surrender announcement on August 14 and continued to destroy Japanese for approximately another week. Among the prisoners captured in Manchuria was the Japanese puppet emperor of Manchukuo, Kang Teh (Henry Pu-yi).

declaration does not comprise any demand which prejudices the prerogatives of His Majesty as a sovereign ruler."

The United States replied on August 11 that "the authority of the Emperor and the Japanese Government to rule the State shall be subject to the Supreme Commander of the Allied Powers," a statement which apparently satisfied the Japanese since they accepted these terms on August 14.

The emperor took another unprecedented step in announcing the news of the surrender to the nation by transcription. There were a few untoward incidents, but nothing serious enough to prevent the surrender broadcast which stunned the populace. The Minister of War, a Field Marshal and his wife, and several other persons of prominence committed suicide. In addition, there were several mass suicides of naval officers, members of patriotic societies, and students.[8]

The actual surrender ceremonies took place aboard the U.S.S. "Missouri" in Tokyo Bay on September 2, 1945, with General of the Army Douglas MacArthur as chief representative of the victors under the title of Supreme Commander for the Allied Powers. The emperor's cousin, Premier Prince Higashi-Kuni, and Mamoru Shigemitsu were the chief Japanese dignitaries at the signing.

Russia and Manchuria

Concessions to Russia. In the course of the Yalta Conference in February, 1945, Marshal Stalin presented Roosevelt and Churchill with the price Russia would require to enter the war against Japan. The terms included the return of Karafuto (southern half of Sakhalin), the acquisition of the Kurile Islands, the independence of Outer Mongolia, joint control between Russia and China over the two big Manchurian railways, the making of Dairen into a free port, and finally, permission for Russia to establish a naval base at Port Arthur. In return for these concessions, the U.S.S.R. would agree to go to war against Japan within ninety days after the defeat of Germany and also promised to sign a pact of alliance and friendship with Nationalist China.

The President and the Prime Minister agreed to Stalin's terms and, it has been stated, also agreed to deliver a considerable amount of supplies and equipment for Russian troops in the Far East.[9] The reasons given for these extremely generous concessions include the following: (1) the

[8] Chitoshi Yanaga, *Japan Since Perry* (New York, 1949), pp. 619 f.
[9] Other concessions made to Stalin at this time were the dismemberment of Poland, the division of Germany into zones, the acceptance of Tito and the abandonment of Mikhailovich in Yugoslavia, together with the granting of two additional places in the General Assembly of the United Nations to Soviet satellites.

atomic bomb was still very much of a question mark; (2) the potentialities of the formidable Japanese Kwantung Army were very impressive; and (3) the cost in American lives of the island-by-island campaign to reach Japan was mounting constantly.[10]

Chiang Kai-shek was kept completely in the dark about what had happened at Yalta until informed by General Hurley on June 15. This delay was due to the fear that the news might leak out prematurely to the Japanese.[11] There was then, of course, nothing the Chinese could do about it except to try to save as much face as possible by ratifying the arrangements. Accordingly, T. V. Soong was sent to Moscow to follow up Stalin's promise to make a treaty with the central government. A thirty-year Sino-Soviet Treaty of Friendship and Alliance was signed on August 14, 1945. China's "full sovereignty" over Manchuria was recognized, and Russia promised to begin to withdraw her troops from Manchuria within three weeks after their entrance and to complete the withdrawal within a maximum of three months. Furthermore, "the Government of the U.S.S.R. agrees to render China moral support and aid in military supplies and other material resources, such support to be given entirely to the Central Government of China."[12]

As bad as the arrangement had seemed originally, it now looked somewhat different to the Nationalists since they had secured Russia's formal recognition. The hopes, however, that Russia might neglect the Communists were quickly dashed, as were those that Russia would materially aid the central government.

SUGGESTED READINGS

For the war, see: Winston S. Churchill, *The Second World War* (Vols. II and VI, Boston, 1949; 1953); Samuel E. Morison, *History of United States Naval Operations in World War II* (Boston, 1947-), a multi-volume work, several volumes of which are on the Pacific War; *United States Army in World War II* (91 vols., Washington, 1947-); United States Navy, *United States Strategic Bombing Survey (Pacific): Interrogations of Japanese Officials* (2 vols., Washington, 1946); United States Strategic Bombing Survey, *The Effects of Strategic Bombing on Japan's War Economy* (Washington, 1946), *Japan's Struggle to End the War* (Washington, 1946), *The Effects of Strategic Bombing on Japanese Morals* (Washington, 1946), *The Effects of Atomic Bombs on Hiroshima and Nagasaki* (Washington, 1946), and *The War Against Japanese Transportation* (Washington, 1947).

See also: Gilbert Cant, *Great Pacific Victory* (New York, 1946); Allan S. Clifton, *Time of Fallen Blossoms* (New York, 1951); John R. Hersey, *Hiroshima* (New

---

[10] *The White Paper*, p. 115.

[11] *Loc. cit.*

[12] The inhabitants of Outer Mongolia ultimately decided their status by a plebiscite on October 20, 1945, which resulted in a vote of 483,291 to 0 for independence! John C. Campbell, *The United States in World Affairs, 1945-1947* (New York, 1947), p. 295n.

THE FAR EAST IN WORLD WAR II

York, 1946); James P. S. Devereux, *The Story of Wake Island* (Philadelphia, 1947); W. F. Halsey and J. Bryan, *Admiral Halsey's Story* (New York, 1947); Cordell Hull, *The Memoirs of Cordell Hull* (2 vols., New York, 1948); Allison Ind, *Bataan* (New York, 1944); Toshikazu Kase, *Journey to the Missouri* (New Haven, 1950); M. Kato, *The Lost War* (New York, 1946); Ernest J. King and Walter M. Whitehill, *Fleet Admiral King; a Naval Record* (New York, 1952); William D. Leahy, *I Was There* (New York, 1950); Walter Millis, ed., *The Forrestal Diaries* (New York, 1951); Robert E. Sherwood, *Roosevelt and Hopkins* (New York, 1948); Edward R. Stettinius, Jr., *Roosevelt and the Russians: The Yalta Conference* (Garden City, N.Y., 1949); Henry L. Stimson and McGeorge Bundy, *On Active Service in Peace and War* (New York, 1948); Harry S. Truman, *Memoirs* (Vol. I, Garden City, N.Y., 1955); United States Department of State, *Foreign Relations of the United States, Japan, 1931-1941* (Washington, 1943), *United States Foreign Policy, 1931-1941* (Washington, 1942), and *Foreign Relations of the United States: The Conferences at Malta and Yalta, 1945* (Washington, 1955); Arthur H. Vandenberg, Jr., ed., *The Private Papers of Senator Vandenberg* (Boston, 1952); J. M. Wainwright, *General Wainwright's Story* (New York, 1946); Charles A. Willoughby and John Chamberlain, *MacArthur, 1941-1951* (New York, 1954); and Ellis M. Zacharias, *Secret Missions* (New York, 1946).

See also: Thomas A. Bisson, *Japan's War Economy* (New York, 1945); Robert J. C. Butow, *Japan's Decision to Surrender* (Stanford, 1954); Herbert Feis, *The Road to Pearl Harbor* (Princeton, 1950); F. C. Jones, *Japan's New Order in East Asia: Its Rise and Fall, 1937-1945* (London, 1954); William L. Langer and S. Everett Gleason, *The Undeclared War, 1940-1941* (New York, 1953); and Charles C. Tansill, *Back Door to War* (Chicago, 1952).

30
CHINA, 1937–1949: THE WAR AND THE TRIUMPH OF THE COMMUNISTS

The Sino-Japanese conflict which exploded in 1937 is discussed elsewhere from the point of view of international relations.[1] It also had tremendous effects on China's internal development, for it prepared the way for the collapse of the Kuomintang and the triumph of the Communists. The war, like a great earthquake, shook the new political, military, and industrial structure of the Nationalists to its very foundations and left it cracked beyond repair. On the other hand, the Communist structure, closer to the earth and grounded in peasant support, was able not only to withstand the war but to expand. And while Nationalist China deteriorated and Communist China grew by infiltration behind the Japanese lines, the third part of China, that occupied by the Japanese, went through a period of life in death.

Occupied China

Between the outbreak of the "China Incident" and the end of 1938, the Japanese gained at least nominal control of a considerable part of China. There followed a long stalemate until the spring of 1944, when the Japanese pushed on into Central China. During the greater part of the war, occupied China comprised about 500,000 square miles, exclusive of Manchuria, which stretched across North China and down the coast, and included most of China's great cities. Japanese control was anchored in these cities and extended along the railway line, but was more shadowy in the countryside where there were local regimes looking toward Chungking, or, more frequently, toward Yenan.

Puppet Regimes in China: The Japanese were loud and clear in their intention not to annex China. They were doing as they had done in Manchuria, generously helping some of their fellow Asiatics to attain "freedom" and participation in Japan's "New Order in Eastern Asia." Their military conquests were followed by the setting up of political

[1] See Chapter 25.

regimes with a Chinese front of shopworn politicians and a Japanese back. The situation was confused by the rivalries between various groups of the Japanese military, each wishing to set up its own tame Chinese regime in the area it had conquered. The Japanese Kwantung army brought together areas in the northwest with a Mongol-Chinese governing council. In Peiping, something called "The Provisional Government of the Chinese Republic" was rigged up with the blessing of the North China Army. After the fall of Nanking in December, 1937, the Central China Army pulled the strings for still another puppet regime. An attempt to bring northern and central regimes together under the leadership of Wu Pei-fu failed. The old war lord refused to serve and died soon after, possibly in consequence of this defiance. One reason for the rather tentative air of Japanese government organization in China in the early war years was the Japanese hope that the Kuomintang itself might repent and agree to join in "The New Order." Not till 1940 did the Japanese organize a rival Chinese government. To head it they caught a big fish, Wang Ching-wei, long "Number Two" in the Kuomintang. Wang had not been a very ardent advocate of resistance to Japan and was resentful of Chiang's leadership in the Kuomintang. Wang realized that the Japanese needed the prestige of his name and bargained for what he thought were good terms, but in the end he was only a super puppet, in constant fear of assassination by patriotic Chinese.[2]

On March 30, 1940, the new regime, a reasonably exact facsimile of the Nationalist Government at Chungking, was established at Nanking. In November, 1940, Japan formally recognized this government and entered into a treaty with it. Wang's regime was well supplied with Japanese advisers and enjoyed the special scrutiny of General Abe, Tokyo's ambassador to Nanking.

Japan and China's Economic Resources

In November, 1940, the Japanese announced with great fanfare the "Greater East Asia Co-Prosperity Sphere," in which Japan, Manchuria, and China were to constitute an economic bloc. In this design, Japan and Manchuria were to be centers of heavy industry, while China was to concentrate on light industry, foodstuffs, and raw materials. Japanese development companies took charge of all sorts of enterprises, and China's businessmen found that if they cooperated there might be small profits for them, while if they did not they would lose out altogether. Japanese exploiters were joined by Chinese racketeers, and the cities under Japanese control suffered badly. "Co-Prosperity" wore no appealing face for

[2] Wang died in 1944, before the end of the war.

most Chinese. Japanese attempts to underwrite political and economic control by "education" through the schools were ineffective.

Nationalist China

Beyond the limits of Japanese army control lay Free China, which embraced about three-fourths of the land surface and about one-half of the population of China. The less developed, less populous, less richly endowed interior provinces were the ones into which Japanese conquest did not penetrate. This area free of Japanese control was divided into two parts: those regions directly under the authority of Chungking, and the Communist regions, which were never really integrated with the Nationalist area. This division grew especially sharp when relations between Chungking and Yenan grew worse, as they did after 1939.

The Chinese Government Moves to the Interior

The course of the war until the end of 1938 determined approximately what areas were to be controlled by each of the three regimes throughout the remainder of the conflict. The Japanese soon established their domination across North China. With the fall of Nanking in December, 1937, the Chinese government moved up-river to Hankow. When the Japanese took Canton and Hankow late in 1938, the Chinese government retreated beyond the gorges of the Yangtze to Chungking with the rallying cry that "those who have blood and breath in them must feel that they wish to be broken as jade rather than remain whole as tile." [3]

The Nationalist government thus left behind the modern China of the treaty ports and took refuge in old, unreconstructed China. Over the ancient city of Chungking hung a fog which proved to be symbolic of the government's experience there. The beleaguered years in Chungking were a great ordeal. The fall of Canton isolated Free China from the outside world, and both Nationalist and Communist China had to survive largely on the strength which they found within themselves.

Economic Problems. The Nationalist government strove to make this backward hinterland into a substitute for the more highly developed areas which had fallen into Japanese hands. The modernized technicians and officials from the coastal areas had brought with them some machines and equipment, but for the most part war materials had to be produced from what lay at hand. Fortunately Southwest China was reasonably

---

[3] *China Year Book*, 1939, pp. 410-11, quoted in H. S. Quigley, *Far Eastern War, 1937-1941* (Boston, 1942), p. 86.

well-endowed with natural resources, though its iron supply was limited, and the Red Basin of Szechwan was a good agricultural area. Transport was rudimentary. To provide a link with the outside world, work was begun on the famous Burma Road. A few large arsenals and many small factories were set up. The Industrial Cooperative Movement, Indusco for short, encouraged many very small productive ventures which added to China's supply of such goods as blankets and tools and did wonders for morale. Indusco was less favored by the government in the later stages of the war when Chungking bureaucrats were suspicious of any popular movement, and its activities were further limited by the inflationary spiral. On the whole, government ownership and financing of industry were more important in Nationalist China in these years than private or cooperative ownership.

Inflation. The great blight of Nationalist China was inflation, of a dizzy and steadily accelerating kind. Heavy costs of war and the shortage of goods resulting from the industrial backwardness of Free China and the cutting of foreign supplies contributed to this problem. Raw materials trickled in over the Burma Road and later over "The Hump," but Nationalist China was almost starved for consumer goods and found only slight relief through smuggling with occupied China.

While these conditions built up the fires under the boiler of inflation, governmental policy did little to relieve the pressure. There was no easy solution: the government faced constantly mounting costs of war and industrial construction and was crippled by the loss of the customs revenue. Its unhappy answer was to issue more paper money. It did grant rice subsidies to government employees and students, but this was a palliative rather than a cure. War taxes might have checked inflation, but corruption soon set in, offenders escaped, and matters grew worse. Officials and army officers, whose fixed salaries shrank in buying power day by day, resorted to unethical practices to stay alive. Commodities were in short supply, prices went steadily upward, and the way to grow rich was to buy and hold foodstuffs and raw materials for speculative profit. The profiteers put their takings into commerce and land, while industry, which was so sorely needed, went begging for investment.

Social Changes. Marked social changes accompanied this painful economic situation. The shift to the interior had struck a hard blow at the new banking and industrial group which had been developing under the Nationalist regime. Groups with fixed incomes—teachers, students, salaried people—were in a desperate pass. On the other hand, merchants flourished and factory workers got on fairly well. In the countryside, the peasants, in theory, should have been less hurt by inflation, but most of them had little to sell at the new fancy prices, while the basic wartime tax, the land tax in kind, bore heavily on them. Meanwhile the landlords and the *nouveaux riches* used their political influence to avoid taxes and bought land with their ill-gotten gains.

Weaknesses of the Chinese Army. The Nationalist Army itself became a major item in the list of socioeconomic problems with which the government could not cope. The Nationalist Army of the later twenties had been a new type of military force in China, led by officers with good training and real patriotic feeling and with a rank and file well disciplined and infused with national spirit. To carry on the war against Japan, the Chinese government needed and might have brought into existence a large army with the same high morale but trained in fighting techniques suited to a poorly armed force facing a highly-mechanized military machine. In 1937 the army could really have become "the nation under arms." Instead, official wariness about arming the peasants, increasing corruption in the officers' corps, general inefficiency, and a disposition to rely on positional warfare instead of guerrilla tactics resulted in an army which was a rabble rather than a military force. Conscription was not equitably enforced: the wealthy bought their way out, while the poor were rounded up like animals and literally dragged away into army service. After the war the Kuomintang was to discover to its sorrow that this sort of army, far from being a bulwark against Communism, was virtually an invitation to its spread.

Intellectuals in Wartime China. In wartime China, teachers and students played a role at once courageous and dispiriting. Japan was intent on destroying or transforming Chinese universities, which had been hotbeds of Chinese nationalism. To escape Japanese control, most Chinese colleges and universities in the coastal area undertook the long trek into Free China. By the end of 1939 there was a concentration of educational institutions in that part of China which had formerly been as backward educationally as economically. There was some consolidation with several institutions sharing one campus; in addition the government set up new institutions to train teachers and technicians. Despite their intense patriotism, in Kuomintang China students did not go into the army: instead they were treated as a precious national resource—the professional people, officials, and experts on whom China would rely in the future.

As time went on, these brave beginnings were blighted. In their flight, the schools had not been able to bring many books or much laboratory equipment, and standards of instruction inevitably declined. The government rice allowances were all that kept students and teachers alive, and both morale and health suffered sorely.[4] The intellectuals were open to official pressure and control of a miserable kind. They had escaped the Japanese thought police only to fall into the hands of Ch'ên Li-fu. Ch'ên, as Minister of Education, set up Youth Corps in the schools and colleges branches of the San Min Chu I, to insure that all thinking was proceeding along orthodox lines. The students, once so valiantly outspoken, were starved and cowed into comparative quiet during the war. In consequence, the intellectuals as a group were alienated from the Kuomintang and listened the more readily to the propaganda of the Communists.

Students and teachers were only a small percentage of the millions of refugees who poured into the interior in the war years. They constituted a problem for the government by increasing the pressure on the meager supply of goods. They were also a great portent of social change. As Chinese from many provinces came together, the rough edges of dialects and customs wore off and the standard pattern of Chinese culture was cracked. These millions of uprooted people were raw material, ready to be worked on by the yeast of new ideas and new types of social organizations.

Nationalist Government During the War

The government of Nationalist China, carried on in the context of these wartime changes, was superficially much the same government machine run by the same group, but it had altered in important ways and steadily lost effectiveness. The shift to the backwoods and the decline of the banker-industrialists and the intellectuals meant that the Kuomintang tended to base its power on the relatively unenlightened landlords and merchants of the hinterland. Had the party secured mass support during the war, it might have been able to ride out the postwar storm as a party of social progress; instead it operated on a narrowed social base and followed policies which, to put it mildly, were shortsighted. Also, the great wave of popular enthusiasm at the outset of the war and the United Front did not lead to a real coalition regime; instead Nationalist and Communist areas remained separate.

In their area the Nationalists maintained institutions of tutelage throughout the war, with a few structural changes. The new organs of leadership were the Supreme National Defense Council and the Military Affairs Committee, of both of which Chiang was chairman. Chiang was, even more than in the years before the war, the apparently indispensable person: the full repertory of posts which he held varied somewhat from time to time during the war period, but among them were those of

[4] Tuberculosis became almost an occupational disease in the colleges.

Generalissimo, President of the National Government, Chairman of the C.E.C. and the Standing Committee of the party, and Chairman of the Executive Yuan. This plenitude of responsibilities made the title of *Tsung-tsai* or Party Leader, conferred on him in 1938, seem a redundancy.

Chiang Kai-shek's Role. In 1937 Chiang had risen to the occasion, accepted the United Front and stood forth as universally accepted symbol and head of China. Thereafter, though many of his associates weakened, Chiang remained resolutely opposed to any compromise with Japan, and thereby built up great moral strength and prestige which only gradually faded after the war. But the time of testing revealed not only Chiang's strength but also his weaknesses. He was determined, sincere, and skilful in politics as played in the Kuomintang, but he was also stubborn, convinced that his leadership was essential to China's welfare, and inadequately educated to face China's problems. He knew little of the West beyond what his American-educated wife could tell him, and her political influence was less than was believed abroad. He also had little idea of the process of social change which had been gathering momentum in China for decades and which did not stop—and could not be stopped—during the war.

The two books which Chiang published during the war caused acute dismay among liberal Chinese and Westerners. At a time when China was the ally of the United States, Great Britain, and other Western states, *China's Destiny* laid the blame for China's woes upon those perennial villains of the piece, the Western powers. Chiang's general view was a sort of simplified version of the opinions of many scholar-officials of fifty years earlier: the traditional institutions of China were true, beautiful, and to be preserved; to them might be added Western technical skills. In *China's Economic Theory* Chiang made the great social thinkers of China's past seem harsh totalitarians, and visualized a China in which the state controlled economic life and the peasants were soldier-farmers on collective farms. In this emphasis on war and agriculture, the ghost of Ch'in legalism walked again. Even the old-line Kuomintang group perceived that Chiang's ideas would produce an unfortunate impression in the West and, although *China's Destiny* was used as a party textbook, no English translation of it was available until 1947.[5]

Throughout the war, Chiang was surrounded by the Kuomintang politicians and generals who had been conspicuous ever since the 1920's. The jockeying for power and influence continued, with Chiang serving

[5] In 1947 there appeared an English translation of *China's Destiny and Chinese Economic Theory* with very critical notes and commentary by Philip Jaffe (New York, 1947). To counter this, an official translation of *China's Destiny* by Wang Chung-hui was issued (New York, 1947).

as "a gyroscope, maintaining Chinese politics on as even a keel as possible."[6] Chiang's inclinations were conservative: among his closest associates were Ho Ying-chin, a military politician who served as minister of war, and Ch'ên Li-fu. The "CC clique" maintained its baleful influence over party and government personnel and education, with a secret police to enforce conformity. Another secret police force was headed by the dreaded General Tai Li.

Tutelage and Democracy. At the outset of the war the Kuomintang party dictatorship had the strength which came from popular support. It was able to bring resistant provincial militarists into line and even executed Han Fu-chu, former warlord of Shantung, for lack of zeal in the defense of his province against Japan. However, as the years went on there were many signs of the government's loss of strength and popularity, and the intensity of secret police action and thought control rose in direct proportion to mounting dissatisfaction. Even these suppressive measures could not stop the ground swell of criticism, which shaped up into a demand for the ending of tutelage and the recognition of the freedoms of speech, publication, assembly, and political organization.

With the postponement in 1937 of the Constituent Assembly, the government reverted to the established procedures of party dictatorship. Perhaps the war was not the time to inaugurate a constitution, but measures looking toward local self-government and the establishment of a coalition regime would have given the government greater popular strength. Early in 1938 the government did take a broader stand by authorizing the formation of the People's Political Council, an advisory body to represent various shades of opinion. It was to consist of 200 persons (later 240), half to be chosen by various groups and half by the C.E.C. of the Kuomintang. The members proved to be mostly good middle class—teachers, officials, and business men. There was a strong stiffening of Kuomintang members, but the Communists and the smaller parties were also represented.

The P.P.C. might have served as a check on dictatorship; it contained some admirable members and was capable of giving advice from which the government could have profited. Actually it was a mere debating society which could make a dent on the party machine only when outside circumstances put the government on the defensive. For example, in 1944, after a series of Japanese victories, the P.P.C. was unusually outspoken and was allowed to hear reports on the current Kuomintang-Communist negotiations from representatives of both delegations.[7]

---

[6] L. K. Rosinger, *China's Crisis* (New York, 1945), p. 55.
[7] The texts of those reports will be found in *The White Paper*, Annexes 40, 41.

The Democratic League. As the P.P.C. became a shadow without substance, a group of small parties, nearly stifled in the Kuomintang one-party atmosphere, tried to find strength in union by forming the Democratic League. The League parties were very small, hardly more than groups of personal associates, which was natural since the Kuomintang allowed no freedom of political organization or propaganda. The six parties in the League were (1) the National-Socialists, rather conservative but in no way connected with the German Nazis; (2) the Young China party, distinctly right wing; (3) the Third Party, made up of those who had continued after 1927 to favor cooperation with the Russian and Chinese Communists; (4) the Rural Education Group, concerned chiefly with the enlightenment of the peasants; (5) the Vocational Education Group, made up of the personnel of a group of well-known vocational schools in Kiangsu; (6) the National Salvation Movement, which had done so much to express the popular desire for national unity in face of Japanese pressure in 1936 and 1937.

At the end of 1939 these groups came together to ask for freedom of speech, assembly, and publication. They first set up the Democratic League early in 1941 as an undercover organization with its base in Hong Kong, where the air was freer than in Chungking, but later in the year made it a public organization. The League worked to reconcile Nationalists and Communists and pressed for liberalization of the government: in this it had the support of many politically conscious Chinese who belonged to no party at all and wanted to see the end of the one-party regime.

Promises of Constitutionalism. Recurrent criticism from the P.P.C., the Democratic League, and liberals in the Kuomintang secured only a series of promises to end tutelage at a specified, but frequently postponed, date. Finally Chiang's New Year's Day message of 1945 pledged that Constitutionalism would be achieved even before the end of the war, and November 12, 1945, was set as the new date for the long-deferred Constituent Assembly. Otherwise there was little progress toward democracy during the war. New regulations for the government of the *hsiens,* issued in 1939, provided for district assemblies which might become training schools of democracy, but they were dominated by the vested interests of old-fashioned Chinese society, the landlords and merchants, and had to deal with *hsien* magistrates who were still appointed, not elected, officials.

At the end of the war, tutelage was still in full effect. Little or nothing had been done to prepare the people to exercise the rights characteristic of a democracy, and many Chinese doubted that the Kuomintang would surrender its monopoly of power except to some similar system which it could still hope to dominate.

Communist China

While the Nationalist Government was weakening, the Chinese Communists flourished like the green bay tree. They expanded their territory, chiefly by military means and at the expense of the Japanese. By the end of 1938 the Communists had extended their influence to areas in northwest and southwest Shansi and to an important base on the Shansi-Hopei-Chahar border, which had a United Front government. The decline in Communist-Nationalist relations which began in 1939 certainly did not stop Communist expansion, which was both an anti-Japanese activity and a form of insurance in case of a postwar clash with the Kuomintang. By the end of the war there were several border areas in North China sufficiently free from Japanese attack for Communist-sponsored governments and schools to function openly. In many areas within the Japanese lines, the Communists had less formally organized guerrilla bases.[8]

Communist Policies. This extension of Communist control under the noses of the Japanese was accomplished by a combination of warfare, propaganda, and practical reform. The Japanese, prepared to carry on positional warfare with a highly trained and well-equipped modern army, were thwarted by China's very backwardness in roads and railways. The Communists, on the other hand, were disposed by both military necessity and ideology to use guerrilla tactics by which they harassed the Japanese endlessly.

The Communist soldiers were well indoctrinated. They were taught to regard themselves as a people's army; they paid for the supplies they got and helped the families upon whom they were quartered. As a result they moved at ease in the countryside and had an admirable popular intelligence service by the grapevine route. The Communists also continued to identify themselves with Chinese nationalism, declaring in the late stages of the war that while the Kuomintang was sitting tight and hoping that the Western powers would win the war, the Communists were opposing the Japanese with undiminished zeal.

The Communists continued the relatively moderate economic policy adopted before the outbreak of the war. They enforced the Nationalist 1930 land law which set a rent ceiling of $37\frac{1}{2}$ per cent, reduced interest rates, and applied a graduated income tax. Absentee and collaborationist

[8] Michael Lindsay, *Notes on Educational Problems in Communist China* (New York, 1950), pp. 9-13.

landlords were still expropriated, but others were left in possession of their holdings subject to legal rent and interest limitations. The Communists did not hesitate to use capitalist incentives of profit as well as socialist incentives to increase production. Mass organizations of farmers, workers, young people, and children were used to spur great production drives. The Kuomintang boycott against the Communist areas meant that the Communists had to achieve self-sufficiency, supplemented only by judicious trade with occupied China. Foreign observers in 1944 thought that the general level of well-being and morale in the Communist areas was higher than in most parts of Kuomintang China. The Communists claimed that they were doing more to fulfill Sun's livelihood principle than the Kuomintang was doing or had done.

Communist Government. The Communists declared themselves to be following political policies which were democratic, in their meaning of the term. Since their holdings were islands of control in supposedly Japanese-held territory, they set up no Communist central government. Each region had a congress elected by all adults, which picked the executive and standing committees. *Hsien* magistrates were elected and worked with elected councils. Each village elected a chairman and a committee. In these elected bodies, the Communists applied a self-denying ordinance by which not more than one-third of the membership could be Communist party members. Although careful to avoid the appearance of party dictatorship à la Kuomintang, they were carrying on a program of tutelage by more subtle means. In the last analysis the Communist Party was in control in Communist China, but it was operating by discussion and persuasion to bring the non-Communists to its way of thinking. In addition to political leadership, the Communists controlled the armed forces, in that almost all officers were party members. The mass organizations used to indoctrinate and activate the rural population were an important part of this structure, in which, although there was only one political party, the nonparty majority supported the party and had an illusion of self-government.

"The New Democracy." This practical social, economic, and political program, "The New Democracy," became the official policy of the Chinese Communist Party in 1940. Mao Tse-tung, chief theoretician of the Chinese Communists, had developed an interpretation of Marxism-Leninism suitable for China. To Mao, socialism for China was still far in future: the immediate goal should be the transformation of "feudalistic" society into "the new democracy." This was not to be the democracy of the West, which the Marxists regarded as simply an instrument of class control; neither could it be the dictatorship of the proletariat, proletarians in China being few and far between. Instead it was to be a United Front regime, including peasants, workers, and "right-minded" capitalists. The government would operate major banks and industries. Agriculture would still be a form of private enterprise, though big land-holdings would be broken up. The government would be characterized by elective institutions with universal suffrage.

The essential contradiction between the existence of a party applying infallible doctrine and an electorate making choices by vote was resolved in practice by the great political skill of the experienced party leadership. Hard experience had taught them a pragmatic approach, and with both ears to the ground they were successful in satisfying the desires of peasants and workers while still adhering to the party line. They viewed democracy as government *for* the people, in which the Communist Party elite, who knew what was best for the masses, would educate them to recognize their best interests.

As its workers in towns and villages, the Communists had been able to recruit many students who, even if they were not actually interested in Communist doctrine, were attracted by the idealism, nationalism, and practical reform program of the party. While in Kuomintang China the intellectuals resented secret police enforcement of conformity, in Communist China intellectuals voluntarily put on the blinders of Marxism under the impression that they were achieving a new mental freedom. Before the end of the war, the Communists were winning support from both the masses and the intellectuals. Even Kuomintang censorship could not prevent the spread of rumor about the very different state of things in the North.

The Breakdown of the United Front

The United Front between Nationalists and Communists began to crack in 1939 and 1940 as Japanese pressure on China lessened. The most painful incident in this revival of hostility between the two parties was an episode in January, 1941, in which the new Fourth Army, formed from Communist elements, came into conflict with Nationalist troops.

Each side blamed the other, but whatever the rights of the case, there was a noticeable cooling off in Nationalist–Communist relations. The Nationalist leadership grew increasingly fearful that, under the guise of anti-Japanese activity, the Communists would rouse a mass revolution— a movement which to them was almost as unhappy a prospect as a Japanese victory. A Nationalist blockade of Communist-held areas in the northwest was established, with Hsianfu as a key fortress and large numbers of Nationalist troops engaged, not in fighting Japanese, but in watching Communists.

After Pearl Harbor, the changes in China's international relations began to affect her domestic policies. The United States was disposed to build up China so that it might be a great power in postwar Far Eastern politics, as the Cairo meeting of Roosevelt, Churchill, and Chiang in December, 1943, showed. At the same time the allies wanted China to be a real fighting partner in the war, whereas Nationalist corruption and inefficiency and the collapse of the United Front actually weakened China's war effort. Japanese victories in the "rice bowl area" of Central China in 1944, coming on top of a wave of foreign and domestic criticisms, had several results. Unity talks were undertaken, both sides presented their views to the P.P.C., and foreign correspondents, who had been barred from the Communist areas by the Nationalist blockade, were allowed to go to Yenan.[9]

The Stilwell Crisis. The obvious interest of the American government in making China a stronger ally did a good deal to stimulate these Nationalist gestures toward reconciliation. However, the Stilwell Crisis [10] in the fall of 1944 exposed some of the traps endangering the American policy of promoting Chinese unity to increase Chinese military strength. Stilwell's proposal that Nationalist and Communist armies be coordinated under his leadership might have made sense militarily, but it was mortally dangerous to Chiang's political control. With Stilwell's recall and the resignation of American Ambassador C. E. Gauss, the American government sent onto the field a new team presumably more acceptable to Chiang, including General Patrick Hurley as ambassador.

The United States and Chinese Political Unification. The new United States effort to encourage unity and reform for the sake of China's efficiency as an ally was a failure. Ambassador Hurley understood his mission in contradictory terms, which, however, simply reflected certain basic contradictions in American policy toward China and certain ambiguities in the position of the Kuomintang. General Hurley tried on the one hand to support Chiang's regime as the government of China and on the other to mediate between Nationalists and Communists with a view to the unification of all Chinese military forces. How could the American government give unqualified support and aid to the Kuomintang as the government of China and at the same time treat it as a faction which must compromise with other factions to achieve "a strong, united and democratic China"? Neither Hurley nor his successors found an answer

---

[9] Several of these journalists put their impressions in books. Among them are G. Stein, in *The Challenge of Red China* (New York, 1945); and H. Forman, in *Report from Red China* (New York, 1945).

[10] See pp. 549-50.

to this paradox. Hurley mediated between the two parties in 1944 and 1945, but outside of arrangements for Communist participation in the Chinese delegation to the U.N.O. meeting in San Francisco, nothing was accomplished. Hurley increasingly supported the Nationalist regime and refused to listen to career diplomats in the American Embassy who tried to tell him that something was rotten in Chungking.[11]

Thus the war ended with United States aid going to Chungking, except for a small American liaison group in Yenan. With conflict between Nationalists and Communists looming as a probability, American assistance to the government of China against a foreign enemy might almost overnight turn into American aid to one of the parties in a Chinese civil war.

General Marshall's Mission

V-J Day set off a wild scramble in which Communists and Nationalists raced to take over occupied China. Chiang called on the Japanese to surrender only to Nationalist forces and even instructed puppet and Japanese troops to keep order pro tem, but the Communists were seizing their opportunity. The United States decided to fly Nationalist armies to key centers and to bring in American marines to North China to help in the repatriation of Japanese. As a result, the Nationalists took over cities and railway lines, but the Communists expanded their control in the countryside—a vital part of their tactics before Japan's collapse.

In August, 1945, Hurley launched peace talks between Chiang Kai-shek and Mao Tse-tung. They agreed on "principles" but no more. The National Assembly, scheduled for November, was postponed, and civil war began again. Then in November Hurley resigned with loud charges that his policy had been sabotaged by career men in the Chungking Embassy. This explosion gave off more heat than light, but cleared the air. In December, 1945, President Truman announced a new formulation of American policy and the appointment of a new special envoy, General George C. Marshall, to carry it out.

United States Policy Statement. The policy statement of December 15, 1945,[12] was an important revelation of the nature of American interest in China's development. It still subscribed to the two conflicting objectives of American policy. The United States continued to recognize the "National Government of China" but stressed the importance of a "strong,

[11] The views of some of these career men are indicated in *The White Paper*, Annex 47.
[12] For the text see *The White Paper*, Annex 62. The chief sources for this treatment of Chinese political and military affairs from 1945 to 1949 are *The White Paper*, *passim*, and the files of *The New York Times*.

united and democratic China." The United States therefore urged a cessation of civil war and the calling of a conference of representatives of major political groups.

The Nationalist regime was not pleased by the American suggestion that the "one party government" should be "broadened to include other political elements." Neither were the Communists made happy by American opposition to the existence of autonomous armies such as that of the Communists. President Truman reiterated the idea that the Chinese should work out their own unification without foreign intervention, but proposed as an incentive that if China moved toward peace and unity along the lines of the message, American economic aid would be forthcoming.

Unification Plans. In January, 1946, the Truman message, General Marshall's great talents as a negotiator, and the deeply felt Chinese desire for peace produced what seemed to be almost miraculous results. On January 10, the Nationalists and Communists announced a cease-fire agreement. A Political Consultative Conference, including representatives of the Kuomintang, the Communist party, the Democratic League, and nonparty Chinese made plans for an interim coalition government to function until the constitution could be adopted by the National Assembly, scheduled to meet on May 5. The 1936 draft was revised and "democratized." In February, a plan for army unification, to be carried out during the next eighteen months, was drawn up. It all seemed too good to be true—as it proved, alas, to be. A few months later, the Nationalists and Communists had returned to their name calling, civil war had flared up, and further mediation by Americans and middle-of-the-road Chinese proved fruitless.

Failure of Unification. What went wrong? It is easier to follow than to interpret the disturbing course of events. In March, the C.E.C. of the Kuomintang met to consider the unification agreements, and there were stormy scenes. The influential right wing haggled over details. They had noted the increasing tension between the United States and the U.S.S.R. and hoped that their undoubted anti-Communism would assure them of American aid, regardless of whether they accepted the unification agreements or not. The reactionaries in the Kuomintang also felt that military settlement, involving the disarmament of the Communists if need be, should precede political settlement. At this stage the Communists still preferred to have political settlement precede military settlement, since they believed that in a free political situation their propaganda and program would soon win them leadership. But until they were sure that the political agreement would stick, they were unwilling to disarm lest their ancient enemies fall upon them. Dissension in the Kuomintang showed that the political compromise did not have the support of the "old guard," the Communists strengthened their military position, and the fat was soon in the fire.

In March, General Marshall returned to Washington to testify in the Pearl Harbor hearings. On his return to China in April he found that the situation had worsened. The Russians, who had overrun Manchuria in August, 1945, had finally evacuated the area with almost indecent haste, taking with them the equipment of Manchurian factories as war booty. The United States flew in Nationalist troops to take over from the Russians, but the Chinese Communists moved ahead too in the wake of the Russians. Marshall managed to bring about a brief truce but the prospects for unity were growing dim. On May 5, at the tomb of Sun Yat-sen, Chiang announced the restoration of the capital to Nanking after the long years of the war, but he was not able to announce a meeting of the National Assembly. It had been postponed again while the Kuomintang continued to hedge on details of coalition government. Another unfavorable omen was the revival of drastic methods to silence critics of the Kuomintang: two leaders of the Democratic League were assassinated in July.

While the plans for a strong, united, democratic China which the United States had sponsored were breaking down, American aid [13] was continuing to come to the government of China, alias the Kuomintang. In July, Mme. Sun said what was in the minds of many Chinese when she urged that the United States withdraw its troops and terminate its aid to the Nationalists lest it underwrite civil war which might lead to an American-Russian struggle with China as the battleground. In the same month, Dr. John Leighton Stuart, for many years president of Yenching University, became American Ambassador to China. The ambivalence of American policy was only too well illustrated by the fact that in August, just as Marshall and Stuart were engaged in important negotiations looking toward a compromise, the sale at bargain rates of a quantity of war surplus to the Nanking government was announced.

The Communists now grew vituperatively critical of American policy: their radio poured forth denunciation of "American imperialism" and of the "Nanking puppets" whom it was manipulating. When the National Assembly finally met in November, Communists boycotted it. From the Democratic League, only the Young China party and the Social Democrats participated. On December 25, 1946, the Assembly adopted a revision of the 1936 draft constitution, to come into effect a year later. In the meantime a "coalition" government (which under the circumstances

[13] See p. 606.

could only mean Kuomintang plus a few Young China and Social Democratic members to save face) would function. Tutelage was supposed to be at an end; but there was no rejoicing, for it was clear that the major experience ahead of China was not constitutional government but civil war.

General Marshall's Withdrawal

In January, 1947, General Marshall returned to the United States to become Secretary of State. His Chinese mission had failed, despite his own very able efforts. There has been a disposition in some quarters to blame not only that failure but all later events in China on the course of American policy in the years from 1944 to 1946. American policy was self-contradictory and thus helped to defeat its own objectives and contributed unintentionally to the victory of the Communists. But, as General Marshall recognized in his parting statement,[14] the major factors causing the breakdown of the negotiations and eventually the collapse of the Kuomintang were internally Chinese. The greatest obstacle to peace was "the complete and overwhelming suspicion with which the Communist Party and the Kuomintang regard each other." More than skilled mediation was needed to establish even the minimum of mutual confidence. As to "the liberals in the Government and in the minority parties" whom Marshall praised, they were limited in influence, and lacking in the military support without which no Chinese political group could survive. Finally, the Kuomintang was no longer able to comprehend and shape the tendency of Chinese development. It had ceased to be a revolutionary party, but China was still a nation in revolution. "The reactionaries in the Government" who, to quote General Marshall, "have evidently counted on substantial American support regardless of their actions" had grievously misjudged the situation. The Kuomintang faced not war, but revolution, and all America's horses and men could not put the Kuomintang back again. The State Department under Marshall's headship realized this well, and American aid to China thereafter reflected American political tensions rather than any conviction on the part of the Truman administration that it could do much good.

The Military and Political Situation 1946–1947

At the time of General Marshall's departure, the leaders of the Kuomintang were still confident of victory. Through early 1947 they continued to make military gains. They had cleared most of the major railways and retaken considerable areas in North China, including Yenan, the Com-

[14] The text of this statement is given in *The White Paper*, Annex 113.

munist capital. However, the Nationalist government was following in the footsteps of Japan in its techniques of war-making: it attached excessive prestige to taking cities, but could not control the countryside around them. Also, it was overextending itself, especially in Manchuria, where it committed its best, American-trained troops, and eventually lost them. The morale of the Nationalist armies was low and the economic situation grew worse, with a budget continuously unbalanced by the costs of civil war. Other debit items on the Kuomintang ledger included continued official corruption and incompetence, peasant resentment against conscription and the land tax in kind, and the dislike of the inhabitants of newly retaken areas for Nationalist civil and military officers who often behaved like carpet baggers.[15]

The Communists, on the other hand, were proceeding on much the same lines which had brought them success during the war, except that they were harsher toward landlords, bitterly anti-American, and drawing closer to the U.S.S.R. They used against the Nationalists the inexpensive, mobile, unsuppressible style of warfare they had used against the Japanese, and, in addition, were increasingly able to oppose the Kuomintang in formal, positional conflict. By the end of 1947 the military balance was shifting: the Communists had isolated Mukden and held the rest of Manchuria, were pushing back government troops in North China, and had built up a force in Central China pointing toward the Yangtze.

Political affairs were also going badly for the Nationalists. The transitional "coalition" regime fooled no one: the Kuomintang still held power in the areas under its control. The student group, that sure barometer of general sentiment, broke out in demonstrations against civil war and in favor of strong economic measures. There was popular loss of faith in the government, which seemed to lack competent statesmanship to meet the crisis. Meetings of the C.E.C. and the State Council in June and July produced nothing more helpful than a declaration that the Communists were in open rebellion. General Wedemeyer's fact-finding mission of that summer did not bring back to the American government an encouraging picture of the Nanking government's progress and left Nationalist stalwarts doubtful of the further extensive aid from the United States which they had been counting on as a way out of their difficulties.[16]

The elections for the new National Assembly, held late in 1947, pro-

---

[15] Taiwan (Formosa) was a case in point. In September, 1945, Chinese forces took over the island. The new governor, Chên Yi, a close associate of Chiang Kai-shek, gave an outstanding demonstration of venality and graft, and in February, 1947, there was a major rebellion which had to be suppressed by force. Face was saved by an investigation which cleared Chên; thereafter a more decent regime was set up. *The White Paper*, pp. 307-10.

[16] For the Wedemeyer report and related documents, see *The White Paper*, Annexes 133, 134, 135.

vided a sad commentary on the coming of "democracy." To maintain the "coalition," the government had promised the little parties blocks of seats out of all proportion to their popular strength. When it became apparent that the voters had not done right by the little parties, the government, in the name of democracy, asked properly elected (and greatly annoyed) Kuomintang members to withdraw in favor of defeated candidates of the little brothers in the coalition.

Events of 1948

Nineteen hundred and forty-eight was a year of disaster for the Nationalists. The new National Assembly met in March in a mood of rebellion against Chiang's leadership and the influence of the C.C. clique. After some show of reluctance, Chiang agreed to run for the presidency and was duly elected, but the Assembly chose as vice-president Li Tsung-jen, one of the Kwangsi generals who had often been at outs with Chiang and was now the white hope of the reform forces. However, the reform movement soon fizzled out. Chiang still controlled the army and the treasury, and the Ch'ên brothers the party machine, and Li was powerless against them.

An effort to halt skyrocketing inflation by setting up a new currency and instituting action against hoarders and profiteers failed and the new gold yuan (dollar) soon went the way of its predecessors. As to the military situation, Chiang, in April, assured the assembly that the Communists would be driven north of the Yellow River in six months: events painfully demonstrated his fallibility as a prophet and as a general.

With their recapture of Yenan in April, 1948, the Communists began a series of impressive victories. So many government officers and soldiers deserted to the Communists, taking their American equipment with them, that the Communists began to refer cheerfully to "Supply Sergeant Chiang." Toward the end of the year, Mukden fell almost without a blow, and the Nationalists lost not only a rich area but their best forces.

Collapse of the Nationalist Government

By the end of the year the Nanking government was in a desperate state. Chiang, who had been put at the head of a Communist list of war criminals, would no doubt be an obstacle to any negotiations with the Communists and his retirement was desired and even expected by many. His eagerly awaited New Year's Day message [17] was a bitter disappointment: he did not retire, and he referred to the possibility of negotiations

---

[17] For the text, see *The White Paper*, Annex 167.

in the tones of one even now willing to forgive and forget if the sinners would return to the fold on the government's terms.

The initiative now rested with the Communists. Their control in the north was rounded out in January by the acquisition of Tientsin and Peking. They were already talking of the creation of a United Front government appropriate to "The New Democracy." It was therefore no surprise that Mao's retort to Chiang's New Year's Day speech was a blast which stated a peace program amounting to unconditional surrender.

Li Tsung-jen as Acting President. On January 26, 1949, Chiang announced that he would retire to his birthplace in Chekiang, leaving Vice-President Li to function as Acting President. It was too late for Li to carry through the reform program on which he had been elected less than a year before. The Kuomintang was far gone in disintegration. On February 5, most of the government offices moved to Canton, and thereafter the "Canton group" were disinclined to cooperate with Li, who remained in Nanking. Li also found it hard to get the backing of the Kuomintang bureaucracy and the Whampoa generals, since Chiang from his retirement constantly interfered in political affairs. The crowning difficulty was that the government treasury and a stockpile of military equipment were shifted to Formosa, where Chiang proposed to make a last-ditch stand. In April a Nationalist delegation went to Peking to negotiate. Although cordially received—so cordially that some of its members went over to the Communists—the members found that the Communist terms were still very stiff, including punishment of the "four families"—Chiang, Soong, K'ung, and Ch'ên, and an unopposed crossing of the Yangtze by Communist forces to "reorganize" Nationalist troops. In the end the Communists prepared a draft agreement, the Nationalist government refused to submit, and at midnight, April 20, Communist troops crossed the Yangtze with almost no opposition. Li and his fellow officials left Nanking on April 23; the Communists took the city the next day.

Nationalist Defeats. Thereafter it was a record of continuing Nationalist defeats. Canton had become the Nationalist capital once more, and Nationalist leaders back in the city where Sun had formulated his principles and Borodin had reshaped the Kuomintang must have had strange reflections indeed. How long the Nationalists could hold out in Canton depended chiefly on how fast the Communists wanted to move. They had been accumulating provinces much more rapidly than they could digest them. The Communist advance halted for a time in the early fall, but on October 15, Canton fell and the Nationalist government shifted to Chungking. Chiang had come to the mainland to inspire the defense, but it was no use. Chungking was lost on November 30. On December 8, Taipei, in

Formosa, became the Nationalist capital. Heaven had withdrawn its mandate, and whatever changes international relations in the Far East might produce, it seemed unlikely that the Nationalists could ever again constitute a government to which the mass of the Chinese people would give their support.

SUGGESTED READINGS

Two translations of Chiang Kai-shek's *China's Destiny,* are available. The official translation is by Wang Ch'ung-hui and has an introduction by Lin Yu-tang (New York, 1947). The other, which also contains Chiang's *Chinese Economic Theories,* has hostile notes and commentary by Philip Jaffe (New York, 1947). For writings of Mao Tse-tung see *China's New Democracy* (New York, 1945) and *Selected Works of Mao Tse-tung* (3 vols., London, 1954). *United States Relations with China with Special Reference to the Period 1944–1949* (Washington, 1949), known as "The White Paper," is full of theretofore secret documents from the files of the Department of State.

Among the many books about China during and since the war, the following are especially helpful: Harold S. Quigley, *Far Eastern War, 1937–1941* (Boston, 1942); two works by Lawrence K. Rosinger, *China's Wartime Politics, 1937–1944* (Princeton, 1945) and *China's Crisis* (New York, 1945); P. M. A. Linebarger, *The China of Chiang Kai-shek* (Boston, 1941); John K. Fairbank, *The United States and China* (Cambridge, Mass., 1958), which discusses recent changes in China against the background of an analysis of Chinese history; Michael Lindsay, *Notes on Educational Policies in Communist China* (Cambridge, Mass., 1950).

Other useful works are: David Nelson Rowe, *China among the Powers* (New York, 1945), a realistic assessment of China's resources; Ch'ien Tuan-sheng, *The Government and Politics of China* (Cambridge, Mass., 1950); Lin Mou-sheng, *Chungking Dialogue* (New York, 1945); Theodore White and Annalee Jacoby, *Thunder over China* (New York, 1946); Benjamin Schwartz, *Chinese Communism and the Rise of Mao* (Cambridge, Mass., 1951).

31

JAPAN SINCE PEARL HARBOR

The choice of General Tojo Hideki as Premier, on October 18, 1941, was an evidence of the political triumph of the extremist faction among the military over those favoring continuing negotiation with the United States and an indication of closer alignment with the Axis powers. Tojo and his advisers believed that the United States was incapable of fighting a prolonged war and could brought to surrender after suffering swift, initial defeats. The Tojo government also deluded itself into believing that Japan's physical and spiritual resources were sufficient to warrant broadening of the scope of the war with China to include the United States, Great Britain, and if necessary, the Soviet Union. Pearl Harbor, December 7, 1941, started the Japanese on the road to disaster.

The Tojo Government

A Totalitarian Regime. During 1942, a year of almost unparalleled victories, Tojo concentrated upon completing the totalitarian political and economic structure which he believed necessary for the conduct of the war. His control over the Army was facilitated by the extensive dossier on officer personnel he had started in 1935 when he was chief of *gendarmerie* in Manchuria. Early in 1942 he organized the Imperial Rule Assistance Youth Corps to assist in eliminating dissident elements. This was followed by the formation of similar organizations for women and for various industries. In the election of representatives to the lower house in the spring of 1942, large contributions from army emergency funds to the campaign expenses of government-sponsored candidates helped to secure a government majority of 381 out of the total house membership of 466.

Not till 1943 did Tojo think it necessary to improve on this demonstration of national solidarity. The Premier's powers were then strengthened so that he had virtually dictatorial authority over the allocation of labor, raw materials, power, and capital. The creation of a Munitions Ministry later that year was an attempt to combine the work of several ministries and thus increase war production, particularly the manufacture of aircraft.

During this year, too, local governments were drawn more completely under the control of the Tokyo government. The Home Minister was empowered to appoint mayors for the cities, and prefectural governors were empowered to approve elected mayors of towns and villages. Finally, in July, 1943, Japan proper was divided into eight districts each with an administrative council to coordinate many financial and economic activities. One of the by-products of the reorganization was the loss by Tokyo of its independent municipal government.

By such methods the Tojo Cabinet tightened its grip on all government agencies. Rigid censorship and the suppression of freedom of speech stifled criticism and overt unrest. In the summer of 1943, Tojo could tell the Emperor that his government had full popular support.

Dissatisfaction with Tojo Cabinet. There is now abundant evidence that this was not true. Shortly after the defeat at Midway, June 5–6, 1942, the *Mainichi*'s headline was "War Cannot Be Won by Bamboo Spears,"[1] an obvious jibe at the government's reliance on "spiritual" superiority instead of the greater attention to scientific warfare and a better supply of planes which the Navy was urging.

Even among ultranationalist groups there was some willingness to consider a negotiated peace. An attempt by Nakano, leader of the *Tohokai*, to induce Tojo to consider a negotiated peace just after the fall of Singapore in February, 1942, failed. In 1943, Nakano was one of the leaders of a plot to overthrow the government: imperial princes and ex-premiers were other participants. When Tojo refused to resign and began the arrest of Diet members suspected of implication in the affair, the plot collapsed. Nakano committed suicide rather than reveal the identity of other leaders. The Tojo government remained in office until July, 1944, by which time it was impossible to conceal the military disasters which had occurred.

Army–Navy Friction

The Koiso-Yonai cabinet which then took office made a serious effort to prosecute the war vigorously. Its main positions were filled by leaders from both branches of the armed services, in recognition of the disastrous effects of rivalry between the Army and the Navy. In some campaigns the Navy had not given the Army proper support; in others, naval personnel had had to do much of the land fighting. Open competition for supplies had added to the friction, and Tojo's open neglect of naval air power had caused bitter resentment in naval circles.

---

[1] See C. Yanaga, *Japan Since Perry* (New York, 1949), p. 608.

Japan Surrenders

By April, 1945, Japan's leaders recognized the necessity for ending the war. The government of Admiral Suzuki which then came into office was expected to prepare the way for a negotiated peace. A definite peace faction headed by Yoshida Shigeru, who was to be one of Japan's postwar premiers, was exerting pressure. The Army arrested Yoshida but significantly was unable to secure his trial and conviction on charges of treason. Mounting military losses, the cabinet's failure to obtain help from the Soviet Union in negotiating peace, and signs of internal collapse formed the prelude to the final disasters of Hiroshima, Nagasaki, and the Russian entry into the war.

An imperial conference called on August 9 voted to accept the unconditional surrender terms stipulated in the Potsdam Declaration, "with the understanding that the said declaration does not comprise any demand which prejudices the prerogatives of his majesty as a sovereign ruler." The reply of the United Nations, while accepting this proviso, stated that the emperor and the Japanese government would both be subject to the Supreme Command of the Allied Powers. An imperial conference on August 14 decided that this answer must be accepted, and on the following day an imperial rescript announcing the surrender was read to the nation.

The Emperor's Responsibility

These events presented the victors with urgent and even dangerous problems. The Japanese propaganda machine had done its work well. The people were not psychologically prepared for surrender. Stunned disbelief was followed by many suicides, including those of War Minister Anami, Field Marshal Sugiyama, and numerous members of patriotic societies and students. How would the Japanese people greet the first army of occupation ever to set foot on Japan's shores?

Another important problem was the Japanese attempt to protect the imperial institution. How were the Allies to appraise the responsibility of the emperor for national policy? It would appear that the emperor took the initiative in calling the August 9 conference and had exercised a decisive influence for peace.[2] To what extent could he be held responsible for the decisions which had led to the war? Was there a danger that he might in the future be the rallying point for a renascent nationalism? Against these perilous uncertainties, the Allies balanced the probability that only an imperial command could effect the wholesale surrender of

[2] See Yanaga, *op. cit.*, pp. 616-23.

Japan's continental and home armies and so obviate the need for long and costly mopping-up campaigns.

A Defeated Nation

A general political, economic, and moral collapse followed the cessation of hostilities. The cumulative effects of the bombing of the home islands made the need for rehabilitation and reconstruction evident.

Until April, 1945, Allied air attacks had been concentrated on industrial targets, with a resulting paralysis of the nation's economy. For example, steel output in 1945 was only 270,000 tons compared with 4,200,000 tons in 1941. The chemical industry was virtually dead. The production of consumers' goods had almost ceased. Interruption of communications between Japan and the mainland had cut off badly needed imports of food. By the fall of 1945 the people faced near starvation.

After April, Allied air attacks shifted to urban centers, in an effort to crack civilian morale. In these raids, 30 per cent of the urban dwellings were destroyed: 241,000 persons were killed, another 313,000 wounded, and more than 8,000,000 affected. The atomic bomb which killed 78,000 persons and demolished four square miles of Hiroshima was a climax to the mass fire attacks on Tokyo and other cities. General apathy, disillusion over the outcome of the war, and a scramble to keep alive were natural first reactions to surrender.

Occupation Policy

These were a few of the facts which confronted the Allied forces as they began in late August, 1945, an occupation of Japan which was to last for more than six years. The Supreme Commander of the Allied Powers (SCAP), General Douglas MacArthur, had even more problems than these. By the terms of the Declaration of Cairo, Japan was to lose Formosa and Korea, important sources of food, and Manchuria and North China, markets and sources of raw materials. The maintenance of even a minimum living standard in Japan would require huge imports of food from the United States. Japan would have little chance to pay for these imports, since its conquests had included many of its former best customers. Bitterness against the Japanese, the general economic chaos after the war, and the need to restore devastated areas meant that it would be some time before these areas would again be open to Japanese economic activity. Moreover, the desire to diversify their own economies through industrialization indicated the likelihood of a permanent loss of markets and sources of raw materials for Japan.

Basic Assumptions. Originally Allied occupation policy put Japan last on the priority schedule for economic recovery. The assumption was that Japan would not again become a strong power in The Far East: China was to be the future bulwark of peace in that area. The original policy also assumed that China and Southeast Asia would be sufficiently stable to permit of normal recovery. Allied planning also reckoned on at least a modicum of cooperation among the Great Powers. As it became evident that none of these assumptions was to be realized, revision of the plan for the occupation of Japan inevitably ensued.

Objectives and Machinery. According to the United States Initial Post-Surrender Policy statement, Japan was to be prevented from becoming again "a menace to the United States or to the peace and security of the world." [3] As quickly as possible a peaceful and responsible Japanese government was to be established, willing and able to support the principles of the United Nations' Charter. In effect this meant the demilitarization of Japan and the elimination of militarist influence from all aspects of the nation's life. This policy also pledged an effort to encourage democracy, individual liberties, and respect for human rights and stated, somewhat cryptically, that "The Japanese people shall be afforded opportunity to develop for themselves an economy which will permit the peacetime requirements of the population to be met." [4]

The formal surrender took place on September 2, 1945, on board the U.S.S. "Missouri" in Tokyo Bay. Only after the Moscow Conference of Foreign Ministers in December could the machinery to implement the surrender and occupation be established. A Far Eastern Commission of eleven nations was to formulate occupation policies which were to be transmitted through the United States government to SCAP. The Allied Council for Japan, composed of representatives of the United States, the Soviet Union, and China, with one representative serving for Great Britain, Australia, New Zealand, and India jointly, was to operate in Tokyo in a consultative and advisory capacity. If any member of the Council objected to a major SCAP proposal there could be no decision until agreement on the question had been reached in the Far Eastern Commission. This machinery differed greatly from that established in Germany, both in that it used the existing government of the occupied country, and in that, despite the representation of the other victorious powers, it evolved into an American-dominated show.

[3] United States Initial Post-Surrender Policy for Japan, Part I.
[4] See Department of State, *Occupation of Japan, Policy and Progress* (Washington, 1946), pp. 9-11.

The Occupation: First Phase, Demilitarization and Democratization

Demilitarization and democratization were the watchwords for occupation policy until the summer of 1947. The Allies were in accord on the necessity for complete demilitarization. This process was virtually completed by March, 1947. The Imperial General Headquarters and War and Navy Ministries were abolished. The remnants of the Japanese navy and air force, army war machinery, and any manufacturing plants used exclusively for war production and arsenals were destroyed. More than six million Japanese soldiers and civilians were repatriated and the former were disarmed. Japan's ability to become an aggressor had been reduced to the vanishing point. Only with outside help could the nation again hope to become a military power.

Actually, demilitarization was carried to such an extreme that self-defense became a problem. Coastal patrol vessels were unable to cope with smuggling and piracy in Japan's home waters, and the police force, decentralized and reduced to 93,000 men, faced difficulty in maintaining order in the event of civil disturbance. Demilitarization was the first occupation policy to be carried out and the only one about which there was little controversy among the Allies.

Democratization, the implementation of the pledge to establish a "peaceful and responsible government," required both Allied and Japanese action. The Allied program rapidly became an American plan, the Japanese reactions to which will be discussed later.

Wide Scope of SCAP Reforms. SCAP immediately issued several directives meant to stimulate political and economic democracy. Political prisoners, including Communists, were liberated, an act which brought a rash of activity by old and new political parties. By the end of 1946, more than sixty parties had been formed. The repeal of the old laws which had throttled discussion encouraged freedom of speech and of the press. Government subsidy of newspapers was banned. Editorial comment was freed. SCAP retained the right to stop the publication of news items likely to disturb law and order: it soon became clear that criticism of SCAP policy was included in this category.

A serious effort was made to build a strong and democratic labor movement. The passage of the Trade Union Law by the Diet in December, 1945, gave the worker the right to join a union and to bargain collectively: it closely resembled the United States Labor Relations Act of 1935. Labor unions before 1945 had been very small and under the strictest sort of government control. By the summer of 1948, almost 50 per cent of the working class had been unionized.

The New Constitution

American Influence. The United States insisted that Japan must have a new constitution. Both Japanese and SCAP headquarters worked for more than a year before the final draft was prepared and then approved by the Diet. The final wording of the preamble—"We, the Japanese people, acting through our duly elected representatives in the National Diet, ...do proclaim that sovereign power resides with the people..."—suggests strongly the prominent role of Americans in the final wording of the document. As early as March, 1946, the emperor gave his approval to the idea of constitutional revision. However, SCAP had to use pressure to get the Japanese to accept the sort of constitution which American advisers to SCAP believed necessary as the basis for democracy in Japan.

Renunciation of War. The constitution renounced war as a sovereign right of the nation and abjured threats or force in the solution of international disputes. The armed services and a war potential were "never" to be maintained.[5] This was a realistic recognition that in the future Japan's war potential would be weak in a world dominated by two great powers. It was also an appeal to the idealism of the Japanese, who, at least temporarily disgusted with militarism, could assume moral leadership by adherence to this statement. Disillusionment was apt to be great, however, should the United States sanction a return to the use of force. Increasing tension between the United States and the Soviet Union after 1947 brought rumors that Japan's man power and industry would be utilized to offset the numerical advantage of Communism in East Asia, and the creation of limited armed services provided for by the Japanese Peace Treaty of 1951 seemed to go against the constitutional renunciation of force.

Popular Sovereignty: Its Practical Meaning. The constitutional determination that the people possessed sovereign power had certain natural consequences. The emperor became a head of state whose principal function was to be the symbol of national unity. All his acts were subject to the advice and approval of the Cabinet, whose members had to be civilians. The Cabinet was made responsible to the Diet, and the majority of its members had to come from the lower house. With a responsible cabinet, the supremacy of the legislative rather than the executive branch of the government was assured. The lower house, the House of Representatives, was given more power than the House of Councillors, which could

---

[5] This clause was the contribution of General MacArthur. See SCAP, *Report of Government Section, Political Orientation of Japan, September 1945 to September, 1948* (2 vols., Washington, 1950), for the role played by General MacArthur and his Government Section in the writing of the constitution.

delay but not reject measures passed by the lower house. The House of Councillors replaced the old House of Peers: both the peerage and the Privy Council were abolished.

The new constitution contained a very comprehensive Bill of Rights, which provided for equal treatment for women, gave a flat guarantee of academic freedom, and established the right of all qualified people to an education. The British and American influence on these articles was very evident.

More Democratic Local Government and a Supreme Court. Local government was strengthened by provision for the popular election of both executive and legislative officers and by giving local governing bodies responsibility for the management of their own affairs. This section of the constitution and the chapter establishing an independent judiciary were distinct departures from previous Japanese experience. The transplantation to Japan of the Supreme Court's power of judicial review was strange to a people accustomed to a government of men rather than of laws.

A Model Document. The new constitution represented the best experience of the Western democracies. From an Occidental viewpoint, the framework for the new government was sound. But Americans were going to have to guard against two temptations: to confuse the framework with the essence of democracy, and to become so enamored of their handiwork that they would not permit its amendment.

The acceptance of this new model constitution by Japan caused many visitors in occupied Japan to believe that in five short years democracy had been adopted. The best machinery had been provided, and on the whole, occupation personnel had been good examples of democracy at work. However, the constitution was apt to be enduring and effective only to the extent that its provisions were or could be associated with Japanese institutions and practices. Any really significant judgment as to the democratization of Japan would have to wait till a later date.

Educational Reforms

The new constitution and the new political and economic program were accompanied by soundly conceived and executed educational reforms. A report by a United States Educational Mission furnished SCAP with the information needed to make changes in Japan's educational system.

An American System Adopted. Compulsory attendance was extended to nine years, almost a year more than the Japanese had averaged before the war. Above the elementary level, an American plan was adopted, with a three-year compulsory junior high school, a three-year senior high school, and a four-year college. An attempt was made to introduce a standard curriculum, so that the same school could provide both general and specialized training. The application of these principles led to demands for new faculties and staff which exceeded available budgets, and in many schools lower standards resulted.

Democracy in Education. Revised courses, new textbooks, and new teaching methods were introduced. Shinto ideology, with its emphasis on the divine origins of Japan and its rulers, was replaced by a realistic historical account. The very nationalistic courses on "morals" gave way to civics and other social sciences. Even in the elementary schools, extracurricular activities which encouraged independent thinking by students became part of the educational pattern.

Admission to higher education was put on a merit basis, with plans for an expansion of university facilities to eliminate the vicious competition of the prewar period. Members of university faculties were no longer to be given government civil service ratings, and the need for financial independence for faculty members and greater faculty control in academic affairs was recognized.

Other Educational Reforms. The excessively centralized control formerly exercised through the Ministry of Education was relaxed in many ways. Elected municipal school boards were made responsible for the local schools. Adult education was encouraged, and great emphasis was put on the development of an adequate library system.

Writing Reform. One basic change, writing reform, was approached hesitantly. A beginning was made in the simplification of the traditional Chinese characters and the native phonetic syllabaries, the learning of which took so much of a student's time. Abbreviations were standardized, archaic grammatical forms were eliminated, and the number of Chinese characters to be learned was reduced to 1,300. Exponents of the use of the Latin alphabet continued to urge the practical merits of this substitution but made little headway.

Altogether the number and scope of the educational reforms constituted an ambitious program. Both here and in political reform, Japan's long tradition of receptivity to new ideas and methods provided the best hope that occupation policies might really take and have abiding effect.

Economic Policy: A Lapse of Two Years

A Subsistence Economy. For almost two years, the economic problems of postwar Japan were relatively neglected. The Allies had declared that the Japanese themselves would have to repair the war damage which they had suffered. SCAP concentrated on destruction of the economic base for Japanese militarism and provisional planning for an economy which would supplement political democracy. General MacArthur was no economist, and the instructions under which SCAP operated put the solution of economic problems at the bottom of the list of objectives of the occupation.

The first statement on reparations, The Pauley Report of 1946, indicated that much of Japan's heavy industry might be moved and the country be left with a bare subsistence economy. Gradually it became clear that political democracy was meaningless without economic hope for the 80,000,000 people crowded into the four main islands of Japan. In view of its commitments elsewhere in the world, the question arose whether the United States would continue to maintain Japan as a ward to the tune of $400,000,000 a year in food and raw materials. The deterioration of Soviet-American relations after 1947 and the collapse of the Nationalist regime in China were additional arguments for more attention to Japan's economic problems.

Land Reform

Both the land reform programs and the first moves to liquidate the *Zaibatsu* were developed by the occupation authorities under the conditions which existed from 1945 to the summer of 1947. The chronology followed in obtaining land reform legislation is typical of the manner in which Japan's occupation legislation was accomplished. SCAP first directed the Japanese government to prepare a land reform program. The Japanese proposals, submitted some time later, did not seem to go far enough, and the occupation authorities suggested changes. The Land Law of October, 1946, was the result. Elected local and prefectural land commissions were given the administration of the law. By the end of 1947, former tenants were able to begin buying land, all land thus acquired to be purchased by the end of 1948.

The Provisions of the New Laws. This law hit especially absentee landlords, who were required to sell all their land to the government. Inflation meant that the land price, based on 1939 values, amounted to confiscation. Under the law, noncultivating resident owners might hold no more than one *cho* (2.45 acres) of land, while a farmer might own and cultivate three *cho*. The law was criticized as perpetuating small farms, but at least the farms were to be significantly less small than they had been.[6]

---

[6] To encourage migration of farmers, these figures were quadrupled for Hokkaido.

Prevailing high food prices also benefited purchasers of farms under the new law. They were able to pay old farm debts and buy the new land in a relatively short time. The Agricultural Land Adjustment Law, which fixed rents for rice paddies and dry fields, required written leases, and improved credit facilities, was designed to ease the condition of tenant farmers.

Effects of Land Reforms. This drastic land reform program was at least outwardly one of the most successful of the reforms. By July, 1948, more than 4,250,000 acres had been purchased, about 3,000,000 of them by former tenants. The tenancy problem had been met for the moment, but agrarian planning had not answered the basic question of "too many people on too little land." Small farms would continue to yield small incomes, to be supplemented by other employment. Legislation could not remedy the shortage of modern machinery and excessive reliance on rice culture.

Pessimists emphasized the number of cases of landlord resistance and the conservatism of the agrarian class. They felt that time would be needed to make the peasant a convinced participant in local government and that the farms still would not be able to produce enough food to feed the nation. Optimists, on the other hand, could point out that only 10 per cent of the land was still farmed by tenants, and that the success of the plan was likely as thousands of Japanese became landowners with a vested interest in the new economic and political scheme.[7]

Economic Deterioration

Although the *Zaibatsu* could not be blamed exclusively for Japan's aggressive foreign policy, the small number, size, and influence of the big financial families invited attack. They had supplied much of the industrial and financial power required by the government before and during the war. They had also acquiesced in and helped with the economic phases of Japanese foreign policy. SCAP advisers believed that without the development of a healthy middle class, small businessmen, labor unions, and farmers would be at the mercy of these financial giants.

Legal Dissolution of the Zaibatsu. In October, 1945, Yasuda, on behalf of the "big four," submitted a plan for the dissolution of the *Zaibatsu*. A Holding Company Liquidation Commission was set up the

---

[7] See J. B. Cohen, *Japan's Economy in War and Reconstruction* (Minneapolis, 1949); E. O. Reischauer, *The United States and Japan* (Cambridge, Mass., 1950); and C. Yanaga, *Japan Since Perry* (New York, 1949), for differing yet authoritative views on Japan during the occupation.

following April which took over for sale to the public the shares of the five largest *Zaibatsu* holding companies. In October, 1946, the assets of the ten wealthiest families were frozen. Next came a capital levy which, with inflation, cut deeply into private fortunes. Income and inheritance taxes designed to prevent concentrations of wealth were adopted. The climax came on December 9, 1947, with the passage of the Economic Deconcentration Law by which Japanese corporations were to be broken up into smaller units, to encourage greater competition. With the promulgation of an antitrust law, the Japanese achieved maximum legislative protection against the *Zaibatsu*.

Problems Created: Industrial Uncertainty. Aside from the question whether this legislation could prevent informal associations of *Zaibatsu* leaders from continuing to control businesses, certain serious problems were apparent. The attacks on the old economic order and the purge of its leaders created an attitude of uncertainty which reduced the efficiency of Japanese industry. In the summer of 1947, industrial production was down to one-third of that of the 1930–1934 base period. The scarcity of raw materials and use of obsolete equipment hurt the morale and efficiency of workers, and no substitute had been found for the banned managerial class.

A New Policy. This policy was abruptly changed. Faced with worsening relations with Soviet Russia and the weakening of China, the United States as early as May, 1947, announced that Japan was to be a base for the reconstruction and recovery of Asia. Occupation policy was to be part of the American plan to contain Communism. By the end of 1949 the dissolution of corporations was virtually halted and in 1949 Japan began to show signs of once more becoming the workshop of the Far East.

Who were to be the owners of former *Zaibatsu* holdings? Originally, labor unions which wanted to buy these properties had been given high priority, but by 1947 the Communists evidently controlled many of the unions. Few persons or groups had the necessary resources to buy, and a trend toward government ownership appeared.

Japanese Reaction to SCAP Policies

What was the Japanese reaction to these allied occupation plans of which an outline has just been presented? The Japanese had long been accustomed to a dual government: now SCAP was the real power behind the scenes. A Japanese cabinet could excuse itself for inaction by pointing out that the real power was in the hands of the Allied Powers. To what extent did the occupation bring quick changes in the Japanese scene? Here the political parties offer a valid field for observation.

Political Parties Revived

In the revival of political parties, Japanese and foreign influences intermingled. Early directives from SCAP encouraged new parties and stimulated the old. The Social Democratic party, which favored the nationalization of industry and included socialists from both extremes, was formed in September, 1945. The Liberal party, most of whose members came from the old *Seiyukai*, advocated a laissez-faire economy and concentration on industrialization. The Progressive party, descended from the prewar *Minseito*, differed from the Liberal party only in advocating more government control of industry. In the plethora of parties, few had new principles or leaders.

The Purges. On January 4, 1946, as the parties were organizing for the first postwar election, the occupation authorities instituted their first purge of political leaders. It barred from office 186,000 people, including practically all experienced public servants who had held office between July 7, 1937, and September 2, 1945. The cabinet had to be reorganized, and the Diet, with 90 per cent of its members disqualified, virtually had to suspend operations. The fate of some individuals was still uncertain. Hatoyama, Liberal party leader, was not banned until he had almost formed a cabinet in May, 1946.

In November, 1946, the purge was extended to those active in local government and leaders in economic and cultural activities. One of the purposes was to stimulate new leadership, but although some new faces appeared, SCAP could not so easily change the character of ultimate control. The attack on the major politicians and bureaucrats was plainly necessary to break their hold on the government. The Japanese, however, failed to see why minor functionaries who had merely done their jobs and had not been part of a great conspiracy should be purged. Who would be left to work for the state?

Elections and Cabinets

One of the major achievements of the occupation was Japan's first postwar election, held on April 10, 1946, with very little corruption by the Japanese or interference from any source. Women voted for the first time: several were elected to the Diet, because many felt they were supposed to vote for their own sex. The voting age was lowered from 25 to 20 years.

Some 27,000,000 people, 70 per cent of the electorate, voted apparently as they had in the past, for individuals rather than for parties and platforms. The result favored the moderate parties: the Liberal party elected 139 members, the Progressive 93, the Social Democratic 93, the Cooperative 14, and the Communist, despite its claims of a large following, only 5. The Diet, which was generally conservative, was led by a Liberal-Progressive coalition cabinet, formed, after the purge of Hatoyama, under Yoshida Shigeru.

A Slight Trend to the Left. In the months following, the political pendulum swung slightly toward the left. The Yoshida government had the unpopular task of passing much of the reform legislation backed by SCAP, including the new constitution. The existence of the coalition depended on the ability of the leaders to reconcile their personal difficulties. As economic conditions remained poor, the government was blamed.

In the April, 1947, election, the Social Democrats became the largest party in the House of Representatives, with a plurality of 143 seats. Katayama, Socialist party leader, became premier after forming an uneasy coalition with the Democratic party, which had been formed by the old Progressive party plus Shidehara's bolters from the Liberal party and had won 126 seats. In this election many candidates ran as independents. Seventy per cent of the members of the House of Representatives were newcomers. The elections for governors and for mayors in cities and towns aroused less popular interest than had the national election.

The Katayama Cabinet. Katayama thus became the first Premier under the new constitution. As Socialist leader, he was pledged to a program of further nationalization of key industries. Disagreements between left- and right-wing members of his party weakened his plans. Even had he been able to obtain a compromise satisfactory to all shades of Social Democrats, it was likely to have been distasteful to the conservative Democrats, partners in the ruling coalition. The Katayama cabinet needed the help of SCAP, yet close cooperation with the occupation authorities was sure to bring charges of subservience. Once more months passed without alleviation of basic economic problems. An outbreak of Communist-initiated labor violence early in the Katayama regime discredited the extreme socialists and led to a sharper cleavage between the Social Democrats and the Democrats. The sessions of the Diet were marked by disorder and inefficiency.

Legislative Achievements. Despite its handicaps and weakness, the Katayama government secured the passage of several important laws. A series of measures was designed to put down and keep down oligarchic domination of Japanese political and economic life. The abolition of the

Home Ministry and decentralization of the police force dealt blows to prewar political machinery. The Economic Deconcentration Law was an attempt to destroy the economic base of the old hierarchy. On the constructive side, the Ministry of Labor was inaugurated, labor standards were improved, and the Supreme Court was completed with the appointment of fifteen judges. Nevertheless, the coalition broke down in February, 1948, and Katayama resigned.

Ashida's Transition Ministry. For a few months, the premiership was held by Ashida, leader of the Democratic party, who managed to form a coalition with the majority of the Social Democrats. Ashida pledged his government to achieve economic recovery but failed, in part because certain keys to industrial development—the revival of Japan's export trade and the rebuilding of its merchant marine—were beyond the control of any Japanese government.

The Democratic Liberal Party Formed. The kaleidoscope of Japanese politics now produced in March, 1948, a new conservative grouping, the Democratic Liberal party, headed by Yoshida and pledged to the restoration of a free economy. Yoshida claimed 169 seats in the lower house for his followers, who had been elected as members of the Liberal party or of the Shidehara clique of the Democratic party. Although Ashida remained as premier till October, this new party foreshadowed his defeat.

Thus, after a year on the opposition bench, Yoshida once more became premier. In the third general election, the last to be held during the occupation, the electors chose 264 of Yoshida's followers, an absolute majority of the 466 seats in the House of Representatives. The Communists also showed a significant gain, from four seats to thirty-five, which brought on anti-Communist activity both by SCAP and by the Yoshida regime. The gains of the two parties at the opposite ends of the political spectrum were achieved at the expense of the middle-of-the-road Social Democratic and Democratic parties. Under Yoshida, Japan at last achieved some degree of economic advance, inflation was brought under control, and the occupation came to an end. Finally a split in the Liberal party, between the adherents of Yoshida and the followers of Hatoyama, who was depurged in 1951, brought the dissolution of the Diet, and in October, 1952, Japan's first post-occupation election was held.

A Democratic Japan?

A description of the political and economic reforms initiated by SCAP through postwar Japanese government and the narration of Japanese political history does not tell the whole story. The degree to which during the occupation old political, social, and economic habits had been replaced by new ones requires thoughtful consideration.

Politics. Even at the end of the occupation period, Japanese politics had retained many of its old characteristics. Party leaders—Shidehara, Yoshida, Ashida, and others—had been prominent before the war, though some had been too "liberal" at that time and had been forced into retirement. Although many new faces were to be seen in the Diet, six years was a very short time in which to develop new leadership.

The political parties themselves traced back to the prewar *Seiyukai* and *Minseito*. The ease with which Shidehara led his faction from the Liberal to the Democratic and then finally to the Democratic Liberal party illustrated the persistent loyalty to leaders rather than to principles. Party discipline and responsibility were still feeble. Party names were meaningless: from the Occidental view the Democratic Liberal party was hardly either democratic or liberal. The purges had removed some of the old leaders, but there were indications that they still controlled the party organizations, which had been preserved largely intact.

Japanese political practices were not admirable. Members of the Diet were unruly, committees were inefficient, dilatory tactics held up important legislation. Scandals concerning war supplies and black market operations involved officials and legislators and shook public confidence. Gangs of hoodlums, many of them ex-servicemen, acted as messengers for political leaders, with the real purpose of establishing party control over the electorate. The position of the former militaristic element in Japanese society remained unsettled. Under these conditions a certain amount of public apathy became characteristic of Japanese political life.

On the other side of the account should be mentioned efforts to break the ties which formerly made independent action by legislators difficult. Members of the Diet were paid salaries supposedly sufficient to free them from having to accept "fees" from interest groups and were given office space and secretarial assistance. With the nation's prewar and war leaders discredited by defeat, this was an important measure to give prestige to and build public confidence in postwar leadership.

Economic Difficulties. The occupation authorities and the Japanese cabinets of the occupation period had difficulty in synchronizing political and economic democracy with economic recovery. SCAP encouraged the unionization of Japanese labor with phenomenal success, even bringing many governmental workers into the union fold. Communist activity in the unions and the development of "workers' control of production," by which workers ran the plants when employers failed to meet their demands, soon raised the question of interference with economic recovery.

The Congress of Industrial Unions, which showed Communist influence, and the Japanese Federation of Labor both organized transport workers. School teachers, tax collectors, and railway and communications workers voted for a general strike for February 1, 1947, which only the direct intervention of General MacArthur prevented. In 1949, in the interest of budgetary economy, SCAP insisted that the Japanese government dismiss about 25 per cent of its employees. This brought on bitter Communist attacks and a resort to force which somewhat discredited the Communists. The dismissals cut across the Japanese tradition that the employer should care for his employees in bad times as well as good. The Japanese obviously did not understand the philosophy of trade unionism. SCAP too had its problems. Trade union violence was a menace to political democracy and to the increased industrial production which SCAP was encouraging during the later stages of the occupation.

Japan after the Occupation

In April, 1952, the Peace Treaty came into effect and Japan recovered its sovereignty. In the years since that date the Japanese have continued to display many of the attitudes and methods which they had developed during their relatively long experience with Western style institutions from the later nineteenth century on and had continued to manifest during the occupation.

Political Developments

When the occupation ended, Yoshida was still prime minister; he remained so until December, 1954. The Liberal party which he headed was full of dissension, and by early 1954 the Yoshida government was obviously weakening. Late in that year, a new party was formed, by the process which had long since become almost a routine of Japanese postwar politics. The Progressives joined with disgruntled Liberals to create a new conservative group, the Japanese Democratic party. Hatoyama,[8] Yoshida's rival in the Liberal party, became the president of the new group, with Shigemitsu of the Progressives as vice-president. In the face of this new alignment, Yoshida resigned, and Hatoyama at last became premier. His government won only 185 seats in the February, 1955, elections, however, and continued in power chiefly because no one could bear to contemplate another general election at the moment. The two wings of the Socialist party, which had hardly been on speaking terms, achieved

[8] Hatoyama suffered a stroke not long before he was depurged in 1951, but recovered sufficiently to be very active politically until the end of 1956. He died early in 1959.

reunification in October. This phenomenon brought together Democrats and Liberals in still another unimaginatively and inaccurately named combination, the Liberal Democratic party. This conservative group, though troubled by internal differences, was able to maintain a clear and substantial majority in the House of Representatives through the first part of 1956. Then a real political crisis developed. Hatoyama's program, which included constitutional revision, greater power for the Ministry of Education, and electoral reform, outraged the Socialists. Seeing no proper parliamentary way of blocking it, they resorted to violence and there was very unedifying rioting in Parliament. In the end, the electoral reform bill was the only major item on Hatoyama's list which did not pass, but in the July elections the voters apparently regarded neither major party as having behaved well and changed the composition of the lower house only to the extent of giving the Socialists a slight increase in number of seats.

Late in 1956, Hatoyama, now on in years and failing in health, turned over the premiership to Ichibashi. He too was old and infirm and early in 1957 gave up the position in favor of Kishi Nobusuke, who had been his foreign minister. Kishi had held a post in the Tojo cabinet, but had not been tried as a war criminal. During his first months in office he retained the cabinet of his predecessor, but in July staged a complete cabinet reorganization, his most notable appointment being that of Fujiyama, a well-known financier, as foreign minister. The Liberal Democratic party continued to be plagued with friction, but preserved sufficient outward unity to carry the elections of May, 1958, on a platform which offered something for all tastes. It favored on the one hand recovery of Okinawa from the United States, ending of nuclear weapons tests, and increase in trade with Peking; and on the other hand, rearmament of Japan, the maintenance of close relations with the United States, and refusal to give formal recognition to the Chinese Communist regime.

The programs of these conservative cabinets of the post-occupation period reflected the persistent ambivalence of Japanese sentiment—the conflicting desires to keep close ties with the United States and to be more independent, to rearm and to avoid the re-emergence of militarism, to industrialize and to preserve economic democracy. Both Yoshida and Hatoyama showed a disposition to modify some of the occupation laws in the direction of recentralization of authority. Among the characteristic measures of the Yoshida regime were a Subversive Activities Prevention program, the revision of labor laws to provide for compulsory arbitration if the dispute seemed to threaten the national economy, more central control of the police force, the reduction of local political autonomy, and the revival of cartel arrangements. On coming into office, Hatoyama expressed his devotion to the not-too-easily reconcilable objectives of holding down the budget and giving generous government help to relieve the housing shortage, but in practice the former goal took precedence over the latter. His plans for constitutional revision resulted in the setting up of a Council for Constitutional Research to suggest changes. Measures to replace elected school boards by appointees of prefectural governors and to strengthen the Ministry of Education in order to check "subversive left-wing tendencies" did not go down well in some quarters. The plan of the Ministry of Education in 1958 to put in a new efficiency-rating scale for teachers brought on violent demonstrations and assertions of an attack on academic freedom. Premier Kishi's attempt, in the fall of 1958, to put through a bill to extend police powers, met with sharp rebuff, both through a Socialist boycott of parliament and a one-day general strike. In many of the measures of the conservative post-occupation regimes, the Socialists and some foreign observers felt that the ghost of the old Japanese state walked again.

Economic Growth

When the occupation ended, Japan still seemed to be in a bad way economically. SCAP's reversal of policy on the economic upbuilding of Japan had not yet shown results. The Korean War brought a temporary boom, because of heavy American purchases in Japan, which was followed by a disillusioning slump when the conflict ended. Reduced in size and deprived of the prewar repertory of raw materials and markets under Japanese control, Japan faced hard problems in the field of foreign trade. Efforts could and would be made to re-establish Japan's trade position in South and Southeast Asia and in Africa. Communist China presented a real riddle. China had in the past been a great outlet for Japanese manufactures, but might no longer be so, since it was industrializing and would be in competition with Japan for raw materials and even for markets. As for the United States, it was to show signs of protectionism and lack of cordiality toward Japanese products.

Nevertheless, by 1956 there were many signs of economic development, symbolized by the construction by Japan in that year of the world's largest oil tanker. Ironically, the *Zaibatsu* had reappeared as the driving force in economic recovery, with special stress on such new enterprises as nuclear power and petro chemicals. By 1958, Mitsui, Mitsubishi, and Sumitomo accounted for one-third of Japan's industrial output and commercial transactions. The *Zaibatsu* had achieved resurrection only in altered form, since the banks now held the strategic position as the only sources of capital, but the industrial and commercial combines still bore a strong family resemblance to their prewar and wartime predecessors.

Both the Hatoyama and the Kishi governments showed great concern to develop new channels for Japanese foreign trade. Kishi visited in South and Southeast Asia, made a sizeable Japanese credit available to

India, and talked of Japan's great interest in programs of economic aid to less developed countries. It was hard to overcome the bitterness and hatred of those who had once been part of the "Greater East Asia Co-Prosperity Sphere," but Japan was making a determined attempt to regain economic leadership in Asia.

Rearmament

The occupation had eventually reversed itself not only on Japanese economic rebuilding but on Japanese armament. In the beginning, the United States had planned for a democratic Japan which was economically and militarily harmless. Under the pressure of world politics, it shifted to the idea of a Japan still democratic, but with revived economic and military strength. Whether the economic and military revival could be achieved without jeopardizing the democracy was a complex question which remained unanswered.

On the issue of rearmament Japanese opinion was seriously divided. In general the Socialists opposed any amendment of the "peace" constitution, and pointed out that rearmament raised the danger of militarism and imposed a heavy burden on Japan's struggling economy. The dominant conservative groups went along with the American desire to rebuild Japan's armed strength, but approached the issue with due caution and at a relatively slow pace. There was general and understandable aversion to the continuance of hydrogen bomb tests.

Yoshida's line in the 1952 elections was "reconstruction before rearmament" but with a bow in the other direction in the form of expressed willingness to develop Japan's capacity for self-defence. In 1953 and 1954, the Yoshida government, with the blessing of the United States, transformed Japan's national security force into national defense forces, which, with American Mutual Security aid and military advice, would grow in five years to over a quarter of a million men. Late in 1955, the United States agreed to provide enriched uranium and Japan set up an Atomic Energy Commission. The ban on former officers of the imperial army was removed, but as a safeguard, the commanding officers of the new forces were put under the direct supervision of the prime minister.

On his accession to power, Hatoyama undertook to meet existing anti-American feeling by attempting to get a peace treaty with the Soviet Union. While a formal treaty proved difficult to negotiate, Hatoyama's visit to Moscow in October, 1956, resulted in a joint declaration ending the technical state of war between the two countries. Russia, which had previously blackballed Japan for membership in the United Nations, changed its tune, and Japan secured not only admission to the U.N. but in 1957 a nonpermanent seat on the Security Council.

Premier Kishi, in 1957, gave great concern to Japan's military development. His trip to Washington led to an American agreement substantially to reduce United States forces in Japan in view of continued expansion of Japan's defense forces. Also, a joint American-Japanese committee was set up to discuss problems arising from and possible modifications of the Mutual Security Treaty of 1951. The efforts of Kishi and his predecessors simultaneously to combine relations with the United States with moves toward an independent course of policy made the Japanese government appear at times to suffer from political schizophrenia, but these contradictions illustrated the difficulties and opportunities which Japan faced as she attempted national recovery in a world split into two hostile camps.

By the end of 1958, Japan's recovery had been spectacular but her future was uncertain. How deeply the war and the occupation had cut into the old pattern was impossible to judge. Japan, throughout its history, had shown a distinctive responsiveness to foreign cultures, and for more than a hundred years had been undergoing "westernization." The occupation and post-occupation periods have constituted the latest stage in the process of Japan's assimilation and naturalization of elements of Western civilization. For a few years the occupation tried to force the pace and deliberately make a cultural revolution in Japan at a speed and in directions which the occupation authorities determined. Now the Japanese are on their own again, and can once more display the unique combination of planned and spontaneous cultural adaptation which has been their hallmark.

SUGGESTED READINGS

Among the most useful general works are: J. B. Cohen, *Japan's Economy in War and Reconstruction* (Minneapolis, 1949); E. W. Martin, *The Allied Occupation of Japan* (Stanford, 1948); E. O. Reischauer, *The United States and Japan* (Cambridge, 1950); and C. Yanaga, *Japan Since Perry* (New York, 1949).

For additional general works and for studies of special phases of the war and postwar period of Japanese history, see: W. M. Ball, *Japan, Enemy or Ally* (New York, 1949); T. A. Bisson, *Prospects for Democracy in Japan* (New York, 1949); H. Borton, *Administration and Structure of Japanese Government,* Far Eastern Series 8 (Washington, 1945); Delmar Brown, *Nationalism in Japan* (Berkeley, 1955); Allan C. Cole, *Japanese Society and Politics* (Boston, 1956); Mark Gayn, *Japan Diary* (New York, 1948); Joseph C. Grew, *Ten Years in Japan* (New York, 1944); John Montgomery, *Forced to Be Free, The Artificial Revolution in Germany and Japan* (Chicago, 1957); Harold Quigley and John Turner, *The New Japan, Government and Politics* (Minneapolis, 1958); United States Department of State, *Occupation of Japan, Policy and Progress* (1946), Publication #2836, Far Eastern Series 22, *The Constitution of Japan* (1947), and *Summation of Non-Military Activities in Japan*—an official 35-volume series which covers the period through August, 1948; H. Wakefield, *New Paths for Japan* (New York, 1948); and Chitoshi Yanaga, *Japanese People and Politics* (Boston, 1956).

32

INTERNATIONAL RELATIONS AND THE FAR EAST, 1945–1950

The Manchurian Issue

Russians Loot Manchuria. Despite their recognition of China's "full sovereignty" over Manchuria, the Russians proceeded to help themselves there to everything they could cart away. They justified their actions on the grounds that such equipment and materials were legitimate war booty. On top of their stripping Manchuria almost bare of its industrial machinery, the Russians took their time about departing. When they finally left all but the Dairen-Port Arthur region, they were replaced by the Chinese Communists who simply took over control, a step facilitated by their having secured through Russian connivance the surrendered military equipment of the Kwantung Army.

The removal of "war booty" by the Russians from Manchuria assumed huge proportions, as the report of the Pauley Mission, which visited Manchuria in June, 1946, revealed. This group found that the total value of industry removed or damaged by the Russians was in excess of two billion dollars. On more than one occasion the American State Department unsuccessfully asked the Russians for an explanation of their actions in Manchuria.

The Moscow Conference. As early as the Moscow Conference of Foreign Ministers in December, 1945, the United States had sought without avail to include on the agenda the question of the transfer of control of Manchuria to the Chinese central government. In their turn the Russians insisted that the question of American troops in North China be discussed at the conference, a demand which the United States honored. The American position was that the United States was simply carrying out its responsibilities towards an ally at whose request American troops were in China. The Russian charge that the United States was interfering in the internal affairs of China was emphatically denied and it was pointed out that the United States sought only to see a unified and united China materialize. Russia's cooperation in that goal was urgently requested.

A communiqué issued at the conclusion of the conference declared that the foreign secretaries "were in agreement as to the need for a unified and democratic China under the National Government, for broad participation by democratic elements in all branches of the National Government, and for a cessation of civil strife." They reaffirmed their "adherence to the policy of noninterference in the internal affairs of China." [1]

The seriousness of the situation in Manchuria was further intensified when the Russians ordered an American naval vessel on official business to leave Dairen, which was then completely under Russian control in violation of their agreement with China. The State Department sent a note to the Russian government on January 3, 1947, calling for the immediate fulfilment of the Sino-Russian agreement on Dairen and the Manchurian railroads. The Russian reply on February 27 indicated that the Russians would implement their agreement but significantly neglected to specify any given time.

Summing up, the Manchurian issue served to put into sharp focus the position of the United States vis-à-vis Russia in the Far East now that the power of Japan had been smashed. Added to the differences separating the two powers in Manchuria and China were the questions of Japan and Korea. The two powers—the United States and the U.S.S.R.—faced one another all the way from the Bering Sea into continental Asia. To the Russians it appeared that it was American policy to maintain Japan, Korea, and China as independent countries outside of the Soviet sphere with the object of making the Pacific into a huge American lake. The U.S.S.R., on the other hand, appeared in American eyes to pursue a policy designed to protect its Far Eastern territories by means of a string of strongholds from the Kuriles to Outer Mongolia and to seek to neutralize as far as possible the strength of the United States in Japan, Korea, and China.[2]

The United States and China, 1945–1950

With the collapse and surrender of Japan, the situation in China was seriously obscure. As strange as it may seem, Nationalist China was not elated by the sudden Japanese capitulation. This lack of enthusiasm was due to the fact that the Nationalist armies were principally in the south and west, whereas the northeastern provinces, which had been held by Japan, would be surrendered to Chinese armies in that area, and they were Communist. This meant that control of the strategic northeastern seaboard would fall into the hands of the Communists unless the United States transported Chiang's forces there. This was done, much to the chagrin of

[1] *The White Paper*, pp. 124 ff.
[2] *Ibid.*, p. 298.

the Communists, who bitterly denounced what they called American interference in China's domestic affairs.

Aid to China. Military lend-lease from the United States to Nationalist China in the period from September, 1945, to October, 1946, amounted to almost $700,000,000 and was nearly as much aid as China had received from the Americans during the entire war period. About half of this amount was expended in transporting Nationalist soldiers to eastern and northern China. In addition, the Export-Import Bank approved credits of $67,000,000 for the first six months of 1946 for China and in the spring earmarked $500,000,000 for possible further credits. American surplus property in China and some of the Pacific islands, originally costing some $825,000,000, was sold to Chiang at a fraction of that amount. UNRRA supplies, chiefly American, to the amount of $535,000,000 were scheduled for delivery during 1946. Impressive as these figures are, they are deceptive because, with the exception of military lend-lease which practically ceased after the middle of 1946, the goods supplied were strictly for civilian relief and reconstruction and thus could affect the military struggle only indirectly. Furthermore, none of the $500,000,000 earmarked by the Export-Import Bank ever reached China.[3]

Charges were made in the United States against the State Department which was accused of interfering unfairly in the Chinese Civil War on the side of Chiang at the expense of China's democratic elements, i.e., the Communists.[4] While all this was transpiring, General George C. Marshall was busily engaged in trying to negotiate a compromise between the Communists and Nationalists in China,[5] a mission described in Chapter 30. Although General Marshall's efforts were unavailing, the State Department maintained a strong interest in the problem.

By the fall of 1947, the Department began the formulation of a program of additional aid within limitations to the government of China. The program was ready for Congress in the spring, at which time President Truman requested $570,000,000 for economic aid to China to cover the

---

[3] John C. Campbell, *The United States in World Affairs, 1945-1947* (New York, 1947), pp. 289 ff.

[4] Many of those charging the American government with intervention in the Chinese Civil War on the side of Chiang overlooked the fact that at a very critical time in that war General Marshall was instrumental in having a ten-month embargo placed on the export of munitions from the United States to China from August, 1946, to May, 1947. *The White Paper*, pp. 354 ff.

[5] During this mission a significant exchange of notes occurred between President Truman and Generalissimo Chiang in which Truman expressed concern over the failure of the Chinese to put their house in order and declared that if genuine progress were not forthcoming shortly, he would have to redefine and explain the position of their government to the American people. Chiang's reply did not satisfy Mr. Truman, who then stated that a speedy end of the civil war would hasten American plans to aid in the rehabilitation of China's industrial and agricultural economy. *The White Paper*, pp. 179 ff.

period from April, 1948, through June, 1949. As the United States was then engaged in trying to check Communism in Europe and the Near East, the House of Representatives favored an omnibus bill which included the Greece-Turkey aid programs, the European Recovery Act, and aid for China. As finally passed by Congress, the Foreign Assistance Act of 1948 allotted to China a total of $463,000,000 for one year, with $125,000,000 of it set aside for military use. The turn of events represented by Congress' decision to grant funds to China for military purposes had not been the intention of the State Department, but the matter was out of its hands. Congress had now taken a momentous step in shaping the China policy of the United States.

United States Policy Debate. The fundamental objective of American policy, however, remained unaltered, but the method of achieving it was changed. The goal continued to be a peaceful, stable, unified China. The policy of mediation in 1946 had not achieved it nor had "the method of cautious noninvolvement" employed during 1947. To many Americans the Communist successes during those years dictated the shift in American policy toward a more energetic position of helping the Nationalists.[6] Other Americans felt differently, and a debate took place in the United States. While it was going on, the Chinese Communists continued to win military victories in rapid succession. Their achievements undermined American prestige in China, and both sides turned more and more against the United States. The Communists were angry because the United States had helped their rivals; the Nationalists were irritated because they felt that the United States had let them down by failing to send adequate assistance. Meanwhile, American policy underwent another shift. The new position was to withdraw virtually from all involvement and to wait and see how matters developed. Accordingly, American naval units and marines were withdrawn from Tsingtao and the military mission was recalled. The implication was that the United States considered China lost and would hereafter base its strategic position on the insular strongpoints of the Philippines, Okinawa, and Japan. By a curious twist of fate, America's recent enemy, Japan, now seemed destined to be the keystone to American Far Eastern policy.

Mao's Hostility Mounts. American hopes that Mao Tse-tung, the Chinese Communist leader, might be another Tito were given a serious setback on June 30, 1949, at the celebration of the twenty-eighth anniversary of the Chinese Communist party. Mao declared that the goal of his party was "the establishment of a people's democracy, led by the working class

[6] John C. Campbell, *The United States in World Affairs, 1947-1948* (New York, 1948), p. 202.

and based on an alliance of workers and peasants." The foreign policy of this "democracy" was henceforth to be based on "alliance with the U.S.S.R., with the countries of the new democracy in Europe, and alliance with the proletariat and masses of the people in all other countries." The Chinese people have learned, Mao went on, that they "must, with no exception, take either the side of imperialism or that of socialism. It is impossible to remain in between the two. There is no third way.... Neutrality is a camouflage and a third way a mirage." As for China's economic relations with imperialist powers, foreign trade was a necessity but not until the destruction of "Chinese and foreign reactionaries" made it possible to carry on relations with foreign states on a basis of "equality, mutual benefit, and mutual respect for territorial sovereignty." [7]

Feeling their success headily, the Communists began to put pressure on the remaining American consular posts in China, an action which the American Embassy in Canton scored. The continued Communist victories and the imminent collapse of the Nationalist cause distressed those Americans who had argued since V-J Day for more effective American assistance to the Nationalists and who were alarmed over the effects Chiang's defeat would have upon the interests and policies of the United States in the Far East. A strong congressional group, long pro-Chiang, began to hurl charges at the State Department in the spring and summer of 1949, holding it largely responsible for the Nationalist debacle and urging that effective American aid could still save Chiang. The State Department, however, backed by President Truman, held firm in its policy despite the mounting severity of these attacks.

The "White Paper." On August 5, the Department answered its critics in the lengthy "White Paper," which reviewed American policy toward China since 1844, with special emphasis on the period since 1944. In the preface Secretary Acheson declared:

> The ominous result of the civil war in China was beyond the control of the government of the United States. Nothing that this country did or could have done, within the reasonable limits of its capabilities could have changed the result; nothing that was left undone by this country has contributed to it. It was the product of internal Chinese forces, forces which this country tried to influence but could not.[8]

This statement indicated that, to all intents and purposes, the State Department, at least as long as Acheson headed it, was convinced that the Chinese Communists had won the civil war, and there was nothing the

---

[7] *Pravda,* July 6, 1949, quoted in Richard P. Stebbins, *The United States in World Affairs, 1949* (New York, 1950), p. 54.
[8] *The White Paper,* xvi.

United States could do about it. The Secretary's policy for the time being was to reiterate the old principles of America's China policy: friendship, the open door, respect for China's independence and its administrative and territorial integrity. To these was added support of United Nations' efforts to maintain peace and security in the Far East. Acheson also made it clear that he held no brief for the Chinese Communists, whom he publicly declared were under a "foreign yoke." On the whole, American Far Eastern policy in 1949 tended to be peripheral to China. It called for greater attention to Japan, Korea, and the Philippines.

Hong Kong and Formosa. There were, however, two Chinese areas which posed major questions in 1949 and which were destined to increase in importance in the years which followed. They were Hong Kong and Formosa. The American press was told by Secretary Acheson that, although the question of a Communist attack on Hong Kong had already been discussed between the Department and British officials, the United States had as yet made no decision relative to American aid. Should any move be made which violated the United Nations Charter and called for action by the Security Council, the United States would take whatever steps its obligations under the Charter required.

Formosa presented a problem which was also rather sticky from the American viewpoint. The apparent determination of the Nationalists to use it for a last stand raised the question of what the United States should do if the Communists attacked. Here again no clear-cut decision was reached.

China and the United Nations. Six weeks after the launching of the new People's Republic of China on October 7, 1949, the Communists called upon the United Nations to expel the Nationalist delegation, and Russia announced that it would no longer recognize that group as China's representatives. Thus began the long, stubborn, and as yet unsuccessful battle to seat the Chinese Communists in the UN.

The United States, placed in a delicate position as a result of moves by the conflicting Chinese groups, chose to play a waiting game and was afforded additional time to consider its future policy as the result of the passage of a resolution by the General Assembly which called for study and report to the Assembly in 1950.

The Angus Ward Incident. The likelihood of American recognition of the Chinese Reds was considerably lessened by the brutal treatment given American Consul Angus Ward in Manchuria. He and his staff had been held in virtual imprisonment in the consulate since the fall of 1948. In May, 1949, the consulate was closed, but the Americans were not allowed to leave. Then on October 24, 1949, Ward and four of his assistants were arrested on a charge of assaulting a Chinese formerly in their employ. They were held incommunicado for more than a month before being tried. American protests and appeals were ignored. As a last desperate measure, Secretary Acheson appealed to thirty nations maintaining diplomatic or consular representatives in China to protest; twelve immediately pledged support.[9] This apparently impressed the Chinese Communists sufficiently to achieve the release of Ward and his associates. Announcement was made, nevertheless, that they had been tried and found guilty and their sentences commuted to deportation. Perhaps to avoid any implications of weakness, Communist authorities seized Ward's deputy, Vice-Consul W. N. Stokes, and ordered him to serve as a witness at a Chinese espionage trial. The entire Mukden consular staff was thereupon, in December, 1949, ordered to leave China. An order issued by the Communists on January 6, 1950, calling for the seizure of the American consular offices in Peking, prompted the United States to order home from Communist China all official personnel whatsoever.[10]

Nationalists Move to Formosa. Meanwhile, the war in China had gone so badly against the Nationalists that Chiang Kai-shek and his principal followers left the mainland and set up their temporary capital at Taipei, Formosa, on December 8, 1949. Except for some sporadic guerrilla activity in the hill country of several provinces, Nationalist opposition to the Communists was limited to a declared naval blockade of the Communist ports and to occasional desultory air attacks. The naval blockade led to a number of incidents involving American ships, all of which happened to belong to the same company, the Isbrandtsen Line. This organization refused to heed the State Department's warning to keep its ships out of Chinese waters and had to suffer the consequences, although the Department did enter protests on the company's behalf with the Nationalists.

United States Stands Aloof. The removal of the Nationalists to Formosa (Taiwan) now raised the question in the United States of what aid, if any, should be furnished to keep it from falling into the hands of the Communists. A campaign to help Chiang enlisted the support of former President Hoover, among others. He urged continued recognition and support of the Nationalists and even recommended United States naval protection for Taiwan, Hainan, and the Pescadores. This prompted President Truman to declare that the United States did not intend to become involved in the Chinese struggle either by using its military forces, establishing bases on Taiwan, or trying to secure special rights or privileges

---

[9] Department of State, *Strengthening the Forces of Freedom: Selected Speeches and Statements of Secretary of State Acheson, February 1949–April 1950* (Washington, 1950), pp. 168-f.
[10] Stebbins, *op. cit.*, pp. 430-31.

there. He also said that no American military aid or advice would be forthcoming but added that economic assistance would continue as long as Congress authorized it.

Thus, as 1950 opened, the United States' official view was that the Communists had won the civil war but that their atrocious behavior in such instances as the Angus Ward case made it increasingly unwise to consider recognizing their regime. The hope was still cherished in official Washington that Chinese nationalism would tire of Russian interference and lead Mao to become another Tito. As for the Nationalists, the administration's attitude was made quite clear by its views on Taiwan.

Sino-Soviet Alliance. American hopes of Mao's emulating Tito were dashed, for the time being at any rate, with the announcement on February 15, 1950, of the signing of a thirty-year Sino-Soviet Treaty of Friendship, Alliance, and Mutual Assistance, followed by a number of related agreements.[11] The main treaty was directed against a repetition of aggression by Japan "or any other state [later revealed to be the United States] which directly or indirectly would unite with Japan in acts of aggression." They pledged themselves to work for an early peace treaty with Japan, to consult mutually on all important international problems of joint interest, and to establish close economic and cultural relations.

The agreements were only partially revealed, but one which was loudly hailed in China called for a credit of $300,000,000 from the Soviets on easy terms. Curiously enough, repayment was to be in part in American dollars. Another agreement supposedly gave China sole control of the Chinese Changchun Railway (formerly the Chinese Eastern) and arranged for the return of Port Arthur within two years and of Dairen contingent upon a Japanese peace treaty. Scientific and cultural cooperation was pledged and quickly implemented by a steady flow of Soviet advisers and technical experts into China.

The military arrangements have largely remained secret, but it is widely believed that the Russians were granted naval and air bases on the Chinese coast. These, together with the Soviets' own Pacific bases, placed the American position in the Far East in considerable jeopardy and, in effect, neutralized the position secured by the United States as a result of the American victory over Japan in 1945.

The Occupation of Japan

It is appropriate at this point to review events following in the wake of that victory by turning our attention to the occupation of Japan. This

---
[11] The details, as published, may be found in Henry Wei, *China and Soviet Russia* (Princeton, 1956), pp. 343-47.

question has already been dealt with in Chapter 31 but several points remain to be discussed here.

The Far Eastern Commission. With the manner in which the occupation of Japan was being carried out by General MacArthur, Supreme Commander for the Allied Powers, there was little if any quarrel on the part of the other nations. There was, however, considerable resentment over the fact that policy was made unilaterally. After some negotiation and compromise, the United States agreed at Moscow on December 27, 1945, to the creation of a Far Eastern Commission in Washington. It was to include representatives of all the Pacific powers which had fought against Japan.[12] The agreement also provided for an Allied Council in Tokyo composed of representatives of the United States, the British Commonwealth, the Soviet Union, and China.

The Far Eastern Commission was designed to formulate "policies, principles, and standards in conformity with which the fulfillment by Japan of its obligations under the Terms of Surrender may be accomplished," and to review directives issued by the Supreme Commander, or any actions, including policy decisions, taken by him. The Allied Council was an advisory body with which the Supreme Commander was to consult on important matters.[13]

In reality, neither the fundamental power of General MacArthur nor the fact that the occupation of Japan was principally an American military undertaking was altered by this new arrangement. MacArthur was merely subject to restraint in certain basic matters, and a handful of British Commonwealth troops were added to the occupation forces. While he was somewhat nettled by this Moscow agreement, MacArthur pledged his cooperation in trying to make it work. What the whole thing boiled down to was that American control continued virtually unabated, but that the other nations could now keep a closer watch on things.

The following spring (1946) the Far Eastern Commission began discussions of a Japanese reparation program based on proposals advanced by the United States. The dilatoriness of the Commission, however, led the American State Department, following a warning of its intentions, to order General MacArthur on April 3, 1947, to begin the removal of certain Japanese plants and equipment to China, the Philippines, the Netherlands East Indies, Burma, and Malaya. Nothing, however, was moved until early the following year.

[12] The United States, Great Britain, the U.S.S.R., China, France, the Netherlands, Canada, Australia, New Zealand, India, and the Philippines. Later additions (1949) were Burma and Pakistan.
[13] Raymond Dennett and Robert K. Turner, eds., *Documents on American Foreign Relations* (Princeton, 1948), Vol. VIII, p. 275.

Because of MacArthur's practice of making informal "suggestions" to the Japanese government, which the latter obediently carried out, there was relatively little work remaining for the Allied Council. Its sessions were marked by the customary Soviet-American disagreements. The Russian member, General Kuzmo Derevyanko, was a particularly rugged and intransigent specimen who took particular pleasure in criticizing the Americans.

Cost of American Assistance. Despite this carping, the occupation appeared to be eminently successful, albeit costly to the American taxpayer. In 1946, Congress granted appropriations of $188,000,000 to supply food and raw materials to Japan; in 1947 some $300,000,000 was set aside; and in 1948 a sum almost two and a half times this amount was provided.

So expensive was American assistance to Japan becoming, that on January 21, 1948, the American member of the Far Eastern Commission announced that the United States would not continue indefinitely to subsidize Japan's economy, although it would give further temporary assistance. In the American view, the Powers should do everything possible to restore Japan to a peaceful and self-supporting condition.

Preliminary Peace Negotiations. General MacArthur, feeling that the occupation had progressed sufficiently, announced on March 17, 1947 that it was time for a peace treaty to be concluded, after which the United Nations should be responsible. The only weak spot, the General conceded, was the economic situation. He pointed out that to remedy this, Japan's production and trade should be restored. Japanese Premier Yoshida did not agree with MacArthur on the desirability of an early end of the occupation; he believed that the United States should remain in Japan after the conclusion of a peace treaty in order to combat Communism and assure peace.[14]

Barely two months later, Dean Acheson, then Undersecretary of State, delivered a speech at Cleveland, Mississippi, in which he defined American policy for the rebuilding of Japan. Acheson declared that Japan should be made the workshop of the Far East, a base upon which the reconstruction and recovery of all Asia would ultimately rest. These remarks were part of the American policy of world reconstruction and the containing of Communism,[15] but they also revealed by implication the trend of United States policy toward China.

These were but two of the more important American feelers being sent out for an early draft of a Japanese peace treaty. On July 11, 1947, United States Ambassador Walter Bedell Smith raised the issue of a preliminary

[14] Campbell, *United States in World Affairs, 1945-1947* (New York, 1947), pp. 261-73.
[15] Chitoshi Yanaga, *Japan Since Perry* (New York, 1949), p. 639.

peace conference for Japan in a discussion with the Russian Foreign Commissar Vyacheslav Molotov. On the same day, identical notes were sent to all ten members of the Far Eastern Commission by the State Department suggesting that a preliminary conference be held in August to discuss terms of peace with Japan. The states so meeting would work out a draft treaty which would then be submitted to all states at war with Japan.

Russian and Chinese Objections Delay Treaty. The American proposal called for decisions by a two-thirds majority on important matters, the veto being eliminated. Of the major powers concerned, Great Britain alone was in accord. Both the Russians and the Chinese were opposed.

The Russians accused the United States of unilateral action in seeking to call a conference without having held prior consultation with Russia, Britain, and China. Nevertheless, the Soviets proposed that a Big Four conference consisting of the Foreign Ministers of the Powers should set a date for a conference. The State Department had no desire for such a procedure; it preferred to include representatives of the various Pacific nations.

China, despite its need for American aid, was alarmed over what it felt was a dangerous trend in American policy toward friendship with Japan, China's long-time enemy. On this point, all Chinese, whatever their political affiliations, appeared united. China leaned toward a four-power meeting wherein all would be equal. Also, if China agreed to the American proposal, there was a chance that the treaty might be drawn up without Russia. This would be a violation of the Sino-Russian Treaty of 1945, which pledged the signatories not to make a separate peace with Japan. For China to do this would irreparably damage her charges that Russia had already violated the treaty.[16]

The Russian and Chinese objections prompted the State Department to indicate on August 21 that conversations aimed at drafting a peace treaty for Japan were to be postponed until late in the fall or even until some time during the next year.

Commonwealth Backs United States Plan. Meanwhile, a British Commonwealth conference on the question of the Commonwealth's attitude toward a Japanese peace treaty was held in Canberra. This meeting gave its approval to the United States proposal that decisions of the eleven-nation peace treaty conference should be by a two-thirds majority. The various conclusions reached by the Canberra Conference were, in general, very close to the American position.

[16] Campbell, *United States in World Affairs, 1947-1948* (New York, 1948), p. 164.

INTERNATIONAL RELATIONS AND THE FAR EAST 609

By the end of September, the prospects for a Japanese peace conference were improving as a result of strong Anglo-American solidarity. A month later the State Department indicated that it was hopeful that work would commence before the end of the year. Unfortunately, Russian and Chinese intransigence remained unshaken, and American hopes began to fade.

United States Revises Its Japanese Policy. With the prospects of a treaty in the near future having dimmed by the end of 1947, the outlines of American policy toward Japan had nevertheless become clear. It was a policy which had undergone sharp changes in the slightly more than two years which had elapsed since the end of the war. Originally taking the position that Japan must be rendered forever weak, the United States, as a result of the attitude shown by the Soviet Union during that period, had come around to the view that Japan could well be made into a buttress against Soviet strength in the Far East. It was gradually being fitted into the American strategic pattern.

American thinking was influenced by such considerations as the belief that Japan's chances of becoming an aggressor within the foreseeable future were extremely remote. Therefore, it was argued that the revival of Japanese industry would not be dangerous. Rather, it seemed to American planners that the continued suppression of Japan's industrial potential could lead only to an unrest that would furnish the Russians with a golden opportunity for exploitation which could conceivably destroy the work of the occupation and the progress toward democratization made by Japan.[17]

Astute Japanese leaders were well aware of American fears and played upon them constantly. A favorite theme, repeated endlessly, was that of the Communist menace. Against it, Japan was prepared to stand four-square with the United States. By 1948, revamped American thinking on the Japanese issue became firmly rooted. In addition to the Communist problem in the Far East, there were such factors as the following to justify and strengthen the new policy: In the first place, the drain on the American taxpayer now amounted to some $400,000,000 a year; this could not continue indefinitely. Secondly, the widespread chaos in East Asia made Japan appear the only stable nation in the area, and the only one whose economic revival was clearly in the best interests of the entire region. Finally, the failure of the nations at war with Japan to agree on a common policy was a factor of importance.[18]

Indicative of the new American attitude is the history of the directive on deconcentration of Japanese industry submitted by the United States to

[17] Yanaga, *op. cit.*, p. 643.
[18] Campbell, *United States in World Affairs, 1948-1949* (New York, 1949), p. 290.

the Far Eastern Commission. This directive, which provided the authority for a widespread reorganization of Japanese industrial companies, became known as FEC-230. It was subject to criticism in the American Congress. One senator, Knowland of California, was particularly upset and declared that its provisions for purging owners and managers of big Japanese concerns were contrary to American "decency and fairness"; he sharply assailed the State Department and called for a complete investigation.[19]

Within a short time, the Secretary of the Army called for the revision of FEC-230, and by the end of 1948 the United States withdrew its support of the directive on the grounds that its major points had already been implemented and its other points had either been already adopted, were unnecessary, or had become outmoded.[20]

Reports Advise Rebuilding of Japan. The case of FEC-230 is but one example of the revised American policy on Japan. An even clearer illustration of this reversal is the Strike Report. This was made in March, 1948, for the United States Army by Overseas Consultants, Incorporated, a group of some thirty engineers headed by Clifford S. Strike. This report recommended that Japan, rather than China, should be selected as the dominant force in the Far East. It called for rebuilding Japan into a sufficiently strong nation to undertake the role of leading Asia. At least five years would be required for the task. It also strongly urged that heavy reductions be made in the stringent reparations bill still facing Japan. The latter recommendation was at sharp variance with that of the earlier American mission headed by Edwin W. Pauley in 1946.[21]

That same month saw the arrival in Japan of Undersecretary of the Army William H. Draper with an economic mission of private citizens headed by Percy H. Johnston. In an interview with the press, Draper declared unofficially that the primary objective of American policy toward Japan was economic recovery. He predicted that Japan would become self-sustaining by 1952 or 1953, and said that an annual grant from the United States would be necessary to accomplish this. He, too, urged a more lenient attitude toward reparations and the deconcentration of Japanese industry and thought that it might be necessary to expand Japan's merchant marine.

The Johnston Report declared that the recovery of Japan was a *sine qua non* for the reconstruction of the economy of the Far East and urged

---

[19] Yanaga, *op. cit.*, p. 643.

[20] For the statement by the American representative on the Far Eastern Commission to that body, December 9, 1948, withdrawing American support of FEC-230, see Dennett and Turner, eds., *Documents on American Foreign Relations* (Princeton, 1950), Vol. X, pp. 163-65.

[21] Yanaga, *op. cit.*, p. 644.

that Congress grant the Army's request for $220,000,000 to begin a new recovery program designed to rebuild Japan in terms of the revised policy and to aid Korea and the Ryukyu Islands. It also recommended that the Japanese merchant marine, now reduced to 20 per cent of its prewar size, should be increased.[22]

On the day that this report was released, President Truman requested Congress for $150,000,000 to aid in the economic recovery of Japan, Korea, and the Ryukyus for a period of one year, beginning July 1, 1948. Congress agreed to set up a revolving credit of $150,000,000 to be used in the three occupied areas for buying American agricultural products and raw materials. In addition, the Export-Import Bank, together with several commercial banks, advanced $60,000,000 in credit to Japan to purchase American raw cotton.

The Johnston Report was opposed in the Philippines but surprisingly was supported by Chiang Kai-shek, who now reversed his previous position. Also Foreign Secretary Bevin of Great Britain, until then quite apathetic toward the Japanese question, called for an immediate Japanese peace conference in a speech before the British Labor Party Conference. Hence, the American policy of reviving the Japanese economy received the strong support of both Britain and Nationalist China.[23]

Extensive Reforms Inaugurated. In July, 1948, General MacArthur urged upon the Japanese government an extensive program embracing such points as taxes, wage stabilization, price control, foreign trade control, food collection, rationing, and balancing the budget. An unwillingness on the part of the Japanese to cooperate led MacArthur, with Washington's approval, to revive a procedure of the early occupation period. This was to issue a SCAP directive incorporating the proposed program. Both the Departments of State and Army in Washington let it be known that they would gauge future requests for funds for Japan by the way in which the Japanese carried out the directive.

Russian protests that the directive (when it was a short time later submitted to the Far Eastern Commission for its information) was of such a fundamental nature that it needed the approval of the F.E.C. were simply ignored by MacArthur.[24]

SCAP now proceeded to free restrictions on Japanese exports to a considerable extent. Trade agreements under which Japan would largely export cotton textiles and import raw materials were made with a number

---

[22] *Report by the "Johnston Committee" to the Secretary of the Army on the Economic Position and Prospects of Japan and Korea and Measures Required to Improve Them* (Department of the Army press release, May 19, 1948).
[23] Yanaga, *op. cit.*, p. 645.
[24] Campbell, *United States in World Affairs, 1948-1949*, p. 295.

of British Commonwealth nations and with Siam and the Netherlands Indies.

Many Doubt Wisdom of Restoring Japan. The issue of expanded Japanese exports was rather harmoniously received by those concerned, but the question of reparations was quite another matter. It was one thing for the United States to undergo an almost complete *volte-face* in its attitude toward reparations, but it was quite another thing for such peoples as the Filipinos and the Chinese, who had suffered so severely at Japanese hands, to be similarly forgiving. They were fearful that the new American policy, strongly influenced by the duel being waged with Russia on a world-wide front, would result in a revival of Japanese military power at their expense.

India was critical of this policy and many Australians and New Zealanders doubted the wisdom of putting Japan back on its feet.

The new program embraced in MacArthur's directive of July, 1948, had begun to take satisfactory shape within a year's time, and Japanese economic recovery showed distinct signs of advancement. Both industrial production and foreign trade increased markedly, although they remained well below prewar levels. As could be expected, occasional hitches developed, particularly in connection with economic stabilization. Whenever an opening presented itself, the Japanese Communists attempted to exploit it through agitation. Their activities had constituted such a nuisance to SCAP that MacArthur's message to the Japanese people on July 4, 1949, implied that this party should be outlawed. Although this was not done, the party's fortunes had already begun to recede.[25]

Russo-American Differences. Despite the diminution of the local Communists' strength, Japan loomed large in the relations between the United States and the U.S.S.R. The latter's refusal to release the approximately 500,000 Japanese prisoners and civilians still in Russian custody hurt the popularity of the U.S.S.R. in Japan. Russia refused to concede that she was holding more than 95,000 prisoners and announced in May, 1949, that some of these would be repatriated during the year. At the end of the year, an American attempt to force this issue to a conclusion in the Allied Council failed through the Russians' recourse to their well-known tactic of walking out, a practice they repeated each time the question was reopened in 1950.

This was but one difference between the two great powers. Their fundamental divergence over the right procedures for negotiating a peace treaty with Japan remained unaltered. The United States decided in 1950, as a result of the continued intransigence of the Soviets, to abandon the

[25] Stebbins, *op. cit.*, pp. 451 ff.

conference method of making a peace treaty with Japan and to seek peace through diplomatic processes, a procedure which no single nation could block.

The Japanese Peace Treaty

Preliminary Negotiations. The actual negotiations began toward the end of the summer of 1950 when many of the nations concerned with the problem of Japan were gathering to attend the United Nations General Assembly in New York. The delegations most directly concerned held frequent consultations. There then followed conferences at various capitals and a number of written exchanges of views. A United States Presidential Mission headed by John Foster Dulles made a world trip, visiting the capitals of the ten nations most directly concerned. In the meantime, the United Kingdom explored the problem within the Commonwealth.

In January, 1951, the United States drafted the principles agreed upon up to this point for the purpose of further study and comment. This draft was then circulated among more than twenty countries.

As the result of its own deliberations, the United Kingdom drafted a text based upon the results of the Commonwealth conferences. In June, the United States and the United Kingdom combined their efforts and drafted a third text. This new text was circulated during the first two weeks of July and kept open for further changes until the middle of August, 1951.

The role of the Soviet Union during all this preliminary work was active but unfavorable. Dulles conferred with Malik several times, and their respective governments exchanged some ten memoranda and drafts. Despite their continued hostility, the Russians accepted the invitation extended by the United States and the United Kingdom as cosponsors to attend a conference at the San Francisco Memorial Opera House to conclude a treaty of peace with Japan. They accepted because they hoped to dislocate the proceedings and possibly prevent the conclusion of a treaty. Gromyko's efforts to disrupt the conference were so fruitless that he walked out in a huff.

The Treaty Signed. Fifty-one nations in all were present at San Francisco for the sessions which lasted from September 4–8, 1951. Burma, India, and Yugoslavia, although invited, did not attend. China and Italy, still technically at war with Japan, were not invited. Of the nations present, all but the U.S.S.R., Czechoslovakia, and Poland signed the treaty, which was of a nonpunitive, nondiscriminatory nature designed to restore Japan to a place of dignity, equality, and opportunity among the nations of the world. Basically the finished document is quite simple and is limited solely to the essentials of peace.

The principal provisions of the treaty follow:

Territory: Japan is reduced to her four main islands together with a few minor ones. She recognizes the independence of Korea and renounces "all right, title and claim" there as well as to the Pescadores, Taiwan, South Sakhalin, the formerly Japanese mandated islands, the Antarctic area, the Spratly Islands, and the Paracel Islands. She promises to agree to any proposal made by the United States to the United Nations that would place under its trusteeship system the Bonin and Ryukyu Islands, including Okinawa.

Security: "Japan accepts the obligations set forth in ... the Charter of the United Nations ... to settle its international disputes by peaceful means ... and to refrain in its international relations from the threat of use of force" and the Allied Powers "confirm" that they will also abide by the Charter in their relations with Japan. They further agree to recognize Japan as "a sovereign nation [which] possesses the inherent right of individual or collective self-defense ... and ... may voluntarily enter into collective security arrangements." It is further stated that "Nothing ... shall ... prevent the stationing or retention of foreign armed forces in Japanese territory under or in consequence of any bilateral or multilateral agreements ... between one or more of the Allied Powers, on the one hand, and Japan on the other." [26]

The interesting thing about these provisions is that Japanese rearmament is allowed although the Japanese Constitution itself outlaws armed forces. This, of course, can be taken care of by the simple device of amending the Japanese Constitution. This portion of the treaty on security also made it possible for the United States to maintain troops in Japan. The two countries signed an agreement at San Francisco on September 8 which gave the United States this necessary authority for an indefinite period.

Reparations: "It is recognized that Japan should pay reparations to the Allied Powers for the damage and suffering caused by it during the war. Nevertheless it is also recognized that the resources of Japan are not at present sufficient, if it is to maintain a viable economy, to make complete reparation for all such damage and suffering and at the same time meet its other obligations." [27] Accordingly, the treaty suggests that countries with claims on Japan could send raw materials to Japan and receive consumer goods and industrial equipment in return.

[26] Department of State, Publication 4330, *Draft Treaty of Peace with Japan* (Washington, 1951), pp. 9-10.
[27] *Ibid.,* p. 16.

These are the chief portions of the treaty, which came into effect in April, 1952. It was ratified by Japan within less than two months, in October, 1951, and by a majority of the other signatories a few months later.

Defense Pacts Signed. Since at least three of the signers were worried about the possibility of a revival of Japanese aggression some time in the distant future, the United States sought to allay their fears by signing treaties of mutual defense with them before the San Francisco Conference. On August 30, the United States and the Philippines signed a mutual defense pact which was followed on September 1 by a similar agreement between the United States and Australia and New Zealand.

United States Far Eastern Policy

In the months prior to the opening of the Korean War in June, 1950, several statements by the President and the Secretary of State expressed important views on United States Far Eastern policy.

Taiwan. On January 5, the President released a statement in which he declared that the United States would not provide military aid or advice to the Chinese forces on Taiwan. The same day Acheson outlined the background of the President's statement. While providing a few reasons for the declaration, he particularly explained a sentence in the President's remarks that had raised question. Truman had stated that "The United States has no desire to obtain special rights or privileges or to establish military bases on Formosa [Taiwan] at this time." The phrase "at this time," said Acheson, should not be interpreted "to qualify or modify or weaken the fundamental policies" of the President's statement. It meant simply that "in the unlikely and unhappy event that our forces might be attacked in the Far East, the United States must be completely free to take whatever action in whatever area is necessary for its own security." [28]

Policy Fundamentals. The real outline of the major principles of United States Far Eastern policy was sketched by Secretary Acheson one week later. The basis of this policy was the identity of interests existing

---

[28] Department of State, *Strengthening the Forces of Freedom. Selected Speeches and Statements of Secretary of State Acheson, February, 1949-April, 1950* (Washington, 1950), pp. 170-73.

As a result of the Korean War, Truman in June, 1950, ordered the United States Seventh Fleet to protect Taiwan from attack but at the same time not to allow an attack on the mainland from the island. That, early in 1951, these orders to keep Taiwan neutralized were still in force is clear from a statement by the fleet's commander, Vice-Admiral Edward B. Struble. *New York Times*, February 21, 1951.

between the people of the United States and the peoples of Asia. The United States, he said, was interested in stopping Communism in Asia because it was inimical to the interests of the peoples of Asia. The way to check this hostile ideology was to assist the Asiatics to realize their own fundamental hopes—efficient administration, adequate educational opportunities, the development of resources and of technical skills. In other words, he stressed the Point Four approach.

The Secretary warned his listeners that no conceivable policy could be formulated to fit the myriad problems of Asia. In China, for example, the United States should avoid any hasty, ill-advised action which would focus the anger of the Chinese people on the United States, an indignation which, if the United States were circumspect, could perhaps be centered on the U.S.S.R. and "its Chinese instruments." The actions of Russia in China, he asserted, "are making plainer than any speech or any utterance or any legislation can make throughout all of Asia what the true function of Communism as an agent of Russian imperialism is."

He did not feel that threats to military security were the most pressing danger in the Pacific area, but nevertheless he pointed out that the United States had a defense perimeter which he held to be "essential under all circumstances"; this was from the Aleutians to Japan, the Ryukyus, and the Philippines. The Ryukyus, he said, would be sought by the United States in time as a trusteeship under the United Nations.[29]

As for the military security of the other areas in the Pacific—including Korea—the Secretary stated that no one could guarantee them against attack. An attack on any one of these places would have to be resisted by the people attacked. The victims of such an aggression would then rely upon the United Nations. These areas were more likely to be the objects of the boring, gnawing tactics of the Communists than of a direct military attack.

Acheson's views were subject to considerable criticism. His statements on China were unpopular with some, while his exclusion of Korea and Taiwan from the defense perimeter of the United States was attacked by others. His failure to mention a Japanese peace treaty or to say anything definite about Indo-China irritated still others.[30]

The Far Eastern Situation Analyzed. Acheson devoted another speech to United States policy toward Asia on March 15, 1950. He reiterated his earlier position that the United States was interested in the peoples of Asia as people. The United States desired only to help them, not to take anything from them. He then stated that a new era was in

---

[29] The United States had already acquired the former Japanese-mandated islands north of the equator as strategic trusteeships.

[30] Stebbins, *op. cit.,* pp. 462-65.

INTERNATIONAL RELATIONS AND THE FAR EAST 617

progress in Asia, made up of two dominant ideas. The first was "revulsion against misery and poverty as the normal condition of life"; the second, "revulsion against foreign domination." These two ideas were joined "in the positive conception of national independence." This was a development toward which the United States was well and friendly disposed; it would be encouraged in the future as in the past.

Tracing briefly the history of modern Asian independence movements, the Secretary attributed the collapse of China's Nationalist government to "its own inherent weakness and the withdrawal of the people's support," a statement which indicated that Acheson intended to cling to his hands-off position on China despite the intensity of the political attacks upon him. On the other hand, his dislike and mistrust of the Chinese Communists remained unchanged. He pictured their seizure of power as a reversal of the true purposes of the Chinese Revolution and saw them forced into the Soviet sphere "as a dependency of the Soviet economy."

As Secretary Acheson pointed out, already a Sino-Soviet Treaty of Friendship, Alliance and Mutual Assistance had been signed (February 14, 1950) which, despite the promises made by the Russians, must eventually convince the Chinese that it does not meet China's real needs and desires. He then proceeded to examine the economic promises made by the Russians. The return of certain Manchurian property to China, Acheson saw as perhaps "a belated admission of a theft which deprived not only China but all of Asia of some two billion dollars worth of productive capacity." Next, the $300,000,000 five-year Soviet credit must be reduced in value to $225,000,000 because of the new 25 per cent devaluation of the ruble. Third, despite the threat of famine in China, food was being taken from China to Russia.

Looking at the political and territorial assurances contained in the treaty, whatever the promises for the future, one thing was crystal clear: the U.S.S.R.'s special rights were an infringement of China's sovereignty, and they (or their equivalent) were held by no other power. The record was clear that United States' friendship for China has been based on the conviction that whoever violates China's integrity is China's enemy and is hostile to American interests. Fifty years of history and World War II had proved that this belief was far more than mere verbiage, Acheson asserted.

Then followed what, in the light of China's later invasions of Korea and Tibet, proved to be a prophetic statement. Acheson stated that there was a prospect that China might become a base for "probing for other weak spots" which the Communists could attack and exploit. Nevertheless, although the United States did not intend to engage in any aggression toward China and intended to remain her friend, China should understand that if she acted aggressively she would be violating the traditions and interests of all free peoples and the United Nations Charter.

Role of the United States. In the matter of Sino-American trade, the United States was willing to continue such relationships if the usual standards of conduct were observed by China. Propaganda to the contrary, the United States did not depend upon its trade with China. Should the present regime think so, time would prove their mistake.

Elsewhere in Asia, the people should understand that the big threat to their freedom and progress came from "Soviet-Communist imperialism and the colonialism it contains." The United States stood ready to help these peoples by aid "appropriate to the particular situation...and within the prudent capabilities of our resources."

The fundamental goal of American foreign policy "is to make possible a world in which all peoples, including the peoples of Asia, can work, in their own way, toward a better life.... We are for something positive, for the most fundamental urges of the human spirit. We are not and must not allow ourselves to appear merely negative, even though that negation is directed against the most corrupting force now operating in the world." [31]

This speech, together with the new attitude toward Japan, served to spell out concretely the form American Far Eastern policy had taken by the spring of 1950. Although it could not be foreseen at the time, in a few short months that policy was to undergo a dramatic change as a result of events in Korea. That country, which had been written off as outside the American defense perimeter, was ordered defended by United States military forces by President Truman on June 27, 1950. What produced this momentous change in American policy?

[31] Department of State, Publication 3817, *United States Policy Toward Asia,* address by Secretary Acheson (Washington, 1950), p. 16.

SUGGESTED READINGS

For China, see: Chih-mai Ch'en, *Kuomintang-Communist Relations: a Historical Survey* (Washington, 1949); Claire L. Chennault, *Way of a Fighter* (New York, 1949); Foster R. Dulles, *China and America: The Story of Their Relations Since 1784* (Princeton, 1946); Israel Epstein, *The Unfinished Revolution in China* (Boston, 1947); John K. Fairbank, *The United States and China* (2d ed., Cambridge, 1958); Herbert Feis, *The China Tangle* (Princeton, 1953); Harold J. Isaacs (ed.), *New Cycle in China: Selected Documents* (New York, 1947); George W. Keeton, *China, the Far East and the Future* (2d ed., London, 1949); Owen Lattimore, *Pivot of Asia: Sinkiang and the Inner Asian Frontiers of China and Russia* (Boston, 1950); Clare Boothe Luce, *The Mystery of American Policy in China* (New York, 1949); Mao Tse-tung, *The Fight for a New China* (New York, 1945); George Moorad,

INTERNATIONAL RELATIONS AND THE FAR EAST

Lost Peace in China (Boston, 1949); David Morris, *China Changed My Mind* (Boston, 1949); Lawrence W. Rosinger, *China's Crisis* (New York, 1945); David N. Rowe, *China Among the Powers* (New York, 1945); Gunther Stein, *The Challenge of Red China* (New York and London, 1945); Joseph W. Stilwell, *The Stilwell Papers,* ed., Theodore H. White (New York, 1948); Anna Louise Strong, *The Chinese Conquer China* (Garden City, N.Y., 1949); Freda Utley, *Last Chance in China* (New York, 1947); United States Department of State, *United States Relations with China: With Special Reference to the Period 1944–1949* (Washington, 1949); Theodore H. White and Annalee Jacoby, *Thunder Out of China* (New York, 1946); Gerald Winfield, *China: the Land and the People* (New York, 1948).

For Japan, see: Suggested Readings for Chapter 33.

For the United States: see appropriate entries above for China. Indispensable is the excellent series sponsored by the Council on Foreign Relations. Called *The United States in World Affairs,* it has been issued annually since 1947. See also: Kenneth Scott Latourette, *The American Record in the Far East, 1945–51* (New York, 1952); John Leighton Stuart, *Fifty Years in China* (New York, 1953); Harold M. Vinacke, *The United States and the Far East, 1945–1951* (Stanford, 1952); and Charles A. Willoughby and John Chamberlin, *MacArthur, 1941–1951* (New York, 1954).

For the U.S.S.R., see: Thomas A. Bailey, *America Faces Russia; Russian-American Relations from Early Times to Our Day* (Ithaca, 1950); Max Beloff, *Soviet Policy in the Far East, 1944–1951* (London, 1953); David J. Dallin, *Soviet Russia and the Far East* (New Haven, 1948); Harold H. Fisher, *U.S.-Soviet Relations in the Far East* (Tokyo, 1954); and E. H. Zabriskie, *American-Russian Rivalry in the Far East* (Philadelphia, 1946).

33

THE KOREAN WAR AND ITS AFTERMATH

Korea

The mountainous peninsula of Korea is an ancient land, called by its people, the "Land of the Morning Calm." It is equal in area to the states of Tennessee and Kentucky combined and has an estimated population of over 31,000,000 (1956 UN figures). Both geographically and politically Korea occupies a most important strategic place in the Far East. It is the center of a vital northeastern Asia triangle. On one side is Siberia, on a second, China, and Japan lies on the third. There is abundant evidence that whenever Korea has been in the hands of a strong military power, that power has been able to control all of northeastern Asia. Until the late nineteenth century Korea was politically and culturally oriented toward China, but by superior force she was swung toward Japan and annexed to that country in 1910.

Korean Independence Pledged. At the Cairo Conference between the United States, Great Britain, and China a statement was issued on December 1, 1943, which declared: "The aforesaid three great powers, mindful of the enslavement of the people of Korea, are determined that in due course Korea shall become free and independent."

Unfortunately for Korea's hopes it was agreed at Yalta in February, 1945, that there should be a joint Russo-American occupation of the country with the Soviets to occupy the north and the Americans to take over the south following the surrender of Japan.

At the Potsdam Conference in August, 1945, the leaders of the Big Three announced that "the terms of the Cairo Declaration shall be carried out," but omitted mention of when this would be done.

Then, when the U.S.S.R. declared war on Japan on August 8, 1945, the declaration said in part; "True to its obligations as an Ally, the Soviet Government has accepted the proposal of the Allies and has joined in the declaration of the Allied Powers of 28 July." This reference was to the Potsdam Declaration, and thus in effect the Soviet government committed itself to support Korean independence.

The Country Divided. Japan's surrender followed quickly, and proposals for the actual arrangements were embodied in an order (subsequently known as General Order No. 1) submitted by the American Secretary of War to the Secretary of State for the consideration of the State-War-Navy Coordinating Committee. The order provided that the surrender of Japanese forces north of 38 degrees north latitude was to be received by the Russians, whereas those south of this line were to surrender to the Americans. This arrangement brought the Korean capital of Seoul and about two-thirds of the country's population within the American sphere.

From the Russian point of view, a division at the 38th parallel had historic significance. In the latter part of the nineteenth century this line had been considered a satisfactory basis on which to divide with Japan spheres of influence on the continent of Asia, although such a division never took place. Furthermore, the Russians naturally desired to have a regime sympathetic with the U.S.S.R. in at least that part of Korea which bordered Russian territory.[1]

Once American forces had entered Korea in September, 1945, it was the United States intention, following the disarmament and repatriation of the Japanese there, to bring about a transfer of governmental power to the Korean people, which would allow the withdrawal of both American and Soviet forces and the establishment by the Korean people of a freely chosen, united, and independent government of their own. In that, the United States was doomed to disappointment, owing to Russian intransigeance.

The American commander in Korea, Lieutenant General John R. Hodge, opened negotiations with the Russian commander to eliminate the artificial border dividing the country and to establish unity in the Korean economy and administration. His efforts proved fruitless, with the result that the United States placed the question of Korea on the agenda of the Moscow meeting of the Council of Foreign Ministers in December, 1945.

The Moscow Agreement. Here it was agreed that a provisional Korean democratic government should be established for all of Korea. The Moscow agreement, which was ratified by the government of China, provided that the United States and Russian commands in Korea should form a Joint Commission which, in consultation with democratic parties and social organizations in Korea, should make recommendations to the Powers for the organization of a provisional Korean democratic government. Such recommendations were to be considered by the Powers prior to

---

[1] Cornelius Osgood, *The Koreans and Their Culture* (New York, 1951), p. 300.

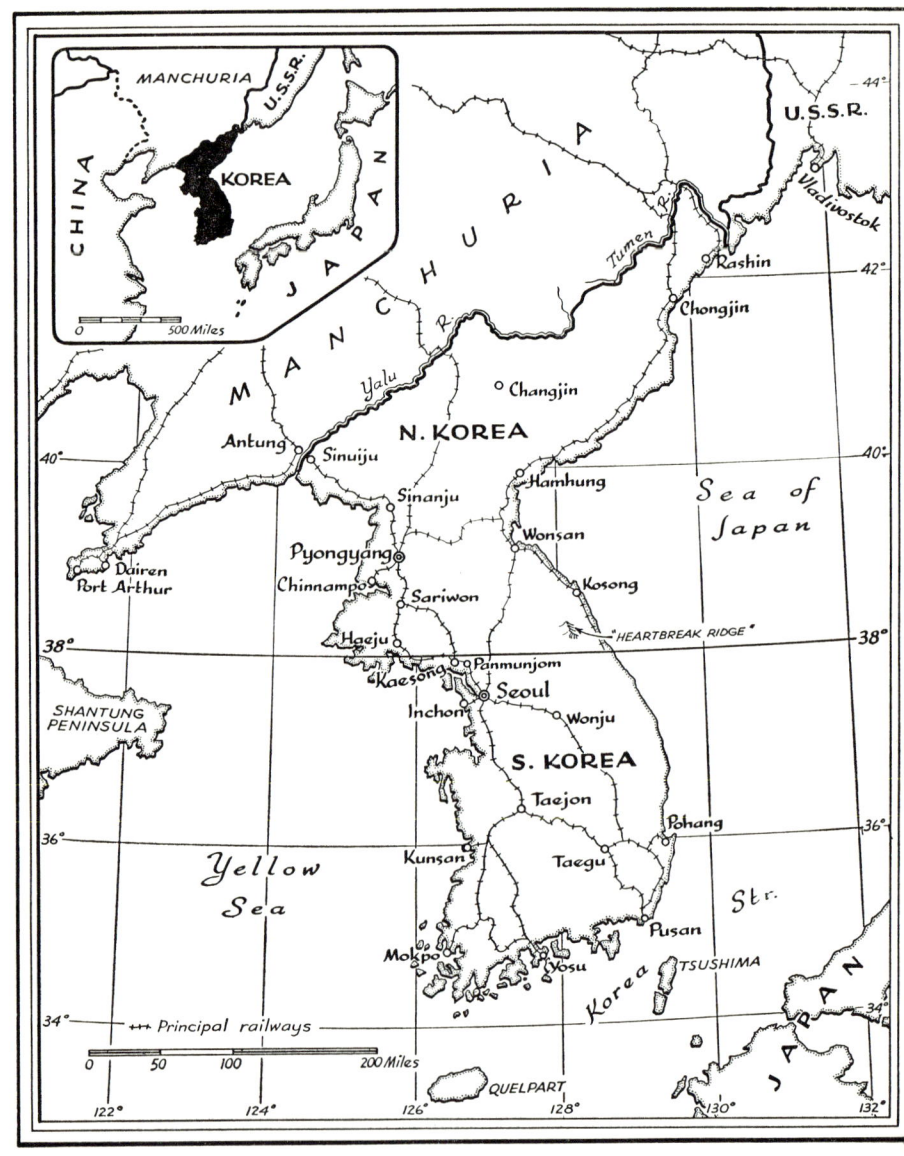

Korea in 1951.

a final decision by the Joint Commission. The latter was also empowered to work out proposals in conjunction with Korean democratic parties and social organizations for helping the Korean people in their progress toward independence. The proposals of the Joint Commission, following consultation with the provisional Korean government, were to be submitted to the joint consideration of China, the Soviet Union, the United Kingdom, and the United States for the working out of a four-power trusteeship agreement for a period not to exceed five years. The Moscow agreement further specified that a meeting of the Russian and American commands in Korea should open within two weeks following the adjournment of the Moscow meeting.

When the news of the trusteeship and the Joint Commission was announced in Seoul on December 28, 1945, there was a work stoppage and mass demonstration bordering on hysteria.

Failure of the Joint Commission. Order having been restored, a joint conference was held, in accordance with the Moscow directive, from January 16 through February 5, 1946, at which the Americans tried hard to remove the barrier of the 38th parallel and provide for the consolidation of Korea as an administrative and economic entity. The only agreements which the Russians would approve, however, were limited to the exchange of mail, the allocation of radio frequencies, and the movement of persons and goods. Even these were not honored, and the United States was able only to secure sporadic exchanges of mail and the occasional exchange of small military liaison teams.

The Joint Commission failed to accomplish anything significant in sessions lasting from March 20 to May 8, 1946, and adjourned. Russian intransigeance continued to block the Americans in the months which followed. Following an indication that the Soviets were now more leniently disposed, the Joint Commission resumed sessions on May 21, 1947, but the results were the same. An American proposal for a Four Power meeting was negated by the Soviets on September 4 on the grounds that such a conference was beyond the scope of the Moscow agreement.[2]

Russia Blocks National Election. In October the United States introduced a draft resolution in the General Assembly of the United Nations calling for the creation of a Korean government on the basis of elections in both parts of Korea to be held under UN observation. The resolution was approved in November and elections were decreed to select a National Assembly which would draft a democratic constitution and establish a national government. Russia refused the UN commission permission to

---

[2] The texts of the American note and the Russian rejection may be found in Department of State, Publication 3305, *Korea, 1945-1948* (Washington, 1948), pp. 43-47.

enter its zone, thereby depriving the North Koreans of their right to participate in a free election.

Two Governments Established. Elections were held in May, 1948, to choose 200 representatives in South Korea under the observation of the United Nations Temporary Commission on Korea. A constitution was drawn up, and a government was established based on democratic foundations. The National Assembly was constituted on a basis of proportional representation, and seats were reserved for representatives who, it was hoped, would one day be elected in the north.[3]

The Russians now proceeded to set up a puppet regime in the north which took the name of the Democratic People's Republic of Korea. This government was described by the United Nations Commission on Korea, which had replaced the Temporary Commission, in a report to the General Assembly on July 28, 1949, as follows:

> The northern regime is the creature of a military occupant and rules by right of a mere transfer of power from that Government. It has never been willing to give its subjects an unfettered opportunity, under the scrutiny of an impartial international agency, to pass upon its claim to rule. The claims to be a people's democracy and its expressions of concern for the general welfare are falsified by this unwillingness to account for the exercise of power to those against whom it is employed.[4]

A lamentable aspect of this division of the country was that it not only denied one-third of the people their freedom but that it split an economic entity. South Korea was principally agricultural whereas in the north lay the major industrial facilities, such as the iron and steel plants and the chemical industry which produced the fertilizers needed in the south. Furthermore, virtually every hydroelectric plant was in the north. This division left the south (the Republic of Korea) without sorely needed fertilizers, hydroelectric power, and the industrial plants basic to its economy. Added to these circumstances was the fact that some two million refugees from the north sorely taxed the south and helped to retard efforts to bolster the economy.

Withdrawal of Occupation Forces. With the formal launching of the new Republic of Korea (ROK), the United States Military Government quickly came to an end in August, 1948. The American occupation furnished some $285,000,000 in grants together with another $25,000,000

---

[3] Any doubts that this election was democratically conducted are set to rest in United Nations, *First Part of the Report of the United Nations Temporary Commission on Korea* (Lake Success, N.Y., 1948), Vol. II, 13-20.

[4] Department of State, Foreign Affairs Outlines, Autumn 1950, No. 24, Publication 3971, *Building the Peace: The Fight Against Aggression in Korea*, p. 4.

THE KOREAN WAR AND ITS AFTERMATH 625

in surplus army goods, such as blankets and clothing, and kept the economy from collapsing.

When on December 12, 1948, the General Assembly of the United Nations formally recognized the Republic of Korea, it reiterated its earlier recommendation that "the occupying Powers withdraw their occupation forces from Korea, as early as practicable." Less than two weeks later, Russia suddenly announced the complete withdrawal of its occupational forces from North Korea, but the puppet regime refused to allow the UNCOK to verify this assertion. However, the claim seems to have been substantially correct in that only a fairly sizable military training mission remained. The United States followed suit more leisurely and, except for the 500 officers and men of the United States Military Advisory Group, completed its withdrawal at the end of June, 1949.

United States Equips Korean Forces. Although the troops had left, American military assistance was to continue. The United States National Security Council decided that the United States should equip a ROK army of 65,000 men, that vessels necessary for a coast guard and arms for these vessels should likewise be made available, that there should be turned over to the Republic of Korea a stockpile of maintenance supplies sufficient to cover six months' replacement and consumption requirements, plus an emergency reserve, and that a USMAG should be responsible for the effective training of the Korean army, coast guard, and police.

The Mutual Defense Assistance Act of 1949 appropriated over $27,000,-000 for aid to Iran, the Philippines, and Korea. Korea's share was $10,200,000. The Korean military-aid program was in the first stages when the North Koreans attacked the south in 1950.

United Nations Action in Korea

South Korea Attacked. On June 25, 1950, at 4 A.M. the defenseless city of Kaesong, located just three miles south of the 38th parallel, was subjected to a sudden assault by troops, tanks, and planes of the so-called Democratic People's Republic of Korea. The initial crossing of the border was supported by some 100 tanks of Russian manufacture. The main attack was down the Pochon-Uijongbu-Seoul corridor. Simultaneously, attacks were launched in the Ongjin Peninsula to the west, against Chunchon in the eastern mountains, and down the east coast road. The North Korean air force covered the amphibious landings and attacked Kimpo Airfield near Seoul. Every phase of the attack clearly indicated long and careful planning.[5]

---
[5] Department of State, Publication 3935, *Action in Korea Under Unified Command, First Report to the Security Council by the United States Government, July 25, 1950*, pp. 1-2.

By contrast, everything about the character and disposition of the ROK army indicated that it was not prepared for this unprovoked attack. The report of an observation team of UNCOK, dated June 24, 1950, bears this out completely.[6] The facts of this report clearly controverted the North Korean broadcast from Pyongyang, late in the morning of June 25, that the Republic of Korea had begun the attack and that the North Korean army was merely acting in self-defense.

United Nations Calls for End of Hostilities. The American government construed the assault as an act of aggression and swiftly brought the matter to the attention of the United Nations by requesting (at 3 A.M. on June 25) an immediate meeting of the Security Council. Within twenty hours after the first official word of the invasion was received in Washington, representatives of ten member nations of the Council had assembled— the eleventh was the Soviet delegate who was absent. A resolution was passed calling for an immediate end to the fighting and requesting the assistance of all members of the United Nations in restoring the peace.[7]

United States Speeds Aid. President Truman authorized General MacArthur to reply favorably to the urgent appeals of the ROK government for ammunition. Within hours, loaded transport planes were flying from Japan under fighter protection, and the United States Seventh Fleet was steaming north from Subic Bay to be on hand in case of need.

On June 26, Truman announced that, in accordance with the call of the Security Council, he had issued orders for United States air and sea forces to give the Korean government troops cover and support, and that the Seventh Fleet had been ordered to prevent any attack upon Taiwan. He revealed that the Chinese Nationalists had been called upon to desist from any air or sea attacks against the mainland and said that the determination of the future status of the island would have to await the restoration of security in the Pacific area, a Japanese peace treaty, or action by the United Nations.

The following day, June 27, the Security Council, by a vote of 7 to 1, with two abstentions and one absence,[8] adopted an American resolution that "Members of the United Nations furnish such assistance to the Republic of Korea as may be necessary to repel the armed attack and to restore international peace and security in the area."

Three days later, President Truman announced that the United States Air Force had been authorized to conduct missions "on specific military

---

[6] U.N. doc. S/1626 quoted in *ibid.*, p. 1.

[7] Department of State, Publication 3922, *United States Policy in the Korean Crisis* (Washington, 1950), p. 16, contains the resolution.

[8] India and Egypt abstained, Yugoslavia was opposed, and Russia was absent.

targets in Northern Korea" and that he had ordered a naval blockade of the whole Korean coast and given General MacArthur the authority to employ "certain supporting ground units."

United Nations Members Send Aid. In addition to the troops of the United States and the Republic of Korea, air and naval units were quickly contributed by Australia, Canada, France, Great Britain, the Netherlands, and New Zealand. Although no ground forces other than American and Korean were supplied until late September, by the end of 1950 eight other nations had contributed troops. In all, troops of sixteen nations joined those of the ROK, while supplies, equipment, and food were sent by forty-nine nations.

On July 7, 1950, by a vote of 7 to 0, with three abstentions and one absence,[9] the Security Council resolved that all nations supplying forces and other assistance in Korea should put them under a unified command headed by the United States, which was also requested to designate the commander. General Douglas MacArthur was appointed commanding general of the forces operating in Korea and directed to use the UN flag.

The Fortunes of War. Driven southward to the sea, the UN forces staged a rally in September, 1950, and regained nearly all of the territory of the Republic of Korea. The rejection of a UN appeal to cease fighting led the UN forces to cross the 38th parallel in October where they mounted an offensive which seemed to signal the defeat of the enemy. At this point, huge Red Chinese armies poured into the conflict and hurled back the outnumbered UN forces. The retreat was stopped south of Seoul in January, 1951, and the UN soon resumed the offensive. By June a line of combat, which extended virtually across Korea above the 38th parallel, became stabilized.

Political Developments. While the military were engaged in their deadly struggle, efforts were made within the United Nations to halt what was styled the "police action" in Korea and which culminated in the branding of Communist China as an aggressor. On January 30, 1951, by a vote of 44 to 7, with eight abstentions, the Political Committee of the General Assembly declared that the Communist government of China "by giving direct aid and assistance to those who were already committing aggression in Korea, and by engaging in hostilities with the United Nations forces there, has itself engaged in aggression." This American resolution had also called for sanctions against Red China, but no sanctions were voted. Nevertheless, an important fact had gone into the record (and remains there to this day): Communist China had been branded an international aggressor.

[9] The abstentions were India, Egypt, and Yugoslavia; the absentee was the U.S.S.R.

Removal of General MacArthur. By the spring of 1951 dissatisfaction with the conduct of the war by General MacArthur began to mount. The General chafed under the restrictions put upon him by his superiors and which denied him the traditional right of "hot pursuit" of the enemy, a restriction giving the enemy airplanes a privileged sanctuary in Manchuria, which MacArthur was forbidden to bomb. In some quarters in the United States, among certain delegations in the United Nations, and in various world capitals, there was increasing apprehension that MacArthur might so broaden the conflict that it would become World War III.

A statement issued by the general on March 24 seemed to confirm these suspicions and fears because it contained the veiled threat of carrying the war into China. This was followed on April 5 by the reading, on the floor of the House, of a letter from MacArthur to minority leader Joseph Martin calling for the opening of a second front in Asia and the use of Chinese Nationalist troops in Korea.

The result was that, on April 11, President Truman relieved General MacArthur of his commands in the Far East on the grounds that, in the President's opinion, the General seemed unable to give adequate support to the policies of both the United States government and the United Nations. On the same day Mr. Truman told the nation in a radio address that he feared MacArthur's policies would certainly lead to a general war if they were followed.

The removal touched off a bitter and extended debate between the supporters of MacArthur and those of Truman. Before a meeting of the joint Senate Committee on the Armed Services and on Foreign Relations, General MacArthur was given an opportunity to air his views. On this occasion, and in many public addresses made later on the question, the General clung steadfastly to his position and was equally strenuously opposed by his critics in the United States and abroad.

Truce Talks. With General Matthew B. Ridgway as the new UN commander, the fighting continued unabated. General Ridgway's suggestion that a cease-fire be discussed finally led to the opening of negotiations on July 10, 1951, at Kaesong.

The site of the talks was shifted to Panmunjom with American Vice-Admiral Joy and North Korean General Nam Il Sung as the chief negotiators. From the beginning of the talks the military situation was restricted to local and indecisive engagements along the stabilized line mentioned above. The talks dragged along until November 27, 1951, when a tentative cease-fire was agreed upon, together with a demilitarized zone to separate the combatants should an armistice be reached.

Despite this promising development, things bogged down again with the result that the negotiations reached an impasse in May, 1952, when the United Nations made an offer which it construed to be "final." The principal stumbling block had been the question of repatriation of prisoners, a commodity with which the United Nations forces were abundantly stocked. The Communists were insistent upon the forced repatriation of these prisoners whereas the United Nations position was that these men should be given the option of deciding for themselves whether or not they desired repatriation.

General Mark Clark had meanwhile succeeded General Ridgway as the UN commander. Since diplomatic negotiations had failed, the only course left appeared to be renewed military pressure. Accordingly, on June 23, 1952, United Nations aircraft staged the heaviest attack yet mounted in the two years of the Korean War. But this onslaught did not seem to awe the enemy, and conditions remained virtually unchanged as the diplomatic and military stalemate continued throughout the year.

The United States and the Two Chinas. One result of the developments in the Korean War was the firming up of the American policy of nonrecognition of Communist China and, as a corollary, warmer friendship for the Nationalist regime on Taiwan. In 1951 military assistance to the Nationalists in the amount of $300,000,000 was approved, and Taiwan continued to be guarded by the United States Seventh Fleet. The administration was at pains to point out, however, that the object was to protect Taiwan, not to consider an attack on the mainland by the Nationalists. Furthermore, it was pointed out that in the eyes of the American government the questions of Taiwan and recognition of the Communists were divorced from the problem of a Korean settlement.

Trade with Communist China. The United States economic relations with Red China had been virtually suspended at the end of 1950, but the American government had become increasingly disturbed over the volume of trade in strategic materials being carried on with that country by members of the United Nations. Consequently, American diplomacy sought to convince the British and others that such trade was inimical to the best interests of the free world. These overtures bore some fruit in 1951.

Since sanctions had never been voted against Red China by the United Nations, the United States reopened the issue and succeeded in securing the adoption of a proposal which placed an embargo by all member states on the shipment of military matériel, petroleum, and "atomic energy materials" to Communist China, and later the list of items prohibited was augmented to include strategic materials.

"The Great Debate." Dissatisfaction in many American circles over the victory of the Chinese Reds in the civil war, coupled with the desultory way in which the Korean War was progressing and resentment over the dismissal of General MacArthur, resulted in the American people holding a full scale debate on American Far Eastern policy during the 1952 presidential campaign. Both General Eisenhower and Mr. Stevenson had determined to visit Korea after the election in the hope of contributing to an armistice which could lead to a satisfactory and lasting peace. Eisenhower publicly made known his intention to visit Korea and following his victory in the election carried out his promise by making a personal inspection of the military situation there on a three-day visit in December. Upon his return to the United States it was clear that he had no magic formula for ending the hostilities honorably, and so the war dragged on as did the seemingly endless talks.

The Korean Armistice. As a consquence of a number of factors, the Reds at last agreed upon an armistice with terms which at least could be accepted by the United Nations. Accordingly, on July 27, 1953, General Mark Clark for the United Nations, Marshal Kim Il Sung, representing North Korea, and General Peng Teh-huai, on behalf of the "Chinese People's Volunteers," signed an armistice agreement on Panmunjom.

The military line of demarcation was set at roughly the 38th parallel. On the east it went into North Korea about three times as far as it dipped into South Korea on the west. The big problem, however, was a familiar one, viz., repatriation of prisoners. This was finally accomplished but only with great difficulty. Operation "Big Switch," as the exchange was called, saw 3,597 Americans repatriated by the Communists along with 7,848 Koreans and 1,300 odd prisoners of other nationalities, including nearly 1,000 Britishers; on the other hand, the UN command returned 70,159 North Koreans and 5,640 Chinese. This exchange was followed by the difficult problem of the prisoners who had refused repatriation. The UN had a total of 22,600 nonrepatriate North Korean and Chinese prisoners, whereas the Communists held a total of 359 nonrepatriate UN prisoners, including 23 Americans. Early in 1954, the UN declared the North Koreans and Chinese prisoners free, and they either entered South Korea or went to Taiwan to join the Chinese Nationalists.

In return for his promise not to oppose an armistice, the United States made several pledges to President Syngman Rhee of the Republic of Korea: (1) economic aid; (2) a sixteen-power (those who contributed forces to the UN command in the Korean War) promise to come to the aid of South Korea in the event the Communists attacked again; (3) a mutual defense pact; and (4) withdrawal from the political conference (which was to follow the armistice) after ninety days, if the latter should prove fruitless at that point.[10]

On the very day the truce was signed (July 27), steps were taken in the United States to speed economic aid as promised. On that same day, the sixteen-nation "Joint Policy Declaration Concerning the Korean Armistice" was signed. The signatories pledged themselves to resume the war should the Communists attack again and warned unmistakably that it might not then be possible to confine hostilities within the frontiers of Korea.[11]

A mutual security pact between the United States and the Republic of Korea was overwhelmingly approved by the United States Senate early in 1954, although a stipulation was added that the United States would not support any moves by the Republic of Korea to unify the country by force.

Finally, the political conference, which was to follow the cessation of hostilities within ninety days, failed to materialize. As a consequence, in March, 1954, at a four-power foreign ministers' conference in Berlin, it was agreed that a Korean Peace Conference be held the following month at Geneva.

The Korean War Assessed. Before considering the results of the Geneva Conference, some assessment of the Korean War is indicated. For one thing, the fighting cost the United States dearly. Some 36,606 Americans were killed and 103,327 wounded. Another 2,953 were listed as missing.[12] In money, the billions of dollars expended do not tell the final story as the costs continue. Second, the war served to stiffen the determination, which earlier was somewhat weak, to refuse Red China recognition, to oppose her entry into the United Nations, and to refuse to see her snatch up Taiwan without opposition. Third, the United States took a new look at Japan and began a move to make that land the key link in the Far Eastern position of the United States. Fourth, the American people, through a series of treaties, found themselves promising to protect not only the Republic of Korea, Japan, and Nationalist China on Taiwan but also the Philippines, Vietnam, Thailand, Australia, and New Zealand.

The Geneva Conference. This meeting opened as scheduled on April 26, 1954. The sixteen nations which had formed the UN command in the Korean War were represented as were the U.S.S.R., North Korea, and Communist China. Added to the Korean problem was the question of the war in Indo-China, which had been draining France of men and treasure for over seven years. The presence of Communist China had been a thorny

[10] Carl Berger, *The Korea Knot* (Philadelphia, 1957), p. 176.
[11] Department of State, *Joint Policy Declaration Concerning the Korean Armistice, Signed at Washington, July 27, 1953* (Washington, 1953), p. 2.
[12] Department of War figures quoted in Samuel F. Bemis, *A Diplomatic History of the United States* (4th ed., New York, 1955), p. 960.

point for some time and caused difficulties right down to the opening session. The United States had been reluctant to permit Red China to be represented and agreed only on the grounds that she was not to be considered one of the sponsoring powers. The U.S.S.R., on the other hand, unsuccessfully sought to gain for her ally the same status enjoyed by the Big Four (United States, Great Britain, France, and Russia).

The first part of the conference was devoted to Korea, but the negotiations proved futile. In June, following weeks of unfruitful discussions, which were characterized by vicious attacks on the United States by the Chinese Communists sparked by Chou En-lai, the UN group and the Republic of Korea reluctantly broke off the talks. The armistice continued, but neither peace nor the democratic unification of Korea had been achieved.

In the Indo-China part of the conference, which is outside the scope of this book, suffice it to say that a partition at the 17th parallel was agreed upon, giving the Communists northern Vietnam, and the question of the future disposition of the south was left to be determined by general elections in 1956. The United States was unwilling to become a signatory to the agreement on Indo-China but, in effect, acquiesced in it.

One result of what was generally conceded to have been a Communist victory was that the United States took the lead in forming a new treaty organization for Southeast Asia, popularly called SEATO (Southeast Asia Treaty Organization) and consisting of the United States, Great Britain, France, Australia, New Zealand, Pakistan, Thailand, and the Philippines.

The First Quemoy Crisis. Although the Chinese Communists had made a number of propaganda speeches directed against Taiwan and American support of the Nationalist government there, they had refrained from any invasion attempts. For their part the Nationalists dreamed of a "return to the mainland" but had likewise refrained from such an ambitious undertaking. The Chiang government, however, had undertaken to bolster its military position on some of the offshore islands it held, notably Quemoy and Matsu. This was apparently done with both the knowledge and encouragement of the United States. The Eisenhower administration upon taking office had lifted the restrictions placed on the Nationalists by former President Truman, who had ordered the Seventh Fleet not only to protect Taiwan but also to prevent any attacks by Chiang on the mainland. The lifting of the restrictions on attack by Chiang now meant that he had been "unleashed," thus enabling him to make attacks against the Communists on the mainland. This action by the new administration in Washington had been followed by a step-up in American military assistance to Chiang.

A few days before the signing of the SEATO pact in Manila, the Chinese Reds suddenly opened a heavy artillery bombardment on Quemoy and Little Quemoy and kept it up for some days, during which two American officers of the USMAG (United States Military Advisory Group) were killed. Chiang's forces retaliated, but the situation soon quieted.

This action created considerable excitement in the United States, and although rumors were rife of a further stiffening of American Far Eastern policy, there were no official announcements of any changes for the time being.

Strengthened Soviet-Chinese Ties. In the fall of 1954, not long after the shooting around Quemoy had quieted down, a top level Soviet delegation headed by Bulganin, Khrushchev, and Mikoyan paid a visit to Peking. The result was that announcements were made of increased Soviet economic aid to its satellite; some mud was thrown at the United States; and a pledge to withdraw from Port Arthur was made by the U.S.S.R. Perhaps the principal value of the visit from the standpoint of the Red Chinese was the seemingly firm and unequivocal promise of backing for the "liberation" of Taiwan by the Russians. Other statements made it appear that the two governments saw eye to eye in the area of foreign policy.

The United States—Republic of China Mutual Defense Treaty. In the light of this formidable solidarity (or what appeared to be), Nationalist China became somewhat uneasy. For the better part of a year, the Nationalists had been hopeful of a mutual defense treaty with the United States. On his return from Manila, where he had negotiated the SEATO pact, Secretary of State John Foster Dulles stopped off at Taipei, the capital of Taiwan, to visit Chiang Kai-shek, and the topic of a defense pact was discussed. Other developments followed, and in December, 1954, a few months later, a Mutual Defense Treaty between the United States and the Republic of China was signed.

Under the terms of the treaty each undertook in the event of an armed attack in the "West Pacific Area" against their respective territories to "act to meet the common danger in accordance with its constitutional processes." How this would be done was omitted. The specific territories were defined as Taiwan and the Pescadores for China and "the island territories in the West Pacific" under "the jurisdiction" of the United States. It will be observed that the numerous offshore islands held by Nationalist China were not included. No duration was set for the treaty, but it could be terminated by either signatory on one year's notice. A supplementary note, whose terms were not immediately revealed, pledged the Nationalists not to undertake any attacks without the prior consent of the United States. On its part, the United States recognized that her ally possessed the "inherent right of self-defense" in the matter not only of Taiwan and the Pescadores but "other territory" (the offshore islands) as well.

One conclusion which astute analysts were quick to draw was that American policy toward the Nationalists now looked somewhat different in at least one very important respect from the first days of the Eisenhower administration, when the "unleashing" of Chiang Kai-shek had been ordered. This was that, instead of being free to attack the mainland, the Nationalists were now quite clearly being discouraged by the Americans.[13]

With respect to the offshore islands, the conclusion seemed to have been put by Secretary Dulles when he declared that the United States was not obligated to defend them but neither did the treaty preclude such action by the United States should it so desire. In other words, a pragmatic policy would henceforth be pursued in respect to these islands, which once again were being subjected to renewed military pressure at the time the mutual defense pact was being negotiated and in the days which followed.

Growing Importance of Japan in American Policy. The fall of China to the Communists in 1949 brought with it a growing awareness in American government circles of the importance of Japan in American Far Eastern policy, but it was the outbreak of the Korean War which made it abundantly clear. As noted in the previous chapter, the United States had moved with celerity to bring about a Japanese Peace Treaty in 1951 and had followed it by signing a mutual defense pact with newly independent Japan. The problems which the re-emergence of her independence brought to Japan proved to be extremely formidable ones. Among them were the following: rearmament; friction resulting from the continued presence of large numbers of American troops; the vital question of the nation's economy; a very high degree of sensitiveness to the Americans' continued experimentation with the H-bomb; difficulties involved in relations with neighboring countries whom she had occupied during World War II; and, in the eyes of the United States, her somewhat apathetic attitude toward the problem of Communism.

Rearmament.[14] The fall of China and the Korean War made it plain to the United States that a serious Communist threat existed in both the Far East and in Southeast Asia. Equally clear was the realization that Japan was the only highly industrialized nation in Asia, possessing indus-

---

[13] Richard P. Stebbins, *The United States in World Affairs, 1954* (New York, 1956), p. 281.

[14] While most of this and the following topics have already been touched upon in Chapter 31, some amplification of them is indicated here.

trial technology, managerial experience, an abundance of technical experts, and a large reservoir of skilled man power. She was also the most stable nation in the area, was seemingly defensible, and had vast experience in adapting Western technology to local conditions.

But to advocate and then implement her rearmament involved both an embarrassing reversal of American policy and a task of awesome proportions from the standpoint of Japanese public opinion. Article IX of the Japanese constitution, itself so patently bearing the marks of "Made in America," stated that "land, sea, and air forces, as well as other war potential, will never be maintained." Yet the Korean War had been underway just two weeks when the occupational forces commenced the rearming of Japan, making Article IX a dead letter. A "Police Reserve" of 75,000 effectives was decreed, ostensibly to replace American troops shipped to Korea from Japan. The name of the new force was changed, for psychological reasons, to the "National Security Force" and it was equipped with various implements of war, including tanks (now styled "special cars").

Meanwhile, the United States frankly conceded that it had been a mistake to disarm the country. To give stature to this confession, Vice-President Nixon went to Japan on an important mission in 1953 and openly revealed that the American haste in disarming Japan had been in error. The following year the Japanese military establishment underwent a further change of name, this time to the "Defense Force," and the emblem on the uniform of the Japanese soldiers, sailors, and airmen was changed from a dove to an eagle.

It was, of course, all very well for the United States to admit a mistake, but the desire on the part of many Japanese to adhere to the decision to remain disarmed, in the hope that their country might never again repeat the tragic experiences of World War II, combined with adroit Communist propaganda against rearmament made the issue a very delicate one in Japanese politics. Notwithstanding the difficulties inherent in their decision, the conservative governments elected to proceed as circumspectly as possible in the task of rebuilding Japan's defunct military establishment—an undertaking in which they were eagerly aided by the United States.

Resentment Toward American Forces and Installations. One feature of Japan's renascent independence was a growing anti-American feeling based on the continued presence of American forces in the country. Although it was widely understood that these forces were there in response to the specific request of the Japanese government, many Japanese were resentful of them and would have been happy to see them go—an attitude which was considerably removed from realism but one which, nevertheless, persisted.

The anti-American irritants were a compound of several factors. Not the least of them was the large number of illegitimate children born to Japanese mothers out of wedlock. These unfortunate youngsters were largely unacceptable to the Japanese people who considered them a source of shame.

Other factors were: the continued retention of extraterritorial rights by the United States; the continuing use of buildings in densely populated areas by the American forces and civilians; the taking over of a considerable portion of desperately needed rural land; and the constant firing activities of the Americans which disturbed Japanese fishing.[15]

The Economy. While American expenditures in Japan in support of Korean War activities produced a considerable economic boom in Japan, it was patent that Japan's economy was in a rather critical condition. Accordingly, the American government took steps to be of assistance. Yet these moves were somewhat removed from solving the problem and were mere palliatives at best. Speeches by Japanese government officials and comments in the press continually called attention to Japan's need to close the critical gap in Japan's unfavorable balance of trade with the United States. These speeches and comments were artfully prone to point out the need which Japan had for trade with Communist China but seemed to agree that this was a step which Japan would be reluctant to take. Numerous references were made to the fact that in prewar days Japanese exports to China, Korea, and Taiwan averaged roughly one-half her annual exports and that this trade had now become insignificant. Her trade to Southeast Asia, on the other hand, had doubled since the war. Accordingly, Japan sought to exploit this area more intensively.

Difficulties with Former Occupied Countries. Militating against the implementation of this objective was the memory of Japan's ruthless occupation of so many of these Southeast Asian nations during World War II. The deep scars left by those years were slow to heal.

Japan's admission to the United Nations was a step in improving relations with Southeast Asia since Japan became a member of the UN Economic Commission for Asia and the Far East (ECAFE). She also participated in the Colombo Plan for Economic Development in South and Southeast Asia. The absence of diplomatic relations with such countries as Burma, Indonesia, and the Philippines, however, retarded economic progress with these lands. The signing of a peace treaty with Burma late

---

[15] Richard P. Stebbins, *The United States in World Affairs, 1953* (New York, 1955), pp. 263 ff. That the United States was conscious of Japan's sensitivity may be seen from the signing of a status of forces agreement in 1953 which gave Japan jurisdiction over American troops committing criminal offenses against non-Americans off duty and off American property.

THE KOREAN WAR AND ITS AFTERMATH 637

in 1954 helped, as Japan promised some $250,000,000 reparations to Burma over the next ten years in machinery, goods, and technical assistance. Efforts to patch up the differences with the Philippines and Indonesia were unavailing for the time being. Her differences with Korea also continued unresolved.[16]

The Hydrogen Bomb. Having been the first victims of the atomic bomb, the Japanese people were extremely (and understandably) sensitive over continued hydrogen bomb experiments in the Pacific. On March 1, 1954, an American test at Bikini produced radioactive fallout with which a Japanese fishing vessel, the *Fukuryu Maru,* came into contact. The entire crew had been exposed, and one member subsequently died as a consequence. Although the United States was not technically responsible, since the ship was well within the danger area, the American government was most generous in its handling of the incident. Yet this generosity was largely overlooked in the hysterical reaction to the affair within Japan—a reaction which was considerably spurred by Communist propagandists whose work was naturally made easy by Japan's national feelings in the matter. Added to her dislike of such a weapon as the bomb was Japan's understandable fear that her vital fishing activities might be seriously impaired and that her national health was likewise in jeopardy.[17]

Communism. Although there was strong American sympathy for the myriad problems faced by Japan in her newly gained independence, there was one critical area in which the United States felt that Japan was noticeably dragging her feet. This was in her rather supine attitude toward the communist threat.

---

[16] Stebbins, *The United States in World Affairs, 1954,* p. 297.

[17] Immediately after the Bikini incident in 1954, the Science Council of Japan appointed an 87 member committee to study the effects of the Bikini hydrogen bomb. As part of the project, a team of scientists sailed for the Bikini area shortly afterwards aboard the survey ship *Shunkotsu Maru* and made an extended on-the-spot survey. The result was the publication two years later of a book containing 200 scientific reports on the effects of the bomb. This 1800-page volume was translated into English by the Society for the Promotion of Science, financed by a subsidy from the government. Some of the papers were devoted to the clinical findings in the cases of the crew members of the *Fukuryu Maru* (Fortunate Dragon) who were hospitalized after being showered with radioactive ash. The results of the autopsy on the dead crew member were also published as were reports on the radioactive rain, snow, and dust recorded in various parts of Japan. *Japan Report,* Vol. II, No. 18 (October 2, 1956), p. 7.

Another example of the many available to point up the persistence of Japan's feelings about the bomb may be gleaned from the report of the Genetics Society of Japan and the Japan Society of Human Genetics, which announced that any amount of radiation, however small, is harmful to the heredity of man. *Japan Report,* Vol. III, No. 5 (April 10, 1957), p. 8.

Japan's feelings were skilfully (and profitably) brought home to a segment of the American public by the release in the United States in the spring of 1959 of a Japanese science fiction motion picture entitled *The H-Man.* This production propagated the thesis that failure to control the bomb experiments would result in the end of human life everywhere.

Fortunately for the American efforts to awaken Japan to this danger, the Socialist Fatherland itself made a substantial contribution in this direction. The persistent Russian refusal to repatriate the some 85,000 Japanese prisoners still held somewhere on the Asiatic mainland and in the Soviet Union served as a painful reminder of the Soviet attitude toward Japan. From the standpoint of the Japanese government there was also a growing realization of the domestic threat to the conservative leaders of the nation which the adroit communist underground in Japan represented.

Although the Russians and the Communist Chinese made a gesture of good will by repatriating some 8,000 prisoners of war in 1953, the negligible proportions of these numbers served merely to call attention to the preponderant total still held captive.

In a further attempt to minimize the ill will which their actions had created in Japan, the Soviets, in 1954, concluded a barter arrangement with the Japanese which quadrupled Japanese exports to the mainland. That such exporting was possible, however, was very largely due to an easement of embargoes which the United States and its allies permitted in East-West trade that year.

As the year drew to a close, steps had been taken by the new Japanese government, which appeared less pro-American than its predecessor, looking toward the resumption of formal ties between Japan and the U.S.S.R.

SUGGESTED READINGS

China

John P. Armstrong, *Chinese Dilemma* (Chicago, 1956); H. L. Bowman, A. Eckstein, P. E. Mosely, and Benjamin Schwartz, *Moscow-Peking Axis: Strengths and Strains* (New York, 1957); Conrad Brandt, Benjamin Schwartz, and John K. Fairbank, *A Documentary History of Chinese Communism* (London, 1952); David Brook, *The United Nations and the China Dilemma* (New York, 1956); Benjamin B. Brown and Fred Greene, *Chinese Representation: a Case Study in United Nations Political Affairs* (New York, 1955); T'ien-fang Cheng, *A History of Sino-Russian Relations* (Washington, 1957); Chiang Kai-shek, *Soviet Russia in China* (New York, 1957); Richard L.-G. Deverall, *Mao Tze-tung* (Tokyo, 1954) (the sub-title is *Stop This Dirty Opium Business! How Red China Is Selling Opium and Heroin to Produce Revenue for China's War Machine*); Joseph Dinwiddie, *Aid to Nationalist China* (New York, 1957); Francis Dufay, *The Star Versus the Cross* (Hong Kong, 1953); Herbert Feis, *The China Tangle* (Princeton, 1953); Charles P. Fitzgerald, *Revolution in China* (New York, 1952); Ying Hsin, *The Foreign Trade of Communist China* (Kowloon, Hong Kong, 1954); Edward Hunter, *Brainwashing in Red China* (New York, 1951); Raja Hutheesing, *The Great Peace* (New York, 1953); Malcom Kennedy, *A History of Communism in East Asia* (New York, 1957); Ping-chia Kuo, *China: New Age and New Outlook* (New York, 1956); Joseph R. Levenson, *Confucian China and Its Modern Fate* (Berkeley, 1958); Werner Levi, *Modern China's Foreign Policy* (Minneapolis, 1953); Michael Lindsay, *China and the Cold War* (Melbourne, 1955); Mao Tse-tung, *On the Protracted War* (Peking,

1954); Mid-West Debate Bureau, *Debate Handbook: Recognition of Communist China* (Normal, Ill., 1954); Frank Moraes, *Report on Mao's China* (New York, 1953); R. C. North, *Moscow and the Chinese Communists* (Stanford, 1953); Amaury de Riencourt, *The Soul of China* (New York, 1958); Fred W. Riggs, *Formosa Under Chinese Nationalist Rule* (New York, 1952); W. W. Rostow et al., *The Prospects for Communist China* (Cambridge and New York, 1954); Benjamin I. Schwartz, *Chinese Communism and the Rise of Mao* (Cambridge, 1951); H. Arthur Steiner, *Maoism: a Sourcebook* (Los Angeles, 1952); Robert Strauz-Hupe et al., *American-Asian Tensions* (London, 1957); Rodger Swearingen, "Techniques of Communist Aggression and the Moscow-Peking Axis," in *Nationalism and Progress in Free Asia* (Baltimore, 1956); Sheng-hao Tang, *Communist China Today; Domestic and Foreign Policies* (New York, 1957); George Taylor, *Formosa* (Cambridge, 1954); S. B. Thomas, *Communist China and Her Neighbours* (Toronto, 1955); United States Department of State, Publication 6198, *Communist China and American Far Eastern Policy* (Washington, 1955); United States Department of State, Bulletin 37, John Foster Dulles, *Our Policies Toward Communism in China* (Washington, 1957); United States Department of State, Bulletin 35, *Question of Chinese Representation in the United Nations; Statements, November 14 and 15, 1956* (by Henry Cabot Lodge, Jr.) (Washington, 1956); John Weston Walch, *Complete Handbook on Recognition of Communist China* (Portland, Me., 1954), and *Supplement on Recognition of Communist China* (Portland, Me., 1955); Richard L. Walker, *China Under Communism* (New Haven, 1955); Henry Wei, *China and Soviet Russia* (Princeton, 1956); Karl A. Wittfogel, *Oriental Despotism* (New Haven, 1957); Yuan-li Wu, *An Economic Survey of Communist China* (New York, 1956).

Japan

Thomas A. Bisson, *Zaibatsu Dissolution in Japan* (Berkeley, 1954); Hugh Borton, *Japan's Modern Century* (New York, 1955); Delmer M. Brown, *Nationalism in Japan* (Berkeley and Los Angeles, 1955); Bernard C. Cohen, *The Political Process and Foreign Policy; the Making of the Japanese Peace Settlement* (Princeton, 1957), "International Aspects of Japan's Economic Situation," in United States Department of State, Publication 6516, *Japan: Free World Ally* (Washington, 1957), and *Japan's Postwar Economy* (Bloomington, Ind., 1958); Jerome B. Cohen, *Economic Problems of Free Japan* (Princeton, 1952); Robert A. Fearey, *The Occupation of Japan, Second Phase, 1948–1950* (New York, 1950); Douglas Haring (ed.), *Japan's Prospects* (Cambridge, 1946); F. C. Jones, *Manchuria Since 1931* (London, 1949); William L. Jorden, "Japan's Diplomacy Between East and West," in *Japan Between East and West* (New York, 1957); *Judgment of the International Military Tribunal for the Far East* (Washington, 1948); Kenneth Scott Latourette, *The History of Japan* (rev. ed., New York, 1957); Baron E. J. Lewe van Aduard, *Japan, from Surrender to Peace* (New York, 1954); Edwin M. Martin, *The Allied Occupation of Japan* (Stanford, 1948); Yale Candee Maxon, *Control of Japanese Foreign Policy* (Berkeley, 1957); John Dickey Montgomery, *Forced To Be Free; The Artificial Revolution in Germany and Japan* (Chicago, 1957); Harold S. Quigley and John E. Turner, *The New Japan: Government and Politics* (Minneapolis, 1956); Edwin O. Reischauer, *Japan—Past and Present* (2d ed., New York, 1953), and *The United States and Japan* (Cambridge, 1951); Edwin O. Reischauer, et al., *Japan and America Today* (Stanford, 1953); Walter J. Robertson, *United States Policy Toward Japan* (Washington, 1954)—speech before Cleveland Council on World Affairs, February 6, 1954; General Headquarters, Supreme Commander for the Allied Powers, *Political Re-*

orientation of Japan, September, 1945, to September, 1948 (2 vols. Washington, n.d.); Robert B. Textor, *Failure in Japan* (New York, 1951); United States Department of State, Publication 4392, *Conference for the Conclusion and Signature of the Treaty of Peace with Japan, San Francisco, California, September 4-8, 1951* (Washington, 1951); United States Department of State, Publication 5138, *The Far Eastern Commission: a Study in International Cooperation, 1945 to 1952* (Washington, 1953); United States Department of State, Division of Northeast Asian Affairs, *United States Relations with Japan, 1945-1952* (New York, 1953); C. Martin Wilbur, "Japan and the Rise of Communist China," in *Japan Between East and West* (New York, 1957); Harry Emerson Wildes, *Typhoon in Tokyo; the Occupation and Its Aftermath* (New York, 1954); and Chitoshi Yanaga, *Japanese People and Politics* (New York, 1956).

Korea

Carl Berger, *The Korea Knot* (Philadelphia, 1957); Jaroslav Jan Brazda, *The Korean Armistice Agreement: a Comparative Study* (Ann Arbor, 1956); Malcom C. Cagle and Frank A. Manson, *The Sea War in Korea* (Annapolis, Md., 1957); John C. Caldwell, *The Korea Story* (Chicago, 1952); Kyong-jo Chong, *Korea Tomorrow, Land of the Morning Calm* (New York, 1956); Henry Chung, *The Russians Came to Korea* (Seoul and Washington, 1947); Mark W. Clark, *From the Danube to the Yalu* (New York, 1954); Major-General William F. Dean, *General Dean's Story* (New York, 1954); John Dille, *Substitute for Victory* (Garden City, N.Y., 1954); Leland M. Goodrich, *Korea: A Study of United States Policy in the United Nations* (New York, 1956); Andrew J. Grajdanzev, *Modern Korea* (New York, 1944); A. Wigfall Green, *The Epic of Korea* (Washington, 1950); Russell A. Gugeler, *Combat Actions in Korea* (Washington, 1954); Charles Turner Joy, *How Communists Negotiate* (New York, 1955); Korea (Republic) Office of Public Information, Statistics Bureau, *Statistics of Damage Suffered During the Korean War, June 25, 1950—July 27, 1953* (Seoul, 1954); George M. McCune and Arthur L. Grey, Jr., *Korea Today* (Cambridge, 1950); Shannon McCune, "The United States and Korea," in Tenth American Assembly, *The United States and the Far East* (New York, 1956); S. L. A. Marshall, *The River and the Gauntlet* (New York, 1953); E. Grant Meade, *American Military Government in Korea* (New York, 1951); Robert Oliver, *Why War Came in Korea* (New York, 1950); *Verdict in Korea* (State College, Pa., 1952), and *Syngman Rhee* (New York, 1954); Cornelius Osgood, *The Koreans and Their Culture* (New York, 1951); Virginia Pasley, *21 Stayed* (New York, 1955); Rutherford M. Poats, *Decision in Korea* (New York, 1954); P. T. Pyun, *Korea—My Country* (Washington, 1953); Richard H. Rovere and Arthur M. Schlesinger, Jr., *The General and the President* (New York, 1951); Robert C. W. Thomas, *The War in Korea, 1950-53* (Aldershot, Eng., 1954); United Nations Department of Information, Background Paper No. 79, *The Question of Korea, 1950-1953* (New York, 1954); United States Congress, Committee on Governmental Operations, *Korean War Atrocities* (Washington, 1954); United States Congress, Senate, Committee on the Judiciary, *The Korean War and Related Matters* (Washington, 1955); United States Congress, Senate Document 74, 83d Congress, 1st Sess., *The United States and the Korean Problem: Documents, 1943-1953* (Washington, 1953); United States Department of the Army, Office of Military History, *Korea, 1951-53* (Washington, 1956); United States Department of State, Press Release 219, *Toward a Free Korea* (Washington, 1954). Speech by John Foster Dulles before 3d Plenary Session of Geneva Conference, April 28, 1954; United States Department of State, Publication

THE KOREAN WAR AND ITS AFTERMATH

5609, *The Korean Problem at the Geneva Conference, April 26—June 15, 1954* (Washington, 1954); United States Department of State, Publication 840, *Statement on Communist Violations of the Truce in Korea* (Washington, 1955); United States Marine Corps, *United States Marine Operations in Korea, 1950–53* (Washington, 1955); William H. Vatcher, Jr., *Panmunjom: The Story of the Korean Military Armistice Negotiations* (New York, 1958); and Melvin B. Voorhees, *Korean Talks* (New York, 1952).

The United States

An indispensable source of accurate information on postwar events is the excellent series sponsored by the Council on Foreign Relations. Called *The United States in World Affairs,* it has been published annually since 1947.

See also entries under preceding headings in the suggested readings for this chapter.

Also the following: Yu-nan Chang, *American Security Problems in the Far East* (Ann Arbor, 1954); Harold H. Fisher, *United States–Soviet Relations and the Far East* (Tokyo, 1954); Kenneth Scott Latourette, *The American Record in the Far East, 1945–51* (New York, 1952); Robert A. Scalapino, "The United States and Japan," in Tenth American Assembly, *The United States and the Far East* (New York, 1956); John Leighton Stuart, *Fifty Years in China* (New York, 1953); United States Department of State, Bulletin 35, *Countering the Soviet Threat in the Far East* (Washington, 1956); United States Department of State, Office of Intelligence Research, Report No. 6870.2, *Chinese Communist World Outlook: Views Regarding the United States* (Washington, 1956); Harold M. Vinacke, *The United States and the Far East, 1945–1951* (Stanford, 1952); William W. Wade (ed.), *United States Policy in Asia* (New York, 1956); Charles A. Willoughby and John Chamberlin, *MacArthur, 1941–1951* (New York, 1954); Allen Suess Whiting, "The United States and Taiwan," in Tenth American Assembly, *The United States and the Far East* (New York, 1956).

U.S.S.R.

Max Beloff, *Soviet Policy in the Far East, 1944–1951* (London, 1953); George B. Cressey, *How Strong Is Russia?* (Syracuse, 1954); Jane Degras (ed.), *Soviet Documents on Foreign Policy* (Oxford, 1951–53); and Aitchen K. Wu, *China and the Soviet Union* (New York, 1950).

34

INTERNATIONAL RELATIONS AND THE FAR EAST, 1955-1960

Communist China

Throughout this entire period the spectre of Red China loomed increasingly large on the international horizon. Chou En-lai and his associates devoted their capable energies to many tasks in the area of foreign policy. Their persistent efforts at "liberating" Taiwan by applying military pressure in the Taiwan Strait against the offshore islands held by the Nationalists, coupled with their anti-American propaganda campaign, brought them perilously close to a denouement with the United States. At the same time their bonds with the U.S.S.R. remained tightly linked. In their dealings with the other Far Eastern and Southeast Asian nations they left nothing untried as they sought by a variety of means to impress them with their growing strength and their present and future importance. Finally, they hammered away with relentless determination and vigor in their objective of gaining admittance into the United Nations.

American Captives. Communist China held prisoner some fifteen United States Air Force personnel who had been shot down and captured during the Korean War together with approximately forty civilians who had been detained in one way or other since 1950. As a result of United Nations efforts, which began late in 1954, four of the fliers were suddenly freed the following spring. That summer the United States agreed to hold talks with Red China at the ambassadorial level in Geneva. A few days after these meetings opened, Peking implemented a speech by Chou, in which he had promised that the remaining airmen would be released, by giving the eleven fliers their freedom. The joy which greeted this act was tempered in the United States by the fliers' revelations that they had been subjected to torture and brainwashing by their captors. By the end of the year, the Geneva talks, combined with the earlier United Nations efforts, had succeeded in securing the release of the majority of the civilians as well. However, late in 1959, some American citizens were still held hostage by the Communists.

The Offshore Islands Problem. In the Geneva talks the refusal of the United States to accept the Chinese suggestion that the American trade embargo against Peking be relaxed was matched by a Communist rejection of an American proposal that the two powers abjure the use of force to secure their international objectives. The American goal in proposing this proposition had been to secure a cease-fire in the Taiwan Strait. As a consequence, the desultory firing there continued, a situation which prompted the United States to cling to the intention it had announced, in a Congressional joint resolution early in 1955, to protect Taiwan.

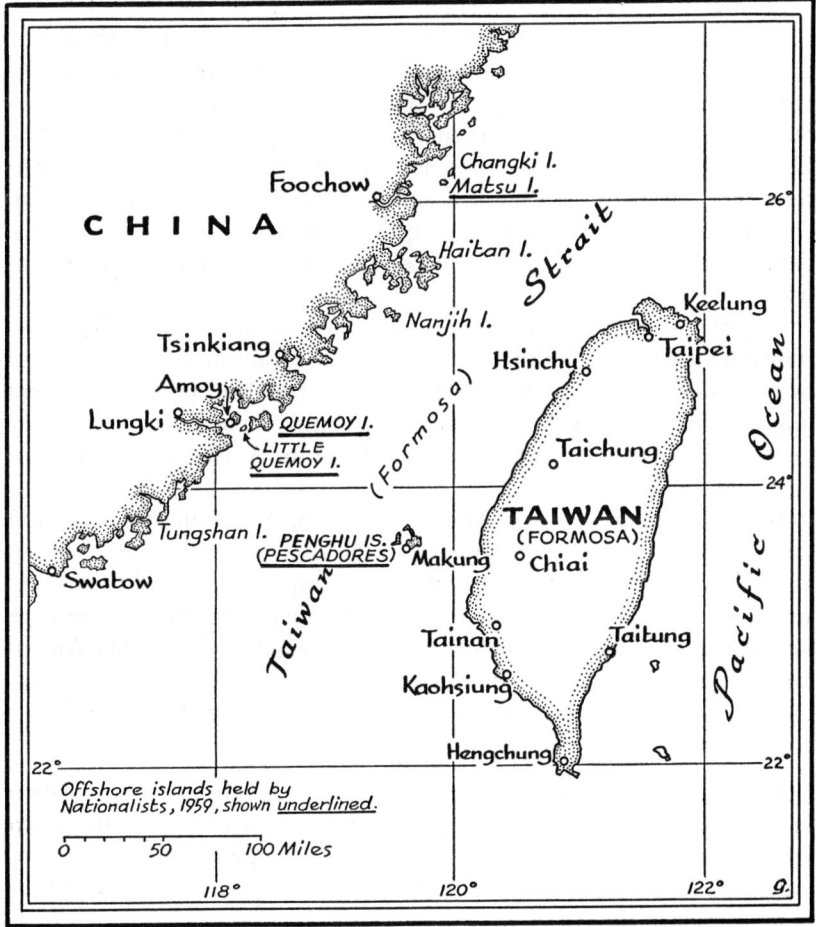

Taiwan and the Nationalist Offshore Islands, 1959

The dangerous problem of the offshore islands quieted down markedly for the next few years only to burst out again in 1958 and 1959 with renewed intensity.

In the late summer of 1958, the Chinese Communists reopened their bombardment of some of the offshore islands. This time their targets were the Matsu Islands off Foochow and the Quemoy group off Amoy. The seriousness of the new attacks was reflected by the proclamation of a state of emergency in Taiwan, where it was widely believed that an invasion was imminent. In this belief they were supported by Peking, which later announced that the real goal was not Quemoy and Matsu but Taiwan itself.

The seriousness of the situation was reflected in the United States, where a public debate took place over what course of action should be charted. One group strongly opposed American involvement despite the 1955 resolution, whereas the other was equally insistent that the United States back the Nationalists even to the point of military action. The Eisenhower administration proceeded circumspectly as far as action was concerned, but both the President and Secretary Dulles took to the air to deliver major addresses underscoring the broadness of the issues and the danger to the free world should the Communists be permitted to have their way.

A proposal from Chou that the suspended ambassadorial talks be resumed with a view to settling the problem of the Taiwan area was accepted by the United States. These meetings, which were held in Warsaw, were unproductive, since the United States constantly proposed a cease-fire only to be met by an equally persistent proposal that the Americans quit Taiwan once and for all.

If the diplomatic conversations were fruitless, American military aid to the Nationalists was most productive. In the vital area of the skies, Nationalist pilots, armed with the best American equipment, showed themselves superior to their adversaries flying Russian planes. An added advantage now possessed by the Nationalists was the presence of the mighty American Seventh Fleet augmented with superb air support. As a consequence, the forces of Chiang managed to hold their positions in the face of heavy bombardments in the summer of 1959.

Peking and Moscow. Long the subject of a good deal of speculation in the West has been the question of how firm were the bonds which linked together Peking and Moscow. Several examples will serve to illustrate that, despite wishful thinking to the contrary, these bonds, at least in the decade of the 1950's, were quite strong.

For one thing, Peking's external trade with the Soviet bloc rose in the five years beginning in 1950 from 26 per cent to 75 per cent of its whole foreign trade. Another was the completion of a key rail link between the capital of Communist China and the Trans-Siberian Railroad, which markedly reduces China's vulnerability to naval blockade.[1] Another important line, scheduled for completion in 1963, will further minimize this vulnerability. Finally is the fact that propaganda speeches emanating from Moscow and Peking revealing identity of interest between the two powers were not infrequently followed by actions implementing the statements and showing that the latter were not mere exercises in rhetoric.

A case in point was the visit to Peking (July 31–August 3) by Soviet Premier Khrushchev. The official announcement following the meeting was purely perfunctory.[2] However, immediately upon his return to Moscow, Khrushchev wrote a letter to President Eisenhower calling for a meeting of the General Assembly of the UN and denouncing the Security Council as useless because of the presence on it of "the political corpse Chiang Kai-shek" instead of "the great Chinese People's Republic." This verbal blast was immediately followed by the reopening of Communist bombardment of the offshore islands. Moreover, Khrushchev had scarcely returned home when it was announced that a new Sino-Soviet agreement providing Soviet technical assistance on a large number of Chinese industrial undertakings had been signed.[3]

Occupation of Tibet. The Chinese Communists had been in power a very short time when they decided to assert authority over the quondam Chinese vassal state of Tibet, which ever since the Chinese Revolution of 1911 had been autonomous.

In 1950 a Chinese Red army invaded the mountainous country in an operation which militarily impressed the world but morally and ethically repulsed it. Tibet was, of course, no match for the tough invaders and fell easily and quickly. The Tibetan leader, the Dalai Lama, initially fled to the Indian border but eventually consented to visit Peking along with the pro-Communist Panchen Lama. The Dalai Lama finally put his approval upon Communist China and in return was permitted to continue his rule subject to Chinese supervision.

The new regime proved too much for the Tibetans, who staged an heroic revolt in 1959 only to be crushed by their oppressors. This time the Dalai Lama made a narrow escape to India where he was given asylum and from whence he has denounced the Communists. The latter,

---

[1] Hollis W. Barber, *The United States in World Affairs, 1955* (New York, 1957), pp. 138 ff.
[2] *New York Times*, August 4, 1958.
[3] John C. Campbell, *The United States in World Affairs, 1958* (New York, 1959), pp. 210 ff., 315 ff.

in defending themselves against Western criticism, have taken the position that they were simply restoring China's rule over territory that had always been Chinese. In other words, this was no concern of the United Nations or any single nation or collection of nations; it was a domestic matter.

The world reaction to the ruthlessness of the Chinese Reds was one which considerably lowered their prestige in many quarters. Their supporters in the West were hard put to justify this slaughter of the Tibetans. In many ways it was a repetition of the Hungarian revolt, so fiercely repressed by the Soviets. It was now plain for all to see that Communist China was a colossus bent on asserting its will regardless of criticism. It was also clear that the American policy of nonrecognition was perhaps deserving of more support than it had previously received either within the United States or abroad.

The Bid for Asian Leadership. The Tibetan episode was merely one instance evidencing the fact that Communist China firmly believed the Machiavellian adage that it is better to be feared than loved. Vituperation, scathing denunciations, displays of power, and downright bad manners have frequently characterized Peking's conduct of foreign relations. Shocking instances of the depths to which Mao and his followers were willing to go in the pursuit of their objectives might be glimpsed from such campaigns as those extorting money from overseas Chinese under threat of imprisonment or death for their relatives on the mainland. Another instance of their barbarism may be seen in their export of narcotics in return for scarce foreign exchange.

But other less drastic means to back their drive to become the recognized leaders of Asia were more customarily employed. These included a tremendous propaganda campaign centered on the official New China News Agency and utilizing such foreign language periodicals as *People's China,* an English language magazine. The reception and careful handling of foreign visitors is another weapon in their drive to impress. Finally, the regime is fond of participating in international conferences, particularly as the host.

Summary. Analysis of Peking's foreign policy in its ten years of rule reveals that Communist China is firmly wedded to a belief in the bipolarization of the world. One side, headed by the U.S.S.R., is unified, strong, and solid. Theirs is the future of the world, and all must work to attain it. On the other side the leadership is in the hands of the United States, a paper tiger but nevertheless the world's leading capitalist state. The Communist objective is complete triumph in this divided world, and the twin foundations of their foreign policy in support of this goal are support for the U.S.S.R. and undying enmity toward the U.S.A.[4] In the ten years that have elapsed since the proclamation of the Chinese People's Republic in October, 1949, there has been no deviation from this policy.

The Republic of China. Against this formidable power, the Republic of China looked somewhat insignificant as it strove to defend itself on Taiwan, an area roughly equal to the combined area of Connecticut, Delaware, and New Jersey[5] and with a population in the main island group of about 10,000,000. Added to these were the offshore islands, numbering about fifty, with a population of perhaps 65,000.

Uncertain though the backing may have been at times, it appeared clear at the end of the period under review that a majority of the American people preferred this regime to that represented by Peking and approved of continued support of both a military and economic nature, up to a point, at least.

Divided Korea. Korea remained a divided country for years following the armistice at the end of the Korean War. The U.S.S.R. and Communist China continued to back the puppet North Korean regime, while the United States stood staunchly behind the Republic of Korea, headed by the old fire-eater President Rhee, who dreamed of unifying the country by force if necessary and who had to be restrained continually by the United States from attempting to invade the north.

Repeated violations of the armistice by the North Koreans and the Chinese Reds led the United States in 1957 to announce that its forces in the Republic of Korea would be equipped with rockets and atomic weapons. The next year the North Koreans attempted to secure an agreement calling for the evacuation of the entire peninsula by all non-Korean troops, a proposal which naturally enough received the ardent backing of Communist China but which was opposed by the sixteen governments which had formed the UN command in the Korean War. The rejection was based on the need still obtaining for free elections to unite Korea under United Nations supervision. The promise was held out, however, that evacuation would take place whenever the requirements set by the General Assembly for a permanent peace had been met.

This refusal to evacuate the UN forces was followed late in 1958 by an announcement from Peking that the entire "Chinese People's Volunteers" had been withdrawn. An invitation was extended to the UN command to do likewise, but no suggestion was made offering to allow the UN to verify the announced withdrawal of the Chinese.

[4] Richard L. Walker, *China Under Communism* (New Haven, 1955), p. 252.
[5] John C. Caldwell, *Still the Rice Grows Green* (Chicago, 1955), p. 311.

There was, however, a reduction of UN forces followed by a vote of the General Assembly, patiently calling once again for the establishment of a unified, independent, and democratic Korea, a resolution which was unsuccessfully opposed by the Soviet bloc. The latter, thanks to the exercise of the veto by the U.S.S.R., was enabled to continue to deny the Republic of Korea membership in the United Nations. As a compromise, the Soviets promised to remove their objections to South Korea if the Western bloc would admit North Korea, a *quid pro quo* the West refused to accept. Thus, the tragic division of Korea has persisted.

Japan

The Shigemitsu Mission to Washington. The fall of Premier Yoshida, who had been at the helm in Japan from 1946 to 1954, was marked by the triumph early in 1955 of Ichiro Hatoyama, who was victorious because of his promise to pursue a more independent policy than that of his pro-American predecessor. Mamoru Shigemitsu, who had served a brief sentence as a war criminal, was chosen by Hatoyama as his foreign minister.

The new government was anxious to secure the return of Japanese territories, the release of the war criminals, a more equitable revision of the 1951 Japanese-American treaty, and the re-establishment of diplomatic relations with the Soviets. In pursuance of some of these objectives, Shigemitsu came to Washington to hold talks with Secretary Dulles in 1955 which were rather disappointing from a Japanese standpoint. The United States did agree to replace the existing Security Treaty with one of "greater mutuality" when Japan had made greater strides toward home defense and ability to contribute to the preservation of international peace and security in the Western Pacific. One measure of success, although a negligible one, was the release of twenty-two war criminals of the 577 still detained in Sugamo prison (210 of whom had been sentenced by the United States).

Japanese-Russian Negotiations. Negotiations looking toward the solution of various outstanding questions between Japan and the U.S.S.R. dragged out for a year and a half before an agreement was reached in October, 1956, but this accord left a number of questions unresolved as far as Japan was concerned. The Japanese objectives in the negotiations had been as follows: the removal of Soviet opposition to Japanese membership in the United Nations; release of the Japanese prisoners of war; the return to Japan of various islands, including Etorofu, Kunashiri, the Habomais, and Shikotan;[6] and certain fishing rights.

---

[6] Etorofu and Kunashiri are in the southern Kuriles, while the Habomai group and Shikotan are located close by, just northeast of Hokkaido.

The interim agreement signed in 1956 did bring about the restoration of diplomatic relations, secured the release of some of the prisoners, and achieved a protocol on trade. The important territorial differences had to await the conclusion of a Japanese-Soviet peace treaty, something which, at this writing, has not been accomplished. Opposition to Japan's entry into the United Nations was removed,[7] and the Soviets also renounced all reparations claims against Japan.

In the years which followed this agreement, which was ratified in December, 1956, the Japanese frequently raised the territorial question with Moscow only to meet with a series of rebuffs. Consistent with her opposition to American experiments with the hydrogen bomb, the Japanese launched formal protests against Russian tests as well.

In 1958, Japan reached an agreement with the Soviet Union in a Moscow conference of the Japan-Soviet Northwest Pacific Fishery Committee and also in negotiations held in Moscow for the Japan-Soviet Trade and Payment Agreement. Negotiations over the important salmon fisheries have remained deadlocked owing to Soviet insistence that the fishery pact be preceded by the signing of a peace treaty between the two countries. This Japan refuses to do because of her view that it would entirely negate Japan's territorial claims. Also unresolved in Japan-Soviet relations is the frequency of seizures of Japanese fishing boats by Soviet patrol boats. Finally, mutually satisfactory terms on cultural and aviation agreements proposed by the Soviets have not materialized.

The Kishi Governments. The Hatoyama government had achieved enough success in its negotiations with the Russians to warrant the feeling that its main mission had been accomplished. Accordingly, Hatoyama resigned and was succeeded by Tanzan Ishibashi, whose illness subsequently caused his replacement by Nobusuke Kishi. Kishi had been forced to serve a three-year sentence by the United States as a war criminal. Notwithstanding, he saw fit to follow a policy of closer cooperation on the whole with the United States instead of the more independent course favored earlier by Hatoyama. Kishi early sought American backing to further Japanese industrial expansion aimed at winning the Southeast Asia market, an area where the bitter memories of the Japanese occupation had finally begun to recede.

In the Southeast Asia area Japan reached a settlement with the Philippines, culminating years of effort. By this agreement, signed in Manila on

---

[7] Japan became the 80th member of the United Nations when the General Assembly unanimously approved the Security Council's recommendation. Her membership took effect on December 18, 1956, ending a four and one-half year wait for which the Soviets were chiefly responsible. In 1958, Japan achieved the honor of membership for a two-year period on the Security Council.

May 9, 1956, Japan agreed to supply the Philippines over a twenty-year period with goods and services worth over a half-billion dollars. In addition the Japanese government guaranteed an additional quarter-billion dollars in credit to be supplied by private Japanese interests. Two years later private Japanese firms again supplied credits ($78,000,000) for additional important Philippine projects. These latter negotiations were capped by an official state visit to Japan by Philippine President Garcia.

Prime Minister Kishi had included Manila on a tour which he had made of Southeast Asia in 1957. Kishi also visited Australia and New Zealand on this tour. Earlier the same year he had made a trip to Burma and several other countries whose wartime treatment at the hands of the Japanese had been extremely unpleasant. In carrying out the reparations program in Burma, the Japanese supplied funds for a variety of important projects and also assisted their former victim by means of the services of Japanese technical experts.

Japan's outstanding reparations arrangements were concluded through agreements with Indonesia and Vietnam in 1958. The Japanese-Indonesian peace treaty and reparations agreement was signed in Djakarta and involved an ultimate expenditure of some $800,000,000 by Japan in Indonesian reconstruction and development. The reparations agreement with Vietnam, signed in Saigon, obligated Japan to pay $39,000,000 over a five-year period. In addition, loans of some $16,000,000 were extended by Japan.

The new favor with which Japan began to be received throughout much of the Far East and Southeast Asia was not reflected in the Republic of Korea, however.

Relations with the Republic of Korea. One irritant in Japanese-Korean relations was the problem of what the Japanese styled the voluntary return of Korean residents of Japan who wished to go back to their former homes in North Korea. The position of the Japanese was that any Koreans who wished to repatriate should be free to go to North Korea if they so desired, whereas the Republic of Korea was strongly opposed to such a move since it would add to the population of the puppet North Korean government.

Another impasse developed over the repatriation of Japanese fishermen detained by the Republic of Korea as a result of the ROK proclamation of 1952 establishing the so-called Rhee Line. This line demarcated a wide zone in the high seas around Korea—at some points over 100 miles from the coast; and Japanese fisherman accused of violating it were seized by the Seoul government and imprisoned. Upon completion of their terms they were permitted to return home, but others had been arrested in the meantime. An agreement was reached at the end of 1957 for the release of all

Japanese fishermen then being held, in return for the release of Koreans arrested in Japan for criminal offenses. All the men were returned by each side with the exception of a few Japanese, at which point the Koreans suddenly resumed their seizures of Japanese fishing boats. In the spring of 1959, Korea was accused of holding over 150 fishing crewmen in prison. Thus, relations between these two nations were poor and showed no immediate prospects of amelioration.

Japan and Communist China. Expended economic relations with Communist China were an openly announced goal of Kishi's. Although he was particularly anxious to see the remaining restrictions on strategic items in such a trade removed, he did not favor recognition of Peking. The trade between Japan and Communist China had reached the modest total of $150,000,000 in 1956 but was on the rise.

All relations between the two countries were suspended, however, on May, 9, 1958, when Chinese Foreign Minister Chen Yi proclaimed a total severance of ties with Japan. This unilateral proclamation was prompted by Peking's dissatisfaction with Japan's position in the matter of a private trade agreement. Various official Communist Chinese organs waged a propaganda campaign calling upon Japan to abandon its "three principles": (1) "hostility" toward the Japanese people themselves, (2) plots to create two Chinas, and (3) prevention of the resumption of normal diplomatic relations between the two countries (Communist China and Japan).

In addition to problems of trade, questions of fisheries and personnel exchange between the two countries continued to create difficulties.

The Security Treaty and Relations with the United States. Although considerably more pro-American than Hatoyama had been, Prime Minister Kishi was most anxious to secure a series of new arrangements in the relations between the United States and Japan. Included in these were: changes favoring Japan in the 1951 Security Treaty between the two countries, the return of administrative control over the Ryukyu and Bonin Islands to Japan, and better economic and trade relations.

These questions were discussed by Mr. Kishi when he visited President Eisenhower in Washington in 1957. As a result of this visit, the United States took steps to commence the reduction of its ground forces stationed in Japan. A contributing factor in this decision was the Girard Case. William Girard was an American soldier who had shot and killed a Japanese woman guilty of trespassing on an American military firing ground in the process of seeking scrap metal for salvage. Public opinion in both countries took a lively interest in the case, which was finally resolved by Japan's jurisdiction being upheld. Girard, who had a Japanese wife, was found guilty of manslaughter, given a suspended sentence, and returned to the United States late in 1957. Early in 1958 the agreed-upon withdrawal of some 35,000 American ground troops was completed.

In the matter of the Ryukus and the Bonins, the American position remained firm. The United States recognized that residual sovereignty over the islands was possessed by Japan but held that as long as conditions of threat and tension existed in the Far East the United States would find it necessary to continue the existing status of American occupation under a United Nations Strategic Trusteeship. The United States pledged itself to continue its policy of improving the welfare and well-being of the inhabitants of the islands and of improving their economic and cultural advancement.

Neither Kishi's visit nor subsequent trips to Washington in 1957 and 1958 by Foreign Minister Fujiyama were able to resolve the economic side of Japanese-American relations.

Despite inability to progress in the economic realm, Japan was enabled to secure the opening of talks on the Security Treaty revision. While no progress had been announced, the talks continued late in 1959, at which time Japan was concentrating on modification of the following six points in the existing pact: (1) According to the 1951 treaty, the United States is granted the right to station troops in Japan without any stipulation obligating the United States to defend the country. Japan hoped a revised treaty would clarify the responsibility of the United States for Japan's defense. (2) The existing pact permits the United States to deploy American troops based in Japan overseas in case the peace and security of the Far East are threatened. There is no stipulation that prior consultation be held with the Japanese government, whose view became that Japan might thus be involved in a war against its wishes. Hence, Japan sought to make it necessary for the United States to hold prior consultations with Japan should the Americans wish to deploy their Japan-based personnel overseas. (3) The deployment and armament of the American forces in Japan may be freely determined by the United States under the 1951 pact, and the United States can thus arm them with nuclear weapons. The abhorrence of the Japanese people for such weapons made it mandatory from Japan's position that a revised treaty include stipulations clarifying this issue. (4) Articles in the present treaty call for the mobilization of United States forces in case of internal disorders and also prohibit Japan from providing a third country with military bases. The Japanese wanted these articles deleted, finding them derogatory to Japanese prestige as an independent country. (5) The preamble of the existing arrangement states that the Security Pact and the United Nations Charter should be mutually compatible, but no provisions were made to this effect. Japan, therefore, hoped that some stipulations of a clarifying nature might be made in this matter.

INTERNATIONAL RELATIONS AND THE FAR EAST 653

(6) The period covered by the treaty and the procedure for its abrogation are not mentioned in the 1951 treaty. The Japanese wanted these points clearly stipulated in a revised treaty.

Thus, despite strong pressure from within Japan itself, as well as from both Moscow and Peking, to renounce the treaty entirely, the Japanese government's position was that the treaty was the key to Japan's foreign relations but that a revision of the 1951 version was clearly indicated.

Trade. The latest available figures for Japanese trade were, on the whole, favorable although the rate of increase over the last two years was infinitesimal. In 1956 there was a 24 per cent increase; in 1957 it was 14 per cent; whereas in 1958 it was but 0.6 per cent. Despite this small increase, however, there was some reason for optimism since imports had fallen 29 per cent in 1958 compared with the previous year.

Offsetting the grounds for optimism for the future was the continuing opposition within the United States, particularly at the state rather than the federal level, of those who feared Japanese imports, a dread which was shared by such elements in Great Britain as the Lancashire cotton interests. Also disconcerting was a Chinese Communist trade drive begun during 1958 and aimed at Southeast Asia with a view to replacing Japanese exports in this area by the simple expedient of underselling them. While it is too early to assess the success of this offensive, it is a sobering and arresting development which calls for close watch, since the effects on Japan could be devastating. This, in turn, would have grave consequences for the United States and the rest of the free world.

The Far Eastern Policy of the United States

As the decade of the 1950's came to a close, there were several clearly recognizable tenets of the Far Eastern policy of the United States which may be conveniently summarized at this point.

Communist China. Despite the presence within the American public of articulate elements advocating the recognition of Communist China and its admittance to the United Nations, it remained the seemingly stronger-than-ever determination of the State Department to refuse recognition. The policy of nonrecognition was based on several factors. In the first place, Communist China remained an aggressor on the books of the United Nations and had given no demonstrable proof of contrition for her actions during the Korean War. Second, the refusal to release all of the American citizens held prisoner by Peking was in itself considered ample justification for nonrecognition were no others present. Third, Peking's close ties with Moscow made it possible to raise the question of whether or not the Chinese Communists were truly independent. Finally, the virulence and truculence of the Hate-America Campaign which Peking was waging both internally and externally made recognition more and more unlikely. There were, of course, other important reasons for refusing recognition, but the foregoing are representative.

Buttressing the determination to refuse recognition and to withhold admission to the United Nations was a growing awareness within American opinion, both official and public, that Communist China was bent upon nothing less than the mastery of East Asia and would pursue any policies whatever designed to secure this ambitious objective.

The Republic of China. Not the least of the reasons impelling the United States to refuse to recognize Communist China was the fact that the United States was allied with the Republic of China, since 1949 based on Taiwan and a number of offshore islands located perilously close to the Chinese mainland. In the gun duels and air and sea skirmishes which took place in 1958 and 1959 between the forces of Peking and Taipei, the United States had, on the whole, stood firmly by its ally despite the fact that such a posture irked many Americans who disliked Chiang and also frightened not a few of the European allies of the United States who feared that a general war might ensue.

There are indications that the firmness of the policy of the Eisenhower administration, as reflected by the late Secretary of State, John Foster Dulles, had successfully come through a searching test. Dulles was also able to secure an official statement from Chiang in late 1958 renouncing any idea of regaining the mainland "by force." Whatever the result, the mere fact that such an announcement could be made represented an achievement for American policy, which was not anxious to involve the United States in war but felt honor-bound to support its ally.

Thus, the prospects were that the United States would continue to supply the Republic of China with both military and economic assistance, together with full support in its fight to hold its seat in the United Nations. This, at any rate, would appear to be the prospect as the decade of the 1960's opens.

The Republic of Korea. Having saved the independence of the Republic of Korea by resort to battle under unfavorable conditions, it would also seem logical that the United States would continue to befriend its courageous ally in its continuing struggle to protect itself from the never-ending Communist threat to the Korean people. Eager as the United States has been to make sure that Chiang Kai-shek refrains from any attack on the mainland, so too have American policymakers sought to restrain the administration of President Syngman Rhee from any adventure which could conceivably reopen the Korean War, now quiescent under an uneasy armistice. In return for a Republic of Korea promise to contain itself and refrain from attack on its countrymen, who are supported by Communist China, the United States continues to work for the economic viability of the South Koreans and to keep them militarily strong enough to resist their rapacious neighbors.

The continued freedom of both Taiwan and the Republic of Korea is important to the United States strategically and diplomatically as the Cold War continues unceasingly.

Japan. The cornerstone of American policy, however, continues to be Japan, but the magnitude of the problems inherent in support of this increasingly nationalistic country is vast.

Wherever consistent with what it deemed the best interests of all concerned, the United States has demonstrated a willingness to be responsive to Japanese requests to make changes in the existing frame of relations between the two countries. In the military area the United States has been prone to prod Japan into taking a greater responsibility for her own defense. Satisfied that the Japanese government has adopted a more realistic attitude in this vital area, the United States agreed to withdraw the greater part of its ground combat troops based on Japan. The Americans, moreover, granted Japan a status-of-forces arrangement which, while the target of much criticism in the United States, was well received and much appreciated by Japan. In addition, greater care in the matter of requisitioning scarce Japanese land and buildings has been exercised by the American personnel in Japan. On the other hand, the United States has decided to keep its air and naval forces up to a high degree of strength in the firm conviction that these forces are indispensable in reducing the threat of renewed aggression by the Communists in the Far East.

In keeping with this feeling, the United States has had to refuse politely but firmly the Japanese requests to regain control over the Ryukyus (including Okinawa) and the Bonins.

While assisting and encouraging Japanese efforts to expand economically in the direction of Southeast Asia and also taking a more lenient view toward lifting embargo restrictions on trade with Communist China, the United States government has been unable to minimize very effectively the barriers against Japanese imports in the United States. President Eisenhower has made it a point to call attention to the dangerous alternatives should the Japanese economy prove not to be viable and has called upon the American people to be more tolerant with respect to Japan's need for foreign trade. His appeals have largely gone unheeded, although he has had some support from academic and press sources.

However, in what might broadly speaking be called the area of culture, the Japanese have enjoyed great success in the United States of recent years. The famous Kabuki dancers were enthusiastically received as have been other Japanese entertainers.[8] Japanese motion pictures, both of an artistic and a popular kind, have been well patronized. Even such relatively unusual fields as *hanga* (woodblock prints) and *ikebana* (the art of Japanese flower arrangements) have had appeal for Americans. And in pursuance of a project close to Mr. Eisenhower's heart, his people-to-people program, American cities have linked themselves with selected Japanese cities in a reciprocal program on the community level.

One wish dear to the vast majority of Japanese, which the United States has not felt advisable to respect, has been the immediate end of nuclear testing. The United States has been entirely sympathetic to Japan's feelings but has held that to cease testing without incontrovertible evidence that the Soviets could be trusted to do likewise would be suicidal, not only for the American people but for the entire free world.

Thus, American policy during the 1950's became increasingly oriented toward maintaining Japan as an independent country, strong enough to defend herself and possessed of a viable economy. In pursuance of these objectives the American government tended to be responsive to Japanese wishes wherever possible in a sincere attempt to convince the Japanese government and people that the United States had no ulterior designs on the country.

The Far Eastern Policy of the U.S.S.R. In a Far East where Communist China's attempts at aggression in Korea were checked by the United States and where the former's repeated threats at "liberating" Taiwan have been thwarted by the United States, what has been the policy pursued by the Soviets?

In general, it would appear that the U.S.S.R. has been quite content in the military sphere to utilize naval bases along the Chinese mainland which, coupled with their own Pacific bases, have enabled the Russians to pose a serious threat with their submarines to American naval supremacy in the vast reaches of the Pacific.

They have demonstrated themselves quite willing to supply planes, tanks, and other war matériel to their allies in both Communist China and North Korea, thereby making possible the aggression of these regimes in Korea and the Taiwan Strait especially. Yet at the same time the Soviets have assiduously avoided direct involvement in the fighting launched by

---

[8] For the first time in history, *Gagaku*, the dancers and musicians of the Japanese Imperial Household, performed outside of Japan. In the spring of 1959 a party of twenty-one artists performed in New York City for a three-week engagement.

their partners, at least in the matter of actually engaging Soviet personnel.

Economically, they have undertaken to provide Peking with the services of countless Soviet technical and scientific experts and to assist their gigantic neighbor in building railroads, bridges, roads, airbases, etc. The *quid pro quo* for this help has been largely in agricultural commodities and other raw materials, items which the Communist Chinese could hardly spare but which they had to supply in lieu of anything else of economic value to the Russians.

Of late years at any rate, Russian policy has been one of full cooperation with their Asiatic communistic brethren. It has been a policy which seems quite content to leave the leadership in East Asian affairs to Peking, and it looks for the foreseeable future as if this policy will be continued. From the Russian standpoint it is easily justified on the grounds that American energies will be drained by their struggle to counter the mounting threat of the Chinese Communists and that the United States' ability in other areas of the global struggle will be so weakened that victory for Socialism in the "protracted conflict" will indeed be inevitable.

In conclusion, events of the decade of the 1950's have demonstrated pretty conclusively that the solidarity of the Peking-Moscow axis is very real and they have rather effectively doomed to disappointment the Western dream that Mao Tse-tung might become "another Tito." Furthermore, the prospects seem rather strong that no lessening of the bonds between Moscow and Peking is in prospect for many years. They need one another and together offer a combination that must give pause to the United States as it seeks to continue to rally the West to face up to the dangers inherent in this situation.

SUGGESTED READINGS

See readings listed for Chapter 33.

35

COMMUNIST CHINA: THE FIRST DECADE, 1949-1959

On October 1, 1949, the Communists inaugurated a new regime for China, the Chinese People's Republic. The reasons for their victory were fairly clear, and some have already been suggested. For many Chinese, acceptance of the Communist regime was essentially a negative choice: they felt that there was no health left in the Kuomintang, and the Communists might as well have their turn.

Founding the "New Democracy"

The Communists had more positive attractions than merely the status of lesser of two evils, however. Perhaps the least decisive of these attractions, except for a few intellectuals, was Marxist-Leninist doctrine. It gave strength to the Communist leadership by providing a definite point of view and promising an assured ultimate triumph; to the mass of the Chinese, however, it had no particular meaning. The Chinese Communists had won not because they were doctrinaire Communists (which the leaders were) but because they were Chinese revolutionaries who had gained leadership of the great surge of agrarian discontent and intense nationalism. The peasants welcomed the Communists for their rural reforms; the intellectuals, for their crusading spirit and zeal for popular well-being—all groups, for their energetic patriotism.

The medal had a darker side, however, to be revealed to the eyes of the Chinese later. The Communists now had on their hands the vast poorhouse which was China and had undertaken to transform it by the magic of Marxism-Leninism into a center of wealth and strength. This involved something which neither prewar Japan nor Nationalist China had been able to achieve: industrialization on a sound base. Land redistribution, which had won the hearts of the poorer peasantry and helped to bring the Communists into power, was a dubious way to agricultural efficiency. Would the Chinese Communists eventually follow the example of the

U.S.S.R. and collectivize agriculture in the hope of making farms into factories of food?

Communist idealism, which so strongly appealed to the intellectuals, was idealism within the framework of a dogmatic, deterministic philosophy. Chinese students and writers had been offended by the clumsy efforts of the Kuomintang to control thought. Would the intellectuals in time find that they must follow the Communist party line or be persecuted as "enemies of the people?" Communist nationalism, that seeming contradiction in terms, was tremendously attractive to a proud people deeply resentful of foreign interference and domination. But this nationalism traded on virulent, distorted versions of American conduct toward China, and simplified, sugar-coated assertions about Russian intentions. However native the Chinese Communist movement was in its history and its practical program, it was aligned in world politics with the U.S.S.R. Would Russia in its dealings with Communist China carry on the traditional Russian imperialist policy in the Far East with Communist China as one of the new galaxy of captive satellites revolving around the Russian sun? These were only a few of the questions which were to be answered as the history of the Chinese People's Republic unfolded.

Initial Successes. During the first phase of their rule of all China, the Communists concentrated on the establishment of their regime and the rehabilitation of the country after the long period of international and civil war. The Political Consultative Council, which was to set up a new government, opened its formal meetings in December, 1949. Its membership and that of the government which it created indicated that many liberal and middle-of-the-road elements had accepted cooperation with the Communists in the "New Democracy." The new government was a cumbersome affair, but the large number of high-sounding posts on councils, ministries, and commissions seemed intended to blazon the united front. In reality, Communist party members were strategically placed in every government body, and real decisions continued to be made in the inner circles of the party. The representatives of the "democratic" groups were to find themselves mere window dressing. The new regime also found it necessary to employ many bureaucrats who had served the Nationalist regime, but looked forward to the day when there would be a sufficient supply of qualified men and women trained in the new system.

The Communists won general popularity by the success of their initial rehabilitation measures. The currency, which had spiralled off into outer space, was made once more responsive to the pull of gravity. Railroads, roads, and irrigation works were repaired. Everywhere there was revolutionary fervor for cleanliness, order, and honesty in public life. The "land reform" procedures were being extended throughout the country. By the outbreak of the Korean War in 1950 almost all of North China and Manchuria had undergone land redistribution; the going was slower in South China, where the regime was new.

The tone of the Communists in this period was relatively mild and benign. The party showed great skill in the arts of persuasion and indoctrination. Mass organizations were launched to bring party propaganda—and control—into the lives of individuals. The first organizations were for groups markedly at a disadvantage in the old order and therefore presumably easy to win to the support of the new—women, young people, and industrial workers. Chou En-lai could find justification for his statement on the first anniversary of the Communist triumph that no government in Chinese history had ever accomplished so much in one year. There were probably only a few pessimistic historians to reflect that the only rival for this place of pre-eminence was the Ch'in dynasty, inspired by that earlier analogue of Communism, Legalism.

Campaigns Against the Opposition. Toward the end of 1950, the Communists began to deserve comparison with the Legalists in methods as well as achievements. Violence took precedence over persuasion in a great drive to enforce conformity and assert the power of the state. This changed tone was observable from the onset of the Korean conflict and grew more intense with the involvement of Chinese "volunteers" in it. The Communists, like other revolutionaries, found the psychology of national emergency a favorable climate in which to unify most of the population in support of the regime. The party pushed against its internal enemies with great harshness and brutality. American imperialism was the scapegoat: to counter it, the Chinese were rallied to cast out "traitors," "spies," and "counterrevolutionaries." Mass hysteria and rampant class struggle flourished, and the tolerant, compromising, adjustable color of the United Front and the "New Democracy" faded.

The first warning to "counterrevolutionaries" was sounded in July, 1950, just after the beginning of the Korean War. In February, 1951, came legislation against them, giving vague definitions of crimes against the state for which the death penalty might be imposed. Throughout 1951 political cannibalism prevailed, especially in rural areas. The cadres held meetings at which, after careful rehearsal, peasants "spoke bitterness" and made accusations. Mass emotion burst out in public trials which were in effect officially sponsored lynching sessions. In response to the violently expressed "will of the people" those denounced as counterrevolutionaries were either executed or sentenced to "reform through labor," while the government confiscated their property. Many committed suicide or fled rather than face this prospect. How many died in this purge is uncertain. Mao is reported to have given, in 1957, a figure of 800,000, but non-Communist estimates run much higher. On October 1, 1951, the second anniversary of the regime, Chou En-lai announced that the terror had done its work of saving the people, but the elimination of "class enemies" went on although at a slower pace, and the regime has continued to "make examples" of them from time to time.

The Five-Anti Campaign. Late in 1951 the emphasis shifted to psychological warfare on certain groups, waged by a method dear to the Communists, that of "campaigns." The Three-Anti Campaign, against corruption, waste, and bureaucratism, was aimed at party personnel and government employees. Out of the Three-Anti Campaign grew the Five-Anti Campaign, designed to cure private business of the sins of bribery, tax evasion, fraud, stealing state property, and stealing state economic secrets. This experience deprived the middle class of any remaining illusion that business could go on somewhat as usual. During the drive on counterrevolutionaries and the Five-Anti Campaign, many businessmen were sent to forced labor camps or lost their property to the government, and the survivors found themselves virtual government functionaries. The Aid Korea, Hate America Campaign exploited the nationalist theme on which the Chinese Communists had played for so many years. Their relative success in the Korean War and the rising status of China in the world won them the grudging support of groups which otherwise would have abominated them. This period also saw the intensified ideological reform movement, in which intellectuals were subjected to "brain washing." After long discussion sessions and revival meetings, Communist style, notable Chinese academicians publicly repudiated their bourgeois, pro-Western past, and expressed hope of salvation through dutiful acceptance of Marxism. A campaign to subordinate religion to Communism involved sharp attacks on Taoist societies, which were especially suspect because of their traditional connection with political dissent. China appeared to have come considerably nearer to 1984 than the official date on the calendar would suggest.

Economic Change. This combination of terror and propaganda generated a climate in which the leadership pushed very rapidly ahead with important social and economic changes. At the end of 1952, the middle and poor peasants held party-inspired celebrations of the "end of feudalism," which was Communist language for the completion of land redistribution. Industrialization was speeded. The great bulk of heavy industry was state-operated; state banks and trading companies were extended. On October 1, 1952, the great theme was praise of China's economic progress. But 1953

From Shabad, Theodore, *China's Changing Map—A Politi*
York: Frederick A. Praeger, Inc., 1956), pp. 26-27.

Communist

cal and Economic Geography of the Chinese People (New
Map by Vaughn S. Gray. By permission of the publisher.

China

was a year in which the regime met setbacks and moved slowly. The pace of land redistribution had been very rapid and had provoked peasant unrest and resistance in some quarters, while in others the new land ownership was accompanied by the manifestation of "bourgeois mentality," which was ideologically distasteful to the Communists. A Five Year Plan was announced, but the goals for 1953 had to be scaled down considerably, in part because Soviet economic aid proved to be less substantial than the Chinese had hoped. The elections for the new National People's Congress were postponed. The census taken in 1953 showed about 600,000,000 Chinese instead of 475,000,000, and even the customary Communist optimism about the advantages of population increase must have been jolted. While the Korean War had been played up as a great victory for China, the regime was relieved to have it end. This was a time, then, of diminished fervor and reduction of pressure. The new condition of things was symbolized by the Five-Too-Many Movement, in which the cadres were made the whipping boys of party policy and rebuked for requiring too many meetings, tasks, forms, and the like.

Consolidation of the Regime

Actually the Communist leadership was consolidating its strength for a great lunge forward toward industrialization and the collectivization of agriculture. The mass organizations were revamped along lines of strict democratic centralism. Regional governments were brought under central control. There was a drive for economy and against "bureaucratism." At the end of 1953 the regime made it clear that the "breather" was over. The new theme was to be "transition to socialism," the watchwords were to be "austerity" and "bitter struggle." The "New Democracy" now approached its end, having had a shorter life than some of Mao's earlier statements had predicted for it.

The Five Year Plan. After its halting start in 1953, the Five Year Plan now moved vigorously toward the ultimate objective of national military and economic power through the development of heavy industry. This implied great changes in agriculture, since only agricultural surpluses could provide the capital accumulation to start heavy industries and to pay for the necessary imports of foreign—chiefly Soviet—machinery. After only a short year in which to settle down with their new farm holdings, the peasants now found themselves being "persuaded" into collectivization. Private businessmen, put on notice in 1954 that their time was running out, danced at their own funeral, complete with firecrackers, as private enterprise officially died in January, 1956.

"Collective" Leadership. A new constitution, appropriate to the "transition to socialism," was adopted in 1954, replacing the Common Program of 1949, under which (so the Chinese were told) the evils of "feudalism, imperialism, and bureaucratic capitalism" had been done away with. The new constitution bore a strong resemblance to the Soviet Constitution of 1936, which had been the token of a similar stage in Russian development. It simply redressed Chinese political windows; actual control remained where it had been, in the closed councils of the party leaders.

The new Chinese government readily endorsed the idea of "collective leadership," which was fashionable in the Communist world after the death of Stalin. After all, in China there had been no such purges at the highest level as had characterized Stalin's dictatorship. Indeed, the first overt break in the unity of the top leadership in China came only with the fall from grace of Kao Kang, who had been chairman of the State Planning Commission and chief administrator of the key Manchurian area, which had been the proving ground for many policies and projects. In 1955 the Chinese people were told that Kao Kang had tried to make Manchuria his private kingdom and that as a result he had been expelled from the party and had subsequently committed suicide. The intellectuals were in trouble again, too. Hu Fêng, well known editor and author, was accused of being a Kuomintang agent and denounced for criticizing the policy of the party toward literature. The inevitable accompaniments of these *causes célebres* were campaigns to enforce party discipline and root out "the cult of personality," more arrests and punishments of counterrevolutionaries and economic saboteurs, and melancholy rounds of criticism, self-criticism, and confessions by artists and litterateurs.

The drive toward industrialization, collectivization, and militarization was intensified. Regulations were announced for the creation of an officers' corps, like that in the Soviet Red Army, a move away from the equalitarianism which had existed in the Chinese Communist forces in the past. The actual situation of Chinese agriculture was still poor; Chinese farmers, whether despite or because of great pressure from their masters, were still operating on a very slim margin and at the mercy of natural calamities. The rounding-up of peasants into cooperatives proceeded with great speed. At the end of 1955, Mao Tse-tung announced a twelve-year plan for agriculture and predicted that three or four years would see the shiftover from the "semi-socialism" of producers' cooperatives to collective farms in the Soviet manner. Implementation of this program was very rapid indeed. By June, 1956, 90 per cent of the agrarian population were apparently in some sort of cooperatives, more than half of them in real collective farms, and the peasants were warned that, in the future, they, unlike their fields, could not lie fallow in the winter, but must do useful tasks in flood prevention and reforestation. Very evidently the peasants would have to continue laboring without rest to support the great industrialization program and to conform to the ideological line of the regime.

Meanwhile the industrialization of China was really under way. At first the Five Year Plan had been shrouded in mystery; only occasionally did official pronouncements shed even a dim light on its specific goals and its progress toward them. In 1955, however, precise and very encouraging data on industrial growth were put before the National People's Congress. In the fall of 1956, the Party Congress was assured that the Plan would be completed on schedule—indeed some of its goals had already been met—and received an outline of the Second Five Year Plan, which would continue the stress on heavy industry but with a promise of some increase in consumers' goods.

Relaxing Controls. The 1956 campaign against the Four Enemies—flies, mosquitoes, sparrows, and rats—seemed to suggest that the regime might focus its attack on its nonhuman opponents and move toward greater moderation in its human relations. In September, 1956, the Eighth National Congress of the Chinese Communist Party met in Peking; the Seventh Congress had met in 1945 in the Yenan days. The Congress exuded pride and confidence. Mao was praised to the skies as the practitioner of "collective leadership," and the friendship of Communist China for Communist Russia was reaffirmed. The Communists seemed victorious, their internal enemies powerless: perhaps they could afford leniency.

There were many indications of a milder approach. For example the Party wooed the intelligentsia, who were encouraged to learn from the capitalist states as well as from the U.S.S.R. and to engage in debate on "academic questions." This tendency to "let one hundred flowers bloom" was confirmed dramatically by Mao Tse-tung's four-hour speech on February 27, 1957, on "The Handling of Contradictions among the People."[1] Mao's contribution to Communist thinking on this occasion was his recognition that in addition to the inevitable "antagonistic contradictions" between the people and their enemies, a society in transition to socialism might show "nonantagonistic contradictions" among the people and between the people and the ruling group. In Hungary, violent handling of such contradictions had turned them into antagonistic contradictions: instead they should be resolved by restraint, persuasion, and "painstaking reasoning." Western readers of the speech found passages in which the spirit of John Milton seemed to have achieved unlikely reincarnation. Mao declared that the true always grows from contact with the false: this is the

---

[1] This speech was not fully reported in the Western press until June, 1957.

law of truth and of Marxism (which presumably are synonymous). Marxism, no hothouse plant, should welcome criticism. The non-Communist democratic parties in China were invited to dwell with the Communist party in "long-term coexistence and mutual supervision." "Let one hundred flowers bloom, let one hundred schools contend!"

At first Western speculation focused on the speech as a revelation of the state of Chinese-Russian relations: Mao, as a top Communist theoretician and leader of a successful independent Communist revolution, seemed to be taking advantage of the Polish and Hungarian crisis to differ with Khrushchev on critical points. But it was also arguable that the clue to the "hundred flowers" doctrine was to be found in China's internal situation. The speech could be viewed as an extensive formulation of that sense of security and inclination toward toleration which the Chinese Communists had already been displaying. Mao could no doubt identify many contradictions in contemporary China. Whether he was justified in regarding them as "nonantagonistic," time was to show. The pressure of the Five Year Plan on the peasants had been severe; agricultural yield was still inadequate, farmers were fleeing to the cities, prices had risen, and rationing had been imposed. Mao's assertion in February that the successfully completed organization of agricultural cooperatives had resolved the major contradiction between socialist industrialization and individual farm economy was distinctly on the optimistic side. The Five Year Plan was hitting snags; May, 1957, brought admissions of waste, inefficiency, and over-concentration on capital development and the suggestion that there should be more local management of enterprises and far more attention to agriculture and the production of consumer goods. Was the Chinese economy in trouble? Perhaps the greatest of all contradictions was that between Marx and Malthus. The revelation of the 1953 census as to the number of Chinese and the annual increment to the population seems to have disturbed even Mao, who in the February 27 speech strayed from the usual Communist line by suggesting the stabilization of the population at about 600,000,000. As to the contradictions between the party and the intellectuals, they had been only too evident for a long time. As Mao put it, "Some of the comrades do not know how to get on with intellectuals." Would Communist lions and academic lambs learn to lie down together in the new era of intellectual give-and-take? There were recognizable contradictions between the leadership and the people, too, contradictions which the Party Rectification Movement, begun in May, 1957, was intended to resolve. Most of the members of the party were relative newcomers, who had joined since 1949, and many of them had settled comfortably into urban bureaucratism. In the winter of 1957-1958, hundreds of thousands of city party members were sent to the country "to reform themselves through labor production" and thus renew their relationship with and understanding of the peasant masses.

Controls Reimposed. The millennium of free speech did not last long. Mao's pledge of immunity to critics brought forth an outburst of criticism. Some of the critics bore down on details and procedures in the way which Mao had expected and was ready to welcome as helpful. Others took the new charter of liberties too literally for their own eventual good and laid hands on the ark of the Marxist covenant by questioning the Communist party, the leadership of the proletariat, the role of the U.S.S.R. in China, and even socialism itself. Mao had pointed out that poisonous weeds might appear as well as lovely blossoms and set standards for telling one from the other. By these standards, which included support of the socialist way and strengthening of the role of the party, many of the criticisms were very poisonous weeds indeed. There were rumors that there were sharp differences within the Chinese collective leadership about Mao's doctrine, and that Liu Shao-chi opposed the "hundred flowers" idea. In any event Chou En-lai told the National People's Congress in late June that the critics had gone too far. Ting Ling, distinguished woman author and long-time party member, was expelled from the party as a rightist. Three ministers of state, members of the Democratic League, who had issued statements of criticism, were dismissed from office on the charge of "betraying the constitution and losing the people's trust." Revolutionary plots were unearthed and the plotters punished. Mao's project for variegated gardening was abandoned and the party turned, in a thoroughly doctrinaire spirit, to the production of a single crop of enthusiastic conformists.

All of this hue-and-cry did not interfere with China's economic march. The Five Year Plan, which reached its end on December 3, 1957, was extolled as having transformed China from backwardness into an industrialized socialist economy. The achievements of the Plan were indeed impressive, but were qualified by some real difficulties. In the opinion of many Western economists, the growth of heavy industry had been achieved at the expense of sound development of agriculture and light industry. The increase in farm output seemed no greater than was needed to care for the increase in population—Chinese farmers were running only fast enough to stay in the same place.

The "Great Leap Forward"

The more difficult part of the journey to the Communist millennium lay ahead. Nineteen fifty-eight was proclaimed as the year of the "great leap forward." Agriculture, the Achilles heel of the regime, was to receive more attention in the form of larger investment in control and irrigation works and greater effort to reclaim waste land, but the major objective was still to be the Communist *idée fixe,* heavy industry. Steel production was encouraged by any means possible. There were great drives for scrap, which was then rendered in tiny blast furnaces everywhere—in fields, in city squares, in family courtyards. If the resulting pig iron was of poor quality, it nevertheless bore witness to the great zeal with which the Chinese were pursuing the widely announced goal of "catching up with Britain."

Collectivization of Agriculture. During the first part of the year there was great propaganda about the desirability of some industrial decentralization with close links between agriculture and manufacture. In midsummer, 1958, came the "leap forward," with a vengeance, in the proclamation of a program of communes for Chinese agriculture. What motives impelled the Chinese leaders to outdistance on the socialist path any other Marxist society? The communes would undoubtedly enlarge the labor force; communal mess halls and child care centers meant that women were "freed" to serve the state by labor outside the home, an old Chinese institution which seemed at this point threatened with extinction. The communes were to have a military character. Every agricultural worker was to be in the militia. Through militarization and the procedures of communal control the peasants could be brought under the sort of discipline which had always been easier to enforce in factories than on farms. In the collective farms there had been considerable variation in economic rewards, since each family was paid in proportion to the work points accumulated by members of the family. This range would be narrowed under a system of fixed wages plus many "free" benefits given to all equally, regardless of labor.

In addition to the economic argument that communes would be more efficient, there was the very powerful doctrinal argument. The experience of 1957 had shown the existence of many "contradictions" in Chinese society: the party had resolved that these contradictions were to be dealt with not by compromise and adjustment but by a rapid move toward Communism in which class and clash would no longer exist. All through the late summer and fall the organization of communes went on. The quantitative results were astonishing. By the end of the year almost all of the 500,000,000 Chinese classified as rural were in communes. Some of the communes were still only blueprints; others were in operation. The regulations varied with the doctrinaire zeal of the organizers: in some, not even a fountain pen could be individually owned. Stark barracks replaced family dwellings, and mess halls, in which the cooking was done by rightists condemned to reform themselves through this sort of menial labor, served meals commonly and understandably regarded as much more truly inedible than the characteristic products of Chinese home cooking. Moreover it was understood that when the communal system was well under way in the countryside, it would be extended to the cities.

Could the Communists pull it off? Were they at last going so sharply against the Chinese grain that the very continuance of their power might be threatened? There were reports of peasant resistance. Prominent officials in Shantung and in Liaoning province in Manchuria were "purged" for obstructing the forward leap in agriculture and industry. The meeting of party leaders in Wuhan in November to discuss the progress of the revolution on the farms may well have been a time for criticism, self-criticism, and even intraparty contradictions. In December a Communist party resolution took a "dizzy with success" line and spoke out against the extremes to which over-eagerness had carried some of the cadres. The peasants must not fear that private property of such kinds as clothing, furniture, small implements, small livestock, and even bank deposits would disappear. The family was not to be extinguished: in housing plans, consideration was to be given to housing members of a family together. The leap forward did not mean that people must work unceasingly: everyone should have at least eight hours of sleep a night, even if this slightly delayed the coming of the new order, and the eight-hour working day should be the standard. Income was to be partly in food and other necessities, but partly also in wages, which seemed necessary to maintain "labor enthusiasm." In December, too, came the interesting announcement that Mao Tse-tung would not continue to serve as chairman of the government. Since he was to remain in the much more important post of chairman of the party, it was possible that he was simply sloughing off ceremonial functions the better to concentrate at this critical juncture on doctrine and policy. As 1958 ended, the regime announced as its great achievement of the year the doubling, as against 1957, of the output of major industrial and agricultural products and looked ahead to the consolidation of the agricultural communes in 1959.

Communism in China—Evolution or Revolution?

Is this revolution, now rolling so far and so fast, more Chinese than Communist or vice versa? When the Communists came into power in China, bitter chagrin and domestic political considerations led many Americans to the easy explanation that China had acquired the revolutionary disease by direct contact with Russia. This theory overlooked the long native pedigree of the Chinese revolution, in which Mao and his associates were the successors, albeit unwelcome ones, of Sun Yat-sen and Chiang Kai-shek. Whereas the earlier revolutionary leaders had included among their models the American and the French revolutions, the Chinese Communists joined with the Russian Communists in the acceptance of Marxism-Leninism, respected the Russian revolution as the first successful Marxist movement, and tried to follow Russian example—and avoid Russian mistakes—at the same time that they insisted, as Chinese nationalists, on the separateness and distinctiveness of their own revolutionary achievements.

Its Roots in Chinese History. Some Western students of Chinese history, struck by the relatively easy triumph of the Communists, have pointed out that in many respects the Chinese Communists seem to continue and fulfill Chinese traditions rather than to contradict and destroy them. By this view, with part—but only part—of which the Communists would concur, Confucian "benevolence" was the opium of the people, used by the scholar-gentry, Confucian by profession but Legalist at heart, as a smoke screen to conceal the essentially exploitative character of the regime: new Communist is old Mandarin writ large.

Without fully accepting this revisionist estimate of the Classical Confucian state, one can acknowledge certain respects in which Communists and Communism have been comprehensible and even acceptable to certain groups of Chinese. Resemblances between the spirit of the Communist regime and that of Ch'in suggest that the two are brothers in totalitarianism and that Chinese Communism may be taken as a modern expression of that Legalist element which has persisted throughout Chinese development. Chinese bred in the Confucian tradition could find in Communist ideas and practices some ingredients more appealing than this resurrection of Legalism, however.[2] The Communist party as an elite could easily be equated with the "superior men" of the old dispensation; Neo-Confucianism had been so truly an orthodoxy that the special place of Marxism was not wholly strange to Chinese intellectuals. The idea of the class struggle gave "scientific" support to the usual attitude of the Chinese gentry—and peasants—toward merchants. Revolution as a technique for social change had the sanction of custom, and the Chinese Communists could and did adopt as their ancestors a whole series of Chinese rebels from the bandits in the great novel the *Shiu Hu Chuan* [3] (reported to be Mao's favorite reading matter) to Sun Yat-sen, who has been regarded by the Commu-

---

[2] See W. W. Rostow *et al., The Prospects for Communist China* (New York, 1954), pp. 135-36.
[3] Translated by Pearl Buck as *All Men Are Brothers* (2 vols., New York, 1933).

nists rather as Jesus is viewed by followers of Mohamet. Marxism-Leninism gained special appeal for nationalistic Chinese through its view of imperialism, which it was popular to regard as the cause of all China's ills. And Mao's "creative deviation" of translating the class struggle into agrarian terms raised up the new style of revolution on the old-fashioned foundation of peasant revolt. In oddly assorted but important ways, Communism tied in with Chinese traditions, both those of orthodoxy and those of revolution.

Its Repudiation of the Past. Nevertheless, for all its links with the past, Chinese Communism is still, for the most part, something new, a far cry from the "stylized traditional autocracy" [4] of the Confucian state and from the rudimentary totalitarianism of Ch'in. The impact of the imported ideology of Marxism-Leninism on Chinese thought and Chinese speech has been remarkable. Marxism has given the Chinese an articulated doctrine and a special vocabulary which have made Sun Yat-sen's *San Min Chu I* look like an eclectic hodgepodge. "Scientific" socialism has meant the abandonment of the dynastic cyclical view of Chinese history in favor of the idea of development through stages. Laggard China was still in the stage of what the Marxists called "feudalism." To Mao and his followers the next inevitable stage would be the simultaneous achievement of industrialism and socialism. With Confucianism outmoded and Sun's gospel shop-worn, Marxism caught the Chinese intellectuals without that necessity of an ordered social life in the Chinese manner, a generally accepted orthodoxy. Thus in some respects it is surprising that the Communists have had to conduct an almost permanent "thought reform campaign" against persistent "bourgeois" ideology.

Marxism brought the disciplined Communist party and provided the doctrine of "democratic centralism" by which, once the party line had been formulated, difference and debate had to give way to acceptance and support. In the use of Marxist doctrine the Chinese leaders have been reasonably but not strictly orthodox. They have at times shown great skill at the sport of rationalizing in Marxist terms policies which can equally well be understood as astute adaptations to Chinese realities. In the late 1950's they seemed to be following a more doctrinaire policy, illustrated by the decision in 1958 to introduce full-scale communization in agriculture and by their "hard line" toward Tito. In the Yenan period and even before, the Chinese Communists had laid down a realistic line, which they were still following in 1949. Though Marxists, they were also vociferous Chinese nationalists. Through Mao's use of the peasants, they had acquired a leadership of the agrarian movement which they could hope to keep

---

[4] Rostow *et al., op. cit.,* p. 21.

through their "land reform" policy of temporary concession to the desire for private property. In the "New Democracy" they presented a united front formula which drew non-Communist Chinese into cooperation with them. But despite all these adjustments, the Communists also launched at Yenan the Ideological Remolding Movement, designed to establish party discipline and democratic centralism, and they had not deviated from commitment to ultimate objectives of a thoroughly Marxist character. In some ways they were using Marxism, but in many ways it had a compulsive force which used them in return.

The methods which the Communists have employed were not a part of the old tradition, any more than was Marxist doctrine. Li[5] has been dethroned from its old position as the key concept in human relations, and violently contrasting procedures for social control now prevail. In essence the Chinese Communists have adopted the techniques of Communist Russia. The Chinese people are subjected to the continuous stimulus of propaganda and indoctrination ("education" in the terminology of the regime) on the one hand, and of terror and pressure on the other, on a scale and with a skill never conceived of by the Confucian state or even by Ch'in.

The Governmental Machinery

During its first decade of control, the Communist regime has operated behind two elaborate political "false fronts," the Common Program of 1949 and the National Constitution of 1954. In the 1949 structure, the supreme organ of government was a fifty-six member Central People's Governing Council. Mao was president of the government, which had six vice-presidents, three Communists and three non-Communists, one of the latter being Mme. Sun Yat-sen. The Administrative Council, headed by Chou En-lai as premier with four vice-premiers, had many responsibilities, including the oversight of a long list of ministries and commissions. It was announced at the outset that in due course a National People's Congress would be formed as the top governing body. The Congress finally met in 1954 and approved a National Constitution, which had been under discussion for almost two years.

The Constitution of 1954. This Constitution, which officially signalized the new stage of "transition to socialism," is still a "united front" document but with more stress on the leadership of the Communist party than there had been in the 1949 program. It contains a Bill of Rights, but only for "the people" as distinct from "their enemies," who are probably the group most in need of rights. The Constitution refers to the "inde-

[5] See p. 56.

structible friendship" between Communist China and the U.S.S.R. and itself neatly demonstrates one aspect of that friendship by being a reasonably exact facsimile of the 1936 Soviet Constitution, though with some suitable variations. There is now a whole network of people's congresses, beginning with small units of government and a system of indirect elections, culminating in the choice of members of the National People's Congress. The National People's Congress, in theory the highest organ, in actuality plays much the same merely formal role as does its equivalent, the Supreme Soviet of the U.S.S.R. The Standing Committee of the Congress has much more real power. For the key positions in the new government the old party stalwarts were promptly chosen. Mao became chairman, Chu Têh vice-chairman, Liu Shao-chi chairman of the Standing Committee, and Chou En-lai head of the State Council. Significantly, it was no longer felt necessary to provide an abundance of titular posts for non-Communist personages.

Communist Party Control. Detailed study of the formal machinery of government does not yield much understanding of its actual operation. Neither Chinese nor Communist traditions would induce much regard for a constitution as the "supreme law of the land," above party and politics. In this dictatorship of the people over their enemies, a small elite group is the self-appointed trustee of the mass dictatorship. The best known and most important members of the inner circle are Mao Tse-tung, Chu Têh, Chou En-lai, and Liu Shao-chi, the only member of the party who is regarded as Mao's peer as a Marxist theoretician. This group has given the outward impression of being singularly united, though in 1957 and 1958 there were rumors that Mao had lost face over the "hundred flowers" venture and Liu Shao-chi's star was in the ascendant. Mao evidently has been the first of equals and has not found it necessary to maintain his position by recurrent purges at the summit *à la* Stalin. However many insignificant "bandits" and "counterrevolutionaries" the Chinese Communist revolution has devoured, only one top leader, Kao Kang, has been eliminated to date. The collective character of the leadership has seemed so strong that Mao's death might well have no such consequences as followed the demise of Stalin, although there might be friction between the old-line military and party veterans, with whom Mao has worked so long, and the new bureaucrats who have laid emphasis on economic planning.

The leadership has exercised control through many channels, of which "government" is only one and certainly not the most important. Each of the top leaders holds posts in numerous organizations. Even Chiang Kai-shek in his prime did not surpass in this respect Comrade Mao, who has held concurrently the positions of chairman of the Republic, chairman of the Council of National Defense, Convener of the Supreme State Conference, and head of the Communist party. The Party is the key organization in the regime. It has grown greatly since the Yenan period and now has a membership of about 12,000,000. There is also a huge bureaucracy. When the Communists first gained control of the whole country, they were constrained to take on and work through any officials of the former government who would serve them. The Three-Anti Campaign and other drives against "bureaucratism" have shown that the regime has not found it easy to constitute a civil service the members of which are both ideologically reliable and technically efficient. Mass organizations are important in shaping public opinion and in detecting and suppressing dissent. They exist for every conceivable group from artists to factory workers. In 1953 they were reorganized along lines of democratic centralism and they all have as their heads party leaders who see that they do not stray from the party line. Residents' committees for urban areas and peasants' associations in the villages provide opportunities to work for the general welfare or to scrutinize and interfere with one's neighbors' lives. There are, of course, instruments of force—a large army, a militia organization into which in 1958 all the able-bodied were enrolled as a part of the communization program, and a secret police, the last less prominent than its counterpart has been at some periods in the history of the U.S.S.R. Basic to the effectiveness of the regime are the "cadres," the young activists, who may or may not be under party discipline. After rigorous training and thorough indoctrination, they are sent out to make the party line a reality in the lives of the masses. They are the shock troops of the regime, which relies heavily on their intelligence, tactical skill, and loyalty. They may also be its scapegoats, who will be denounced for "adventurism" (going too fast) or "bureaucratism" (not going fast enough) if matters do not go well. Every major revolution has seen their fellows, but the Chinese Communist movement has gone further than perhaps any other comparable movement in organizing and exploiting the zeal of picked young people to project its program. Through this whole repertory of organizations and agencies, the will of the regime has penetrated into villages, into homes, and into individual minds. Private doctrines, private fortunes, and private lives are all intolerable to it. The old days in China when the emperor was far away and the peasant could till his fields with little awareness of his rulers are gone without a trace.

Communism's Impact on Chinese Society

The regime which has just been sketched has put its greatest emphasis on the transformation of Chinese life through the simultaneous development of industrialization and socialization. Industrialization has been a long-standing objective of Chinese reformers, dating back to China's nineteenth century contacts with the West. The Communists are determined on a degree of industrialization sufficient not only to make China the leading industrial state in Asia but to put China on a par with the major powers of the West. Nationalism as well as Marxism spurs this drive, since an industrialized China presumably will be strong and independent. The changes which this great movement toward socialization and industrialization have made in the status and roles of key groups in Chinese society can be used as the framework for an analysis of some of the major developments of the first decade of "Red China."

The Bourgeoisie. The bourgeoisie can suitably be discussed first, as the group most evidently out of step with the new long, fast march. It had also been out of step in the old regime, where the landlord had been exalted and the businessman held down. Contact with the West had stimulated the emergence of a new pattern of manufacture and trading. Capitalists had played an important role in the period before 1937, but the war had hit them hard, and the only real industrial center which the Communists inherited was the Japanese-made establishment in Manchuria. China in 1949 had no equivalent of the Japanese *zaibatsu*, and the Communists could create major industries which would be state-controlled from the start. On coming into power, the Communists took over the large-scale economic enterprises, such as the textile industry and the banking and commercial enterprises in the former treaty ports. To smaller businessmen, the "New Democracy" may not at first have seemed too ominous: granted that the bourgeoisie were to live on borrowed time, the regime seemed willing to lend it in tolerable quantity.

This initial period of the peaceful coexistence of the bourgeoisie with a government dedicated to its ultimate destruction proved to be very brief. In the violent attack on counterrevolutionaries which accompanied the Korean War, many of the middle class were denounced as enemies and saboteurs. Few could hope to be found innocent of all of the offenses against which the Anti-Five Campaign was directed—bribery, tax evasion, fraud, stealing state property, and stealing state economic secrets. Execution or suicide disposed of many; others were sent to "reform by labor," in which phrase "reform" meant brainwashing and "labor" meant forced labor on great water-conservancy projects on the Huai and Yellow Rivers, the Communist equivalent of the building long before of the Great Wall and the Grand Canal. The state moved rapidly toward complete control of economic life. Close restrictions and supervisions hemmed in the mercantile group. Joint public-private organizations marked the transition to state enterprise. By 1952 the government controlled 90 per cent of all loans through the People's Bank, and monopolized dealings in agricultural and industrial commodities.[6] The First Five Year Plan meant for the residual middle class further shrinkage of their "life-space." The end came with the New Year celebration of the termination of private enterprise in 1956. State enterprise and joint public-private enterprise and the business class had become mere agents and functionaries of the state.

The Urban Workers. What have been the fortunes of the urban proletariat, that group so important in Marxist theory and so insignificant in Chinese fact? In the 1920's the Chinese Communists had tried to work with and through the proletariat. Later Mao had turned from this orthodox but ineffective procedure to the organization of the peasantry as a revolutionary force. Thereafter the urban workers had played almost no part in the rise of Communism, a circumstance which did not, however, keep the Communists in 1949 from proclaiming the proletariat as the vanguard of the revolution. Communist plans for industrialization, of course, called for an immense growth, both in quality and in quantity, in the ranks of skilled labor. The propaganda agencies extolled the virtues of factory work. Women were released from their traditional bonds so that they could add to the labor force, a process which reached its climax with the communization of agriculture in 1958. Fringe benefits, Soviet style, were offered—nurseries, vacations, rest homes, insurance. Soviet technicians were employed. Universities became primarily technical institutes. In many ways the workers were being paid more in prestige than in cash or comfort, however. They were organized into the All-China Federation of Trade Unions, which, like organizations of its kind, dispensed both exhortation and control. Working hours were long and what spare time there was went to special technical training or the endless indoctrination sessions which the workers came to call "fatigue meetings." Real wages remained low. The regime took up the system of piece-work wages in factories as an incentive, but at the end of 1958, workers on this basis, after long discussion, "spontaneously" denounced the system as bad and bourgeois. For many workers life must still have seemed "bitter struggle," with only the Communist millennium ahead to give it point and promise.

The Peasants. The peasants are the most important group for the future of the regime. They exist in tremendous and steadily increasing quantity. At the end of the 1950's they were numbered at better than 500,000,000. For the Communist leadership, the peasants are both an economic and a political problem. Many peasants were early supporters of the Communists, attracted not by the long-range prospect of Communism, but by the imme-

[6] Rostow, *op. cit.*, p. 242.

diate accomplishment of land redistribution. The expropriation of the property of the landlords and "rich peasants" and its transfer to "middle" and "poor" peasants (fine distinctions which were clear only to Marxist doctrinaires) gave the Communists a temporary tactical advantage but did not provide a likely foundation for socialism. In extending and confirming private property in land, the regime risked retrogression into old-fashioned Chineseness. Its redistribution of land was in itself no more a fundamental social change than had been the changes in land titles which had come with each new dynasty in the long Chinese historical record. Moreover, the Communists proposed to make a community which was industrialized as well as socialized, and the road to industrialization obviously ran through the countryside. Would private ownership of land provide greater stimulus than collectivization to the production of the agricultural surpluses necessary to endow the new industries? If the regime must choose, which would take precedence in its policy toward the peasants, political control through collectivization or even communization, or economic incentive through the preservation of elements of private enterprise?

During the first period of Communist control of all China, land reform was pushed. It became in 1951 and 1952 a bloody business as the Communists unleashed terror in the countryside. By 1953 it seemed expedient to give the peasants a moment of relaxation. The cadres were rebuked for having gone too fast, while the peasants were urged merely to form mutual aid teams as a simple experience in cooperation. There were many signs, however, that the Communists would not let the peasants rest in the enjoyment of the land which they had acquired from their erstwhile betters. Even after land redistribution, farms were tiny; even with the most powerful psychological and economic incentives, agricultural efficiency was not likely on this pattern. The Five Year Plan necessitated agricultural production at something above the minimum subsistence level to provide the capital accumulation with which to launch heavy industry and to pay for the importation of foreign, chiefly Soviet, machinery. The regime, therefore, at the end of 1953 began the first of a series of dramatic moves, first into cooperatives, then into collectives, and finally, in 1958, into full communes. Here the Communists met head-on the old durable society of China, and which would win, the irresistible force or the immovable object, was still at the end of the 1950's uncertain.

Pressures of Population

The facts of Chinese demography complicate the agricultural issue. Each year adds about 13,000,000 Chinese to the 600,000,000 revealed in the 1953 census. Communist measures for the improvement of sanitation and health and the control of flood and famine have simply reduced the death rate and aggravated the problem. On one point the views of old-fashioned Chinese and of pedantic Marxists have oddly agreed—opposition to birth control. The birth control campaign which followed Mao's speech of February 27, 1957, was half-hearted by Communist standards, and before long vigorous advocates of population restriction were accused of defeatism. It is not in good Marxist taste to admit that the inevitable triumph of Socialism may be thwarted by an excess of people: the official Communist attitude is that the growth of population is an asset, not a liability.

Collectivization: Curse or Cure? Redistribution of population has been used as a partial answer to some of the problems which redistribution of land could not solve. Many Chinese have been shifted to the new industrial centers on what used to be the thinly settled frontiers, such as Lanchow, Paotow in Inner Mongolia, and the Sungari region. The Communists have boasted that newly found or exploited natural resources and reclaimed waste land can take care of an almost infinite number of human beings, each by his labor producing value, but this optimism is not shared by most Western students of Communist China. Population growth even stands in the way of the mechanization which might contribute to increased food supply. Chinese agriculture, which has always depended on extravagant use of human labor, now can use human labor in unprecedented and increasing amount. In 1956, in the full flush of enthusiasm over collective farming, the regime put money into elaborate farm machinery only to find that it put men out of work. Moreover, the nature of China's topography and the technique of cultivation of such major products as rice are inconsistent with the organization of large farms on which tractors and combines can deploy. When in March, 1958, Chairman Mao himself demonstrated the virtues of a new simple double-edged plow, he demonstrated what degree of mechanization is feasible—and probably also called to the memory of elders the old days when the Son of Heaven inaugurated the agricultural year by turning a furrow.

These problems of incessant population increase and the unsuitability of certain modern agricultural techniques have not moved the Communist leadership to moderation. Even Khrushchev's admission in 1953 that collectivization had not stimulated production in Eastern Europe seems to have been no deterrent. A petty bourgeois peasantry might be fatal to the realization of the socialist state; a collectivized or communized peasantry, even if initially less efficient, could be held under closer control, forced to disgorge to the state more of what it did produce, and remolded to total enthusiasm for the new order. It was possible, of course, that in the long run an unwillingly communized peasantry might wreck the prospects for socialism by outright rebellion, but the leaders seemed willing to take that risk.

The great drive for collectivization began in 1954. With it, logically enough, came a reorganization of taxation and grain requisitioning, the establishment of a state monopoly of trade in the principal products of the farms, and rationing. In 1954 neither the peasants nor the forces of nature were too cooperative. In fact, in this and the following years, flood and famine served overtime as explanations for the failure of agriculture to move ahead at the expected speed. The earlier objective of a 30 per cent increase in agricultural production under the First Five Year Plan was cut to 17 per cent. Measures had to be taken to keep distressed peasants from moving to the cities, and the cadres were exhorted to change the attitude of the farmers toward productivity. During 1955 the rounding up of peasants into collectives proceeded with great rapidity. Mao, in his "hundred flowers" speech, declared his faith in collective agriculture, but the persistent lag in farm yield suggested that many peasants did not share his view. Even Mao's statement that the state would hold taxes and grain collections at their current level must have been only cold comfort to farmers still existing on a margin of the slimmest sort. The Five Year Plan was hailed as a great success on its conclusion at the end of 1957, but there was reason to believe that the increased production of agricultural goods was no greater than was needed to keep pace with the production of babies. As the Second Five Year Plan began, agriculture was still the Achilles' heel of the regime. Experiments with full communes in the spring of 1958 went well enough to move the leadership to the institution of communes for the whole agricultural sector in the summer. This extremist measure left not only the capitalist states but the other countries of the Communist bloc gasping. The "lao pai hsing" had not been too quick at learning new tricks. Would life in communes transform them simultaneously into efficient food producers and ideal citizens of the Socialist state?

Education and Intellectual Life

The Communists have, of course, been intent on changing Chinese education and intellectual life. In the years just before the Communist take-over, the Chinese intellectuals were rudderless. The old Confucian tradition had lost its efficacy and the gospel of Sun Yat-sen had proved inadequate. Into this ideological vacuum Communism might hope easily to make its way. The rudimentary "thought control" measures of the Kuomintang had been irritating rather than effective, and had succeeded only in alienating many of the educated group. When the Communists offered a united front for national reform and welfare, the intellectuals listened readily enough. Indeed in 1949 the first reaction of many of the Peking intelligentsia to the Communists was disturbingly uncritical.[7]

The non-Communist intellectuals were not long to enjoy cooperation with the new government on terms agreeable to them, however. As a British journalist has shrewdly observed of the Communist effort to change the Chinese intellectual type, "If any parallel to the new discipline in China can be found, it is perhaps that in England in the seventeenth century as the result of Puritanism."[8] Heretofore China had not been noted for the production of fanatics: now the Chinese literati found that both total zeal and total submission were demanded of them. Both the older Chinese humanistic tradition and the more recent attachment to Western European and American ideas were to be extirpated. The ordeal of the Chinese intellectuals has been one of the most notorious aspects of Communist control. Here, as in their dealings with other groups, the Communists fitted the punishment to what was in their eyes the crime. Just as the landlords had to surrender their property, so the intellectuals had to surrender their minds. They were subjected to the process which has become widely known as "brain-washing." Under constant surveillance, and after interminable revival meetings, Communist style, intellectuals publicly confessed their past errors. Willingness to denounce Hu Shih and to abjure his influence became the sign of the achievement of Marxist grace. It was easy to whip up student denunciations of teachers whom the Communists wished to eliminate. Many lost their posts for having been "corrupters of youth" and some were sent to reform through labor.

However, either the ideological reform of 1951–1952 failed of complete success or else the regime has continued to need scapegoats, for the Communists have continued the struggle against "bourgeois thinking" (i.e., any ideas not on the "line" of the moment). In 1955 Hu Fêng, a Chinese literary figure with long-standing party membership, was held up to his fellow writers as a horrible example for having argued that good writing did not have to be political in purpose. In 1956 and 1957 there was a shift to a milder approach. Chou En-lai set the new line in the summer of 1956 by calling for more confidence in intellectuals and more incentives for intellectual achievement. Most of the academicians, despite their recantations, were still not regarded as "progressive" in their thinking; in fact repression had bred fear and apathy rather than original thought. But competent and convinced scientists and technicians were desperately

---

[7] See Derk Bodde, *Peking Diary: A Year of Revolution* (New York, 1950), p. 121. This work contains the valuable first-hand impressions of an American sinologist who was in Peking from August, 1948, to August, 1949.

[8] Guy Wint, *Spotlight on Asia* (London, 1955), p. 115.

needed in the Five Year Plan, and the Party now announced a great effort to enroll in its ranks by 1962 one-third of the top-level intellectuals. The imperfect indoctrination of even the student group was shown by mass student demonstrations in the fall of 1956, stirred up by dissatisfaction with job assignments and by a sympathy with the Hungarians which did not conform to the official approval of Russian intervention in Hungary. Mao's speech of February, 1957, continued to counsel party members in the direction of liberalism: for example, they were advised to avoid dogmatism in their criticisms of literary works and scientific theories. Few university people joined the outright critics in 1957, however, apparently suspecting that the new freedom was simply a scheme to smoke out opponents of the regime. In summary, the older Chinese literati, for all their troubles, seem not yet to have been reshaped beyond all recognition. They have managed to preserve some independence of mind, and the regime, so long as it still needs their talents, may be expected to vary its strategy of pressure with inducement.

In the meantime the Communists have been working to produce a new generation of government officials, scientists, and technicians on whom they can rely in their drive to reshape Chinese society. From the beginning, the regime has made a strong appeal to the idealism and ambition of the young, who, like many of their elders, were disillusioned with the Kuomintang. The schools have been made over in an effort to make them the matrix of the new society. A reorganization of the educational system in 1952 reduced sharply the number of institutions of higher learning, merging a number of well-known colleges, such as Yenching and Tsinghua. Most of the universities in China today are specialized technical institutes. Chinese students, in complete contrast to their forerunners, have gone over to virtual adoration of science, especially that queen of the sciences, Marxism-Leninism, on the ground that there is no question that science cannot answer. As in Russia, the tone of the school system has varied from time to time, from extreme "permissiveness" to a recent emphasis on quality and discipline to produce the skills needed in economic development. In 1958 Liu Shao-chi was endorsing boarding schools even for young children as the truly socialist pattern of education. The Communist regime has been atacking the perennial problem of mass education. While universal schooling is recognized as a goal, it is at present beyond both the capacity and the desire of the government, since young people are badly needed for "glorious" labor in fields and factories. The most notable gesture of the regime in the direction of mass literacy has been the endorsement of an alphabetic system of writing which is, very gradually, to supersede the old ideographic script. If this change is ever accomplished, it will mark an even more effective break with the cultural tradition of the past than Ch'in Shih Huang-ti was able to achieve with the "Burning of the Books."

Treatment of Religious Groups

The dealings of the Communists with religious bodies constitute a significant theme in the history of the new order. Christianity was obviously liable to Marxist denunciation not only as an opiate for the people but also as a manifestation of Western imperialism. At first the Communists seemed tolerant, and missionaries hoped they could carry on; but the Hate-America Campaign of the Korean War period was accompanied by an attack on Protestantism, and, more harshly, on Catholicism. Many Christians suffered in the terror of 1951-1952. At the same time, Chinese Christians were assured that they could practice their religion if they denounced and cast off their foreign connections. Christianity has been allowed to continue in China on condition of subservience to the regime. Buddhism, far from vigorous long before the Communists gained power, has certainly not enjoyed the favor of the new government. The temples were treated as landlords during land redistribution and lost their holdings. Buddhism, like Christianity, could escape trouble only by becoming a tame organization under Communism's control. Taoism suffered more direct persecution than did Buddhism. The Communists, aware of its historical association with rebellion, moved to stamp it out. Of all the organized religions in the area of Chinese Communist control, only Lamaist Buddhism in Tibet seemed in a position to stave off Communist domination.

Treatment of Minority Groups

The relative effectiveness of the resistance of Tibetan Lamaism to Chinese Communist pressure has sprung in large part from its status as the religion of a distinct national group. At least 60,000,000 inhabitants of Communist China are members of minority groups. The Communists have inherited the long-standing hostility of these peoples toward the Han Chinese and during the past decade have had to face minority rebellions of the traditional sort. Official Communist policy has included both solicitude for the cultural autonomy of the minorities and warnings, backed up on occasion by force, against going far in the direction of "regional nationalism." In 1950 the Communists "liberated" Tibet and joined it to China, but the marriage has not been very harmonious. Attempts to transform Tibetan society ran into determined opposition from the Tibetan theocracy. Even a Communist announcement in 1958 of the deferment of further attempts at socialization, including the inauguration of communes, did not prevent vigorous Tibetan resistance, the flight of the Dalai Lama, and the institution of closer Chinese control early in 1959.

As might be expected from the history of their relations with the Chinese,[9] both those of Chinese physical stock in the Northwest and the non-Chinese Moslems of Sinkiang have been very troublesome. In Sinkiang, separatist tendencies among the Uighurs, a Moslem Turkic group, led to a series of risings in 1956, 1957, and 1958. In 1958 the Communist leadership moved vigorously to bring Sinkiang into line. The Sinkiang Communist party was purged of "Moslem chauvinists" who had been plotting to restore "feudalism." Chinese immigration into Sinkiang was encouraged and a ten-year plan to turn the region into a major base of industry and agriculture was announced. The Chinese Moslems of the Kansu area who had shown violent opposition to Chinese Communist rule were warned in 1958 that the Koran was a religious document, not a political guide, and that the China's People's Republic was not a federal state. Nevertheless, the regime has deferred to the strength of minority feeling by organizing autonomous regions at the provincial level in Inner Mongolia, in Sinkiang, in Kwangsi for the Chuangs, and in Ninghsia for the Chinese Moslems.

The Nationalist Regime on Taiwan

During the past ten years the world has observed and debated the phenomenon of two governments, each claiming ecumenical authority over China. One of them controls all of the mainland, the other only one province, the island domain of Formosa, or Taiwan. On December 8, 1949, Taipei in Taiwan was proclaimed the capital of the Nationalist government. About 1,500,000 Nationalist supporters, over 500,000 of them soldiers, came to the island. From the first, the Nationalists talked bravely of an early return to the mainland as soon as the mass of the Chinese people discovered the true character of the Communists and rose against them. As the years passed, this vision of the recovery of China *irredenta,* which has been a Nationalist article of faith, has retreated before the Nationalists like a mirage, and practical necessity has impelled them to develop in Formosa a long-term political and economic system.

Problems of the Taiwan Government. Initially the auspices were poor. The native Taiwanese, who make up four-fifths of the island's population of approximately 10,000,000, were not willing hosts to the remnants of the Kuomintang: they had bitter memories of their experience with the

---

[9] See pp. 219-20.

first Nationalist postwar governor, Chên Yi.[10] The great majority of the Taiwanese were Chinese in blood, but fifty years of Japanese rule had cut them off from the great convulsions and changes of China in the early twentieth century. The mainland Chinese now descended on them as a ruling group. The Kuomintang dominated the government; the Peace Preservation Corps (the security police) hunted down enemies of the regime; the philosophy and practice of one-party rule, not really terminated by the "democratic" constitution of 1947, was transplanted.

The governmental arrangements on Taiwan were curious and confusing. Taiwan played two roles in the Nationalist political structure. The Nationalist regime was still in its own eyes the government of all China: Formosa was at the moment all of China which the government controlled. The elected institutions of the national government operated in and on Taiwan alone. On the other hand, Formosa, as a province of China, also had a provincial government. At first the mainland Chinese controlled at both levels of government, to the irritation of the Taiwanese, while the Kuomintang monopoly of government posts angered those members of the small political parties who had come to Taiwan rather than cooperate with the Communists. The impeachment proceedings against Premier O. K. Yui early in 1958 could be taken as one overt demonstration of strain and dissatisfaction. The government responded to criticism by relaxing and liberalizing some of its practices. In the local administration, at the *hsien* level, and in the provincial government, Taiwanese came to hold the great majority of posts and of seats in elected bodies. Their integration with the mainlanders has also been advanced by their conscription into the army. Two small political groups, the Young China group and the Democratic Socialist party, were allowed to exist though they did not come to constitute an effective political opposition. The perennial subject for speculation about the Nationalist government on Taiwan was what would happen when Chiang Kai-shek disappeared from the scene. Ch'en Ch'eng, who became vice-president in 1954 and also premier in 1958, was the apparent heir apparent. Chiang's announcement that he would not ask a waiver of the constitutional limitation so that he could have a third term as president beginning in 1960 suggested that the government would soon have to demonstrate that it was something more than an emanation of the prestige, influence, and political skill of the Generalissimo.

Record of the Chiang Government. In their economic policy in Taiwan, the Nationalists have shown that, unlike the Bourbons, they have learned something from disaster and exile. Land reform in Formosa has been a considerable success. The famous Land Law of 1930, not well

[10] See p. 493.

enforced on the mainland until the advent of the Communists,[11] has been put into effect. A maximum size for landholdings has been set, and government land has been sold cheaply. The result has been an increase of from 50 to 75 per cent in the proportion of land being farmed by its owners. The American-sponsored Joint Committee on Rural Reconstruction has encouraged better methods of cultivation and better safeguards for health in the villages. The government has carried on extensive development in irrigation works and in maintenance and exploitation of the island's timber resources. The Nationalist government has also pushed a program of industrialization for Taiwan, implemented through a series of Four Year Plans, reminiscent of the Five Year Plans of the Communists. Here, as in other aspects of their program in Taiwan, it has been evident that the Nationalists have studied the successes of their Communist enemies, and have not been above adopting Communist procedures which might build up their own strength. Taiwan has prospered during the past decade, and the standard of living on the island is distinctly superior to that on the Communist mainland.

Nevertheless the Nationalists must struggle to overcome economic difficulties many of which ironically resemble the troubles which confront the Communists. The Nationalists, too, have a population problem: the annual increase is more than 3 per cent. Less than one-third of the land surface of the island is arable, and almost all of that has been under intensive cultivation for a long time. The large army of over 600,000 has drawn heavily on Taiwan's wealth. Even with American support, about half of the Nationalist government's expenditures has gone to the maintenance of its military establishment. There has been a chronic deficit, offset only by American aid.

In Taiwan the Nationalists have kept alive traditional Chinese culture as it has been affected by Western European and American influences. Many academicians came to Taiwan with the Nationalist government, and one university, five independent colleges, and a teachers' training institution testify to lively interest in higher education. Vocational, scientific, and technical education has been stressed to provide qualified personnel for industrialization. Taiwan has an impressive literacy rate of close to 85 per cent, thanks in part to the educational program of the Japanese during their period of control.

The Nationalist government in Taiwan stands as a demonstration to all Asiatic peoples that economic progress can be achieved in a non-Communist social system. But the tremendous scope and dramatic speed of the Communist movement on the mainland draw all eyes. How does the Chinese Communist account stand at the end of the first decade?

[11] See p. 433.

Communist China: The Record to Date

In the column headed "Achievements" is a formidable list. The old Chinese social, political, and economic pattern gave cohesion to the lives of several hundred million people. The Communist regime has broken this quantitative record by establishing its authority over the largest group of human beings ever brought under a single sovereignty. More than that, it proposes to transform the way of life of this quarter of the human race by prosecuting with appalling energy and apparent success a program of change which make even the Russian revolution seem a small enterprise. As one commentator observed early in the 1950's, "The myth, formerly accepted by many people, that no regime could organize and discipline the Chinese people, seems to have been exploded."[12] Characteristic institutions of the old dispensation have been either smashed, badly dented, or transmogrified. Private property has given way to socialism. The loyalties which formerly focused on the family have been transferred to the socialist state and the revolutionary process. Of course, not all of the disruption of the inherited social order is the work of the Communists. It had begun as result of the earlier contact with the West. The drastic changes in present-day China can be viewed as a process of heterodox westernization, the vehicle of which is the European doctrine of Marxism, as transmuted in another non-Western society, that of Byzantine Russia, which, like China, first took on Western European coloration before being dyed with the red of Communism.

Under the Communists, what used to be called "Changeless China" has been dragged and persuaded into changes both more extensive and more rapid than those which have been effected in the U.S.S.R. in over forty years. While there has been miscalculation, waste, and inefficiency, the rising level of industrialization and socialization in China suggests that the 1958 slogan, "Catch up with Britain in fifteen years" must be taken as more than a mere propaganda line designed to get from the Chinese the last ounce of effort. China, formerly synonymous with military weakness, can now send out, instead of great masses of human beings under inadequate arms, the modern forces which conspicuously broke the Chinese nineteenth-century precedent of always losing wars to Westerners by carrying the Korean War to a stalemate. This productive, forward-looking, powerful China is the "image" which the regime impresses on its subjects and the goal toward which it urges and forces them. In so doing, it can summon to its support that deep-rooted feeling of superiority bred of China's great past and bitterly frustrated in the later Manchu period and

[12] A. Doak Barnett, "Social Controls in Communist China" in *Far Eastern Survey*, Vol. XXII, No. 5 (April 22, 1953), p. 45.

the early years of the republic. China is once more the Middle Kingdom, although now giving off cultural radiations of a very different sort from those which emanated from the earlier imperial regime.

While the Communists have in an amazing number of ways and to an astonishing extent been able to remold China to their will, they have certain critical problems, as yet unsolved and perhaps insoluble. The chief of these have already been referred to—a gigantic population which increases at such a rate that a total of 1,000,000,000 Chinese is in prospect; a repertory of natural resources, including arable land, which may not be adequate to sustain an industrial establishment of top rank; an economic dependence on the Soviet Union, which, however, is lessening; a procedure compounded of executions, punishments, psychological probing, drives, campaigns, and the inducement of a sort of mass hysteria and hypnosis which may overshoot the utmost limits of human toleration. Government by adjustment and decorum has yielded to rule by terror and propaganda.

But has the Communist violation of human integrity and individuality proceeded so far, especially through the communization program, that the handwriting is already on the wall for the Communists, though not yet clearly visible? The Communists hold and use with unequalled skill all of the instruments of force and influence; they have considerable popular support, especially from the young; they have bent if not broken the intellectuals; they have been reshaping public opinion; they have a leadership still apparently united; and they can point to achievements which appeal to Chinese pride. The phrase used by a British correspondent suggests the tone of China in the late 1950's: everywhere he saw "discipline, drabness, and dedication."[13] Sporadic trouble with the national minorities and unorganized local risings by groups of peasants are not sufficient to unseat the regime. Despite persistent Kuomintang reports of extensive resistance, there has been little likelihood that Heaven would soon withdraw the mandate from the Communists, and less likelihood that it would thereupon confer it upon the Nationalists. The Chinese Communists seem to combine the fanatic extremism of the Jacobins with the formidable durability of the Bolsheviks. Yet both the Chinese Communists and their opponents might well reflect on Crane Brinton's analysis of the result of four great attacks of the revolutionary fever, the English, American, French, and Russian—"that they indicate that in general many things men do, many human habits, sentiments, dispositions cannot be changed at all rapidly, that the attempts made by the extremists to change them by law, terror and exhortation fail, that the convalescence brings them back not greatly altered."[14]

[13] Walton A. Cole, editor of Reuter's, quoted in *New York Times*, February 23, 1958.
[14] Crane Brinton, *The Anatomy of Revolution* (New York, 1957), p. 277.

SUGGESTED READINGS

Observers' accounts of the Chinese Communist regime of course vary with the competence and point of view of the observer. Among the more interesting are Derk Bodde, *Peking Diary: A Year of Revolution* (New York, 1950), the work of an American student of Chinese philosophy; two works by Indian journalists, Raja Hutheesing, *The Great Peace* (New York, 1953, and Frank Moraes, *Report on Mao's China* (New York, 1953); two accounts by British newspapermen, James Cameron, *Mandarin Red* (London, 1955), and Guy Wint, *Spotlight on Asia* (London, 1955); an account by a Canadian journalist, Gerald Clark, *Impatient Giant: Red China Today;* and a French account, Robert Guillain, *600 Million Chinese* (New York, 1957).

Among the useful scholarly works are W. W. Rostow *et al., The Prospects for Communist China* (New York, 1954); Michael Lindsay, *Notes on Educational Policies in Communist China* (Cambridge, Mass., 1950), and *China and the Cold War* (Carlton, Victoria, Australia, 1955); Richard L. Walker, *China under Communism: The First Five Years* (New Haven, 1955); Ygel Gluckstein, *Mao's China* (Boston, 1955); Ronald Hsia, *Economic Planning in Communist China* (New York, 1955); Peter Tang, *Communist China Today: Domestic and Foreign Policies* (New York, 1957); John K. Fairbank, *The United States and China* (rev. ed., Cambridge, Mass., 1958), which discusses recent events in China against the background of an analysis of Chinese history.

On Taiwan under the Nationalists see F. W. Riggs, *Formosa under Chinese Nationalist Rule* (New York, 1952); George W. Barclay, *Colonial Development and Population in Taiwan* (Princeton, 1954).

INDEX

Abe, General N., 557
Acheson, Dean: China policy, 560-65, 615-17; Far East policy, 615-18
Adachi, 513, 515
Adams, H. A., 199
Adams, John Quincy, 173, 186
Adams, William, 161
Aigun, Treaty of, 348
Ainslie, Dr., 183
Ainus, 89-90, 92
Alaska: United States acquisition, 331-32; World War II and, 547, 551
Aleutians, in World War II, 547, 552
Alexander III, Tsar, 349
Alexieff-Tseng Agreement, 274, 302
Alexiev, Cossack adventurer, 347
All-China Peasants' Union, 434
Allied Council for Japan, 581, 606-7, 612, 636
Alvarez, explorer, 152
Amau Statement, 455-56, 471-72
American China Development Co., 303
American Revolution, 186
Amerika Soki (General Account of America), 197
Amherst, Lord, 164
Amur River, 346-47, 407
Analects, The, 66, 67
Anami, Japanese politician, 579
Andaman Islands, 546
Anfu clique, 391, 392, 397
Anglo-Japanese Alliance, 274-75, 277, 302, 351ff, 443ff
Anglo-Japanese Treaty of Commerce and Friendship, 201
Anking, 214, 460
Annam, French power in, 288
Anshan Works, 15
An Tê-hai, 223
Anti-Comintern Pact, 408
Aoki-Kimberley Treaty, 272
Arabs, early Chinese contacts, 149-50
Araki, Sadao, 514
"Argonaut," 182
"Arrow" War, 176-78
Arsenals, Chinese, 231
Arthur, Chester A., 291, 333
Ashida, Japanese politician, 591-92

Ashikaga shogunate, 102-5; Chinese relations during, 143-45; economic situation during, 118; rivalry of Buddhist sects, 134
Asia: Buddhism in, 72; central melting pot, 5; early Chinese cultural influences, 30; mineral resources, 85-88; United States policy, 615-18 (*see also* United States Far Eastern policy). *See also* separate Asiatic countries
Association for the Worship of God, 208, 212
Atom bomb, 550, 552, 580, 596, 637
Attu Island, 552
Aulick, John H., 193
Australia: in World War I, 359; in World War II, 546; Japan policy, 612; Korea attitude, 627; naval-bases policy, 443; United States mutual-defense treaty, 615
Austria-Hungary: Chinese relations, 368-69; Japanese relations, 201

Baikal, Lake, 403
Baker, Newton D., 470
Bakufu, 100-101, 243
Balfour, Lord, 374, 444
Banking system, Japanese, 524-25
Bataan, 546
Belgium: Chinese relations, 299, 303; in the Washington Conference, 441; Japanese relations, 201
Beniowski, Graf von, 185
Bergsmark, D. R., 82
Bevin, Ernest, 611
Biddle, James, 191
Bikini, 637
"Black pottery" culture, 24
Block printing, 31
Blücher, General, 414, 415
Bogue, Treaty of the, 173
Bolsheviks (*see* Communists)
Bonin Islands, 193, 258, 329; in World War II, 614; Japanese claim, 269, 614, 651-52, 655
Book of Changes, The, 66
Book of History, 66
Book of Mencius, 66
Book of Poetry (Book of Odes), 66, 298
Borah, William E., 469-70

691

Borodin, Michael, 414-15, 416, 422ff, 575
Boxer Rising, 296-99, 313; foreign powers in, 274, 339, 352; indemnity settlement, 367, 369, 376
Brinton, Crane, 688
British Commonwealth of Nations: in Japanese Occupation, 608-9; in Japanese peace treaty, 608, 613-15, 636-38
British North Borneo, 546
British Supreme Court for China, 286
Bronze Age, 10, 23, 24-25
Bryan, William Jennings, 365
Buddhism, 31, 68-69; cultural influence, 143; history of, 30, 71-73; Japanese, 94, 136-41, 241, 538; political involvement, 99, 106-7, 139-40, 297; sects, 139-40, 244; Soga family and, 94-95; "Three Treasures" of, 137; in Red China, 683
Buir Nor, Lake, 406
Buriats, 346
Burlingame, Anson, 178-79, 235; Chinese mission, 332-33
Burma: British annexation, 288; in Japanese peace, 606, 613, 637; in World War II, 546, 550
Burma Road, 486, 548, 559
"Burning of the Books," 28, 68, 683
"Burying of the Scholars," 68
Bushido, 147, 242
Butler, Nicholas Murray, 470
Byrnes, James F., 555

Cairo, Declaration of, 580
Cairo Conference (1943), 548-49; Korea in, 568, 620, 621
California, 333, 342-43
Cambaluc, 32
Cambodia, 488
Canada, Korea attitude, 627
Canal Zone, Korean annexation and, 280
Canberra Conference, 608-9
Canton, 17; Communists capture, 575; foreign trade and, 168-72, 175-77, 326, 328; Japanese and, 460, 478, 558; Republican government in, 391, 393; schools in, 234; Sun Yat-sen's government in, 413-15; Treaty of, 175
Canton Delta, 7, 12
Canton-Hankow railway, 303, 383-84
Capitalism, in Japan, 245; in China, 51
Carolines, the, 378
Caron, Francis, 184
Catholic Church: in China, 153-56, 174-75, 235-36; in Japan, 114-17, 159-60; in Korea, 291; in Red China, 683
Cécille, Rear Admiral, 184

Central America, Japanese trade, 533
Ch'ahar Province, 457, 458; under Japan, 473
Ch'angan, 31
Chang Chih-tung, 227, 229-33, 308, 310, 312ff; army reform, 317; death, 383; railway negotiations, 384
Changchun, 449, 453
Chang Hsueh-liang, 402, 425, 448, 455; kidnaping of Chiang Kai-shek, 438-39; nonresistance policy, 449, 450
Chang Hsün, 369, 391
Changkufeng, 407
Chang Tso-lin, 370, 401, 402, 414, 446ff; Japanese support of, 511-12; Kuomintang period, 420, 423ff; opposition to Anfu, 392, 393
Chapdelaine, Abbé, 176
Chefoo Convention, 286
Chekiang, 12, 460
Chemulpo, 276
Ch'ên, Eugene, 423
Ch'ên brothers, 574, 575
Ch'en Ch'eng, 685
Ch'ên Kuo-fu, 430
Ch'ên Li-fu, 430, 561, 563
Ch'ên Pao-chên, 308
Chên Yi, 573, 651, 684
Ch'i, 27
Chia Ch'ing, Emperor, 164, 206
Ch'iang Hsüeh Hui, 308
Chiang Kai-shek, 387, 511; books written by, 562; Cairo conference, 548, 568; dominance achieved, 422, 425, 574; head of Whampoa, 415; Japanese policy after World War II, 611; Japanese war and, 459-61; kidnaping of, 438-39; leadership, 662-63; New Year's Day speech, 564, 574-75; North China separatist problem, 458; Quemoy crisis, 632; railway dispute, 402; relations with United States, 488, 548-50, 569-70, 590-91, 600n, 604, 633; role of, 562-63, 574-75, 674-75; Sino-Japanese war, 561-63; Soviet and, 404, 409-10; Taiwan government, 604, 685-86; Yalta Conference, 620
Chiang Kai-shek, Mme., 425, 438, 549
Ch'ien Lung, 33
Chih Kang, 179
Chihli, 297, 315, 352
Ch'in, 27, 671-72
Chin, 27
China: agriculture (*see* Chinese agriculture); armies (*see* Chinese armies); art in, 74; at Versailles, 375-79; Christianity in (*see* Christianity in China); Civil

INDEX 693

War (*see* Chinese Civil War); commerce (*see* Chinese commerce); Communism in (*see* Chinese Communists); culture (*see* Chinese culture); dynasties (*see* Chinese dynasties); economy (*see* Chinese economy); extraterritorialities in, 273-74, 292, 376, 465, 548; finance reforms, 323-24; foreign imperialism in, 273, 283-84, 351-53; foreign relations (*see* Chinese foreign relations); Four-Power Consortium, 278; geography, 6-15; history (*see* Chinese history); in Anglo-Japanese alliance, 275; influence on Japan, 93-94, 96; in Japanese peace treaty, 608, 612; in Treaty of Portsmouth, 277-78; Japanese concessions in, after Russian war, 277-79; Japanese extraterritorial privileges, 272; Japanese iron imports from, 534; Japanese occupation, 556-59; Japanese relations (*see* Chinese-Japanese relations *and* Sino-Japanese War); Marshall's mission to, 569-72; Meiji Policy, 256-57; Moscow Conference and, 598-600; Nanking puppet regime, 484-85; Nationalists (*see* Chinese Nationalists *and* Nationalist China); navy, 230-31, 316-17; opium problem in, 167-73, 320-22; people of (*see* Chinese people); People's Republic (*see* Chinese People's Republic *and* Chinese Communists); philosophy (*see* Chinese philosophy); political institutions (*see* Chinese political institutions); Portugal's claims, 152-54; railway problems, 277, 349ff, 362, 370-72, 401-3, 465; religion (*see* Chinese philosophy); Republic (*see* Chinese Republic); Revolution (*see* Chinese Revolution); social institutions (*see* Chinese social institutions); United States policy (*see* United States-China relations); Washington Conference and, 441-46; westernization, 230-34; World War I and, 358, 359-60, 366-78; World War II in, 547-51

China Incident (1937) (*see* Sino-Japanese War)

China Merchants' Steam Navigation Company, 232

China's Destiny, Chiang Kai-shek, 562

China's Economic Theory, Chiang Kai-shek, 562

China's Sorrow (*see* Huang Ho)

Chinchow, 466

Chinda, Viscount, 376

Ch'in dynasty, 27-28, 150; philosophies during, 68

Chinese agriculture: agrarian discontent, 50, 207, 433; Chou period, 26; collectivization in Communist China, 659, 664-65, 667, 669-70, 678-80; crops, 11, 49-50; farming characteristics, 46-50; Kuomintang proposals for improvement, 433; population distribution, 17; regional differences, 9-14, 49-50; rivers' influence, 6-8; soil maintenance, 49

Chinese armies: arsenals, 231; Peiyang force, 386; provincial, 387; war lord forces, 392; westernization, 230-34; 316-17

Chinese Changchun Railroad, 605

Chinese Civil War: during the '20's, 463-65; events of 1948, 574-75, 600-601; period of 1946-47, 572-74; Soviet and, 410; two-government period, 391-93; United States and, 599-605. *See also* Chinese Communists; Chinese Nationalists

Chinese commerce: Canton's role in, 12; communications, 231-33; early, 29, 51, 149, 394; foreign trade relations, 52, 149, 164; opium issue, 166-73; post-reconstruction outlook, 79; rivers and, 7-8; transportation, 51-52

Chinese Communists, 565-67, 658-89, 670-73 (*see also* Chinese People's Republic); anti-Japanese united front, 436-39, 566-67, 575; beginnings, 395; civil war, 569-76; doctrines of, 434-35; early leaders, 434; economic policy, 565-66; in Manchuria, 598-99; Kuomintang and, 429, 433-36, 459-60, 549; military and political situation, 1946-47, 572-74; military tactics, 565; move to the northwest, 435-36; nationalism issue, 435; "new democracy" of, 566-68, 575; peasant-movement leadership, 433-34; police, 565-66; propaganda, 561, 566-67, 646; reform measures, 50, 564-65; relations with Japan, 595, 651; relations with Chinese Nationalists, 565-72, 574-75, 643-44; relations with Soviet Union, 554-55, 633, 644-46; relations with U.S., 568, 599-605, 617-18, 642-48, 653-54; Sino-Soviet Alliance, 605-17; student elements, 567; Sun Yat-sen period, 413-15; technique of war, 572, 574; trade relations, 629; United Nations and, 642; war-time organization, 564, 586; writing reform, 60, 682-83

Chinese culture: archaeological records of early, 23-25; art, 73-75; birthplace of Chinese civilization, 10; education, 53, 54, 59-60, 62-63, 229-30, 311, 314-16, 396; effect on cohesion of Chinese life, 76; emphases in, 19-20; geographic influences, 4-20; in early Republic period, 395-96; influence on Japan, 30, 103, 134-36, 137-

694 INDEX

Chinese culture—*cont.*
38, 142-45; language, 58-62; legends of early, 22-25; literature, 59, 63-65, 307, 396; Ming period, 32; Nationalist educational system, 430-31, 560-62, 686; New Life movement, 431; non-scientific quality, 75-76; printing in, 65; spoken language, 61-62; Red China, 687-88; Sung age, 31; superiority attitudes, 227; T'ang age, 31; Western culture and, 226-30, 233-34, 687-88; writing, 25, 26, 29, 58-61, 396, 682-83

Chinese dynasties: Ch'in, 27-28; Chou, 22, 26-27; Han, 28-29; histories of, 64; Hsia, 22; Manchu (Ch'ing or Ta Ch'ing), 33-34; Ming, 32; Shang, 22, 23, 24-26; Sung, 31-32; Ta Ch'ing (Manchu), 33-34; Tang, 31; Wei, 30

Chinese Eastern Railway, 277, 349ff, 465; Russian Revolution and, 370-72 (*see also* Chinese railways); Russo-Chinese disputes over, 401-3; Russo-Japanese conflict over, 404-8

Chinese Eastern Railway Company, 294-350

Chinese economy: business practices, 50-51; Chou period, 26-27; currency reforms, 322; during Japanese war, 558-59; family income, 48; foreign financing, 303-4, 339; in early Republic period, 394; inflation, 559; land ownership, 48; living standards, 52-53; rebellion-inciting elements, 207; resources for industry, 15; rivalry with Japan, 527, 533; Sino-Japanese war, 557-58; Spanish dollars, 153; Sun Yat-sen's program, 419; Taiping program, 211; taxes, 217; U.S.S.R. and, 617-18; westernization of, 233-34

Chinese foreign relations: anti-Bolshevik movements of the powers, 371-72; Boxer Rising and, 296-99; Burlingame mission to the west, 332; deterioration of, 283-86; during Taiping movement, 214, 215, 217-18; Dutch, 153, 167, 299; early European contacts, 151-57; English (*see* English-Chinese relations); equal treatment of foreigners policy, 326-28, 332, 338; extra-territorialities, 273-74, 292, 376, 447, 465, 547; foreign concessions after Japanese defeat, 293-96; foreign financing and, 303-4, 356, 376; foreign study plan, 316; French, 153, 174, 176ff, 284-86, 288, 295, 300, 303; German, 294, 295; international consortium, 441-42; isolation policy, 154-56; Italian, 295; Japanese (*see* Chinese-Japanese relations); Korea (*see*

Korea); loss of dependencies, 286-93; monarchy restoration and, 366-67; most-favored-nation policy, 328; open door, 299-300, 338-39, 351, 444; pattern for concessions, 293; Portuguese, 152-54; pre-European, 149-50; railway, 383-84; Russian (*see* Russo-Chinese relations); Spain, 153; Sun Yat-sen and, 419; tariff autonomy, 426, 447, 465; unequal treaties, 401, 463ff; United States (*see* United States-China relations); Yüan Shih-k'ai and, 387, 390

Chinese history: early, 22-44; feudal, 26; Hundred Days of Reform, 308-11; Manchu reform, 313-24; Mongol period, 31-32; outlying regions, 13-14; reform movement of 1898, 306-13; rivers' influence on, 6-8; Six Dynasties, 29, 30; Taiping Rebellion, 175-76, 195, 206-19; the Warring States, 27; Three Kingdoms, 29-30; Tientsin massacres, 284-86; Tz'ŭ Hsi regency, 222-26; year of decadence, 236-37

Chinese-Japanese relations, 277-79; Boxer treaty, 299; Chinese students in Japan, 316; during World War I, 359-66, 368-78; early trade relations, 103, 105; following defeat of China, 349-51; Hay notes and, 300; Japanese aggression in, 453, 455, 456-61; Japanese occupation of China, 556-57; Japanese Peace Treaty, 608, 613; Japanese politics and China, 511-20; Japan's liberal decade, 442; Japan's privileges in China, 292; Korea in, 157-58; Liu Ch'iu Islands issue, 286-87 (*see also* Ryukyus); Manchurian crisis, 447-51; reparations, 606; separatist efforts by Japan, 458; Shidehara policy, 446; treaties, 201; Twenty-One Demands, 360-66; wars, 158, 446-71, 476-82, 556-76

Chinese Mixed Court, 286

Chinese Nationalists: army weaknesses, 560; democracy and, 429-32; "Double Five" constitution, 432; furtherance of national principle, 428-29; government moves to Chungking, 558; governmental structure, 426-28; Industrial Cooperative Movement, 559; intellectual uniformity efforts, 560-62; Japanese pressure on, 429, 452; Land Law of 1930, 433; livelihood measures, 433; military victory in north, 425-26; provisional constitution, 431-32; railway interests, 448; revival of Communism and, 433-36; seizure of Chinese Eastern Railway, 402; Soviet aid to, 410; student demonstrations, 437; successes against Communists in south, 435-36; united front

INDEX 695

and, 436-39; warlordism after 1928, 428-29. *See also* Kuomintang *and* Nationalist China

Chinese people: banditry background, 50; birth rate, 53; concentrations of, 7-8, 11, 17, 47; diet, 17, 52; emigrant, 20; family discipline, 54-55, 396; farm population, 46; health conditions, 52-53; landed gentry, 54; merchants, 54; numbers of, 15-17, 53; physical make-up, 17-18; regional differences, 18; scholar-officials, 54, 63; standard of living, 52-53; women, 55, 210, 396

Chinese People's Republic, 409, 436, 575-76, 603, 617, 647, 658-89; achievements, 687-88; American captives, 642; American Policy of non-recognition, 629, 642, 646; anti-American campaigns, 571, 660-61, 683; attempted invasion of Taiwan, 643-44; bid for Asian leadership, 646; "brainwashing," 681; campaigns against the opposition, 660-61; Chinese Nationalists and, 659; "collective" leadership, 665-66; collectivization of agriculture, 46, 659, 664-65, 667, 669-70, 678-80; communism in China, 670-73; Communist party control, 674-75; consolidation of the regime, 664-68; economic changes, 661-62; education and intellectual life, 680-83; Five-Anti Campaign, 661; Five Year Plan, 14, 50, 664, 666-67, 678, 680, 682; foreign policy, 646-47; founding the "New Democracy," 658-64; Geneva Conference, 631-32; governmental machinery, 566, 673-75; impact of communism on Chinese society, 675-78; industrialization, 659-61, 664-66, 669, 677; land reform, 658-61, 664, 673, 678; National Constitution of 1954, 673-74; occupation of Tibet, 645-46; offshore islands problem, 643-44; peasants, 677-78; Political Consultative Council, 659; population problems, 664, 667, 678-80, 688; Quemoy crisis, 632-33; religion, 661, 683; secret police, 675, 688; Soviet Union and, 659, 688; treatment of minority groups, 683-84; urban workers, 677

Chinese philosophy: ancestor-worship, 26; Boxer theories, 296-97; Buddhism (*see* Buddhism); Christian religion and, 234-36; Classical period of, 27; Confucianism (*see* Confucianism); in Ch'in period, 68; reform ideas, 395-96; impact of communism on social institutions, 675-78; religion during the Six Dynasties, 30; Sun Yat-sen's, 415-21; Taiping, religious elements, 207-19; T'ang and Sung periods, 31-32

Chinese political institutions: basic elements, 34; boards, 36; civil service examinations, 41-43, 55; Communist organization, 566; corruption, 40; criminal law, 166; dependencies, 38; dictated by Boxer victors, 299; early foreign relations, 36; emperor, 34-35, 43; financial system and, 39; Grand Council, 35-36; Grand Secretariat, 35; Hanlin Academy, 36, 226, 234; *hsien*, 427-28, 564, 566, 685; Japanese occupation and, 556-57; Japanese use of, 96-97, 100; Kuomintang, 415; law, 38-39; legal reforms, 322-23; Manchu, 33; military system, 39-40, 217; Nationalist, 426-28, 432; People's Republic (*see* Chinese People's Republic); personal quality of, 430; political parties, 388; preparations for parliament, 319-20; provinces, 36-38; regional armies, 217; revolutionary societies, 383; revolutionary theory and, 43, 212, 218; scholar-bureaucracy, 35-36, 40; student movement and, 397; Taiping version, 211; taxes, 573; westernization of, 317-20; *yuan*, 427; Yüan Shih-k'ai and, 389-90

Chinese Progress, 311

Chinese railways, 232; Chinese Eastern (*see* Chinese Eastern Railway); foreign involvement, 295-96, 303-4; issue in revolution of 1911, 383-84; Knox plan, 304; nationalization, 384; popular hatred of, 296; Russian negotiations, 293-94

Chinese Republic: beginnings of, 385-86; Constitutional Compact, 389; constitutions of, 388; early factionalism, 388; military dictatorship in north, 393; monarchical movement of 1915-16, 366-67; Nationalist movement origins, 393; "Temple of Heaven" constitution, 389, 393; two-government period, 391-93; war lord period, 390-94; Yüan Shih-k'ai presidency, 385-90

Chinese revolution: agrarian discontent and, 50; attempted "second revolution," 389; civil war of early republic, 391-93; events of 1911, 381-85; examination principle and, 418; family system decay, 55; livelihood principle, 419; October 10 incident, 384; organizing groups, 383; principle of democracy, 417-19; principle of nationalism, 416-17; rise of Kuomintang, 413-15; role of peasantry, 434; secret societies, 55, 383; social confusion, 386; student movement, 383, 397; theory of right, 43, 100, 381-82; three-stage theory, 419-20

INDEX

Chinese social institutions: family, 53-56; *kotow*, 164, 178; landlordism and tenancy, 48; *li* concept, 56; Manchu-Chinese discrimination, 323; rebellion-inciting elements, 207; secret societies, 55; social rank, 53-54, 211
Chinese Turkestan (*see* Sinkiang)
Ch'ing, Prince, 225, 303
Ch'ing dynasty, 3, 156; art of, 74; declining power, 206-7; history of, 64; philosophy during, 69; Tz'ŭ Hsi regencies, 222-26
Ch'ing Hai, 14
Ch'in Shih Huang-ti, 683
Ch'in-wên, 228
Ch'i Shan (Kishen), 171-72
Chita, 294, 373, 399
Chonin, economic transformation, 521
Chosen (*see* Korea)
Chosen, Bank of, 510
Choshu clan, 269; in Tokugawa overthrow, 249, 252
Chou An Hui, 366
Chou dynasty, 22, 26-27
Chou En-lai, 674, 681; foreign policy, 632, 642, 644; premier of Red China, 660, 661, 673, 674, 681
Chou Li, 211
Christianity in China, 174-75; Boxer Rebellion and, 296-99; early missions, 32, 150-56; early Republic hopes, 393; effect on foreign relations, 283, 284-86; land disputes, 284-85; persecutions of, 156; Taiping movement, 207-19. See also Catholic Church *and* Protestant Church in China
Christianity in Japan, 105, 538; early success, 159-60; first arrival and exclusion of, 114-17; Nestorian, 150; proscription of, 112
Ch'u, 27
Chuang Tzŭ, 70
Chuang Tzŭ, Book of, 70
Chuenpee, Convention of, 172
Chu Hsi, 69
Ch'un, Prince, 319, 323; regency, 382-83
Ch'un Ch'iu, 66
Ch'ung Hou, 287
Chungking, 12, 460; American embassy damaged, 491; Chinese Nationalists in, 557, 558; Communist capture, 575-76; Taipings in, 213
Chung Kuo, 3
Chung Wang, 213-15
Chung Yung, 66
Churchill, Winston: Cairo Conference, 568; Yalta Conference, 620
Chusan Islands, 171, 172
Chu Teh, 434, 674

Chvostov, Lieutenant, 185
Clans, in Tokugawa overthrow, 249, 252
Clark, General Mark, 629, 630
Classic of Filial Piety, 66
Classic of the Way and Its Power, The, 69
Cleveland, Grover, 334, 335
Coal: in China, 15; in Japan, 86-87
Cochin China, 288
Coffin, Reuben, 193
Co-hong, 165, 173
Colbert, French Minister, 184
Colombia, Korea and, 280
Columbo Plan for Economic Development in South and Southeast Asia, 636
Communists: in China (*see* Chinese Communists); in Japan, 591-93, 612; United States policy on, 615-18
Compact of Naha, 199
Competition, in Japanese economy, 530
Confucian classics, 65-66, 137
Confucianism, 27, 30, 31; attitude toward Western culture, 227-28; Buddhism and, 73; development of, 28-29; history of, 66-69; influence on the Taiping movement, 210, 211; in Japan (*see* Confucianism in Japan); literature of, 65-66; reform movement interpretation, 306-13; social responsibility theory, 41
Confucianism in Japan, 93, 134, 136-38; eighteenth century, 141; emphasis on family, 104; loyalty encouraged by, 112
Confucius, 66
Confucius as a Reformer, K'ang Yu-wei, 307
Constitutional Compact, 358, 366
Convention of Chuenpee, 172
Convention of Shimonoseki, 203
Coolidge, Calvin, 462, 465
Cooper, Mercator, 190
Coral Sea, Battle of, 547
Corregidor, 546
Cossacks, Siberian expansion, 345-48
Cotton, in Japanese economy, 533
Cressey, G. B., 88
Crimean War, 347, 348
Cushing, Caleb, 173-74, 328
Czechoslovakia, 613
Czechs, 372, 399

Daigo II, Emperor, 102
Daimyo, 111, 128; decline and transformation, 240-50, 254, 256; economic transformation, 521
Dai Nippon, 142
Dairen, 292; in Yalta Conference, 553; Japanese gain, 276; Russia and, 294, 351, 598-99, 605

INDEX

Dalai Lama, 645, 684
Dalny (see Dairen)
Dan, Takuma, 513
Davidov, Lieutenant, 185
Davis, John W., 191
Dawes, Charles G., 467
Democracy, Japanese approach, 499-520, 582-97
Democratic League of China, 564, 571, 668
Democratic Liberal party, in Japan, 591
Democratic party, in Japan, 591
Democratic People's Republic of Korea (see North Korea)
Democratic Socialist party, Nationalist China, 685
Denmark, 201
Dennett, Tyler, 332
Depression, Japanese economy and, 449, 532-35
Derevyanko, K., 607
Deshima, Dutch in, 161, 182, 183
Dewey, Commodore George, 337
Dewey, John, 395
Dezhniev, Cossack adventurer, 347
Doctrine of the Mean (Chung Yung), 66
Doeff, Dutch factor, 183
Dominicans, in China, 155
Doolittle, James H., 547, 551
Draft Constitution, Chinese, 571-72
"Dragon," 201
Draper, William H., 610
Dull, Siberian railway proposal, 349
Dulles, John Foster: relations with Japan, 613, 648; relations with Nationalist China, 633-34, 644, 654
Dutch-Chinese relations, 153, 167, 299
Dutch East India Company, 161
Dutch East Indies (see Netherlands Indies)
Dutch Harbor, Alaska, 547
Dutch-Japanese relations, 161, 182, 183, 203; cultural aspects, 147; early trade, 115, 161

East Hopei Autonomous Council, 458
Edo: Japanese capital at, 111; manufacturing importance, 126; Perry's mission and, 194; Treaty of, 220. See also Tokyo
Einosuke Moriyama, 198
Eisenhower, Dwight D.: Far Eastern policy, 630, 654; Japanese policy, 651; Nationalist China policy, 632, 634, 644-45, 654
Elder Statesmen (Genro), 264-66, 502-6, 518
Elgin, Lord, 201
Elliot, Captain Charles, 166-72
"Emperor," 201
English-Chinese relations, 295, 548-49; "Arrow" War, 176-78; Burma sovereignty, 288; Canton anti-foreign incidents, 175-77; Communists and, 603; during Taiping Rebellion, 215; early difficulties, 153, 163-64; first war, 166-70; German banking agreement and, 303; Hay policy and, 300-302; Margary affair, 286; memorandum of 1926, 464; most-favored-nation policy, 173-75; opium problem, 166-73, 321, 327; trade restrictions, 164-66. See also Great Britain and Extraterritoriality
English East India Company, 161, 165-67, 182
English-Japanese relations, 161, 272, 607-9, 611-12; early trade, 115, 182-83; early treaties, 201; first Japanese mission to Europe, 204; post-Perry, 202-4
"Epoch of the Warring Country," 103
Etoile Belge, 349
Everett, Alexander H., 191
Ever-Victorious Army, 214, 215, 218
Extraterritoriality: Chinese-Japanese conflict over, 447; in China, 273-74, 292, 376, 465, 548; in Japan, 269-73. See also separate countries

Far Eastern Advisory Committee, 454, 478-79
Far Eastern Commission, 581, 606-7, 610, 611
Far Eastern Republic, 373, 399-400
Fêng Kuo-chang, 370, 391
Fengtien, 302
Fêng Yü-hsiang, 420, 422, 423ff, 428, 429; in the early Republic, 392, 393
Feng Yün-shan, 209
Feudalism, in Japan, 104ff, 109-11, 119, 127ff, 239-44, 253-68
Fifteen-Passenger Bill, 333
Fillmore, Millard, 193, 194
Fisheries, 355, 405, 408-9, 411, 649, 651
Five Classics of Confucianism, 65-66
Five-Power Naval Treaty, 443
Foochow, 17, 231, 597
Foote, Captain, 177
Forged Classics of the Wang Mang Period, K'ang Yu-wei, 306
Formosa (Taiwan), 286; Cairo Conference on, 548; Japan and, 78, 84, 256-58, 273, 292, 637; Nationalist government on, 604-5, 575-76; neutralized, 615n, 684-86; opium problem, 321; railway, 232; United States policy, 330, 562, 564-65, 615, 616-18, 626-27. See also Taiwan
Four Books of Confucianism, 65-66
Four Power Consortium, 278-79
Four-Power Treaty, 443, 483

698 INDEX

France: Annam affair, 288; at the Washington Conference, 441ff; Chinese relations, 174, 284-86, 295, 300, 303, 563; in Four Power Consortium, 278-79; Japanese relations, 184, 201, 204, 272, 273, 482, 488; Korea attitude, 289, 627; naval limitation and, 475
Franciscans: in China, 151-52, 155; in Japan, 115
Fudai daimyo, 111, 124
Fujiwara family, 96, 98-99, 101, 243; Mitsui connection, 528
Fujiyama, Japanese leader, 594, 652
Fujiyama, 80
Fukien, 12, 18

Galen, General, 414, 415
Gama, Vasco da, 152
Gauss, Clarence E., 550, 568
Gautama, 71
"General Account of the Republican Government States, A," 197
General Principles of Reconstruction, Sun Yat-sen, 416
Geneva Conference, 631-32, 642
Genro: origin, 264-66; political role, 502-6, 518
Genroku culture, 146-47
George, Henry, 419
George III, King, 33, 163, 164
Germany: Chinese relations, 294, 295, 299-302, 303; early Japanese relations, 201, 272, 273; Far East relations in World War I, 358, 362, 367ff; in Four Power Consortium, 278-79; Japanese alignment with, 456-57, 484, 486, 545; treaty relations with Soviet Union, 410-11
Girard, William, 651-52
Glynn, James, 191-92
Gobi Desert, 13
Go-Daigo, Emperor, 140
God-Worshippers religion, 208-19
Golden Horde, 150
Goodnow, Professor, 390
Gordon, Charles, 215
Gordon, Peter, 183
Grand Canal, 12, 31
Grand Memorial, 307-8
Grant, Ulysses S., 287
Great Britain: at the Washington Conference, 441, 442-46; Cairo Conference, 620; Chinese sphere understanding, 351-52; early Japanese relations, 272; Far East relations in World War I, 358, 365, 368, 374; Formosan attitude, 330; Hawaiian interest, 331; in Four Power Consortium, 278-79; in Yalta Conference, 553; Japanese aggression in China and, 468, 469, 479, 486, 489; Japanese Alliance, 274-75, 277; Korea attitude, 627; naval limitations and, 474-76. *See also* English-Chinese relations *and* English-Japanese relations
Greater East Asia Co-Prosperity Sphere, 551, 557-58
Great Wall, 28, 457
Greece, Korea attitude, 627
Gresham, Walter, 272
Grew, Joseph C., 476, 481, 483, 492, 497
Gromyko, Andrei, 613
Gros, Baron, 176
Guadalcanal, 547, 551
Guam, 546, 551
Gutzlaff, Dr. Karl, 187

Hague Peace Conference, 280
Hainan: in United States-China policy, 604; Japanese in, 482, 545
Hakka, the, 18, 207ff
Hakodate, 199, 200
Hamaguchi, 512, 514
Han dynasty, 28-29; philosophies during, 68, 70-73
Han Fu-chu, 563
Hangchow, 11
Hanihara, Ambassador, 442, 444
Hankow, 11, 17; Japanese in, 446, 460, 478; Nationalist capital in, 423, 460, 558. *See also* Wuhan cities
Hankow-Chengtu railway, 303
Hanlin Academy, 36, 227, 234
Hanoi, 487
Hanyang, 11, 460 (*see also* Wuhan cities)
Hanyehping iron and steel works, 233, 361
Hara, Japanese politician, 505-9, 514
Harbin, 404
Harriman interests, 278
Harris, Townsend, 200, 202, 248, 330
Hart, Sir Robert, 232
Hasegawa, Admiral, 478
Hatoyama, Ichiro, 589-90, 593-94, 596, 648-49, 651
Hawaii, 469; early United States interest in, 329, 331; naval base at, 443; United States annexation of, 335-36
Hay, John, 178; China policy, 273, 300-302; open door doctrine, 339, 352
Hayashi, Premier, 459, 518
Hayes, Rutherford B., 333
Hermit Kingdom (Korea), 289
Heusken, C. J., 202

INDEX

Hidetada, 112, 124
Hideyori, 108, 124
Hideyoshi, Toyotomi, 105ff, 159, 160; Christianity and, 114-15, 116; Korean invasion and, 289
Hieizan monasteries, 106-7, 140
Higashi-Kuni, Prince, 553
Hioki, 364
Hirado, 126
Hiranuma, Baron, 481
Hirohito, Emperor, 505n; surrender to Allies, 552-53, 579-80
Hiroshima, atom bombing, 550, 552, 579, 580
Hirota, Ambassador, 404, 455, 456; cabinet, 515, 517; on the bombing of Nanking, 478; on naval limitation, 476
Hirota-Karakhan Agreement, 408
Historical Memoirs, Ssŭ-ma Ch'ien, 29
History of the Former Han Dynasty, Pan family, 29
Hizen clan, 249, 252
Hodge, John R., 621
Hokkaido, 78, 184; Ainus of, 89-90; climate, 81, 84; coal fields, 86; farms, 82; forests, 84, 85; Japanese take, 269; petroleum fields, 88
Hokusai, artist, 146
Holcombe, A. N., 427
Honan Province, 207, 232, 308, 460
Hong Kong, 12, 17, 169; attempt to poison foreigners in, 177; ceded to British, 172, 173; in United States China policy, 603; in World War II, 546; Japanese pressure on, 486; Kuomintang boycott, 421; naval base at, 443; opium depot, 168
Honshu, 78, 80, 81; forests, 84, 85; government, 98; hydroelectric power in, 88
Hoover, Herbert, 467-71, 604
Hopei-Ch'ahar Political Council, 458
Hopei Province, 458, 473
"Hornet," U.S.S., 547
Horvat, General, 371, 372
Ho Shên, 206
Hosso Buddhism, 140
Ho Ying-chin, 458, 563
Hsia dynasty, 22
Hsianfu, 31, 438, 567
Hsiao Chên, Empress (Tz'ŭ An, Empress Dowager), 222-25
Hsiao Ch'in (*see* Tz'ŭ Hsi, Empress Dowager)
Hsiao Ching, 66
Hsien Fêng, Emperor, 222
Hsi K'ang, 14
Hsinking, 449, 453

699

Hsüan T'ung, Emperor, 369, 382, 385 (*See also* Pu-yi)
Hsün Tzŭ, 68
Huai River, 6, 11
Huang Ho, 6; influence on Chinese culture, 10-11
Hu Fêng, 665, 681
Hughes, Charles E., 444, 445, 462
Hughes, William Morris, 378
Hu Han-min, 422
Hulbert, Homer B., 280
Hull, Cordell, 545; policy on Japanese aggression, 471-74, 477-95
"Hump," 548
Hunan Braves, 213, 217
Hunan Province, 207, 232, 308
Hundred Days of Reform, 308-11
Hun Empire, 29
Hungarian revolution, effects of, 666-67, 682
Hung Hsiu-ch'üan, 207-19
Hu provinces, 315
Hurley, Patrick, 550, 554, 568-69
Hu Shih, 60, 396, 681
"Hyacinth," 170
Hydroelectric power, Japanese, 86-88
Hydrogen bomb, 637, 649
Hypothec Bank of Japan, 531

Ichibashi, Premier, 594
Iemitsu, shogun, 112, 113, 124
Iemochi, shogun, 249, 250
Iesada, shogun, 247-49
Ieyasu, 103, 105, 106; Christianity and, 116; foreign trade under, 115, 124, 161; rule of, 108-12
Ignatieff, General, 178, 348
I Ho Ch'üan secret society, 296
I Ho Yüan, 225
Ii, shogun, 202
Ikko sects, 106-7
Ili, region of, 220, 287
Immigration Act of 1924, 462
Imperial Maritime Customs, 232, 324; foreign control of, 283-84
Imperial Party, Japan, 503
Imperial Post, Chinese, 232
Imperial Rule Assistance Association, 518, 577
Imperial University, 234
India: Buddhism in, 72; Chinese Communist relations, 645; early Chinese contacts, 149; in Anglo-Japanese Alliance, 277; in World War II, 546, 550; Japan policy, 527, 533, 596, 612, 613; opium trade, 320, 321

INDEX

Indo-China: in World War II, 545-46, 550, 631-32; Japanese pressure on, 486, 487, 490-91; United States policy, 640, 616
Indonesia, 650; relations with Japan, 637 (*see also* Netherlands Indies)
Indusco, 559
Industrial Bank of Japan, 531
Industrial Cooperative Movement (Indusco), 559
Ingersoll, David, 187
Inner Mongolia, 356, 361ff; Japanese in, 406, 556, 684
Inoue, Ki, 263, 513
International Banking Consortium, 441-42
Inukai, 513, 515
Iron ore, in China, 15
Ise Bay, 80
Ishibashi, Tanzan, 649
Itagaki, 502-6; Restoration politics, 252, 258-68
Italy: at the Washington Conference, 441ff; Chinese relations, 295; Japanese relations, 201, 271, 486, 545; naval limitation and, 475; Tripartite Treaty, 410
Iterup, 349
Ito, Marquis, 352, 499-503; mission abroad, 263; Resident-General in Korea, 279-80; Restoration politics, 252, 257, 263, 268; unequal treaties and, 270
Iwakura: Restoration politics, 252, 257-58, 262; unequal treaties and, 270; western mission, 253, 261
Iwasaka, Mitsubishi founder, 528
Iwojima, 551

James, Huberty, 297
Japan: admission to U.N., 596, 636; after the occupation, 593-97; aggression in China, 353, 466-71, 476-77, 556-57; agriculture (*see* Japanese agriculture); Allied Council for Japan, 581; anti-American feeling, 635-36; army-navy friction, 578; "burden of responsibility" attitude, 455-56, 471-72; Chinese reforms and, 318-19; Chinese relations (*see* Chinese-Japanese relations); constitutions of, 260-68, 583-84; culture (*see* Japanese culture); demilitarization, 582; development of internal commerce, 126-27; early foreign trade, 103, 115-16, 124; economy (*see* Japanese economy); family in, 104, 120; fishing interests, 85, 355; foreign relations (*see* Japanese foreign relations); geography, 78-88, 92-93; history (*see* Japanese history); hydrogen bomb, 637; militarism (*see* Japanese militarism); modernization, 236-37, 252-68, 269-81; occupation policy, 580 (*see also* Japanese occupation); people of (*see* Japanese people); Perry mission and its effects, 196-98, 201-4; philosophy a guide to government, 95-96; politics of (*see* Japanese politics); post-Russian War conditions, 354-55; primogeniture developed, 104; rearmament, 634-35; religion (*see* Japanese religion); Siberia evacuated by, 399; social progress, 537-44; social rank, 104, 127; social significance of popular drama, 147; surrender, 551, 553, 569, 579-80; transportation, 119; Tripartite Treaty, 411; United States Occupation, 580-93, 605-13, 615-16, 655-56; world depression in, 449, 532-35; World War I and, 358-66, 372-78, 577-80; World War II and, 495-97, 545-53, 577-93
Japan Advertiser, 473
Japan, Bank of, 524-25, 529
Japan Current, 81, 187
Japan Steel Manufacturing Company, 529
Japanese agriculture: agrarian unrest, 105, 118, 122, 123, 129; basic problems of, 82-83; crops, 83, 119-20; farm size, 82-83; human element in, 83; intensive nature, 83-84; in war economy, 535-37; land reform, 97; lumber resources, 84-85; Occupation and, 586-87; pre-Meiji, 244-45; rainfall, 81-82; self-sufficiency in, 119-20; soil maintenance, 83
Japanese Alps, 80
Japanese Communists, 612, 637-38
Japanese constitutions, 260-68, 683-84
Japanese culture: architecture, 134, 142; Bushido in, 243; Chinese influence, 30, 92ff, 103, 134-36, 137-38, 142-45, 157; education, 135-36, 539-42, 584-85; family in, 239-41, 542; feudalism and, 239-44, 253-68; Genroku, 146-47; government regimentation in, 241-43; individualism discouraged in, 148; isolation and, 142, 147; language, 541; literature, 142-45, 146-47, 197-98; native period, 141-42; post-Meiji, 542-44; religion and, 132; tea-drinking, 143-44; Tokugawa period, 145-47; Westernization, 597; writing, 59, 91, 134-35, 157, 585
Japanese Diet, 265-67
Japanese economy: after the Korean War, 636; after the Occupation, 595-96, 610-12; banking system, 524-25; capitalism in, 245; diversification, 533; feudalistic nature, 119, 127, 128-29; financial problems, 128, 130; fishing in, 85, 649, 651; govern-

INDEX

ment investment in, 525, 530-31; guild system, 123-26; hydroelectric power, 86-88; imperialism in, 534-35; industrial development, 85-90, 126-27, 525-37, 609-12; labor in, 526-27, 535; land titles annulled, 97; lumber resources, 84-85; modernization, 521-37; money economy, 127; monopolistic privileges, 125-26; monopoly, 530; Occupation policy, 587-88, 607-11; paternalism in, 526-27; Perry's expedition and, 130-31; population pressure, 119-21; post-World War II, 607, 614-18, 623-25; raw-material problem, 527; rearmament, 596-97, 614; reparations and, 630, 638; rice economy, 119-20, 122; SCAP and, 614; tariffs, 122-23, 270, 272-73; Tokugawa period, 118-31, 244-47; trade, 595, 653, 655-56; trade unions, 588, 592; United States assistance, 630; war and, 531, 535-37

Japanese foreign relations: Anglo-Japanese Alliance, 274-75; axis alignment, 456-57, 481; Boxer Rising and, 274, 339, 352; Chinese (*see* Chinese-Japanese relations); Communist China, 595, 651; domestic politics and, 249; Dutch (*see* Dutch-Japanese relations); earliest foreign contacts, 105, 157-58; emigration attitude, 341, 462; extraterritoriality in, 269-73; Four Power Consortium in, 279; France in, 184, 201, 203, 204, 272, 273; Germany in, 201, 272, 273, 545; Great Britain (*see* English-Japanese relations); Italy in, 271, 545; Korean relations (*see* Korea); Meiji period, 253, 256-58; Mexico in, 271-72; Mongol contacts, 158-59; naval limitation and, 474-76; Philippines, 649-50; pirates, 159; Portuguese, 159, 160, 201; Russian (*see* Russo-Japanese relations); seclusion policy, 161, 187; Siam in, 272, 488, 635; Spanish, 160-61, 201; tariffs in, 270, 272-73; Tokugawa policies, 181-92, 248-49; trade treaties, 201; treatment of castaways, 191; unequal treaties in, 269-73; United States relations (*see* United States-Japanese relations); U.S.S.R. neutrality pact, 545; Versailles and, 376-79; Washington Conference, 441-46; World War II peace treaty, 583, 593, 613-15

Japanese governments: Kishi government, 649-50; Tojo government, 577-78

Japanese history: Ashikaga period, 103-5; Chinese influence, 93-94, 96; early chronicles of, 91-92; European arrival and expulsion, 114-17; Fujiwara period, 98-99; internal disorders of the 16th century, 106-8; mythological background, 92; prehistoric, 91-92; Soga period, 94-96; Tokugawa shogunate, 108-17, 238-50; Yamato clan in, 92-93

Japanese militarism, 457-58; defeat and, 577-80; education and, 539-41; political strength, 504-5; pre-Meiji, 239; religion and, 537-39; Sino-Japanese War and, 274

Japanese occupation, 580-93, 605-13, 615-16; Allied Council, 606; American economic aid, 596, 607, 609; demilitarization, 582; democratization, 582-84; economic policy, 585-88, 595-96; economic deterioration, 587-88; educational reforms, 584-85; elections and cabinets, 589-91; Far Eastern Commission, 606-7; government, 589-92; land reform, 586-87; Mutual Security Treaty of 1951, 597; new Constitution, 583-84; political parties, 589, 592; preliminary peace negotiations, 607-8; reaction to SCAP policies, 588-89; rearmament, 596-97; rebuilding Japanese industry, 610-11; reforms, 611-12; reparations, 586, 606-7, 614-15; Russo-American differences, 612-13; SCAP, 579, 580-81, 582, 588-89; U.S. policy revised, 609-10; Zaibatsu liquidated, 586

Japanese Peace Treaty of 1951, 583, 593, 613-15; British Commonwealth and, 608-9; preliminary negotiations, 607-8, 613-14; Russian and Chinese objections, 608; signing, 613-14

Japanese people: agrarian discontent, 105, 118, 122, 123, 129; farm population, 82-83; fishing interests, 85; merchant-artisan class, 123-26; middle class in Meiji reforms, 245-47; movement from farms to urban area, 122-23; nobility, 263; origins of, 89-90; peasant conditions, 127, 244-45, 255-56; physical characteristics, 90; "picture brides," 342; population trends, 89, 119-21; regulation under the Tokugawa, 110-11; social ranks, 93, 128; women, 104, 142

Japanese politics, 499-520; anti-foreign laws, 185; approach toward democracy, 499-520, 580-97; aristocracy in, 110, 263; army-navy relations, 519-20; *bes* in, 93; cabinet voting, 504-5; Chinese influence in, 92, 100; clans in, 92-93; daimyo, 111-12; Diet, 589-92; education for office-holding, 100, 136; extraterritoriality in, 269-73; feudalistic nature, 104, 105-6; fief regulations, 111-12; *han* in, 104; imperial institution, 95, 98, 99, 108-10, 139, 243-44, 579, 587; Meiji reforms, 245-47, 522ff,

702 INDEX

Japanese politics—*cont.*
  539-44; military in, 99, 112, 274; Occupation, 580-93, 605-13; parties, 589, 592; political divisions, 106; political theory, 138, 139, 147, 242; postwar, 592-95; rearmament, 634-35; reforms, 96-97; shoguns, 101; slaves, 93; suffrage, 509, 589; suppressive institutions, 113-14; tax system, 105, 120; unequal treaties in, 248-50, 269-73; uniformity in government, 113; Zaibatsu in, 530, 586
Japanese religion, 91, 103, 107, 241, 252; Buddhism, 136-37, 138-41, 241, 252; Chinese influence, 93-94; Christianity (*see* Christianity in Japan); Confucianism, 136-38; divine origin beliefs, 92; Kamikaze element, 159; militarism and, 537-39; Shinto, 94, 95, 132-37, 140-41, 252
Japanese-Soviet relations, 596, 637-38
Jehol, 455
Jenchuan, Treaty of, 291
Jenghiz Khan, 150
Jenks, Professor, 322
Jesuits: in China, 154-56; in Japan, 114-16
Jimmu Tenno, 92
Jingo, Empress, 157
Jiyuto party, 259-60, 266, 267, 499
Jodo Buddhism, 140
John Company (*see* English East India Company)
John of Monte Corvino, 151-52
John of Plano Carpini, 151
Johnson, Andrew, 179
Johnston, Percy H., 610-11
Johnston Report, 610-11
Joint Commission, Korean failure, 645-47
Joy, Admiral, 628
Jung Lu, 224, 230, 282; death, 314; reform and, 309, 311-12

Kabu, 124, 125
Kaesong, 625, 628, 659
Kagoshima, 126, 159; bombardment, 249, 269; British burn, 203; foreign learning in, 521
K'aifêng, 460
Kaiping-Peking railway, 232
Kaishinto party, 259-60, 266
Kamakura, 102, 140
Kamakura shogunate, 100-102
Kamatari, 98
Kamchatka, 347
Kamikaze, 159
Kana, 142
Kanazawa (Yokohama), 79, 552; Treaty of, 199

K'ang Hsi, Emperor, 33
Kang Teh (*see* Pu-yi, Henry)
K'ang Yu-wei, 234, 238, 391; in the 1911 revolution, 383; reform efforts, 306-14, 316
Kansu, 220
Kao Kang, 665, 674
Karafuto (*see* Sakhalin)
Kashgar, 287
Katayama, Japanese politician, 590-91
Kato, Baron Takaaki, 442, 506, 509-11, 514
Katsura, 503, 504
Kearny, Lawrence, 327
Kegon Buddhism, 140
Keiki (Yoshinobu), 250
Kellogg, Frank B., 464-65
Kellogg-Briand Pact, 467
Kenseikai party, 506, 509-11; Mitsubishi and, 528
Kenseito party, 502
Ketteler, Baron von, 297, 299
Khabarov, 347
Khabarovsk, 347
Khiton dynasty, 150
Khrushchev, Nikita, 633, 644, 667, 679
Kiakhta, Treaty of, 163
Kiangnan Arsenal, 231
Kiangsi, 434, 435
Kiaochow, 351, 358, 364
Kiaochow Convention, 294
Kido, Restoration politics, 252, 257
Kim Il Sung, Marshall, 630
Kim Koo, 645
King, Charles W., 187, 189-90, 192
Kishen (Ch'i Shan), 171-72
Kishi, Nobusuke, 594-95, 597, 651
Kiying, 174
Kiyoura, politician, 505, 509
Knowland, William F., 610
Knox, Philander C., 278, 304, 355
Kobe, 79
Kochi, 184
Kodo-ha, Japanese army group, 519
Koiso, Japanese politician, 578
Kojiki, Motoori, 91, 142, 242
Ko Lao Hui (Elder Brothers), 55
Kolchak, Admiral, 371-72
Komei, Emperor, 248
Konoe, Prince Fumimaro, 481, 486, 514; as premier, 491, 492, 517-19; in the China War, 459
Koo, Wellington, 376ff, 420
Korea, 580; American aid to, 611, 625; anti-foreign feeling, 291; area, 620; Cairo Conference on, 548-49, 568, 620, 621; Chinese

domination and loss of, 289-92; country divided, 621, 647-48; early Chinese influence, 30, 158; failure of Joint Commission, 623; foreign relations, 289-92; geography of, 289; history of, 288-92; independence pledged, 620-21; Japanese interest and dominance in, 93, 157-58, 290-92, 341, 354-56; Japanese sovereignty over, 74, 84, 269, 273-81, 341; Japanese wars, 108, 160; maps, 643; Meiji problems, 257-58; Moscow agreement, 621-23; North Korea, 624-25; partition of, 631, 647-48; people of, 289, 620; Potsdam Conference, 620; Protestant Church in, 291; Republic of (*see* South Korea); Russo-Japanese conflicts in, 350; South (*see* South Korea); treaties, 201, 290, 291; two governments established, 624; United Nations forces in, 647-48; United States policy and, 595, 616, 620-21, 650-51, 654-55; U.S.S.R. in, 552n, 623-24; withdrawal of occupation forces, 624-25; writing in, 59
Korean War, 620-41; armistice, 630-31; cost to U.S., 631; effect on Japan, 595; Geneva Conference, 631-32; MacArthur in command, 627; military action, 627; political developments, 627; removal of MacArthur, 628; truce talks, 628-29; United Nations action, 625-29; violations of the armistice, 647-48
Koryo dynasty, 289
Kowloon, 178, 295
Koxinga, 153
Krasnoschekoff, Alexander M., 373
Kuang Hsü, Emperor, 224; death, 382, 383; Edict of 1898, 309-10; Hundred Days of Reform and, 308-11
Kublai Khan, 32, 150, 151
Kung, H. H., 430
Kung, Prince, 223ff, 234
K'ung family, 575
K'ung Fu Tzǔ (Confucius), 66
K'un Lun Range, 8
Kunming, 574
Kuomintang, 383, 557; abortive second revolution, 389; Communists and, 413-15, 549, 570-72; corruption, 573; divisions in, 421-26, 430; ideology, 415-16; Nationalist-Communist split, 423-26; 1937-49, 561-62; northern campaign, 422-23; organizing of, 388; political structure, 415; student movement, 397, 429; thought control, 563, 680; on Taiwan, 684-85; United States views on, 599-605; World War I and, 369, 370. *See also* Chinese Nationalists
Kuo yü (national speech), 61

Kuriles, 78, 258; in Yalta Conference, 553; Japanese claim, 269, 348-49
Kurino, diplomat, 272
Kuropatkin, 353
Kuroshio (current), 81, 187
Kurusu, Saburo, 493ff
Ku wên, 228
Kwanami, Japanese actor, 144
Kwangchow-wan, 295
Kwangsi, 12, 295; lawlessness in, 207; rebellion, 367, 437, 684
Kwangtung, 12, 18, 207, 295
Kwanto Plain, 80
Kwantung Army, 407, 513, 515, 557; Mukden incident, 449
Kwantung Leased Territory, 278, 354
Kweichow, 12, 18
Kyoto, 99, 142, 202; craftsmen of, 126; Ear Mound at, 160; foreigners expelled from, 202; standards of living in, 103
Kyushu, 78; climate, 81, 82; coal fields, 86; forests, 84; government of, 98; people of, 89-90

Labor-Farmer party, Japanese, 511
"Lady Pierce," 199
"Lagoda," 191, 192
Lagréné, Théodose de, 174
Lamsdorff-Yangyu Convention, 302
Lang, Captain, 231
Lansing, Robert, 374, 441
Lansing-Ishii Agreement, 374, 444
Laos, 488
Lao Tzǔ, 69
"Lawrence," 191
"Laws of the Military Houses," 112
Laxman, Adam, 185
Lay, Horatio Nelson, 231
League of Nations: China's appeal to, 478-79; Japan's resignation, 454; Manchurian crisis, 405, 449-55, 467; Versailles Treaty and, 377, 378. *See also* separate countries
Learn, Chang Chih-tung, 227, 310
Legalism, 27-28, 68, 71
Legge, James, 229
Lena River, 346
Liang Ch'i-ch'ao, 228, 307, 308, 310-11, 383; in the Republic, 385, 389, 390
Liaotung Peninsula, 274, 350, 351; Japan's sovereignty, 276, 278, 292, 354; restored to China, 293
Liberalism, Japanese, 258-59, 499-520
Liberal Party, in Japan, 589-91
Li Chi, 66
Li Hsiu-ch'êng, 213-15

Li Hung-chang, 225, 311, 314, 317; Nienfei uprising and, 219; reform and, 228ff; Russian negotiations, 287, 293-94; Taiping movement, 214, 215, 217
Li Lien-ying, 225
Liliuokalani, Queen, 335
Li-Lobanov Treaty, 294, 350
Lin Tsê-hsü, 168-71, 230
Li Ssŭ, 28
Li Tsu-ch'eng, 155
Li Tsung-jen, 437, 574; acting president, 574-75
Liu Ch'iu Islands (*see* Ryukyus)
Liu K'un-i, 232, 313
Liu Ming-ch'uan, 219, 228, 232, 233
Liu Shao-chi, 668, 674, 682
Livadia, Treaty of, 287
Li Yüan-hung, 367, 369, 384, 390-91, 393
Lloyd George, David, 365, 377, 378
Lodge, Henry Cabot, 336
Loess, 9, 10, 15, 24
Lolo, the, 18
London Missionary Society, 164
London Naval Conference, 474, 475
London naval treaties, 449, 476, 512, 515
Long, John D., 33
Long March, the, 409
Louza Police Station incident, 463
Lowell, President of Harvard, 470
Lu, state of, 66
Lu Cheng-huang, 376
Lukouchiao Incident, 459
Lu Yung-t'ing, 370
Lytton, Lord, 450
Lytton Commission, 405, 470; Manchurian investigation, 450, 453-54; report of, 470

Macao, 168; in World War II, 546; Portuguese occupation of, 152-53
MacArthur, Douglas: as SCAP, 605-13; Japanese surrender, 553; Korea command, 626-28; Occupation command, 580-97, 606-7, 611; removed from command, 628
Macartney, 153, 163, 182
MacDonald, Ranald, 192, 198
MacNair, H. F., 415
"Maine," sinking of, 336
Mainichi, Osaka, 529, 578
Makin Island, 551
Makino, Baron, 376, 379
Malaya: in World War II, 496, 546, 606; Japanese mines in, 534
Malik, Jacob, 613
Manchouli, 406
Manchukuo, 411, 469, 515, 517-20; establishment of, 451-53; Japanese manufacturing in, 533; Soviet and, 406, 407, 552n; United States protests on, 473
Manchuria: Angus Ward incident, 603-4; anti-Bolshevik conflicts in, 371, 405; Cairo Conference on, 548; Chinese-Japanese conflicts over, 447-51, 466-71; Chinese relations, 38, 425, 447-51, 571, 573; Communists take over, 571-73; economy of, 557; geography of, 13; Japanese designs on, 359, 360-61, 362ff, 374; Japanese paramountcy in, 78, 277-81, 404-8; looted by Soviets, 598-99, 617; Moscow Conference and, 598-99; people of, 20; reasons for value, 448; Russia in, 274, 275, 294, 302, 351-56; Russo-Chinese disputes over, 401-3; Russo-Japanese secret agreement on, 355-56; Russo-Japanese war theater, 276; Soviet Russia in, 552n, 571-72, 598-99, 617, 641; Yalta Conference and, 553
Manchurian Incident (1931), 513
Manchus, 3-4; Confucianism under, 69; conquest of China, 155-56; early history, 13, 20; fall of, 381-85; intermarriage attitudes, 19; military establishments, 39-40; political organization, 35-44; Russian clashes in Siberia, 347. See *also* Ch'ing dynasty
Mandarin dialect, 61
"Manhattan," 190
Manifesto of the Kuomintang, The, Sun Yat-sen, 416
Manjiro, Nakahama, 196-98
Manyogana, 135
Mao Tse-tung: agricultural policy, 665; collapse of Nationalist government, 569, 574-76; foreign policy, 569, 601-2, 646; "hundred flowers" speech, 666-68, 680, 682; president of People's Republic, 666-67; purges of class enemies, 661; role of, 666, 670-71, 674; strong ties between Soviet and, 657, 667; theories of, 566, 667, 672, 677; United Front movement, 438
Marco Polo, 32, 151, 160
Marco Polo Bridge, 459, 477
Marcus Aurelius, 149
Marcy, William L., 331
Margary Affair, 286
Marianas, 378
Mariinsk, 348
Marshall, George C., mission to China, 569-72, 600
Marshall, Humphrey, 329
Marshall Islands, 378, 551

Martin, Joseph, 628
Martin, W. A. P., 234, 311
Marx, Karl, 73, 419, 566-67
Matahei, artist, 146
Matsu Islands, 632, 644
Matsukata, Japanese politician, 499, 506-7, 524
Matsuoka, Yosuke, 411, 457, 486
McCalla, Captain, 297
McKinley, William, 336-37
Meiji, Emperor, 250, 505n; Charter Oath, 260-61
Meiji Restoration, 204; economic sequels, 521-37; events leading to, 238-50; foreign relations, 256-58, 269-81; social sequels, 537-44
"Memorial," Tanaka, 472
Mencius, 67-68, 138
Meng Tzŭ (Mencius), 67
Meriken Shinshi (New Account of America), 197
Merinkai, the, 473
Mexico, 201
Miao, the, 18, 207, 208
Midway, Battle of, 547, 578
Midway Island, 546, 547
Mikawa Province, 106
Mikoyan, 633
Minamoto family, 99, 100-102
Mineral resources: Chinese, 14-15; Japanese, 85-88
Min faction, Korean, 290
Ming dynasty, 32, 143; Christianity and, 152, 155; overthrow of, 155
Minobe, Professor, 515-16
Mino-Owari, 80
Minseito party, 511-19; after World War II, 618, 622; Mitsubishi and, 528; origin, 259-60
"Mississippi," U.S.S., 193
"Missouri," U.S.S., 551, 553, 581
Mitsubishi, house of, 514, 528, 595
Mitsubishi Shipbuilding and Engineering Co., 528
Mitsui, house of, 123, 127, 246; political involvement, 513, 514; range of interests, 528-29, 595
Mitsukuri Seigo, 197
Mohammedans, Chinese, 149-50, 219-20; physical characteristics, 19, 20
Mohism, 27, 71
Molotov, V.: in Japanese peace treaty, 608; in Moscow Conference, 555
Mongolia: geography of, 13; government under China. 38; people of, 20; Russia in, 274, 275, 287, 352. *See also* Inner Mongolia *and* Outer Mongolia
Mongol People's Republic, 411; Japanese border clashes, 406, 407; Soviet defense of, 406
Mongols, 19; attack Japan, 158-59; Japanese claims to lands of, 406; rule in China, 31-32, 150-52
Monroe, James, 186
Montoku, Emperor, 98
Moriyama, Einosuke, 198
"Morrison" expedition, 187-90
Morrison, Robert, 164
Morrow, Dr. James, 193
Moscow Conference of Foreign Ministers, 581, 598-99, 621-23, 645-46
Moslems, in Red China, 684
Mo Ti (Mo Tzŭ), 71
Motoori, Norinaga, 242
Mukden, 17, 573, 574; Chinese-Japanese bombing incident, 449; Japanese defeat Russians at, 276; Russia in, 274
Munich Agreement, 480
Murasaki, Lady, 142
Muraviev, Nicolai, 347-48
Muscat, 187
Mutō, General, 515
"Mutsu," 443
Mutsuhito, Emperor (Meiji), 250, 260-61, 505n

"Nadezhda," 185
Nagasaki, 79, 126, 159, 200; atom bombing, 550, 552, 579, 580; early Russian contacts, 185
Nagoya, 79
Naha, Compact of, 199
Nakahama, Manjiro, 196-98
Nakano, Japanese politician, 578
Naka-no-Oye, Prince, 96
Nakatomi-no-Kamatari, 96
Namamugi Affair, 282
Nam Il Sung, 628
Nanking: anti-foreign uprising in, 285; Communist occupation, 557, 558, 571; "incident" of 1927, 465; Japanese and, 459, 460, 478, 484-85, 598; republican government in, 385, 388; Taiping movement in, 210, 211, 213, 215, 218; Treaty of, 172-73, 327
Napier, Lord, 165
Nara, 142
Narcotics, 646
National Assembly of China, 388ff, 574
National Cooperative Party, 590-92

National Council of the Chinese Republic, 388-89
National Defense Act, United States, 486-87
National People's Congress, 664, 666, 668, 673-74
National Salvation Fund, 366
National Salvation Movement, 437, 564
National-Socialist Party of China, 564
Nationalist China: American economic aid, 570, 571, 573, 600-601, 629; anti-foreign sentiment, 463-65; anti-Japanese unity, 458-60; area, 559; army, 573; Cairo meeting, 568; Canton group, 575; civil war, 569-70; collapse of government, 574-76; Communist-Nationalist relations, 565-72; Constitution promised, 564-65; corruption, 559, 574; culture, 560-61, 686; Democratic League, 564; economic aids to, 570, 571, 573, 600-601, 629; economic policies, 558-59, 685-86; fight U.S.S.R. in Manchuria, 571; Four Year Plan, 686; government, 557, 561-65, 684-85; inflation, 559, 574; intellectuals in China, 560-61; Japanese surrender, 599; Japan's recognition of, 447; Marshall's mission, 569-72; military and political situation, 1946-47, 572-73; move to Chungking, 558-61; move to Formosa, 575, 604, 684-85; National Assembly, 573-74; population problems, 686; reform movement, 574; secret police, 563; social changes, 559-560; territory, 558, 647; tutelage and democracy, 563; Taiwan government, 684-85; unification efforts of U.S., 569-72; United Front failure, 567-68; United States policy, 615-18, 654, 684-86; weakness of the army, 560; World War II, 569. *See also* China; Chinese Nationalist; Kuomintang; Taiwan
Naval limitation efforts, 442-43, 474-76
Neale, B., 202
Nelson, Donald M., mission to China, 549, 586
Neolithic culture in China, 23, 24
Nerchinsk, Treaty of, 156-57, 347
Nesselrode, Russian politician, 347
Nestorianism, 150
Netherlands: China relations, 153, 167, 299; Korea attitude, 627; Washington Conference and, 441. *See also* Dutch-Japanese relations
Netherlands Indies: in World War II, 545-46; Japan and, 485, 487-89, 533, 606
Nevelskoy, Admiral, 347-48
Newchwang, 274
New Fourth Army, 410, 567

New Guinea, 546-47, 551
New Life Movement, 431, 456
Newspaper Press Ordinance of 1876, 262
New Zealand: Japan policy, 612, 615, 627; Korea attitude, 627; naval bases, 443; United States mutual defense treaty, 615
Nichiren Buddhism, 140
Nicholas II, Tsar, 293, 349
Nicobar Islands, 546
Nienfei uprising, 218-19
Nihon Shoki, 91, 92, 142
Nikolaevsk, 347
Nine-Power Customs Convention, 444
Nine-Power Treaty (1922), 444, 453, 467, 469, 479
Nineteenth Route Army, 452
Ninghsia, 684
Nishihara Loans, 370
Nishi-Rosen Protocol, 351
Nixon, Richard, 635
Nobi Plain, 80
Nobunaga (Oda), 105-7; Buddhist foes, 139, 140; foreign relations under, 159-60; Jesuits and, 114
Nō drama, 144-47
Nomonhan, 407-8
Nomura, Admiral, 489ff, 545
Norinaga (Motoori), 242
North China, 573, 580
North Korea: government established, 624-25; war with South Korea, 625-32, 647-48
North Manchuria Railway, 406
Norway, 201

O'Conor, British diplomat, 288
Okada, Admiral, 514-16
Okhotsk, Sea of, 346
Okhotsk Current, 81
Okinawa, 199, 551, 594, 601
Okubo: Restoration politics, 252, 257, 261; unequal treaties and, 270
Okuma, 499-506; Mitsubishi and, 528; Restoration politics, 252, 255, 259-68
Omsk, 372
One Thousand Character Movement, 60, 396
Onin War, 105
Opium traffic, 167-73; Manchu reforms, 320-21; United States attitude, 327, 333
Opium War, 166-73
Organic Law of Chinese Nationalists, 426-28
Osaka: Dutch School, 522; manufacturing importance, 126
Outer Mongolia: Japanese border clashes, 406; Russian dominance in, 294, 355, 356; Soviet-Chinese struggle, 400-401; Yalta

INDEX 707

Conference and, 553. *See also* Mongolia and Mongolian People's Republic
Outline of National Reconstruction, An, Sun Yat-sen, 416
Overseas Consultants, Ltd., 610
Owari Province, 106
Oyashio (Current), 81

Pai Chung-hsi, General, 437
Pai hua, literary style, 60
"Painted pottery" culture, 24
Pakche, 93
Paleolithic culture, in China, 23-24
"Panay," U.S.S., 460, 480
Pan family, 29, 64
Panmunjom, 628, 630
Paotingfu, 299
Paotingfu Military Academy, 386
Paper-making, 150
Papua, 547
Paracel Islands, 545, 614
Paris, Pact of (Kellogg-Briand), 403, 465, 468ff, 479
Paris, Treaty of (Spanish-American War), 337
Paris Peace Conference, 376
Parker, Dr. Peter, 187, 330
Patriotic Public Party, 258
Pauley, Edwin W., 586, 598, 610
"Pax Tartarica," 32
Peace Preservation Law, 507, 509-11, 516, 684
Peace Preservation Ordinance, 262
Pearl Harbor: first United States use of, 335; Japanese attack, 460-61, 496-97, 546
Pearl River, 171
Pei Ho, 6
Pei hua, 396
Pei Wang, 213
Peiyang army, 317, 386, 391
Peking, 17, 292, 575, 644; Boxer rising in, 297-98; Burma Convention, 288; looting of, 298-99; Republican government at, 388, 392-93; schools in, 234; Sikkim Convention, 288; Treaty of (1925), 403-4
Peking dialect, 61
Peking Field Force, 230
Peking man, 23-24
Peking-Mukden railway, 448
Peleliu, 551
Pellew, Fleetwood, 182
People's Political Council of Nationalist China, 563-64, 568
People's Republic of China (*See* Chinese People's Republic; Chinese Communists)
Perestrello, Rafael, 152

Perouse, Comte de la, 184
Perry, Matthew C., 238-51; mission to Japan, 130-31, 192-96, 198-200; Pacific expansion and, 329-30
Peru, 201
Pescadores Islands, 153, 604; Cairo Conference and, 548; in United States China policy, 604, 614, 633-34; Japan gains, 273, 292
Petroleum: China, 15; Japanese, 88
Petropavlovsk, 348
"Phaeton," 182
Philippine Rehabilitation Act, 606
Philippines: Insurrection, 337; Japanese iron imports from, 534; Japanese relations, 606, 612, 637, 649-50; naval bases understanding, 443; Spanish conquest, 160; United States acquires, 336-38; United States defense policy and, 615; United States relations, 340, 625; World War II and, 545
P'ing-An Kuo, 219
Poland: in Japanese peace, 613
Political Consultative Council of Communist China, 598
Polo, Marco, 32, 151, 160
Polos, the, 151
Port Arthur, 292; in Yalta Conference, 553; Japan gains, 276, 353; Russia and, 294, 351, 598, 605
Porter, Commodore, 186
Portsmouth, Treaty of, 276-77, 302, 340, 341, 354, 408
Portugal: Chinese relations, 152-54, 167; Japanese relations, 105, 159, 160, 201; Washington Conference and, 441
Postal Union, 232, 271
Potsdam Conference, 552; Korea in, 620
Potsdam Declaration, 552-53, 579
Poulo Condore, 288
P'o-yang, Lake, 7, 11
Poyarkov, Vasily, 346-47
Pratt, Zadoc, 190
"Preble," U.S.S., 191
"Prince of Wales," H.M.S., 546
"Principles of the Constitution," 319
Printing, Chinese, 15, 150
Progressive Party, in Japan, 589
Protestant Church in China, 164; Boxer war treaties, 299; influence on Hung Hsia Ch'üan, 208; missions, 171, 229, 234-36; United States interest in, 327
Protestant Church in Korea, 291
"Providence," 182
Provisional Government of the Chinese Republic, 556
Pruyn, Robert H., 202

Putiatin, Count, 178, 185, 195
Pu-yi, Henry, 369, 382, 452, 453, 552n
Pyongyang, 626

Quemoy crisis, 632-33, 644

Raffles, Stamford, 183
Records of Ancient Things, 91
Red Banner Army, 407
Red Basin of Szechuan, 12, 559
Red China (*see* Chinese Communists; Chinese People's Republic)
Reinsch, Dr. Paul, 374
Reischauer, R. K., 132, 242
Republic of China, 647 (*see also* Nationalist China)
Republic of Korea (*see* South Korea)
"Repulse," H.M.S., 546
"Return," 182
Review of the Times, 229
Rezánov, Nicolai de, 185
Rhee, Syngman, 630, 654-55
Ricci, Matteo, 154
Rice, 50, 83-84, 119-20, 122
Richard, Dr. Timothy, 229, 308
Richardson, Charles L., 202
Richardson incident, 249
Ridgway, Matthew B., 628
Roberts, Edmund, 187
Roberts, I. J., 208
Rock Springs incident, 333
Rogers, John, 289
Romulo, Carlos P., 629, 658
Roosevelt, Franklin D., 568; at Yalta, 553; Cairo Conference, 548; China relations, 548-50; Far Eastern policy, 471-74, 477-95; on the Washington Conference, 446; "quarantine" speech, 479
Roosevelt, Theodore: Japanese relations, 342-43; Korea and, 279-80; mediates Russo-Japanese War, 276; Philippine acquisition, 336-37; Portsmouth Treaty and, 340, 353
Root-Takahira Agreement, 277, 343, 485
Ruggieri, Michele de, 154
"Rules of the Imperial Court and the Court Nobles," 112
Rural Education party, 564
Russell, Bertrand, 395
Russia: Anglo-Japanese Alliance and, 275-76; Bolshevist Revolution, 370-71; Chinese relations (*see* Russo-Chinese relations); eastern railway policies, 349-51; Four Power Consortium and, 279; in Boxer Rising, 274; Japanese relations (*see* Russo-Japanese relations); Korea and, 289; Manchuria and, 351, 352; Revolution of 1905, 354; Siberian expansion, 345-48. *See also* Union of Soviet Socialist Republics
Russian-American Company, 185, 347, 348
Russian-Korean Bank, 350
Russian Maritime Province, 399
Russo-Chinese Bank, 302, 350
Russo-Chinese Convention (1902), 302
Russo-Chinese relations: agreement of 1898, 351; agreement of 1902, 353; Anti-Japanese policies, 350; border problems, 156-57, 220, 287; during Japanese aggression in China, 409-10; during Russo-Japanese War, 302-3; during World War I, 370-73; Hay notes and, 300; Ili incident, 287; in International Consortium, 356; Kuomintang influence, 413-15; Outer Mongolia issue, 400-401; railway disputes, 401-3; Russian infringements of Chinese sovereignty, 293-94, 295; Siberian conflicts, 347-48; Soviet in, 400, 409, 465-66; treaties, 163, 177, 178, 302. *See also* Union of Soviet Socialist Republics
Russo-German Treaty of Nonaggression, 408-9, 483
Russo-Japanese Agreement of 1925, 463
Russo-Japanese Fisheries Convention, 355
Russo-Japanese relations, 272, 274; after Japan's defeat of China, 349-51; agreement of 1925, 463; early contacts, 184, 272; fisheries agreements, 355, 405, 408-9, 411; Inner Mongolia agreement, 356; Manchurian crisis, 404-8; Nishi-Rosen Protocol, 351; North China border clashes, 406-8; post-Russian Revolution, 403-9; pre-World War II friendliness, 410-11; Putiatin expedition, 195; Sakhalin question, 399-400
Russo-Japanese War, 275-77, 339, 352-56
Ryukyus, 78, 184, 256-58, 269; in Japanese peace, 611; in United States policy, 614, 616, 651-52; Japanese sovereignty over, 283-84; Perry in, 193, 194

Saigo, Restoration politics, 252, 255, 257, 258, 524
Saigon, 288
St. Petersburg, Treaty of, 287
Saionji, Marquis, 376, 503-5, 513, 515, 518
Saipan, 551
Saito, Admiral, 475, 514ff
Sakai, 126
Sakhalin, 78, 184, 276, 347, 348, 354, 411; in Japanese peace, 614; Japanese interests in, 269, 354; Japanese occupation, 399-400, 403, 404, 463; Russia in, 185, 348-49, 552n, 553; Yalta Conference and, 553

Sakurada Affair, 202
Samurai, 128; decline and transformation, 240-50, 254-56, 521
San Chao (Three Doctrines), 66, 69
Sandwich Islands (*see* Hawaii)
San Francisco Conference (on Japanese peace treaty), 613, 615
San Ho Hui (Triad Society), 55
Sanjo, Restoration politician, 252
Sanmen Bay, 295
San Min Chu I, Sun Yat-sen, 416, 425; Communist use of, 434-36; Youth Corps, 565
Sansom, G. B., 90, 144
Sarawak, in World War II, 546
Satsuma clan, 107, 202, 203, 269; foreign trade, 521; industrial enterprise, 526; in Tokugawa overthrow, 249, 252
Satsuma rebellion, 255, 257-58, 524
Savo Sea, battle of, 547
Sayings of Confucius, 66
SCAP, 579, 580-83, 588-89; democratization effort, 582; Occupation function, 581
Schaal, Adam, 156
Seigo, Mitsukuri, 197
Seiyu-honto party, 508-11
Seiyukai party, 503-19; after World War II, 589, 592; Mitsui support, 529; origin, 259-60
Sekigahara, Battle of, 111
Semenov, Captain, 371, 373
Seng-ko-lin-ch'in, 212, 219
Seoul, 160, 621, 625, 627
"Settsu," 443
Seventeen Articles Constitution, 95-96
Seward, William H., 329, 331-32
Seymour, Sir Edward, 297
Shang period, 10, 22; culture of, 23-26
Shanghai, 7, 11, 17; boycott against Japan, 450; British control in, 286; Communist conquest of, 597; foreign holdings, 295-96; Japanese aggressions, 452, 468, 478; Kuomintang capture, 424; Louza incident, 463; schools in, 234; Taiping Rebellion and, 214-15
Shanghai Municipal Council, 296
Shanghai-Woosung railroad, 232
Shansi, 458, 473
Shantung, 458, 563; Boxer origins in, 296; Chinese-Japanese conflict over, 444; German seizure of, 294; Japanese and, 368, 473, 511; Versailles handling of, 375-79
Shantung Treaty (1922), 444, 445
Shensi, 220; Communists at, 409, 436
Shidehara, Baron, 422, 449, 509-13; China

policy, 446; Manchurian incident, 449; post-War politics, 592
Shigemitsu, Mamoru, 553, 593, 648
Shih Chi, Ssŭ-ma Ch'ien, 29, 64
Shih Ching, 64
Shih Huang Ti, 27, 28
Shih Ta-k'ai, 209-13
Shikoku, 78, 81, 89; government, 98
Shimadzu family, 107
Shimoda Convention, 199, 200
Shimonoseki, 203; bombardment, 249, 269; Convention of, 203; Treaty of, 274, 292, 307
Shimpoto party, 499
Shin Buddhism, 140
Shingon monks, 139-40
Shintoism, 94-95, 132-37, 252; revival, 140-41; Sect and State, 537
Shiozawa, Admiral, 468
Shogun, office of, 101
Shotoku, Prince, 95-96, 137
Shufeldt, R. W., 291
Shun Chih, Emperor, 156
Siam (*see* Thailand)
Sian Incident, 409, 458
Siberia: Allied intervention in, 371-73, 399; Cossack expansion in, 345-47; Japanese and, 406, 445, 463, 508, 511; railway conflicts, 349-51
Sibir, 345
Sidotti, Father, 181
Sikkim, British protectorate, 288
Silk, in Japanese economy, 531-33
Silk Route, 5, 14, 29
Sinanthropus Pekinensis, 23-24
Singapore, in World War II, 546
Sinkiang (Chinese Turkestan), 14, 20, 220, 684; Communist control in, 576; Ili dispute, 287; Russian-Chinese contention over, 401-2
Sinnan Islands, 482
Sino-Japanese Military and Naval Agreements (1918), 371
Sino-Japanese Tariff Agreement of 1930, 447
Sino-Japanese War (1894), 268, 273-74, 291-92
Sino-Japanese War (1937) (China Incident), 458-61, 517-20, 556-76; Communist accomplishments in, 565; dykes cut during, 6; resistance under the Nationalists, 556-57; Russian reaction to, 349-50; united front in, 436-39
Sino-Soviet Treaty (1924), 402
Sino-Soviet Treaty of Friendship and Alliance (1945), 605, 608

Sino-Soviet Treaty of Friendship, Alliance, and Mutual Assistance (1950), 617
Si River, 7
Six Dynasties period, 30
Slovaks, 399
Small Swords group, 219
Smith, Walter Bedell, 607
Social Democratic Party, in Japan, 589, 591
Social Democrats, of China, 571-72
Socialist Party, in Japan, 591
Society for the Diffusion of Christian and General Knowledge (SDK), 229
Society for National Rejuvenation, 308
Soga, Amako, 95
Soga, Inami, 94
Soga family, 94-96, 134, 135
Solomon Islands, 546, 547
Soochow, 11, 17, 461
Soong, Mei-ling (Mme. Chiang Kai-shek), 425, 438, 549
Soong, T. V., 423, 554, 575; in Nationalist movement, 422, 425, 428
Soong family, 422n
South China Reform Association, 308
Southeast Asia, 649-50; Communist threat, Japan and, 595
Southeast Asia Treaty Organization (SEATO), 632
South Korea: attack on, 625-26; government established, 624; relations with U.S., 624-27, 630-31; removal of General MacArthur, 628; truce talks, 629; United Nations action in, 626, 627; United States sends aid, 626-27; United States withdraws forces, 624-25; war with North Korea, 620-32 (see also Korean War)
South Manchurian Railway, 278, 351, 448, 449; Mitsui interest, 529
Spain: China and, 153, 299; Japanese relations, 160-61, 201; war with United States, 336-37
Spratly Islands, 482, 545, 614
Spring and Autumn Annals, 66
Ssŭ-ma Ch'ien, 29, 64
Stalin, J. V.: at Yalta, 553; Japanese relations, 441
Steel, in Japanese economy, 533-34
Sterling, Sir James, 201
Stilwell, Joseph, 547-50, 568
Stimson, Henry L.: Chinese policy, 465, 466-71; letter to Senator Borah, 469-70; Manchurian crisis, 451
Stokes, W. N., 604
Straight, Willard, 279
Strike, Clifford S., 610
Strike Report, 610

Strokonov commercial firm, 345
Stuart, John L., 571
Su, General, 405
Sugiyama, Field Marshal, 297, 579
Sui dynasty, 31
Suiko, Empress, 95
Suiyuan, 458, 473
Suleiman, Sultan, 219
Sumitomo, house of, 528, 595
Sun Chia-ku, 179
Sun Fo, 422ff
Sungari River, 347, 404
Sung Confucianism, 227
Sung dynasty, 31-32, 150; philosophies during, 68-69
Sun Yat-sen, 36, 38, 306, 316, 370, 383, 566, 571, 575, 671-72, 680; at outbreak of revolution, 385; Canton government, 391, 393; death, 420, 421; exile in Japan, 389; ideology of, 415-21; Nationalist interpretation of program, 426-33; Soviet period, 413-15; student support, 397
Sun Yat-sen, Mme., 423, 424, 571, 673
Supreme Commander for Allied Powers (see SCAP)
Su Shun, 222, 223
"Susquehanna," 193
Suzuki, Admiral, 514; heads "surrender" government, 579
Sweden, 201
Switzerland, 201
Szechuan Province, Chinese Nationalists in, 295, 384, 559

Ta Ch'ing dynasty, 3, 14, 33-34
Taft, William Howard, 303
Taft-Katsura Memorandum, 279, 341
Tai Li, 563
Taipei, capital of Nationalist China, 573n, 575-76, 604, 684
Taiping dynasty, 207-19
Taiping Rebellion, 175-76, 195, 206-19; decline of, 212-19; divergencies among followers, 216; purge of leaders, 213
T'ai P'ing T'ien Kuo, 209
Taira family, 100
Taiwan, 614; American forces on, 654; Communist attacks on, 643-44; defense of, 633-34; Nationalist regime on, 604-5, 684-86; United States policy, 615, 684-86. *See also* Formosa; Nationalist China
Taiwan, Bank of, 510
Taiwan Development and Tea Producing Company (Mitsui), 529
Takahashi, Japanese politician, 508, 516, 535

INDEX

Takauji, 102
Takla-makan Desert, 14
Taku forts, 298, 299
Tale of Gengi, The, Lady Murasaki, 142
Tali, revolt in, 219
Talien-wan (*see* Dairen)
Tanaka, Baron, 472-73, 511-14; Positive Policy in China, 446-47
"Tanaka Memorial," 472
Tang dynasty, 31
Tangku Truce, 455, 457, 458
Tannu Tuva, 401
Tan Ssŭ-t'ung, 308, 310, 311
Taoism, 27, 30, 31, 68ff; Buddhism and, 73; in the Boxer Rising, 297; in Red China, 683
Tao Kuang, Emperor, 206
Tao Tê Ching, 69, 70
Tarim Basin, 14, 29
Teiseito party, 259-60
Tenchi, Emperor, 96, 98, 136
Tendai monks, 139-40
Terauchi, Premier, 503, 504, 506; Resident-General in Korea, 281
Textiles, in Japanese economy, 526, 533
Thailand (Siam), 49, 187, 201, 272; in World War II, 545, 546; Japanese pact with, 488; Japanese trade, 612
Third Party, of Nationalist China, 564
Three-Anti Campaign, 675
Three Kingdoms period, 29-30
Three Principles of the People, The, Sun Yat-sen, 416, 425, 434-36
Tibet, 20, 288; British influence, 295; Chinese invasion of, 617, 645-46, 683-84; geography of, 14; government under Chinese control, 38
Tientsin, 17; 575; Communists capture, 596; massacres, 235, 284-86; Treaties of, 177-78, 179, 284, 332, 348; World War I effects in, 369, 370
T'ien Wang (*see* Hung Hsiu-ch'üan)
Timor, in World War II, 548
Tinghsien experiment, 431
Ting Ling, 668
Tinian, 551
Tobolsk, 345
Togo, Admiral, 354
Togo, Foreign Minister, 492ff
Tohokai, political group, 578
Tojo, Hideki, 492ff; government, 577-78
Tokugawa, Prince, 442
Tokugawa family, 108-17
Tokugawa period, 86, 89, 90; Buddhist support, 140-41; culture under, 145-47; economic affairs, 118-31, 244-47, 521-22; end of, 238-50; foreign contact policies, 181-92; foreign innovations, 522
Tokyo: bombings of, 547, 551-52, 580; Chinese revolutionary organizations in, 383; rainfall in, 81; Treaty of, 350. *See also* Edo
Tokyo Mutiny, 516, 519
Tong Hak uprising, 291
Tongking, 288, 295
Tosa clan, in Tokugawa overthrow, 249, 252
Tosei-ha, Japanese army group, 519
Toyoda, Admiral, 491
Tozama daimyo, 111-12, 124
Trade Association Decree (of Japan), 125
Trade Union Law (Japan), 582
Trans-Siberian Railway, 293-94, 349-51, 371
Treaties: Japanese tariff convention of 1866, 204; of Aigun, 348; of the Bogue, 173; of Canton, 175; of Commerce and Friendship, Anglo-Japanese, 201; of Edo, 200; of 1880, United States-China, 333; of Jenchuan, 291; of Kanagawa, 199; of Kiakhta, 163; of Livadia, 287; of Nanking, 172-73, 327; of Nerchinsk, 156-57, 347; of Paris, 337; of Peking, 292, 403-4; of Portsmouth, 302, 354, 408; Republic of China Mutual Defense Treaty, 633-34; of St. Petersburg, 287; of Shimonoseki, 292, 307; Sino-Russian Treaty of 1945, 608; Sino-Soviet Alliance of 1950, 605, 617; of Tientsin, 177-78, 179, 284, 288, 332, 348; of Tokyo, 350; of Versailles (*see* Versailles, Treaty of); of Wanghia, 174, 328; of Whampoa, 174
"Trenton," 291
Triad Society, 55, 207
Tripartite Pact (Germany, Italy, Japan), 410, 545
Truman, Harry: China policy, 569-70, 599-605; Far East postwar policy, 611; Korean policy, 626; removes MacArthur, 628
Tsai T'ien (Kuang Hsü), 224
Ts'ao Ao, 390
Ts'ao Kun, 392, 393
Tsêng, Marquis, 287
Tsêng Kuo-chüan, 214, 215
Tsêng Kuo-fan, 213, 227, 228, 230, 231, 315; in the Taiping movement, 214, 215, 217, 218; Nienfei uprising, 219
Tsinan, Communist capture, 575; incident in, 447, 511
Tsinan-Tsingtao Railway, 44, 359, 447
Tsingling Range, 8
Tsingtao, 294, 359
Tsingtao-Tsinan Railway, 44, 359, 447

Tsinghua, 682
Tso Tsung-t'ang, 219, 230ff, 287; in the Taiping movement, 214, 215, 217, 220
Tsunayoshi, 181
Tsushima, 354; Battle of, 276
Tuan, Prince, 299, 313; support of the Boxers, 297
Tuan Chi-jui, 391, 393, 397, 420; in World War I, 368, 370
Tuan Fang, 323, 382, 384
Tukhachevsky, Marshal, 407
T'ung Chih, Emperor, 223-24, 382
T'ung-mêng Hui, 383
Tungpei Army, 438-39
T'ung River, 7
T'ung-t'ing Lake, 7, 11
Tunguses, 346
Tung Wang, 209, 212, 213
T'ung Wên Kuan, 227, 229, 234, 311
"Tutuila," U.S.S., 491
Tuva Autonomous Republic, 401
Twenty-one Demands, 360-66
Tyler, John, 174, 328
Tz'ŭ An, Empress Dowager, 222-25
Tz'ŭ Hsi, Empress Dowager, 35, 179; Boxer Rising and, 296-99; death, 382; period of regency, 222-26; reform movement, 313-14, 318-20

Ugaki, General, 513
Uighurs, 684
Unequal treaties: Chinese, 173-75, 463; Japanese, 248-50, 269-73; Russia's yielding of, 401; United States offer to negotiate, 464-65
Union of Soviet Socialist Republics (U.S.S.R.): Axis negotiations with, 410-11; Communist China and, 601-3, 605, 633, 644-46, 656-57, 687-88; Far East after the Revolution, 399-400; Far Eastern policy, 656-57; Far East in World War II, 550, 552-56; Geneva Conference, 631-32; Japanese neutrality pact, 545; Japanese occupation, 588, 608; Japanese Peace Treaty, 608, 613-14; Japanese relations, 583, 586, 596, 648-49; Korean truce talks, 628-29; Korean war, 620-41; Manchuria looted by, 571, 598-99; Moscow Conference, 581, 598-99, 621-23; purge of 1937, 407; railroad issue in Far East, 401-3; second Five-Year Plan, 405; United States relations, 471, 579; World War II, 550, 552-56, 579; Yalta Conference, 553, 620
United Front in China, 567-68
United Nations: action in Korea, 625-29; Charter, 581, 603, 618; Chinese civil war, 603; Commission on Korea, 623-24; Japanese membership, 636, 648; Japanese Peace Treaty, 613-15; Korea becomes a member, 625; Korean war, 623-25; meeting at San Francisco, 569; Red China's bid for membership, 603
United States: Alaska purchase, 331-32; annexation of Hawaii, 335-36; anti-Chinese feeling in, 333-34; Australian mutual defense treaty, 615; British relations, 351; China relations (see United States-China relations); first American-Oriental treaties, 187; growth of Pacific policy, 326; Hay's "open door" and Russia, 352; in Four Power Consortium, 278-79; in Russo-Chinese relations, 274; on Yalta Conference, 553-54; Japanese interests, 247-50; Japanese iron imports from, 534; Japanese relations (see United States-Japanese relations); Korea activity, 620-41, 654-55; Korea-Japanese policy, 279-80; Korea negotiations with Soviet Union, 628-29; Korean relations in nineteenth century, 289ff; New Zealand mutual defense treaty, 615; Philippine Mutual defense treaty, 615; Philippine relations, 336-38; Soviet Union relations, 471, 570-71; World War II in Far East, 545-53. See also United States Far Eastern policy
United States-China relations, 547-51, 556-76, 599-605, 643, 647, 654; Burlingame sets policy, 178-79; Cairo meeting, 568; Communist relations, 603-5, 642-48, 653-54; during the Chinese Revolution, 463-65; during Sino-Japanese War, 334; during Taiping Rebellion, 214; early American trade with China, 165, 170-71; economic aid, 570; early F. D. Roosevelt administration policies, 471-74; exclusion troubles, 333-34; extraterritoriality negotiations, 465; Hay negotiations, 300-302; historical commercial aspects, 326-29; immigration restrictions, 333; international consortium, 356; Japanese aggression and, 477-95; Marshall's mission, 569-72; Mutual Defense Treaty, 633; 1945-50, 599-605; open door policy, 299-300, 338-39, 351, 444, 480-81; opium crisis, 169-71; peace efforts after World War II, 568-69; promotion of wartime unity by United States, 567-69; student relations, 316; tariff autonomy and, 426, 465; territorial integrity policy, 301, 329, 330, 332, 338-39; trade treaties, 173-79. See also United States Far Eastern policy

INDEX 713

United States-Chinese Communists relations, 604-5, 642-48; Angus Ward incident, 603-4; policy of non-recognition, 653-54

United States Far Eastern policy, 615-18, 653-56; anti-Bolshevik efforts of World War I, 371-73; at Versailles, 376-79; before Korean War, 615-18; broadening character of, 485; Burlingame sets policy, 178-79; cessation of trade with Japan, 411; China, 1945-50, 599-605; Chinese Civil War and, 463-65; cooperation with the League of Nations, 467; defense pacts, 615; during depression years, 471-74; early history of, 326-43; economic sanctions, 468-69, 470, 486-87; expansionist period, 338-43; fundamental principles statement of Secretary Hull, 477; growing importance of Japan, 634; in Manchurian crisis, 451, 454, 466-71; Japanese Occupation policy, 605-13; Japanese peace treaty initiative, 613-15; Japanese treaty abrogated, 482-87; Japan's Twenty-One Demands, 365-66; Korea, 647-48; Korean War, 629-32; Lansing-Ishii Agreement, 374-75; Manchuria and, 352, 598-99; Manifest Destiny period, 336; monarchy restoration in China and, 367; moral embargo against Japan, 483-84; Mutual Defense Treaty with Nationalist China, 633-34, 647; Nanking puppet regime protected, 484-85; naval limitation policy, 441-46, 474-76; 1945-50, 598-619; 1955-60, 642-57; nonrecognition of aggressor theory, 467-68; open door policy, 299-300, 338-39, 351-52, 444, 480-81; opposition to Russian influence in Nationalist China, 463, 465-66; Pacific Navy maneuvers of 1935, 475; pre-war negotiations with Japan, 489-95; sacredness of treaties policy, 469; Washington Conference, 441-46, 474-76; World War I developments, 462. *See also* United States, United States-China relations, *and* United States-Japanese relations

United States-Japanese relations, 247, 339, 545, 577-97, 609-10, 655-56; after Russo-Japanese War, 340-43; American policy for rebuilding Japan, 607-8; Biddle expedition, 191; Boxer war treaty, 299; demilitarization and democratization of Japan, 582; economic aid, 596, 607; early contacts, 185-86, 271, 272; early F. D. Roosevelt Administration, 471-74; Far Eastern Commission, 581; first American consulate in Japan, 200; first tourists in Japan, 199-200; Gentlemen's Agreement, 342, 462; immigration issue, 341-43, 462; in United States defense policy, 614, 616; Japanese aggression in China and, 477-95; Japanese interpretation of open door, 480-81; Japanese mission to United States in 1860, 204; Korea in, 341; "Manhattan" expedition, 190; "Morrison" expedition, 187-90; Mutual Security Treaty of 1951, 597, 651-53; naval limitation dissatisfactions, 474-76; Perry expedition, 192-96, 198, 202-4; Pratt resolution, 190-91; surrender, 579; Shigemitsu mission to Washington, 648; trade treaties, 200; whaling interests, 186. *See also* United States Far Eastern policy

United States-Soviet relations: Far East, 599; Japanese occupation, 612-13; Japanese Peace Treaty, 608, Korean War, 621-24

Universal Postal Union, 232, 271

Urga, 400

Ussuri River, 347, 348

Vasco da Gama, 152

Versailles Treaty, effect on China, 392; Japanese reaction, 509; racial equality issue, 378-79; Shantung question, 375-79

Victoria, Queen, 287

Vietnam, 632, 650

Viviani, Ambassador, 374

Vladivostok, 293, 294, 348, 372

Vocational Education party, 564

"Volage," H.M.S., 170

Waardenar, Dutch factor, 183
Wakatsuki, 509-14
Wake Island, 546, 551
Waldersee, Count, 298-99
Wallace, Henry A., 549
Wamping, 459
Wang, Dr. C. T., 376ff
Wang An-shih, 31
Wang Ching-wei, 485, 557; in the Kuomintang, 422ff, 428, 429
Wanghia, Treaty of, 174, 328
Wang Kwoh Kung Pao, 229
Wang Mang, 28, 29, 307
Wan Li, Emperor, 154
Ward, Angus, 603-4
Ward, Frederick Townsend, 214-15
War Lords, 390-94
Warring States Period, 27
Washington Conference, 373, 462; purpose and accomplishments, 441, 442-46
Washington Naval Treaty, 474-75, 515
Watanabe, general, 516
Webster, Daniel, 193
Wedemeyer, Albert C., 573; succeeds Stilwell, 550

Wei dynasty, 30
Weihaiwei, 295
Wêng T'ung-ho, 225, 229, 309
Wên li, 59, 60, 63, 396
Westernization: China reaction to in late nineteenth century, 226-30; early Chinese Republic period, 394-97; Japan, 597; K'ang Yu-wei's sponsoring of, 306-13; Manchu reforms, 312-24; methods of penetration in China, 228-30; Sino-Japanese contrasts, 236-37
Whaling industry, 186, 331
Whampoa Military Academy, 168, 387, 415, 430, 575
White Lotus Society, 156, 206, 207
White Paper, The, 569, 573n, 600n, 602-3
William, Maurice, 419
Williams, Dr. S. Wells, 187, 189
Williamson, missionary, 285
Wilson, Woodrow, 339, 376, 387; at Versailles, 377-78, 379; Chinese policy, 441; Consortium policy, 279
Witte, Sergei, 293-94, 349, 351, 353
Wo Jên, 227, 234
World War I: China in, 358, 359-60, 366-78, 391, 392; Japan in, 358-66, 372-78
World War II: Far East in, 545-72; Japan in, 78, 85, 577-88
Written Chronicles of Japan, 91
Wu, Dr. C. C., 376
Wuchang (Wuhan City), 11, 460
Wuhan cities, 11, 233, 384, 423-24
Wu K'o-tu, 24
Wu Pei-fu, 392, 393, 420, 423, 551
"Wyoming," U.S.S., 203

Xavier, St. Francis, 114, 154, 159

Yakoob Bey, 220
Yakutsk Province, 346
Yalta Conference, 553-54, 620
Yamagata, 502-7, 514
Yamaguchi, unequal treaties and, 270
Yamamoto, 495, 503, 505, 509
Yamato, 92-93, 95, 142
Yangchow, 212-13
Yang Hsiu-ch'ing, 209-13
Yangtze River, 7, 11-12, 558

Yap, 378
Yap-Guam cable, 444
Yap Treaty, 444-45
Yasuda, house of, 528
Yellow River (Huang Ho), 6, 10-11
Yen, Dr. Y. C. (James), 60, 396, 431
Yenan, 409, 436, 459, 558, 568, 569, 572, 666; communist recapture, 574
Yenching University, 571, 682
Yên Fu, 231
Yen Hsi-shan, 423ff, 429
Yenisei River, 346
Yermak, Cossack adventurer, 345-46
Yi dynasty, 289
Yin Ju-ken, 458
Yokohama, 79, 552
Yokohama Specie Bank, 524
Yonai, Admiral, 514, 578
Yoritomo, 99, 100-102
Yoshiaki, 106
Yoshida, Shigeru, 579, 590-93, 596, 607, 648
Yoshifusa, 98
Yoshihito, Emperor, 505n
Yoshimitsu, 103, 140
Yoshimune, 113, 119, 122, 147, 240
Yoshinobu (Keiki), 250
Young China Party, 564, 572, 685
Yuan Ming Yüan, 225
Yüan Shih-k'ai, 290, 291, 311ff, 323; as president of China, 358, 364, 366; attempts to restore monarchy, 389-90; imperial ambition, 366-67; in 1911 revolution, 382, 385; in the Republic, 385-90; reform activities, 316, 317
Yüeh Fu, 431-32
Yugoslavia, 613
Yui, O. K., 685
Yung Cheng, Emperor, 156
Yung Wing, 229, 231
Yünnan, 12, 18, 295; Moslem outbreaks in, 219; rebellion and, 367

Zaibatsu, 532; Occupation and, 586-88; liquidated, 586-88, 595; political role, 515, 517; rise of, 527-30; war interest, 534-35
Zen Buddhism, 103, 140, 244; support of Nō drama, 145

DATE DUE

MAR 19 '68